READER'S DIGEST
ATLAS
OF
CANADA

Reader's Digest

The Reader's Digest Association (Canada) Ltd., Montréal

ACKNOWLEDGMENTS

PROJECT EDITOR: Andrew R. Byers

ART DIRECTOR: John McGuffie

ASSISTANT ART DIRECTOR: Lucie Martineau

DESIGNER: Cécile Germain

RESEARCH EDITOR: Wadad Bashour

PICTURE EDITOR: Rachel Irwin

COPY PREPARATION: Joseph Marchetti,
   Gilles Humbert

CONTRIBUTING RESEARCHERS: Robert Ronald,
   Jennifer Lee Thomas

MAP RESEARCHER: Michelle Pharand

EDITORIAL ASSISTANCE: Elizabeth Eastman

PRODUCTION: Holger Lorenzen

COORDINATOR: Susan Wong

CARTOGRAPHY:
   Schwerdt Graphic Arts Ltd.
   (MapArt)

Special Consultants

J. S. Beckett
Director
Fisheries Research Branch
Department of Fisheries and Oceans
Ottawa

Dr. Andrew Burghardt
Professor Emeritus of Geography
McMaster University
Hamilton

Dr. Leonard Guelke
Professor of Geography
University of Waterloo

Dr. C. Richard Harington
Research Scientist (Quaternary Zoology)
Canadian Museum of Nature
Ottawa

Dr. Stephen Kumarapeli
Professor of Geology
Concordia University
Montreal

Dr. Gordon MacEachern
Former President
Agricultural Economics Research Council
   of Canada
Ottawa

Dr. Jag Maini
Special Adviser
Sustainable Development
Canadian Forest Service
National Resources Canada

Jayson Myers
Chief Economist
Canadian Manufacturers' Association
Toronto

David Phillips
Chief Climatologist
Environment Canada
Downsview, Ontario

Dr. Dale Russell
Research Scientist (Fossil Vertebrates,
   Dinosaurs)
Canadian Museum of Nature
Ottawa

Dr. John E. Udd
Director
Mining Research Laboratories
Natural Resources Canada
Ottawa

Dr. P. B. Waite
Professor Emeritus of History
Dalhousie University
Halifax

Reader's Digest thanks the companies, libraries, and government departments that provided information for *Atlas of Canada*. Reader's Digest especially thanks Statistics Canada, the source of the facts and figures appearing in the book.

The credits and acknowledgments that appear on page 176 are hereby made part of this copyright page.

Canadian Cataloguing in Publication Data

Main entry under title:

   Atlas of Canada
   ISBN 0-88850-248-6

1. Canada—Maps. I. Reader's Digest Association (Canada).

G1115.R43 1995   912.71   C94-900722-6

Printed in Canada

95 96 97 98 / 5 4 3 2 1

CONTENTS

Portrait of the Nation covers the principal themes of Canada's geology, geography, history, society and economy. Each theme is treated in a self-contained two-page unit, the headings of which are given here. Under each heading, the main topics are listed, followed by references to related subjects on other theme pages and in *Facts About Canada*.

OF THE NATION

A Nation of Superlatives

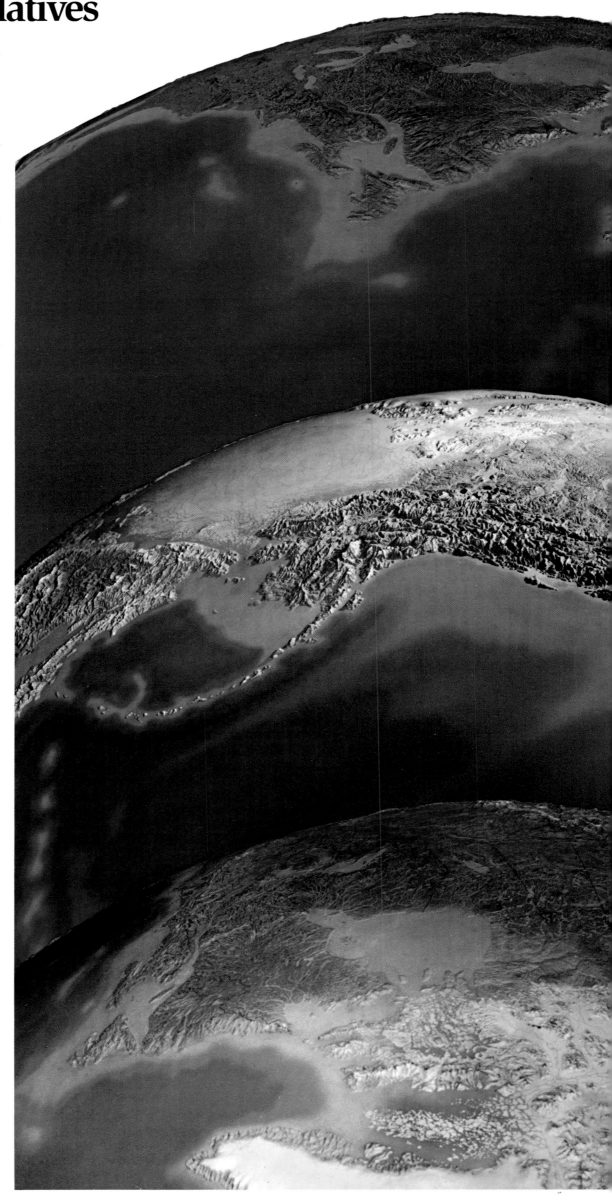

He shall have dominion also from sea to sea, and from the river
unto the ends of the earth.   —Psalms 72:8

"When you see this country for the first time, all of it . . . you
say to yourself, 'My God, is all this ours!' "
                              —Hugh MacLennan, *Two Solitudes*

From a geographic viewpoint, Canada bulks large. With a land
area of 9,970,610 square kilometres, our nation spreads over half
a continent, covering nearly 7 percent of the earth's surface. The
largest country in the Western Hemisphere, Canada rests on the
Americas like a giant capstone.

Ours is the largest country in the world after Russia. Only
Australia, Brazil, China and the United States rival Canada in
territorial extent. But there is no other nation that could not
be accommodated comfortably within Canada's boundaries.
France and Germany could be fitted into the interior of Quebec,
leaving room for Austria, the Czech Republic and Poland. Belgium, the Netherlands, and Luxembourg together would not
cover the area occupied by New Brunswick.

More than 4600 kilometres separate Cape Columbia on Ellesmere Island, Canada's northern extremity, from Point Pelee,
Ontario's southernmost tip. From a northern perspective, Canada's only neighbor, the United States, with which it shares an
8892-kilometre-long boundary, almost disappears from view.

Even greater than the north-south span of Canada is the
distance from east to west. St. John's on the Atlantic Ocean is
5047 kilometres from Victoria on the Pacific. Alberta is as far to
the west of Newfoundland as Germany is to the east. Vancouver
is closer to Mexico City and the Arctic coast than it is to Halifax.
The vastness of this nation, stretching from sea to sea, captured
the imagination of the Fathers of Confederation, inspiring Sir
Samuel Leonard Tilley of New Brunswick to suggest "Dominion" for Canada's baptismal name.

The physical diversity of the country is remarkable: towering
mountains, great plains, fertile lowlands, northern wilderness,
and tundra. Few nations can match Canada's abundance of minerals, forests, and bodies of waters. The lakes, scattered so lib-
erally across the land, contain some of the world's greatest
stores of fresh water.

Our majestic rivers—pathways of the fur trade and settlement—are set amid landscapes of ineffable beauty, which
evoke sentiments of grandeur and abundance. The most famous
of our national waterways, the St. Lawrence–Great Lakes, is a
key setting in Canadian history. Along this route the nation had
its origins, as adventurers and missionaries penetrated the interior of the continent.

But Canada's landforms have combined with its climate to
confine development. Beyond the narrow band of settlement
along the country's southern edge looms the rugged Canadian
Shield, which thrusts down to the St. Lawrence River between
Lake Ontario and Montreal, and the Arctic islands.

Four-fifths of Canada has never been settled permanently. Of
all the provinces, only Prince Edward Island is completely inhabited. The largest unbroken tract of mixed rural and urban
settlement is the Prairies, which account for slightly more than
6 percent of Canada's area. Most of the nation's 27 million people live in urban areas that take up 1 percent of the land, with
the heaviest concentration located in the industrial heartland
stretching from Quebec to Windsor.

Yet the distances separating Canada's major urban centres are
immense. In no other country, except Australia, is there a comparable scattering of centers of population without continuous
settlement. Therefore, development of transportation systems,
particularly the railways, has been of special importance in
Canada's history. Only that epic of nation-building, the Canadian Pacific Railway, stretching 27,487 kilometres across prairie
and forest, mountain and muskeg, from the Maritimes to the
Fraser delta, made a "dominion from sea to sea" truly possible.
To seal this bond, nearly a century later, came the Trans-Canada
Highway between Victoria and St. John's, at 7307 kilometres the
world's longest national road.

*The three global views at right present Canada as it might be seen from
high above the North Atlantic (top), the mid-Pacific (middle), and the high
Arctic (bottom). Bounded by these three vast bodies of water, Canada has
the longest ocean coastline in the world: 243,792 kilometres.*

*On the Atlantic shore, the direct distance between the Bay of Fundy and
Hudson Strait (separating northern Quebec and Baffin Island) is about
1600 kilometres. But the true measure of this shoreline, with its numerous
estuaries, inlets and capes, is 10 times as great. Facing eastward to Europe and northward to Greenland, Atlantic Canada is bypassed by the Gulf
Stream which warms the coast of northern Europe. The chill Labrador
Current, flowing down from between Baffin Island and Greenland, meets
the Gulf Stream off the coast of Newfoundland. Canada's Atlantic coast
was the first to become known to Europeans. Norse explorers briefly
settled the northern tip of Newfoundland in the 11th century. Five hundred
years later, when European exploration began in earnest, the French
explorer Jacques Cartier discovered the St. Lawrence—the gateway
to the interior of North America.*

*Canada's Pacific coast was charted by the Royal Navy in the 18th century.
Here the mountain ranges rise sheer from the sea, creating a formidable
barrier to the interior. The length of this precipitous shore is 7022 kilometres. For most of its distance it is deeply indented by fjords and studded
with islands, the largest of which are Vancouver Island and the Queen
Charlottes. This coastline, warmed by the Alaska Current, is temperate
and, except for sheltered inlets, its waters are ice-free. The 30,000-
kilometre-long coastline of the Arctic and Hudson Bay is the longest in
Canada and, because the ocean is perpetually covered with drifting ice,
the least accessible. Locked in the Arctic ice is one of the world's largest
archipelagoes, with a land area of over 1,330,000 square kilometres. The
centuries-old search for a passage through these hazardous waters ended
in 1906 with the successful voyage of Roald Amundsen. Today icebreakers
and other vessels with modern navigation aids make the passage from
Baffin Bay to the Beaufort Sea possible in late summer and early autumn.*

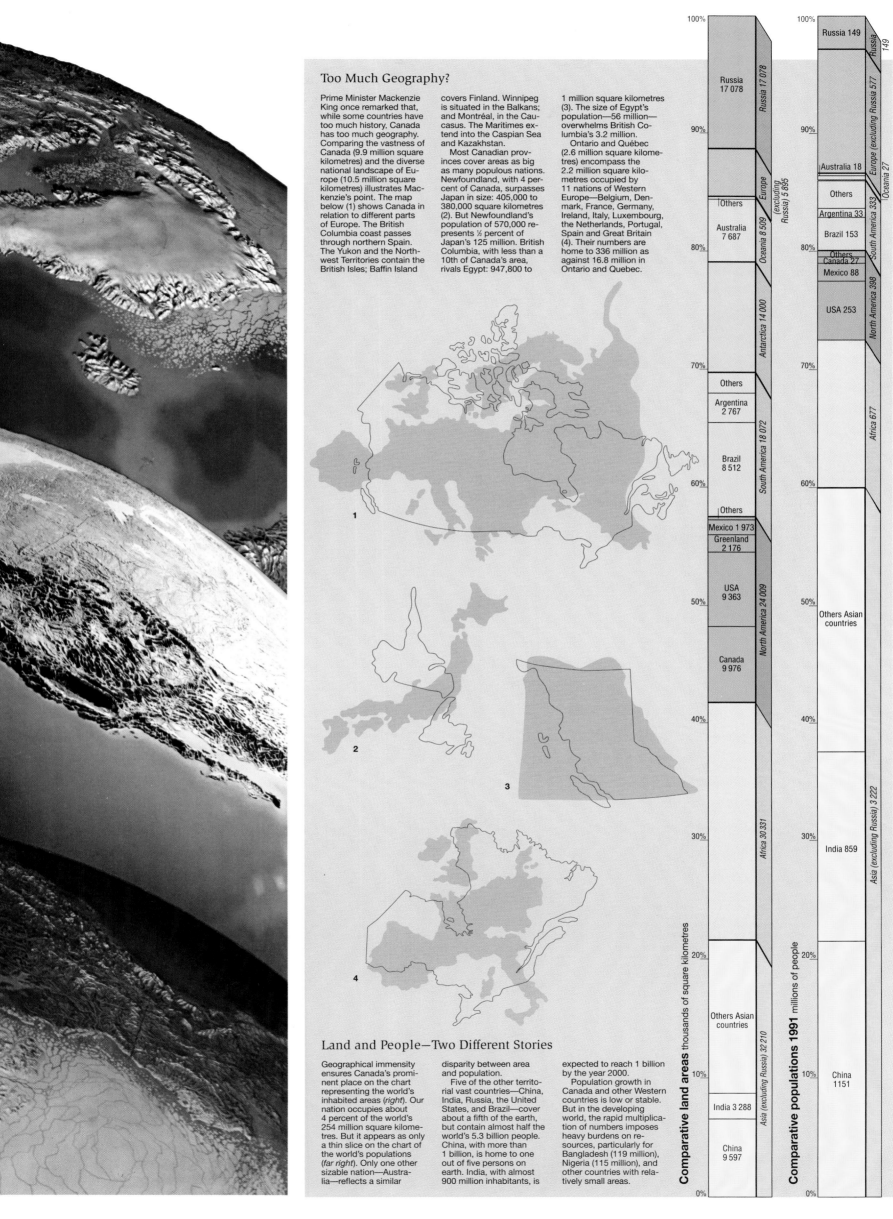

Too Much Geography?

Prime Minister Mackenzie King once remarked that, while some countries have too much history, Canada has too much geography. Comparing the vastness of Canada (9.9 million square kilometres) and the diverse national landscape of Europe (10.5 million square kilometres) illustrates Mackenzie's point. The map below (1) shows Canada in relation to different parts of Europe. The British Columbia coast passes through northern Spain. The Yukon and the Northwest Territories contain the British Isles; Baffin Island covers Finland. Winnipeg is situated in the Balkans; and Montréal, in the Caucasus. The Maritimes extend into the Caspian Sea and Kazakhstan.

Most Canadian provinces cover areas as big as many populous nations. Newfoundland, with 4 percent of Canada, surpasses Japan in size: 405,000 to 380,000 square kilometres (2). But Newfoundland's population of 570,000 represents ½ percent of Japan's 125 million. British Columbia, with less than a 10th of Canada's area, rivals Egypt: 947,800 to 1 million square kilometres (3). The size of Egypt's population—56 million—overwhelms British Columbia's 3.2 million.

Ontario and Québec (2.6 million square kilometres) encompass the 2.2 million square kilometres occupied by 11 nations of Western Europe—Belgium, Denmark, France, Germany, Ireland, Italy, Luxembourg, the Netherlands, Portugal, Spain and Great Britain (4). Their numbers are home to 336 million as against 16.8 million in Ontario and Quebec.

Land and People—Two Different Stories

Geographical immensity ensures Canada's prominent place on the chart representing the world's inhabited areas (right). Our nation occupies about 4 percent of the world's 254 million square kilometres. But it appears as only a thin slice on the chart of the world's populations (far right). Only one other sizable nation—Australia—reflects a similar disparity between area and population.

Five of the other territorial vast countries—China, India, Russia, the United States, and Brazil—cover about a fifth of the earth, but contain almost half the world's 5.3 billion people. China, with more than 1 billion, is home to one out of five persons on earth. India, with almost 900 million inhabitants, is expected to reach 1 billion by the year 2000.

Population growth in Canada and other Western countries is low or stable. But in the developing world, the rapid multiplication of numbers imposes heavy burdens on resources, particularly for Bangladesh (119 million), Nigeria (115 million), and other countries with relatively small areas.

Comparative land areas thousands of square kilometres

Asia (excluding Russia) 32 210
- China 9 597
- India 3 288
- Others Asian countries

Africa 30 331

North America 24 009
- Canada 9 976
- USA 9 363
- Greenland 2 176
- Mexico 1 973
- Others

South America 18 072
- Brazil 8 512
- Argentina 2 767
- Others

Antarctica 14 000

Oceania 8 509
- Australia 7 687
- Others

Europe (excluding Russia) 5 895

Russia 17 078

Comparative populations 1991 millions of people

Asia (excluding Russia) 3 222
- China 1151
- India 859
- Others Asian countries

Africa 677

North America 398
- USA 253
- Mexico 88
- Canada 27
- Others

South America 333
- Brazil 153
- Argentina 33
- Others

Europe (excluding Russia) 577

Oceania 27
- Australia 18
- Others

Russia 149

The Making of Our Land

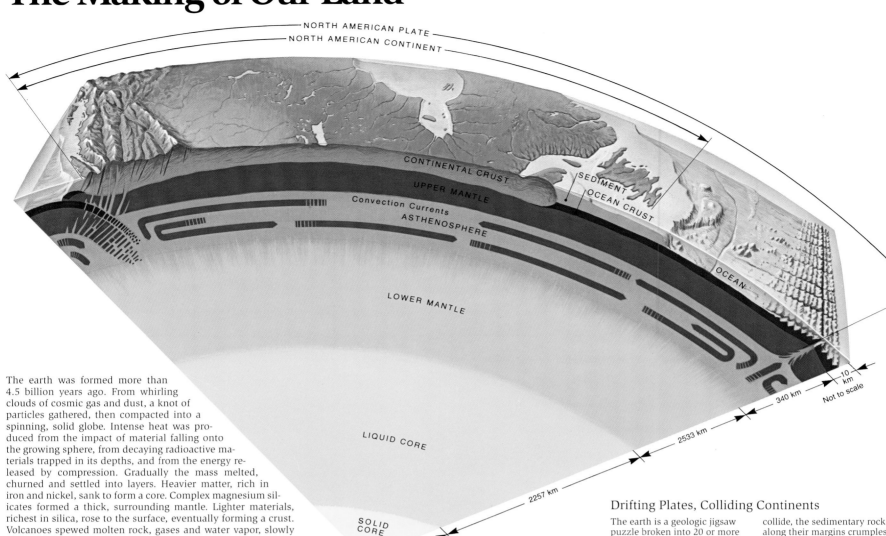

NORTH AMERICAN PLATE
NORTH AMERICAN CONTINENT

CONTINENTAL CRUST
UPPER MANTLE
Convection Currents
ASTHENOSPHERE
SEDIMENT
OCEAN CRUST
OCEAN

LOWER MANTLE

LIQUID CORE

SOLID CORE

10 km
Not to scale
340 km
2533 km
2257 km
1231 km

The earth was formed more than 4.5 billion years ago. From whirling clouds of cosmic gas and dust, a knot of particles gathered, then compacted into a spinning, solid globe. Intense heat was produced from the impact of material falling onto the growing sphere, from decaying radioactive materials trapped in its depths, and from the energy released by compression. Gradually the mass melted, churned and settled into layers. Heavier matter, rich in iron and nickel, sank to form a core. Complex magnesium silicates formed a thick, surrounding mantle. Lighter materials, richest in silica, rose to the surface, eventually forming a crust. Volcanoes spewed molten rock, gases and water vapor, slowly giving birth to land, air and seas.

The slow sorting of the earth into layers is still going on. At the earth's center, the inner core burns at a white-hot 5000°C, but pressures up to 3.5 million times the normal surface atmospheric pressure compress it to a solid ball. The molten outer core flows around it, rippling with currents caused by the earth's rotation. This fluid core behaves like a dynamo, turning the earth into a gigantic magnet with north and south poles. The solid mantle is composed of three zones: a rigid lower layer; the soft asthenosphere, eddying slowly like liquid simmering in a pot; and a rigid upper layer. The upper layer of the mantle together with the crust forms the rigid lithosphere: a thin, brittle layer some 100 kilometres thick which floats on the asthenosphere. The lithosphere is cracked into a mosaic of huge plates of irregular size and shape. The crust includes the continents and ocean basins—less than one percent of the earth's bulk. The continental crust, largely composed of relatively light granitic rock up to 35 to 80 kilometres thick, floats higher in the asthenosphere than the heavier ocean floors. Basaltic ocean crust averages only 7 to 8 kilometres in thickness, but sags to form deep basins that fill with seawater.

Our restless planet is never still. Over billions of years, parts of it have been uplifted, then ground flat again, washed by seas and sculpted by erosion, thrust up into belts of rugged mountains and worn down into plains and gently rolling hills.

The Violent Birth of the Continents

Some 200 million years ago, the continents formed one landmass, *Pangaea* (Greek for "all lands"), with what is now Canada at its northwest corner. About 135 million years ago this continent began ripping apart, dividing into southern Gondwanaland and northern Laurasia, which included an embryonic North America ("Laurentia"). As the Atlantic Ocean developed, Canada's east coast pulled apart from southern Europe, and North America swiveled before separating from Scandinavia.

The jigsaw-puzzle fit of both sides of the Atlantic and the similarity of fossils and mineral deposits on widely separated continents support the theory of continental drift. Scientists have found proof that seafloors are older the farther they are from mid-ocean rifts. This enables them to map how the earth's oceans grew, and to determine in which direction and how fast each plate is moving.

200 million years ago

135 million years ago

65 million years ago

→ Plate movement
～ Spreading rift
≈ Subduction zone
— Transform fault
- - - Uncertain or generalized boundary

Drifting Plates, Colliding Continents

The earth is a geologic jigsaw puzzle broken into 20 or more plates up to 100 kilometres thick, all driven by forces in the asthenosphere. Earthquakes and volcanoes outline the plate boundaries and give awesome testimony to the forces beneath our feet.

Where plates pull apart, as at the mid-Atlantic rift, molten rock oozes up onto the seafloor, creating 3 centimetres of new bottom each year. Where plates push together—off Canada's west coast, for example—one may be forced under the other, eventually to soften in subduction zones and melt in the hot interior. The westward-creeping American plate is bulldozing over the small Juan de Fuca and Explorer plates. Molten rock from the descending plate edge once fueled active volcanoes throughout British Columbia, and its heat produced a solid granite spine 2000 kilometres long underlying the Coast Range. Where two continents collide, the sedimentary rock along their margins crumples and is pushed up into mountain peaks. Some 250 million years ago, such continental collision produced the Appalachians of eastern Canada. At certain plate boundaries, called transform faults, plates grind past each other, triggering earthquakes. California's San Andreas Fault is one of these.

Ocean floor spreading pushes Canada and Europe farther apart by 3 centimetres a year. At the same time, the Pacific plate is shrinking, and British Columbia and Japan draw 12 centimetres closer every year. In 42 million years, if this drift continues, North and South America will separate, Africa will break apart, the Mediterranean will be squeezed into a large lake and California west of the San Andreas Fault—including Los Angeles—will have drifted off to a point somewhere off the west coast of Canada.

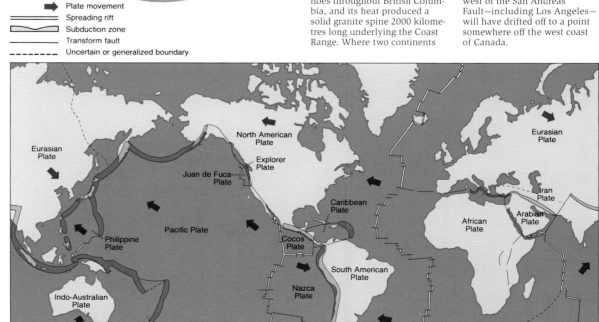

Eurasian Plate
North American Plate
Explorer Plate
Juan de Fuca Plate
Philippine Plate
Pacific Plate
Caribbean Plate
Cocos Plate
Nazca Plate
South American Plate
Indo-Australian Plate
Eurasian Plate
Iran Plate
Arabian Plate
African Plate
Scotia Plate
Antarctic Plate

Pent-Up Pressures That Cause Quakes

Plate movements, where rock grinds against rock, create immense pressures. Ninety-five percent of earthquakes occur at plate boundaries such as the Pacific "Ring of Fire," the rest along inland fault lines. Sometimes the rock masses move imperceptibly. When they resist, pressures may build. Rock bends until pent-up strain overcomes friction, then moves suddenly and violently—an earthquake. There are more than a million quakes each year, 300 in Canada.

Parts of Québec and British Columbia lie in zones most susceptible to quakes, but damage would be most severe in major cities, in coastal areas vulnerable to tidal waves from offshore quakes, and in areas where loose, clay-based soils may shift or even liquefy. Earthquakes measuring seven or more on the Richter scale, powerful enough to bend steel rails and topple all but the strongest buildings, have happened in Canada (see map), although never in densely settled areas. Large and small, all quakes are monitored, since repeated shuddering is a clue that the pressure is building.

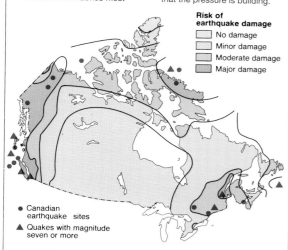

Risk of earthquake damage
- No damage
- Minor damage
- Moderate damage
- Major damage

● Canadian earthquake sites
▲ Quakes with magnitude seven or more

Platforms
- Interior
- Arctic
- Hudson
- St. Lawrence

Canadian Shield
- Superior
- Slave
- Nutak
- Churchill
- Bear
- Southern
- Grenville

Orogens
- Innuitian
- Appalachian
- Cordilleran

▲ Volcanoes
— Normal fault
▲▲▲ Thrust fault

Coastal shelves and plains
- Arctic
- Atlantic
- Pacific

Our Seventeen Provinces

Canada has 17 geologic provinces or landform regions. The nucleus of the continent is the Canadian Shield, the ancient, eroded landmass cradling Hudson Bay. The Shield's seven provinces formed during three surges of mountain-building over 2 billion years. Near its edges, the Shield disappears under the plateaus, plains and lowlands of the four platform provinces, built from layers of sediments. At the Shield's edges are belts of unstable younger mountains—the three orogen provinces. In the youngest orogen, the Cordilleran, a few lines of fracture, called faults, one side of the break may sink downward (normal fault), or overlap the other (thrust fault). Molten rock oozes upward along cracks in older rock and then solidifies to form dikes. Near the collision zone between two plates, uplift builds mountains such as the Rockies. Farther from plate boundaries, the earth is quieter. The flat grasslands of the Prairies, the hills of the Shield and the broad, submerged continental shelf beneath Newfoundland's Grand Banks show that forces of erosion may be winning.

volcanoes remain. Although all are dormant, several Canadian volcanoes may have erupted as recently as 200 years ago. On the fringes of the orogens, new sediments are accumulating in the continental shelves of the three coastal provinces.

Erosion and Uplift Transform the Land

Wind, rain, and frost gnaw at the Canadian landscape, working to level it. Rocks split from jagged peaks, then shatter; boulders slowly disintegrate. Grains of sand are ground to silt. The loose, eroded sediments are pounded by rains and peppered by grit-laden winds. Streams and rivers carry them to the sea. While these forces are constantly wearing down the land, others are rebuilding it. As rock is worn away, other rock moves up to replace it. More rock pushes from the sides, sometimes causing warping and fracturing. At such

YOUTH

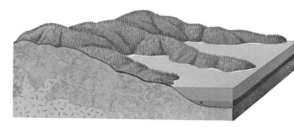

MATURITY

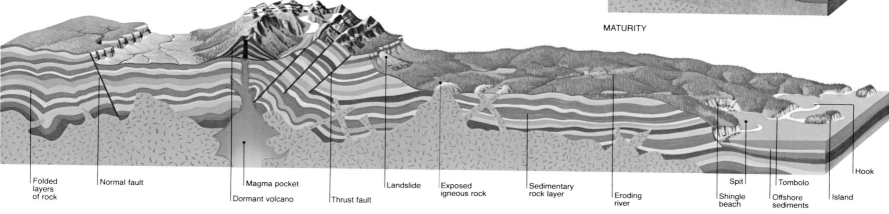

Folded layers of rock | Normal fault | Magma pocket | Dormant volcano | Thrust fault | Landslide | Exposed igneous rock | Sedimentary rock layer | Eroding river | Spit | Shingle beach | Tombolo | Offshore sediments | Island | Hook

Sandstone, Gneiss and Granite: The Three Phases of Rock Formation

SEDIMENTARY rock—shales, limestones and sandstones—is formed from particles of other rock, or from the fossil shells of tiny marine animals. They accumulate in layers, often trapping larger plant and animal fragments, and are compressed and cemented together by water-soluble minerals. Forming at or near the earth's surface, they make up only 8 percent of the crust, but 75 percent of its topmost layer. As surface rocks, they erode easily and are ground back to loose sediments. The sculpted coulees and hoodoos of western Canada's badlands show how poorly sandstones and shales resist erosion.

METAMORPHIC or altered rocks are formed when older rocks, chiefly sedimentary, are baked by volcanic heat, or are buried deep in the earth and steeped in hot, chemically active groundwater. These new rocks may form without melting, but the process takes millions of years. Minerals separate into bands of long, stretched-out crystals; pebbles flatten; crystals lock together. Metamorphized marbles, granites and gneisses lie in mountain belts and in the Canadian Shield.

IGNEOUS or fire-formed rocks harden from magma (melted older rock), rising from 40–60 kilometres underground. If the magma reaches the surface while hot and still liquid, it is called lava. Magma may also be forced through cracks in older rocks to harden as sheets or vertical dikes. Larger masses may crystallize underground in coarse, grainy blocks. Eventually all are exposed as softer surrounding rocks wear away.

However rocks form, most contain silica and a few other minerals. The photographs (*right*) show a silica compound as it might appear at each major step of the rock cycle—as sandstone, gneiss and granite.

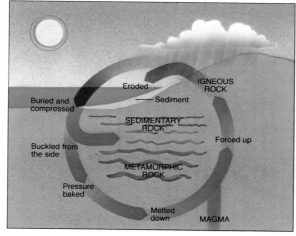

Eroded
Buried and compressed
Sediment
IGNEOUS ROCK
SEDIMENTARY ROCK
Buckled from the side
Forced up
METAMORPHIC ROCK
Pressure baked
Melted down
MAGMA

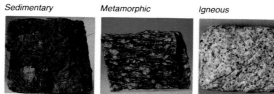

Sedimentary | *Metamorphic* | *Igneous*

OLD AGE

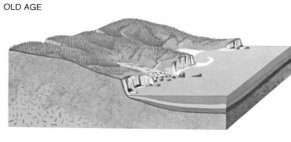

Where Restless Waves Carve and Age an Ever-Changing Shoreline

These views show a slowly sinking coast. In the seacoast's youth, river-carved valleys have been drowned by rising sea levels to form deep bays and estuaries, while the sea pounds against former inland hills. Waves gnaw at steep promontories, cut cliffs on their seaward sides, and flush away rock and soil. A coast of this type provides excellent natural harbors. As the seacoast matures, headlands slowly erode, and sandbar spits and crescents of shingle beach are built from sediments sorted by the sea. More sediment accumulates in the shallow, sheltered waters of the bay.

As the seacoast ages, sandbars may transform bays into silt-choked lagoons, and eventually into tidal mud flats. Parts of New Brunswick's coast have reached this stage. Relentless pounding by waves breaks up offshore islands and washes them away. Eventually the sinking coastline will be worn nearly straight, far inland from the original shoreline.

The Panorama of Ages Past

Peeled back, the layers of Canada's surface should reveal the rocks of earlier ages as neat chapters of geologic history. But the layers were seldom left in peace. Molten rock pierced and tilted them. Folding and faulting sandwiched and inverted them. Parts of Canada rose and sank, and whole pages of the story were destroyed by erosion. Piecing together this fragmentary record, geologists have drawn speculative maps of Canada in past ages: a drifting land rent by earthquakes, engulfed by oceans, uplifted by mountain building and worn down by wind and water.

The history of life is also written in the rocks, in remnants called fossils. Mineral-rich groundwater may petrify plants, bones, and shells, turning them to stone. Shells often leave their imprints in casts or molds. Animal remains have been preserved in dry caves or acidic peat bogs. These remains provide clues to our planet's past and the evolution of its life.

The story begins with the first stirrings of life in Precambrian seas, where organic molecules joined to form amino acids—building blocks of life—and finally living cells. As the fossil record shows, the road was long and tortuous: the evolution of single-celled organisms from organic compounds took far longer than the development from single cell to Homo sapiens. Early life, cradled by warm, shallow seas, burgeoned in the Cambrian Period some 550 million years ago. Species diversified and, following evolutionary trends toward complexity and specialization, eventually spread from sea to land.

Each era had its own most successful types. The hard-shelled trilobites and other arthropods of the Paleozoic were dominant for 300 million years. They were superseded by the reptiles of the Mesozoic, whose rule on earth lasted 150 million years. When the dinosaurs fell 65 million years ago, they were succeeded by the more efficient and adaptable warm-blooded animals of the Cenozoic, which quickly diversified to fill niches left empty. As the once-unified continents slid farther apart on their moving plates, each landmass drifted through its own sequence of environmental changes. Over the epochs and the Ice Age, modern mammals evolved, joined at last by recent immigrants to North America—human beings.

THE RIBBON OF TIME
The entire span of earth's history is divided into four unequal portions called eras—the Precambrian, stretching from earth's formation to 570 million years ago; the Paleozoic ("ancient life"); Mesozoic ("middle life"); and Cenozoic ("recent life"). Each is further divided into periods and epochs, including the Pleistocene, or Ice Age, and the Holocene, the last 10,000 years. Life has evolved slowly since the first single-celled organisms appeared in the late Precambrian. If this time scale were compressed into a single day, humans would appear only in the final few seconds.

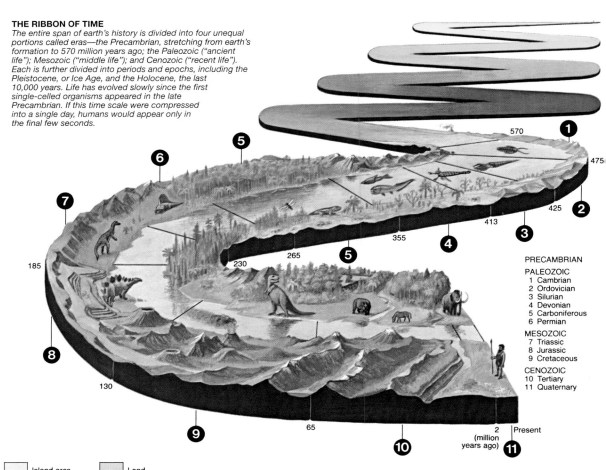

PRECAMBRIAN
PALEOZOIC
1 Cambrian
2 Ordovician
3 Silurian
4 Devonian
5 Carboniferous
6 Permian
MESOZOIC
7 Triassic
8 Jurassic
9 Cretaceous
CENOZOIC
10 Tertiary
11 Quaternary

| Marine deposits | Ocean | Terrestrial deposits | Island arcs | Land |

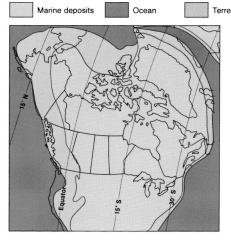

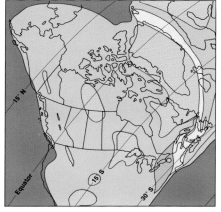

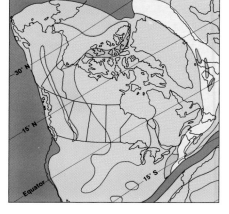

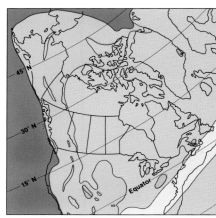

Early Cambrian (550 million years ago). Continental shields, low and barren, drifted about the globe, and climates were mild during the Cambrian Period. In a burst of evolution, animals with hard parts began replacing simple, soft-bodied organisms. In warm, shallow seas swam the earliest invertebrates: crustaceans and mollusks, worms and jellyfish. The similarity of fossils found in western Europe and North America's east coast supports the theory of continental drift.

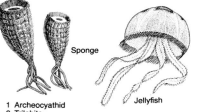
Sponge
Jellyfish

1 Archeocyathid
2 Trilobite
3 Arthropod
4 Annelid worm
5 Sea cucumber

Late Ordovician (440 million years ago). As North America slowly rotated toward Eurasia, shallow tropical seas flooded the continents. An arc of volcanic islands along Canada's east coast preceded the uplift of an eastern mountain chain. Two marine animal groups dominated the period: bryozoans, plantlike creatures of various shapes from stems to mosslike colonies; and brachiopods or "lamp shells," once numbering 30,000 species. In placid shallows appeared jawless fishes, the first vertebrates.

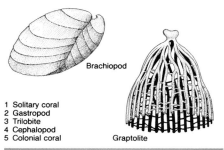
Brachiopod
Graptolite

1 Solitary coral
2 Gastropod
3 Trilobite
4 Cephalopod
5 Colonial coral

Late Devonian (360 million years ago). The triumph of the vertebrates began with the Devonian "age of fishes." Five classes had evolved: the jawless fishes, represented today only by lampreys and hagfishes; the jawed armored fishes and spiny sharks, both extinct; the true sharks, skates and rays; and the bony fishes. On land, small plants and rootless trees crowned with leaflike fronds sprouted in abundance. Lush swamps left a legacy of coal, oil, and natural gas which underlies much of North America. Forests teemed with air-breathers, such as spiders, ancestral dragonflies and some 800,000 species of insects that survive today.

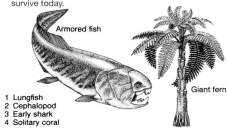
Armored fish
Giant fern

1 Lungfish
2 Cephalopod
3 Early shark
4 Solitary coral

Permian (230 million years ago). The drifting continents came together to form the single supercontinent Pangaea. A jarring collision with northern Africa uplifted North America's east coast, where volcanoes towered over baking deserts. Previously isolated faunas came into contact, causing competition and widespread extinctions. The union of the continents drained shallow seas, exposing continental shelves and reducing favored marine environments. As marine species waned, land-dwelling amphibians and reptiles such as Dimetrodon (*below*) diversified.

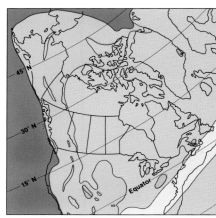
Conifer
Cordaites

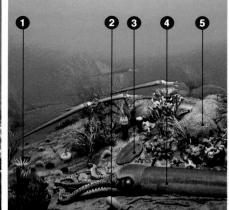

The Climatic Pendulum

Fossil evidence shows that world temperatures have swung many times during past ages (*below*). The coalfields of British Columbia, Saskatchewan, and Nova Scotia, and the oil reserves of Alberta are evidence of a much warmer and wetter climate during several past epochs; southern Ontario's moraines and drumlins mark the paths of great glacial ice sheets that covered North America in other ages.

These temperature changes were never large, but the earth's climate is so finely tuned that a shift of a few degrees could upset the balance. A rise of 5°C would melt polar ice caps, drowning the continents; a 5°C fall could lock the earth in an ice age. Fluctuations are normal—scientists calculate that ice ages have occurred at least four times in the last billion years, perhaps coinciding with some greater galactic cycle.

Earth's climate is influenced by even minute variations in solar activity, atmospheric conditions and shifts in the earth's orbit or tilt, as well as developments on its surface. In the Precambrian, seas were shallow and landmasses low, and both precipitation and the sun's warmth spread easily around the globe. The uplift of mountain ranges and the draining of vast inland seas in later ages brought about today's complex weather patterns and diverse climatic zones.

Canada's climate has swung more drastically than the chart indicates. Propelled by sluggish currents in the upper mantle, North America has drifted through various latitudes, from the equator to the North Pole.

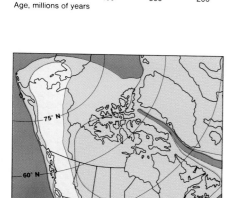

Dikes, Faults, and Dormant Volcanoes

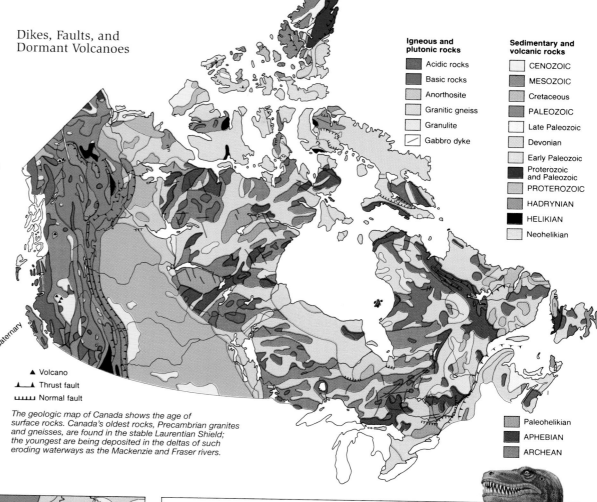

Igneous and plutonic rocks
- Acidic rocks
- Basic rocks
- Anorthosite
- Granitic gneiss
- Granulite
- Gabbro dyke

Sedimentary and volcanic rocks
- CENOZOIC
- MESOZOIC
- Cretaceous
- PALEOZOIC
- Late Paleozoic
- Devonian
- Early Paleozoic
- Proterozoic and Paleozoic
- PROTEROZOIC
- HADRYNIAN
- HELIKIAN
- Neohelikian

- Paleohelikian
- APHEBIAN
- ARCHEAN

▲ Volcano
⊥⊥⊥ Thrust fault
⊔⊔⊔ Normal fault

The geologic map of Canada shows the age of surface rocks. Canada's oldest rocks, Precambrian granites and gneisses, are found in the stable Laurentian Shield; the youngest are being deposited in the deltas of such eroding waterways as the Mackenzie and Fraser rivers.

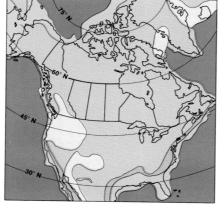

Late Jurassic (150 million years ago). The age of reptiles began as the great landmass of Pangaea began the slow breakup into the continents of today. Dinosaurs evolved in bewildering variety: long-necked vegetarians such as Brachiosaurus (*below*), fierce predators, leather-winged gliders, bizarre creatures with bony armor. They found living room and plentiful food supplies on Jurassic plains and in widespread tropical jungles dominated by tall conifers, delicate tree ferns and mosses, and palmlike cycads.

Early Tertiary (50 million years ago). In North America, the Rockies rose, high plains formed in the Midwest, and forests gave way to spreading grasslands. Oaks, maples and hickories joined the rich forests of pines, palms and cycads. Huge lakes flooded the plains, teeming with perches, gars, and other forerunners of modern freshwater fishes. The 100-million-year reign of the dinosaurs had ended abruptly. In their place emerged a new group: warm-blooded mammals, such as Uintatherium and primitive horses (*below*), descendants of shrewlike Jurassic ancestors. On North American plains roamed ancestral hyenas, marmots, squirrels, and Smilodectes, an early primate.

Ischyrotomus
(marmot)

Mesonyx
(hyena)

When Reptiles Ruled

The Mesozoic Era was an age of giants, especially in subtropical North America where dinosaurs grew to unprecedented size—ranging in length up to 25 metres. Reptiles, unlike earlier species, were not dependent on water for reproduction, and moved freely inland. Most were vegetarians, browsing on the lush greenery of cypress swamps and conifer forests; others preyed on their more peaceable cousins. Tyrannosaurus rex stood 6 metres high, the largest predator ever to walk on land, and had teeth the size of railway spikes. Apatasaurus was 15 metres long and weighed as much as 10 large elephants.

Giant reptiles also ruled the seas, including the seaway that bisected the continent. Long-necked plesiosaurs sculled slowly along the surface. Below swam marine lizards called mosasaurs, fishlike ichthyosaurs and giant turtles.

Suddenly, 65 million years ago, the dinosaurs were gone. Their extinction—whether from climatic change, continental drift, competition from mammals, or celestial phenomenon such as an impacting comet—remains one of nature's greatest mysteries.

Struthiomimus

Albertosaurus

Triceratops

Lambeosaurus

Alberta's Red Deer Badlands (left), once a land of forests and floodplains, now yield fossil treasures. Here roamed the beaked "ostrich-mimic" Struthiomimus; the ferocious predator Albertosaurus; horned Triceratops; and duck-billed Lambeosaurus, whose skeleton (above) was unearthed near Manyberries, Alta.

How the Ice Age Shaped Canada

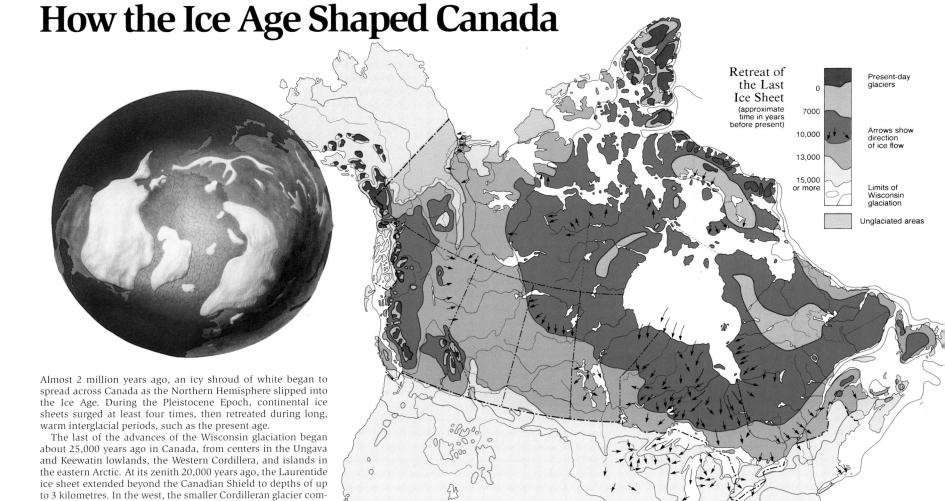

Almost 2 million years ago, an icy shroud of white began to spread across Canada as the Northern Hemisphere slipped into the Ice Age. During the Pleistocene Epoch, continental ice sheets surged at least four times, then retreated during long, warm interglacial periods, such as the present age.

The last of the advances of the Wisconsin glaciation began about 25,000 years ago in Canada, from centers in the Ungava and Keewatin lowlands, the Western Cordillera, and islands in the eastern Arctic. At its zenith 20,000 years ago, the Laurentide ice sheet extended beyond the Canadian Shield to depths of up to 3 kilometres. In the west, the smaller Cordilleran glacier complex stretched from the Rockies to the Pacific. The glaciers met, and for centuries formed a vast barrier from coast to coast.

Both coming and going, the ice reshaped Canada. Advancing slowly but irresistibly, it ground rocks into pebbles and pebbles into clay, and bulldozed tremendous quantities of rock and earth over the land. As temperatures warmed and the ice retreated at a sluggish 30 kilometres per century, embedded debris was exposed and dropped in the wake of the melting mass. Ice-gouged river channels and lake bottoms flooded with meltwater, and many of today's familiar landmarks were created or re-exposed—the Great Lakes, Niagara Falls, Lake Winnipeg, and Atlantic Canada's rocky coast.

The Ice Age also influenced animal life in Canada. The growing ice sheets and intense cold squeezed life zones southward into narrowing bands, and withdrew water from the oceans, lowering the global sea level by 120 metres. A land connection emerged where now the Bering Strait separates Asia from North America. Earlier plate movements had raised the Panamanian Isthmus, creating a land link to South America. Animals—including people—could now migrate between the continents.

Why the Ice Came; Will It Return?

Slowly, during the late Tertiary, temperatures veered downward. In the North, ice caps grew larger as winter snowfall outpaced summer melting. Under the pressure of its own weight, the ice spread from centers in Canada, Greenland, Northern Europe, and Siberia.

Scientists can only speculate why the earth's climate suddenly shifted. Continental drift, which affects ocean and atmospheric circulation, and the amount of solar radiation reaching the earth may have initiated the cooling trend. Perhaps the sun briefly dimmed, either from its own internal processes or from the passing of an interstellar dust cloud. Other theories include shifts in the earth's orbit or tilt, meteorite impact, the position of the solar system, and polar wandering.

The earth may be due for another glacial advance. Some scientists believe that today's warmer weather is only an interglacial reprieve, and that the ice may surge again within 10,000 years.

Beringia—An Natural Haven for Ice Age Animals

Across the Bering and Panamanian continental links coursed a two-way traffic of Ice-Age animals. Moose, wapiti, musk-ox, brown bear, wolf and other species came from Eurasia; ground sloths and armadillos arrived from South America. Some indigenous species, such as ancestral camels and horses, migrated north and south to other continents, but died out in North America.

During the Ice Age, Beringia —named for the Bering Strait— included the Yukon, Alaska, and northeastern Siberia. Mountains sheltered it from the North American ice sheets, and a Eurasian climate kept it relatively dry. The grasslands of the Yukon and Alaska offered a haven for people and beasts, some of which are depicted in greater-than-life concentration at right.

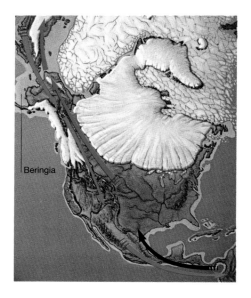

Beringia

1 Arctic ground squirrel
2 Caribou
3 Brown lemming
4 Red fox
5 Horse
6 Badger
7 Saiga antelope
8 Dall sheep
9 Arctic fox
10 Alaskan tundra hare
11 Lynx
12 Helmeted musk-ox (female and calf)
13 Large-horned bison
14 Helmeted musk-ox (male)
15 Ground sloth
16 People
17 Moose
18 Woolly mammoth
19 Great North American short-faced hare
20 Wolf
21 Wolverine
22 Grizzly bear
23 American cat
24 Musk-ox
25 Wapiti (American elk)
26 Camel
27 American mastodon
28 Scimitar cat

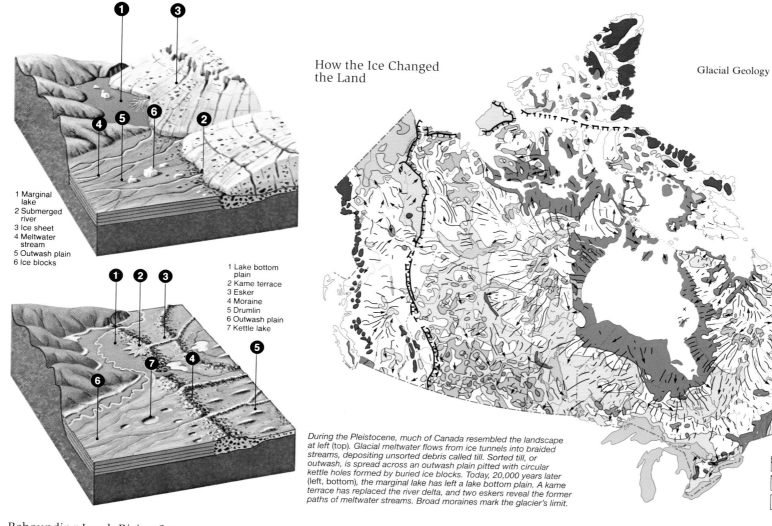

How the Ice Changed the Land

1 Marginal lake
2 Submerged river
3 Ice sheet
4 Meltwater stream
5 Outwash plain
6 Ice blocks

1 Lake bottom plain
2 Kame terrace
3 Esker
4 Moraine
5 Drumlin
6 Outwash plain
7 Kettle lake

Glacial Geology

- Existing glaciers
- Unglaciated areas
- Areas in part unglaciated
- Areas once covered by seas
- Areas once covered by glacial lakes
- Outwash plains
- Eskers, kames
- Ribbed or hummocky terrain
- Moraines

210 Direction of glacial flow (generalized)

Western limit of Laurentide ice sheet

Eastern limit of Cordilleran ice sheet

During the Pleistocene, much of Canada resembled the landscape at left (top). Glacial meltwater flows from ice tunnels into braided streams, depositing unsorted debris called till. Sorted till, or outwash, is spread across an outwash plain pitted with circular kettle holes formed by buried ice blocks. Today, 20,000 years later (left, bottom), the marginal lake has left a lake bottom plain. A kame terrace has replaced the river delta, and two eskers reveal the former paths of meltwater streams. Broad moraines mark the glacier's limit.

Rebounding Land, Rising Seas

Millions of tonnes of ice covered Canada during the Wisconsin glaciation—a burden so massive that it pushed the rock foundations of the crust down into the plastic mantle on which they float. For every 3.6 metres of ice above it, the crust sagged approximately one metre.

Relieved of this tremendous burden as glaciers receded, the crust began to spring back to its present position. This rebound is still going on (below, left). The north shore of Lake Ontario is rising above the south

shore at the rate of 10 centimetres per century. Hudson Bay, where the ice first accumulated and disappeared last, will eventually reemerge as dry land.

Glaciers also alter nature's balance by locking up vast amounts of water as ice. Today's glaciers hold less than 2 percent of the earth's water supply (below, right); Pleistocene ice sheets held more than 5 percent—an extra 40.5 million cubic kilometres. Sea levels dropped by some 120 metres, draining much of the shallow continental shelves.

As the ice waned, meltwater swelled rivers and lakes, altering drainage patterns and raising sea levels. Glacial Lake Agassiz once covered most of southern and central Manitoba and filled the Red River valley of Minnesota and North Dakota. (Lake Winnipeg is a remnant, as is the flat, fertile soil of the Prairies.) The sediments of other ancestral lakes, into which glacial streams and the newly exposed land drained, form the lake plains of the Great Lakes region today, including all of southwestern

Ontario. Bond Lake, north of Toronto, was left by a single block of melting ice.

The most spectacular monument to the action of the ice is the Great Lakes. All four glacial advances played a part in producing them, each gouging the basins deeper until the earth's largest bodies of fresh water were formed. Niagara Falls was born as receding glaciers revealed a channel between Lakes Erie and Ontario. Erosion will eventually reduce the falls to low cataracts.

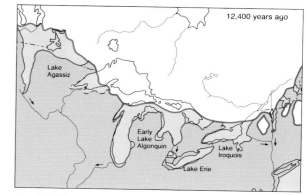

About 12,400 years ago, the ancestral Great Lakes discharged to the south—down the Illinois River to the Mississippi.

210 Maximum height of post-glacial rebound (in metres above present sea level)

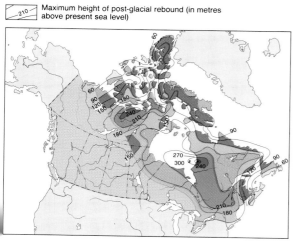

Distribution of the World's Water

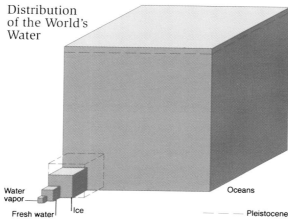

Water vapor
Fresh water
Ice
Oceans
Pleistocene

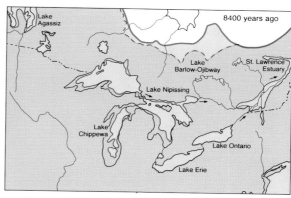

By 8400 years ago, drainage patterns had changed and the lakes discharged to the sea via the St. Lawrence estuary.

Anatomy of a River of Ice

Snow crystals

Firn (granular snow)

Glacier ice

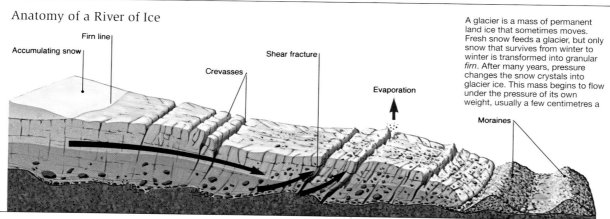

Firn line
Accumulating snow
Crevasses
Shear fracture
Evaporation
Moraines

A glacier is a mass of permanent land ice that sometimes moves. Fresh snow feeds a glacier, but only snow that survives from winter to winter is transformed into granular firn. After many years, pressure changes the snow crystals into glacier ice. This mass begins to flow under the pressure of its own weight, usually a few centimetres a

day, but sometimes "galloping" at 10 to 100 times its normal rate. Above its firn line, which advances and retreats in response to climate, the glacier grows. Below, it wastes away as new snow evaporates or tumbles down in avalanches. The upper surface, rent with crevasses, flows slightly faster than the lower portion, which grinds against the land. Rockslides pile rubble on the advancing glacier; beneath, pieces of bedrock are plucked, locked in the ice and dragged along. Gradually, the debris is plowed forward into moraines. Near the glacier's rubble-choked snout is the ablation zone, or area of melting.

13

The Forces That Control Our Climate

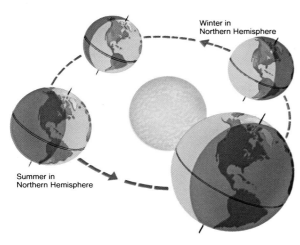

Winter in
Northern Hemisphere

Summer in
Northern Hemisphere

The earth has two motions that affect climate. Once a day, it rotates on its axis; once a year, it revolves around the sun. At any time during its daily rotation, half the globe faces the sun and half is in darkness. The west-to-east movement also steers the world's winds and ocean currents.

The annual trip around the sun accounts for the seasons. Because the earth is tilted on its axis, the amount of light—and heat—reaching any area changes with the time of year. When the North Pole slants away from the sun, it is winter in the Northern Hemisphere: daylight hours are shorter, and the sun's rays strike at the greatest angle.

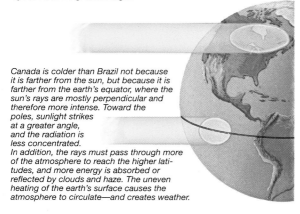

Canada is colder than Brazil not because it is farther from the sun, but because it is farther from the earth's equator, where the sun's rays are mostly perpendicular and therefore more intense. Toward the poles, sunlight strikes at a greater angle, and the radiation is less concentrated. In addition, the rays must pass through more of the atmosphere to reach the higher latitudes, and more energy is absorbed or reflected by clouds and haze. The uneven heating of the earth's surface causes the atmosphere to circulate—and creates weather.

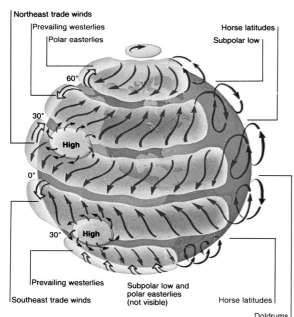

Northeast trade winds
Prevailing westerlies
Polar easterlies
Horse latitudes
Subpolar low
60°
30°
High
0°
30°
High
Prevailing westerlies
Subpolar low and polar easterlies (not visible)
Southeast trade winds
Horse latitudes
Doldrums

Great Rivers of air

The earth's average temperature is a mild 14°C, but actual temperatures vary widely: flowers bloom all winter in Victoria, but the sun barely shines in Inuvik.

Canada loses more heat to space each year than it receives from the sun. Despite this loss, the weather does not get colder and colder each year because the circulation of the atmosphere constantly redistributes heat.

Hot air in the tropics expands and rises, creating a low-pressure area around the equator (the hot, humid doldrums). Heavier, cooler air from high-pressure areas to the north and south sweeps in toward the equator, producing the steady, gentle trade winds.

Warm equatorial air cools as

it flows toward the poles. Around latitude 30° N and S it begins to sink to earth, creating belts of alternating calm air and weak breezes called the horse latitudes. Here, centered over the oceans, are large "cells" of high pressure where air spirals outward. On the eastern side of the cells the air flows toward the equator; on the western side it flows poleward, joining the changeable westerlies.

Heavy, frigid polar air flows toward the equator. Areas where polar easterlies and prevailing westerlies clash—the subpolar lows—are among the stormiest on earth.

The earth's spin deflects the movement of all air currents—in the Northern Hemisphere to the east, and in the Southern Hemisphere to the west.

Climate affects every aspect of life in Canada. Fogs shrouding the coast of Newfoundland often disrupt fishing and shipping for days. Toronto can be a steam bath in July, a deep freeze in January. Heavy rainfalls produce lush forests that supply jobs in logging for more than a fifth of British Columbia's work force. The Canadian climate—its sun and rain, blistering heat and bone-chilling cold—is a combination of the four main factors that control our climate: the sun, the earth's position in space, the earth's atmosphere and its landforms.

The sun is one natural resource man will never exhaust. In billion years this thermonuclear furnace will still radiate as much energy as it does today. Most of the radiation disappears into space, but the amount reaching this planet—about one two-billionth—provides more energy in a minute than all mankind uses in a year. The earth itself influences the climate by its orbit, its tilt and its daily rotation. These factors determine how much sunlight—and heat—the earth receives, and where.

The atmosphere plays a crucial role in regulating climate. Heat is distributed unequally about the earth, and the atmosphere's attempt to redistribute it, through massive movements of air, results in the daily phenomenon called weather, which is unpredictable and ever-changing. (Climatologists now say climate—the average weather pattern observed over many years—is also changing, dynamic, and variable.) The atmosphere's thin veil shuttles water vapor about the globe, and insulates the earth from the cold of space and the scorching rays of the sun.

The earth's mountains, plains, lakes, and oceans also influence climate. Canada's vast size and varied landscape result in weather that swings from one extreme to another. One summer day is warm and breezy, the next oppressively hot and humid. In a few hours, winter's blue skies and crisp, clean air can give way to bitter cold and howling winds. But just when the weather makes Canada seem uninhabitable, it turns delightful again. This is the climate Canadians endure—and appreciate.

The Atmospheric Engine

Although solar rays travel 150 million kilometres to reach the earth, barely half penetrate the protective blanket that surrounds the planet. Averaged worldwide, the atmosphere's ozone, water vapor and dust absorb about 17 percent of the sun's rays (1), including most of the lethal ultraviolet rays. Approximately 32 percent of the rays are returned unused to space. Some are scattered by dust (2), but most bounce off the upper surface of clouds (3). The earth's surface reflects an average 2 percent of the sun's

rays (4), but actual amounts vary with ground cover. A dense forest soaks up almost all the sunlight that reaches it; fresh snow may reflect 90 percent.

About 19 percent of the sun's direct rays are finally absorbed by the earth (5). A further 28 percent reach the ground as

diffused light, filtered through clouds (6) or dust (7).

Once absorbed, the sun's rays are converted to heat, which warms the earth and is radiated into the atmosphere. Some heat energy escapes into space (8), but most is captured by water vapor and carbon dioxide (9), then reradiated

back to earth (10). Meanwhile, winds (11) and ocean currents (12) redistribute the sun's warmth.

About a third of the heat is lifted into the atmosphere (13), either by air currents or by evaporation (see Water's Endless Cycle, opposite page).

Eventually, every ray of sunlight the earth receives is radiated back into space (14). But before this energy leaves the atmosphere, it has changed from light to heat to motion—the winds and water currents.

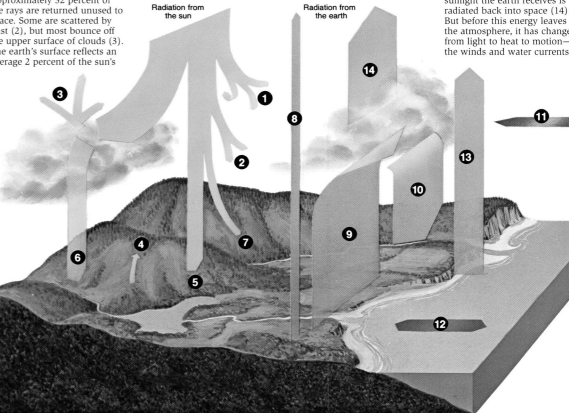

Radiation from the sun

Radiation from the earth

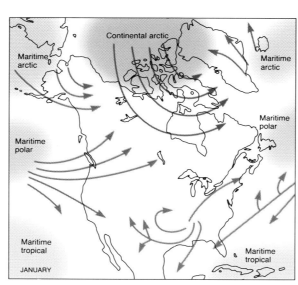

JANUARY

Winds carry great bodies of air across land and sea. Each air mass has uniform temperature and moisture throughout, taking these characteristics from the area over which it forms—usually a vast landmass or an ocean.

In the maps above, colored areas show the sources of air masses that affect Canada; arrows indicate their most frequent direction of wind flow. Winter winds transport continental arctic air masses to much of Canada,

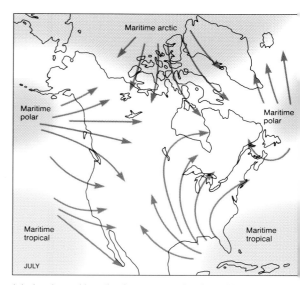

JULY

bringing clear, cold weather. In summer, cool, moist maritime arctic air sweeps down to provide relief from heat waves. Mild, humid maritime polar air delivers rain and snow to the Rocky Mountains, and occasional fog and cloud to the east coast of Canada. Maritime tropical air from the Pacific Ocean seldom reaches Canada, but to the east, warm, humid air masses from the Gulf of Mexico sometimes bring snowstorms in January and hot, muggy weather in July.

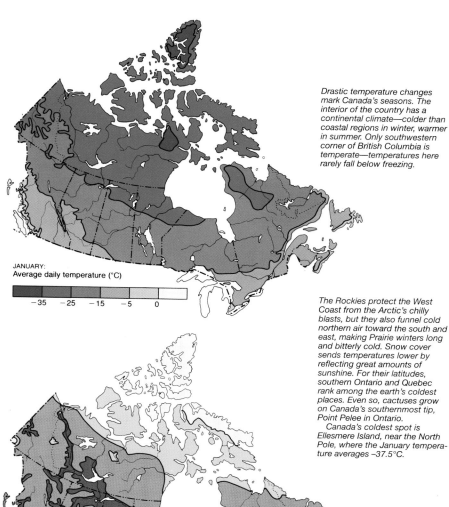

JANUARY:
Average daily temperature (°C)

-35   -25   -15   -5   0

Drastic temperature changes mark Canada's seasons. The interior of the country has a continental climate—colder than coastal regions in winter, warmer in summer. Only southwestern corner of British Columbia is temperate—temperatures here rarely fall below freezing.

The Rockies protect the West Coast from the Arctic's chilly blasts, but they also funnel cold northern air toward the south and east, making Prairie winters long and bitterly cold. Snow cover sends temperatures lower by reflecting great amounts of sunshine. For their latitudes, southern Ontario and Quebec rank among the earth's coldest places. Even so, cactuses grow on Canada's southernmost tip, Point Pelee in Ontario.

Canada's coldest spot is Ellesmere Island, near the North Pole, where the January temperature averages –37.5°C.

JULY:
Average daily temperature (°C)

5   10   15   20

Water's Endless Cycle

The amount of water on earth is approximately 1.36 billion cubic kilometres. Water in ice caps and glaciers may remain frozen for centuries, but the rest of the world's supply, in oceans, lakes, rivers, and the atmosphere, is constantly recycled.

The water cycle transforms salt water (97 percent of the earth's water) into fresh. Water evaporates from the oceans, and the circulation of the atmosphere sweeps moist air over land. There the water vapor condenses and falls as rain or snow.

Some precipitation evaporates while falling; some is caught by vegetation and held until it evaporates. Water in the soil either evaporates or is taken in by plants, which transfer it to the air (transpiration).

As runoff, some water joins streams, rivers, and lakes; some seeps down to become groundwater. Both eventually drain to the sea.

Water vapor helps redistribute the sun's warmth. Tropical heat causes much evaporation. The resulting water vapor, transported poleward, carries with it heat. As it cools and condenses, great quantities of heat are released.

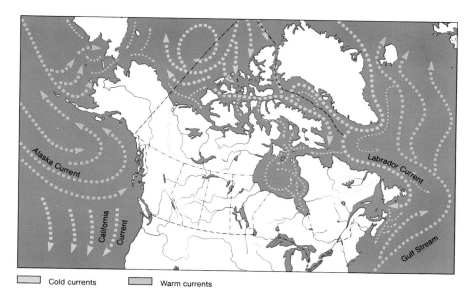

Alaska Current
California Current
Labrador Current
Gulf Stream

Cold currents   Warm currents

The Weather-Making Oceans

Water heats up more slowly than land but retains its warmth longer. Thus oceans can absorb heat in tropical zones and transfer it, by means of ocean currents, to cooler lands. Both wind and the earth's rotation push ocean currents on their global journeys. The earth's spin causes the currents to move in great circular eddies.

The Alaska Current tempers the climate of British Columbia and Alaska. Huge masses of warm water bring mild winters unusual for such high latitudes.

The climate in the Atlantic Provinces is harsher than that of the West Coast, since prevailing winds blow much of the mild maritime air out to sea. The Labrador Current brings frigid Arctic water—and icebergs—past Baffin Island to Labrador and Newfoundland. Off the Grand Banks, the current collides with the warm Gulf Stream and fog results.

Smaller bodies of water also affect climate. The Great Lakes and Hudson Bay moderate winter temperatures in adjacent areas by warming the air. But additional moisture due to evaporation is transported to land, and heavy snowfalls result.

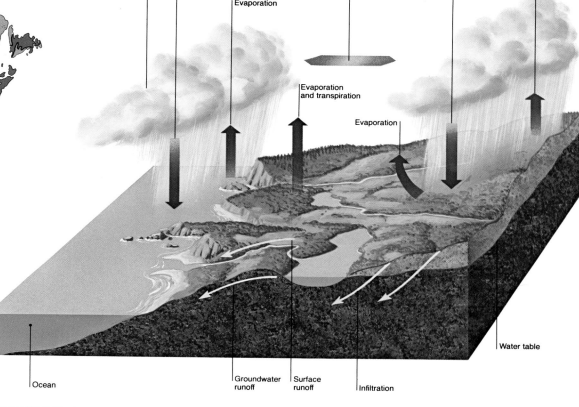

Condensation
Precipitation
Evaporation
Moist air
Precipitation
Evaporation
Evaporation and transpiration
Evaporation
Ocean
Groundwater runoff
Surface runoff
Infiltration
Water table

Patterns of Rain and Snow

Canada's heaviest precipitation falls on the Pacific and Atlantic coasts. (Figures for precipitation—rain and snow—are the sum of total rainfall plus one-tenth the depth of freshly fallen snow.) Parts of British Columbia receive more than 3200 millimetres a year. The mountains here wring so much moisture from the air that on their leeward sides, in the rain shadow, luxuriant forests give way to sagebrush and cactus.

The rain shadow effect also produces occasional droughts on the Prairies. However, this region's heaviest rainfall usually comes in May and June, when wheat needs it most.

Most precipitation in the Arctic—Canada's driest area—falls in summer showers. Winter snowfall is surprisingly light.

Moist air from exotic climes—the Gulf of Mexico and Caribbean Sea—causes abundant rain and snow to fall on most of eastern Canada.

Average annual precipitation (mm)

200   400   800   1600   2400

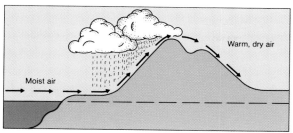

Moist air   Warm, dry air

The Ingredients of Precipitation

Precipitation occurs when moist air is lifted and cooled, causing water vapor to condense and fall. Three common conditions produce precipitation over land. The first is brought about by the earth's landforms. Here *(above)* a moisture-laden wind encounters a mountain and is forced upward. The air cools as it rises, and precipitation results. On the lee side of slopes, the air descends, warms and is able to hold more water. This often brings a dramatic reduction in rainfall—the rain shadow effect.

Second, a layer of cold air can trigger precipitation. Since cold air is denser than warm air, it remains close to the ground. Warm air colliding with it is pushed upward and rain occurs where the two air masses meet.

Uneven heating of the ground often causes air to rise spontaneously—a third cause of precipitation. The sun warms a field, for instance, more quickly than it does a forest. A balloon of hot air begins to rise, cooling as it ascends. Condensation then releases heat, which sends the balloon even higher, until cold air causes moisture to fall as rain.

The Zigs and Zags of Our Weather

Weather lore has been passed from generation to generation through stories and proverbs, some less reliable than others. No one would really pack his winter coat away if the groundhog missed its shadow on February 2, or buy more heating oil according to the layers of an onion. But often there is more than a grain of truth in weather lore, legend, and litany. It is true, for example, that "the moon with a circle brings water in her beak." High cirrus clouds—which can form a halo around the moon or sun when ice crystals scatter light—are usually forerunners of rain or storm.

Scientific forecasting started to replace folklore in the 19th century. A network of stations across Canada began to issue storm warnings in the 1870s. When widespread telegraph lines made distributing information easier, forecasts were printed in morning newspapers. Ship's captains and, later, airplane pilots especially needed reliable weather reports.

Computers, their memory banks loaded with data from around the world, now help predict the weather. Satellites send pictures of cloud formations from vantage points in space. But science has not made us masters of the weather. Farmers still plant, irrigate, and harvest according to reports of rainfall, drought and frost. Construction workers stop pouring concrete when the temperature dips below freezing. Even the baseball manager's choice of a pitcher is influenced by weather: curve-balls are more easily thrown when air pressure is high; low pressure is better for fastballs. Unable to control the weather, neither can man predict it with much certainty. Although he can be reasonably sure of tomorrow's weather, long-range forecasts—even a week ahead—are still beyond man's grasp.

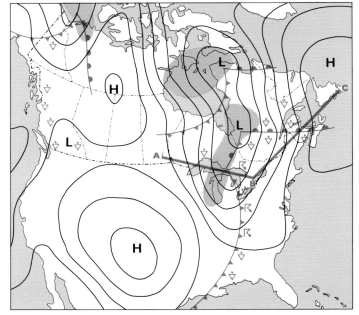

H	Center of high pressure
L	Center of low pressure

Warm front

Cold front

Stationary front

Trowal

Rain showers

Thunderstorm

Continuous precipitation

Fair Weather or Foul? Reading a Weather Map

At least four times a day, more than 250 observers across Canada record atmospheric pressure, cloud cover, winds, precipitation, temperature and humidity: information used to compile a weather map, and to make the next day's forecast.

Differences in the weather are the result of different air masses. Generally, cold air sweeps down from the north, warm air moves up from the south; moist air comes from the ocean, and dry air from the land. Most weather changes occur along the fronts where two air masses collide. Cold air is heavy; when it meets warm air, it nudges—or shoves—the warm air aloft. Clouds that appear when rising air cools and condenses may produce rain, snow or thunderstorms.

A weather map's curving black lines, called isobars, link all points of equal pressure, the

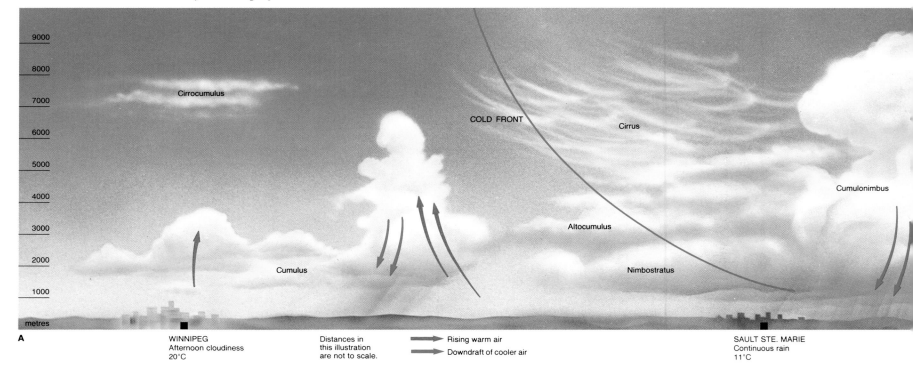

WINNIPEG	Afternoon cloudiness 20°C

Distances in this illustration are not to scale.

→ Rising warm air
→ Downdraft of cooler air

SAULT STE. MARIE
Continuous rain
11°C

Days of Warmth and Sunshine

Canadians must cope with cold and snow, sealing homes against chilly blasts and venturing out in heavy clothes. Despite a love for winter sports, most Canadians welcome the warmth and sunny skies of summer.

Temperature is a good indicator of vacation weather: in high summer, that period when the daily maximum is above 18°C, swimming and other outdoor recreations are popular. The

map of annual hours of bright sunshine shows Canada's sunniest spots. July is the sunniest month for most of Canada.

In coastal British Columbia, a long, mild summer with gentle breezes brings ideal boating weather to the Strait of Georgia. But farther north is Canada's cloudiest city, Prince Rupert, where the sun shines an average 120 hours in July—and 24 hours in December.

The Prairies have long, hot summers. Canada's highest temperature ever was recorded here in 1937: 45°C at both Midale and Yellow Grass, Sask.

Uncomfortable, humid heat occurs mostly in the large cities of the East. Ideal cottage country is found around the Great Lakes and the thousands of smaller lakes in southern Ontario and Quebec. Summers here are usually warmer than anywhere else in Canada.

In the Atlantic provinces, warm days are fewer due to the icy Labrador Current, and skies are dimmed by fogs that roll in off the ocean. Parts of northern Canada have no high summer at all: despite 24-hour sunshine, cold northern seas and permafrost keep the summer months chilly.

Days of Rain and Storm

Rain revives parched gardens, but spoils picnics and sometimes washes topsoil away. When a thunderstorm breaks, nature can be truly destructive. Lightning sparks forest fires that destroy half a million hectares of trees in Canada each year; deluging rains, combined with snowmelt, can cause peaceful waterways such as the St. John and Red rivers to flood thousands of homes.

Most thunderstorms occur in summer, triggered by heat that

causes moist, unstable air to rise. Rainy periods vary throughout Canada. The Pacific Coast has pronounced wet and dry seasons. During sodden Vancouver winters, rain falls a third of the time, and the ground is seldom dry.

Thunderstorms are rare on the West Coast, but frequent during hot Prairie summers. Those with hail are so common in Alberta that the area between

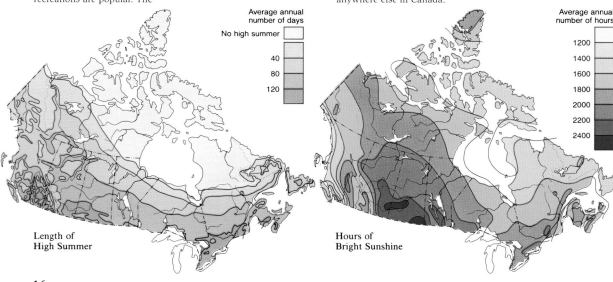

Length of **High Summer**

Average annual number of days

No high summer

40
80
120

Hours of **Bright Sunshine**

Average annual number of hours

1200
1400
1600
1800
2000
2200
2400

Days With **Precipitation**

Average annual number of days

80
120
160
200
240

same way lines on a contour map join points of equal elevation. Winds blow along the isobars. The closer the lines, the stronger the winds.

The arrival of a high-pressure area generally means sunny weather. Low-pressure areas, or depressions, bring unstable, rising air currents that cause rain and snow. Much of Canada's unsettled weather is brought by vast depressions advancing from west to east.

The map at left describes the weather on an actual June day; the illustration below depicts that weather between Winnipeg and St. John's. A weak low-pressure area lies over the West Coast—"weak" because a lack of isobars indicates that pressure is almost uniform throughout. Skies are clear over all three Prairie provinces—weather usually associated with a high. Cumulus clouds over Winnipeg are caused by afternoon heat and warm air billowing upward.

Much of Ontario and Quebec is experiencing bad weather from

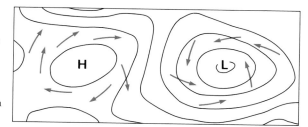

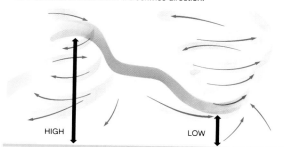

Low-pressure areas are also called cyclones — not tropical storms, but depressions that bring changeable weather. Winds whirl around a pressure system; in the Northern Hemisphere, they spiral counterclockwise toward the center of a cyclone. An anticyclone is a high-pressure system where winds whirl outward in a clockwise direction.

a large trough of low pressure. Two low-pressure centres can be seen over Quebec; a third is forming over Sault Ste. Marie. A thunderstorm rages in this area, where warm and cold air masses meet. Air shoots upward, then is dragged downwind to form an anvil-shaped thunderhead on the ominous cumulo-nimbus clouds. Behind the thunderstorm, the air is cold and a continuous rain falls from low, gray nimbostratus clouds. Farther west, altocumulus and cirrus clouds dim the sky.

Cloud formations could act as a storm warning to observant Montrealers, now enjoying warm, humid weather with mostly clear skies. Wispy cirrus clouds mean increasing moisture aloft, and signal possible rain. Most of the Maritimes is experiencing intermittent showers associated with a warm front. Altocumulus clouds threaten to bring showers to Charlottetown, while St. John's, under the influence of a high-pressure area, has sunny skies.

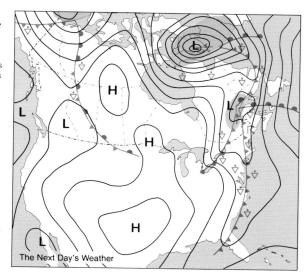

The Next Day's Weather

In 24 hours the high-pressure area over the Prairies provinces has shifted east, bringing clear weather to northern and central portions of Ontario. The low-pressure centre that formed yesterday over Sault Ste. Marie has merged with the low pressure over central Quebec, causing rain over Gaspé and the St. Lawrence's north shore. A trowal—"trough of warm air aloft"—in the deep low over Baffin Island is also producing precipitation.

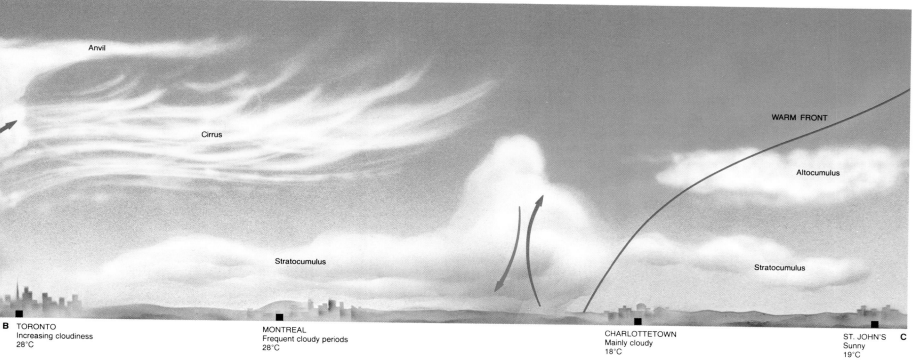

Anvil

Cirrus

WARM FRONT

Altocumulus

Stratocumulus

Stratocumulus

B TORONTO
Increasing cloudiness
28°C

MONTREAL
Frequent cloudy periods
28°C

CHARLOTTETOWN
Mainly cloudy
18°C

ST. JOHN'S **C**
Sunny
19°C

Calgary and Edmonton is called "hailstone alley." Tornadoes also occur: 60 to 100 are reported each year, most in the Prairies and southern Ontario. Hurricanes cause occasional damage, but few reach Canada with their destructive power intact.

Winters are dry on the Prairies, but in southern Ontario and Quebec both long dry and long wet spells are rare. Southwestern Ontario has the most thunder and lightning: more than 30 days a year.

Though rainfall increases toward the east, the number of thunderstorms drops. Remnants of hurricanes may travel up the Atlantic coast, but Newfoundland averages only two to six thunderstorms a year.

The Arctic has the fewest days of rain; in some areas, thunderstorms have never been recorded. Here dryness and low temperatures keep air stable.

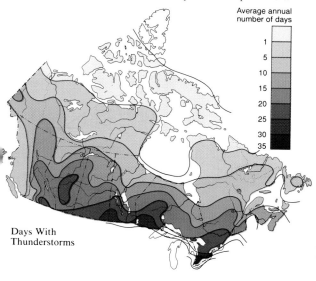

Days With
Thunderstorms

Average annual
number of days

	1
	5
	10
	15
	20
	25
	30
	35

A Change in the Weather: Man Versus Nature

Man has always longed to change the weather. In early days he modified his environment by huddling around fires and making clothes to keep warm. Modern man, having learned how to predict at least short-term weather, now seeks ways to change it.

Besides devising such creature comforts as central heating and air-conditioning, man is also trying to modify weather for the benefit of agriculture. He plants rows of trees to shield crops from wind, or sets out smudges when frost threatens his orchards. The most ambitious venture is rainmaking: injecting silver iodide into clouds to provide nuclei for raindrops. But its success is still hard to measure. In Alberta, where hailstorms destroy crops every year, meteorologists have studied the use of cloud seeding to suppress hail. The technique may also modify thunderstorms.

Scientists conceive of long-range plans to change the earth's climate permanently. But even if their plans could be carried out, the consequences must first be predicted. Weather is the result of subtle interactions of oceans, atmosphere, landforms and living creatures. A change in one element would surely change the whole.

Upside-Down Air Causes Urban Pollution

Winds usually disperse polluted air. But when cool air is trapped near the ground by a layer of warm air—a phenomenon known as temperature inversion—pollutants can accumulate. Toronto often suffers from smog while windier cities on the Prairies enjoy cleaner air.

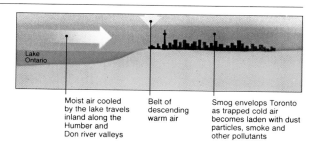

Lake Ontario

Moist air cooled by the lake travels inland along the Humber and Don river valleys

Belt of descending warm air

Smog envelops Toronto as trapped cold air becomes laden with dust particles, smoke and other pollutants

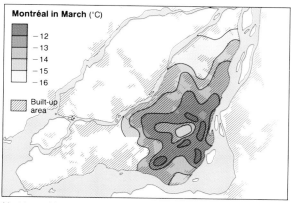

Montréal in March (°C)

	−12
	−13
	−14
	−15
	−16

Built-up area

Most large cities create a heat island—a stationary envelope of warm air. Heat escapes from buildings, is released by car exhausts and spewed out of factories. Bricks and concrete retain warmth longer than trees and soil: Mount Royal Park (above) remains a cool basin.

Man's greatest influence on the weather is unintentional. Polluted air reflects the sun's rays and cools the earth. Acid rain, carrying chemicals emitted by industry, harms forests and crops, and destroys aquatic life in lakes. Burning fossil fuels release carbon dioxide, causing the atmosphere to trap more heat radiated from the earth, and raising temperatures.

Long-term weather changes are still impossible to predict. Perhaps cooling caused by air pollution and heating caused by carbon dioxide will cancel each other out. A temperature increase of only a few degrees could melt polar ice caps and cause wide-scale flooding. But colder temperatures could devastate Canadian crops.

Living with Snow

"A few acres of snow" is how Voltaire described Canada. Summer always comes, but for many months snow does predominate, influencing our economy, recreation and culture. From back-breaking work with a shovel to the sophisticated equipment that keeps airport runways clear, countless dollars and hours of effort are spent in overcoming snow. Millions of dollars more are spent enjoying snow: on snowmobiles, ski vacations and the latest in winter fashions.

Despite the quantities of snow Canadians must deal with, few people know much about it. Most know which kind of snow is good for snowballs or skiing, but the English language, born in a moderate climate, has no way to express it. The Inuit, whose lives are linked with snow, have found words to describe it. For them, the snow that collects on trees is *qali*; snow on the ground, *api*; and dense, wind-packed snow, *upsik*. *Tumarínyiq* is their word for ripple marks sculpted by the wind. They know how snow varies in texture from place to place, and use this knowledge to survive for centuries in the Far North.

Though most southern Canadians don't think of snow as use-ful, like the Inuit they would find life difficult without it. Farmers appreciate the insulating value of snow, which limits frost penetration. Snow also acts as a natural fertilizer, spreading nourishing minerals over the soil. Pulp and paper companies make use of snow in the North to build thousands of kilometres of snow roads each winter. Some northern communities, isolated during summer, are easily accessible by snowmobile in winter. In spring, the melting of snowfields irrigates farms and replenishes town and city reservoirs. Animals use snow for its insulating qualities: many make their winter homes in snug burrows beneath its surface. And some creatures enjoy snow for its own sake. Bears and otters delight in snowslides; mink and weasels leap in and out of snowbanks like dolphins in water.

Snow transforms drab, leafless landscapes into scenes of still and silent beauty. Seldom is it white: it glitters on a cold, bright day, lies dull gray under overcast skies or urban grime, or deep purple in a shadowed drift. Snow is always changing, from a light shawl of delicate flakes to a mass of icy pellets. Each spring it melts; just as inevitably, it falls again next winter.

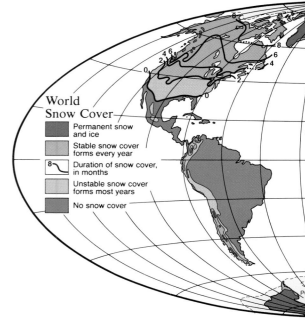

World Snow Cover
- Permanent snow and ice
- Stable snow cover forms every year
- Duration of snow cover, in months
- Unstable snow cover forms most years
- No snow cover

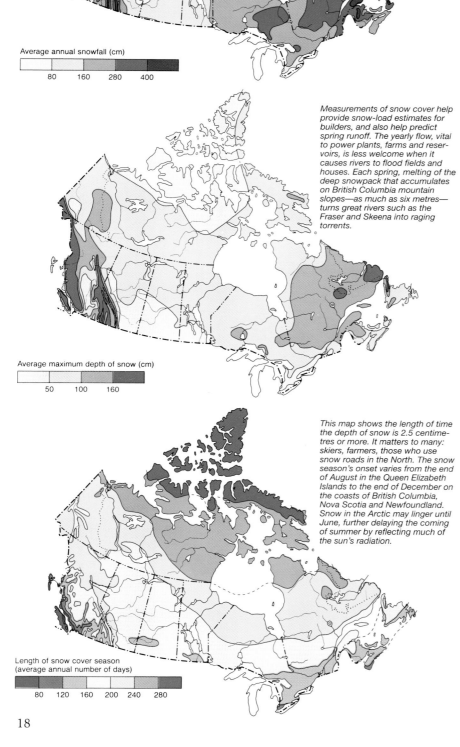

A snowfall map is never exact, since snow is difficult to measure. It drifts and blows, or melts as it hits the ground. Annual snowfalls in any one location vary widely: more snow may fall in one day than fell in the entire previous winter. An area southeast of Kitimat has the highest snowfalls: an average 1071 centimetres a year. Far to the north, on Ellesmere Island, Eureka has only 38 centimetres of snow a year—but it falls year-round.

Average annual snowfall (cm)
80 160 280 400

Measurements of snow cover help provide snow-load estimates for builders, and also help predict spring runoff. The yearly flow, vital to power plants, farms and reservoirs, is less welcome when it causes rivers to flood fields and houses. Each spring, melting of the deep snowpack that accumulates on British Columbia mountain slopes—as much as six metres—turns great rivers such as the Fraser and Skeena into raging torrents.

Average maximum depth of snow (cm)
50 100 160

This map shows the length of time the depth of snow is 2.5 centimetres or more. It matters to many: skiers, farmers, those who use snow roads in the North. The snow season's onset varies from the end of August in the Queen Elizabeth Islands to the end of December on the coasts of British Columbia, Nova Scotia and Newfoundland. Snow in the Arctic may linger until June, further delaying the coming of summer by reflecting much of the sun's radiation.

Length of snow cover season (average annual number of days)
80 120 160 200 240 280

Blizzards, Chinooks and an Arctic Semidesert

Canada's highest and lowest snowfalls occur in British Columbia. Parts of Vancouver Island's mild west coast often get less than 30 centimetres of snow a year, and rain soon clears the ground. Entire winters may pass without snow cover.

But when moist air from the Pacific Ocean is forced up by coastal and interior mountain ranges, record snowfalls result. Near Revelstoke, 2446 centimetres of snow fell during the winter of 1971-72.

Glaciers grow from snow that accumulates from one year to the next. Many form in Canada's loftiest range, the St. Elias Mountains of northwestern British Columbia and the Yukon, where snowfields lie year-round.

Snowfall on the Prairies is comparatively light, but blizzards—with bitter cold, high winds and driving snow—are common. Southwestern Alberta is often released dramatically from winter's grip by the wind known as a chinook (also called a "snow eater"). Warm, dry air from the Rockies can suddenly raise temperatures 20 degrees.

The Great Lakes trigger heavy snowfalls. Moisture evaporating from these vast bodies of water rises, condenses over the cold terrain, and deposits a belt of deep snow downwind. But southwestern tip of Ontario has a low annual snowfall: mild temperatures often bring rain instead of snow.

Both southern Ontario and Quebec lie in the path of most major winter storms crossing

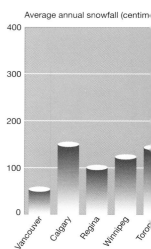

Average annual snowfall (centim
400
300
200
100
0
Vancouver Calgary Regina Winnipeg Toron

Most Canadian cities must wage campaigns against snow each winter. Fredericton snow is often heavy and wet, and Québec plows must negotiate steep, narrow streets; in Saskatoon, light snow is blown into hard, packed drifts. Montreal spends more than $54 million to clear almost 1995 kilometres of streets, while Vancouver spends an average $1,000,000 on 1385 kilometres.

The heavy work is done in a long procession: plows and graders scrape the snow into windrows; a blower scoops it up and discharges it into trucks, which haul the snow away to dumps or sewers. Despite this army of machines, few winters pass without one blizzard that strands airline passengers, jams traffic and brings unscheduled school holidays.

Salting the roads eases winter transportation in some cities, but creates other problems. Salt can harm plants and trees and contaminate water supplies; it also causes millions of dollars worth of damage by corroding vehicles.

Winter's Many Faces, Delightful and Destructive

Canadian winters shape Canadian living. Car owners spend millions each year on snow tires, antifreeze and repairs to salt-rusted vehicles. A Canadian invented the snowmobile: a tracked power toboggan that cruises over snowbanks. Canadians also pioneered the development of snowplows, making winter highway and rail travel possible.

Canadian architects design for a northern climate. A structure's exterior walls must be insulated against bitter cold, its roof solid enough to withstand heavy snow loads.

To aid construction, the Canadian building code provides estimates of snow loads across the country. Climatic records are used to determine the most likely maximum depth of snow. The weight of this much snow is calculated, using an average density, and to this is added the weight of any rain the snow might absorb—a particular hazard in spring.

Certain structures create snowdrifts. Porches or balconies beside higher roofs can collapse from collected snow. Poor design of large buildings may produce winds that deposit snow in towering piles that obstruct walks and entrances. Snow fences are sometimes used to collect snow before it reaches traveled areas, although barriers placed too close to a road can make drifting worse.

Engineers in Canada are studying snowdrift patterns. They build scale models of buildings, then simulate drifting with fine white sand carried by water as wind would carry snow. Their tests solve problems with existing buildings and help design new structures better suited to Canadian winters.

Snow load in a sheltered area

Wind

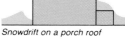

Snowdrift on a porch roof

Accumulation beside a snow fence

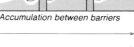

Accumulation between barriers

Snowdrifts can form wherever wind speed drops. Above, an obstacle such as a wall or building disrupts the wind flow, causing turbulence on its leeward side. Here downdrafts produce snow accumulation.

Fragile Works of Art in Ice

Snow crystals form when water vapor in the atmosphere freezes around microscopic particles such as dust or salt. Like human fingerprints, no two crystals are alike. Most are hexagonal, but few are perfectly symmetrical.

In cold, dry weather, snow crystals are usually small, simple plates or columns. Crystals formed in warmer, moister clouds sprout intricate branches. Hundreds may stick together to form huge, feathery snowflakes. Other crystals, battered by winds, land as ragged fragments.

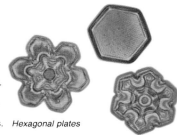

Hexagonal plates

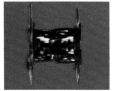

Stellar crystal

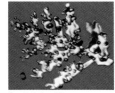

Hexagonal columns   *Needles*   *Spatial dendrite*   *Capped column*   *Irregular crystal*

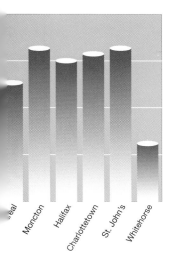

North America. Eastern Canada's heaviest snowfall occurs north of the Gulf of St. Lawrence, where moist air is forced upward by steep slopes. Snow accumulates here because of constant low winter temperatures; in parts of central Quebec and Labrador snow may lie two metres deep by March.

Although snowfall is high in much of Atlantic Canada, the ocean's warming influence brings frequent mild spells to the coast, melting snow or causing precipitation to fall as rain.

The treeless tundra of the Northwest Territories actually has one of Canada's lowest snowfalls, and snow drifts so much that ground is often bare. Despite long, cold winters, the air in the semidesert Arctic islands holds too little moisture to produce much snow.

Wildlife in Winter: Adapt, Migrate or Sleep

Winter is a hard season for most animals. Water is scarce; snow covers food caches and makes travel difficult. Many die of cold or starvation, or fall victim to hardier predators.

The snowshoe hare is designed for snow country. It skims over deep snow on wide, heavily furred feet, with a white winter coat for camouflage.

Moose are adapted to winter in another way: long, stiltlike legs permit them to wade through all but the deepest snowbanks. Deer usually spend winter months grouped together in yards—treed areas where snow is trampled down—where they browse on trees and shrubs. If severe weather confines them too long, many die of starvation.

Some animals cope with winter by hibernation, entering a sleeplike state in which their body temperatures drop, their heartbeat and breathing rates slow down, and their need for food is drastically reduced.

Other creatures survive winter by finding shelter in snow. Mice, shrews and voles dig snowy tunnels which hold their body heat and deflect harsh winter winds. In this damp, silent world the temperature remains just below freezing, no matter how frigid the air above.

Animals whose habits or anatomy cannot adapt to snow find a way to avoid winter altogether: each fall millions of birds and butterflies migrate to southern skies.

Moose

Cottontail rabbit

White-footed mouse   *Masked shrew*   *Meadow vole*

Snow cleared from the streets must be put somewhere else. Montréal, with more snow than any other large city in North America, has three ways to dispose of it. Some of the snow is dumped into the St. Lawrence River, some into sewers through special chutes, and the rest, piled in vacant lots, is left to the sun and rain. The last is the slowest method: outside Ottawa, such piles often linger until June, as dirt and debris slow down melting while valuable land goes unused. Salt and garbage in snow dumped into rivers can also cause environmental problems.

When blizzards sweep the Prairies, tales are told of pioneer farmers who perished midway between house and barn. Even now a traveler stranded in a blizzard may be in danger. But the greatest loss of life from snow is due to avalanches. In Canada, most occur in British Columbia's interior mountain ranges, where average snowfalls can exceed 900 centimetres. A single slide—carrying as much as 22,000 tonnes of snow—can strip a mountainside of trees.

Concrete snowsheds cover the Trans-Canada Highway at danger spots; earth dams and barriers of rubble divert small slides. At Rogers Pass, one of the world's worst avalanche zones, winter observers watch for dangerous buildups. Then an artillery crew fires howitzer shells into unstable snow to trigger a controlled avalanche.

Victims of a heavy snowslide once stood little chance of survival, but today many people who work or ski in avalanche-prone areas wear electronic beacons that will help searchers to locate them if buried.

Avalanche! Treacherous snow thunders down a slope in the Yukon's St. Elias Mountains. A slide may be set off by an earth tremor, falling cornice (overhanging drift) or skiers' weight.

The pleasures of the season: Striking out for the wilderness (above), a skier seeks winter's snowy solitude. Right, riders glide along one of the many extensive snowmobiling trails found throughout Canada.

Skiers keep a watchful eye on winter weather, lamenting warm, moist winds or light rainfall that covers slopes with a hard, unskiable crust. Heavy snowfalls and long winters make two areas in Canada ideal for alpine skiing: the high slopes of British Columbia and Alberta, and the rolling hills of Quebec's Eastern Townships and Laurentian regions. Cross-country skiing can be enjoyed wherever snow lies several centimetres deep—almost anywhere in Canada in winter.

Man can modify ski conditions. When snowfall is insufficient, ski-area owners make their own, spraying a mixture of air and water on the slopes. Near Saskatoon, Mount Blackstrap, a 91-metre-high mountain, was man-made for the 1971 Canada Winter Games.

Canadians are said to spend more on skiing than on snow removal. Snowmobiling is another popular sport that consumes vast sums of money. Snowshoes are one less expensive way to explore the tranquil beauty of a winter landscape.

But however they do it, many Canadians find some way to make fun in the snow.

Natural Regions: The Five/Far West

Canada's vast landscape contains natural "provinces" as distinctive as its political divisions: the coastal rain forest, interior plateau and towering mountains of the Western Cordillera; the patchwork grasslands; the evergreen arch of the boreal forest; the diverse mixed forest of the East; and the harsh, treeless tundra of the Far North.

Occasionally, climate, soil and topography draw clear boundaries, as in southwestern Alberta where the high spine of the Rocky Mountains soars above the grasslands. More often, natural provinces blend together in transition zones called *ecotones*, which abound in plants and animals from adjoining regions.

Each province is composed of ecosystems—associations of plants and animals living in a relationship not only to each other, but also to the rocks and soil. Ecosystems may be as small as a Pacific tidal pool brimming with more than 40 species of plants and animals, or as vast as the boreal forest, dominated by a dozen types of trees throughout its 6000-kilometre span.

Each type of organism has a role essential to the entire community. Through photosynthesis, green plants transform water, oxygen, minerals and the sun's energy into living matter that provides food for animals. Herbivores (plant eaters) consume this vegetation and are, in turn, consumed by carnivores (meat eaters) in a sequence of eating and being eaten known as the food chain. Since most organisms consume more than one type of plant or animal, simple chains combine to form complex food webs. Even when an organism dies, it remains part of the community. Bacteria and other microorganisms decompose dead organic matter and return its minerals to the soil, where they again become available to plants.

Canada's natural regions began to assume their present character about 10,000 years ago when belts of flora, like fauna, shifted north in the wake of receding glaciers. Tundra vegetation colonized the Arctic barrens, while conifers covered the boreal forest and much of the western Cordillera. Seeds of broadleaved and evergreen trees were carried by wind and water from southern refuges to form the mixed forest of eastern Canada. Grasses invaded the Prairies and thrived in clay soils—once the beds of glacial lakes.

The landscape was dominated by large mammals, most of which migrated from Siberia to Alaska across the Bering land link. Yet, within a few thousand years of the last glaciation, some 70 percent of this megafauna—the ground sloths, mammoths, mastodons, native camels and horses—had vanished. Most species were unable to adapt to climatic changes at the end of the Pleistocene. Man, another recent immigrant to North America, may have accelerated these extinctions by hunting large herbivores into oblivion, depriving carnivores of prey.

Man's impact is still being felt. Grasslands, where 60 million bison once thundered, are now checkered with farms and ranches. Man's imprint, in the form of oil rigs, pipelines and mines, has even scarred Canada's last frontier, the North. Parks and sanctuaries—about 7 percent of Canada's total area—preserve much of what remains of its primeval landscapes.

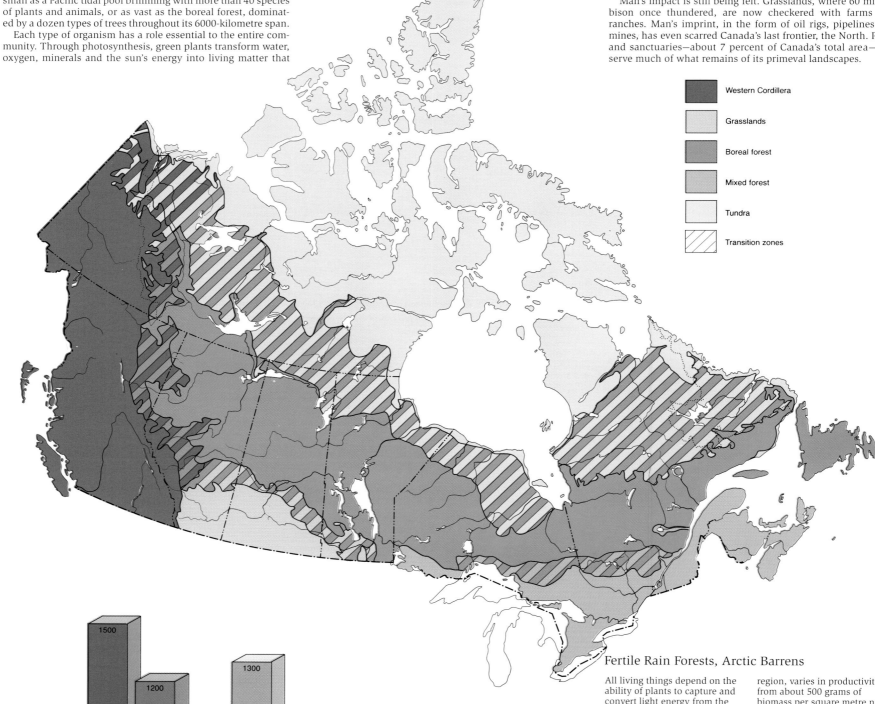

Legend:
- Western Cordillera
- Grasslands
- Boreal forest
- Mixed forest
- Tundra
- Transition zones

Estimated net primary productivity of Canada's major ecosystems (grams/m²/year)

West Coast rain forest	1500
Deciduous forest	1200
Mixed forest	1000
Boreal forest	1300
Grasslands	500
Continental shelf	500
Tundra and alpine tundra	350
Open ocean	150 / 130

Fertile Rain Forests, Arctic Barrens

All living things depend on the ability of plants to capture and convert light energy from the sun into biomass, or living matter. Canada's natural regions vary in productivity, due mainly to differences in climate and soil, and currents and light penetration in the ocean.

The graph (*left*) illustrates the amount of biomass, estimated in grams per square metre, produced annually by Canada's natural regions. Most of this biomass is plant tissue, less than 1 percent of which is converted into animal tissue by herbivores in the first link of a food chain. The rest dies and decays; its energy is lost to the environment as heat. Canada's most productive region, the humid coastal forest of the western Cordillera, yields about 10 times more biomass annually per square metre than the Arctic tundra. The boreal forest, Canada's largest natural region, varies in productivity from about 500 grams of biomass per square metre near the tundra to about 1300 grams in the coniferous forests of northeastern British Columbia and northwestern Alberta.

Oceans cover three-quarters of the earth's surface, but contribute only about a quarter of its biomass yield. Shallow, nutrient-rich continental shelves produce abundant sea life, but the deep, open ocean is as barren as a desert. Pockets of productivity called fishing banks yield twice as much as other parts of the continental shelf and four times as much as the high seas. At the Grand Banks off Newfoundland, where the cold Labrador Current and the warm Gulf Stream mix, plankton upwells and nourishes cod, herring, mackerel and haddock. Yet, only a few hundred kilometres southeast, the Atlantic yields less than the Arctic.

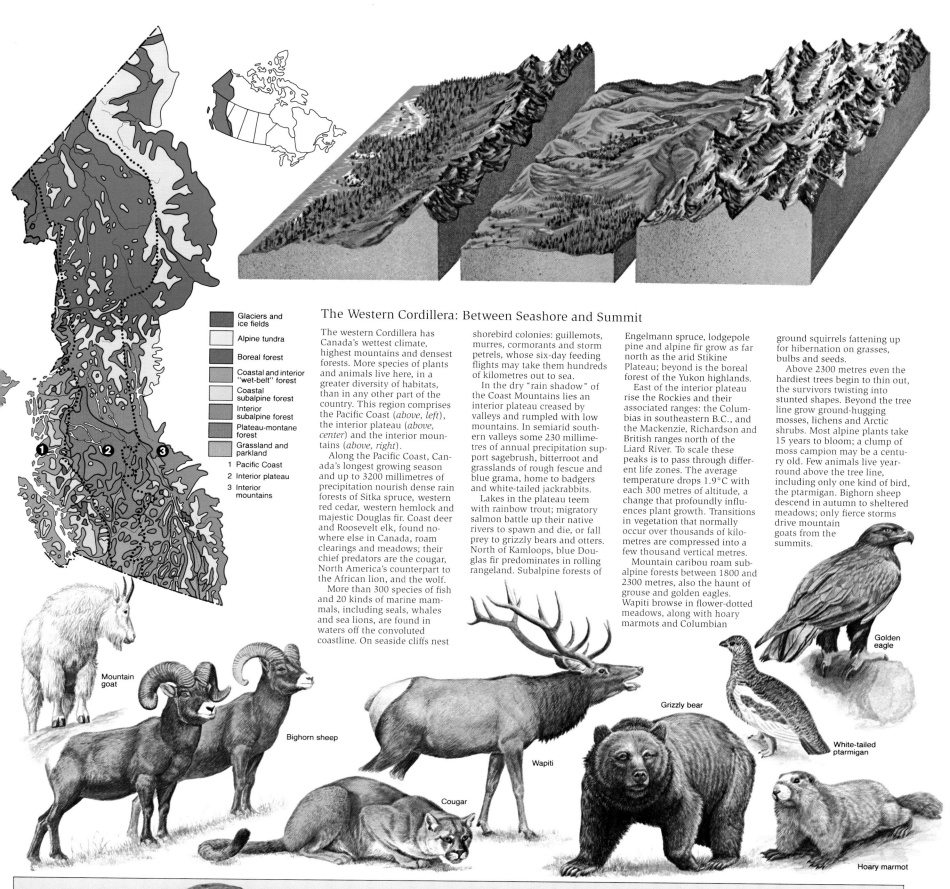

The Western Cordillera: Between Seashore and Summit

The western Cordillera has Canada's wettest climate, highest mountains and densest forests. More species of plants and animals live here, in a greater diversity of habitats, than in any other part of the country. This region comprises the Pacific Coast (*above, left*), the interior plateau (*above, center*) and the interior mountains (*above, right*).

Along the Pacific Coast, Canada's longest growing season and up to 3200 millimetres of precipitation nourish dense rain forests of Sitka spruce, western red cedar, western hemlock and majestic Douglas fir. Coast deer and Roosevelt elk, found nowhere else in Canada, roam clearings and meadows; their chief predators are the cougar, North America's counterpart to the African lion, and the wolf.

More than 300 species of fish and 20 kinds of marine mammals, including seals, whales and sea lions, are found in waters off the convoluted coastline. On seaside cliffs nest shorebird colonies: guillemots, murres, cormorants and storm petrels, whose six-day feeding flights may take them hundreds of kilometres out to sea.

In the dry "rain shadow" of the Coast Mountains lies an interior plateau creased by valleys and rumpled with low mountains. In semiarid southern valleys some 230 millimetres of annual precipitation support sagebrush, bitterroot and grasslands of rough fescue and blue grama, home to badgers and white-tailed jackrabbits.

Lakes in the plateau teem with rainbow trout; migratory salmon battle up their native rivers to spawn and die, or fall prey to grizzly bears and otters. North of Kamloops, blue Douglas fir predominates in rolling rangeland. Subalpine forests of Engelmann spruce, lodgepole pine and alpine fir grow as far north as the arid Stikine Plateau; beyond is the boreal forest of the Yukon highlands.

East of the interior plateau rise the Rockies and their associated ranges: the Columbias in southeastern B.C., and the Mackenzie, Richardson and British ranges north of the Liard River. To scale these peaks is to pass through different life zones. The average temperature drops 1.9°C with each 300 metres of altitude, a change that profoundly influences plant growth. Transitions in vegetation that normally occur over thousands of kilometres are compressed into a few thousand vertical metres.

Mountain caribou roam subalpine forests between 1800 and 2300 metres, also the haunt of grouse and golden eagles. Wapiti browse in flower-dotted meadows, along with hoary marmots and Columbian ground squirrels fattening up for hibernation on grasses, bulbs and seeds.

Above 2300 metres even the hardiest trees begin to thin out, the survivors twisting into stunted shapes. Beyond the tree line grow ground-hugging mosses, lichens and Arctic shrubs. Most alpine plants take 15 years to bloom; a clump of moss campion may be a century old. Few animals live year-round above the tree line, including only one kind of bird, the ptarmigan. Bighorn sheep descend in autumn to sheltered meadows; only fierce storms drive mountain goats from the summits.

Glaciers and ice fields
Alpine tundra
Boreal forest
Coastal and interior "wet-belt" forest
Coastal subalpine forest
Interior subalpine forest
Plateau-montane forest
Grassland and parkland
1 Pacific Coast
2 Interior plateau
3 Interior mountains

Mountain goat
Bighorn sheep
Cougar
Wapiti
Grizzly bear
Golden eagle
White-tailed ptarmigan
Hoary marmot

Turbulent Life Between the Tides

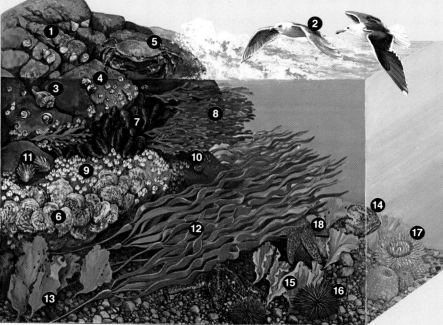

Where the sea meets the land, life is linked to the rise and fall of tides. Along the shore are three distinct habitats: the splash zone, high on the rocks; the intertidal zone, where tides ebb and flow twice daily; and the subtidal zone, usually covered with water.

Plants and animals in these turbulent realms have adapted to battering waves, exposure to air and submersion. Organisms anchored to rocks depend on the sea to bring water-borne food. Some creatures are active at low tide when their prey is exposed; others take refuge in shallow tide pools that seldom dry up.

Marine life on the west coast, whose habitat is warmed by the Alaska Current, is more varied than in any other temperate waters. There are some 90 types of North Pacific starfish, but only about 20 varieties at similar latitudes in the Atlantic, which is chilled by the Labrador Current.

Splash Zone
Life here relies on spray for its seawater needs, and tough coverings to withstand lengthy exposure to air. The checkered periwinkle (1) obtains oxygen directly from the air; its young develop, complete with shell, inside the female's shell. This snail eats minute blue-green algae which it scrapes from rocks with an abrasive, tonguelike radula that is longer than the periwinkle's body. Glaucous gulls (2) patrol shores for dire whelks (3) and turban snails (4); gull eggs and shore crabs (5) often fall prey to minks. Black oyster catchers open the shells of mussels and oysters with a chisel-like bill.

Intertidal Zone
Resisting pounding surf is the key to survival here. Olympia oysters (6) cement themselves into dense colonies; females release 100 million eggs two or three times a year into the hostile sea, but few offspring survive. Sticky threads anchor California mussels (7) among rubbery fingers of bladder wrack (8). Acorn barnacles (9) spend three months as floating larvae, then attach their shells to rocks. Four plates atop the shell close to retain moisture when the tide is out; when submerged, the plates open and the barnacle sweeps in plankton with its feathery feet. The shell of the chiton (10) is composed of eight plates that allow the mollusk to curl into a protective ball. The chiton grazes over its base rock and, although sightless, always returns to the same spot before daylight; the limpet (11) has similar feeding habits.

Subtidal Zone
Broad-bladed ribbon kelp (12) sprout from rocks patched with sea lettuce (13); rootlike holdfasts anchor kelp, whose fronds stream in and out with the surf. Sculpins (14) lurk among the purple layer (15). Sea urchins (16), anchored with hundreds of sucker-tipped feet, swivel threatening spines to confront attackers. Tentacles of the green sea anemone (17)—in appearance more floral than animal— capture prey with poison-tipped stingers. A purple starfish (18) pries open shellfish with suction-cup feet, inserts its stomach and digests the prey within.

Natural Regions: Grasslands, Boreal Forest

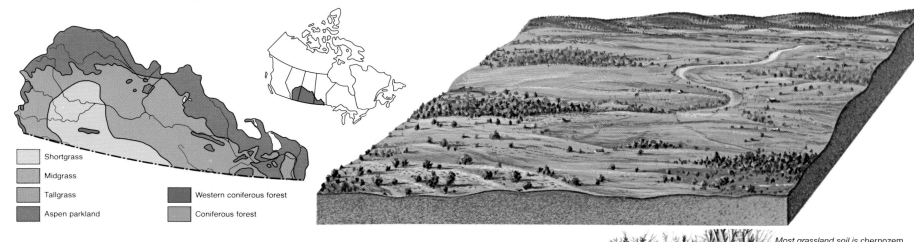

- Shortgrass
- Midgrass
- Tallgrass
- Aspen parkland
- Western coniferous forest
- Coniferous forest

The Patchwork Grasslands

Climate and soil define four grassland regions: shortgrass, midgrass and tallgrass prairie, and aspen parkland where plains yield to boreal forest.

The shortgrasses—mainly blue grama, wheatgrass and needle-grass—grow to half a metre in light-colored, often sandy soil with 250 millimetres of annual precipitation. Sagebrush, buck-brush and hay grass stabilize the semiarid Great Sand Hills of southwestern Saskatchewan.

In the midgrass prairie, 400 millimetres of precipitation and dark brown soil support more luxuriant, metre-high western wheatgrass, needle and thread, and little bluestem.

Tallgrasses up to 2.5 metres high once flourished in the rich, black topsoil of southern Manitoba. Patches of big bluestem and Indian grass still grow along roadsides and in river valleys.

Trembling aspen predominates in the parklands; Manitoba maple and bur oak are scattered throughout moist regions of eastern Saskatchewan and southwestern Manitoba. Silvery lupine, bunchberry and lodge-pole pine—common in Rocky Mountain foothills—grow in the cool, moist Cypress Hills.

Balsam fir and white spruce, usually found in the boreal forest, carpet much of Manitoba's Riding Mountain.

Large animals of the grasslands survive on the margins of cultivated land, or like the bison, in parks and sanctuaries. Mule deer, pronghorn antelope and sharp-tailed grouse find refuge in badlands and sandhills. Burrowing rodents such as the ground squirrel are found throughout the region; their tunnel systems have several entrances as protection from badgers, weasels and coyotes.

Waterfowl offer the most spectacular wildlife displays. More than eight million potholes and sloughs provide breeding grounds for half of North America's ducks, geese, swans and pelicans.

Most grassland soil is chernozem (Russian for "black earth"). Its layers, or horizons, usually consist of a surface mat of humus; a layer of topsoil mixed with roots, dead plant matter and microorganisms; and a mineral horizon of lime particles.

The tallgrass prairie and aspen parkland have black, humus-rich soil laced with fibrous roots that absorb water and nutrients from moist clays in the subsoil.

Midgrass prairie soil is relatively shallow. The mineral horizon, mixed with clay, is within reach of metre-deep root systems.

Humus-poor sandy soil about a half-metre deep lies below the shortgrass prairie. The lime layer marks the depth to which rainwater and roots penetrate. Below, the subsoil is permanently dry.

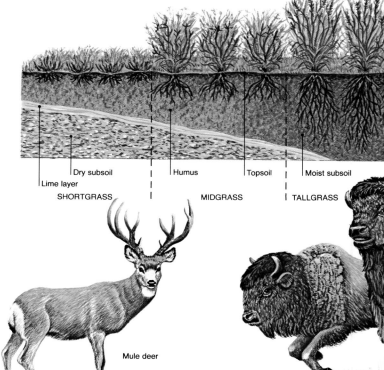

Lime layer | Dry subsoil | Humus | Topsoil | Moist subsoil

SHORTGRASS | MIDGRASS | TALLGRASS

Mule deer

Bison

Coyote

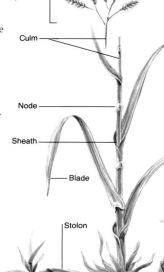
Richardson's ground squirrel

Sharp-tailed grouse

Pelican

Pronghorn antelope

Mallard

Flexible, Durable Grass

More than 100 grass species carpet Canada. Typical features are shown in a single stylized plant (*right*).

Spikelets of grass flowers are exposed only once for pollination—usually for an hour—when temperature, humidity and sunlight trigger the opening of a protective capsule.

Hollow stems (culms) and solid joints (nodes) give grasses strength and flexibility. Leaves grow at the nodes; the sheath wraps around the stem and unfurls a narrow blade.

Root systems penetrate the soil to a depth of up to six metres. Tallgrasses usually reproduce by underground stems called rhizomes; short- and midgrasses propagate by surface runners called stolons.

Spikelet
Culm
Node
Sheath
Blade
Stolon
Roots
Rhizome

A Calendar of Wildflowers

From spring until autumn's first frost, wildflowers brighten the tawny grasslands and mark the passing of the seasons with distinctive hues.

Amid the melting snows of April, the downy buds of the prairie crocus appear and unfold delicate lavender petals. The smooth blue beardtongue blossoms on dry slopes in May; in moist areas, the golden bean adds its fragrant yellow blossoms. Birds, rodents and deer feed on the seeds of the prairie sunflower, a two-metre-high annual that blooms in June.

By midsummer, eastern Prairie thickets are ablaze with wild bergamot. The western red lily highlights meadows and open woodlands with flame-red flowers. On foothill slopes, late summer brings gaillardia's distinctive flower head—a purplish disc surrounded by yellow petals.

The blazing star's dense clusters of rose-purple flowers spike sandy hillsides from July to September. In early autumn many-flowered asters spangle the grasslands with white or pinkish blossoms that usually face the same direction.

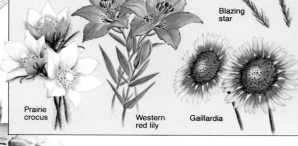
Many-flowered aster
Blazing star
Prairie crocus
Western red lily
Gaillardia
Prairie sunflower

Wild bergamot
Golden bean
Smooth blue beardtongue

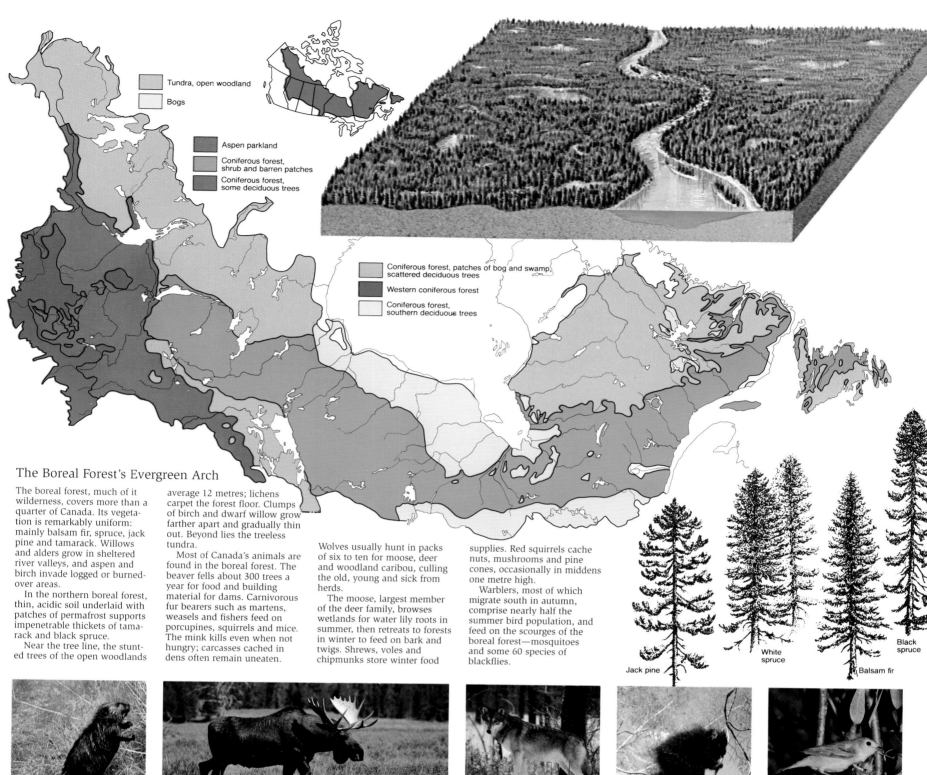

Tundra, open woodland

Bogs

Aspen parkland

Coniferous forest, shrub and barren patches

Coniferous forest, some deciduous trees

Coniferous forest, patches of bog and swamp scattered deciduous trees

Western coniferous forest

Coniferous forest, southern deciduous trees

The Boreal Forest's Evergreen Arch

The boreal forest, much of it wilderness, covers more than a quarter of Canada. Its vegetation is remarkably uniform: mainly balsam fir, spruce, jack pine and tamarack. Willows and alders grow in sheltered river valleys, and aspen and birch invade logged or burned-over areas.

In the northern boreal forest, thin, acidic soil underlaid with patches of permafrost supports impenetrable thickets of tamarack and black spruce.

Near the tree line, the stunted trees of the open woodlands average 12 metres; lichens carpet the forest floor. Clumps of birch and dwarf willow grow farther apart and gradually thin out. Beyond lies the treeless tundra.

Most of Canada's animals are found in the boreal forest. The beaver fells about 300 trees a year for food and building material for dams. Carnivorous fur bearers such as martens, weasels and fishers feed on porcupines, squirrels and mice. The mink kills even when not hungry; carcasses cached in dens often remain uneaten.

Wolves usually hunt in packs of six to ten for moose, deer and woodland caribou, culling the old, young and sick from herds.

The moose, largest member of the deer family, browses wetlands for water lily roots in summer, then retreats to forests in winter to feed on bark and twigs. Shrews, voles and chipmunks store winter food supplies. Red squirrels cache nuts, mushrooms and pine cones, occasionally in middens one metre high.

Warblers, most of which migrate south in autumn, comprise nearly half the summer bird population, and feed on the scourges of the boreal forest—mosquitoes and some 60 species of blackflies.

Jack pine   White spruce   Balsam fir   Black spruce

Beaver

Moose

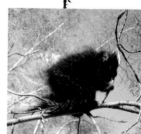

Wolf

Porcupine

Yellow warbler

Life in a Bog: Cold, Wet and Acidic

Most of Canada's 1.3 million square kilometres of wetlands are found in the boreal forest, where Ice Age glaciers gouged countless stagnant, water-filled depressions.

Bogs are the most common type of wetland in northern forests. These poorly drained patches of land are pocked with pools of open water colonized by floating plants such as the water lily and pondweed. The remains of these aquatic species form a fine, soft layer called a "false bottom" which gradually rises as sediment accumulates.

Reeds, sedges and marsh cinquefoil grow in the shallows; buckbean sends "runners" along the surface to form a floating mat. Sphagnum, a moss that absorbs 20 times its weight in water, fills the spaces between plants. The mat thickens and may form hummocks and ridges that support shrubs such as leatherleaf, Labrador tea, sweet gale and bog rosemary, which are less tolerant of water. Scattered clumps of black spruce and tamarack grow between the bog and the surrounding forest of spruce, balsam fir and birch.

Different zones of vegetation—sedge, sphagnum, shrubs and trees—deposit distinctive types of peat, occasionally to a depth of 30 metres. This partially decomposed organic matter releases acids that stain bog water brown.

The landscape is brightened with orchids: dragon's tongue, lady's slipper, spotted coralroot, grass pink, and tway-blade orchid, which takes years to flower.

Carnivorous pitcher plants and round-leaved sundews obtain nutrients from insects. Down-pointed bristles on the inner surface of pitcher plant leaves trap insects, which drown in a mixture of rainwater and enzyme-rich secretions. The plant then digests its victim. Sundew leaves have hundreds of sticky red hairs that entangle insects. The plant then slowly closes, suffocating its prey.

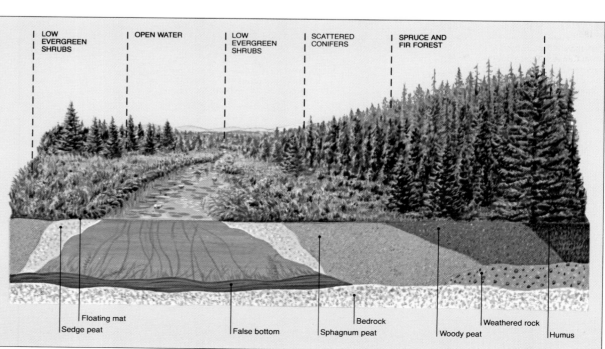

LOW EVERGREEN SHRUBS   OPEN WATER   LOW EVERGREEN SHRUBS   SCATTERED CONIFERS   SPRUCE AND FIR FOREST

Floating mat

Sedge peat   False bottom   Sphagnum peat   Bedrock   Woody peat   Weathered rock   Humus

Natural Regions: Eastern Forest, Tundra

The Mixed Forest: Woodlands and Wetlands

Almost none of the original mixed forest that confronted Canada's pioneers survives today. Agriculture and urban sprawl have swallowed most of the woodlands; logging, mining and fire have altered much of the rest.

Hardwoods more typical of the United States grow in southwestern Ontario, including hickory, sassafras, pawpaw and tulip tree—species found nowhere else in Canada.

In the Great Lakes-St. Lawrence region, sugar maple and beech dominate mature forests; red and white oak, basswood, white elm and black cherry thrive in younger woodlands. Coniferous species, mainly white and red pine and eastern hemlock, are scattered throughout stands of deciduous trees.

The Acadian forest of the Maritimes has hardwoods similar to those in the Great Lakes-St. Lawrence region. Boreal trees, especially red and black spruce and balsam fir, fringe the coastlines and carpet the highlands of Cape Breton Island and the Gaspé Peninsula.

Wildlife in the mixed forest is most abundant in freshwater marshes and wooded swamps. Plankton-rich waters and aquatic plants such as cattails, duckweed and loosestrife anchor food chains and sustain wetland creatures. The sleek otter pursues sunfish, minnows and game fish such as perch and bass. Painted turtles sun on mossy rocks and logs. The bobcat prowls wetland margins for rabbits and rodents, and earns its reputation for ferocity when treed or cornered.

Thousands of monarch butterflies congregate at Point Pelee on Canada's southernmost tip each autumn before flying south. The region also shelters the opossum, Canada's only marsupial. This mammal, which has changed little in 70 million years, bears up to 20 young, and nourishes them for about six weeks in a pouch.

Deciduous trees

Deciduous trees; scattered conifers

Deciduous and coniferous trees

Conifers; scattered deciduous trees

Conifers

Monarch butterfly

Opossum

Swainson's hawk

Arctic tern

Brant

Otter

Bobcat

Largemouth bass

Midland painted turtle

Migration by Land, Stars, Sun and Sound

Two thirds of North America's 660 bird species migrate in twice-yearly journeys along four main flyways. More than 200 species pass over Point Pelee, where the Mississippi and Atlantic flyways overlap.

No one is certain why birds migrate, but food shortages are a factor. Most species fly much farther than necessary to avoid winters that the stay-at-homes survive. The arctic tern wings 35,000 kilometres on round trips between the polar regions.

How they migrate is also a mystery. Birds sense changes in the length of daylight and add layers of fat to fuel their impending flights. Night migrants are believed to navigate in part by the stars. Nestlings learn the rotation of the heavens, and later recognize constellations. Day migrants steer by the sun, and follow coastlines, mountain ranges and rivers.

Orientation may also involve ultraviolet and polarized light, even the earth's magnetic field in combination with gravity. Homing pigeons can hear infrasound, noise that carries vast distances in the atmosphere. The sound of breakers on a distant shore may guide a seabird to a tiny mid-ocean island.

Migration is risky. In North America, 100 million waterfowl wing south each fall. Only 40 million return. Hunters kill 20 million; the rest succumb to predators, accidents and disease.

White trillium

Highbush cranberries

Tulip tree flower

Swainson's hawk

Semipalmated sandpiper

Brant

Arctic tern

To Europe

To South America via Europe and Africa

PACIFIC FLYWAY

CENTRAL FLYWAY

MISSISSIPPI FLYWAY

ATLANTIC FLYWAY

To South America and Antarctica

Urban Animals: The Wildlife Among Us

The wildlife that most Canadians encounter is found in our cities, where animals thrive in seemingly hostile environments. The familiar rock dove, or pigeon, has been urbanized since the time of ancient Egypt, and lives in parks and downtown areas, where it flourishes on human handouts. Nighthawks nest on flat roofs, the urban equivalent of gravelly beaches; city lights allow them to hunt all night, rather than just at dawn and dusk. Gray squirrels, notorious panhandlers in parks, seem to prefer man-made nesting boxes to natural cavities in trees. The Norway rat prowls waterfronts and rundown neighborhoods, feeding mainly on garbage.

Some species prefer residential areas and suburbs. Winter feeding stations attract chickadees, grosbeaks, blue jays and house wrens. Aggressive species such as starlings and sparrows pirate nests from woodpeckers and bluebirds. Gardens provide bountiful larders of vegetables and tender greens for cottontail rabbits and woodchucks. The garter snake, one of the few urbanized reptiles, slithers after wood frogs in moist, shady nooks. Moles furrow lawns, gardens and golf courses for grubs and earthworms. Raccoons and skunks raid garbage cans at night and during the day den in trees, garages, culverts and chimneys.

The Tundra's Brief Season of Life

North of the tree line, as far as the Arctic Ocean, lies the tundra, a vast plain carpeted with sedge and grass hummocks and mats of dwarf willow and birch. Glaciers and rock deserts, hospitable only to avens, lichens and saxifrage, cover much of the Arctic islands.

The tundra receives about 250 millimetres of annual precipitation—scarcely more than deserts—but frozen ground (permafrost) prevents drainage and leaves a sodden summer landscape. But from June until August, a sun that never sets unfolds almost 900 species of flowering plants. The arctic poppy flowers and goes to seed in less than a month. Willows and sedges start summer growth while still buried in metre-deep snowbanks.

Timing is also crucial for the birds that congregate here in summer from all over the Western Hemisphere. Mating often occurs during migration; eggs are laid by mid-June so parents can rear offspring in time for the August exodus.

The tundra shelters tremendous concentrations of wildlife. Prince Leopold Island hosts a vast seabird colony in summer; for a few days each year thousands of beluga whales calve in the warm shallows of Cunningham Inlet on Somerset Island. Between 300,000 and 500,000 caribou in five main herds wander between summer feeding grounds on the tundra, then winter in the sheltered boreal forest. Musk-oxen, found mainly in the Arctic islands, graze in valley meadows, then shift in winter to windswept hummocks and mountain slopes with light snow cover.

Polar bears winter along oceans and bays near the breathing holes of ringed seals. The walrus uses its tusks to rake the bottom for shellfish, open breathing holes in the ice, haul itself up on floes and fight enemies—polar bears on land and killer whales at sea.

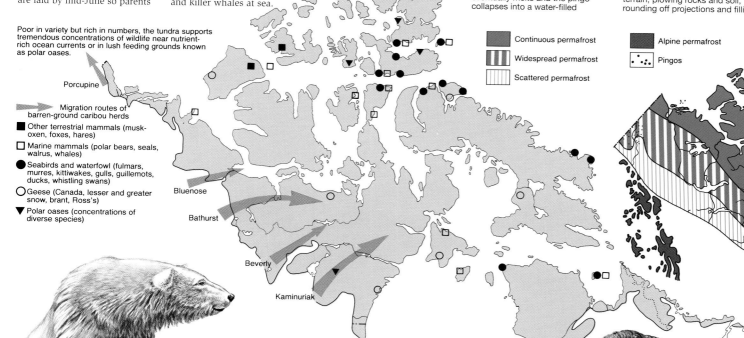

Pingos (1) are formed when pockets of water are trapped in permafrost. The water freezes, expands and is forced to the surface by pressure from the surrounding permafrost. Pingos rise in conelike mounds 3 to 45 metres high. Cracks develop at the summit; the exposed ice core (2) eventually melts and the pingo collapses into a water-filled crater (3). Solifluction (4), or "soil creep," occurs when water-logged soil, propelled by gravity and frost action, "slides" downhill on the underlying permafrost. This slumping—occasionally violent, but usually sluggish—occurs on inclines as gentle as two percent and gradually transforms the terrain, plowing rocks and soil, rounding off projections and filling in hollows. Intense cold contracts the soggy tundra soil, and forms fissures that fill with water during spring thaws. Repeated freezing and thawing expands the openings. Eventually, after some years, this produces networks of geometric fractures called polygons (5). The more severe and rapid the freeze-up, the larger the polygon; some are 90 metres across.

Poor in variety but rich in numbers, the tundra supports tremendous concentrations of wildlife near nutrient-rich ocean currents or in lush feeding grounds known as polar oases.

Porcupine

Migration routes of barren-ground caribou herds
■ Other terrestrial mammals (musk-oxen, foxes, hares)
□ Marine mammals (polar bears, seals, walrus, whales)
● Seabirds and waterfowl (fulmars, murres, kittiwakes, gulls, guillemots, ducks, whistling swans)
○ Geese (Canada, lesser and greater snow, brant, Ross's)
▼ Polar oases (concentrations of diverse species)

Bluenose
Bathurst
Beverly
Kaminuriak

Continuous permafrost
Widespread permafrost
Scattered permafrost
Alpine permafrost
Pingos

Polar bear
Ringed seal
Walrus
Musk-ox

The Lichen— Two Plants in One

Deserts, mountain peaks, tundra: lichens grow almost anywhere, often where nothing else can survive. These primitive rootless plants need no soil, few minerals and little moisture and sunlight.

A lichen is two primitive plants in one: an alga and a fungus that combine in a beneficial relationship called mutualism. The fungus lacks chlorophyll to produce its own food, but absorbs moisture vital to the millions of algal cells enmeshed in its tangled network of strands. The algae, in turn, photosynthesize food for the entire organism.

Lichens have a variety of appearances. Crustose lichens are crusty mats embedded in wood and rocks by tiny threads that penetrate as much as one centimetre. Foliose lichens attach small, leafy lobes to rocks, soil and trees with a rootlike anchor called an umbilicus. Fruticose lichens include trumpet-shaped fairy cups, red-capped British soldiers and reindeer moss, which forms spongy mats 25 centimetres thick in open woodlands near the tree line and provides winter fodder for caribou.

Lichens remain dormant during drought and intense heat and cold. Even in hospitable climates they grow slowly—at most one millimetre a year—but steadily; some colonies are thought to be 4000 years old.

Reindeer moss

British soldiers

Fairy cups

The Power of Permafrost

An "active layer" of shallow tundra soil thaws each spring; below lies permafrost, ground frozen year-round. Almost half of Canada, including mountain summits in the Western Cordillera and eastern Arctic islands, lies within zones of continuous or discontinuous permafrost.

Permafrost is formed when the ground temperature, determined mainly by air temperature, soil, drainage and snow cover, remains below 0°C. Ground temperature is usually 1° to 5° warmer than the average air temperature, so permafrost extends to areas with an average temperature of about –1°C. The colder the ground, the deeper the permafrost. At Hay River, N.W.T., a ground temperature slightly below freezing produces patches of permafrost 1.5 to 15 metres deep. Resolute, N.W.T., with an average ground temperature of –13.3°C, rests on permafrost about 400 metres deep.

Permafrost and powerful frost action, called "cryoplanation," shape the Arctic landscape more than erosion. Cryoplanation forces soil to the surface in circular frost boils, or fractures the terrain into polygons—geometric scars that cover hundreds of square kilometres. Permafrost melts when its insulating mantle of vegetation is removed, and the ground fractures and slumps.

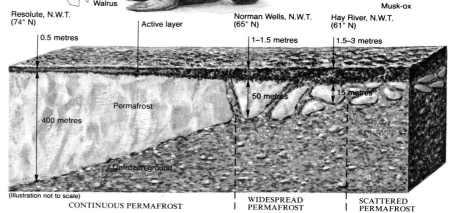

Resolute, N.W.T. (74° N)
Active layer
0.5 metres
Permafrost
400 metres
Unfrozen ground
(Illustration not to scale)
CONTINUOUS PERMAFROST

Norman Wells, N.W.T. (65° N)
1–1.5 metres
50 metres
WIDESPREAD PERMAFROST

Hay River, N.W.T. (61° N)
1.5–3 metres
15 metres
SCATTERED PERMAFROST

Our Great Outdoors

To Canada's early settlers, the wilderness was a place of hardship and an inexhaustible source of raw materials, land and wealth. But the land had another face, as author-pioneer Susanna Moodie observed in 1853: "Beautiful—most beautiful in her rugged grandeur is this vast country. How awful is the sublime solitude of her pathless woods! What eloquent thoughts flow out of the deep silence that broods over them." Today, much of that grandeur has been cleared and cut, mined, dredged and dammed. Only about 10 percent of the provinces can be considered truly wild. The picture brightens when the North is included, but there too, wilderness is shrinking in the wake of industry and development.

Hundreds of hiking trails and canoe routes, 36 national parks or reserves, some 1288 provincial parks and scores of wildlife refuges and wilderness areas seek to preserve what remains of Canada's wildlands. They comprise a majestic array of landscapes: the wave-sculpted shore of Vancouver Island, northern Saskatchewan's mosaic of rivers and lakes, the twisted shapes of Alberta's Red Deer Badlands, Cape Breton's rugged highlands and the exotic plant and animal life where Point Pelee juts into Lake Erie.

More than 13 million visitors to our national parks each year present a challenge: how to welcome visitors and still preserve the parks. New parks are one answer: since 1970 some 120,800 square kilometres have been added to our national park system alone. Another answer is to make better use of parks. Interpretive programs, museums, special exhibits, canoe routes, hiking trails and self-guiding nature trails transform visitors into participants, and broaden the park experience beyond a blurred vision through a speeding car window.

A Guide to Canada's Parks

From more than 1438 parks and historic sites preserved across Canada, the map at right locates a selection: 36 national parks, 55 national historic sites, 74 provincial parks (about 5 percent of the total), 21 wildlife refuges and bird sanctuaries and 20 heritage rivers. These are special places, set aside to preserve unique and irreplaceable samples of the nation's wild lands and historical heritage. Most are open year round, and many offer recreations such as camping, hiking, boating, fishing, winter sports, and nature study. Types of recreation vary with the park and the season.

- Ⓝ National Park
- ㉒ Provincial Park
- ⑱ National Historic Site
- ▬ Trans-Canada Highway
- National or provincial wildlife preserve
- National or provincial bird sanctuary
- Canadian Heritage Rivers

Our Heritage Rivers: White Water, Quiet Water

Canada was shaped by its rivers. Through the forest and across the Prairies they beckoned, north to furs and fortunes and west to the Pacific. By the late 19th century the millstream had become a part of Canadian life. Today, rivers generate power, irrigate fields and provide water for industry and growing cities.

Other rivers have escaped dams, dikes and impound ments and provide a valuable resource in their wild state. Such waterways as the Mattawa, Missinaibi and Yukon are living museums of natural and human history. Canoeists challenge the rapids of others, such as the Nahanni and Moisie. Still others—the Winisk, Coppermine and Thelon—snake northward to the Arctic Ocean in a wild panorama of rock, water, tundra and sky.

A first step toward the protection of our rivers was taken in 1971-73, when Parks Canada surveyed 72 of Canada's historic, scenic and recreational waterways (*20 are mapped at right*). Instead of trappers and fur traders, they now attract campers, boaters, fishermen and naturalists.

The 80-kilometre West Coast Trail passes Tsuiat Falls, 11-kilometre Long Beach and Barkeley Sound—the "Graveyard of the Pacific"

Map labels

A 56-kilometre trail climbs 1140-metre Chilkoot Pass as it retraces the gold-rush "Trail of '98" between Skagway, Alaska, and Dawson, Yukon

Volcanic-shaped pingos, huge mounds of solid ice, are common in the Mackenzie Delta

Some 800,000 thick-billed murres and 100,000 kittiwakes nest on sheer cliffs along the northwest coast of Bylot Island

Canada's highest peak, 5959-metre Mount Logan, towers over the world's largest non-polar icefields in Kluane National Park

Boaters pass rock walls up to 900 metres high in Nahanni's First Canyon, where two headless bodies were found in 1908. Virginia Falls' twin chutes tumble 90 metres

This 55,931-square-kilometre preserve of tundra and boreal forest was established to protect the musk-ox, a relic of the Ice Age. Also in the sanctuary are caribou, Barren Ground grizzly, moose and lemming

Rugged backcountry trails lead to Mount Edziza, a 2787-metre dormant volcano that last erupted 1400 years ago

In Wood Buffalo National Park is the last remaining herd of 1500 wood bison. More than a million ducks and geese populate the Peace-Athabasca Delta in summer

The remains of 35 dinosaur species have been unearthed in Alberta's Red Deer River Valley.

IVVAVIK, VUNTUT, Kendell Island Bird Sanctuary, Banks Island Bird Sanctuary, AULAVIK, Bylot Island Bird Sanctuary, Peel River Game Reserve, McArthur Game Reserve, Kluane Game Reserve, KLUANE, Queen Maud Gulf Bird Sanctuary, Thelon Game Reserve, NAHANNI, Mackenzie Bison Sanctuary, WOOD BUFFALO, GWAII HAANAS, Wilmore Wilderness Park, JASPER, ELK ISLAND, PRINCE ALBERT, Wildcat Hill Wilderness Area, White Goat Wilderness Area, Siffleur Wilderness Area, MOUNT REVELSTOKE, BANFF, GLACIER, KOOTENAY, YOHO, Purcell Wilderness Conservancy, PACIFIC RIM, RIDING MOUNTAIN, WATERTON LAKES, GRASSLANDS

Provincial Parks—Picnic Sites to Primeval Domains

Canada's provincial parks range in size from a few hectares to many thousands of square kilometres. They protect wild lands and habitats, and provide outdoor recreation for millions of visitors each year. Many have a small entry charge and, where applicable, a camping fee. There are numerous private camping and picnic grounds in the Yukon and Northwest Territories, but no areas that correspond to provincial parks. Most of Nova Scotia's fine parkland is divided between provincial wildlife areas and two national parks. Prince Edward Island has an extensive system of recreation areas from day-use-only picnic sites to campgrounds.

Mount Robson (B.C.)

Dinosaur (Alta.)

Cypress Hills (Sask.)

Algonquin (Ont.)

	British Columbia														Alberta							Saskatchewan										Manitoba									Ontario											
Camping																																																				
Hiking																																																				
Boating																																																				
Fishing																																																				
Winter activities																																																				

#	Park
1	Strathcona
2	Garibaldi
3	Golden Ears
4	Manning
5	Kokanee Glacier
6	Mount Assiniboine
7	Wells Gray
8	Mount Robson
9	Bowron Lake
10	Tweedsmuir
11	Naikoon
12	Mount Edziza
13	Atlin
14	Muncho Lake
15	Kwadacha
16	Lac Cardinal
17	Winagami Lake
18	Long Lake
19	Crimson Lake
20	Peter Lougheed
21	Dinosaur
22	Writing-on-Stone
23	Cypress Hills, Alta.
24	Cypress Hills, Sask.
25	Moose Mountain
26	Buffalo Pound
27	Duck Mountain
28	Greenwater Lake
29	Narrow Hills
30	Meadow Lake
31	Lac La Ronge
32	Grass River
33	Clearwater
34	Duck Mountain
35	Turtle Mountain
36	Spruce Woods
37	Hecla
38	Grand Beach
39	Whiteshell
40	Lake of the Woods
41	Quetico
42	Sleeping Giant
43	Polar Bear
44	Nagagamisis
45	Missinaibi Lake
46	Lake Superior
47	Mississagi
48	Killarney
49	Algonquin
50	Presqu'ile

A Place to Grow in Canada's Wildlife Preserves

The original purpose of national and provincial wildlife preserves was to protect game animals and birds, especially migratory waterfowl, from the devastating effects of a growing society. Now a wider view of the role of wildlife refuges has emerged. Legislation has dealt not only with game animals but with all threatened wildlife, including Canada's endangered species (*right*).

Improving or expanding our wildlife habitats involves more than buying up pristine land. Much of the property is overgrazed, logged, drained or burned, requiring investment in dams, fences, reforestation and other expensive rehabilitation.

Roadless and resortless, wildlife refuges may restrict visitors to daylight hours or ban them completely so that the fauna will not be disturbed. But for the most part these wild lands are open and beckoning.

MARINE LIFE
Acadian Whitefish
Aurora Trout
Salish Sucker
Beluga
(St. Lawrence
River population)
Beluga
(Ungava
Bay population)
Beluga
(SE Baffin
Island/Cumberland
Sound population)
Bowhead Whale
Right Whale
Sea Otter
(Pacific Coast)

BIRDS
Eskimo Curlew
Harlequin Duck
Kirkland's Warbler
Loggerhead shrike
Mountain Plover
Peregrine Falcon (*Anatum*)
Piping Plover
Sage Thresher
Spotted Owl
Whooping Crane

MAMMALS
Eastern cougar
Peary Caribou (Banks Island)
Peary Caribou (High Arctic)
Vancouver Island Marmot
Wolverine

REPTILES AND AMPHIBIANS
Blue racer
Lake Erie water snake
Leatherback Turtle
Small-mouthed salamander
Blanchard's cricket frog

Eskimo curlew

Lake Erie water snake

Wilderness "Unimpaired": the National Parks

Some 218,902 square kilometres of the Canadian landscape are preserved in 36 national parks and reserves. By law these areas are "dedicated to the people . . . for their benefit, education and enjoyment" and must remain "unimpaired for future generations." As pressures on the national parks increased, the federal government—in cooperation with the provinces—has responded by creating more parks and reserves (17 since 1968).

Our parks range from the oldest, Banff, to one of the newest, Auyuittuq (the world's first park north of the Arctic Circle); from the world's largest park, 27,700-square-kilometre Wood Buffalo, to Canada's smallest, the 400-hectare St. Lawrence Islands park, which set in the Thousand Islands. There are the rugged coastal cliffs of such eastern parks as Terra Nova, Gros Morne (*right*) and Cape Breton Highlands; parks fronting lovely beaches, especially the Prince Edward Island and Pacific Rim; and the great parks of the Prairie grasslands and western mountains.

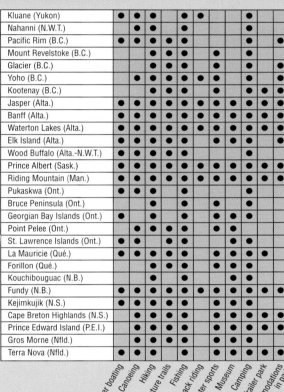

Mantling Auyuittuq is the 5720-square-kilometre Penny Ice Cap. Among 38 bird species are the endangered peregrine falcon and whistling swan

AUYUITTUQ

Dewey Soper Bird Sanctuary

The world's largest goose colony protects one million Canada geese, lesser snow geese and black brants

Arctic hare and Newfoundland caribou inhabit this park, named for 806-metre Gros Morne Mountain. Tidal pools teem with sea urchins, sponges and sea anemone

TERRA NOVA
Exploits
GROS MORNE
Avalon
Wilderness Area   Wilderness Area
MINGAN ARCHIPELAGO

Polar bears, arctic foxes and caribou roam the park, one of the world's most southerly extensions of arctic tundra

Canoeing is popular in Chibougamau Provincial Park, where the Chamouchouane River plunges 33 metres over Chaudière Falls and churns through a series of rapids. Pike, trout, walleye, otter and beaver inhabit the many lakes

Akimiski Island Bird Sanctuary

FORILLON
CAPE BRETON HIGHLANDS
PRINCE EDWARD ISLAND
Plaster Rock-Renous Game Refuge
Kedgwick Game Management Area
KOUCHIBOUGUAC
Chignecto Game Sanctuary

La Mauricie has campsites, beaches, wilderness and wildlife areas, and 154 lakes. A 23-kilometre scenic road divides the park
LA MAURICIE

Canaan Game Management Area
FUNDY
St. Croix
Lepreau Game Management Area
KEJIMKUJIK
Tobeatic Game Sanctuary

In Kejimkujik are Indian petroglyphs and one of Canada's most varied reptile and amphibian populations

PUKASKWA

Coves and inlets cut into steep sandstone cliffs along 13-kilometre shoreline of Fundy National Park. Beachcombers can explore coves and tidal pools; amateur naturalists can watch for some of the park's 160 bird species

French
GEORGIAN BAY ISLANDS   ST. LAWRENCE ISLANDS
Fathom Five National Marine Park

Along the Bruce Peninsula are eroded limestone "flowerpots," rare orchids and 400-million-year-old fossils embedded in shale bluffs

BRUCE PENINSULA

POINT PELEE

Some 250 bird species have been sighted on the 17-kilometre sandspit at the southernmost tip of mainland Canada, also a haven for rare plants and animals

	Power boating	Canoeing	Hiking	Nature trails	Fishing	Horseback riding	Winter sports	Museum	Camping	Trailer park	Accommodations in park
Kluane (Yukon)	●	●	●		●	●		●	●		●
Nahanni (N.W.T.)	●	●	●		●						
Pacific Rim (B.C.)	●	●	●	●	●			●	●		●
Mount Revelstoke (B.C.)			●	●	●		●	●			●
Glacier (B.C.)			●	●			●	●	●		●
Yoho (B.C.)		●	●	●	●			●	●		●
Kootenay (B.C.)		●	●	●	●	●		●	●		●
Jasper (Alta.)	●	●	●	●	●	●	●	●	●	●	●
Banff (Alta.)	●	●	●	●	●	●	●	●	●	●	●
Waterton Lakes (Alta.)	●	●	●	●	●	●	●	●	●	●	●
Elk Island (Alta.)	●	●	●	●	●		●	●	●	●	●
Wood Buffalo (Alta.-N.W.T.)	●	●	●		●				●		
Prince Albert (Sask.)	●	●	●	●	●	●	●	●	●	●	●
Riding Mountain (Man.)	●	●	●	●	●	●	●	●	●	●	●
Pukaskwa (Ont.)		●	●	●	●				●		
Bruce Peninsula (Ont.)			●	●	●				●		
Georgian Bay Islands (Ont.)	●		●	●	●				●		
Point Pelee (Ont.)		●	●	●	●			●			●
St. Lawrence Islands (Ont.)	●	●	●	●	●			●	●		●
La Mauricie (Qué.)	●	●	●	●	●		●		●	●	●
Forillon (Qué.)	●	●	●	●	●	●	●	●	●		●
Kouchibouguac (N.B.)			●	●	●				●		●
Fundy (N.B.)	●	●	●	●	●		●	●	●	●	●
Kejimkujik (N.S.)	●	●	●	●	●		●		●		●
Cape Breton Highlands (N.S.)	●	●	●	●	●			●	●	●	●
Prince Edward Island (P.E.I.)	●	●	●	●	●			●	●	●	●
Gros Morne (Nfld.)			●	●	●			●	●		●
Terra Nova (Nfld.)	●	●	●	●	●			●	●	●	●

	Québec											N.B.	N.S.			P.E.I.			Nfld.				
	La Vérendrye	Papineau-Labelle	Mont-Tremblant	Mastigouche	Saint-Maurice	Laurentides	Chibougamau	Mistassini	Port-Cartier/Sept-Îles	Mont-Orford	Matane	Mont Carleton	Mactaquac	Boylston	Five Islands	Mira	Risser's Beach	Brudenell River	Green Park	Strathgartney	Sir Richard Squires	Pistolet Bay	Fitzgerald's Pond
Camping	●	●	●	●	●	●	●		●	●	●	●	●	●	●	●	●	●	●	●	●	●	●
Hiking	●	●	●	●		●				●	●	●	●		●					●	●	●	●
Boating	●	●	●	●	●	●	●	●		●		●	●	●	●	●		●			●	●	●
Fishing	●	●	●	●	●	●	●	●		●	●	●	●	●	●	●		●			●	●	●
Winter activities	●	●	●		●	●																●	

51 La Vérendrye
52 Papineau-Labelle
53 Mont-Tremblant
54 Mastigouche
55 Saint-Maurice
56 Laurentides
57 Chibougamau
58 Mistassini
59 Port-Cartier/Sept-Îles
60 Mont-Orford
61 Matane
62 Mont Carleton
63 Mactaquac
64 Boylston
65 Five Islands
66 Mira
67 Risser's Beach
68 Brudenell River
69 Green Park
70 Strathgartney
71 Sir Richard Squires
72 Pistolet Bay
73 ...
74 Fitzgerald's Pond

National Historic Sites: Preserving Our Past

Our national historic sites commemorate people, places and events that have shaped Canada's history. Historians, archeologists and anthropologists are active in the excavation and restoration of these sites. Fur-trade posts such as Lower Fort Garry have been restored with care; historic houses, rebuilt and refurnished in the styles of centuries past. The Fortress of Louisbourg, built in 1720 and abandoned for two centuries, is Canada's biggest historical reconstruction. The 52-square-kilometre park includes some 50 buildings, the blackened shells of other structures and huge stone fortifications. These sites are more than monuments and museums. Many have costumed guides and sound-and-light shows recreating the past. In all, there are 129 national historic sites, of which 55 are listed here. (Farwell's Trading Post is not a designated site.)

Fort Lennox (Que.)

1 Fort Rodd Hill
2 *St. Roch*
3 Fort Langley
4 Fort St. James
5 Dawson City Buildings
6 S.S. *Keno*
7 Rocky Mountain House
8 Fort Walsh
9 Farwell's Trading Post (near Fort Walsh)
10 Fort Battleford
11 Batoche
12 Fort Espérance
13 Lower Fort Garry
14 Prince of Wales Fort
15 York Factory
16 Fort St. Joseph
17 Fort Malden
18 Woodside
19 Fort George
20 Queenston Heights and Brock's Monument
21 Butler's Barracks
22 Bethune Memorial House
23 Kingston Martello Towers
24 Bellevue House
25 Battle of the Windmill
26 Fort Wellington
27 Rideau Canal
28 Fort Témiscamingue
29 Sir Wilfrid Laurier NHS
30 Coteau-du-Lac
31 Fort Chambly
32 Fort Lennox
33 Forges du Saint-Maurice
34 Fortifications of Québec
35 Artillery Park
36 Cartier-Brébeuf National Historic Site
37 Maillou House
38 St. Andrews Blockhouse
39 Carleton Martello Tower
40 Port Royal
41 Prince of Wales Martello Tower
42 Fort Edward
43 Fort Anne
44 York Redoubt
45 Halifax Citadel
46 Grand Pré
47 Fort Beausejour
48 Province House
49 Fort Amherst
50 Alexander Graham Bell NHS
51 Fortress of Louisbourg
52 Castle Hill
53 Cape Spear
54 Signal Hill
55 L'Anse aux Meadows
56 Port au Choix

The First Canadians

Ice-age glaciers created a land link between Siberia and Alaska, providing a means of passage for the first immigrants to North America. But scholars disagree as to when man first traversed it. Finds in the Yukon's Old Crow Basin—ice-free during most of the Pleistocene Period—support a date of at least 27,000 B.P. (before present). Evidence from Alberta may push that date back even farther, perhaps to 40,000 B.P.

Whenever they came, the first Canadians were neither explorers nor settlers nor adventurers. They were hungry nomads following the game upon which their survival depended. These ancestors of today's Indians and Inuit needed intelligence and imagination to adapt to the wondrous, variegated new continent. They had to learn to live on frozen tundra, in forests, on grassy plains and high mountains, and along rugged coastlines.

To survive in these environments, the people developed weapons and techniques for hunting, learned to farm and forage, and used the natural medicines the earth provided. They built dwellings—from simple windbreaks to huge wooden buildings—for many climates, and watercraft for everything from river travel to whale hunting. Clothing was made from the skins of animals, and even woven tree bark. Tools were essential, and were fashioned from rock, wood, bone and copper.

As the people spread over the continent, languages and lifestyles developed which were as diverse as those of Europe. Indians of the Subarctic and the Plains, where game was plentiful, became hunters. The rich resources of the sea made fishing a mainstay of West Coast and maritime Woodland tribes. When workable soil and ample water were available, as in the wood-

lands of southern Ontario, several tribes turned to farming. They and other groups acted as middlemen in the exchange of goods among tribes.

Social and political structures also varied. Iroquoians of the populous Eastern Woodlands felt intense tribal loyalty, but the concern of nomads in the sparsely populated Subarctic did not extend beyond the family. The Inuit were an egalitarian people; among the West Coast tribes, individuals were rigidly ranked by lineage and wealth. Despite this remarkable diversity, the Indians and Inuit existed in rare harmony with their environment, holding that all living things—plants as well as animals—had souls and were to be shown respect. They had a basic appreciation of the interdependence of all living things—an attitude still only dimly understood by modern man.

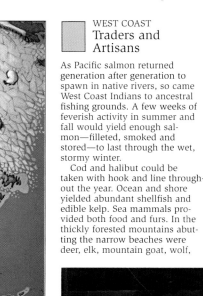

Across an Arctic Bridge Glaciers penetrated deep into the Northern Hemisphere during the Pleistocene, locking up so much water that sea levels dropped some 120 metres. Beringia, the land bridge between Siberia and Alaska (lightly shaded area in map above), vanished and reappeared with the ebb and flow of the glaciers, but was exposed for two extended periods: between 34,000 and 30,000 B.C. and again between 26,000 and 11,000 B.C. Migrating Asian hunters followed such game as mammoths and caribou down ice-free corridors (arrows) to the heart of the continent, perhaps as early as 40,000 years ago.

25,000 B.C.	Caribou bone scraper, Yukon—earliest evidence of man in North America.	*Caribou bone scraper*
10,000	Paleo-Indians hunt giant ice-age mammals.	
8000	Ancestors of Subarctic Indians move north in wake of receding ice sheet.	
7000	First settlements along Pacific Coast.	
4000	Last of the ice-age megafauna disappear.	*Stone mortar and pestle*
2000	Copper is mined on the upper Great Lakes.	*Copper blade*
2000	First wave of immigration to Arctic (Small Tool Tradition) begins.	*Bone harpoon head*
1000	Pottery made in eastern Canada.	
A.D. 300	Village Tradition settlements begin to dot Prairies.	*Reed duck decoy*
500	Beans, maize and squash cultivated in Eastern Woodlands.	
1000	Thule—ancestors of present-day Inuit—replace Dorset culture across Arctic.	*Ivory snow goggles*
1400	West Coast tribes establish vast trade network.	
1600	Mohawk, Oneida, Onondaga, Cayuga and Seneca form powerful Iroquois confederacy.	*Carved owl's head*

WEST COAST
Traders and Artisans

As Pacific salmon returned generation after generation to spawn in native rivers, so came West Coast Indians to ancestral fishing grounds. A few weeks of feverish activity in summer and fall would yield enough salmon—filleted, smoked and stored—to last through the wet, stormy winter.

Cod and halibut could be taken with hook and line throughout the year. Ocean and shore yielded abundant shellfish and edible kelp. Sea mammals provided both food and furs. In the thickly forested mountains abutting the narrow beaches were deer, elk, mountain goat, wolf,

Kwakiutl

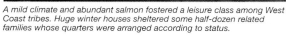

A mild climate and abundant salmon fostered a leisure class among West Coast tribes. Huge winter houses sheltered some half-dozen related families whose quarters were arranged according to status.

bear, beaver and marten. Cedar grown huge in the mild, damp climate made dugout canoes up to 22 metres long in which paddlers would hunt whales or trade with neighboring tribes. Cedar posts and beams framed houses 20 metres wide and more than 90 metres long. The wood, easily split with stone tools, made planks to sheath houses; its shredded bark was woven into rain cloaks, mats and conical hats.

So much wealth so easily obtained left time for artistic expression. Brightly colored designs and stylized animal forms were woven into blankets of dog and goat hair. Festive and utilitarian objects of wood were decorated with elaborate, carved designs: this sculpture in wood is one of Canada's finest arts.

Because the Coastal people had an abundance of necessities, seaboard trade centered on luxuries. The Nootkas offered whale products, for example, in exchange for ceremonial canoes built by the Haidas of the Queen Charlotte Islands. Slaves—considered the ultimate sign of wealth—were a major item of barter. There was also much trade with the tribes of the interior, the Kwakiutls and Tlingits acting as middlemen.

No occasion was more important among most West Coast Indians than the potlatch, an elaborate ceremony given by one clan to humble another. Such ceremonies offered the hosts an opportunity to display their wealth—thus confirming their status—through lavish gifts and the destruction of valuable possessions.

PLATEAU
Fishermen and Foragers

Wedged between the Coast Mountains and the Continental Divide, the interior Plateau formed a cul-de-sac into which migrant people of various languages and customs moved over many centuries.

The Columbia and Fraser rivers were the arteries of this landlocked region. They were the avenues of trade and travel and, in season, a source of food in migrating salmon. Their banks provided homesites for countless small tribes speaking dialects of four major languages.

Most Plateau people spent

Spears in hand, Plateau Indians fish for salmon on the Columbia.

summers in lodges constructed of bulrush mats layered over cottonwood frames. In winter they lived in semiunderground earthen lodges, entered by way of a notched log ladder through a central roof opening. Early spring found them combing the

ground for wild carrots, wild onions, bitterroot and camas root. The starchy bulb of the camas (a variety of lily) was eaten raw, roasted, or pulverized into cakes, which were boiled. Fish, berries and game completed the Plateau diet. The cold climate and poor soil prevented widespread agriculture..

Trade thrived throughout the river-laced Plateau region. Dugouts brought merchants from the West Coast bearing sea otter pelts, decorative shells and baskets; along with material goods, they passed on their love of wealth, status and power. Plateau traders paddled pine and cottonwood dugouts downstream to barter fur pelts, copper, jadeite and herbs with coastal tribes.

Most Plateau groups had few, if any, political ties outside their loosely organized villages; their culture was essentially a patchwork quilt with the pieces provided by their neighbors. Religion, dress, customs, housing—all reflected regions bordering the Plateau.

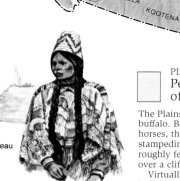

Plateau

PLAINS
People of the Buffalo

The Plains Indians lived off the buffalo. Before the use of horses, they hunted on foot, stampeding the buffalo into a roughly fenced enclosure or over a cliff—a buffalo jump.

Virtually every part of the buffalo was utilized. Meat was dried on racks and made into jerky, or pounded together with fat and berries to make pemmican, a concentrated, high-protein food carried on the trail. Hides were made into leggings, dresses and moccasins. Skins taken in autumn and winter, when the hair was long and thick, served as blankets and robes. Buffalo hair, woven, became strong rope; loose, it stuffed cradleboards, moccasins

Copper

ARCTIC
Survivors in an Icy Realm

From the eastern tip of Siberia, across Alaska and Canada to Greenland, Inuit territory stretched more than 8000 kilometres. Their homeland was the tundra: rocky, rolling plains bearing little vegetation other than mosses, lichens and low-lying bushes; a bitter, snow-bound world in winter, a mosquito-infested quagmire in summer.

Along the Arctic Coast, seals, whales and walruses were hunted with spear and lance. Fish was an important food, especially when meat supplies ran low. The land yielded other game—from caribou and an occasional polar bear to burrowing voles and lemmings. Birds were snared with seal-thong nets or felled by darts, sticks and stones.

Blubber, meat and fish were eaten when raw (and most nutritious), and partially digested lichen from a caribou's stomach was a delicacy. Driftwood—the only wood available—was carved and pegged to make harpoons and sleds. Where there was no wood, caribou antlers were pieced together. In an emergency, Inuit built sleds of frozen fish or hides—sleds which could be eaten if necessary.

As autumn waned, many Inuit gathered in groups of 100 or more on the sea ice to build winter snowhouse villages. When stormbound, an entire village might gather in a large snowhouse to take part in a drum dance, watch wrestling matches or witness a shaman's attempt to quell a storm.

The Inuit had 100 words for various types of snow but not one word for chief. Power lay in the community's acceptance or rejection of its members. There were no bad hunters, just "unlucky" ones. When all luck ran out, people died.

Intensely spiritual, all Inuit shared an unshakable belief in the supernatural, and their daily lives were directed by concerns over human and animal souls, monsters and deities. They relied on shamans and medicine men to protect them from evil spirits.

Despite their constant struggle for survival, the Inuit lived life one day at a time, with constant cheerfulness that puzzled early European explorers—but for which the Inuit had an explanation: "If you knew what horrors we often have to live through, you would understand why we are so fond of laughing."

Evidence of the antiquity of Northern art, this shaman's mask (left) dates back 1000 years. Ivory goggles (below) shielded eyes from the sun's glare, preventing snow blindness. In a 19th-century engraving (bottom), a lone Inuit hunter sits patiently beside a seal hole, watching for signs of his prey. He would then harpoon the seal sight unseen and chop the hole large enough to land it.

Labrador

Canada in 1500

By 1500, Indian population patterns in Canada were well established. The map (left) locates major tribal groups at the beginning of the 16th century. Names within each color-coded cultural zone place the Indians according to historical evidence. Because of shifting of tribes, some locations are only approximate. Groups often moved from place to place as climate changed, game migrated or dwindled, or hostile neighbors threatened—a situation that accelerated as European settlement spread.

PER

CENTRAL

ARIBOU

PEWYAN

Naskapi

LABRADOR

NASKAPI

CREE

R E E

MONTAGNAIS

MICMAC

MALECITE

OJIBWA

ALGONQUIN

Assiniboine

BOINE

HURON

TOBACCO

NEUTRAL   IROQUOIS

BEOTHUK

Large animals were easy prey to Subarctic hunters on snowshoes.

Iroquois

SUBARCTIC
Nomads of the Northern Forest

Athapaskan-speaking tribes of the western Subarctic were nomadic hunters whose lives revolved around the caribou. They ate its flesh, made tools from its bones and antlers, and converted its skin into clothing and shelter. During spring and fall, hunting was a communal effort. Large numbers of caribou were driven into surrounds—corrals of wooden posts—or killed at river crossings.

When traveling, the band carried the entire camp on its backs. Women and children shouldered loads of up to 60 kilograms while men ranged through the woods in constant search of game.

Like the Woodland Algonkians farther south, Algonkians of the eastern Subarctic fished, foraged and hunted a variety of game. Meat and fat were used for food, bones for making implements. From hide, women sewed clothing, using tendons as thread. Moose and caribou stomachs were made into cooking pots, and glands were valued as medicine. From the wood, bark and roots of trees were made canoes and conical wigwams, snowshoes and toboggans.

In winter, three or four families frequently trekked and camped together. In summer, several groups hunted and fished cooperatively. During such gatherings, berry picking, dancing, storytelling and gambling alternated with the tanning of hides and construction of birchbark canoes.

and pillows. At birth, the Indian was often swaddled in the soft skin of a young calf; in death, a buffalo robe became his shroud.

Without buffalo skins there could have been no tepees. Not only was the tepee a movable dwelling, it was also a sacred place. The floor was the earth on which the Indians lived; the sides, vaulting to a peak, the sky. The tepee's roundness was a reminder of the sacred life circle, with no beginning or end, and behind the hearth, in even the most modest of tepees, was an earthen altar where incense was burned and prayers intoned.

Tribes left the open grasslands in late autumn, setting up winter camps along broad, timbered river valleys and scattering their tepees among the trees. Men drove buffalo into hobbling snowdrifts or stalked deer and elk. But severe winters thwarted even small-game hunting, and when dried meat and pemmican ran out, there was starvation.

In summer, when life was easy, the Plains people gave thanks to the Great Spirit through such rituals as the Sun Dance, which included feats of endurance and self-mutilation.

Flailing furiously with webbed sticks, Plains Indians play a version of today's lacrosse.

EASTERN WOODLANDS
Woodsmen and Warriors

As early as A.D. 1000, eastern Canada's woodlands began to show signs of human activity. There were green squares of maize and tobacco, as well as patches of ground farmed into sterility and abandoned. Fishing camps dotted the riverbanks, and hunting paths were hardened into well-trodden trails.

By the 1600s, two Indian language groups dominated the region: Algonquian and Iroquoian. The realm of the Algonquian tribes stretched from Lake Superior to the Atlantic. These tribes—Ojibwa, Algonquin, Micmac, and Malecite—warred with the Iroquoians, whose base south of the Great Lakes and the St. Lawrence extended into southern Ontario.

The life for the Algonkian-speaking tribes matched the seasons. In winter, they hunted deer, caribou and moose; in spring and summer, they ate fish, beaver and the flesh and eggs of birds, and gathered roots and berries, drying the surplus for periods of shortage; and in the fall, they returned to hunting.

Coastal, lake and river tribes also found a bounty in shellfish and marine mammals.

By contrast, the Iroquoian-speaking peoples, such as the Hurons of southern Ontario, lived in villages and depended heavily on agriculture. They cultivated beans, maize and squash—the "Three Sisters" — and tobacco, which had profound religious significance. These tribes made good use of materials at hand: clay, wood and bark for cooking utensils; bark for torches, canoes, dishes, wigwams and longhouses.

Warfare was a part of life for the Iroquoians. Although their battles involved small raiding parties, local rivalries were deep-rooted and intense. In the raids, enemies were slain, and captives and goods were taken. Prisoners might be tortured and killed, but they were often adopted into the captors' tribe to replace men who had died.

Birchbark canoes and wigwams identify a Woodland Indian camp of the 19th century.

29

Exploration From Sea to Sea

"Between Spain and India there is a small sea which may be crossed in a matter of a few days." So wrote Christopher Columbus, planning his 1492 voyage westward to Asia. Like most knowledgeable men of his time, Columbus believed that the world was round. But no one knew its size. He calculated that a mere 4400 kilometres of ocean lay between Europe and Asia. In fact, the distance was 16,000 kilometres—and a vast obstacle, the North American continent, blocked the way.

Legends hint at much earlier visits to the unknown continent: pilgrims from Britain in A.D. 75, the sixth-century missionary Saint Brendan seeking a "land of promise," Irish monks living along the St. Lawrence toward the end of the ninth century. Certainly Norwegian Vikings had reached North America 500 years before Columbus, but their settlements disappeared and Europe had forgotten the New World.

In the 15th century, the dream of a sea route to the spices, silks and jewels of the Orient lured Europe's kings and merchants to send explorers westward into the Sea of Darkness. These riches were available in Middle East markets, but Arab traders and Italian middlemen controlled all trade routes. By the late 1400s, better ships and navigation aids had made long ocean voyages possible. The new Portuguese caravels combined Arab lateen (triangular) sails for speed with the deep, sturdy hull of North European trading ships. Instruments that helped determine latitude gave sailors confidence on the sea.

Adventurers set out across the Atlantic and found, not Asia, but North America. Columbus believed until his death that he had reached the East Indies. In the summer of 1497 John Cabot, a Venetian in the service of England's Henry VII, became the first explorer since the Vikings to set foot on this continent. His exact landfall is not known. It may have been Cape Breton Island. But it was no land of silks and spices. His reports of the teeming Grand Banks fishing grounds, however, brought European fishing vessels to Canada's coast in the following years. Still convinced he had found Asia, Cabot set out again in 1498 in search of Japan, but never returned.

Gaspar Corte-Real, sailing from Portugal, landed in Labrador in 1501. His three ships separated near the Strait of Belle Isle, and Corte-Real was never seen again. In 1524 Giovanni da Verrazzano, in the service of France, landed near Cape Fear, North Carolina, and sailed north to Newfoundland. Gradually an accurate view of the new continent's coast emerged. But it was not until Jacques Cartier, sent by Francis I of France, landed on Canadian shores in 1534 that Newfoundland was discovered to be an island. On his second visit, in 1535, the existence of the St. Lawrence River—the key to the interior—became known.

The search for ways around or through the continent took explorers and traders farther inland as the New World revealed its real riches: furs. Rival European traders fighting for new territory moved gradually westward. But the exploration of Canada was to take three centuries to complete. Not until 1793, when the young Scottish fur trader Alexander Mackenzie reached the Pacific overland from Montreal, was the country finally crossed from sea to sea.

John Cabot's discovery of Canada and the Grand Banks in 1497 made him England's hero. "He goes dressed in silk," wrote a contemporary, "and these English run after him like mad." But Henry VII, who had hoped for gold, not fish, was less impressed. He paid Cabot £10. Cabot set out again, in 1498, to find the Orient, but never returned.

Jacques Cartier was contemptuous of the land (probably Labrador) he first saw in 1534, describing it as "the land God gave to Cain." In 1535 he discovered the St. Lawrence, and traveled 1300 kilometres up what he thought was a waterway to the Orient to the Iroquois village of Hochelaga, where eventually Montréal would grow.

A Race for Furs—and a Continent Spanned

No silks or spices filled the holds of European ships returning from the new land. Explorers found only fish off Canada's shores, and the search for a passage to Asia continued. Only slowly did Europe realize that the furs for which fishermen bartered with the Indians could be as valuable as the riches of the Orient.

Led by the visionary Samuel de Champlain, the French returned to North America in the 17th century. Champlain traveled inland from the St. Lawrence, charting much of the Great Lakes region. In 1615 he followed the waterways to Georgian Bay, pioneering the main fur-trade route to the West.

Traders, missionaries and explorers extended the horizons of New France. In 1672 the Jesuit Charles Albanel traveled north to Hudson Bay. Fur trader René-Robert Cavelier de La Salle traced the Mississippi to the Gulf of Mexico, and in 1682 claimed its enormous watershed in the name of Louis XIV. In the early 1700s, Pierre de La Vérendrye and his sons reached the Prairies, establishing a chain of trading posts as they went.

Meanwhile, the English Hudson's Bay Company was establishing a stronghold in the north. Pierre-Esprit Radisson

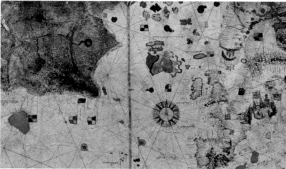

Using John Cabot's information, Columbus's shipmate Juan de la Cosa drew the first map (left) depicting North America in 1500.

Cabot 1497
Corte-Real 1501
Verrazzano 1524

and Médard Chouart des Groseilliers, disenchanted with the French governor in Québec, had found backers in the court of England's Charles II for their scheme to take furs out by sea from the great uncharted "Bay of the North." In 1670 the company was granted a trade monopoly in the bay.

Company policy was to trade only from its bayside posts, but individuals roamed the interior to persuade Indians to desert French traders and bring their furs to the bay. In 1691 Henry Kelsey reached the plains of northern Saskatchewan. In 1754 Anthony Henday, a company laborer, became probably the first white man to see the Canadian Rockies.

The HBC was forced to abandon its "long sleep by the Frozen Sea" when aggressive Scots traders moved into Quebec after the British con-

quest and allied themselves with French-Canadian *voyageurs* to take over the French trade. Its monopoly thus challenged, the HBC sent traders inland. Indian reports of vast copper deposits sent Samuel Hearne to the Coppermine River in 1771. He was the first white man to reach the Arctic Ocean by land.

As competition sharpened, the Montreal traders joined forces in 1787 to form the North West Company. Seeking a passage through the Rockies, Nor'Wester Alexander Mackenzie discovered the river that bears his name in 1789. In 1793 he reached the Pacific—the first European to cross the continent.

In the race for new sources of fur, in a double line of advance from Montréal and Hudson Bay, the Canadian West had been explored and mapped.

Through Arctic Ice—Triumph and Tragedy of a Legendary Passage

By the mid-1500s, explorers had found that the land barrier separating Europe from Asia presented a continuous coastline from the Arctic to Cape Horn. The remote, stormy Strait of Magellan to the south was Spanish territory. English explorers headed north into Arctic waters.

Adventurer Martin Frobisher, sent by Queen Elizabeth I, pioneered the search for a navigable, ice-free route around the north of the continent in 1576. He sailed west to Baffin Island and discovered Frobisher Bay, an inlet he mistakenly hoped was a strait leading to Asia.

Henry Hudson's ill-fated 1610 voyage took him through Hudson Strait to discover Hudson Bay (which he thought was the Pacific), before his mutinous crew set him adrift in a small boat.

Concluding that there was no way out of Hudson Bay to the west, William Baffin circumnavi-

gated Baffin Bay in 1616. This took him farther north than anyone else was to go for more than two centuries. On his return he discovered Lancaster Sound, but the importance of his discovery was not recognized. Only in the 19th century was this proven to be the entrance to the passage.

After wintering in James Bay

in 1631, Thomas James wrote a grimly discouraging account of his experiences. "In all probability," he concluded, "there is no northwest passage to the south sea." His backers gave up.

Two hundred years passed before the Royal Navy resumed the task. After the Napoleonic wars, Britain had men and ships to spare,

and in 1819 Arctic ice conditions were favorable. In that year Lieut. Edward Parry sailed into Lancaster Sound, through Barrow Strait and Viscount Melville Sound, farther west than anyone before him.

The most significant of 19th-century British Arctic ventures, the Franklin expedition, ended in tragedy. Sir John Franklin and his men were never heard from again after they left England in 1845. In the futile search for the Franklin party, however, most of Canada's Arctic coastline was charted, and much of the Arctic archipelago added to the map.

A route through the polar ice cap had now been revealed, but remained to be proved navigable. In 1903-06 Norwegian Roald Amundsen, in his converted fishing smack, Gjoa, made his way in ice-strewn waters through Lancaster Sound and the maze of Arctic islands into the Beaufort Sea. The Northwest Passage had finally been conquered.

HMS Investigator in pack ice north of Banks Island during Comdr. Robert McClure's unsuccessful 1850-54 search for the Franklin expedition.

Canada From the West

Canada's Pacific coast was all "uncertainty and conjecture" in 1778 when **Capt. James Cook** (*right*) anchored in Nootka Sound and became the first European to go ashore. Cook had surveyed the St. Lawrence and made his reputation as a mathematician and astronomer. He volunteered to search for a waterway through North America from the Pacific, eventually concluding that it did not exist.

Capt. George Vancouver, a 20-year-old midshipman on Cook's voyage to the Pacific, made a second survey of the coast in 1791-95, exploring inlets Cook had missed. In June 1793, he discovered the outlet of the Bella Coola River, just seven weeks before Alexander Mackenzie reached the same spot, and by 1795 had disproved the theory of a low-latitude Northwest Passage.

eputation for daredevil manship gained **Martin bisher** the blessing of Queen zabeth I for his expedition to d the Northwest Passage. ling into a large body of er off Baffin Island in July 76, he confidently named it robisher's streytes." His aits, however, proved to be y a bay, and later voyages came futile treasure hunts.

In December 1770, **Samuel Hearne,** a 24-year-old clerk for the Hudson's Bay Company, was sent on a 1400-kilometre trek to locate a northern river and its rumored wealth of copper. In July 1771, he discovered the Coppermine River—where copper was present but scarce—and continued on to become the first to reach the Arctic Ocean overland.

Hoping to blaze a fur-trading trail across the Rockies to the west coast, Scots-born **Alexander Mackenzie** followed an outlet from Great Slave Lake in 1789. When he found that it led instead to the Arctic Ocean, he named the river Disappointment. But in 1793, he finally succeeded in reaching the Pacific by land via the Peace and Parsnip rivers.

In 1819, while seeking the Northwest Passage, British naval officer **Edward Parry** forced his ketches *Hecla* and *Griper* into Lancaster Sound and beyond. Stopped by ice at Melville Island, he had nevertheless gone farther west than anyone before him. Parry's Arctic exploration methods and survival techniques became standard procedure.

Sir John Franklin's ships *Erebus* and *Terror* left England in 1845 to search for the Northwest Passage, but were never seen again. In the hunt for Franklin and his men, 40 search parties charted thousands of kilometres of Arctic coastline. In 1859, a message found in a cairn on King William Island told of Franklin's death in 1847.

In 1903-06, sailing with a six-man crew, Norwegian **Roald Amundsen** realized the goal of generations of explorers when he fought his way through shallow waters, drifting ice and dense fogs to navigate the Northwest Passage. In 1911 he became the first to reach the South Pole. But in 1928, while leading a rescue party in the Arctic, Amundsen vanished.

The major routes of more than four centuries of Canadian exploration are shown here in three phases. Only the most significant expeditions have been mapped, and where a succession of explorers followed the same route, only one is shown. The first globe traces the discovery and exploration of North America's east coast in the 15th and 16th centuries. (Because of conflicting evidence, early routes are approximate.) The center globe shows early searches for the Northwest Passage, and the exploration of the interior as far west as the Prairies. West coast expeditions, later searches for the Northwest Passage, and the charting of the Canadian North are mapped below.

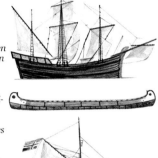

John Cabot's historic 1497 voyage was made in the barque Matthew, less than 23 metres long, with canvas that included a triangular sail copied from Arab spice traders. Improved navigation aids had made the crossing possible.

Birchbark canoes, from 5 to 10 metres long, carried explorers into Canada's interior on waterways unnavigable to conventional craft.

Roald Amundsen's Gjoa, the first ship to sail the Northwest Passage, was a converted herring smack 22 metres long and 3 metres wide. Packed with scientific instruments and supplies for the voyage, Gjoa barely rode above the waterline, but made the passage where larger ships had failed.

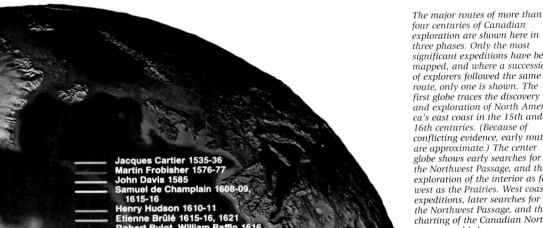

Jacques Cartier 1535-36
Martin Frobisher 1576-77
John Davis 1585
Samuel de Champlain 1608-09, 1615-16
Henry Hudson 1610-11
Etienne Brûlé 1615-16, 1621
Robert Bylot, William Baffin 1616
Thomas James 1631-32
Médard Chouart des Groseilliers 1654-56
Pierre-Esprit Radisson, Médard Chouart des Groseilliers 1659-60
René-Robert Caveller de La Salle 1669, 1678-80
Charles Albanel 1672
Henry Kelsey 1689, 1690-92
William Stuart 1715
Pierre de La Vérendrye 1731-41
Louis-Joseph, François de La Vérendrye 1742-43

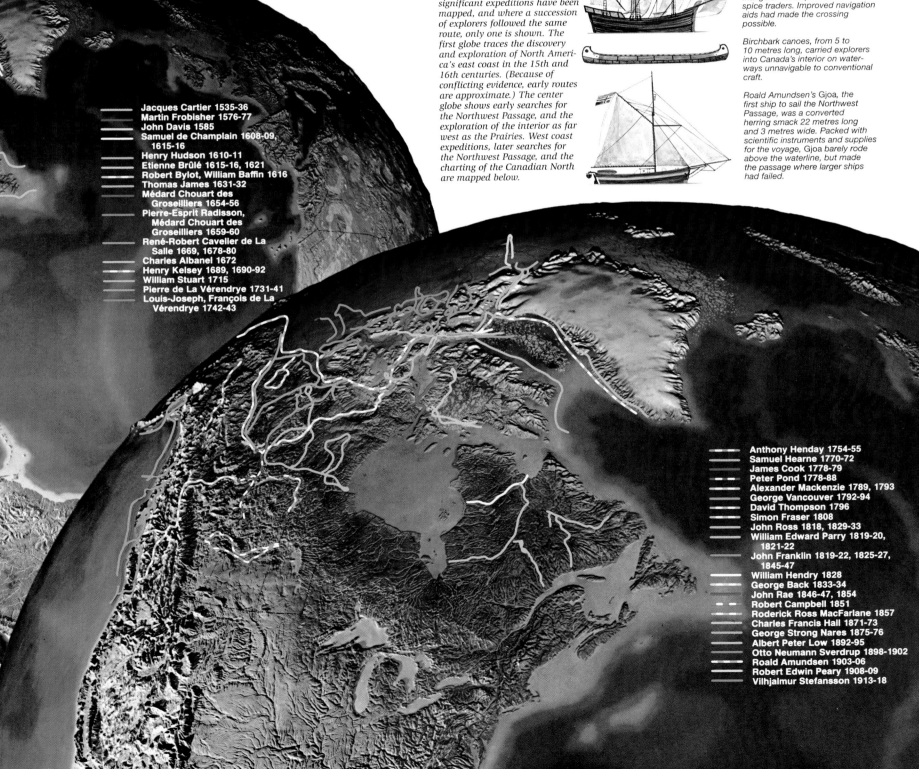

Anthony Henday 1754-55
Samuel Hearne 1770-72
James Cook 1778-79
Peter Pond 1778-88
Alexander Mackenzie 1789, 1793
George Vancouver 1792-94
David Thompson 1796
Simon Fraser 1808
John Ross 1818, 1829-33
William Edward Parry 1819-20, 1821-22
John Franklin 1819-22, 1825-27, 1845-47
William Hendry 1828
George Back 1833-34
John Rae 1846-47, 1854
Robert Campbell 1851
Roderick Ross MacFarlane 1857
Charles Francis Hall 1871-73
George Strong Nares 1875-76
Albert Peter Low 1892-95
Otto Neumann Sverdrup 1898-1902
Roald Amundsen 1903-06
Robert Edwin Peary 1908-09
Vilhjalmur Stefansson 1913-18

A New World Settled, a New Country Founded

The people of present-day Canada had little say in deciding the shape of their country. The settlements, from which Canada and the United States of America evolved, started off perched on the Atlantic shores and worked their way west. As this westward expansion went on, the boundary developed sector by sector. Treaties were made—and boundaries settled—between the United States and a distant Britain interested mainly in the fur-trading routes to the west and north. By the time Canada became a Confederation, her southern boundaries had been fixed from coast to coast.

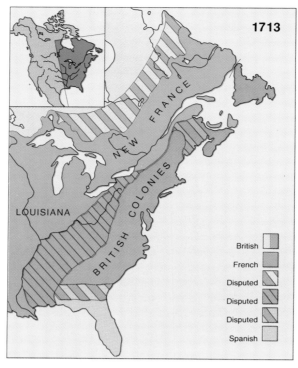

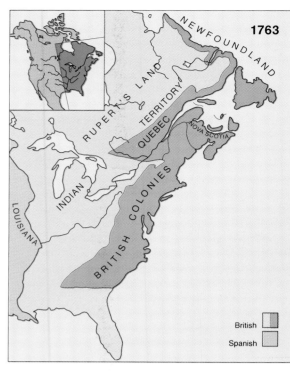

1713

British
French
Disputed
Disputed
Disputed
Spanish

1763

British
Spanish

Struggle for Survival—The Age of New France

France's empire in the New World began in 1605 with the tiny colony of Port Royal in Nova Scotia. Three years later Samuel de Champlain built his *Habitation* at Québec, its great shadowing rock a symbol of his determination and a destination for Indians traveling downriver with pelts to barter.

By 1700, Indians were trading 100,000 beaver pelts each year

Both Acadia, on the Atlantic, and Canada, along the St. Lawrence, were founded as fur-trading ventures. The quality of northern furs, the Grand Banks cod fisheries, territorial claims laid for France by Jacques Cartier, Spanish and English strength in the south—all led to the choice of a New France in the north. But as England and France warred in Europe, the territories France had chosen began to be contested.

As early as 1613, a party of English raiders from Virginia burned Port Royal. In 1627 the monopolistic Company of One Hundred Associates was set up to govern New France, promising to defend the colony and to send 200 settlers each year. But the next year, freebooting Englishmen intercepted the Company's first convoy of settlers and supplies and besieged Québec, forcing Champlain to surrender. Québec was returned to France in 1632 but the Company, interested only in fur profits, neglected colonization. The tiny settlements, isolated and poorly defended,

were frequently attacked by Iroquois tribes. Alienated by Champlain's support of their Algonkin and Huron enemies, the Iroquois had become allies of the English. Their hostility to the French was the cause of the death by torture of six Jesuit missionaries.

When Louis XIV established royal government in New France in 1663 there were fewer than 3000 inhabitants. He set up a sovereign council composed of a governor, the bishop, an intendant (administrator), and five colonists. Jean Talon, the first intendant, arrived in 1665. To spur immigration, he paid passages and provided land, supplies and tools. Bachelors were penalized—denied fishing, hunting and trapping rights—while parents of 10 or more children received 300 livres ($750) a year. Talon imported "king's girls" — orphans and farmers' daughters—to become wives and mothers. By 1673 the population had more than doubled.

Seigneurs, "persons of rank," were granted waterfront land, which they had to fill with tenant farmers. New France's first professional fighting force, the *Troupes de la Marine*, arrived from France in 1683 and, along with the colonial militia, checked the Iroquois threat for a time. Talon started a shipbuilding industry and a brewery, and encouraged farmers to grow hops, and hemp for thread, cloth, rope and sails.

Farms in New France were laid in narrow strips so that each seigneurial tenant had river frontage. Cool in summer and warm in winter, farmhouses were made of stone with metre-thick walls for stability. Steep gable roofs limited snow buildup; dormers were added as growing families needed top stories for bedrooms.

But the furs demanded by European fashion remained the economic backbone of the colony—and many of New France's young men defied government and church decrees to take to the forest as *coureurs de bois.* They traded with Indians, and their forays into the interior opened up the country. Montréal became the great entrepôt for the fur trade. Annual fairs were established, and bartering, feasting and brandy attracted hundreds of Algonkins, Hurons and Ottawas with their pelt-laden canoes.

By the 1680s the empire claimed by France extended beyond Lake Superior, and down the Mississippi to the Gulf of Mexico. But it was thinly held and most of its

inhabitants lived along the St. Lawrence between Québec and Montréal. The English colonies to the south, by contrast, had a population of 250,000. Their farmers and merchants enjoyed a flourishing trade with Europe and the West Indies. They had year-round access to the sea and a range of climates that favored varied and plentiful crops. To the north of New France, the English Hudson's Bay Company, formed in 1670, had claimed the whole of the Hudson Bay drainage basin as its territory.

The great imperial struggle for the continent began in 1689, when England joined a European alliance against Louis XIV. In North America, English and French colonists used Indian allies in guerrilla attacks on each other's forts and settlements. Québec withstood a siege in 1690, but this series of wars went badly for France. The Treaty of Utrecht in 1713 gave the Hudson Bay territory, Newfoundland and mainland Acadia to England. Some 1700 Acadians were forced to choose allegiance to the British Crown or exile. Most chose to stay on the fertile Fundy lowlands.

Left with an unpopulated Cape Breton Island as the last Atlantic approach to New France, the French built the Fortress of Louisbourg to protect it. The French fortress was captured by New England forces in 1745 but was returned three years later. The British founded Halifax in 1749 to rival Louisbourg.

Formidable but undermanned, isolated fortress Louisbourg guarded New France's Atlantic approach

The thirteen colonies had a population of 1.2 million by 1750; New France, only 55,000. But the English, hemmed in along a strip of Atlantic coastline, were prevented from

expanding beyond the Appalachians by France's claim to the midwest. The decisive conflict came with the Seven Years' War (1756-63).

Both the French and the British reinforced their colonial armies for this climactic struggle. France sent one of its ablest generals, the Marquis de Montcalm, as commander-in-chief. But the British sent more troops, their regulars numbering 23,000 in 1757, as opposed to 6800 for the French. Louisbourg fell to the British in June 1758. A year later, Gen. James Wolfe arrived off Quebec with 168 ships. On Sept. 13, 1759, he led his men up an undefended cliff to the Plains of Abraham and took the city. Both Wolfe and Montcalm were killed. Montreal's frail defenses fell a year later. In 1762 Louisiana was ceded to Spain, and in 1763, the Treaty of Paris made Canada a British colony. New France was no more.

Montcalm's death in 1763 sealed the fate of New France

1600	1610	1620	1630	1640	1650	1660	1670	1680	1690	1700	1710	1720	1730
	• Port Royal founded, first successful settlement				• Maisonneuve brings first colonists to Montréal		• Royal government established at Québec 1665		• La Salle claims Louisiana for France		• Iroquois sign peace treaty with New France		• French begin construction of Fortress Louisbourg
			• Kirke brothers capture French convoy in Gulf of St. Lawrence		• Iroquois destroy Jesuit missions to the Hurons; five priests martyred		• Hudson's Bay Company founded		• Lachine Massacre triggers new series of Iroquois raids		• Port Royal surrenders for last time to English		First road from Québec to Montréal, Chemin du Roi, opened
• Québec founded by Champlain			• English capture Québec					• La Salle builds Griffon, first ship launched on Great Lakes		• Frontenac dies			
• First Jesuits arrive in New France						• Laval becomes first bishop of Québec							
• Recollet missionaries arrive in New France		• Treaty of St. Germain-en-Laye restores Québec to France					• Jean Talon becomes first Intendant of New France, Canada's earliest sponsored immigrants, the filles du roi, arrive		• British capture Port Royal but fail to take Québec			• A 12,000-man British force from Boston out to conquer Québec is shipwrecked in the Gulf of St. Lawrence	First Canadian iron foundry, Les Forges du Saint-Maurice, established at Trois-Rivières
• Port Royal sacked by Virginians			• Champlain dies at Québec							• French attack and destroy British settlements in Newfoundland	• Treaty of Utrecht cedes Hudson Bay, Newfoundland and mainland Acadia to Britain		
• Louis Hébert and family, first settlers at Québec			• Port Royal re-established at present-day Annapolis, N.S.										
							• Frontenac appointed Governor of New France						
• James VI of Scotland grants Nova Scotia to Sir William Alexander							• Fort Frontenac (Kingston) founded		• Treaty of Ryswick restores Acadia to France				

32

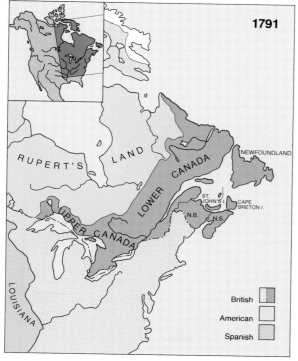

1791

NEWFOUNDLAND

RUPERT'S LAND

LOWER CANADA

UPPER CANADA

LOUISIANA

ST. JOHN'S I.
CAPE BRETON I.
N.B. N.S.

British
American
Spanish

Metis massacred 20 outmaneuvred Red River settlers and Assiniboia Governor Robert Semple at Seven Oaks in 1816

1866

NEWFOUNDLAND

RUPERT'S LAND

CANADA

N.B. N.S.
P.E.I.

British
American

British North America—Colony to Confederation

Following the Treaty of Paris, some 60,000 French Canadians faced life in a continent that was British from the Gulf of Mexico to Hudson Bay. They were under military government until 1774, when the British Parliament's Québec Act granted them political rights and religious freedom as Catholics, and confirmed the system of French civil law and seigneurial land ownership.

After the outbreak of the American Revolution in 1775, British regulars and Canadian militia stood against invading American armies. When a second Treaty of Paris ended the war in 1783, the first boundary between Canada and the United States was fixed from the Atlantic to Lake of the Woods. Americans who supported the British during the revolution called themselves Loyalists. Others branded them traitors and hounded them off their land. Some 50,000 Loyalists fled northeast, to found New Brunswick, or north into the St. Lawrence Valley and the Great Lakes region. Their new land was forbidding and lonely—"the roughest I ever saw," said one. Those transported into the "Western Settlements" of Québec lived in tents until they could build log cabins. Difficult adjustments had to be mad between two quite different peoples and their legal, religious and social systems. The problem was partly solved in 1791 by the division of Québec

into Lower and Upper Canada, each with its own legislature and legal system.

By 1812, a half-million people were spread thinly over the Maritimes, and Lower and Upper Canada. In that same year, the vast plains of the West received their first European settlers as the Red River Settlement was established by the philanthropic Earl of Selkirk. But this venture angered the Metis, the mixed descendants of Indians and French and Scots fur traders, who considered the region their own. The new colonists also came into conflict with the North West Company, whose main trade route crossed Selkirk's land. Attacks on settlers by Metis and Nor'Westers resulted in the death of 20 settlers at the Seven Oaks Massacre in 1816. Reprisals followed. Five years later the Nor'Westers merged with the

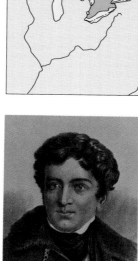

Lord Durham found "two nations warring" in Canada and proposed change in his 1839 report

Hudson's Bay Company. The Red River Settlement survived, grew and prospered.

After the indecisive War of 1812, British North America experienced an expansion of

trade with Britain, the West Indies and the Mediterranean countries. The timber trade and shipbuilding flourished. Upper Canada had 2000 sawmills by 1845 and British North America's merchant fleet grew into the third largest in the world. Montréal and Québec were busy commercial centers. York (renamed Toronto in 1834) grew into the business center of Upper Canada. Halifax was a major seaport and garrison town; Saint John, the trading center of a prosperous New Brunswick.

But the growing colonies were still ruled by governors accountable only to the British government. Executive councils controlled administrative appointments, banking and land grants. Unrest grew as Maritimers and Canadians became dissatisfied with the colonial constitutions and social structure.

Demands for reform were intense in both the Canadas. In Upper Canada they were prompted by abuses in government and the courts, and the power of the Anglican Church. In Lower Canada the struggle was also a social and religious one, French Canadians fighting for control of an English Executive Council. In 1837 armed rebellions broke out in both provinces. They were put down by British troops and militia—but they dramatized the need for change.

Lord Durham was sent out in 1838 to report on the rebellions and to suggest solutions. His

1839 *Report on the Affairs of British North America* led to the union of Upper and Lower Canada in 1841, and to the introduction of responsible government—but not before this latter goal was achieved in Nova Scotia. There, editor-orator Joseph Howe led a long battle against the local oligarchy and the British government. In 1848 his province formed the first responsible government in the overseas Empire. In the same year the Province of Canada also achieved responsible government, and by 1855, so had Newfoundland, Prince Edward Island and New Brunswick. In 1858 the Crown Colony of British Columbia was created.

Lord Durham had written that, "The North American colonist needs some nationality of his own," and now there was serious consideration of union among the colonies. When the American Civil War broke out in 1861, unease over the threat of an American invasion increased. At the same time, Britain, increasingly reluctant to spend money on the defense of British North America, was encouraging its colonies to move toward union and self-government.

In June 1864, a coalition of the Liberal-Conservative and Reform parties in the Province of Canada was formed to promote a confederation of all the colonies. The Maritimes, already considering their own union, were doubtful. At the Charlotte-

town Conference in 1864, Canada held out to the Maritimers the prospects of an intercolonial railway, assumption of their public debts, allowance for new debts, legislatures for local affairs, representation by population in an elected House of Commons and Maritime representation equal to that of the Canadas in an appointed Senate. But no resolution was passed.

In October of that year, the Québec Conference elaborated the Confederation scheme, and in 1865, the Canadian legislature voted in favor of it. Opposition was growing in the Maritimes, particularly Nova Scotia—but the British government wanted the colonies to unite.

The threat from the United States seemed greater after the North's victory in the Civil War in 1865. And in 1866, the Fenian Brotherhood made armed attacks across the border from New York State in an effort to foment rebellion against British rule. These attacks convinced some doubters in New Brunswick and Nova Scotia that Confederation was necessary to their survival.

The British Parliament passed the British North America Act in 1867, and on July 1, the new country came into being with four provinces: Nova Scotia, New Brunswick, Québec and Ontario—"One Dominion under the Name of Canada."

Some 14,000 Loyalist refugees landed at Saint John in 1783

Rough-hewn but practical, a typical Upper Canadian homestead was built of squared logs cleared from the fields. Other lumber went into snake fences that were "horse-high, bull-strong and skunk-tight." A settler might take three years to clear 30 acres. Until they were pulled, burned or rotted, stumps made one-third of the cleared land useless.

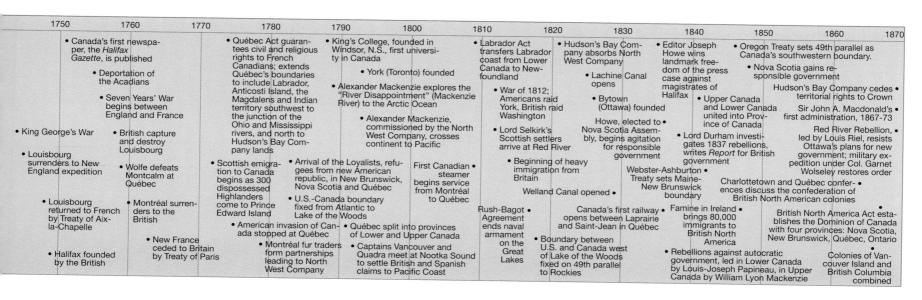

1750	1760	1770	1780	1790	1800	1810	1820	1830	1840	1850	1860	1870
	• Canada's first newspaper, the *Halifax Gazette*, is published		• Québec Act guarantees civil and religious rights to French Canadians; extends Québec's boundaries to include Labrador, Anticosti Island, the Magdalens and Indian territory southwest to the junction of the Ohio and Mississippi rivers, and north to Hudson's Bay Company lands	• King's College, founded in Windsor, N.S., first university in Canada		• Labrador Act transfers Labrador coast from Lower Canada to Newfoundland	• Hudson's Bay Company absorbs North West Company	• Editor Joseph Howe wins landmark freedom of the press case against magistrates of Halifax	• Oregon Treaty sets 49th parallel as Canada's southwestern boundary.			
	• Deportation of the Acadians			• York (Toronto) founded						• Nova Scotia gains responsible government		
				• Alexander Mackenzie explores the "River Disappointment" (Mackenzie River) to the Arctic Ocean		• War of 1812; Americans raid York, British raid Washington	• Lachine Canal opens			Hudson's Bay Company cedes territorial rights to Crown		
	• Seven Years' War begins between England and France							• Bytown (Ottawa) founded	• Upper Canada and Lower Canada united into Province of Canada	Sir John A. Macdonald's first administration, 1867-73		
• King George's War				• Alexander Mackenzie, commissioned by the North West Company, crosses continent to Pacific		• Lord Selkirk's Scottish settlers arrive at Red River	Howe, elected to Nova Scotia Assembly, begins agitation for responsible government	• Lord Durham investigates 1837 rebellions, writes *Report* for British government	Red River Rebellion, led by Louis Riel, resists Ottawa's plans for new government; military expedition under Col. Garnet Wolseley restores order			
• Louisbourg surrenders to New England expedition	• British capture and destroy Louisbourg		• Scottish emigration to Canada begins as 300 dispossessed Highlanders come to Prince Edward Island	• Arrival of the Loyalists, refugees from new American republic, in New Brunswick, Nova Scotia and Québec	First Canadian steamer begins service from Montréal to Québec		• Beginning of heavy immigration from Britain		• Webster-Ashburton Treaty sets Maine-New Brunswick boundary	• Charlottetown and Québec conferences discuss the confederation of British North American colonies		
• Louisbourg returned to French by Treaty of Aix-la-Chapelle	• Montréal surrenders to the British		• American invasion of Canada stopped at Québec	• U.S.-Canada boundary fixed from Atlantic to Lake of the Woods		• Rush-Bagot Agreement ends naval armament on the Great Lakes	• Welland Canal opened	• Canada's first railway opens between Laprairie and Saint-Jean in Québec	• Famine in Ireland brings 80,000 immigrants to British North America		British North America Act establishes the Dominion of Canada with four provinces: Nova Scotia, New Brunswick, Québec, Ontario	
• Halifax founded by the British	• New France ceded to Britain by Treaty of Paris		• Montréal fur traders form partnerships leading to North West Company	• Québec split into provinces of Lower and Upper Canada			• Boundary between U.S. and Canada west of Lake of the Woods fixed on 49th parallel to Rockies	• Rebellions against autocratic government, led in Lower Canada by Louis-Joseph Papineau, in Upper Canada by William Lyon Mackenzie			Colonies of Vancouver Island and British Columbia combined	
				• Captains Vancouver and Quadra meet at Nootka Sound to settle British and Spanish claims to Pacific Coast								

Triumphs and Trials of Nationhood

1867

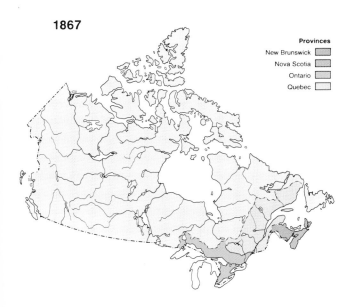

Provinces
New Brunswick
Nova Scotia
Ontario
Quebec

1873

Territories
Northwest Territories

Provinces
New Brunswick
Nova Scotia
Ontario
Quebec
Manitoba
British Columbia
Prince Edward Island

1895

Territories
Northwest Territories
District of Keewatin

Provinces
New Brunswick
Nova Scotia
Ontario
Quebec
Manitoba
British Columbia
Prince Edward Island

On July 1, 1867, the new Dominion of Canada was born. Its first prime minister was Sir John A. Macdonald who, apart from a five-year break, was to remain in power until his death in 1891. But the Dominion he was to govern was incomplete. Prince Edward Island and Newfoundland had refused to join, the vast prairie lands to the west and north belonged to the Hudson's Bay Company, and British Columbia seemed remote.

The first step toward forming a nation from sea to sea was the acquisition of the Northwest Territories from the Hudson's Bay Company. Manitoba, carved out of this area, became the fifth province in 1870. British Columbia, promised a railway link to the east, joined Confederation a year later. Prince Edward Island came into the Dominion in 1873 after a federal promise to establish permanent communication with the mainland and to assume the island's crippling railway debts.

The West now had to be governed and protected. American fur traders had begun to

After 30 months and three conferences, the Fathers of Confederation created the new four-province country which became, by royal proclamation, "One Dominion under the Name of Canada." On July 1, 1867, in Ottawa, Scots-born Sir John A. Macdonald (standing, center) was sworn in as Prime Minister with his cabinet.

Two rival groups, in Toronto and Montréal, applied for the charter. The Montrealers were awarded the contract—until it was revealed that they had subsidized Macdonald's reelection in 1872. The ensuing Pacific Scandal brought down the Conservative government in 1873.

Under the new Liberal government of Alexander Macken-

The CPR's Pacific Express, Canada's first transcontinental passenger train, arrived at Port Moody, B.C., from Montréal on July 4, 1886.

move into the Canadian Prairies, and after the Cypress Hills massacre in May 1873, when Montana wolf hunters killed a group of Assiniboine Indians, the North West Mounted Police were organized. Treaties were negotiated with Plains Indians for their land. In September 1877, leaders of the Blackfoot Confederacy, the last of the Prairie Indians to surrender their lands, signed Treaty No. 7 and ceded 130,000 square kilometres of what is now southern Alberta to the federal government.

The railways were the links that united the young nation. The Intercolonial Railway between Halifax and Québec went into operation in July 1876. As for the transcontinental route to British Columbia, the Macdonald government, realizing that the estimated costs of more than $100 million would consume much of Canada's available capital, decided to allow a private company to build the railroad.

zie, government-supervised construction began between Fort William, Ont., and Winnipeg. Five years later the Conservatives were returned to office, but progress on the railway was hampered by lack of funds. Finally, in February 1881, a private company was

formed—the Canadian Pacific Railway. The CPR's dynamic general manager, William Cornelius Van Horne, achieved what had been thought impossible. Regular service was inaugurated on June 28, 1886, when the Pacific Express left Montréal for Port Moody, B.C. It arrived at noon on July 4, six days and 4652 kilometres from Montréal.

The CPR enabled the government to transport troops west to defeat the combined Métis-Indian forces in the Northwest Rebellion of 1885. The Métis leader, Louis Riel, had demanded self-government and recognition of their title to the land, proclaiming a provisional government and threatening the North West Mounted Police with a "war of extermination."

The execution of Louis Riel stirred great controversy. The government was caught between those who demanded Riel's death and others who felt that the government had provoked the rebellion.

The Conservatives, in power for 24 of the Dominion's first 29 years, fell in 1896 on the Manitoba Schools Question. Roman Catholics felt that the province's "nondenominational" schools were a Protestant system in disguise. But the federal Tories

were divided on the issue and in 1896 they were beaten by the Liberals under Sir Wilfrid Laurier.

During his 15-year administration, Laurier presided over a dramatic transformation of Canada's economy. Technological change improved communications. Industrial development, begun in the 1880s and spurred by Macdonald's National Policy, encouraged a shift of population toward cities. Canada's urban population grew from 30 to 46% of entire population between 1891 and 1911. At the close of the Laurier era, Canada had established a solid manufacturing base.

This era was also an age of massive immigration to the West. Canada's population in 1901 was 5.4 million. Ten years later, it was 7.2 million, with the largest growth in western Canada. In 1913 alone, more than 400,000 immigrants arrived, and many went west to take up farming. On the treeless grasslands toward the U.S. border, the settlers built houses of sod—"prairie shingles." Wheat production leaped from 56 million bushels in 1901 to 231 million in 1912. In 1905 the two new prairie provinces of Alberta and Saskatchewan were created. The borders of Ontario, Manitoba and Québec were extended north in 1912, but the Québec–Labrador boundary remained unsettled until 1927.

This buoyant era ended, however, in 1914, when the British Empire went to war against Germany. In October of that year, 33,000 Canadian troops sailed overseas; at least 400,000 others were to follow. By 1917, the rate of Canadian casualties—10,000 at Vimy Ridge alone—caused a crisis at home. The toll of dead and wounded was outstripping enlistments, and Sir Robert Borden's Conservative government introduced conscription. By the end of the war in 1918, more than 60,000 Canadians had died.

Ottawa was chosen as Canada's capital in 1857. Two years later, ground was broken for the Parliament Buildings.

1870	1875	1880	1885	1890	1895	1900	1905	1910	1915	1920	1925
					Canada-Alaska boundary fixed •		• Provinces of Alberta and Saskatchewan formed		• Britain declares war on Germany. More than 30,000 Canadian volunteers leave for England	• First administration of Arthur Meighen (Cons.)	
• British Columbia, promised transcontinental railway in ten years, joins Confederation	Second Macdonald administration			• Manitoba law abolishes denominational schools and use of French as legislative language, creates nondenominational school system		• Yukon District becomes a separate territory				First administration of W. L. Mackenzie King	• Old Age Pension Act
	• British dominion over Arctic islands passes to Canada				• Canadian soldiers take part in Boer War	• Northwest Territories divided into Mackenzie, Keewatin and Franklin districts	• World War I		King-Byng Affair •
Administration of Alexander Mackenzie, first Liberal prime minister		• 15,000 Chinese laborers imported to work on the Canadian Pacific Railway				Early-maturing Marquis wheat introduced		• Ontario, Manitoba and Québec boundaries extended north to present limits	Second administration of W. L. Mackenzie King
• Manitoba becomes the fifth province	• Blackfoot Confederacy last of Indian tribes to surrender prairie lands in exchange for reserves	• Secessionist government elected in Nova Scotia, but fails to take action	Series of short-lived Conservative governments, headed successively by John Abbott, John Thompson, Mackenzie Bowell and Sir Charles Tupper	• Doukhobors settle in the West	First manned flight in British Empire, at Baddeck, N.S., by J. A. D. McCurdy	Canada, as separate state, signs Treaty of Versailles ending World War I	Québec-Labrador boundary settled by Privy Council
• Intercolonial Railway opened between Halifax and Québec	• Wheat first exported from Manitoba to Britain	• Canadian Pacific Railway completed		*Empress of Ireland* sinks in St. Lawrence, 1015 die	Union government led by Borden	• Bankrupt railroads amalgamated into publicly owned Canadian National Railways
• District of Keewatin created from part of Northwest Territories	• First use of secret ballot in federal general election	• Northwest Rebellion erupts over land and hunting grievances; Louis Riel forms provisional government, but yields to military force and is hanged	• Sir John A. Macdonald dies	Administration of Sir Wilfrid Laurier (Lib.)	Mariner Joseph-Elzéar Bernier affirms Canadian sovereignty in Arctic by erecting a plaque on Melville Island	Conservative administration of Sir Robert Borden	• Drs. F.G. Banting and C.H. Best discover insulin
• Prince Edward Island enters Confederation			• Heavy immigration from Europe until World War I		Royal Canadian Navy formed	Halifax explosion kills nearly 2000 people and levels north end of city	• Conscription and personal income tax introduced	• Group of Seven officially formed
• North West Mounted Police formed		• First Ukraine settlers arrive	• Klondike Gold Rush	Battles of Vimy Ridge, Hill 70, Passchendaele •	Royal Canadian Air Force created	• Canada signs Halibut Treaty with U.S.—first bilateral treaty signed independently of Britain
											• Wall Street Crash marks beginning of ten Depression years

Slabs of sod, held together by wheatgrass roots and often thatched with grass, made the first homes of many Prairie settlers.

Borden accompanied British leaders to Versailles and took an active part in the peace-making of 1919. At his insistence, Canada signed the peace treaties separately and with that, achieved its first significant recognition as an autonomous nation, a status ultimately confirmed by the Statute of Westminster in 1931.

The postwar years brought economic expansion and social change. Automobiles became common. Women received the vote. Prohibition, introduced temporarily during the war, was gradually lifted by the introduction of government-owned liquor stores. At home and abroad, stock markets soared—and their crash in 1929 led to the Great Depression.

The Conservatives, under R. B. Bennett, defeated the Liberals in 1930 but inherited mass unemployment. By 1933, one quarter of the labor force was out of work. Trade and the gross national product declined. A major exporter of raw materials, Canada was badly hit by falling foreign demand. The world price of wheat plummeted, and a series of devastating droughts in 1931 and 1934 ruined thousands of western farmers. Mackenzie King's Liberals, reelected in 1935, started an inquiry into constitutional powers, for the Depression was demonstrating that the federal government lacked the power to deal with such an emergency. However, by the time a Royal Commission recommended changes in 1940, the country was again at war.

Canada made its own declaration against Germany on September 10, 1939, seven days after Britain. With a population of only 11 million, Canada gathered together a military force of 1,086,343 men and women. Some 42,000 Canadians were killed during the war.

Canadian soldiers fought in Hong Kong and Western Europe. The Royal Canadian Navy helped convoy merchant ships through a North Atlantic infested with U-boats. The Royal Canadian Air Force became one of the Allies' largest. Under the British Commonwealth Air Training Plan, Canada trained 131,553 airmen at 97 flying schools across the country.

After the war, Canada assumed a middle-power role in the world. A strengthened sense of nationhood emerged at home. Canadian citizenship was proclaimed in 1947. The

Supreme Court of Canada became the court of last resort when appeals to Britain's Privy Council were abolished in 1949. Mackenzie King retired in 1948 after 22 years as prime minister—a British Commonwealth record—and was succeeded by Louis St. Laurent, who welcomed Newfoundland as the tenth province in 1949.

Oil discoveries provided a major impetus to the Canadian

NUNAVUT

In June 1993, the Canadian parliament passed a bill creating the new Arctic territory of Nunavut, which will come into existence officially on April 1, 1999. Nunavut—"our land" in Inuktitut—embraces 2 million square kilometres and is home to 22,000, whose numbers include 17,000 Inuit.

economy in the immediate postwar years. In February 1947, Leduc No. 1 came in south of Edmonton, the first major indication of Alberta's huge reserves of oil and natural gas. Iron ore was exploited in Ungava, along the Québec–Labrador boundary, and the need to facilitate ore shipments spurred the construction of the St. Lawrence Seaway. The most controversial project was a natural gas pipeline from Alberta to Montréal, the financing of which became a hotly debated issue and contributed to the St. Laurent government's fall in 1957. John Diefenbaker, Canada's first western prime minister, led the Tories back to power and, in an election the following year, obtained a huge majority: 208 out of 265 Commons seats.

The 1960s saw a resurgence of nationalism in Quebec, characterized by the development of a separatist movement and the emergence of a new pro-Confederation group led by Pierre Elliott Trudeau. After the federal Liberals, led by Lester B.

Pearson, were returned to office in 1963, they appointed a Royal Commission on Bilingualism and Biculturalism to examine the whole field of French–English relations, then took its advice by initiating measures to expand federal government services in French for French-speaking Canadians. When he replaced Pearson in 1968, Trudeau continued this policy, and the Official Languages Act of 1969 promoted the use of French in the federal public service.

Separatist strength grew in Québec, culminating in the triumph of the Parti Québécois under René Lévesque in the provincial election of 1976.

Canadians who stormed Vimy Ridge gave the British Empire its first major victory in World War I.

Lévesque had told the voters of Québec he would seek a special mandate before taking any steps toward separation from Canada but, in May 1980, some 60% of Québec voters rejected "sovereignty-association."

Trudeau's administration, beset by the nation's problems of inflation and unemployment, fell when the 1979 national election, which brought the Conservatives under Joe Clark to power. Clark's government fell nine months later over the proposed budget, and the Trudeau administration was returned with a strong majority in February 1980.

Trudeau proposed "patriation" of the constitution, which would eliminate British approval for Canadian amendments to the British North America Act 1867. Trudeau's proposed reforms were approved by all provinces except Québec. The revised constitution, which included the Charter of Rights and Freedoms, took effect on April 17, 1982.

A major recession took hold during the early 1980s. By

1983, 14 percent of the Canadian workers had no jobs—the highest unemployment rate since the 1930s. John Turner became Liberal leader and prime minister when Trudeau retired in June 1984, but he lost the federal election in September 1984 to Brian Mulroney. The Conservatives took 211 seats, the largest majority in the history of Canada's parliament.

Canada's economy rebounded in the late 1980s; the unemployment rate fell to 7.3% by 1989. In 1987, Canada and the United States agreed to reduce tariffs between the two countries over a ten-year period. The free-trade pact was the main issue of the 1988 federal election, which produced a second Conservative majority government. The pact became law on January 1, 1989. Three years later, Canada, the U.S., and Mexico signed the North America Free Trade Agreement (NAFTA), which built on the earlier agreement.

Hope of gaining Québec's approval of the constitution grew in the late 1980s. In August 1987, the prime minister and all the premiers, meeting at Meech Lake, Qué., agreed on major reforms, which all provinces had to ratify by June 1990. The Meech Lake Accord collapsed when Manitoba and Newfoundland failed to meet the June deadline. Further constitutional reforms were included in the Charlottetown Accord of August 1992, but it was rejected by 54 percent of Canadian voters in a referendum held in October 1992.

Beleaguered by the constitutional impasse and a serious economic recession, Mulroney resigned in early 1993. His successor, Kim Campbell, Canada's first woman prime minister, lost her seat in the federal elections of October 1993, as did all but two Conservatives. The Liberals under Jean Chrétien won a majority government, with the remainder of the seats going to new political groupings, the Bloc Québécois and the Reform Party.

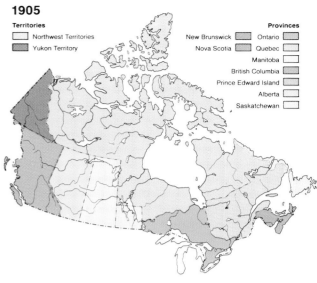

1905

Territories	
Northwest Territories	
Yukon Territory	

Provinces			
New Brunswick		Ontario	
Nova Scotia		Quebec	
		Manitoba	
		British Columbia	
		Prince Edward Island	
		Alberta	
		Saskatchewan	

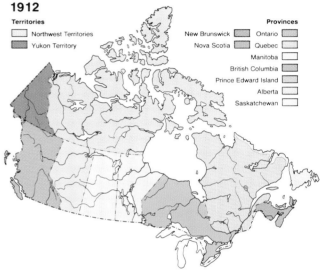

1912

Territories	
Northwest Territories	
Yukon Territory	

Provinces			
New Brunswick		Ontario	
Nova Scotia		Quebec	
		Manitoba	
		British Columbia	
		Prince Edward Island	
		Alberta	
		Saskatchewan	

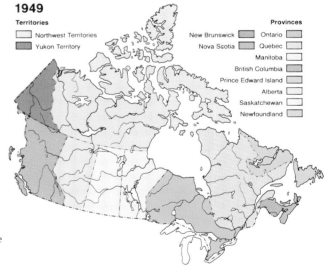

1949

Territories	
Northwest Territories	
Yukon Territory	

Provinces			
New Brunswick		Ontario	
Nova Scotia		Quebec	
		Manitoba	
		British Columbia	
		Prince Edward Island	
		Alberta	
		Saskatchewan	
		Newfoundland	

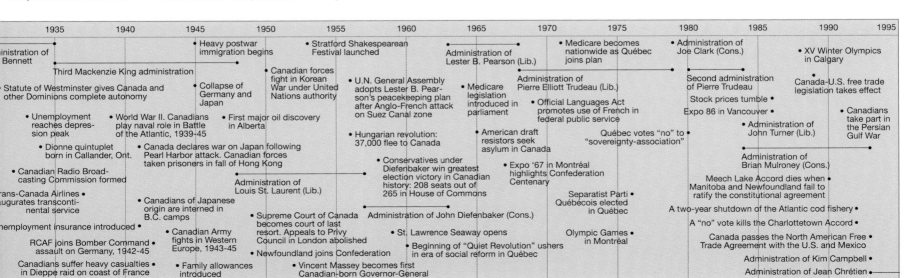

Working Our Land: the Farms

Only one eighth of Canada's land is suitable for agriculture. On this small area along the southern border, farmers raise a variety of produce: apples and asparagus, cattle and wheat, grapes to make wine and sunflowers for oil, potatoes for chips and hogs for *tourtière*.

Though only 4 percent of Canada's labor force works on the farm, this country was settled by farmers. Indians were the first to cultivate the soil. They cleared land by cutting trees and burning the stumps, then planted hills of corn, beans and squash. In the rich soil and mild climate of southwestern Ontario, Indians grew tobacco for religious ceremonies and barter.

The first Europeans to reach these shores were more interested in fish and furs than farming. But once settlements were established, food was needed. The first white farmer, Louis Hébert, came to New France in 1617 and cleared ten acres of forest with axe, pick and spade to plant grain and a vegetable garden for Champlain's colony at Quebec.

Early in the 19th century, agriculture had spread to the Prairies with the Selkirk colony—a group of Scottish farmers—

in Manitoba's Red River valley. Late in the century, waves of immigrants moved west and agriculture boomed. The government lured prospective farmers with pamphlets printed in 20 languages and distributed across the United States and Europe. A man could earn a homestead—160 acres of empty prairie—with three years' clearing, breaking and residence.

The Canadian Pacific Railway also encouraged immigration, to help fill its trains and sell its real estate in the West. Advertisements touted "25,000,000 acres of the richest soil, the healthiest climate, and the cheapest farming land in the world." Photographs depicting this paradise were always taken in summer. Though bitter Prairie winters tested their fortitude, those early settlers took possession of a vast expanse of deep topsoil which had been covered for centuries with a dense growth of mixed grasses. Layer upon layer of decaying vegetation had produced a fertile, water-retentive soil, ideal for growing wheat.

Pioneer farmers struggled against wind, hail, frost and drought, insects, weeds and disease. But above all there was the weary isolation of frontier life. To fight loneliness, farm families

formed close-knit groups, gathering for harvest bees, barn raisings, religious meetings, community suppers and sports days.

Agricultural fairs became a necessary social event. Farmers exhibited their finest crops, fattest sows and strongest draft horses; competed in plowing matches and tugs-of-war; and traded advice with neighbors. Farm women displayed their best quilts, preserves and baked goods. Today, these fairs give many city dwellers their only glimpse of rural Canada.

Many time-honored farming methods have gone the way of the hand-held plow and milking stool. Where once a farmer tethered his bull through a ring in its nose, today's cattle breeder houses high-priced livestock in a spotless barn, where they are monitored by closed-circuit television and even vacuumed every day. Maple sap, once collected in galvanized buckets and drawn by wagon to the sugarhouse, now flows through plastic tubing to a central vat. In place of horses, farmers ride tractors equipped with tape decks and air-conditioning. But no matter how sophisticated their methods, farmers still have one thing left to worry about: the weather.

Canadian Born and Bred

One of Canada's greatest agricultural achievements helped to open up the West. In the early 1900s, the Prairies were accessible by rail, but a short growing season made farming risky. Then, in 1904, a chemist at the Dominion Experimental Farm in Ottawa discovered a

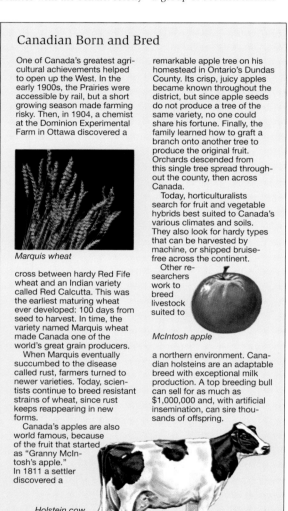

Marquis wheat

cross between hardy Red Fife wheat and an Indian variety called Red Calcutta. This was the earliest maturing wheat ever developed: 100 days from seed to harvest. In time, the variety named Marquis wheat made Canada one of the world's great grain producers.

When Marquis eventually succumbed to the disease called rust, farmers turned to newer varieties. Today, scientists continue to breed resistant strains of wheat, since rust keeps reappearing in new forms.

Canada's apples are also world famous, because of the fruit that started as "Granny McIntosh's apple." In 1811 a settler discovered a

Holstein cow

remarkable apple tree on his homestead in Ontario's Dundas County. Its crisp, juicy apples became known throughout the district, but since apple seeds do not produce a tree of the same variety, no one could share his fortune. Finally, the family learned how to graft a branch onto another tree to produce the original fruit. Orchards descended from this single tree spread throughout the county, then across Canada.

Today, horticulturalists search for fruit and vegetable hybrids best suited to Canada's various climates and soils. They also look for hardy types that can be harvested by machine, or shipped bruise-free across the continent.

Other researchers work to breed livestock suited to

McIntosh apple

a northern environment. Canadian holsteins are an adaptable breed with exceptional milk production. A top breeding bull can sell for as much as $1,000,000 and, with artificial insemination, can sire thousands of offspring.

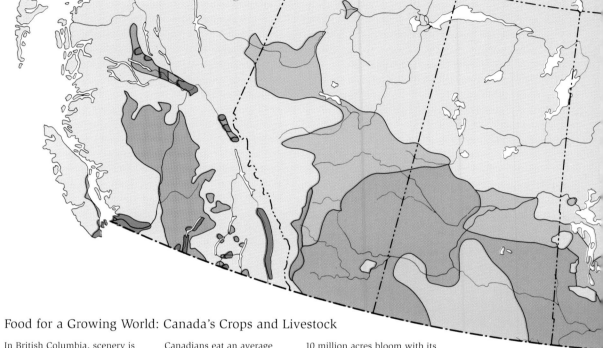

Food for a Growing World: Canada's Crops and Livestock

In British Columbia, scenery is plentiful but land to grow food is scarce. Less than 5 percent of the province is good farmland. However, Canada's longest growing season makes the area ideal for raising vegetables and fruit. Irrigation has transformed the arid Okanagan Valley into lush orchards.

Great herds of dairy and beef cattle once grazed the interior foothills of B.C. and Alberta. Beef cattle still roam these regions, but most are prepared for market by feedlot finishing—"finished" on a rich diet of feed grains that increases an animal's weight by a kilogram a day.

Canadians eat an average 33.8 kilograms of beef per person each year. We prefer grain-fed beef, and Alberta's source of cattle feed is nearby in Prairie grainfields. "Canada's breadbasket" is a vast tract of land where long summer days, moderate temperatures and limited rainfall produce some of the world's best wheat. The level land is ideally suited to the heavy machinery that makes large-scale grain farming profitable.

Wheat, barley, oats and rye grow well here. A newer crop is oilseed, such as rape and flax. Few farmers planted canola in the 1950s; today more than

10 million acres bloom with its bright yellow flowers.

Since milk is difficult to transport long distances, most of dairy farms are located near urban markets in southern Ontario and Quebec. Ontario also has the most livestock farms, many of them highly mechanized "food factories" where hogs and chickens are raised. The southern region's rich soil and mild temperatures favor high-value crops, such as corn, grapes and tobacco. Many Quebec farms raise both livestock and field crops. But more than half the province's farms are dairy farms, producing milk

and supplying ingredients to butter and cheese factories.

Both Ontario and Quebec grow apples, but neither province's crop is as famous as that of Nova Scotia's Annapolis Valley. In other parts of Nova Scotia are dairy, livestock and poultry farms, while potatoes grow well in the slightly acidic red soil of New Brunswick and Prince Edward Island. Farmers in Newfoundland, where the soil is rocky and the climate harsh, keep a few cattle or sheep, or grow cool-weather vegetables.

Prairie Gold—From Kernel to Kitchen

After choosing a variety suited to local soil and climate, a Prairie wheat farmer sows his crop in May, as soon as threat of frost is past. The steel blades of a tractor-drawn disker comb furrows eight centimetres deep

into which seeds are dropped every 2.5 centimetres. With enough rain, green shoots appear within a week. Most farmers rely on chemicals to fertilize the soil and kill weeds. During the summer they make two or more applications.

Harvesting begins in mid-August, when the tall, golden

stalks are heavy with kernels. Timing is crucial: late summer wind or rainstorms can be harmful; hail, frost or tornadoes disastrous.

Some farmers cut wheat with a swather and lay it in metre-wide windrows to dry and harden in the sun. Others harvest with a combine (*below*):

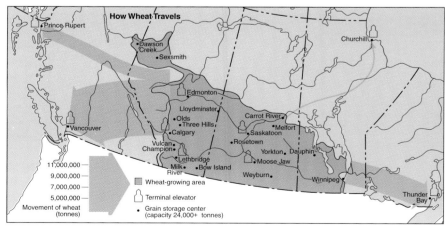

1 Header
2 Sickle
3 Auger
4 Gathering system
5 Processing system
6 Distribution auger
7 Flow fan
8 Grain bin
9 Chaff spreader
10 Straw spreader

How Wheat Travels

Prince Rupert · Dawson Creek · Sexsmith · Churchill · Edmonton · Lloydminster · Olds · Three Hills · Carrot River · Melfort · Vancouver · Vulcan · Champion · Calgary · Saskatoon · Rosetown · Yorkton · Dauphin · Lethbridge · Milk River · Bow Island · Moose Jaw · Weyburn · Winnipeg · Thunder Bay

11,000,000
9,000,000
7,000,000
5,000,000
Movement of wheat (tonnes)

□ Wheat-growing area
⌂ Terminal elevator
• Grain storage center (capacity 24,000+ tonnes)

the self-propelled machine that revolutionized grain farming when it was developed in Canada in 1938. The combine cuts the stalks, threshes the wheat (knocks the kernels from the head), separates the grain from the stalks, cleans it by screening out chaff and delivers grain ready for storage.

Most Prairie wheat is trucked to grain elevators, where it is weighed and graded. From there it travels by boxcar to West Coast ports, Churchill or Thunder Bay, where it is stored in huge terminal elevators, or poured into ships bound for eastern Canada or foreign ports.

Canada's chief customers are China and western European nations, such as Great Britain and Italy. Russia and other eastern countries are also major buyers of our wheat.

More than a quarter of the crop is consumed here, as livestock feed and a substantial part of Canadians' diets.

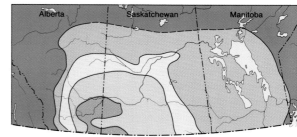

Canada's climate determines the crops grown here: hardy plants such as potatoes and wheat, bred to mature before fall's early frost. The map of the growing season (left) shows the length of time temperatures average more than 5.6°C. Above, the water deficit map illustrates the Prairies' worst problem. Some regions need as much as 300 millimetres more rain for crops to develop. Despite irrigation, drought still threatens many crops.

Water Deficit (mm)
300
230
180
130
80
25

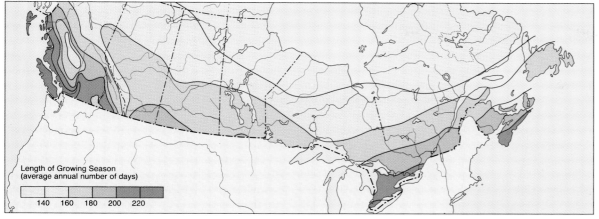

Length of Growing Season
(average annual number of days)

140 160 180 200 220

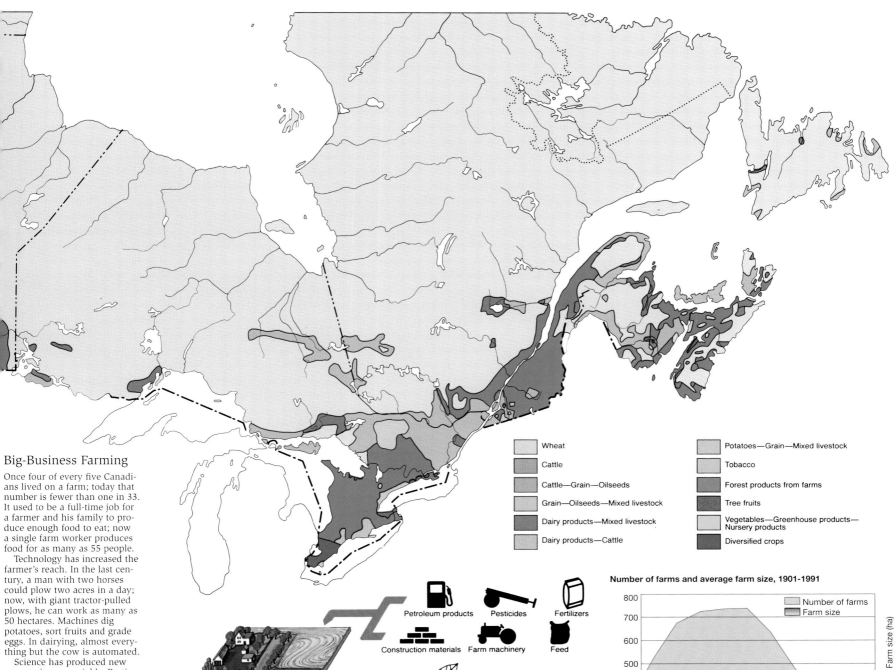

Wheat		Potatoes—Grain—Mixed livestock
Cattle		Tobacco
Cattle—Grain—Oilseeds		Forest products from farms
Grain—Oilseeds—Mixed livestock		Tree fruits
Dairy products—Mixed livestock		Vegetables—Greenhouse products—Nursery products
Dairy products—Cattle		Diversified crops

Big-Business Farming

Once four of every five Canadians lived on a farm; today that number is fewer than one in 33. It used to be a full-time job for a farmer and his family to produce enough food to eat; now a single farm worker produces food for as many as 55 people.

Technology has increased the farmer's reach. In the last century, a man with two horses could plow two acres in a day; now, with giant tractor-pulled plows, he can work as many as 50 hectares. Machines dig potatoes, sort fruits and grade eggs. In dairying, almost everything but the cow is automated.

Science has produced new ways to increase yields. Pesticides limit the ravages of insects and weeds; chemical fertilizers, hybrid seeds and new farming methods have more than doubled wheat yields per acre.

In the process of modernization, agriculture has changed from a way of life to big business. One trend is toward fewer and bigger farms. Because it does not pay to use costly equipment on small areas, farmers must expand to compete. Specialization is also more profitable. Most successful farmers concentrate on large-scale livestock raising or a single crop. High land prices, machinery and equipment discourage part-time farming. Farmers must follow price and market trends as closely as businessmen or investors.

Increasing mechanization, specialization and huge investment link agriculture and industry more closely. Farmers are big consumers of fuels, chemicals and building materials. Yearly sales of farm machinery total $1.25 billion. In turn, farms supply fruit, vegetables, cereals, dairy products, meat

and animal by-products, such as hides for shoes and chemicals for medicines. The food and beverage industry—Canada's largest employer—provides 221,704 jobs. Transporting farm products supports railways, shipping firms and ports.

Some critics feel that modern farming practices are destroying

the land. Heavy machines compact the earth so that water cannot penetrate. Pesticides kill many nutrient-producing—as well as harmful—microorganisms in the soil. Increasing use of pesticides is needed to protect the single-crop farm, which are more vulnerable to infestation or disease than a

farm with a variety of crops.

Farmers have always left some fields idle in summer to let land regenerate nutrients and moisture. Now it appears plant foods are leached away during this season, forcing farmers to add more fertilizer. As the soil deteriorates, it holds less water; thus, valuable top-

soil drifts away. Even more soil is lost, as cities encroach upon farmland. The fertile Niagara Peninsula, situated in Canada's most populous area, is slowly being engulfed by roads and buildings. Will we someday be forced to choose between homegrown produce and housing developments?

Petroleum products Pesticides Fertilizers

Construction materials Farm machinery Feed

Wool, fibers Tobacco

Meat By-products (hides, chemicals)

Dairy products Eggs

Cereals, flour Malt Fruit, vegetables Edible oils

Number of farms and average farm size, 1901-1991

Number of farms
Farm size

('000) 800 700 600 500 400 300 200 100

Farm size (ha) 250 200 150 100 50

1901 1911 1921 1931 1941 1951 1961 1971 1981 1986 1991

Working Our Land: The Forests

The forests that cover half of Canada present some of the country's most familiar landscapes: shadowed woods thick with evergreens, lightened here and there by gleaming trunks of white birch; the flaming foliage of autumn maples; the slender stems and flickering leaves of an island of aspens in a sea of grass. Traditionally, wood has been the country's greatest source of wealth. Even today, thousands of Canadians depend on wood and wood products for their livelihood.

As Canada's forests are almost all publicly owned, every Canadian holds eight hectares of productive forest land. The forests are administered by the provinces, which lease them to lumber and pulp and paper companies. In the past, when Cana-

da's trees grew thick and tall at every doorstep, loggers cut without a thought for the future. But a tree that can be felled in minutes takes 50 to 100 years to grow. Nevertheless, Canada still has thousands of hectares of untouched forest.

Forests supply more than wood. They provide habitats for wildlife and recreational havens from the tumult of city life. But trees must be cut. Wood is an essential raw material for everything from houses to hockey sticks, telephone poles to writing paper. As logging costs rise and conservation problems become more apparent, foresters are more aware of the need for responsible harvesting and reforestation. Well-planned logging roads need not gouge and erode the soil. If harvested areas are

shaped to blend with natural landforms, the visual impact of clear-cutting is minimized. Planting and cultivation can vastly increase the yield from accessible areas. Short rotation crops, such as hybrid poplars, produce logs in less than ten years.

As the demand for forest products grows, better use is made of wood. For example, Canada's pulp and paper, as well as its wood panel products, are manufactured from the residue and waste material from lumber production.

Loggers, naturalists and vacationers may never be entirely compatible. But farsighted management can provide Canadians with forests that yield not only jobs and products, but also a beautiful, living natural resource.

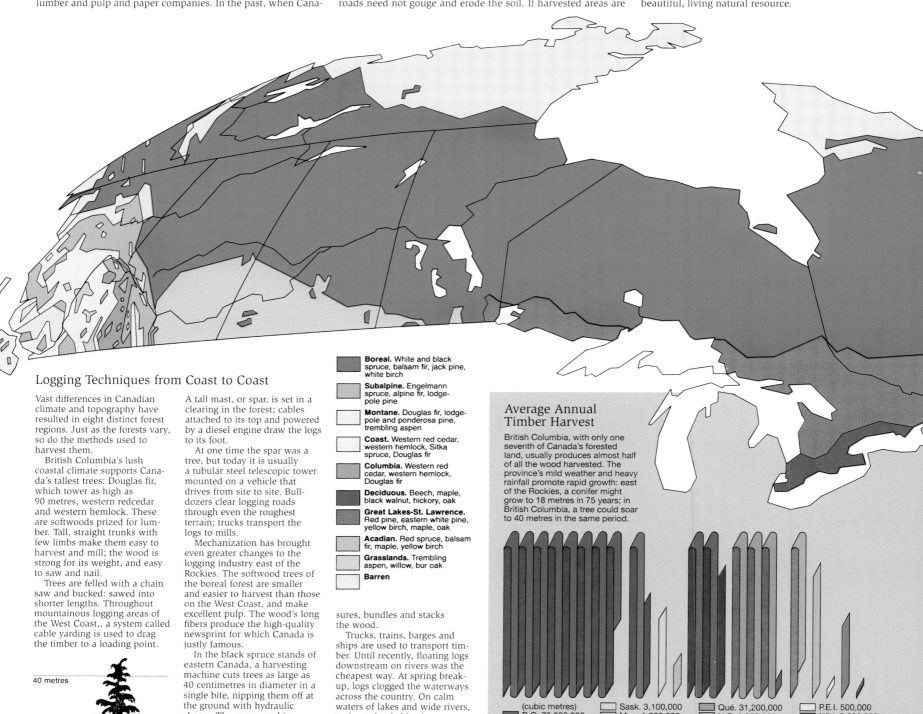

Boreal. White and black spruce, balsam fir, jack pine, white birch

Subalpine. Engelmann spruce, alpine fir, lodgepole pine

Montane. Douglas fir, lodgepole and ponderosa pine, trembling aspen

Coast. Western red cedar, western hemlock, Sitka spruce, Douglas fir

Columbia. Western red cedar, western hemlock, Douglas fir

Deciduous. Beech, maple, black walnut, hickory, oak

Great Lakes-St. Lawrence. Red pine, eastern white pine, yellow birch, maple, oak

Acadian. Red spruce, balsam fir, maple, yellow birch

Grasslands. Trembling aspen, willow, bur oak

Barren

Logging Techniques from Coast to Coast

Vast differences in Canadian climate and topography have resulted in eight distinct forest regions. Just as the forests vary, so do the methods used to harvest them.

British Columbia's lush coastal climate supports Canada's tallest trees: Douglas fir, which tower as high as 90 metres, western redcedar and western hemlock. These are softwoods prized for lumber. Tall, straight trunks with few limbs make them easy to harvest and mill; the wood is strong for its weight, and easy to saw and nail.

Trees are felled with a chain saw and bucked: sawed into shorter lengths. Throughout mountainous logging areas of the West Coast,, a system called cable yarding is used to drag the timber to a loading point.

A tall mast, or spar, is set in a clearing in the forest; cables attached to its top and powered by a diesel engine draw the logs to its foot.

At one time the spar was a tree, but today it is usually a tubular steel telescopic tower mounted on a vehicle that drives from site to site. Bulldozers clear logging roads through even the roughest terrain; trucks transport the logs to mills.

Mechanization has brought even greater changes to the logging industry east of the Rockies. The softwood trees of the boreal forest are smaller and easier to harvest than those on the West Coast, and make excellent pulp. The wood's long fibers produce the high-quality newsprint for which Canada is justly famous.

In the black spruce stands of eastern Canada, a harvesting machine cuts trees as large as 40 centimetres in diameter in a single bite, nipping them off at the ground with hydraulic shears. The same machine severs the branches, cuts the trunk into sections, and mea-

sures, bundles and stacks the wood.

Trucks, trains, barges and ships are used to transport timber. Until recently, floating logs downstream on rivers was the cheapest way. At spring break-up, logs clogged the waterways across the country. On calm waters of lakes and wide rivers, tugboats hauled log booms to the mills. Many provinces no longer permit this.

Average Annual Timber Harvest

British Columbia, with only one seventh of Canada's forested land, usually produces almost half of all the wood harvested. The province's mild weather and heavy rainfall promote rapid growth: east of the Rockies, a conifer might grow to 18 metres in 75 years; in British Columbia, a tree could soar to 40 metres in the same period.

(cubic metres)			
B.C. 78,600,000	Sask. 3,100,000	Qué. 31,200,000	P.E.I. 500,000
Alta. 13,600,000	Man. 1,600,000	N.B. 9,200,000	Nfld. 2,800,000
	Ont. 24,300,000	N.S. 4,200,000	Yukon and N.W.T. 210,000

40 metres

25 metres

20 metres

Western hemlock: *Important to British Columbia. Strong white wood used for pulp and in flooring, siding, crates and plywood*

White spruce: *Light, resilient wood used in construction. White color of pulp produces the finest newsprint*

Jack pine: *Moderately hardwood used in construction, siding and pulp. Also good for railway ties, posts and mine timbers*

Balsam fir: *A staple of the pulp and paper industry. Also used for construction, plywood and packaging, and as Christmas trees*

White birch: *Strong, fine-textured, whitish wood that makes excellent plywood. Solid birch used in furniture and cabinets*

Sugar maple: *Valuable hardwood used in furniture, flooring and plywood. Sap is boiled down to make maple syrup and sugar*

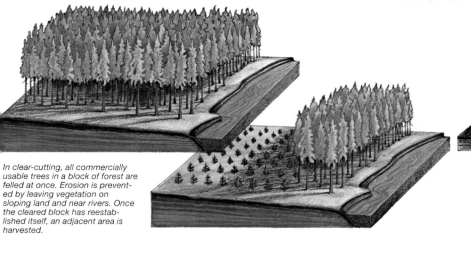

In clear-cutting, all commercially usable trees in a block of forest are felled at once. Erosion is prevented by leaving vegetation on sloping land and near rivers. Once the cleared block has reestablished itself, an adjacent area is harvested.

In selection cutting, only individually chosen trees of a desired size and species are felled. The practice is usually confined to mixed forests of hardwoods and softwoods of uneven ages; less than 20 percent of Canada's trees are harvested this way. Natural reseeding usually ensures regeneration. Harvesting expenses are greater, since care is needed to avoid damaging trees left standing.

Cash Crop or Renewable Resource?

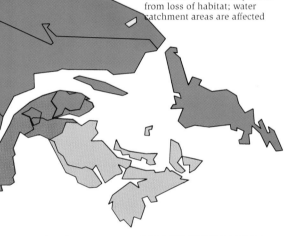

Most trees in Canada are harvested by clear-cutting: all the timber in an area—which may be as large as 60 hectares—is cut down and removed. This method is widely used in the boreal forest, where natural stands often consist of a single species of uniform age. After the cutting, bare ground may be prepared for new growth by burning the slash (debris) and applying herbicides, or by scarification: breaking up the surface to expose mineral soil. Adjacent stands of trees may then reseed the site naturally, but the resulting forest may not be of commercial value. Seeding or replanting by hand or machine, though expensive, does ensure the growth of usable species.

Careless clear-cutting can be disastrous. Wildlife may suffer from loss of habitat; water catchment areas are affected when forests disappear. Removing trees from the banks of waterways can bring soil erosion, flooding and silting of streams and rivers.

Selection cutting—harvesting single trees or small groups of trees—disturbs the environment less but is not always practical. When an area's tree cover is not fully removed, new growth must be capable of developing in shade. Trees that are not shade-tolerant, including many softwoods, fare poorly under these conditions.

But thinning by selection cutting does benefit remaining trees, allowing them more sunlight, water and nutrients. The practice also preserves scenic forest landscapes and wildlife habitats.

The forest industry tries to maintain a *sustained yield* of wood, ensuring new growth by replacing harvested trees. However, these efforts at reforestation have not made up for past wastefulness. Wood for mills must be hauled greater and greater distances to fill demands. *High-yield* forestry would improve the situation, but more money must be devoted to silviculture, or "farming" trees. Better soil preparation, planting of healthy seedlings from the best parent trees, weeding, thinning and fertilizing can more than double forest yields—and ensure supplies of wood for future generations.

Making the Most Out of Wood

Almost half the wood cut in Canada is used for lumber. More than 800 sawmills across the country slice and plane softwoods like spruce, hemlock and Douglas fir, and hardwoods such as birch and maple, to produce boards of varying dimensions. Each year Canada exports enough lumber to construct 1.6 million single detached houses.

Other primary wood products are plywoods, shingles (mostly cut from easy-splitting western redcedar) and veneers. Further processing turns wood into prefabricated buildings as well as a wide range of products for house construction, such as moldings, kitchen cabinets, doors, and sashes.

As costs rise, the wood products industry finds way to use wood that once was wasted. Some is sold for pulp chips or fuel. Sawdust and wood shavings are coated with adhesive and pressed into sheets to form cheap, sturdy particleboard for cabinet and furniture cores. Waferboard, made from wood flakes, is as strong as plywood.

The pulp and paper industry, long one of Canada's leading manufacturers, provides an endless stream of wood pulp, paperboards, paper products such as boxes and bags, as well as by-products such as turpentine, rayon and artificial sponges. The most important product is newsprint: our pulp and paper mills turn out an impressive 28 percent of the world's supply.

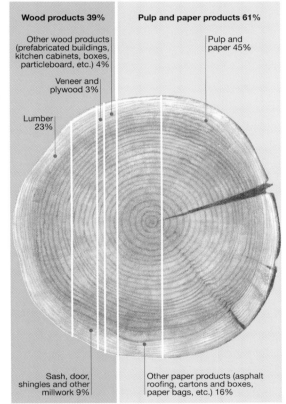

Percentage Value of Forest Products

Wood products 39%

Other wood products (prefabricated buildings, kitchen cabinets, boxes, particleboard, etc.) 4%

Veneer and plywood 3%

Lumber 23%

Sash, door, shingles and other millwork 9%

Pulp and paper products 61%

Pulp and paper 45%

Other paper products (asphalt roofing, cartons and boxes, paper bags, etc.) 16%

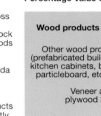

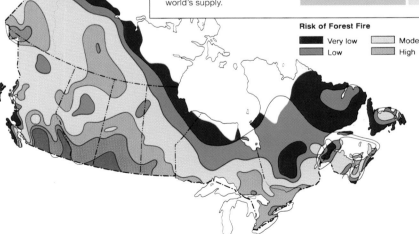

Risk of Forest Fire

- Very low
- Low
- Moderate
- High
- Very high
- Extreme

The Life of a Lumberjack

Canada's earliest pioneers considered trees an obstacle rather than a resource. Settlers used some wood for fuel and for building cabins and boats, but most trees were simply destroyed in giant bonfires as the land was cleared for farms. Then, late in the 18th century, the Royal Navy began to buy Canada's wood. Tall white pines proved ideal for ships' masts. Square timbers—massive logs with straight-hewn sides—were also shipped overseas.

Soon the woods around the St. John, Miramichi and Ottawa rivers rang with the sound of axes. But felling trees was brutal work. Loggers worked in pairs, taking alternate swings at tree trunks perhaps two metres in diameter. Skilled axmen could predict a tree's fall with amazing accuracy.

A shantyman's winter home was a "camboose," a crowded log cabin without windows or chimney. A fire blazed in the center of the floor: some of the smoke—and much of the heat—escaped through a hole in the roof. Amusements were few, and cooks served the same meal three times a day: bread, pork, beans and tea.

Shantymen at season's end, released with pockets full of cash from their dangerous, back-breaking labor, wreaked havoc in town. Some acquired enduring reputations, such as Joe Montferrand (called Joe Mufferaw by the English), a brawling raft foreman from Montréal. Agile, belligerent and strong as a bear, Montferrand could kick so high that he left heel marks on tavern ceilings with his hobnailed boots.

By 1860, massive white pines were becoming scarce in eastern Canada, and loggers were forced to cut smaller trees or other species—or to move west, where giant Douglas fir still stood. In 1866, a mill was built at Valleyfield, Québec, which ground wood into pulp for paper. Canada was on its way to becoming the world's greatest producer of newsprint.

Enemies of the Forest

Fires caused by lightning were part of the forest cycle long before man's arrival, periodically removing overmature trees to clear the way for vigorous new growth. Many plants flourish in direct sunlight and the mineral-rich soil left by fire.

But nature's way is not always convenient to man. Each year fires in Canada may destroy as much as a million hectares of trees and cause untold damage to soils and wildlife. Lightning sets off only one quarter of the fires; most are caused by man—with a smouldering cigarette butt or untended campfire.

Fire risk can be reduced by prescribed (deliberate) burning of slash and by closing the woods to the public in times of high fire hazard. The map above combines information on temperature, humidity, wind speed and rainfall to gauge forest fire risk.

Some forest fires are fought on the ground, by men pumping water from tanks on their backs or clearing fire lines and trenches to halt the progress of an advancing blaze. Aircraft are used to bomb some conflagrations in the wild with tankfuls of water scooped from nearby lakes or rivers.

Pests take their toll of Canada's trees. Several defoliating insects are quite destructive to forests. These insects and bark beetles destroy about 50 million cubic metres of wood annually. To curb these pests, scientists are searching for biological pest controls, such as viruses, bacteria or parasitic insects.

Diseases also cause the loss of another 50 million cubic metres of wood annually. In its slow procession across the country, Dutch elm disease has killed many of the stately shade trees that once lined the streets of cities and towns in eastern Canada.

Infrared, or false-color, photography can be used to detect forest damage not visible to the naked eye. Since chlorophyll in healthy trees is a strong reflector of infrared, variations in chlorophyll content show up in aerial photographs. Above, healthy early autumn foliage on deciduous trees ranges from magenta to pink to yellow in infrared colors. A plantation of healthy red pines appears reddish, but a small patch of bright yellow-green (circled) reveals a stand of damaged trees.

Working Our Waters: Fishing

John Cabot, returning to England from the New World in 1497, told of a sea so thick with fish that they could be dipped out of the water with a net. This was the vast range of submerged plateaus and plains that stretches 1600 kilometres between Cape Cod and Labrador. Over these submarine fields, fertilized by great rivers and enriched by nutrients churned up by Atlantic currents, swarm billions of fish. On the Pacific Coast, the fishing grounds cover a rich continental shelf that stretches about 100 kilometres from land. Inland, Canada's freshwater fisheries are dispersed over myriad lakes and rivers.

From these vast resources Canadian fishermen annually harvest more than one million tonnes of fish, such as cod, herring, salmon, lobster and scallops. Until recently, Canada ranked among the top ten fishing nations in the world, and the fishing industry provided some 130,000 people with full or seasonal employment. In 1990, Canada was the world's second largest fish exporter, selling 86 percent of its catch abroad, largely to the United States, Japan and the European Community.

Since the late 1960s, the fishing industry has faced stiff competition on world markets, and the constant danger of overfishing in coastal waters. Dwindling stocks and a declining fishing industry prompted Canada to extend its offshore limits from 22 to 370 kilometres in 1977. On the Pacific Coast, the Salmonid Enhancement Program was launched in 1977 to reverse declines in salmon stocks, the mainstay of the West Coast fishery.

In 1992, a steep decline in the levels of groundfish—particularly cod—prompted the federal government to curtail cod fishing off the east coast of Newfoundland and Labrador. The ban—imposed to allow time for the recovery of cod stocks—dealt a serious economic blow to the Atlantic Coast. The federal government gave financial aid to those affected by the ban.

A growing trend is the development of aquaculture, or fish farming. An aquaculture of salmon, oysters and other fish exists in New Brunswick and Prince Edward Island. Other successful aquaculture operations include trout-farming on the Prairies and salmon "ranching" in British Columbia.

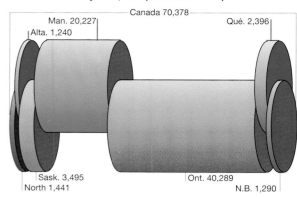

Freshwater catch by value, 1992 (thousand dollards)

Canada 70,378

Man. 20,227
Alta. 1,240
Qué. 2,396
Sask. 3,495
North 1,441
Ont. 40,289
N.B. 1,290

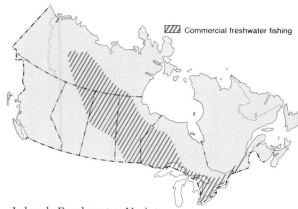

▨ Commercial freshwater fishing

British Columbia: Salmon Story

The five species of Pacific salmon—chinook, chum, coho, pink and sockeye—dominate Canada's Pacific fishery, accounting for more than 45 percent of British Columbia's $416 million in 1992.

Fish of "mysterious comings and goings," salmon are hatched in cold, clear rivers often hundreds of kilometres from the sea, then spend up to a year, depending on species, in freshwater lakes. As fingerlings, salmon enter the Pacific and gain weight rapidly in the rich waters of the open ocean. They return to their native rivers to spawn and die. (Unlike the Pacific species, the Atlantic salmon may spawn more than once.) Only one in a thousand eggs will produce a salmon that will reach maturity.

Herring, which is a pelagic fish like salmon, contributes more than 10 percent of the total landed value of Pacific fishery. Groundfish—halibut, redfish, and hake—are a valuable catch. Clam, crab, shrimp and other shellfish also provide substantial fishing revenue.

Most West Coast fishing is carried on within sight of land. But even small boats, highly powered and equipped with sophisticated mechanical gear, navigational aids and fish-finding sonar, travel great distances along the coast following the seasonal movements of fish. Most of the catch is canned; the remainder is sold fresh, frozen or mild-cured.

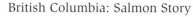

- ● Pacific salmon
- ● Pacific herring
- — 200-mile limit

Value (thousand dollars)

191,800

51,547

21,525
19,413

* Excluding queen crab

12,416
11,203

Salmon | Herring | Clams | Halibut | Crab* | Shrimps

Catch (tonnes)
3851
3355
4577
4254

34,587

64,259

Trolling: Tall poles reaching up from behind the wheelhouse and bow identify Pacific trollers (left). Baited hooks or lures are dragged behind the boat, their depth controlled by the speed of the boat or by large sinkers called cannonballs. When a fish strikes, the line is drawn in by a power "gurdy," or reel. The catch, mostly chinook and coho salmon, is gutted, cleaned and stored in ice.

Sockeye salmon (sea-run)
Oncorhynchus nerka
24 in. (610 mm). 5 lb. (2.3 kg)

Male sockeye in spawning colors

Female sockeye in spawning colors

Lake whitefish
Coregonus clupeaformis
15 in. (381 mm). 1.5 lb. (0.7 kg)

Inland: Freshwater Variety

Canada's streams, rivers and lakes, which comprise half the world's available fresh water, also support important commercial fisheries. More than a dozen species are taken, with whitefish, yellow perch and walleye accounting for half the total landed value. Locally important species include Manitoba saugers, Ontario lake trout and Quebec eels.

In summer, the inland lakes are fished with gill and pound nets, and with a variety of craft from canoes to 15-metre Lake Winnipeg whitefish boats. In winter, fishing with gill nets set through the ice is an important seasonal activity. The inland catch is processed at shore stations with icing, cooling, grading and storage facilities. Most of the catch is marketed fresh or frozen.

Commercial inland fishing has declined or disappeared in certain areas. This problem is not caused by lack of fish, but by environmental and economic factors. Chemical pollutants—some of them transported from central Canada and the United States as acid rain—have contaminated stocks in many lakes and rivers. Low profitability has also plagued small-scale and part-time operations of many inland fishermen.

Gill netting: The gill net (left) is "set" in the water to form either a fixed or drifting wall of fine nylon netting. It is buoyed by floats on the top line, weighted by lead sinkers on the bottom line, and marked by a surface buoy. Fish attempting to swim through the net are caught by their gills and entangled.

Walleye
Stizostedion vitreum
16 in. (406 mm). 1.5 lb. (0.7 kg)

Yellow perch
Perca flavescens
7 in. (178 mm). 8 oz. (0.2 kg)

Total Canadian catch, 1992: 1,293,273 tonnes

Nfld.	283,203
P.E.I.	47,372
N.S.	429,930
N.B.	127,653[1]
Qué.	71,429[1]
Ont.	20,406[2]
Man.	10,133[2]
Sask.	3,029[2]
Alta.	1,393[2]
B.C.	297,152
North	1,573[2]

Total landed value, 1992: $1,470,650

Nfld.	$199,121
P.E.I.	$79,715
N.S.	$511,592
N.B.	$106,140[1]
Qué.	$91,277[1]
Ont.	$40,289[2]
Man.	$20,227[2]
Sask.	$3,495[2]
Alta.	$1,244[2]
B.C.	$416,127
North[2]	$1,441

[1] Combined sea and freshwater figure
[2] Freshwater

Totals	Landed value ($000)	Metric tonnes
Freshwater	70,384	38,697
Sea	1,400,266	1,254,576

- ● Lobster
- ● Cod
- ● Scallops
- ● Atlantic herring
- — 200-mile limit

Out of the Water: Tonnes and Dollars

Prince Edward Island dwarfs Ontario in the chart (*left*) representing the provinces' contribution to Canada's total 1992 fish production.

The Atlantic provinces and Québec supply more than 75 percent of the fish landed in Canada, worth about two-thirds of the total landed value. Lobsters—less than 4 percent of the Atlantic catch—bring in a third of the landed value.

Inland fishery is dispersed across seven provinces and the number of tonnes of fish taken is low. However, the relatively high value of fresh water fish makes inland commercial fishing profitable.

Pacific salmon is British Columbia's major contribution to the market: 5 percent of the national catch, worth 13 percent of the landed value.

Value (thousand dollars)

316,986
152,991
100,634
28,060
29,389
27,872

Cod
Herring and sardines
Small flatfish
Scallops
Redfish
Lobster

Catch (tonnes)

41,827
48,685
92,078
99,365
187,526
215,750

Atlantic: A Declining Bounty From the Deep

More than 30 kinds of fish, shellfish and marine mammals are harvested from the waters of the North Atlantic.

Traditionally, the most valuable catches have been cod and lobsters. But a steep decline in cod stocks prompted a federal ban on the cod fishery in 1992.

Taken with cod are other species of groundfish—so called because they feed on the sea floor. These species include haddock, pollock, hake, cusk, redfish, and the flatfishes. Shellfish are clams, quahogs, oysters and scallops. Herring dominate the catch of schooling ("pelagic") and estuarial fish.

Traditional shore fishery is carried on within 20 kilometres of land, using traps, handlines and trawl lines with baited hooks. Mackerel and herring are landed with seine, trap and gill nets; lobsters are trapped in "pots." Special rakes are used to gather oysters; scallops are harvested with dredges. Offshore, trawlers and draggers tow huge otter trawls (*below*) or other nets. Long-liners haul thousands of baited hooks.

About three quarters of the catch is chilled or frozen. Curing or canning are the other main fish-processing methods.

Lobster trap: *Hydraulic winches and echo sounders have replaced brawn and intuition in lobster fishing, but the basic trap (left) remains little changed. Lobsters enter the "pot" lured by bait in the first compartment or "kitchen." The entrance is a funnel of netting that allows entry but prevents exit. Passing through a second hole to the "bedroom," the lobster is trapped.*

Purse seine: *One end of the long, small-meshed purse seine (left) is secured to a small skiff. The seiner then "shoots" the net as it encircles a school of fish, returning to the skiff, where the two ends of the seine are brought together. The purse line is tightened, drawing the bottom of the net together to form a huge bag where the fish are trapped. The seine is then hauled aboard.*

Otter trawl: *Groundfish on both coasts are often taken by trawlers, or "draggers," using the otter trawl (below): a long, wedge-shaped net that narrows into a "cod end." Two "doors" keep the mouth of the trawl open as it is towed along the ocean floor, scooping up fish. As the trawl is drawn in, the fish are forced into the cod end, which is hoisted onto the ship's deck and emptied.*

Lobster
Homarus americanus

Giant scallop
Placopecten magellanicus

Atlantic herring
Clupea harengus harengus
To 17 in. (431 mm), 1.5 lb. (0.7 kg)

Atlantic cod
Gadus morrhua
25 in. (635 mm), 5 lb. (2.3 kg)

Redfish
Sébastes marinus
12 in. (304 mm), 2 lb. (0.9 kg)

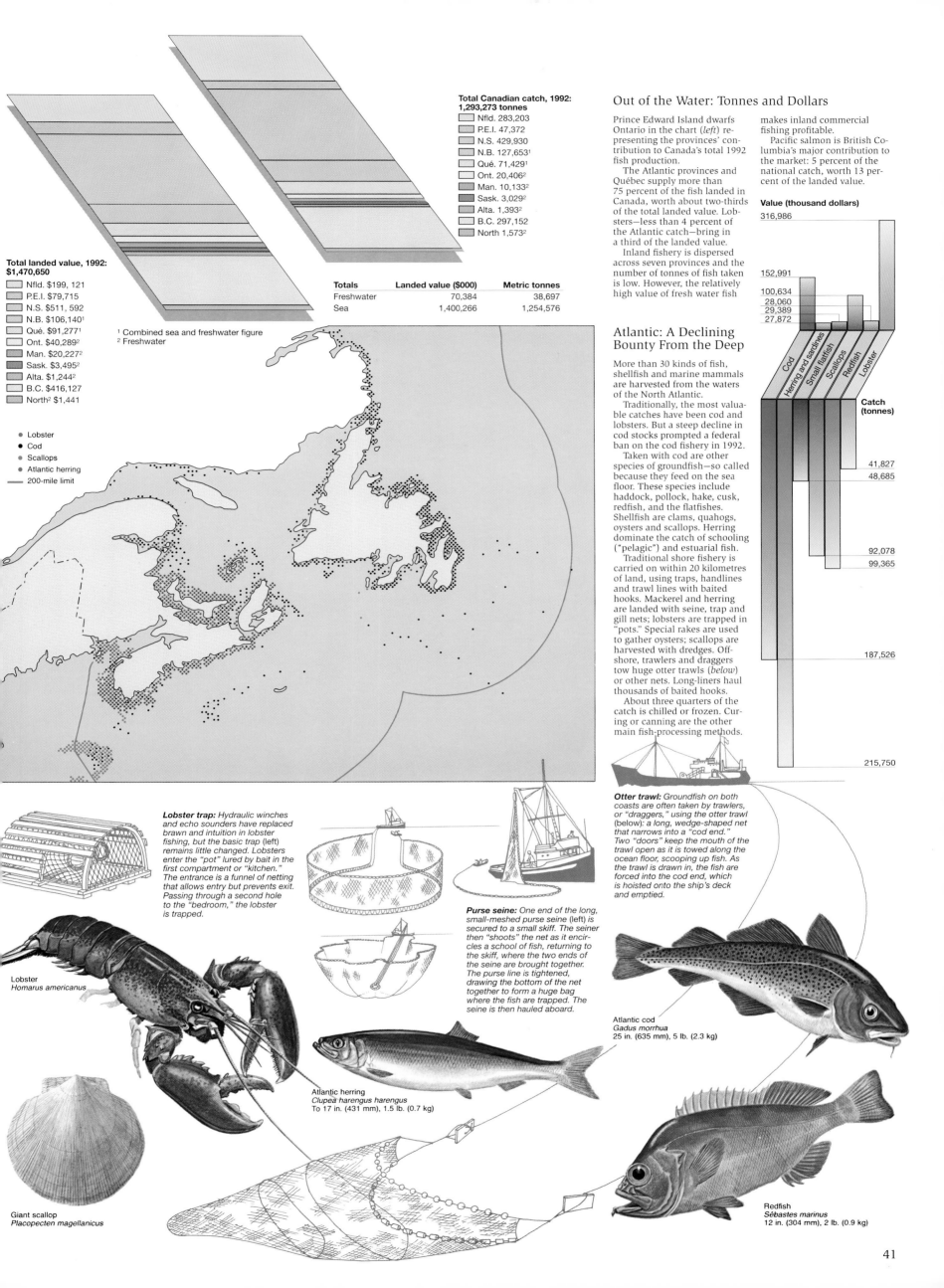

Working Our Land: Mining

Mining in Canada dates back almost 1000 years, to Norsemen who dug iron ore from a bog near present-day L'Anse aux Meadows, Nfld., and forged it into crude tools. Five centuries later, Jacques Cartier mined what he thought were diamonds and gold near Quebec City; in France, the minerals were found to be quartz and iron pyrite. In the 1570s, Martin Frobisher also confused pyrite with gold, and shipped tonnes of worthless "blacke stone" to England from mines on Baffin Island.

An accidental discovery ushered in Canada's modern mining era. In 1883, workmen blasting a route for the Canadian Pacific Railway through northern Ontario ripped into copper and nickel deposits near Sudbury. This bonanza spurred other discoveries nearby: silver at Cobalt; gold at Kirkland Lake and Timmins; and, in the 1920s, copper and gold in Quebec's Abitibi region.

Today, the industry is nationwide and employs 138,000 workers to prospect, mine and smelt 60 kinds of minerals. Canada is third in total production among leading producers, and ranks first in the mining of zinc and uranium; second in asbestos, nickel and potash; third in aluminum; fourth in copper and silver; and fifth in lead and gold.

Mining is risky and expensive. Canadian oil companies spend millions every year drilling exploratory oil and natural gas wells, but few prove commercially successful. It costs an average $400-500 million to find a mineral deposit rich enough to mine, and may take up to six years of planning and construction before ore is extracted. Remote mines once required townsites, but flying in miners to work on site for short periods is a growing trend.

New mines also require transportation links to refineries and markets. Most of the new railroad construction in Canada since World War II has been associated with mineral development. The huge iron-ore deposits first reported along the Quebec-Labrador border in 1894 achieved economic importance only in the 1950s, after completion of the St. Lawrence Seaway, a 560-kilometre railway and ports to handle 200,000-tonne freighters.

Mining is a once-only harvest, but Canada seems blessed with a rich supply of most minerals. At 1993 consumption rates, estimated reserves of iron ore will last more than 240 years; uranium, 50 years; copper, 48 years. New reserves are added as discoveries and technology, along with higher prices, turn low-grade, less accessible deposits into producing mines.

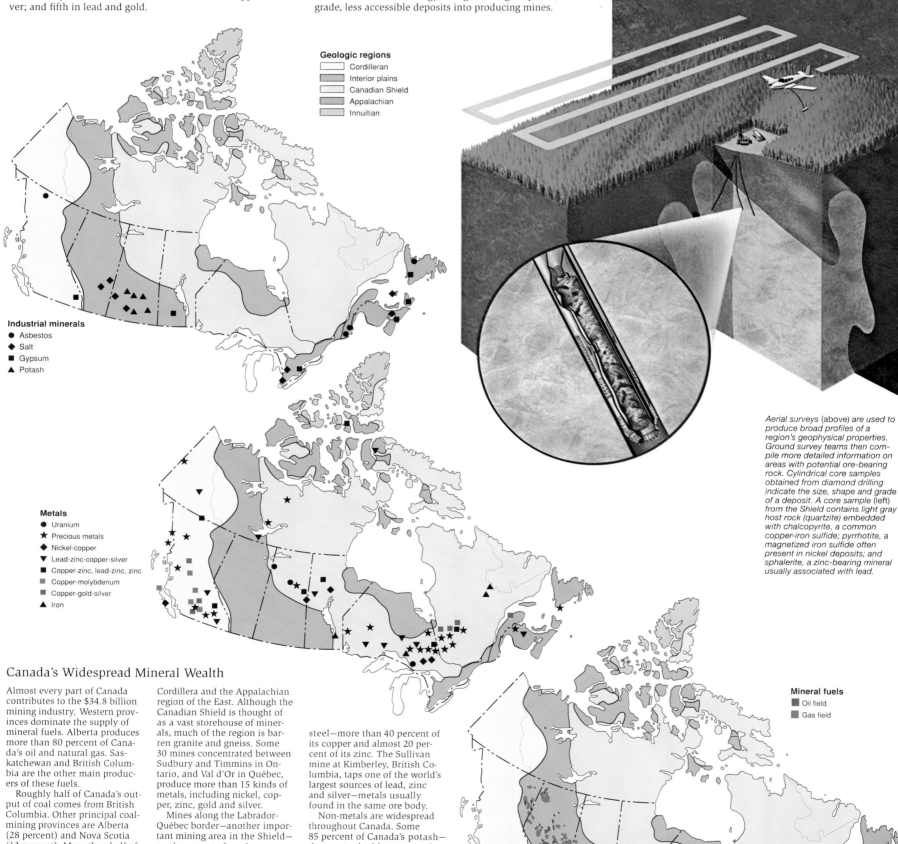

Geologic regions
- Cordilleran
- Interior plains
- Canadian Shield
- Appalachian
- Innuitian

Industrial minerals
- ● Asbestos
- ◆ Salt
- ■ Gypsum
- ▲ Potash

Metals
- ● Uranium
- ★ Precious metals
- ◆ Nickel-copper
- ▼ Lead-zinc-copper-silver
- ■ Copper-zinc, lead-zinc, zinc
- Copper-molybdenum
- Copper-gold-silver
- ▲ Iron

Mineral fuels
- Oil field
- Gas field

Aerial surveys (above) are used to produce broad profiles of a region's geophysical properties. Ground survey teams then compile more detailed information on areas with potential ore-bearing rock. Cylindrical core samples obtained from diamond drilling indicate the size, shape and grade of a deposit. A core sample (left) from the Shield contains light gray host rock (quartzite) embedded with chalcopyrite, a common copper-iron sulfide; pyrrhotite, a magnetized iron sulfide often present in nickel deposits; and sphalerite, a zinc-bearing mineral usually associated with lead.

Canada's Widespread Mineral Wealth

Almost every part of Canada contributes to the $34.8 billion mining industry. Western provinces dominate the supply of mineral fuels. Alberta produces more than 80 percent of Canada's oil and natural gas. Saskatchewan and British Columbia are the other main producers of these fuels.

Roughly half of Canada's output of coal comes from British Columbia. Other principal coal-mining provinces are Alberta (28 percent) and Nova Scotia (13 percent). More than half of Canada's uranium—used to power nuclear plants—comes from northern Saskatchewan; the other major source of uranium is Ontario.

Metal ores are found in the Canadian Shield, the Western Cordillera and the Appalachian region of the East. Although the Canadian Shield is thought of as a vast storehouse of minerals, much of the region is barren granite and gneiss. Some 30 mines concentrated between Sudbury and Timmins in Ontario, and Val d'Or in Québec, produce more than 15 kinds of metals, including nickel, copper, zinc, gold and silver.

Mines along the Labrador-Québec border—another important mining area in the Shield—produce most of our iron ore. British Columbia and northern Ontario supply the rest. Canada ranks seventh in world iron-ore production.

The Western Cordillera yields 97 percent of Canada's molybdenum—used to strengthen steel—more than 40 percent of its copper and almost 20 percent of its zinc. The Sullivan mine at Kimberley, British Columbia, taps one of the world's largest sources of lead, zinc and silver—metals usually found in the same ore body.

Non-metals are widespread throughout Canada. Some 85 percent of Canada's potash—the most valuable non-metal—is mined in Saskatchewan. About 95 percent of our asbestos comes from southwestern Québec. Nova Scotia produces two thirds of our gypsum; and Ontario supplies two thirds of our salt.

The Search for Deposits; Getting Out the Ore

Mining companies locate anomalies (geologic irregularities that may contain minerals) using federal and provincial geophysical maps and through exploration. Deposits are then pinpointed with aerial and surface surveys. The density, magnetism and conductivity of rocks, recorded by magnetometers, gravimeters and other electromagnetic instruments, determine the depth and composition of an ore body buried beneath barren rock. Geochemical surveys trace concentrations of minerals from soil, water and plants to a deposit. Geobotanists look for "indicators": vegetation patterns and individual plants affected by minerals. Natural radiation from uranium, for example, sometimes produces local mutations: blueberries with unusual shapes, and white flowers on normally purple fireweed.

The illustration (*left*) shows a typical mine working a metal-bearing ore body (1). Vegetation, soil and barren rock are removed, and the exposed ore is recovered from an open-pit mine (2). The rock is loosened with explosives, scooped into trucks by electric shovels, and transported to a primary crusher (3).

When the cost of removing the overburden and waste rock exceeds the value of the recovered ore, an underground mine (4) may be developed. A shaft (5) houses the mine's elevator for workers, machinery and ore. Tunnels, called drifts (6), branch off the shaft and parallel the ore body; crosscut tunnels (7) intersect the deposit. In this type of mine, ore is usually loosened with explosives from stopes, or working areas, between the levels. The broken rock is transported to a primary crusher (8). An ore skip (9) hoists the rock to the surface, where conveyors (10) transport it to a storage pile (11). Another conveyor system (12) feeds a secondary crusher (13) that reduces the ore to pebble size; grinding mills pulverize the ore to a sandlike consistency. A concentrator (14) separates the ore from waste minerals, or tailings, which are pumped to a storage pond (15). The mineral concentrate is then shipped to smelters for further refining.

Other mine structures include maintenance shops (16), warehouses, offices and a ventilation shaft (17), which supplies fresh air to the mine and doubles as an emergency exit.

In the past mining meant abusing the land. Today stringent environmental laws in most parts of our country demand the reclamation of sites stripped of vegetation by decades of mining and smelting activity. One such desertlike site (above), shown as it appeared in the mid-1960s, was located near the 380-metre-high superstack at Inco's Sudbury plant. The main steps of reclamation involved adding some 20 tons of limestone to neutralize the acidity of the site and, then, fertilizer and special seed mix to increase nutrient levels. Once vegetation was established, the site was planted with pine seedlings. The dramatic transformation achieved by this method of reclamation can be seen in the photograph of the same site (left), which was taken in the early 1990s.

Rocks to Riches

Mining contributes about 10 percent of Canada's Gross Domestic Product. Mineral fuels represent roughly 55 percent of total production value (*right*); major metals, 30 percent; and non-metals (potash, asbestos, sulfur, peat, and gypsum), 6 percent; and structural materials, 6 percent. The value of all structural materials (cement, sand and gravel, lime, stone and clay products) is slightly higher than that of gold.

Alberta has been a leading mineral producer in Canada since 1960 (*left*); mineral fuels account for 97 percent of the total value of provincial output. Six metals—nickel, gold, copper, zinc, uranium and silver—contribute almost two thirds of Ontario's diversified output.

Alberta (46.3%)
Ontario (14.5%)
British Columbia (10.7%)
Québec (8.4%)
Saskatchewan (8.1%)
Manitoba (3.1%)
Newfoundland (2.2%)
Northwest Territories (2.1%)
New Brunswick (1.2%)
Nova Scotia (1.2%)
Yukon (1.1%)
P.E.I. (less than 1%)

Oil 30%
Natural gas 15%
Gold 7%
Copper 6%
Nastural gas byproducts 6%
Coal 5%
Nickel 5%
Iron 4%
Zinc 4%
Cement 2%
Potash 2%
Uranium 1%
Asbestos less than 1%
Others 13%

Rx for the Environment: Recycling and Reforestation

Canada's 500 mines disturb about 70,000 hectares, or .007 percent of the land. The effects of mining are often widespread: acidic mine water contaminates rivers and lakes; dust and gases from refining and smelting pollute the air. Roads, railways and townsites essential to mineral development cause upheaval in remote regions.

Today mining firms prepare studies to assess the environmental and social impact of a project. Moreover, most provinces require that the land be returned as closely as possible to its original state. In Alberta, for example, a program in coal-mining areas has regenerated 1800 of 6800 hectares on the plains, and more than 3200 of 5144 hectares in the foothills.

Strict regulations have also led to innovative antipollution controls and a cleaner environment. Special bacteria neutralize acidic mine water and turn soluble iron into an insoluble form, which settles out in holding basins. After the addition of limestone, the neutralized, iron-free water is returned to the environment. Some large mines recycle up to three-quarters of the 60 million litres of water used daily at large operations.

Canadian mines process more than 430 million tonnes of rock. Most of this output is waste, or tailing. For example, 50 tonnes of copper ore yield only a tonne of the refined metal. Some of the tailings are used to support underground mines, but most are stored in ponds, which dry up and eventually become barren. Reforestation is a successful method used to reclaim land ravaged by the effects of mining. At Sudbury, Ont., Inco—long a pioneer in reclamation—plants tens of thousands of pine seedlings on local wasteland. The firm uses the warm and protective conditions of abandoned mine shafts to grow the seedlings, which are brought to the surface for planting every spring.

Made in Canada: Primary Products, Finished Goods

A single glove means jobs for at least 60 Canadians. They tan, cut and stitch hides. They spin cotton into thread and weave thread into lining, assemble sewing machines, cast steel into girders, mix cement for the factory walls and lay asphalt for the roof. Manufacturing employs 1.8 million people, produces some 10,000 different items, and accounts for roughly 20 percent of all Canadian production.

Before Confederation, Canada fueled the industrial revolutions of Great Britain and the United States with such raw materials as lumber and furs, and looked abroad for finished goods. Sir John A. Macdonald's National Policy of protective tariffs and the success of the railways encouraged domestic manufacturers to compete with foreign companies for a larger share of Canadian markets.

The prosperity of the early 20th century brought a great de-

mand for investment to exploit mineral wealth and to build electric power plants and factories, especially for automobiles and electrical appliances.

With the Great Depression of the 1930s, investment plummeted and unemployment rose to include one in four Canadians. Full recovery did not come until the advent of World War II, when massive government spending on war materials brought a new surge of economic vigor. Canadian production increased dramatically: agricultural products, 40 percent; iron and steel, 100 percent; aluminum, 500 percent.

After World War II, the economy began a great new wave of peacetime growth. Although British Columbia and the Prairies have made gains in manufacturing since the 1950s, more than 75 percent of the country's manufacturing is concentrated along lower Great Lakes and the St. Lawrence River, bounding the

populous industrial centres of the northeastern United States.

The post-war period has been marked by higher manufacturing productivity. Output increased two thirds faster than other sectors of the economy, while the number of manufacturing jobs fell in proportion to the size of the labor force. Today more people work in services than goods production. Since the 1970s, high technology such as computers has played an increasingly vital role in manufacturing. Toronto, Ottawa, Kitchener-Waterloo and Montréal are the main Canadian centres for electronics. In the field of telecommunications, Canada is a world leader.

During the 1980s, Canada's exports shifted from natural resources to manufactured goods, such as machinery and equipment. The recessions of 1981 and 1991 dealt serious blows to Canadian manufacturing—particularly in Ontario and Quebec. A slow recovery in this sector was underway by the mid-1990s.

A GUIDE TO CANADIAN MANUFACTURING

Canada's six economic regions and their key local factories, regional industries and industrial giants are located on the map at right. The goods they produce—from paper and petroleum to light bulbs and potato chips—are grouped within 23 industrial classifications which are listed below and symbolized on the map.

- The North
- British Columbia
- The Prairies
- Ontario
- Québec
- Atlantic provinces

- Automobiles
- Chemicals
- Dairy products
- Electrical and electronic products
- Fabricated metals
- Fertilizers
- Foods and beverages
- Furniture
- Leather products
- Machinery
- Meats
- Primary metals
- Printed matter
- Processed fish
- Processed fruits and vegetables
- Pulp and paper
- Refined oil
- Rubber products
- Ships
- Textiles
- Tobacco
- Transportation equipment
- Varied products

The North

Remote and sparsely settled, the Yukon and Northwest Territories have few manufacturing companies. Still, some of Canada's most prized goods—gold, furs, native art and handicrafts—are made here. Local sawmills provide the poles, piling and lumber for the region's mines. Petroleum refineries in Whitehorse and Norman Wells produce gasoline, stove oil, and diesel and industrial fuels for local markets.

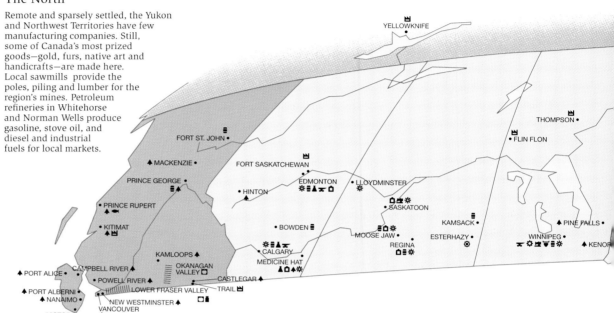

British Columbia

As its forests tower over British Columbia's landscape, so the forest industry dominates provincial manufacturing. Pulp and paper, lumber, veneer and plywood mills account for more than half of provincial production, and employ four in ten of B.C.'s manufacturing workers. From the province's mills comes a quarter of Canada's supply of pulp and paper.

The railway opened eastern markets to British Columbia's raw materials in the late 19th century. Primary manufacturing, particularly sawmills, spread rapidly. Improvements in technology and transportation—larger oceangoing ships, freight airplanes and container handling—raised the level of British Columbia industry to a world scale and made foreign trade profitable.

British Columbia is one of Canada's most active exporting provinces. More than $18 billion worth of manufactured goods are shipped from its ports. The province's leading exports include lumber, pulp, coal, newsprint and fish products.

Vancouver—a major trade gateway to the Pacific—is Canada's third largest manufacturing center. The city's diverse industries include machinery,

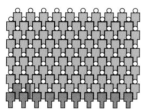

Percentage of regional labor force employed in manufacturing

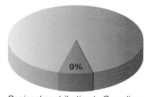

9%

Regional contribution to Canadian manufacturing

motor vehicles and appliances.

Resource-based and single-industry "company towns" are characteristic of British Columbia's manufacturing. Towns such as Powell River depend on pulp and paper mills. Trail's smelters and refineries process locally mined silver, lead and zinc ores. Kitimat's massive aluminum complex and its wealth of hydroelectric power have helped to bring billions of dollars of new industry into the province in pulp and paper, fishing and tourism.

The Prairies

Land grants and rail links opened Canada's West to settlers in the late 19th century. Burgeoning Prairie towns provided new markets for the products of British Columbia's sawmills, Ontario's tool factories and Nova Scotia's iron and steel mills.

Until the World War I, Winnipeg was the dominant industrial and commercial centre of the Prairies and the hub of the western transportation network. By the late 1920s, industries, such as meat processing, flour milling, brewing and printing had spread across the Prairies. Regina, Saskatoon, Calgary and Edmonton began to produce goods for local markets.

After World War II, western expansion was accelerated by rich resource discoveries—oil and natural gas in Alberta, and potash in Saskatchewan. Such large-scale extraction industries attracted workers and investors, and spurred the growth of related industries.

Soaring symbols of oil-fueled progress, Calgary and Edmonton grew from frontier garrisons into urban centers in less than a century. By the 1990s, more than 350 companies in Calgary alone are involved in the petroleum industry. Refineries and petrochemical plants have

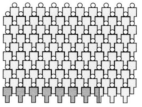

Percentage of regional labor force employed in manufacturing

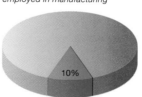

10%

Regional contribution to Canadian manufacturing

attracted such dependent industries as plastics and textiles.

In Manitoba, manufacturing is the largest industry. Saskatchewan—once a wheat-producer with little industry—has become the world supplier of processed potash for agriculture and industry. A giant plant in Esterhazy is the largest in the province. Regina and Saskatoon, whose populations tripled between 1951 and 1991, have diversified into manufacturing of steel pipes, cement, chemicals and fertilizers.

Ontario

Automobiles, electronic goods, foodstuffs—all come from Ontario, which produces 53 percent of Canada's manufactured goods. Ontario makes 80 percent of Canada's motor vehicles, 60 percent of its electrical and electronic products, and more than half of its chemical products, furniture, machinery, plastic and rubber products.

In the industrial heartland of southern Ontario, more than half Canada's manufacturing labor force, working in half of its factories, turns out most of Canada's manufactured goods.

No other province offers Ontario's spectrum of attractions to manufacturing industries: a large skilled labor pool; a major consumer market; raw materials; hydroelectric power; and superb air, rail, road and water links for transportation.

Along the north shore of Lake Ontario, stretching east from Niagara Falls, is the province's "Golden Horseshoe" of plants extending up the St. Lawrence to Cornwall. Major manufacturing centers around the lake include St. Catharines, Hamilton, Oakville, Toronto, Oshawa, Belleville, Kingston and Brockville. The concentration extends west from Toronto to Windsor and includes Brantford, Lon-

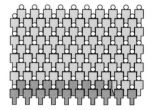

Percentage of regional labor force employed in manufacturing

53%

Regional contribution to Canadian manufacturing

don, St. Thomas and Chatham.

In Hamilton, where lake freighters unload coal and iron ore, half the manufacturing work force is employed by three steelworks. Canada's ninth largest urban centre produces about 80 percent of the country's steel. Some of the processed iron ore remains in Hamilton, where metal fabricating industries make tools, furnaces, wire and stamped metal plates. The production chain continues through transportation and appliance manu-

Acres of machinery grind wood chips, then roll and dry pulp at a Powell River newsprint mill, one of the world's largest. About 1450 workers oversee this capital-intensive manufacturing process.

Packers slaughter, dress, split into sides and hang beef in this refrigerated room at a Winnipeg meat plant. A government inspector later grades each side before it is butchered.

At a Hamilton mill, steelmakers control the processing of the molten metal as it passes from giant ladles to the continuous caster, which produces uniform, cut-to-length steel slabs.

Les Forges du Saint-Maurice (left), *Canada's first heavy industry, produced stoves, plowshares, tools and anchors by 1738. At peak production, 300 men worked around the clock, many on six-hour shifts stoking the cold-air blast furnaces. The forges closed down in 1883 when the supply of local bog iron ran out.*

Most pre-Confederation manufacturers employed fewer than five workers per shop and supplied local markets with furniture, shoes, flour and farm equipment. Industry was dependent on water for power and transportation; millponds and riverside factories were part of the 19th-century landscape.

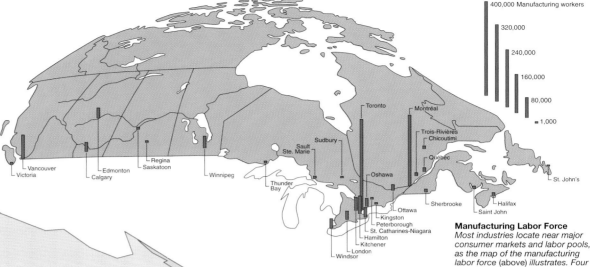

Manufacturing Labor Force
Most industries locate near major consumer markets and labor pools, as the map of the manufacturing labor force (above) illustrates. Four out of five Canadian workers live between Windsor and Québec. Of the remaining 20 percent, three quarters live in the West and the rest in the Atlantic Canada. Southern Ontario and the Montréal area of Québec form the northern part of the populous North American industrial heartland around the Lower Great Lakes. Across this "invisible border" with the United States flows a two-way traffic in raw materials and finished goods. In British Columbia, manufacturers look overseas to Pacific markets. Prairie manufacturers have turned increasingly to markets in upper mid-western United States.

...acturers, who use stamped steel parts in products ranging from toys to truck bodies.

Toronto, Windsor, St. Cathrines, Kitchener and London are large consumers of iron and steel. Metal plate, fabricated metal, machinery and automobile-parts makers dominate manufacturing in these cities.

Sarnia's oil refineries—Canada's largest—have attracted such related industries as plastics, fertilizers, pharmaceuticals, paints, soaps, cosmetics and industrial chemicals.

Toronto has about half the province's manufacturing facilities. Products include machinery; transportation equipment; electrical, rubber, wood and plastic products. Raw material shortages and sluggish specialized markets—devastating to single-industry centres—have less impact on Toronto's diverse economy. Since the late 1970s, Toronto—with Ottawa and Kitchener-Waterloo—has become a high-tech centre.

Dotted across northern Ontario are pulp and paper mills. The area's other important primary manufacturing industry is metal refining, located near Sudbury.

Québec

Québec, the second most important manufacturing province, produces roughly 24 percent of the country's manufactured goods. The province's major industry is paper and allied products, followed by transportation equipment. Other important products include primary metals, chemicals and fabricated metal products. Key provincial industries also include petroleum refining, phamaceuticals, iron ore and asbestos processing.

Industrial growth in Québec coincided with the decline of small family farms in the 19th century. Labor-intensive industries such as textiles, clothing and furniture making attracted rural people to Montréal, Québec, and Trois-Rivières.

Maritime trade and cheap power further encourage Québec's growth. Port-oriented

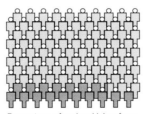

Percentage of regional labor force employed in manufacturing

24%

Regional contribution to Canadian manufacturing

industries using imported raw materials mushroomed along the St. Lawrence River. Québec added paper mills and garment factories. Generating stations

attracted large textile factories, pulp and paper mills, and aluminum plants.

By World War II, electrical power had replaced steam, and electrometallurgy offered new industrial prospects. After the war, huge mining development at Chibougamau, Matagami, Schefferville, Gagnon, Wabush, Labrador City and Lake Allard produced gold, silver, copper, lead, zinc, and iron for Québec's metalworks.

Today, about 50 pulp and paper mills in Québec make 30 percent of Canada's pulp and newsprint. Twenty percent of Canada's fabricated metals are made in Québec.

Montréal's industries, ranging from food and beverage companies and pharmaceutical firms to makers of appliances and transportation materials and equipment, account for half of Québec's work force, factories and output. One of the city's largest employers is the clothing industry, which is vulnerable to seasonal slumps and unpredictable markets.

Atlantic Provinces

The Atlantic Provinces have traditionally looked to the sea. In the mid-1800s, 200 shipyards exported $2.5 million worth of vessels. From nearly 2000 sawmills came lumber for boats, barrels and casks.

But from 1876 to 1900, the export of ships dropped 90 percent as iron replaced wood in hulls and steam engines made canvas sails obsolete. Textile and diary plants did spring up in Nova Scotia and Prince Edward Island, however. And by the end of the 19th century, growing New England markets sought Maritime processed fish. Investments in Cape Breton iron and steel mills led to new rolling mills and wire-, nail- and bolt-making facilities.

For a time, Sydney's iron and steel mills were the country's largest, and eastern wool, cotton and canvas mills prospered. But by the 1920s, Ontario factories had overshadowed eastern mills. Hamilton's steel mills were outproducing Sydney's. The Maritime textile industry was eroded by Québec's.

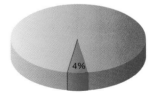

Percentage of regional labor force employed in manufacturing

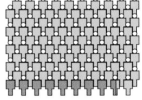

4%

Regional contribution to Canadian manufacturing

In recent times, provincial governments in Atlantic Canada have sought to stimulate industrial growth. Food processing in particular has enjoyed relative prosperity. The pulp and paper industry has expanded to meet British and American newsprint demands. And energy resources and the promise of offshore oil are attracting new industry to Newfoundland—traditionally one of Canada's "have-not" provinces.

In recent years the use of robotic operations has helped to speed production in the car industry. Two Oshawa plants can process more than 2,000 cars daily, but require only a small staff for the purpose of maintenance.

Lightning-fast fingers attach zippers; others stitch on buttons; still more sew the seams of pants at this Montréal garment factory. Piecework means speed and precision in such a labor-intensive industry.

Skilled packers at this Blacks Harbour sardine cannery in New Brunswick sort, clean and pack 2000 sardines an hour. The filled tins are sealed and sterilized automatically.

Canada and the World

Although Canada became a self-governing country in 1867, its real declaration of independence is the Statute of Westminster, which defined the status of the British Dominions as "autonomous communities" in 1931. This declaration recognized an evolution that had taken place in the British Empire in the 20th century, with Canada conspicuously in the vanguard. In the first 50 years of nationhood, Canada's interests were subordinated to those of Britain. In 1914, when Britain declared war on Germany, Canada was automatically at war, too. However, emboldened by this country's sacrifices in that war, the Canadian delegates to the peace conference insisted on signing the Treaty of Versailles in 1919 as representatives of a separate state.

The League of Nations accepted this claim to sovereign status and admitted Canada to its ranks. In 1923 Canada signed its first treaty, the Halibut Fisheries Treaty with the United States, without Britain's cosignature. It sent its first diplomats to Washington, Paris and Tokyo in 1927. Canada made its own declaration of war in 1939 and played a leading part in the founding of the United Nations in 1945. When Canada repatriated its constitution in 1982, British influence had long vanished.

After World War II, Canada retained its Commonwealth connection, while broadening its international role. Today Canada is a major source of aid to underdeveloped nations within the Commonwealth—and beyond. It participates in the Organization of American States (OAS), the Organization for Economic Cooperation and Development (OECD), and other international agencies. Canadians have taken an active part in UN welfare-promoting and peacekeeping activities. While serving at the UN General Assembly, Lester B. Pearson won the Nobel Peace Prize for defusing the Suez Canal crisis in 1956.

At the end of World War II, Canada had marshaled the third-strongest navy and fourth-strongest air force among the Allied powers. But Canada reduced its armed forces after 1945 and chose the path of collective security by joining the United States and Western Europe in the NATO in 1949.

As a nation of vast and varied resources, and relatively small population, Canada has always been a major trading nation. Our traditional trading partners have been Great Britain and the United States. Although trade with other nations has grown substantially in the last 40 years, three-quarters of our exports go to the United States. This trade pattern has been reinforced by the North American Free-Trade Agreement (NAFTA), which came into effect in 1994, linking Canada, the United States and Mexico in the world's largest free-trade zone.

Ottawa is the center of the world in this Lambert Equal Area projection. It reveals that the shortest route from Ottawa to Singapore is over the North Pole, and that a direct route from Ottawa to Tokyo passes over the Yukon. Concentric circles on the map make it clear that Honduras is as close to Ottawa as Whitehorse, that Brasilia is slightly closer than Hawaii, and that the most distant capital in the world is Canberra, Australia.

Goods, Services, and the Wealth of Nations

Canada enjoys one of the highest material standards of living in the world. With highly productive labor force of 14 million people, the Canadian economy ranks the seventh largest among the affluent industrial nations of the world. The total Gross Domestic Product (GDP)—the value of all our goods and services produced in the country—was $680 billion in 1993. Only the United States, Japan, Germany, France, Italy and the United Kingdom (in that order) surpassed this figure.

The chart below compares per capita GDP of selected nations. Distributing the value of the world's goods and services would provide each person with about $3700—roughly equal to the present per capita GDP of Mexico, but 30 times greater than that of Mozambique.

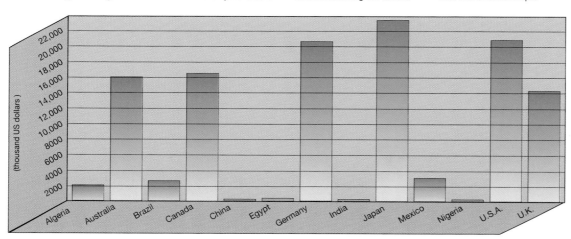

(thousand US dollars): 22,000 / 20,000 / 18,000 / 16,000 / 14,000 / 12,000 / 10,000 / 8000 / 6000 / 4000 / 2000

Algeria · Australia · Brazil · Canada · China · Egypt · Germany · India · Japan · Mexico · Nigeria · U.S.A. · U.K.

Imports and Exports: Autos, Lumber, and Wheat for Aircraft, Computers, and Footwear

One half of all the goods produced in Canada is shipped abroad. The world's top exporter of paper, nickel, and uranium, Canada is among the world's first six trading nations—and one of only four countries that export more than they import. Because national income levels closely follow exports, trade is essential to Canadian prosperity.

For 200 years, Canada's major trading partners have been Great Britain and the United States. Since 1882, the United States has been more important in terms of total trade. But Britain remained the foremost market for Canadian exports until the late 1940s.

The trade between Canada and the United States is greater than that between any other two countries in the world. Since the Canada–U.S. Automotive Products Agreement of 1965, motor vehicles and parts have remained Canada's most profitable exports, accounting for about one out of every four export dollars earned. Canada's traditional major exports—fabricated materials, such as lumber, newsprint, and chemicals, and raw materials, such as wheat, metals and crude petroleum—bring in much of the rest. In effect, these goods are exchanged for a wide range of manufactured imports, from aircraft to computers, and farm machinery to footwear, which help Canada to maintain its high material standard of living.

Imports to Canada (million dollars)		Exports from Canada (million dollars)
96,397	U.S.A.	118,421
2751	Mexico	770
715	Brazil	620
4102	United Kingdom	3012
3551	Germany	2161
2668	France	1339
514	Russian Federation	1263

Imports to Canada (million dollars)		Exports from Canada (million dollars)
131	Israel	118
542	Saudi Arabia	286
10,757	Japan	7412
2649	Taiwan	952
2447	China	2132
2008	South Korea	1405
954	Australia/New Zealand	734

This global projection, centered on Canada, depicts the breadth of the nation's external ties. Diplomatic and consular representation keeps Canada in touch with almost every other country. Our membership in the Commonwealth of Nations, NATO, OAS, and our UN peacekeeping role and foreign aid programs have all forged substantial links around the world.

*The **North Atlantic Treaty Organization (NATO)** comprises 16 countries in North America and Europe, bound together for mutual defense under a treaty signed, partly at Canada's instigation, in 1949. Since the end of the cold war in 1989, Canada's NATO commitment has been broadened to further our political, economic, and scientific links with Europe.*

PAPUA–NEW GUINEA

SOLOMON ISLANDS

AUSTRALIA

NAURU

VANUATU

KIRIBATI

TUVALU

•Canberra

FIJI

WESTERN SAMOA

TONGA

NEW ZEALAND •Wellington

10,500 km
12,000 km
13,500 km
15,000 km
16,500 km
18,000 km

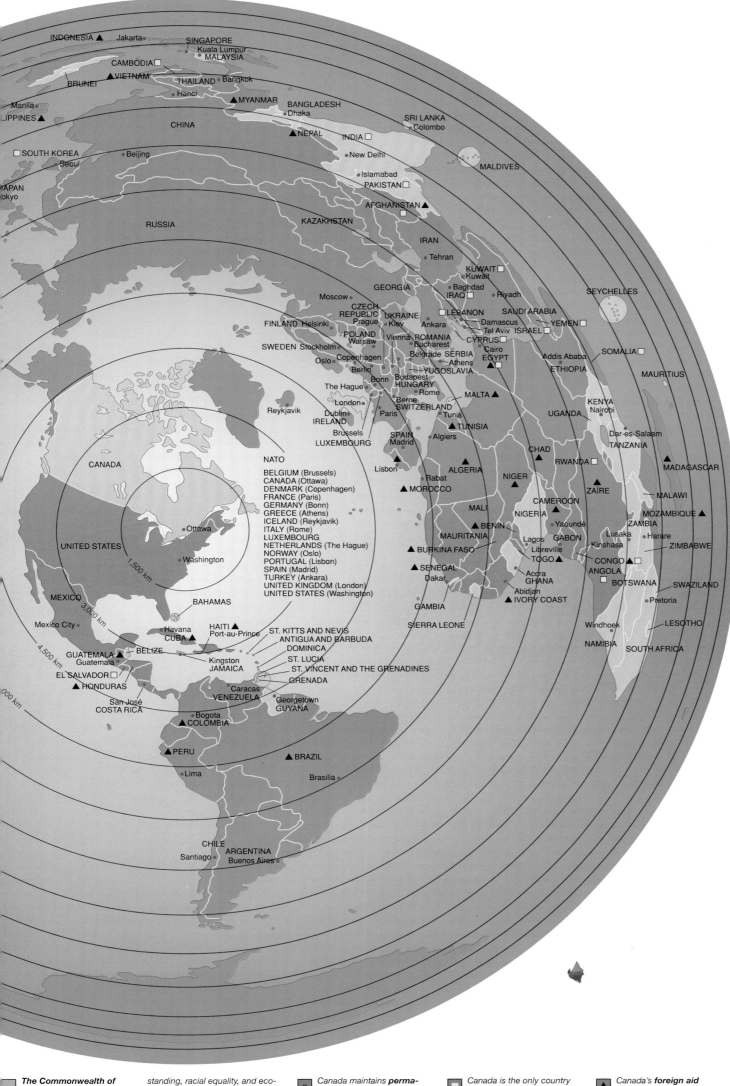

Foreign Aid and Investment

Canadian money—either as external aid or as business investment—finances projects in more than 140 countries. Two thirds of this foreign aid, amounting to $1.9 billion, goes directly to the governments of recipient countries, in the form of food, building materials, industrial and agricultural equipment, or technology. The Canadian International Development Agency (CIDA) distributes another 43 percent of its funds among some 58 international organizations, many of which are United Nations agencies. This money helps to finance programs undertaken by organizations such as UNICEF (the United Nations International Children's Emergency Fund) and the World Bank.

Canada's foreign aid program was initiated in 1950 as part of the Commonwealth's Colombo Plan. For the 14 million Canadians at that time, the $200,000 worth of wheat donated to India, Pakistan and Sri Lanka represented a penny-a-person sacrifice. By the late 1980s, Canada's donations to more than 70 countries had climbed to more than $110 from each person.

Direct Canadian investment in business abroad has also increased significantly, jumping from more than $13 billion in 1977 to $94.4 billion in 1991. The United States was the largest beneficiary of these investment dollars ($54.6 billion), followed by Great Britain ($11.3 billion), Bermuda ($2.6 billion), and Australia ($2 billion).

Foreign Aid

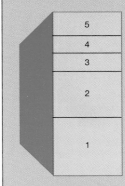

1. Africa 36%
2. Asia 27%
3. Caribbean,
   Latin America 11%
4. Other countries 11%
5. Other forms
   of aid 15%

Foreign Investment

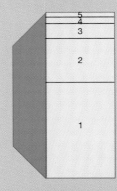

1. United States 58%
2. Europe 25%
3. Pacific Rim 10%
4. Caribbean,
   Mexico 5%
5. Other countries 2%

The Commonwealth of Nations is a loosely structured voluntary association of 50 independent states, most of which were once colonies or dependencies of the British Empire. The Commonwealth embraces one quarter of the world's area and a similar proportion of its people. The organization is pledged to furthering peace, social understanding, racial equality, and economic development. The heads of the Commonwealth governments meet periodically to discuss matters of common concern. The member governments hold some 50 conferences yearly on such topics as education, science and health. Canada provides development assistance to 42 out of 50 Commonwealth nations.

Canada maintains **permanent representatives** in more than 80 countries. They are called ambassadors or, in the case of the Commonwealth, high commissioners. Some 20 Canadian consulates are located in cities other than national capitals. There are also more than 80 trade offices in countries where Canada has commercial interests.

Canada is the only country in the world to have participated in all of the **United Nations peacekeeping missions** undertaken since World War II. In recent years, Canadian troops or official military observers were stationed in El Salvador, Mozambique, the Middle East, along the India–Pakistan border, and in the former Yugoslavia.

Canada's **foreign aid** also extends beyond the Commonwealth countries to other nations. For example, some Latin American states and former French colonies in Africa are significant beneficiaries as Canada expands its cultural and trade ties. This map pinpoints some of the countries that have received Canadian aid in recent times..

FACTS A

BOUT CANADA

The Nation and the Provinces

CANADIAN SUPERLATIVES

Largest island: Baffin (N.W.T.), 507,451 km²

Longest river: Mackenzie, 4241 km

Largest lake within Canada: Huron (Ont.). Area in Canada: 39,473 km². (Total area of the lake, including United States area: 63,096 km²)

Highest mountain: Mount Logan (Yukon), 5959 m

Highest lake: Chilco (B.C.), 1171 m

Rainiest place: Ocean Falls (B.C.), 4386.8 mm/year

Highest waterfall: Della Falls (B.C.), 440 m (more than one leap)

Greatest waterfall by volume: Niagara Falls (the Canadian Horsehoe Falls, Ont.), 5365 m³/second

Largest metropolitan area: Edmonton (Alta.), 11,396.7 km²

Longest bridge: The Pierre Laporte Suspension Bridge, Québec (Qué.), 668 m

Longest tunnel: Macdonald Railway Tunnel at Rogers Pass (B.C.), 14.6 km

Highest dam: Mica, Columbia River (B.C.), 244 m

Coldest city: Yellowknife (N.W.T.). Mean annual temperature: −5.4°C

Warmest city: Vancouver (B.C.). Mean annual temperature: 10.4°C

Northernmost point: Cape Columbia, Ellesmere Island (N.W.T.), 83°07′N

Northernmost town: Grise Fiord, Ellesmere Island (N.W.T.), 76°25′N

Southernmost point: Middle Island, Lake Erie (Ont.), 41°41′N

Southernmost town: Pelee Island South (Ont.), 41°45′N

Westernmost point: Yukon/Alaska border 141°W

Westernmost town: Beaver Creek (Yukon), 140°52′W

Easternmost point: Cape Spear (Nfld.), 52°37′W

Easternmost town: Blackhead, St. John's South District (Nfld.), 52°39′W

Highest city: Rossland (B.C.), 1056 m

Highest town: Lake Louise (Alta.), 1540 m

Highest tide: The Bay of Fundy at Burntcoat Head (N.S.), 14.25 m (mean spring range)

AREA OF THE PROVINCES AND TERRITORIES

Province or territory:	Land (km²)	Freshwater (km²)	Total (km²)	Percent of total area
Newfoundland	371,690	34,030	405,720	4.1
Prince Edward Island	5660	—	5660	0.1
Nova Scotia	52,841	2650	55,490	0.6
New Brunswick	72,090	1350	73,440	0.7
Québec	1,356,790	183,890	1,540,680	15.5
Ontario	891,190	177,390	1,068,580	10.7
Manitoba	548,360	101,590	649,950	6.5
Saskatchewan	570,700	81,630	652,330	6.5
Alberta	644,390	16,800	661,190	6.6
British Columbia	929,730	18,070	947,800	9.5
Yukon Territory	478,970	4480	483,450	4.8
Northwest Territories	3,293,070	133,300	3,426,320	34.4
CANADA	9,215,430	755,180	9,970,610	100.0

POPULATION BY PROVINCE (thousands)

Province or territory	1961	1971	1981	1986	1991
Newfoundland	458	522	567.7	583.3	568.5
Prince Edward Island	105	112	122.5	126.6	129.8
Nova Scotia	737	789	847.4	873.2	899.9
New Brunswick	598	635	696.4	710.4	723.9
Québec	5259	6028	6428.4	6540.3	6895.9
Ontario	6236	7703	8625.1	9113.5	10,084.9
Manitoba	922	988	1026.2	1071.2	1091.9
Saskatchewan	925	926	968.3	1021.3	988.9
Alberta	1322	1628	2337.7	2375.3	2545.5
British Columbia	1629	2185	2744.5	2889.2	3282.1
Yukon	15	18	23.2	23.5	27.8
Northwest Territories	23	35	45.7	52.2	54.6

CANADA'S POPULATION: Past and future growth

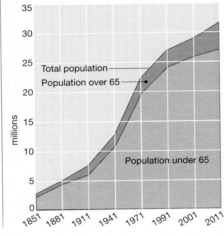

CANADA'S POPULATION: Geographic distribution (1986)

Selected parallels of latitude	Population	%
South of 49°	17,827 382	70.4
Between 49° and 54°	6,898 501	27.3
Between 54° and 60°	505 222	2.0
North of 60°	78 226	0.3

Selected distances North of Canada–USA border		
0-150 km	18,218 596	72.0
151-300 km	3,394 247	13.4
301-600 km	2,630 864	10.4
Over 600 km	1,065 624	4.2
Total Canadian population	**25,354 064**	**100.0**

CANADA'S TIME ZONES

(map showing: PACIFIC STANDARD TIME, MOUNTAIN STANDARD TIME, CENTRAL STANDARD TIME, EASTERN STANDARD TIME, ATLANTIC STANDARD TIME, NFLD. STANDARD TIME)

ALBERTA

One of the wealthiest of Canada's provinces, Alberta was named after Queen Victoria's daughter, the wife of the Marquis of Lorne, governor-general from 1878 to 1883. The French explorer Pierre de La Vérendrye was probably the first European to set foot in Alberta in 1751. In 1754, Anthony Henday was sent by the Hudson's Bay Company to establish contact with the Blackfoot Indians. By 1774, Peter Pond had established a trading post on Lake Athabasca. But it was not until the District of Alberta was created in 1882, and the railway pushed through, that a steady flow of immigrants came from Europe, the United States and eastern Canada. Marquis wheat, and oil and natural gas development have contributed to the province's prosperity.

Capital: Edmonton
Motto: *Fortis et liber* (Strong and free)
Flower: Wild rose (also known as prickly rose)
Date of entry into Confederation: September 1, 1905
Total area: 661,190 km²
Percentage of Canada: 6.66%
Length of boundaries: 3926 km
Length of coastline: 0 km

Population (1991): 2,545,553
Percentage of national population: 9.3%
Urban population (1991): 79.8%
Population density (1991): 3.8/km²
Per capita prov. income (1992): $27,714

Selected events: Banff Festival of the Arts (July-August); Calgary Stampede (July); Klondike Days, Edmonton (July); Medicine Hat Exhibition and Stampede (July); Whoop-Up Days, Lethbridge (July).

Historic sites: Cochrane Ranche, Cochrane; C. Ora Card Home, Cardston; Fort Edmonton; Fort George/Buckingham House, Elk Point; Fort Macleod Museum; Fort Saskatchewan Museum and Historic Site; Fort Whoop-Up; Frank Slide Interpretive Centre; Head-Smashed-In Buffalo Jump Interpretive Centre, near Fort McLeod; Heritage Park Historic Village, Calgary; Historic Dunvegan; Rocky Mountain House National Historic Site; Rutherford House, Edmonton; Stephansson House Historic Site, Markerville; Ukrainian Cultural Heritage Village; Victoria Settlement Provincial Historic Site, Smoky Lake.

Natural attractions: Banff National Park; Crowsnest Pass; Cypress Hills Interprovincial Park; Dinosaur Provincial Park; Dinosaur Trail, Red Deer River valley near Drumheller; Dry Island Buffalo Jump Provincial Park; Elk Island National Park; Jasper National Park; Kananaskis Country; Waterton Lakes National Park; Willmore Wilderness Park; Wood Buffalo National Park; Writing-on-Stone Provincial Park.

BRITISH COLUMBIA

Exploration of Canada's most westerly province brought Britain and Spain close to war. Spaniards were in the area as early as 1774. Captain Cook visited the coast in 1778. In 1792, Captain Vancouver was sent by the Royal Navy to survey the territory a year before Alexander Mackenzie reached the Pacific overland. Spain withdrew in 1795 and, by 1821, the Hudson's Bay Company controlled the territory. Vancouver Island and the mainland became two separate crown colonies, but were joined in 1866. Five years later, the united colonies joined Confederation on the promise of a railway. Immigration surged when the Canadian Pacific Railway was completed in 1886, and again after the Prairie drought of the 1930s and during World War II. Queen Victoria christened the province in 1858, changing the proposed name of New Caledonia to avoid confusion with a French island of the same name in the South Pacific.

Capital: Victoria
Motto: *Splendor Sine Occasu* (Splendor without diminishment)
Flower: Pacific dogwood
Date of entry into Confederation: July 20, 1871
Total area: 947,800 km²
Percentage of Canada: 9.5%
Length of boundaries: 30,801 km
Length of coastline: 25,730 km
Population (1991): 3,282,061
Percentage of national population: 12%
Urban population (1991): 80.4%
Population density (1991): 3.5/km²
Per capita prov. income (1992): $25,114

Selected events: Abbotsford International Airshow (August); Bathtub Race, Vancouver (July); Billy Barker Days, Quesnel (July); Chemainus Festival of Murals (July-August); Pacific National Exhibition, Vancouver (August-September); Peach Festival, Penticton (July); Vancouver Sea Festival (July).

Historic sites: Barkerville Historic Town; Bowron Lake Provincial Park; Cottonwood House Provincial Historic Park;

the CPR "Last Spike" cairn, Eagle Pass, Craigellachie; Fort Langley National Historic Site; Fort Rodd National Historic Site; Fort Steele Heritage Town; Fort St. James National Historic Site; 'Ksan Indian Village, Hazelton; North Pacific Cannery Village and Museum, Port Edward; *St. Roch* National Historic Site, Vancouver; Maritime Museum, Vancouver.

Natural attractions: Cathedral Grove, MacMillan Provincial Park; Della Falls, Strathcona Provincial Park; Garibaldi Provincial Park; Glacier National Park; Golden Ears Provincial Park; Gulf Islands; Harrison Hot Springs; Hell's Gate Airtram, Boston Bar; Kootenay National Park; Manning Provincial Park; Mount Revelstoke National Park; Naikoon Provincial Park; Okanagan Valley; Pacific Rim National Park; Queen Charlotte Islands; Sasquatch Provincial Park; Stanley Park, Vancouver; Tweedsmuir Provincial Park; Wells Grey Provincial Park; Yoho National Park.

MANITOBA

Cree, Salteaux and Assiniboines inhabited the area now known as Manitoba when the first European, Sir Thomas Button, wintered on Hudson Bay in 1612. Fur trading soon began and in 1670, Charles II of England granted the entire watershed to the Hudson's Bay Company. York Factory, the province's oldest permanent settlement, was founded in 1684. In 1812, Lord Selkirk brought Scottish crofters to the Red River valley near present-day Winnipeg to provide agricultural products for the fur traders. In 1869, Canada purchased the land for 300,000 pounds, and in 1870, Manitoba became Canada's fifth province. Manitoba was once known as "Lake of the Prairies"; its name may be derived from two Indian words: *Minne Toba*, meaning "water prairie." English- and French-Canadians, British, Icelandic, Ukrainian and Mennonite peoples were the main settlers before 1900.

Capital: Winnipeg
Motto: None
Flower: Prairie crocus
Date of entry into Confederation: July 15, 1870
Total area: 649,950 km²
Percentage of Canada: 6.5%
Length of boundaries: 4063 km
Length of coastline: 917 km
Population (1991): 1,091,942
Percentage of national population: 4%
Urban population (1991): 72.1%
Population density (1991): 1.7/km²
Per capita prov. income (1992): $21,535

Selected events: Canadian National Ukrainian Festival, Dauphin (July-August); Canadian Turtle Derby, Boissevain (February); Festival du Voyageur, Winnipeg (February); Flin Flon Trout Festival (June); Folklorama, Winnipeg (August); Icelandic Festival of Canada, Gimli (August); Northern Manitoba Trappers' Festival, The Pas (February); Pioneer Days, Steinbach (July-August); Red River Exhibition, Winnipeg (June); Royal Manitoba Winter Fair, Brandon (March).

Historic sites: Eskimo Museum, Churchill; The Forks National Historic Site, Winnipeg; Gimli Historical Museum; Hecla Island Heritage Home Museum; Lower Fort Garry National Historic Site; Mennonite Heritage Village, Steinbach; Margaret Laurence Home, Neepawa; Prince of Wales' Fort National Historic Site, Churchill; St. Michael's Ukrainian Orthodox Church, Gardenton.

Natural attractions: Baldy Mountain, Duck Mountain Provincial Park; Hecla Provincial Park; International Peace Garden; Nopiming Provincial Park; Oak Hammock Marsh Wildlife Management Area and Conservation Centre; Riding Mountain National Park; Sandilands Provincial Forest; Spruce Woods Provincial Heritage Park; Turtle Mountain Provincial Park; Whiteshell Provincial Park.

NEW BRUNSWICK

French-speaking settlers were the first European inhabitants in New Brunswick. Verrazano and Cartier explored the coast in the 16th century, and Champlain established the first Canadian settlement on Île Ste. Croix in 1604. France relinquished its control to Britain in 1713 and, in the wake of the American Revolution, United Empire Loyalists streamed in. In 1784, the area was separated from Nova Scotia, becoming the colony of New Brunswick in honor of the British king, George III, whose family name at the time was Brunswick. In the 1800s thousands of immigrants came from Britain. Saint John is the oldest incorporated city in Canada, and Mount Allison University in Sackville was the first university to confer a degree on a woman, in 1875.

Capital: Fredericton
Motto: *Spem Reduxit* (Hope was restored)
Flower: Purple violet
Date of entry into Confederation: July 1, 1867
Total area: 73,440 km²
Percentage of Canada: 0.7%
Length of boundaries: 3079 km
Length of coastline: 2269 km
Population (1991): 723,900
Percentage of national population: 3.3%
Urban population (1991): 47.7%
Population density (1991): 9.9/km²
Per capita prov. income (1992): $18,529

Selected events: Acadian Festival, Caraquet (August); Atlantic Waterfowl Celebration, Sackville (August); Chocolate Festival, St. Stephen (August); Lobster Festival, Shediac (July); Loyalist Days, Saint John (July); Salmon Festival, Campbellton (July).

Historic sites: Acadian Historical Village, near Caraquet; Fort Beausejour National Historic Site; Hartland Covered Bridge (the world's longest); Kings Landing Historical Settlement, near Fredericton; Martello Tower, Saint John.

Natural attractions: Fundy National Park; Grand Falls; Grand Manan; Kouchibouguac National Park; Magnetic Hill, near Moncton; Mount Carleton Provincial Park; The Rocks Provincial Park; Roosevelt-Campobello International Park; Sackville Waterfowl Park; Sugar Provincial Park.

NEWFOUNDLAND

The oldest English dependency in the New World and possibly the home of the first European child born in North America, Snorri Karlsefni (b. 1013), is the youngest province of Canada. Newfoundland's history is a blend of legend and high adventure. The Vikings established a temporary settlement at L'Anse aux Meadows at the end of the 10th century. Bristol merchants from England were engaged in lucrative fishing off the Grand Banks as early as 1481. In 1502 King Henry VII referred to the island as "newe founde launde." Morris Dancers from England performed in St. John's in 1583, but it was only in 1610 that the first organized colony was established by John Guy at Cupids on Conception Bay. In 1855, it became a self-governing dominion and, in 1949, joined Confederation.

Capital: St. John's
Motto: *Quaerite prime Regnum Dei* (Seek ye first the Kingdom of God)
Flower: Pitcher plant
Date of entry into Confederation: March 31, 1949
Total area: 405,720 km²
Percentage of Canada: 4.1%
Length of boundaries: 33,478 km
Length of coastline: 28,964 km
Population (1991): 568,474
Percentage of national population: 2.1%
Urban population (1991): 53.6%
Population density (1991): 1.5/km²
Per capita prov. income (1992): $15,890

Selected events: Conception Bay Folk Festival, Harbour Grace (July); Hangashore Folk Festival, Cornerbrook (July); Newfoundland and Labrador Folk Festival, St. John's (August).

Historic sites: Cape Spear National Historic Site; Castle Hill National Historic Site, Placentia; L'Anse aux Meadows National Historic Site; Port au Choix National Historic Site; Signal Hill National Historic Site, St. John's.

Natural attractions: Conception Bay; Gros Morne National Park; La Manche Provincial Park; Long Point, near Twillingate; Terra Nova National Park.

NOVA SCOTIA

It may be that Celtic monks from Iceland settled on Cape Breton Island in 875 A.D., and the Norseman Thorfinn Karlsefni lived for a time around 1008 on the mainland coast. Historians agree that John Cabot visited Nova Scotia in 1497, and Portuguese fishermen likely wintered there. But the first permanent settlement was built in 1605, when Monts and Champlain founded the *habitation* at Port Royal. One year later, Champlain encouraged the formation of Canada's first social club, the "Ordre de Bon Temps". In 1621, Nova Scotia was granted to Sir William Alexander for settlement, and his charter bears the name "New Scotland" in Latin. In 1848, it was the first British colony to have responsible government. English, Germans, Scots and Loyalists were the main settlers. Possessor of a great seafaring tradition, Nova Scotia is still called "the wharf of North America."

Capital: Halifax
Motto: *Munit Haec et Altera Vincit* (One defends and the other conquers)
Flower: Mayflower
Date of entry into Confederation: July 1, 1867
Total area: 55,490 km²
Percentage of Canada: 0.6%
Length of boundaries: 7613 km
Length of coastline: 7582 km
Population (1991): 899,942
Percentage of national population: 3.3%
Urban population (1991): 53.5%
Population density (1991): 16.2/km²
Per capita prov. income (1992): $19,530

Selected events: Digby Scallop Days (August); Gaelic Mon, St. Ann's (August); Maritime Old Time Jamboree, Dartmouth (July); Nova Scotia Fisheries Exhibition and Fishermen's Reunion, Lunenberg (September); Seafest, Yarmouth (July).

Historic sites: Alexander Graham Bell National Historic Site, Baddeck; Annapolis Royal Historic Gardens; *Bluenose II*, Halifax; Cape Breton Miners Museum, Glace Bay; Fisheries Museum of the Atlantic, Lunenberg; Fort Anne National Historic Site and Museum, Annapolis Royal; Fortress of Louisbourg National Historic Site; Grand Pré National Historic Site; Halifax Citadel National Historic Site; Maritime Museum of the Atlantic, Halifax; North Hills Museum, Granville Ferry; Port Royal National Historic Site; Springhill Miners' Museum.

Natural attractions: Annapolis Valley; Bras d'Or Lake; Cabot Trail; Cape Breton Island National Park; Five Islands Provincial Park; Giant's Causeway, Brier Island; Kejimkujik National Park; Margaree Valley, Cape Breton Island; The Ovens, Lunenburg; Peggy's Cove; Nova Scotia Provincial Wildlife Park, Shubenacadie.

ONTARIO

An old Iroquois word meaning "the shining waters," Ontario has one quarter of all the available fresh water in the world. In the early 17th century, Étienne Brûlé, a lieutenant of Samuel de Champlain, explored as far as western Ontario before he was killed by the Hurons. Henry Hudson claimed the northern part for the British Crown in 1610. In 1791, the province of Upper Canada was formed, and William Lyon Mackenzie was instrumental in gaining power for the legislative assembly following an unsuccessful rebellion in 1837. English, Germans, Dutch, Scots, Irish and runaway slaves from the United States were Ontario's earliest immigrants, and since 1881 other Europeans have added their heritage to this prosperous province.

Capital: Toronto
Motto: *Ut Incepit Fidelis Sic Permanet* (Loyal she began and loyal she remains)

SURFACE AREA: The largest countries

Rank	Country	Area (thousand km²)
1.	Russia	17,070
2.	CANADA	9970
3.	China	9597
4.	United States	9363
5.	Brazil	8512
6.	Australia	7687
7.	India	3288
8.	Argentina	2767
9.	Kazakhstan	2717
10.	Sudan	2506
11.	Algeria	2382
12.	Zaire	2345
13.	Greenland	2175
14.	Saudi Arabia	2150
15.	Mexico	1973
16.	Indonesia	1905
17.	Libya	1760
18.	Iran	1648
19.	Mongolia	1565
20.	Peru	1285
21.	Chad	1284
22.	Niger	1267
23.	Angola	1246
24.	Mali	1240
25.	Ethiopia	1222
26.	South Africa	1221
27.	Colombia	1141
28.	Bolivia	1098

POPULATION: Canada and the world

Rank	Country	Population (Jan. 1, 1991)	Density/ km²
1.	China	1,171,000,000	122.01
2.	India	843,930,861	256.70
3.	United States	248,709,873	25.35
4.	Indonesia	191,170,000	98.58
5.	Brazil	150,368,000	17.67
6.	Russia	148,800,000	8.72
7.	Japan	124,491,000	334.40
8.	Pakistan	115,524,000	154.85
9.	Nigeria	112,163,000	121.42
10.	Bangladesh	108,000,000	750.01
11.	Mexico	87,836,000	44.53
12.	Germany	80,372,000	219.74
13.	Vietnam	71,267,000	216.25
14.	Philippines	62,868,000	209.56
15.	Turkey	60,777,000	77.86
16.	Italy	57,052,000	189.40
17.	Thailand	56,923,000	110.75
18.	France	56,614,000	103.49
19.	United Kingdom	56,467,000	231.37
20.	Iran	55,762,000	33.84
21.	Egypt	54,688,000	54.61
22.	Ukraine	52,000,000	86.14
23.	Ethiopia	49,883,000	40.82
24.	South Korea	43,268,000	439.34
25.	Burma	42,561,000	62.91
26.	Spain	38,872,268	77.00
27.	Poland	38,300,000	122.49
28.	Zaire	36,672,000	15.64
29.	South Africa	36,070,000	29.54
30.	Colombia	33,613,000	29.51
31.	Argentina	32,370,298	11.69
32.	Tanzania	28,359,000	30.00
33.	Morocco	27,575,000	61.75
34.	CANADA	27,296,859	2.73
35.	Sudan	25,941,000	10.35
36.	Kenya	25,905,000	44.46
37.	Algeria	25,660,000	10.77
38.	North Korea	23,193,000	192.41
39.	Romania	22,760,449	95.83
40.	Peru	22,465,000	17.48

Flower: White trillium

Date of entry into Confederation:
July 1, 1867

Total area: 1,068,580 km²

Percentage of Canada: 10.7%

Length of boundaries: 6265 km

Length of coastline: 1211 km

Population (1991): 10,084,885

Percentage of national population:
36.9%

Urban population (1991): 81.8%

Population density (1991): 9.4/km²

Per capita prov. income (1992): $26,148

Selected events: Blossom Week, St. Catharines (May); Canadian National Exhibition, Toronto (August); Fergus Highland Games (August); Festival of Festivals, Toronto (September); Glengarry Highland Games, Maxville (August); International Sailing Regatta, Kenora (July-August); Kitchener-Waterloo Oktoberfest (October); Maple Syrup Festival, Elmira (April); Miners' Festival, Cobalt (August); Shaw Festival, Niagara-on-the-Lake (April-November); Stratford Festival (May to mid-November).

Historic sites: Bytown Museum, Ottawa; Dundurn Castle, Hamilton; Fort George, Niagara-on-the-Lake; Fort Henry, Kingston; Fort St. Joseph National Historic Site; Fort Malden National Historic Site; Historic Fort Erie; Historic Naval and Military Establishments, Penetanguishene; Laurier House, Ottawa; Martyrs' Shrine, Midland; Muskoka Pioneer Village, Huntsville; Nancy Island Historic Site, Wasaga; Oil Museum of Canada, Oil Springs; Parliament Buildings, Ottawa; Petroglyphs Provincial Park; Sainte-Marie among the Hurons, Midland; Serpent Mounds Provincial Park; Sharon Temple; Stephen Leacock Memorial Home, Orillia; Uncle Tom's Cabin Historic Site, Dresden; Upper Canada Village, Morrisburg.

Natural attractions: Awenda Provincial Park; Algonquin Provincial Park; Bruce Peninsula National Park; Fathom Five National Marine Park; Georgian Bay Islands National Park; Jack Miner's Bird Sanctuary, Kingsville; Kakabeka Falls, Kakabeka Falls Provincial Park; Killarney Provincial Park; Lake of the Woods; Lake Superior Provincial Park; Manitoulin Island; Niagara Falls; Ouimet Canyon Provincial Park; Point Pelee National Park; Pukaskwa National Park; Quetico Provincial Park; Sandbanks Provincial Park; Sleeping Giant Provincial Park; St. Lawrence Islands National Park.

PRINCE EDWARD ISLAND

Canada's smallest and most densely populated province is an island of picturesque beauty. The Micmac Indians called it *Abegweit*, a "home cradled on the waves." The French established an outpost in 1663 and named it Île St. Jean. Conquered by the British in 1758, it was renamed St. John's Island, and later Prince Edward Island after Edward, Duke of Kent, father of Queen Victoria. Loyalists settled here during the American Revolution, and Scottish settlers, led by Lord Selkirk, arrived in 1803. Agriculture, tourism and fishing are the Island's main industries today.

Capital: Charlottetown

Motto: *Parva Sub Ingenti* (The small under the protection of the great)

Flower: Lady's slipper

Date of entry into Confederation:
July 1, 1873

Total area: 5660 km²

Percentage of Canada: 0.1%

Length of boundaries: 1260 km

Length of coastline: 1260 km

Population (1991): 129,765

Percentage of national population: 0.5%

Urban population (1991): 39.9%

Population density (1991): 22.9/km²

Per capita prov. income (1992): $16,546

Selected events: Charlottetown Festival (June to September); Georgetown Days (July); Lobster Carnival and Livestock Exhibition, Summerside (July); Old Home Week Celebration, Parkdale (August).

Historic sites: Acadian Pioneer Village, Mont-Carmel; Anne of Green Gables Museum at Silver Bush House; Basin Head Fisheries Museum; Green Park Provincial Historic Park; Fort Amherst/Port La Joye National Historic Site and Museum; Orwell Corner Historic Village; Province House National Historic Site, Charlottetown.

Natural attractions: Prince Edward Island National Park; Strathgartney Provincial Park.

QUÉBEC

An Indian settlement, Stadacona, was the site of the trading post founded by Champlain in 1608 and called "Québec": an Indian name meaning "the place where the water narrows." In 1642, a French civil servant, Sieur de Maisonneuve, organized a settlement on the site of an older Indian village, Hochelaga. Today it is Montréal, Canada's second largest metropolis. By 1663, "Canada" had become a province of France, following the Seven Years' War, and 100 years later it was ceded to Britain. In 1791, the territory was divided into Lower and Upper Canada (Québec and Ontario). Reunited in 1841, it was once again separated in 1867. In the late 18th and 19th centuries, there was an influx of Loyalist and British settlers, but this province remains uniquely French in character.

Capital: Québec

Motto: *Je me souviens* (I remember)

Flower: Iris

Date of entry into Confederation:
July 1, 1867

Total area: 1,540,680 km²

Percentage of Canada: 15.5%

Length of boundaries: 20,683 km

Length of coastline: 13,773 km

Population (1991): 6,895,963

Percentage of national population:
25.3%

Urban population (1991): 77.6%

Population density (1991): 4.5/km²

Per capita prov. income (1992): $21,964

Selected events: Carnaval de Québec, Québec (February); Carnaval-Souvenir, Chicoutimi (February); Festival des Couleurs, Mont-Tremblant (September to October); Huitaine de Gaieté, Roberval (July); Just for Laughs Festival, Montréal (July); Montréal Jazz Festival (June to July); Québec International Summer Festival, Québec (July); World Film Festival, Montréal (August); Saint-Jean-Baptiste Day (June 24).

Historic sites: Artillery Park National Historic Site; Cape Redoubt, Québec; Château de Ramezay, Montréal; The Citadel, Québec; Coteau-du-Lac National Historic Site; The Forges of St-Maurice National Historic Site, Trois-Rivières; Fort Chambly, Chambly; Fort Lennox National Historic Site; Hôtel-Dieu Augustine Museum; *La Grande Hermine*, Cartier-Brébeuf National Historic Site, Québec; National Battlefields Park, Québec; Val-Jalbert Historic Village.

Natural attractions: Baie-Saint-Paul; Cap Tourmente National Wildlife Area; Eastern Townships; Forillon National Park; Gaspé Peninsula; Gatineau Park; Île aux Coudres; Île Bonaventure and Percé Rock Park; Îles de la Madeleine; Île d'Orléans; Lac St. Jean; La Mauricie National Park; Métis Gardens; Mingan Archipelago National Park; Montmorency Falls; Parc d'Aiguebelle; Parc de la Gaspésie; Parc du Mont-Tremblant; Saguenay Marine Park; Saguenay Provincial Park.

SASKATCHEWAN

Half of the improved land in Canada is located in Saskatchewan, whose name derives from *Kisiskatchewan*, a Cree word meaning "the river that flows swiftly."

Paleo-Indians may have roamed here 20,000 years ago; later it became the home of the Chippewa, Blackfoot and Assiniboines. Samuel Hearne set up Cumberland House in 1774 for the Hudson's Bay Company, but within a century the fur-trading era had ended. Beginning in 1872, settlers were lured by free land, and in 1882, Pile of Bones—later called Regina—was founded beside a vast midden of buffalo bones.

Capital: Regina

Motto: None

Flower: Western red lily

Date of entry into Confederation:
September 1, 1905

Total area: 652,330 km²

Percentage of Canada: 6.5%

Length of boundaries: 3571 km

Length of coastline: 0 km

Population (1991): 988,928

Percentage of national population: 3.6%

Urban population (1991): 63%

Population density (1991): 1.5/km²

Per capita prov. income (1992): $20,138

Selected events: Buffalo Days Fair, Regina (August); Prince Albert Exhibition (July to August); Regina Waskimo Winter Festival (February); Saskatoon Exhibition (July); Yorkton Short Film and Video Festival (May).

Historic sites: Batoche National Historic Site; Cannington Manor Provincial Park; Cumberland House Provincial Historic Park; Fort Battleford National Historic Site; Fort Carlton Provincial Historic Park; John Diefenbaker's boyhood home, Wascana Centre, Regina; Last Mountain House Provincial Historic Park; Moose Mountain Provincial Park; Motherwell Homestead National Historic Park; RCMP Museum, Regina; St. Victor's Petroglyphs Provincial Park; Wanuskewin Heritage Park, Saskatoon; Wood Mountain Post Historic Site.

Natural attractions: Buffalo Pound Provincial Park; Cypress Hills Interprovincial Park; Grasslands National Park; Lac la Ronge Provincial Park; Lake Diefenbaker; Meadow Lake Provincial Park; Prince Albert National Park; Qu'Appelle River valley and the Fishing Lakes.

YUKON TERRITORY

In 1825, the Arctic coast of the Yukon Territory was visited by the British explorer Sir John Franklin on one of his expeditions to locate the Northwest Passage. During the 1830s and 1840s, Hudson's Bay Company fur traders mapped the interior. In 1870, the company lost its fur-trading monopoly, and the region became part of the Northwest Territories. Miners began to enter the area in the 1870s. In August 1896, the gold rush began when George W. Carmack made a big strike on Bonanza Creek, a tributary of the Klondike River, and thousands of prospectors poured into the area. The Yukon was declared a separate territory in 1898. But the goldfields began to decline within a decade. During World War II, the Yukon revived with the construction of the Alaska Highway and other military projects. Mining, tourism, and renewable resource development are the Yukon's economic mainstays.

Capital: Whitehorse

Motto: None

Flower: Fireweed

Date of entry into Confederation: June 13, 1898

Total area: 483,450 km^2

Percentage of Canada: 4.8%

Length of boundaries: 4409 km

Length of coastline: 343 km

Population (1991): 27,797

Percentage of national population: 0.1%

Urban population (1991): 58.8%

Population density (1991): 0.06/km^2

Per capita income (1990): $35,731

Selected events: Discovery Days, Dawson City (August); Sourdough Rendezvous, Whitehorse (February).

Historic sites: Dawson; Old Log Church, Whitehorse; *S.S. Keno* National Historic Site, Dawson; *S.S. Klondike* National Historic Site, Whitehorse.

Natural attractions: Ivvavik National Park; Kluane National Park.

NORTHWEST TERRITORIES

The first Europeans to explore this region were the Vikings who visited the eastern Arctic from their settlements in Greenland. During the late 16th century the English explorer Martin Frobisher visited the Arctic Islands in a search for the Northwest Passage. Samuel Hearne and Alexander Mac-kenzie traveled through the northern interior in the late 18th century. The Hudson's Bay Company spurred exploration and development by setting up fur-tradings posts in the early 19th century. The Canadian government bought out the Hudson's Bay Company in 1870. The Arctic Islands lying north the Canadian mainland were annexed in 1880. At present, the area is divided into five administrative regions: Fort Smith, Inuvik, Kitikmeot, Keewatin, and Baffin. A territorial referendum, held in November 1992, approved the land-claim settlement required for the creation of a new territory, known as Nunavut (Inuktitut for "our land") in the eastern Arctic. Its official start-up is set for April 1, 1999.

Capital: Yellowknife

Motto: None

Flower: Mountain avens

Date of entry into Confederation: July 15, 1870

Total area: 3,426,320 km^2

Percentage of Canada: 34.4%

Length of boundaries: 165,389 km

Length of coastline: 161,764 km

Population (1991): 57,600

Percentage of national population: 0.2%

Urban population (1991): 36.7%

Population density (1991): 0.02/km^2

Per capita income (1992): $39,259

Selected events: Caribou Carnival, Yellowknife (March); Delta Daze, Inuvik (October).

Historic sites: Qaummaarvit Historic Park; Northern Life Museum, Fort Smith; The Prince of Wales Northern Heritage Centre, Yellowknife.

Natural attractions: Aulavik National Park (Banks Island); Auyuittuq National Park; Ellesmere Island National Park Reserve; Nahanni National Park Reserve; Old Crow Flats (Vuntut National Park); Wood Buffalo National Park.

THE GOVERNORS GENERAL OF CANADA

VISCOUNT MONCK (1867-68)

Sir Charles Stanley, 4th Viscount Monck, played a major role in the Confederation of the British North American colonies and served as the first governor general of the Dominion of Canada on July 1, 1867. He had to tread a fine line in fulfilling his new job, respecting the powers of the new government without compromising the prerogatives of the Crown.

Born in 1819 and educated at Trinity College, Dublin, he entered the British House of Commons in 1852 and served as Lord of the Treasury in the Palmerston cabinet. In 1868, he returned to Ireland, where he was lord lieutenant of County Dublin for 20 years. He died there in 1894.

BARON LISGAR (1868-72)

Baron Lisgar was governor general during the Red River Rebellion of 1870, and the Fenian border raids, where his wisdom and administrative experience aided in the resolution of these conflicts. In a fishing-rights dispute with the United States, however, Baron Lisgar made little effort to defend Canada's interests, as his overriding concern was to maintain good relations between London and Washington. As a result, the 1871 Treaty of Washington on fishing and navigational rights was highly favorable to the United States.

A thoughtful, practical man, he was born into an Irish family in India in 1807. He led a relatively secluded life as governor general, but did undertake several official tours. He died in Ireland in 1876.

THE EARL OF DUFFERIN (1872-78)

Canada's third governor general, Frederick Temple Blackwood, the Earl of Dufferin, was a charming and enthusiastic man who inaugurated a period of vitality and enterprise at Rideau Hall. Though he used his eloquence to advance the cause of Canadian unity, he ran into conflict with the Canadian government. In 1875 the earl exercised his right of clemency by lifting the death sentence imposed on Louis Riel's adjutant general, who had been accused of murdering Thomas Scott. Justice Minister Edward Blake opposed the earl's acting without the advice of the Canadian cabinet. As a result of this conflict, future governors general were instructed to act on the advice of their Canadian ministers.

Born in 1826, Dufferin had a noteworthy career in the British public service. In Canada, he and his remarkable wife, Hariot, hosted countless parties, cultural events and sport activities. In 1875, he persuaded Quebec citizens to preserve their city walls, then threatened by demolition.

After his departure from Canada in 1878, Dufferin served as Britain's ambassador to Russia, Turkey, Italy and France, and as viceroy of India. He died in 1902.

THE MARQUESS OF LORNE (1878-83)

Sir John Douglas Sutherland Campbell, the Marquess of Lorne, was the husband of Queen Victoria's daughter Louise. Their chief influence was in the field of arts and letters: they helped found the Royal Canadian Academy of Arts, from which grew the National Gallery of Canada, and the Royal Society of Canada.

In 1878, Lorne took Prime Minister Sir John A. Macdonald's advice by dismissing Lieutenant Governor Letellier de Saint-Just of Québec, although Lorne personally disagreed with the decision. Again, to enhance the position of the governor general above politics, he approved the creation of the office of high commissioner to represent Canada's interests in London. Born in 1845, son of the Duke of Argyll, he succeeded to his father's title in 1900. He died in 1914.

THE MARQUESS OF LANSDOWNE (1883-88)

A controversial figure, Henry Charles Keith Petty-Fitzmaurice, 3rd Marquess of Lansdowne, was a member of the Gladstone cabinet from 1868 to 1872, and in 1880 was appointed Secretary for India. He resigned from that post over a disagreement with Gladstone about Irish Home Rule.

Lansdowne's vice-regency was an eventful time for Canada: in the spring of 1885, the second Riel Rebellion erupted in the Northwest, followed by a fisheries dispute with the United States, but Lansdowne was able to intercede on Canada's behalf with the British Colonial Office. In his farewell speech in 1888, he noted with pride the "peaceful progress of industry, education and art" during his tenure. He was viceroy of India from 1888 to 1893, and served from 1900 to 1905 as foreign secretary. Born into Irish nobility in 1845, he died in 1927 at Clonmore, Ireland.

BARON STANLEY OF PRESTON (1888-93)

Sir Frederick Arthur Stanley was born in 1841, the younger son of the British Prime Minister, the Earl of Derby. A man of tact and good judgment, he was a Member of Parliament and held several cabinet posts, including that of Colonial Secretary, before coming to Canada.

Baron Stanley's term in Canada was marked by his strong support of Canadian culture and sports: he is particularly remembered for his institution of the Stanley Cup. After his departure, Baron Stanley served as lord mayor of Liverpool and as first chancellor of the University of Liverpool. He died in 1908.

THE EARL OF ABERDEEN (1893-98)

Upon their arrival in Canada, John Campbell Gordon, 7th Earl of Aberdeen, and his wife declared their goals to be to "sweeten and elevate public life" and became involved in social and philanthropic work. Lady Aberdeen founded the YWCA in Ottawa, the Canadian branch of the Boys' Brigade (which served both Christian and Jewish children), the Ottawa Maternity Hospital, the National Council of Women and the Victorian Order of Nurses. She also organized relief for famine victims in India, clubs for newsboys and the prison reform movement. Lord Aberdeen withheld approval in 1896 of what he called some "lame duck" political appointments, though it cost him the friendship of Prime Minister Sir Charles Tupper.

Born in 1847, Lord Aberdeen was lord lieutenant of Ireland, before and after his term in Canada. He was raised to Marquess of Aberdeen and Temair in 1915, and died in 1934.

THE EARL OF MINTO (1898-1904)

Gilbert John Elliott, the 4th Earl of Minto, came to Rideau Hall as a veteran of the Russo-Turkish War of 1877, the Afghanistan War of 1879 and the Egyptian campaign of 1882. A military man, he was a staunch supporter of Canadian participation in the Boer War. His chief interest as governor general, however, lay in the establishment of a system of national parks. He also urged the government to safeguard Indian culture and to redress injustices that had been dealt to the native peoples. As well, he persuaded the government to build the Public Archives in Ottawa. From 1905 to 1910 Lord Minto was viceroy of India. He died in 1914.

EARL GREY (1904-11)

Albert Henry George Grey, 4th Earl Grey, started a movement for the preservation of the Plains of Abraham as a national park, and for the restoration of the Fortress of Louisbourg. He also donated the Grey Cup, the nation's premier football trophy, led a campaign for better treatment of tuberculosis, presided over the 1905 ceremonies creating the provinces of Saskatchewan and Alberta, and established the Department of External Affairs in 1909.

Born in 1851, Grey was elected to the British House of Commons in 1880 and entered the House of Lords in 1894. An ardent imperialist and lifelong friend of King Edward VII, Grey regarded Canadians as unenthusiastic about the Empire, but he supported the growth of Canadian nationalism. He died in 1917.

THE DUKE OF CONNAUGHT (1911-16)

The first royal governor general was Prince Arthur, the Duke of Connaught and Strahearn, third son of Queen Victoria, and husband of Princess Louise Margaret of Prussia. During World War I, the duke was active in auxiliary war services and charities, while his wife worked for the Red Cross. His daugher lent her name and helped to raise the "Princess Pat" regiment (Princess Patricia's Canadian Light Infantry), which distinguished itself in both world wars.

As the number of casualties mounted during the war, life at Rideau Hall grew increasingly austere. Nearly all the members of the duke's household staff were killed. The duke presented a memorial window to St. Bartholomew's, the parish church across the park, to commemorate them. He died at Bagshott Park, Surrey, England in January 1942, the last surviving child of Queen Victoria.

THE DUKE OF DEVONSHIRE (1916-21)

The last governor general to be appointed without the Canadian prime minister's consultation, Victor Christian William Cavendish, Duke of Devonshire, arrived in time for the conscription crisis of the First World War. Conscription was enforced, and a bitter controversy followed, but Devonshire was careful not to interfere in domestic political matters. He gained the confidence of Prime Minister Sir Robert Borden through simple dignity, wisdom and geniality. He had a special interest in Canadian agriculture and was also a great hockey fan.

Born in 1868, he began working in business and reading law in London. Elected to Parliament in 1891, he succeeded to the dukedom in 1908, then served as first lord of the Admiralty before his appointment to Canada. When he returned to Britain in 1921, Devonshire was appointed colonial secretary. He died in 1938.

BARON BYNG OF VIMY (1921-26)

Julian Hedworth George Byng was the central figure in the King-Byng Crisis of 1926. He refused to dissolve Parliament when

Prime Minister Mackenzie King wanted to evade a vote on a motion of censure. Byng instead called on Arthur Meighen to form a government. When Meighen failed to gain a majority, Byng granted his request for dissolution. King fought and won the ensuing general election on the grounds that Byng had meddled in politics. Historians have generally agreed, however, that he was justified in refusing King's request.

A career soldier, Byng gained renown as commander of the Canadian Corps at Vimy Ridge in 1917. He was elevated to the peerage in 1919. When Byng returned to Britain in 1926, he was created viscount and promoted to field marshal. From 1928 to 1931 he was commissioner of the London Metropolitan Police. He died in 1935.

VISCOUNT WILLINGDON OF RATTON (1926-31)

Viscount Willingdon, a diplomat by experience and temperament, was an ideal governor general at a time when Canada was taking the final steps toward autonomy. These years saw the opening of Canada's first foreign diplomatic missions and the definition, in the Statute of Westminster (1931), of the British Dominions as fully autonomous states.

Born Freeman Freeman-Thomas in 1866, Willingdon was lord-in-waiting to King George V from 1911 to 1913. From 1913 to 1924 he was governor of Bombay and Madras respectively. After leaving Canada in 1931, Willingdon returned to India as viceroy. He died in 1941.

THE EARL OF BESSBOROUGH (1931-35)

Sir Vere Brabazon Ponsonby, the 9th Earl of Bessborough, arrived in Canada in the midst of the Depression and voluntarily refunded a tenth of his stipend. Despite the economic difficulties of the time, the Bessboroughs initiated the Dominion Drama Festival and generally encouraged the arts.

That same year witnessed the creation of the Canadian Radio Broadcasting Corporation, the forerunner to the CBC. A shy man with a high sense of duty and a stiff manner, the Earl of Bessborough was less popular than his French wife, Roberte de Neuflize. The newspapers criticized him for rebuking the mayor of Toronto on the grounds that the latter had been discourteous to him, the King's representative.

Born in 1880, he entered business life in London. A Member of Parliament from 1913 to 1920, he served in France and at Gallipoli (Turkey) during World War I. He succeeded to the earldom in 1920. Bessborough returned to London's business world in 1935. During the Second World War, he set up a division to aid French refugees in Britain. He died in 1956.

BARON TWEEDSMUIR OF ELSFIELD (1935-40)

Lord and Lady Tweedsmuir had little interest in "society," preferring the company of intellectuals. Together they established a proper library at Rideau Hall and instituted the governor general's Awards for literature. Born John Buchan in 1875, the son of a clergyman, Tweedsmuir was himself a writer of distinction who published histories, biographies, and popular thrillers. His best-known thriller, *The Thirty-Nine Steps*, was published in 1915 and served as the basis of a 1935 film by Alfred Hitchcock. During World War I, he was a *Times* correspondent in France. From 1927 to 1935, he represented the Scottish universities in the House of Commons.

Devoted to the cause of Canadian unity, Tweedsmuir spoke eloquently against religious and racial barriers, publicly deploring narrow provincial policies that ignored the nation as a whole. Conscious of the prestige of his position, he traveled extensively. In 1939, King George VI and Queen Elizabeth made a tour of Canada; World War II broke out the same year. The strain of these events put great pressure on Tweedsmuir's frail health: he died in Montréal on February 11, 1940—the first governor general to die in office.

THE EARL OF ATHLONE (1940-46)

The Earl of Athlone arrived in Canada early in World War II, at a time when many were calling for a Canadian governor general. But Athlone and his wife, Princess Alice, were a dignified couple who helped to provide needed stability during the war years. They showed great interest in Canada's war effort, inspecting military bases and training schools, and visiting hospitals and factories.

Born Prince Alexander of Teck in 1874, Athlone was a career soldier who joined the British Army in 1894 and served in the Boer War and World War I. In 1917 he relinquished his German title and was made Earl of Athlone. He was promoted to major general in 1923, when he began an eight-year term as governor general of South Africa. Lord Athlone died in London, England, in January 1957.

VISCOUNT ALEXANDER OF TUNIS (1946-52)

The last British governor general appointed to Canada, Sir Harold Alexander came here with a secure reputation as one of the greatest military leaders in his country's history. Commissioned in 1910, he commanded a battalion and was wounded in World War I. A major general when World War II broke out, Alexander commanded the 1st Division in France and directed the evacuation of Dunkirk in 1940—he was the last man to leave the beach. He was commander in chief in the Middle East in 1942 and in 1943 led the invasion of Italy. In 1944, following the capture of Rome, he was made field marshal. For the next two years, he was the Supreme Allied Commander in the Mediterranean, after which he was raised to the peerage.

In Canada, Lord and Lady Alexander made long, arduous tours of the country, but lived a simple and informal private life away from the glare of publicity. After leaving Canada, Alexander served as Minister of Defence in the last Churchill cabinet. He died in 1970.

VINCENT MASSEY (1952-59)

Long before he became the first Canadian-born governor general, Vincent Massey was one of the nation's most eminent public servants. He opened the Canadian legation in Washington in 1926, becoming the first diplomat to represent this country in a foreign land. From 1936 to 1947 he was high commissioner in London. From 1949 to 1951 he was chairman of the Royal Commission on National Development in the Arts, Letters and Sciences, whose report led to the creation of the Canada Council.

Born in Toronto on February 20, 1887, Massey studied at the University of Toronto and at Oxford. He became a history professor at the University of Toronto in 1913, then entered the Canadian public service. His autobiography, *What's Past is Prologue*, appeared in 1963. Massey died on December 30, 1967, at his home near Port Hope, Ontario.

GENERAL GEORGES-PHILIAS VANIER (1959-67)

A handicapped veteran with a distinguished war record, General Georges Vanier displayed remarkable energy in the role of governor general. He traveled widely, kept in touch with the life of the nation at many points and, in 1964, called a national conference that resulted in the creation of the Vanier Institute of the Family.

Born in Montréal on April 23, 1888, Georges Vanier graduated from Laval University as a lawyer. His destiny was changed by World War I, during which he lost his right leg. From 1925 to 1928 he commanded Quebec's famous Royal 22nd Regiment, and then became Canada's representative on the Permanent Advisory Commission of the League of Nations for Military, Naval and Air Questions. From 1931 to 1938 Vanier was secretary at the Office of the Canadian High Commissioner for Canada in London. In 1939 he became Canadian minister to France, returning home after the fall of France in 1940 to command the Quebec Military District. In 1943 he was named Canadian minister to the Allied governments-in-exile in London, and Canadian representative to the French Committee of National Liberation the same year. In 1944 he was named ambassador to France, serving in that post for nine years. One of the most widely admired men ever to serve as governor general, he died at Rideau Hall on March 5, 1967.

ROLAND MICHENER (1967-74)

Roland Michener began his term as governor general by introducing the Order of Canada, the first exclusively Canadian system of honors for exemplary merit and achievement. He became the Order's first chancellor and principal companion.

Born in Lacombe, Alberta, on April 19, 1900, Michener was educated at the University of Alberta. He served in the Royal Air Force in 1918. In 1920 he went to Oxford as a Rhodes scholar, and began practicing law in Toronto four years later. In 1945 Michener was elected to the Ontario Legislature, where he held a provincial cabinet position (1946-48). From 1953 to 1962 he was an MP and served as the speaker of the House of Commons (1957-62). In 1964, he was appointed Canada's high commissioner to India.

The first governor general to pay state visits to other countries, he was well suited to this task by his wide background in law, politics and diplomacy. His personal interests were sports and physical fitness. Michener retired from his post in 1974 and settled in Toronto. He died in 1991.

ENGLISH AND FRENCH MONARCHS OF CANADA

FRENCH

François I	1515-1547
Henry II	1547-1559
François II	1559-1560
Charles IX	1560-1574
Henry III	1574-1589
Henry IV	1589-1610
Louis XIII	1610-1643
Louis XIV	1643-1715
Louis XV	1715-1774

ENGLISH

Henry VII	1485-1509
Henry VIII	1509-1547
Edward VI	1547-1553
Mary I	1553-1558
Elizabeth I	1558-1603
James I	1603-1625
Charles I	1625-1649
Charles II	1660-1685
James II	1685-1688
William III	1689-1702
Mary II	1689-1694
Anne	1702-1714
George I	1714-1727
George II	1727-1760
George III	1760-1820
George IV	1820-1830
William IV	1830-1837
Victoria	1837-1901
Edward VII	1901-1910
George V	1910-1936
Edward VIII	1936-1936
George VI	1936-1952
Elizabeth II	1952-

INTENDANTS OF NEW FRANCE

Jean Talon	1665-1668, 1670-1672
Claude de Bouteroue	1668-1670
Jacques Duchesneau	1675-1682
Jacques de Meulles	1682-1686
Jean Bochart de Champigny	1686-1702
François de Beauharnois	1702-1705
Jacques Raudot	1705-1711
Antoine Denis Raudot	1705-1710
Michel Bégon	1710-1726
Claude Thomas Dupuy	1726-1728
Gilles Hocquart	1731-1748
François Bigot	1748-1760

GOVERNORS OF ACADIA

By the 1713 Treaty of Utrecht, France ceded mainland Acadia to England. It became the British colony of Nova Scotia. Civil government was established in 1749, and there were seven governors from that date until 1786, when Nova Scotia came under the jurisdiction of the governor at Québec.

Edward Cornwallis	1749-1752
Peregrine Thomas Hopson	1752-1753
Charles Lawrence	1756-1760
Montague Wilmot	1764-1766
William Campbell	1766-1773
Francis Legge	1773-1776
John Parr	1782-1786

EARLY GOVERNORS

FRENCH

Samuel de Champlain	1612-1629, 1633-1635
(New France under British occupation)	1629-1632
Charles Huault de Montmagny	1636-1648
Louis d'Ailleboust de Coulonge	1648-1651
Jean de Lauzon	1651-1656
Pierre de Voyer, vicomte d'Argenson	1658-1661
Pierre Dubois, baron d'Avaugour	1661-1663
Augustin Saffray, chevalier de Mézy	1663-1665
Daniel de Rémy de Courcelle	1665-1672
Louis de Buade, comte de Frontenac	1672-1682, 1689-1698
Joseph-Antoine Lefebvre de La Barre	1682-1685
Jacques-René de Brisay, marquis de Denonville	1685-1689
Louis-Hector, chevalier de Callière	1699-1703
Philippe de Rigaud, marquis de Vaudreuil	1703-1725
Charles, marquis de Beauharnois	1726-1747
Jacques-Pierre Taffanel, marquis de La Jonquière	1749-1752
Ange, marquis Duquesne de Menneville	1752-1755
Pierre de Rigaud, marquis de Vaudreuil-Cavagnal	1755-1760

BRITISH

James Murray	1764-1766
Sir Guy Carleton	1768-1770, 1774-1778
Frederick Haldimand	1778-1784
Sir Guy Carleton, Lord Dorchester	1786-1791 1793-1796
Robert Prescott	1797-1799
Sir James Henry Craig	1807-1811
Sir George Prevost	1812-1815
Sir John Coape Sherbrooke	1816-1818
Duke of Richmond	1818-1819
Lord Dalhousie	1820-1828
Lord Aylmer	1831-1835
Lord Gosford	1835-1838
Lord Durham	1838-1838
Sir John Colborne	1838-1839
Charles Poulett Thomson (Lord Sydenham)	1839-1841
Sir Charles Bagot	1842-1843
Sir Charles Metcalfe	1843-1845
Lord Cathcart	1846-1847
Lord Elgin	1847-1854
Sir Edmund Head	1854-1861
Lord Monck	1861-1867

JULES LÉGER (1974-79)

A few months into his term as governor general, Jules Léger suffered a stroke that impaired his ability to speak and partially paralyzed his left arm. He offered to resign but was asked by the federal government to remain. After his convalescence, he traveled across the country, meeting people on the job, presenting citizenship certificates personally to new Canadians, and issuing written messages to the press. His main concern was preserving Canadian unity, and he showed great interest in contemporary trends.

Born in St. Anicet, Québec, on April 4, 1913, Léger studied law at the University of Montréal and won a doctorate from the Sorbonne. He was assistant editor of *Le Droit* in Ottawa for a year before joining the Department of External Affairs. From 1943 to 1947 he served with the Canadian legation in Chile, and in 1948 acted as adviser to the Canadian delegation to the United Nations General Assembly. In 1950, he was made assistant under secretary of state for External Affairs. Three years later he was appointed ambassador to Mexico. Promoted to under secretary of state for External Affairs in 1954, he was in that post for four years. Later he was ambassador to Italy, France, Belgium and Luxembourg. Admired for his courageous battle against his illness, Léger stepped down as governor general in 1979 and died in 1982.

EDWARD SCHREYER (1979-1984)

Edward Richard Schreyer was born in Beausejour, Manitoba, on December 21, 1935. He studied at the University of Manitoba, and at one point considered professional baseball as a career. Instead, he graduated with a master's degree in political science and economics, and taught at St. Paul's College in Winnipeg. In 1960, he married Lily Schulz.

Schreyer became the youngest member of the Manitoba Legislature when first elected in 1958. Seven years later, he won the seat for Springfield in the House of Commons. Schreyer did not like Ottawa, however: he returned home to become leader of the New Democratic Party in Manitoba and then premier of the province from 1969 to 1977. His government amended the Public Schools Act to permit full-time instruction in either English or French, and he championed Ottawa's efforts to promote bilingualism.

In January 1979, Schreyer became the first governor general from the West. His tenure of Rideau Hall was marked by a friendly and informal atmosphere, his four young children enlivening the official residence. After stepping down as governor general, Schreyer served as Canadian high commissioner in Australia (1984-88). Since his return to Canada, Schreyer has held teaching posts at the University of Winnipeg, the Simon Fraser Institute, and the University of Victoria.

JEANNE SAUVÉ (1984-1990)

Jeanne-Mathilde Sauvé, née Benoit, was born in Prud'Homme, Saskatchewan, on April 26, 1922. She grew up and was educated in Ottawa and Paris. In 1948, she married Maurice Sauvé and went with him to Paris.

In 1952, Jeanne Sauvé began a career as a journalist. She was elected Liberal MP for the Montreal riding of Ahuntsic (1972-79) and the Quebec riding of Laval-des-Rapides (1979-84). Under Prime Minister Pierre Trudeau, she became the first female French-Canadian cabinet minister. She served as Minister of State for Science and Technology (1972-74), Minister of the Environment (1974-75), and Minister of Communications (1975-79). As the first female speaker of the Commons (1980-84), she reformed the internal administration of Parliament. In June 1984, she became first female governor general of Canada. During her tenure, Sauvé adopted a more formal approach than the style of her predecessor. Jeanne Sauvé died in 1993.

RAY HNATYSHYN (1990-1995)

Ramon John (Ray) Hnatyshyn was born in Saskatoon, Saskatchewan, on March 16, 1934. Trained as a lawyer, he entered federal politics as a Conservative MP in 1974. Under Joe Clark, he was Minister of Energy, Mines and Resources (1979-80). In 1984, he became Opposition House Leader. He also served the Mulroney administration as Government House Leader, Minister of Justice, and attorney general.

ROMÉO LEBLANC (1995-)

The first governor general from Atlantic Canada, Roméo LeBlanc was born in Memramcook, New Brunswick, on December 18, 1927. He worked as a professor and broadcast journalist before becoming press secretary to prime ministers Pearson and Trudeau. He served as a Liberal MP from 1972 to 1984. Under Trudeau his cabinet posts included fisheries and public works. He was appointed to the Senate in 1984 and was Speaker when named governor general. LeBlanc is the first francophone from outside Québec to hold this office.

THE PRIME MINISTERS OF CANADA

SIR JOHN A. MACDONALD

Born in Glasgow, Scotland, on January 11, 1815, John Alexander Macdonald arrived in Canada five years later. The son of a cotton broker, he was articled to a young Kingston lawyer at the age of 15 and called to the bar in 1836. He made a name for himself by acting for the defense in unpopular cases, and, because of his wit and graciousness, acquired a reputation as a dandy as well. He married his cousin, Isabella Clark, in 1843. The following year, he was elected Tory representative for Kingston to the Legislative Assembly, a seat he would hold almost continuously until his death in 1891. He became receiver general in the Draper administration in 1847 and later attorney general for Upper Canada. He played a leading role in the formation of the Great Coalition of 1864, which led to Confederation three years later. He was the chief architect of the union of Canada and became Canada's first Prime Minister.

During Macdonald's first administration (1867-73), Manitoba, British Columbia, and Prince Edward Island joined Canada. The Intercolonial Railway linking Halifax and Québec was built by 1871. Plans were drawn up for the CPR, which was completed during his second administration.

Macdonald lost the 1873 elections over the Pacific Scandal, but was returned to power five years later. In 1879, he introduced a system of protective tariffs known as the National Policy. Macdonald remained leader until his death. An adroit political opportunist, he was master of the art of managing people and considered ethical niceties subordinate to political necessity. He died on June 6, 1891.

ALEXANDER MACKENZIE

Alexander Mackenzie was born on January 28, 1822, near Dunkeld, Scotland, and came to Canada at the age of 20. A builder and contractor by trade, he married Helen Neil in 1845. From 1852 to 1854, he was the editor of the *Lambton Shield*, a crusading reform newspaper that failed after a Tory minister sued for libel.

Mackenzie entered politics to support his brother's ambitions, but was himself elected to the Legislative Assembly in 1861. A good organizer and a strong debater, he won a seat in the House of Commons six years later. He reluctantly became leader of the Liberal Party in 1872. Sir John A. Macdonald's defeat the following year made him Prime Minister.

In 1874 he introduced a bill that led to the creation of the North West Mounted Police. He served as public works minister while in office, and applied himself, to the point of illness, to the building of the CPR. Mackenzie's administration saw the creation of the Supreme Court of Canada and the Auditor General.

A cautious, strict man of stubborn honesty, he lacked Macdonald's bold imagination and breadth of vision. He was defeated in the 1878 election, but remained party leader for another three years, despite the Liberals' protests. After stepping down, Mackenzie stayed on as a member of Parliament until his death on April 17, 1892, in Toronto.

SIR JOHN J.C. ABBOTT

The son of an English missionary, John Abbott was born on March 12, 1821, at St. Andrews, Lower Canada (later Québec). He enrolled as a student in McGill's law faculty at the age of 22, and became its dean in 1855. Elected as the Conservative member for Argenteuil (Québec), Abbott sat in the House of Commons for 14 years. In 1862, he served briefly as solicitor general. In 1887 he was named to the Senate; that same year he was also elected mayor of Montreal.

Abbott was closely involved with the construction of the Canadian Pacific Railway and played a key role in the Pacific Scandal. A reluctant Prime Minister, he was pressed into service as a "caretaker" when Macdonald died in 1891. However, Abbott resigned the following year due to failing health. Canada's first native-born prime minister died in Montreal on October 30, 1893.

SIR JOHN S.D. THOMPSON

John David Sparrow Thompson was born on November 10, 1844, in Halifax, Nova Scotia. He left school at 15 to article as a student-at-law and was called to the Bar in 1865. Early in his career, he worked as a reporter for The Nova Scotia House of Assembly. In 1870 he married Annie Affleck, with whom he had five children. A dedicated public servant, he served as chairman of the Board of School Commissioners in Halifax before being elected to the House of Assembly as the Conservative member for Antigonish in 1877. The following year he was made attorney general of Nova Scotia, and in 1882 he became premier. In the election later that year, however, the Conservatives were defeated, and while he retained his seat, he resigned soon after to become judge in the Nova Scotia Supreme Court.

Macdonald persuaded Thompson to become Canada's Minister of Justice in 1885. Two years later, he played a major role in negotiating Atlantic fishing rights with the United States. He became Prime Minister following Abbott's resignation and was responsible for bringing a great deal of new legislation before Parliament.

A politician of great ability and high character, Thompson won the respect of his fellow legislators and countrymen. His premature death occurred in December 1894. He had been at Windsor Castle in England, just after having been sworn in as member of the Privy Council, when he suddenly collapsed. All mourned the lucid, puckish, faithful John Thompson.

SIR MACKENZIE BOWELL

Born in Suffolk, England, on December 27, 1823, Mackenzie Bowell came to Canada with his father in 1833. Soon after, he was apprenticed to the publisher of the *Belleville Intelligencer*, a job he kept until the age of 18, when he left to attend school in Upper Canada. Six months later, he returned to the position of foreman at the paper. In 1847, he married Harriet Louise Moore, and, around the same time, bought the *Intelligencer*. He founded the Belleville Rifle Company, and became a member of the Orange Order, a fraternal group hostile to French Canadians and Roman Catholics, and eventually became its grand master.

Bowell ran as the Conservative candidate for Belleville in 1863 and lost, but four years later won a federal seat for Hastings North and sat in Parliament until 1892. He was appointed to the Cabinet as Minister of Customs in 1878, where he implemented the National Policy. He served as Minister of Militia under Sir John Abbott and as Canada's first Minister of Trade in the Thompson administration. In 1892 he was appointed to the Senate, and two years later became Prime Minister following Thompson's sudden death. His Cabinet forced his resignation over the Manitoba schools crisis, but he remained in the Senate from 1896.

Noted for his penchant for arguing and capacities as critic, Bowell was nevertheless considered a mediocre administrator. He died in Belleville, Ontario, on December 10, 1917.

SIR CHARLES TUPPER

The eldest son of a Baptist minister, Charles Tupper was born in Amherst, Nova Scotia, on July 2, 1821. He studied medicine at Edinburgh University, graduated at the age of 22, and practiced in rural Nova Scotia. In 1846 he married Frances Amelia Morse. He was elected to Nova Scotia's House of Assembly in 1855 as the Tory member for Cumberland County. Two years later, Tupper was appointed provincial secretary. He became Premier of Nova Scotia in 1864, and helped to plan the Charlottetown Conference that led to Confederation.

Tupper lost the provincial election of 1867, and rather than press a claim for high office in the newly formed Macdonald's government, sat as a private member in the House of Commons. In 1870 he entered the Cabinet, then became president of its Privy Council. He was Minister of Inland Revenue in 1872 and Minister of Customs the following year. In 1878, he was appointed Minister of Public Works and was responsible for building the transcontinental railway. As Minister of Finance in 1887, he helped negotiate the Canada–U.S. fishing treaty, for which he was rewarded with a baronetcy the next year. He served as Canada's high commissioner in London from 1883 until 1896, when he became secretary of state.

Tupper took over as Prime Minister in 1896, but lost the federal election three months later. He remained leader of the Conservatives until after the elections of 1900, where the party again faced defeat. He died at Bexley Heath, England, on October 30, 1915.

SIR WILFRID LAURIER

Wilfrid Laurier, the son of a land surveyor, was born in St. Lin, Québec, on Nov. 20, 1841. He graduated from McGill with a law degree in 1864, and practiced in Montréal for two years before moving to Arthabaska because of his health. While there, he also edited Le Défricheur, which folded in 1867. The following year he married Zoë Lafontaine. He was elected to the Quebec legislature in 1871, but resigned three years later to represent Drummond-Arthabaska as a Liberal Member of Parliament. In 1877 he was appointed Minister of Inland Revenue, and that same year made a speech that has since become a classic statement of Canadian liberalism. The Liberals made him party leader in 1887.

A brilliant orator, handsome, stately, and charming, Laurier won wide acclaim. When he was elected Prime Minister of Canada in 1896, he assembled a distinguished cabinet. The country entered into the "Sunshine Years": the economy flourished, and thanks to an aggressive immigration policy, the population soared.

Laurier furthered the cause of Canadian autonomy from Great Britain. British troops were withdrawn from Canadian soil and the militia came under Canadian command; the Navy was founded and Canada won the right to negotiate its own trade treaties. In 1909 the Department of External Affairs was established.

Laurier was reelected in 1900, 1904 and 1908, but was defeated over the issue of trade reciprocity with the United States in 1911. He supported Canada's war commitment in 1914, but would not enter into a coalition with Sir Robert Borden over the conscription issue in 1916. In the elections of the following year, he won Québec but lost the rest of the country. Laurier remained in the House of Commons as leader of the Opposition until his death on February 17, 1919.

SIR ROBERT BORDEN

Born June 26, 1854, at Grand Pré, Nova Scotia, Robert Laird Borden was teaching classics and mathematics at a local school at the age of 14. In 1874, he entered law school in Halifax and was called to the bar four years later. He married Laura Bond in 1879. By 1882, he was a junior partner in the largest legal practice in the Maritimes. He entered politics out of a sense of public duty, winning the seat for Halifax in the House of Commons in 1896, and became Conservative leader in 1901. As Prime Minister from 1911 through the war years, he insisted that Canada have a voice in the conduct of the war.

In 1917 Borden formed a coalition without Laurier and won the federal election over the conscription issue. At the Paris Peace Conference following World War I, he won the right of separate representation for Canada.

Borden resigned from government in 1920 because of poor health. He had been chancellor of McGill University from 1918 to 1920, and from 1924 to 1930 he served in the same capacity at Queen's University in Kingston, Ontario. He died on June 10, 1937, in Ottawa.

ARTHUR MEIGHEN

Born June 16, 1874, near Anderson, Ontario, Arthur Meighen studied mathematics at the University of Toronto, where he graduated with First Class Honours in 1896. He then taught school for a year, but quit over disagreements with the trustees. After investing in a small business that later failed, he moved to Manitoba, where he again taught for a time. He then studied law, was called to the bar in 1903, and steadily became a successful and prosperous lawyer. The following year he married Isabel Cox.

He was elected to the House of Commons in 1908 as the Conservative representative for Portage la Prairie and was appointed solicitor general five years later. He entered the Privy Council, became secretary of state, and in 1917, Minister of the Interior. Despite opposition from the Cabinet, Borden appointed Meighen his successor in July 1920. The new Prime Minister became leader of the Opposition less than eighteen months later, when the Conservatives lost the 1921 election.

Meighen was restored briefly to power when the governor general, Lord Byng, asked him to form a government in 1926. But this administration became involved in a crisis over parliamentary procedure. The Conservative Party called an election, which it lost only three months later.

Meighen returned to a career in investment banking in 1926. He made a brief reappearance in federal politics, but lost a by-election in 1942. He returned to Toronto, where he died on August 5, 1960.

WILLIAM LYON MACKENZIE KING

The grandson of the 1837 reform leader William Lyon Mackenzie, King was born December 17, 1874, in Kitchener, Ontario. A graduate of the University of Toronto, he studied sociology at Harvard and worked for a year in Chicago. He was appointed deputy minister of Laurier's newly created Labour Department in 1900, and was elected the Member of Parliament for Waterloo eight years later. From 1909—the same year that he was awarded his Ph.D.—to 1911, he was Minister of Labour. He succeeded Laurier as Liberal leader in 1919 and became Prime Minister with a minority government two years later. The Liberals barely made it to power in 1925, and resigned one year later only to return in three months by means of a forced election. Except for the 1930 election, which King lost by misjudging the severity of the Depression, he was to remain Prime Minister for a total of 22 years, returning in 1935 and serving until 1948. During that long period, he played a role in the Allied war effort and prevented a breach between English and French Canadians over conscription.

In 1948, he passed the party leadership on to Louis St. Laurent. King, a lifelong bachelor who believed in the supernatural and visited mediums, died at Kingsmere, Québec, in July 1950.

RICHARD BEDFORD BENNETT

Richard Bennett was born on July 3, 1870, in Hopewell, New Brunswick. The son of a shipbuilder, Bennett became a schoolteacher, then principal, before he was 20, then studied law at Dalhousie University in Halifax. He began his practice in Chatham, New Brunswick, and was elected to its town council in 1896. The following year he moved to Calgary, where he became a successful corporation lawyer. He was elected to the Northwest Territories Legislature in 1898, and in 1909 won a seat in the Alberta Legislature. He resigned two years later to sit in the Commons as the Conservative representative for Calgary East. He served briefly as Minister of Justice and attorney general in 1921, and in 1926, as Minister of Finance. He was chosen party leader in 1927 and, after the onset of the Depression, won the federal election by a landslide in July 1930.

Until 1934, the Bennett government adopted a laissez-faire approach to the Great Depression. Early in 1935, Bennett changed direction, proposing legislation on minimum wages, maximum hours, pensions, price controls and unemployment and health insurance. The Bennett administration saw the creation of the Canadian Wheat Board, the Bank of Canada, and the forerunners of both the Canadian Broadcasting Corporation and Air Canada.

Bennett lost the 1935 election but remained the leader of the Opposition until 1938, when he retired in Surrey, England. He was later appointed to the British House of Lords as Viscount Bennett. He died in England on June 26, 1947.

PARTY REPRESENTATION BY REGIONS 1957–1993

Region	1957	1958	1962	1963	1965	1968	1972	1974	1979	1980	1984	1988	1993
CANADA													
Liberal	105	40	100	129	131	155	109	141	114	147	40	83	176
Conservative	112	208	116	95	97	72	107	95	136	103	211	169	2
New Democratic	25	8	19	17	21	22	31	16	26	32	30	43	9
Social Credit	19	—	30	24	14	14	15	11	6	0	—	—	—
Bloc Québécois	—	—	—	—	—	—	—	—	—	—	—	—	54
Reform	—	—	—	—	—	—	—	—	—	—	—	—	53
Other	4	—	—	—	2	1	2	1	0	0	1	—	1
ONTARIO													
Liberal	21	15	44	52	51	64	36	55	32	52	14	43	98
Conservative	61	67	35	27	25	17	40	25	57	38	67	46	0
New Democratic	3	3	6	6	9	6	11	8	6	5	13	10	0
Reform	—	—	—	—	—	—	—	—	—	—	—	—	1
QUEBEC													
Liberal	62	25	35	47	56	56	56	60	67	74	17	12	19
Conservative	9	50	14	8	8	4	2	3	2	1	58	63	1
Social Credit	—	—	26	20	9	14	15	11	6	0	—	—	0
Bloc Québécois	—	—	—	—	—	—	—	—	—	—	—	—	54
Other	—	—	—	—	—	—	—	—	—	—	—	—	1
ATLANTIC													
Liberal	12	8	14	20	15	7	10	13	12	19	12	20	31
Conservative	21	25	18	13	16	25	22	17	17	13	25	7	1
New Democratic	—	—	1	—	—	—	—	1	2	0	—	—	0
WESTERN													
Liberal	10	1	7	10	9	27	7	13	3	2	2	8	26
Conservative	21	66	49	47	46	25	42	49	60	49	61	48	0
New Democratic	22	5	12	11	12	16	19	6	18	26	17	33	8
Social Credit	19	—	4	4	5	—	—	—	—	0	—	—	—
Reform	—	—	—	—	—	—	—	—	—	—	—	—	52

LOUIS ST. LAURENT

Louis St. Laurent was born in Compton, Québec, on February 1, 1882. He received a classical education at St. Charles-Borromée Seminary, and then studied law at Laval University. After refusing a Rhodes scholarship, he began his career in 1905, the year he married Jeanne Renault. He had a flourishing law practice and lectured at Laval. He became head of the Quebec Bar in 1929 and president of the Canadian Bar Association the following year.

In 1941, he was asked to join King's cabinet, where he served as Justice Minister and attorney general. Toward the end of the war, he acted as Prime Minister whenever King left the country, and was appointed chairman of the Canadian delegation to the founding conference of the United Nations. After the war, he became secretary of state for External Affairs and was one of the original advocates of the North Atlantic Pact.

He was chosen as King's successor in 1948; soon after, he was elected Prime Minister. He brought Newfoundland into Confederation in 1949, saw the St. Lawrence Seaway built and the Trans-Canada highway begun, and established the Canada Council. He helped to make the Supreme Court the final court of appeal and to establish Canada as a respected international power. St. Laurent lost the 1957 elections, retired the same year, and died in Québec on July 25, 1973.

JOHN GEORGE DIEFENBAKER

Born in Grey County, Ontario, on September 18, 1895, John Diefenbaker moved with his family to rural Saskatchewan in 1903. He studied at the University of Saskatchewan, where he distinguished himself as both an orator and a practical joker, and went off to war in 1916. Later he became a lawyer, creating a reputation for himself as a brilliant criminal defense counsel. He ran for Parliament in 1925 and again the following year, losing both times. In 1929 he married Edna Bower. After successive attempts to win office, he finally became Member of Parliament in 1940, then Conservative leader 16 years later. Two years after his wife's death in 1951, he married Olive Palmer.

In 1957, Diefenbaker was elected Prime Minister of Canada. He introduced the Bill of Rights in 1960 and set up federal agencies to help both the western and Atlantic provinces. He also moved to expel South Africa from the Commonwealth. He initiated grain sales to mainland China and maintained trade and diplomatic links with Cuba after the 1961 Missile Crisis.

Despite having united the West into a coherent political force, he was defeated in 1963 due to his inability to build support in Québec, as well as by his uncertainty over defense issues.

Diefenbaker then became leader of the Opposition until he lost the party leadership in 1967. "The Chief" continued as a vigorous and outspoken Member of Parliament until his death in August 1979.

LESTER BOWLES PEARSON

Son of a Methodist minister, "Mike" Pearson was born in Toronto on April 23, 1897. He began studying at the University of Toronto, but enlisted in 1915. He was awarded a degree in history in 1919, then attended Oxford, where he distinguished himself as an athlete. He returned to teach history at the University of Toronto in 1923 and married Maryon Elspeth Moody two years later.

At the age of 32, he joined Canada's infant foreign service. He was appointed first secretary to the high commissioner in London in 1935, was posted to the Canadian embassy in Washington in 1941 and became ambassador to the United States four years later. He played an important role in establishing the United Nations.

In 1946 he returned to Canada as under secretary for External Affairs; two years later he was appointed Minister for External Affairs. He served as both president of the United Nations General Assembly and chairman of the NATO council in 1952. He won the Nobel Prize for Peace in 1957.

The Liberal leader from 1958, Pearson won both 1963 and 1965 elections with a minority government. His administration introduced Medicare and the Canada Pension Plan, and legislated today's Canadian flag during the Centennial. Pearson resigned in 1968 and died in Ottawa on December 27, 1972.

PIERRE ELLIOTT TRUDEAU

Born into a wealthy Montréal family on October 18, 1919, Pierre Elliott Trudeau attended Jean de Brébeuf College and studied law at the University of Montréal. After being called to the bar, he studied political economy at Harvard, Paris and London, and traveled widely. He entered Parliament as the Liberal member for Mount Royal in 1965. Two years later he was Justice Minister and attorney general. He succeeded Lester Pearson as Liberal Party leader in 1968, winning a decisive victory in the federal election that year.

In 1970, the October Crisis erupted in Québec, and Trudeau invoked the emergency War Measures Act to maintain order. The elections in 1972 resulted in a minority government for the Liberals, and revealed regional hostilities growing out of cultural and economic differences. In 1974, Trudeau regained a strong majority. The Liberals lost in the 1979 contest, but returned to power early in 1980. In May 1980, Trudeau led the federalist forces to victory in Quebec's referendum on sovereignty-association.

During the 1970s the Trudeau administration had been responsible for the Official Languages Act, early recognition of Communist China, temporary wage and price controls, and extension of offshore fishing limit to 200 miles (370 kilometres).

The second Trudeau administration saw major constitutional reform. In 1982, Trudeau won a two-year effort to give Canada its own constitution, which incorporated a charter of rights and freedoms. The 1982 Constitution Act permitted Canada to amend its own constitution without appeal to the British government. But Trudeau's triumph was marred by Québec's unwillingness to sign the constitution. His National Energy Policy led to a dispute with the West, notably Alberta.

In 1984 Trudeau embarked on a worldwide peace initiative, traveling to more than 40 countries to call for an end to the nuclear arms race. In June 1984, he retired from politics, eventually joining a Montreal law firm. He kept a low profile but went public to voice his opposition to the Meech Lake and Charlottetown accords.

JOE CLARK

Charles Joseph Clark was born in High River, Alberta, on June 5, 1939. He attended the University of Alberta and Dalhousie, and was national president of the Progressive Conservative Student Federation from 1963 to 1965. In 1967, Clark served as advisor to Davie Fulton and executive assistant to Robert Stanfield for the following three years. First elected to the House of Commons in 1972, he succeeded Stanfield as Conservative party leader four years later.

Clark served as Prime Minister of Canada for only six months following the Conservative victory in the federal elections of June 1979. His minority government fell, over its first budget, and he was defeated at the federal election of February 1980. He subsequently became the leader of the Opposition.

In 1983, Clark lost the Conservative leadership to Brian Mulroney. When Mulroney became Prime Minister in September 1984, Clark joined the Cabinet as Minister of External Affairs. In 1991, Clark became the minister responsible for constitutional affairs, with the task of finding a formula for amending the Constitution Act of 1982. The following year, after intense negotiations, Clark and the provincial premiers agreed on the Charlottetown Accord. This constitutional agreement was rejected by the majority of voters in an October 1992 referendum. Clark retired from politics in the fall of 1993.

JOHN TURNER

John Napier Turner was born in Richmond, Surrey, England, on June 7, 1929. After his father died when he was two years old, he returned with his Canadian-born mother to Canada in 1932. He attended Ottawa private schools and graduated from the University of British Columbia in 1949. He went to Oxford University as a Rhodes scholar and also attended the University of Paris. He was called to the Québec bar in 1954 and practiced law in Montréal.

Turner was first elected to the Commons in 1962. He became Minister of Consumer and Corporate Affairs in Pearson's Cabinet in 1967. Under Trudeau, Turner served as Minister of Justice and Finance Minister. After a disagreement with Trudeau over wage and price controls, Turner left the government in 1975 and joined a Toronto law firm.

Turner won the Liberal leadership after Trudeau resigned in February 1984. In June, Turner became Prime Minister and called an election for the following September. After a disorganized campaign, the Liberals were dealt a crushing defeat by the Progressive Conservatives under Brian Mulroney. Turner, however, won his own seat in Vancouver Quadra. In 1988, the Liberals opposed the Conservatives' free-trade legislation and forced an election on the issue. The election ended with another Conservative victory. Turner remained the Liberal leader in 1989. In June 1990, he was succeeded by Jean Chrétien.

BRIAN MULRONEY

Martin Brian Mulroney was born in Baie Comeau, Québec, March 20, 1939. He received a B.A. from St. Francis Xavier University. He studied at Laval and joined a Montreal law firm in 1965, where he specialized in labor negotiations. He made an unsuccessful bid for the leadership of the Progressive Conservative Party in 1976. The following year, he joined the Iron Ore Company of Canada, and subsequently became its president.

At the 1983 Conservative leadership contest, Mulroney defeated Joe Clark, and won a federal seat in a Nova Scotia by-election. The following year, Mulroney led the Conservatives to a landslide victory, and captured the Québec seat of Manicouagan. Mulroney's initiatives during his first term

CANADA AT WAR—FROM BOER WAR TO THE KOREAN CONFLICT

Canada's first army, a small volunteer force, was established a decade before Confederation. Until then, British North America depended entirely on British garrisons comparable in strength to the regular U.S. Army. In 1870, Britain began to withdraw its forces, leaving only the naval bases and a few soldiers at Halifax and Esquimalt, B.C., until the formation of the Royal Canadian Navy in 1910. In 1871, two batteries of Canadian artillery were formed, and in 1883, cavalry and infantry units were raised.

Between 1899 and 1902, 7300 Canadians fought in the Boer War at the battles of Paardeberg, Wolve Spruit and Leliefontein. There were 476 Canadian casualties, including 224 dead.

Together with Britain, Canada entered World War I on Aug. 4, 1914, and the first Canadian contingent, 30,808 strong, sailed for England on Oct. 3. By August 1916, four Canadian divisions were fighting in Europe, and in 1917 the army experienced its first major victory, at Vimy Ridge. In June of that year, the Canadian Corps was placed under its first Canadian commander, Lt.-Gen. Sir Arthur Currie. By August 1918, the Canadians, along with other Allied forces, were finally on the advance. When the Armistice came in November, they were in Mons, Belgium.

World War I claimed the largest number of Canadians of any war: 59,544 fatalities and 172,950 wounded from the Army; 225 dead from our small Navy; and 1600 killed from among those serving with the British Royal Flying Corps and the Royal Naval Air Service.

Canada entered World War II on Sept. 10, 1939. The Navy was in action on convoy routes from the beginning; the 1st Division went overseas before the end of 1939; and Air Force units were posted to Britain in 1940. The whole population was mobilized for a prodigious war effort, which included the manufacture of 16,000 aircraft, 1000 ships, 8000 small craft, 50,000 tanks and gun carriers and 800,000 army trucks.

The Royal Canadian Navy grew from 1585 men at the start of the war to 106,522 men and women during the war and, by the end of the war, had a fleet of 404 warships and 566 auxiliary vessels. The Navy's main role was the protection of Allied shipping in the North Atlantic, but it also saw action in European waters and the Pacific.

Canadian troops fought in the unsuccessful defense of Hong Kong against the Japanese in December 1941, and led the raid on the French coast at Dieppe in August 1942. The next year, the 1st Division took part in the invasion of Sicily and fought its way up the Italian mainland with the British 8th Army. By the end of 1943, there was a Canadian Corps in Italy. The 3rd Division stormed ashore at Normandy in June 1944, and soon the 1st Canadian Army, commanded by Lt.-Gen. H.D.G. Crerar, became operational on the Western front. Canadian soldiers fought their way along the coast of the English Channel during the Allied offensives of 1944 and 1945, and were largely responsible for the liberation of the Netherlands in 1945.

Canada's air force became the fourth largest among the Allied Powers during World War II. Canadian airmen fought in the Battle of Britain, patrolled the north Atlantic and joined in the massive bomber assault on Germany from 1942 to 1945. The largest Canadian formation overseas was the No. 6 R.C.A.F. Group, attached to the R.A.F. Bomber Command.

Canadian forces also fought in the Korean War, 1950-53. A destroyer flotilla, dispatched to Korean waters in July 1950, remained on duty there throughout the war. One R.C.A.F. transport squadron assisted in the trans-Pacific airlift of supplies, and a small number of combat pilots saw duty with the United Nations. On the ground, a Canadian brigade was in action under UN command.

were the Meech Lake Accord—designed to rectify Québec's refusal to sign the 1982 constitutional reform—and a free-trade agreement with the United States.

At the 1988 federal election, in which free trade was the main issue of public debate, Mulroney won another majority. The free-trade legislation came into effect in January 1, 1989. The Meech Lake Accord, however, died in June 1990 when the provincial legislatures of Manitoba and Newfoundland failed to ratify it. Mulroney's popularity began to fall after the failure of Meech Lake, and hit an unprecedented low with the implementation of the Goods and Services Tax in 1991.

The following year, Mulroney attempted to find a new constitutional agreement to replace the Meech Lake Accord. In August 1992, the federal government and the provinces agreed on the Charlottetown Accord. At a referendum, held two months later, voters rejected the accord. In February 1993, Mulroney announced his retirement from office. He was succeeded by the newly elected leader of the Conservative Party, Kim Campbell.

KIM CAMPBELL

Avril Phaedra (Kim) Campbell was born on March 10, 1947, at Port Alberni, British Columbia. After earning a political science degree from the University of British Columbia in 1969, she attended the London School of Economics (1970-73). In 1983, she received a law degree from the University of British Columbia.

In 1986, Campbell became a policy adviser for the Social Credit Party. The following year, she won a seat in the provincial legislature, but lost a bit to become Social Credit leader. In 1988, Campbell turned her energy to the federal sphere and the Progressive Conservative Party. She resigned her provincial seat and was elected to the House of Commons, representing Vancouver Centre.

During her years in the Mulroney administration, Campbell held the portfolios of Indian Affairs and Northern Development (1989), Justice (1990) and Defence (1993). As Justice Minister, she successfully dealt with issues such as gun control and sexual abuse. In 1993, after Mulroney announced his intention to retire, Campbell successfully ran for the Conservative leadership and became Prime Minister in June. Four months later, Campbell and the Conservatives went down to defeat. The party won only two seats in the Commons, and Campbell herself lost her seat. She resigned as the leader of the Conservative Party on December 13, 1993.

JEAN CHRÉTIEN

Joseph-Jacques Jean Chrétien was born at Shawinigan, Québec, on January 1, 1934. After studying law at Laval University, he was called to the Quebec bar in 1958. He was first elected to the House of Commons as a Liberal for the Québec riding of St. Maurice in 1963.

During Prime Minister Pearson's administration, Jean Chrétien was appointed parliamentary secretary to the Minister of Finance and Minister without Portfolio. Under Prime Minister Trudeau, Chrétien's cabinet posts included: Indian Affairs and Northern Development (1968-74), Finance (1977-80), and Justice (1980-82).

Chrétien was the first French-Canadian Minister of Finance. As Minister of Indian Affairs and Northern Development, he created 10 national parks. As Minister of Justice, he played a key role in the preparation of the 1982 Constitution Act, which also included the Charter of Rights and Freedoms.

In 1984, Jean Chrétien ran second to John Turner in the leadership race for the Liberal Party. Although he retained his seat in the 1984 election, he resigned from the House of Commons and returned to his law practice in 1986. After becoming Liberal leader in 1990, he was reelected by the riding of Beausejour, New Brunswick, in a by-election on December 10 of that year. Chrétien led the Liberal Party to a sweeping victory in the federal election on October 25, 1993.

NOTABLE CANADIANS OF THE PAST

Milton Acorn (1923-1986): Poet, winner of the governor general's Award for his collection, *The Island Means Minago* (1975).

Emma Albani (1848-1930): Opera singer.

François Amyot (1904-1962): Six times Canadian canoeing champion, Olympic gold medalist (1936).

Brother André (1845-1937): Religious mystic; builder of a shrine to Saint Joseph on Mount Royal, Montréal.

Sir Frederick Banting (1891-1941): Physician and scientist, winner with Dr. J.J.R. Macleod of the 1923 Nobel Prize for the discovery of insulin.

Marius Barbeau (1882-1974): Ethnologist, folklorist, a collector of traditional texts and songs of French Canadians and native peoples.

Big Bear (d. 1888): Chief of the Plains Cree Indians during the Northwest Rebellion, 1885.

Julia Beckwith (1796-1867): Novelist, published the first novel in Canada, *St. Ursula's Convent* (1824).

Archibald Stansfeld Belaney (alias *Grey Owl*) (1888-1938): Wildlife conservationist and author of *Tales of an Empty Cabin* (1936) and other books.

W.A.C. Bennett (1900-1979): Social Credit Premier of British Columbia (1952-1972).

Roloff Beny (1924-1984): Photographer.

Charles Herbert Best (1899-1978): Biochemist, codiscoverer of insulin with Sir Frederick Banting and Dr. J.J.R. Macleod.

Norman Bethune (1890-1939): Surgeon, inventor, and organizer of the world's first mobile blood-transfusion service.

William Avery (Billy) Bishop (1894-1956): World War I air ace; Victoria Cross winner.

J. Armand Bombardier (1907-1964): Inventor of the snowmobile.

Jordi Bonet (1932-1979): Painter, muralist, and sculptor.

Paul-Emile Borduas (1905-1960): Painter and author.

Henri Bourassa (1868-1952): Politician, founder and editor of the Montréal newspaper, *Le Devoir* (1910).

Marguerite Bourgeoys (1620-1700): Founder of the Montréal Congregation of Notre-Dame.

Ignace Bourget (1799-1885): Roman Catholic Bishop of Montréal (1840-1876).

Joseph Brant (1742-1807): Mohawk chief and principal chief of the Six Nations Indians, whom he led on the British side during the Seven Years' War.

Jean de Brébeuf (1593-1649): Jesuit missionary and martyr.

Samuel Bronfman (1891-1971): Industrialist, president of Distiller's Corporation-Seagram's Ltd. (1928-1971).

Tommy Burns (1881-1955): Boxer, Canada's only world heavyweight champion (1906).

Morley Callaghan (1903-1990): Novelist, short-story writer, broadcaster, winner of the Governor General's Award for *The Loved and the Lost* (1951).

Franklin Carmichael (1890-1945): Artist, member of the Group of Seven.

Emily Carr (1871-1945): Painter, author of *Klee Wyck* (1941).

Noël Chabanel (1613-1649): Jesuit missionary and martyr.

Floyd Chalmers (1898-1993): Editor, publisher, patron of the arts.

Médard Chouart, sieur des Groseilliers (1618-1696): Fur trader and explorer.

Lionel Conacher (1900-1954): Canada's all-round athlete of the first half century.

Ralph Connor (pen name of Charles W. Gordon) (1860-1937): Clergyman, author of *Glengarry School Days* (1902).

Donald Creighton (1902-1979): Historian, author of *The Commercial Empire of the St. Lawrence* (1937).

Octave Crémazie (1827-1879): Poet, the "father of French-Canadian poetry."

Henry Crerar (1888-1965): General, commander in chief, 1st Canadian Army, World War II.

Sir Samuel Cunard (1787-1865): Halifax merchant and shipowner, founder of the Cunard Steamship Lines.

Sir Arthur Currie (1875-1933): General, commander of the Canadian Corps, World War I.

Louis Cyr (1863-1912): Weight lifter and legendary strongman.

John Dafoe (1866-1944): Editor in chief of the *Winnipeg Free Press* (1901-1944).

Antoine Daniel (1601-1648): Jesuit missionary and martyr.

Mazo De La Roche (1879-1961): Novelist, playwright, author of the 24 *Jalna* novels.

Etienne Desmarteau (1877-1905): Canada's first Olympic gold medalist (hammer throw, 1904).

Adam Dollard des Ormeaux (1635-1660): Pioneer leader massacred by Iroquois at the Long Sault, 1660.

Sir James Douglas (1803-1877): Governor of Vancouver Island (1851-1863) and British Columbia (1853-1864).

Gabriel Dumont (1838-1906): Military leader of the Northwest Rebellion of 1885.

Maurice Duplessis: (1890-1959): Union Nationale Premier of Québec (1936-1939; 1944-1959).

Timothy Eaton (1834-1907): Merchant, founder of T. Eaton and Company (1869).

Betty Farrally (1915-1989): Co-founder of the Royal Winnipeg Ballet.

John Fisher (1912-1981): Broadcaster and publicist.

Sir Sandford Fleming (1827-1915): Civil engineer, inventor of international standard time and designer of Canada's first stamp.

Terry Fox (1958-1981): "Marathon of Hope" runner.

Simon Fraser (1776-1862): Fur trader and explorer.

Barbara Frum (1937-1992): Radio and television journalist.

Northrop Frye (1912-1991): Literary critic, university professor, editor, author of *Fearful Symmetry* (1947) and *Anatomy of Criticism* (1957).

Hugh Garner (1913-1979): Writer, author of *Cabbagetown* (1950).

Charles Garnier (1606-1649): Jesuit missionary and martyr.

Abraham Gesner (1797-1864): Doctor, geologist, author, inventor of kerosene (1852).

George (Mooney) Gibson (1880-1967): Baseball star.

James Gladstone (1887-1971): Canada's first Indian senator.

Charlies Gorman (1897-1940): Speed skater, world champion (1926-1927).

Glen Gould (1932-1982): Pianist, writer, broadcast and recording artist.

René Goupil (1608-1642): Jesuit martyr.

Lorne Greene (1915-1987): Radio broadcaster, stage and television actor.

Lionel Groulx (1878-1967): Historian.

Sir Casimir Gzowski (1813-1898): Civil engineer, financier; builder of the Grand Trunk railway from Toronto to Sarnia.

T.C. Haliburton (1796-1865): Judge and author of humorous fiction under the pseudonym Sam Slick.

Edward (Ned) Hanlan (1855-1908): Six times world rowing champion.

Lawren Harris (1885-1970): Artist, member of the Group of Seven.

Louis Hébert (d. 1627): Canada's first farmer.

John Hirsch (1930-1989): Theatre director, headed the Stratford Festival (1981-1985).

C.D. Howe (1886-1960): World War II federal cabinet minister; contributed to establishing the Canadian Broadcasting Corporation.

Joseph Howe (1804-1873): Nova Scotia journalist and politician.

Bruce Hutchison (1901-1992): Author of *The Unknown Country* (1942) and *The Incredible Canadian* (1952).

Kenneth Irving (1901-1992): Industrialist, founder of the Irving family empire.

A.Y. Jackson (1882-1974): Artist, member of the Group of Seven.

Diamond Jenness (1886-1969): Anthropologist, author of *The Indians of Canada* (1932).

Isaac Jogues (1607-1646): Jesuit missionary and martyr.

Pauline Johnson (1862-1913): Métis poet, author of *Flint and Feather* (1912).

Frank (or Franz) Johnston (1888-1949): Artist, member of the Group of Seven.

Claude Jutra (1930-1986): Filmmaker, director of *Mon Oncle Antoine* (1971).

Paul Kane (1810-1871): Artist, best known for paintings of Indians and the West.

Cornelius Krieghoff (1815-1872): Artist.

Father Albert Lacombe (1827-1916): Roman Catholic missionary to the Canadian West.

Jean de La Lande (d. 1646): Jesuit missionary and martyr.

Margaret Laurence (1926-1987): Novelist, author of *The Stone Angel* (1964).

Calixa Lavallée (1842-1891): Composer of "O Canada."

François-Xavier Laval-Montmorency (1623-1708): First Roman Catholic bishop of Québec.

Pierre de La Vérendrye (1685-1749): Fur trader and explorer.

Stephen Leacock (1869-1944): Humorist, educator and author.

Roger Lemelin (1919-1992): Novelist and scriptwriter, author of *Les Plouffe* [*The Plouffe Family*, in English] (1948).

René Lévesque (1922-1987): Journalist, Parti Québécois Premier of Québec (1976-85).

Arthur Lismer (1885-1969): Artist, member of the Group of Seven.

Gweneth Lloyd (1901-1993): Ballet director, choreographer, co-founder of the Royal Winnipeg Ballet.

Arthur Lower (1889-1988): Historian, author of *Colony to Nation* (1946).

J.E.H. MacDonald (1873-1932): Artist, member of the Group of Seven.

Sir Alexander Mackenzie (1764-1820): Fur trader and explorer.

William Lyon Mackenzie (1795-1861): Politician, leader of Upper Canada's Rebellion of 1837.

Hugh MacLennan (1907-1990): Novelist, author of *Two Solitudes* (1945) and *The Watch that Ends the Night* (1959).

Agnes Macphail (1890-1954): First woman Member of Parliament (1921-1940).

Nellie McClung (1873-1951): Author, feminist and suffragette.

John McCrae (1872-1918): Physician and poet, author of *In Flanders Fields*.

J.A.D. McCurdy (1886-1961): Air pioneer; made the British Empire's first airplane flight, in the *Silver Dart* (1909).

James McGill (1744-1813): Montréal merchant and philanthropist.

James McGuigan (1894-1974): Archbishop and cardinal.

Norman McLaren (1914-1987): Director of animated films.

R.S. (Sam) McLaughlin (1871-1972): Manufacturer and philanthropist; first president of General Motors of Canada (1918-1945).

Marshall McLuhan (1911-1980): University professor, communications theorist, author of *The Gutenberg Galaxy* (1962) and *Understanding Media* (1964).

Raymond Massey (1896-1983): Actor of stage, film and TV.

Honoré Mercier (1875-1937): Lawyer and politician; Liberal Premier of Québec (1887-1891).

Lucy Maud Montgomery (1874-1942): Novelist, best-known for *Anne of Green Gables* (1908).

Susanna Moodie (1803-1885): Writer, author of *Roughing It in the Bush* (1852).

Emily Murphy (1868-1933): Author and the British Empire's first woman magistrate.

Leonard Warren Murray (1896-1972): Rear admiral, commander in chief, Canadian Northwest Atlantic, World War II.

James Naismith (1861-1939): Professor of physical education, inventor of basketball (1891).

Alden Nowlan (1933-1983): Poet, winner of the 1967 Governor General's Award for his collection, *Bread, Wine and Salt*.

Sir William Osler (1849-1919): Physician and author.

Louis-Joseph Papineau (1786-1871): Politician, the leader of the French-Canadian reformers, *les Patriotes*, during the rebellion of 1837.

Wilder Penfield (1891-1976): Neurosurgeon, founder of the Montreal Neurological Institute.

Mary Pickford (1893-1979): Star of silent films, known as "America's Sweetheart."

Poundmaker (1826-1886): Cree Indian chief; took part with Métis leader Louis Riel in the Northwest Rebellion (1885).

Pierre Radisson (1636-1710): Fur trader and explorer.

Kate Reid (1930-1993): Actress at the Stratford Festival, on Broadway, and on radio and television.

James Armstrong Richardson (1885-1939): Financier, pioneer in Canadian aviation development.

Louis Riel (1844-1885): Métis leader of the Red River and Northwest rebellions (1870, 1885).

Fanny (Bobbie) Rosenfeld (1903-1969): Sportswriter and athlete; voted Canada's best woman athlete of the half century.

Gabrielle Roy (1909-1983): Novelist, author of *Bonheur d'ocassion* [*The Tin Flute*, in English] (1945).

Adolphus Egerton Ryerson (1803-1882): Methodist minister and educator.

F. R. Scott (1899-1985): Poet, professor of law, winner of Governor General's Award for *Collected Poems* (1981).

Laura Secord (1775-1868): Heroine of the War of 1812 (1813).

Hans Selye (1907-1983): Medical researcher, known for his work on the effect of stress on individuals and groups.

Robert Service (1874-1958): Poet and novelist of the North, best known for *Songs of a Sourdough* (1907).

Ernest Thompson Seton (1860-1946): Artist, naturalist and author.

Gordon Sinclair (1900-1984): Journalist, radio and television personality.

Joey Smallwood (1900-1991): Journalist, politician, Premier of Newfoundland (1949-1972).

Sir Sam Steele (1849-1919): Mounted police, soldier.

Vilhjalmur Stefansson (1879-1962): Arctic explorer.

George Stephen, 1st Baron Mount Stephen (1829-1921): Banker, first president of the Canadian Pacific Railway.

Emily Stowe (1831-1903): Canada's first woman doctor and a leading suffragette.

Kateri Tekakwitha (1656-1680): Christian convert, first Indian to be named venerable by the Roman Catholic Church.

Yves Thériault (1915-1983): Novelist, author of *Agaguk* (1958).

David Thompson (1770-1857): Geographer and explorer; the first white man to descend the Columbia River.

Tom Thomson (1877-1917): Painter.

Harold Town (1924-1990): Artist, whose works include paintings, murals, drawings, sculpture, illustrated books.

Catharine Parr Traill (1802-1899): Author of *The Backwoods of Canada* (1836).

Joseph Burr Tyrrell (1858-1957): Geologist, explorer and historian.

Sir William Van Horne (1843-1915): President and chairman of the board of directors of the Canadian Pacific Railway.

Fred Varley (1881-1969): Artist, member of the Group of Seven.

Garfield W. Weston (1908-1978): Food merchant, manufacturer.

John Tuzo Wilson (1908-1993): Geophysicist, professor, best known for his contribution to the understanding of plate tectonics.

Adele Wiseman (1928-1992): Novelist, winner of the Governor General's Award for *The Sacrifice* (1956).

The Physical Environment

Natural areas of Canadian significance

1. **Northern Ellesmere Island:** The high plateau surrounding Lake Hazen is the site of mountains reaching 2590 m, the highest in the Arctic islands. Ellesmere Island National Park Reserve, established in 1992, covers a 39,500-km² area in this northerly region of Ellesmere Island.

2. **Axel Heiberg Island:** This 43,178-km² island is indented by fjords that are ice-bound most of the year. The west coast is dominated by a range of ice-capped mountains, the second highest in the Canadian Arctic archipelago (up to 2290 m).

3. **Fosheim Peninsula:** An excellent example of a high Arctic ecosystem, the landscape of this peninsula on the west coast of Ellesmere Island has rolling hills and a mild climate for the latitude (80° N).

4. **Bylot Island—Eclipse Sound:** Bylot Island, separated by Pond Inlet and Eclipse Sound from the northeastern coast of Baffin Island, has mountains rising to 1830 m. This 11,067-km² island is a sanctuary for greater snow geese and other seabirds.

5. **Western Borden Peninsula:** Precambrian and Paleozoic bedrock have given this peninsula on Baffin Island a varied topography, including a vast polar desert with little vegetation.

6. **Creswell Bay:** Rock deserts and diverse rock types along this bay on Somerset Island have produced many floral varieties.

7. **Banks Island:** The terrain of the most westerly island in the Canadian Arctic archipelago varies from a ravined Devonian

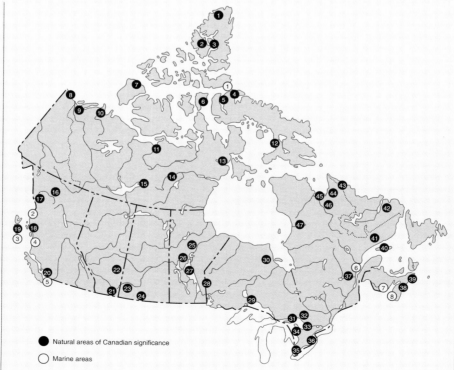

● Natural areas of Canadian significance

○ Marine areas

plateau to coastal lagoons and supports the most vigorous musk-oxen population in the Arctic. The island, with an area of 70,028 km², is the site of a bird sanctuary. Aulavik National Park, established in 1992, occupies an area of 12,275 km² in the northeastern corner of the island.

8. **Northern Yukon:** This area of diverse environments is of critical importance as the habitat for Arctic mammals and birds. Two national parks—10,168-km² Ivvavik (established in 1984) and 4,400-km² Vuntut (established in 1993)—preserve these wildlife habitats.

9. **Caribou Hills—Napoiak Channel:** At the easterly edge of the Mackenzie River delta, the hills level off to a rolling plateau some 150 to 240 m high. In this area, land and sea support a wide variety of plants and animals.

10. **Horton—Anderson rivers:** Brock River canyon, 16 km long with vertical walls up to 110 m, and the Smoking Hills with their burning bituminous beds are features of the area.

11. **Bathurst Inlet:** South of Coronation Gulf, Bathurst Inlet is a submerged rift valley. Wilberforce Falls (50 m) are the highest north of the Arctic Circle.

12. **Foxe Lowlands:** The Great Plain of Koukdjuak on Baffin Island supports the largest goose colony in the world.

13. **Wager Bay:** Situated off Ross Welcome Sound north of Hudson Bay, Wager Bay is a submerged rift valley that penetrates 160 km into the Canadian Shield.

14. **Thelon Game Sanctuary:** Remarkable for its variety of tundra vegetation and concentration of wildlife, the Thelon Game Sanctuary, with an area of 38,850 km², protects the largest surviving mainland population of musk-ox.

15. **East Arm, Great Slave Lake:** Artillery Lake lies across the transition zone between taiga and tundra and supports diverse flora and fauna.

16. **Spatsizi Plateau:** The plateau is part of the more extensive Stikine Plateau and contains the headwaters of the Stikine River, one of the most spectacular in northern British Columbia.

(Continued on next page)

17. **Mt. Edziza—Coast Mountains:** Lava flows, cinder cones and breccia pipes are found near 2787-m-high Mt. Edziza, a composite volcano. Colored, altered lavas coat the Spectrum Range.

18. **Northern coast of British Columbia:** A diverse biological and geological region representative of the Pacific coast.

19. **Queen Charlotte Islands:** Plants that occur nowhere else in the world are evidence of a Pleistocene glacial refuge on the Queen Charlotte Islands.

20. **Gulf Islands—Saltspring Island—Cowichan Estuary:** Located in the Strait of Georgia, the Gulf Islands have a remarkable biological diversity.

21. **Milk River:** Adjacent to the Canadian–U.S. border in southeastern Alberta, the area is a rolling prairie incised by the Milk River. On the sheltered canyon's faces is found one of the largest collections of Indian rock carvings in Canada.

22. **Suffield:** This Alberta region, containing ancient Indian cairns, tepee rings and medicine wheel sites, has tremendous archaeological potential.

23. **Cypress Hills:** The prairie of southern Alberta and Saskatchewan is broken here by the Cypress Hills, a flat-topped, forested plateau rising some 600 m from the surrounding area. This 2,600-km² region is the highest point between the Rocky Mountains and Labrador. Alberta and Saskatchewan preserve portions of this region in the Cypress Hills Interprovincial Park.

24. **Grasslands:** The Val Marie–Killdeer area of southern Saskatchewan is broken by the bizarre landforms of the Killdeer badlands. Dinosaur remains were discovered here in 1874. The 450-km² Grasslands National Park, established in 1975, comprises two separate blocks of land, which contain mixed-grass prairie and habitats for rare, endangered species.

25. **Churchill River:** This forested Precambrian lake country is the site of aboriginal rock paintings considered sacred.

26. **Little Limestone Lake:** In the northern part of the Manitoba lowlands, the area has varied landforms such as flood plains, sinkholes, and meandering rivers.

27. **Long Point:** Both Silurian and Ordovician geological themes are found here. This Lake Winnipeg area is famous for migrating raptors, waterfowl and shorebirds.

28. **Bloodvein River—Atikaki:** The area of eastern Manitoba displays an outstanding example of lake and stream geology.

29. **Northern Lake Superior islands and peninsulas:** The area includes the Sleeping Giant, Ontario's highest vertical cliffs, 11 km long and rising to 300 m. Nearby Ouimet Canyon is a 110-m-deep gorge, 150 m wide and 3 km long.

30. **Attawapiskat River—Akimiskitwin Island Area:** This northern Ontario region along James Bay spans several transitional zones and has excellent examples of delta vegetation and marine ecology.

31. **Manitoulin Island:** Lying in northern Lake Huron, Manitoulin is said to be the largest freshwater island in the world.

32. **French River:** The river's forested mouth on Lake Huron is one of the most spectacular stretches of the Great Lakes.

33. **Parry Sound:** Several rare plant species and virtually every species of wildlife in the region are found here.

34. **Bruce Peninsula:** The rugged peninsula is on an extension of the Niagara Escarpment cuesta. Bluffs rise 90 m above the Georgian Bay shoreline.

35. **Point Pelee:** Canada's southernmost point is a haven for birds. A large part of the point is below water level and marshy.

36. **Long Point:** The fragile sand-based ecosystems of this Lake Erie peninsula can be duplicated nowhere else in Canada. The marshes and shoreline represent an important migratory bird area.

37. **Saguenay Fjord:** Linking the Gulf of St. Lawrence and the lowlands around Lac Saint-Jean, the fjord has a diversity of land and marine resources. Escarpments here reach 460 m high. Saguenay Marine Park preserves the fjord and the adjacent St. Lawrence estuary.

38. **Cape La Have:** Three major marine ecosystems of the Nova Scotia coast are represented: brackish waters, exposed outer beaches and cold-water reefs.

39. **Ship Harbour:** The stretch of Nova Scotia coast has boulder beaches, rocky islands, coves, drumlins, saltwater marshes, sand dunes, bogs and barren islands.

40. **Anticosti Island:** At the mouth of the Gulf of St. Lawrence, this 8000-km² island has postglacial terraces caused by upward movements of the continent and changing sea levels.

41. **Manitou River:** The topography of this region in remote eastern Quebec is characteristic of the Canadian Shield with highlands, valleys, cliffs and lowlands. Areas more than 910 m in elevation display tundra landscapes.

42. **Mealy Mountains:** The 7680-km² region of Labrador has a marine environment, coastal plains and a rugged plateau crowned by 1100-m peaks.

43. **Torngat Mountains:** The mountains in Labrador and Quebec are the highest in eastern Canada, with peaks over 1520 m.

44. **George River Area:** The area in northern Quebec is a 352-km corridor surrounding the George River from Lac de la Hutte Sauvage to Ungava Bay. Evidence of ancient human occupation has been unearthed from archaeological sites.

45. **Koksoak River Area:** The 13,800-km² region, bounded by Ungava Bay, the Whale River watershed and La Baie aux Feuilles, has 19-m tides.

46. **Caniapiskau Area:** A variety of flora and fauna species in this part of northern Quebec represent taiga and tundra.

47. **Richmond Gulf:** In a transitional zone between boreal forest and Arctic tundra, the Richmond Gulf coastline on Hudson Bay has spectacular features including cliffs more than 460 m high.

Marine Areas

1. **Lancaster Sound Marine Area:** This body of water between Baffin and Devon islands is critical to the reproduction and survival of seabirds.

2. **Dundas Islands Marine Area:** Northwest of Prince Rupert, this area consists of a cluster of rugged islands including Dundas, Zayas, Baron, Dunira and Melville.

3. **Queen Charlotte Islands (Southern Moresby Island) Marine Area:** The area is renowned for its diversity of invertebrates and seaweed.

4. **Calvert Island—Hunter Island Marine Area:** The area includes Calvert, Hunter, Goose, and other islands. With their exposed coastlines, Calvert and Goose islands have diverse flora and fauna.

5. **Gulf Islands Marine Area:** An archipelago dominated by a mild, dry, Mediterranean-type climate. Wave action has worn the coastal sandstone into striking caves.

6. **Tadoussac—Les Escoumins Marine Area:** The last remaining refuge of the declining population of beluga whales.

7. **Deer Island Archipelago Marine Area:** Cold saline water supports abundant zooplankton life, while islands and islets shelter seabird colonies.

8. **Brier Island Marine Area:** One of the richest biological areas in the Bay of Fundy, with undisturbed shoreland bogs that support a variety of unique Atlantic flora and fauna.

INTERNATIONALLY RECOGNIZED HERITAGE SITES IN CANADA

This list includes a number of protected natural and cultural sites that have received designations under the World Heritage Convention (UNESCO), the Man and the Biosphere Programme (UNESCO), the Ramsar Convention, and the Western Shorebird Reserve Network. The Ramsar Convention encourages the protection of wetland habitats, about 24 percent of which are found in Canada. In all, the Ramsar sites listed below embrace some 130,000 km², the largest area so designated of any country.

International designation	Sites	International designation	Sites
World heritage sites	**Natural sites**	Ramsar sites (cont'd)	Mary's Point, New Brunswick
	Gros Morne National Park, Newfoundland		Shepody Bay, New Brunswick
	Kluane National Park Reserve, Yukon		Cap Tourmente, Québec
			Baie de l'Île-Verte, Québec
	Wood Buffalo National Park, Alberta/Northwest Territories		Lac Saint-François, Québec
	Canadian Rocky Mountains (Banff, Jasper, Kootenay, and Yoho national parks, and Mt. Assiniboine, Mt. Robson, and Humber provincial parks), Alberta and British Columbia		Long Point, Ontario
			Lake St. Clair, Ontario
			Polar Bear Provincial Park, Ontario
			Southern James Bay, Ontario
	Dinosaur Provincial Park, Alberta		Point Pelee National Park, Ontario
	Nahanni National Park Reserve, Northwest Territories		Delta Marsh, Manitoba
	Cultural sites		Oak-Hammock Marsh Wildlife Area, Manitoba
	Anthony Island, Queen Charlotte Islands British Columbia		Last Mountain Lake, Saskatchewan
	Head-Smashed-In Buffalo Jump, Alberta		Quill Lakes, Saskatchewan
	L'Anse aux Meadows National Historic Park, Newfoundland		Whooping Crane Summer Range, Alberta and Northwest Territories
	Historic District of Québec City, Québec		Peace-Athabasca Delta, Alberta
Biosphere reserves	Waterton Lakes, Alberta		Hay-Zama Lakes, Alberta
	Riding Mountain, Manitoba		Beaverhill Lake, Alberta
	Long Point, Ontario		Polar Bear Pass, Northwest Territories
	Niagara Escarpment, Ontario		Queen Maud Gulf, Northwest Territories
	Mont St. Hilaire, Québec		Rasmussen Lowlands, Northwest Territories
	Charlevoix, Québec		McConnell River, Northwest Territories
Ramsar sites	Grand Cordroy Estuary, Newfoundland		Dewey Soper, Northwest Territories
	Malpeque Bay, Prince Edward Island		Alaksen, British Columbia
	Chignecto, Nova Scotia		Old Crow Flats, Yukon
	Musquodoboit Harbour Outer Estuary, Nova Scotia	Western hemisphere shorebird reserves	Shepody Bay, New Brunswick
	Southern Bight-Minas Basin, Nova Scotia		Minas Basin, Nova Scotia

PRIMARY LAND COVER IN CANADA

Land cover class	Predominant cover in the class	Area[a] (km², 000s)	% Canada Total[b]
Forest and taiga	Closed canopy forest and/or open stands of trees with secondary occurrences of wetland, barren land, or others	4456	45
Tundra/sparse vegetation	Well-vegetated to sparsely vegetated or barren land, mostly in arctic or alpine environments	2303	23
Wetland	Treed and non-treed fens, bogs, swamps, marshes, shallow open water, and coastal and shore marshes	1244	12
Freshwater	Lakes, rivers, streams, and reservoirs	755	8
Cropland	Fenced land (including cropland and pasture land), hedge rows, farms, and orchards	658	6
Rangeland	Generally nonfenced pasture land, grazing land; includes natural grassland that is not necessarily used for agriculture	203	2
Ice/snow	Permanent ice and snow fields (glaciers, ice caps)	272	3
Built-up	Urban and industrial land	79	1
Total		**9970**	**100**

[a] Includes the area of all land and freshwater. [b] Rounded to the nearest percent.
NOTE: Data for this table are derived from satellite imagery and may deviate slightly from other sources of data.

LAND ACTIVITY IN CANADA

Land activity class	Predominant activity in the class	Area (km², 000s)[a]	% Canada Total[b]
Forestry	Active forest harvesting or potential for future harvesting	2440	24
Recreation and conservation	Recreation and conservation within national, provincial and territorial parks, wildlife reserves, sanctuaries, etc.	708	7
Agriculture	Agriculture on improved farmland (cropland, improved pasture, summer fallow) and unimproved farmland	678	7
Urban/industrial	Residential and industrial activities of urban environments	72[c]	1
Other activities	Includes hunting and trapping, mining, energy developments, and transportation	6072	61
Total		**9970**	**100**

[a] Includes the area of land and freshwater. [b] Rounded to the nearest percent. [c] Includes only the 25 major metropolitan areas.

HIGHEST POINTS IN CANADA

Province and point	Elevation (m)
NEWFOUNDLAND	
Torngat Mountains	
Mount Caubvick (Mont d'Iberville)	1652
Cirque Mountain	1568
Mealy Mountains	
Unnamed peak (53°37' 58°33')	1176
Kaumajet Mountains	
Bishops Mitre	1113
Long Range Mountains	
Lewis Hills	814
Gros Morne	806
PRINCE EDWARD ISLAND	
Highest point (46°20' 63°25')	
Queen's County	142
NOVA SCOTIA	
Highest point (46°42' 60°36')	
Cape Breton Highlands	532
NEW BRUNSWICK	
Mount Carleton	817
Wilkinson Mountain	785
QUEBEC	
Monts Torngat	
Mont d'Iberville (Mount Caubvick)	1652
Les Appalaches	
Mont Jacques-Cartier	1268
Mont Gosford	1192
Mont Richardson	1185
Mont Mégantic	1105
Les Laurentides	
Unnamed peak (47°19' 70°50')	1166
Mont Tremblant	968
Mont Sainte-Anne	800
Mont Sir-Wilfrid	783
Monts Otish	
Unnamed peak (52°19' 71°27')	1135
Collines Montérégiennes	
Mont Brome	533
ONTARIO	
Ishpatina Ridge	693
Ogidaki Mountain	665
Batchawana Mountain	653
Tip Top Mountain	640
Niagara Escarpment	
Blue Mountains	541
Osler Bluff	526
Caledon Mountain	427
MANITOBA	
Baldy Mountain	832
Highest point in Porcupine Hills	823
Riding Mountain	610
SASKATCHEWAN	
Cypress Hills	1468
Wood Mountain	1013
Vermilion Hills	785
ALBERTA	
Rocky Mountains	
Mount Columbia	
(on Alta.-B.C. boundary)	3747
North Twin	3733
Mount Alberta	3620
Mount Assiniboine	
(on Alta.-B.C. boundary)	3618

Province and point	Elevation (m)
Mount Forbes	3612
South Twin	3581
Mount Temple	3547
Mount Brazeau	3525
Snow Dome (on Alta.-B.C. boundary)	3520
Mount Lyell (on Alta.-B.C. boundary)	3504
Mount Athabasca	3491
BRITISH COLUMBIA	
St. Elias Mountains	
Fairweather Mountain	
(on Alaska-B.C boundary)	4663
Coast Mountains	
Mount Waddington	4016
Rocky Mountains	
Mount Robson	3954
Mount Columbia	
(on Alta.-B.C. boundary)	3747
Mount Clemenceau	3642
Mount Assiniboine	
(on Alta.-B.C. boundary)	3618
Mount Goodsir: North Tower	3581
Mount Goodsir: South Tower	3520
Snow Dome (on Alta.-B.C. boundary)	3520
Selkirk Mountains	
Mount Sir Sandford	3522
Cariboo Mountains	
Mount Sir Wilfrid Laurier	3520
Purcell Mountains	
Mount Farnham	3481
Monashee Mountains	
Torii Mountain	3429
YUKON	
St. Elias Mountains	
Mount Logan (highest point in Canada)	5959
Mount St. Elias	
(on Alaska-Yukon boundary)	5489
Mount Lucania	5226
King Peak	5173
Mount Steele	5067
Mount Wood	4838
Mount Vancouver	
(on Alaska-Yukon boundary)	4785
Mount Macaulay	4663
Mount Hubbard	
(on Alaska-Yukon boundary)	4577
NORTHWEST TERRITORIES	
Mackenzie Mountains	
Unnamed peak (61°51' 127°42')	2773
Mount Sir James MacBrien	2762
Ellesmere Island	
Barbeau Peak	2616
Baffin Island	
Mount Odin	2147
Devon Island	
Summit Devon Ice Cap	1920
Franklin Mountains	
Cap Mountain	1577
Mount Clark	1462
Pointed Mountain	1405
Nahanni Butte	1396
Banks Island	
Durham Heights	732
Victoria Island	
Unnamed peak	655

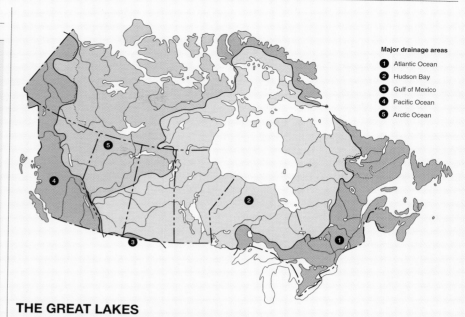

Major drainage areas
- ❶ Atlantic Ocean
- ❷ Hudson Bay
- ❸ Gulf of Mexico
- ❹ Pacific Ocean
- ❺ Arctic Ocean

THE GREAT LAKES

Lake	Elevation (m)	Length (km)	Breadth (km)	Maximum depth (m)	Total area (km²)	Area on Canadian side of boundary (km²)
Superior	184	563	257	405	82,100	28,700
Michigan	176	494	190	281	57,800	—
Huron	177	332	295	229	59,600	36,000
St. Clair	175	42	39	6	1210	490
Erie	174	388	92	64	25,700	12,800
Ontario	75	311	85	244	18,960	10,000

Rivers and their tributaries	Length (km)
Winnipeg (to head of Firesteel)	813
English	615
Fairford (to head of Manitoba Red Deer)	684
Churchill (to head of Churchill Lake)	1609
Beaver (to outlet of Beaver Lake)	491
Severn (to head of Black Birch)	982
Albany (to head of Cat)	982
Thelon	904
Dubawnt	842
La Grande-Rivière (Fort George River)	893
Koksoak (to head of Caniapiscau)	874
Nottaway (via Bell to head of Mégiscane)	776
Rupert (to head of Témiscamie)	763
Eastmain	756
Attawapiskat (to head of Bow Lake)	748
Kazan (to head of Ennadai Lake)	732
Grande rivière de la Baleine	724
George	565
Moose (to head of Mattagami)	547
Abitibi (to head of Louis Lake)	547
Mattagami (to head of Minisinakwa Lake)	443
Missinaibi	426
Harricana/Harricanaw	533
Hayes	483
Rivière aux Feuilles (Leaf)	480
Winisk	475
Broadback	450
Rivière à la Baleine	428
Rivière de Povungnituk	389
Innuksuac	385
Petite rivière de la Baleine	380
Arnaud	377
Nastapoca	360
Kogaluc	304

FLOWING INTO THE ATLANTIC OCEAN

Rivers and their tributaries	Length (km)
St. Lawrence River	3058
Nipigon (to head of Ombabika)	209
Spanish	338
Trent (to head of Irondale)	402
Ottawa River	1271
Gatineau	386
Rivière du Lièvre	330
Saguenay (to head of Peribonca)	698
Péribonca	451
Mistassini	298
Chamouchouane	266
Saint-Maurice	563
Manicouagan (to head of Mouchalagane)	560
Rivière aux Outardes	499
Romaine	496
Betsiamites (to head of Manouanis)	444
Moisie	410
St-Augustin	233
Richelieu (to mouth of Lake Champlain)	171
Churchill (to head of Ashuanipi)	856
Saint John	673
Little Mecatina	547
Natashquan	410
Bersimis	386
St-François	280
Exploits	246
Eagle	233
Miramichi	217

PRINCIPAL LAKES

Province and lake	Area (km²)
NEWFOUNDLAND AND LABRADOR	
Smallwood Reservoir	6527
Melville	3069
NOVA SCOTIA	
Bras d'Or	1099
QUEBEC	
Mistassini	2335
Manicouagan Reservoir	1942
Gouin Reservoir	1570
à l'Eau-Claire	1383
Bienville	1249
Saint-Jean	1003
ONTARIO	
Nipigon	4848
Lake of the Woods (total 4,349)	3150
Seul	1657
Abitibi	931
Nipissing	832
Simcoe	744
Rainy (total 932)	741
MANITOBA	
Winnipeg	24,387
Winnipegosis	5374
Manitoba	4624
Southern Indian	2247
Cedar	1353
Island	1223
Gods	1151
Cross	755
SASKATCHEWAN	
Athabasca	7935
Reindeer	6650
Wollaston	2681
Cree	1434
La Ronge	1413
ALBERTA	
Clair	1436
Lesser Slave	1168
BRITISH COLUMBIA	
Williston	1761
Atlin	775
YUKON TERRITORY	
Kluane	781
NORTHWEST TERRITORIES	
Great Bear	31,328
Great Slave	28,568
Nettilling	5542
Dubawnt	3833
Amadjuak	3115
Nueltin	2279
Baker	1887
La Martre	1776
Yathkyed	1449
Kasba	1341
Aberdeen	1100
Napaktulik Lake	1080

PRINCIPAL RIVERS

Rivers and their tributaries	Length (km)
FLOWING INTO THE PACIFIC OCEAN	
Yukon (mouth to head of Nisutlin)	3185
(international boundary to head of Nisutlin)	1149
Porcupine	721
Stewart	644
Pelly	608
Teslin	393
Columbia (mouth to head of Columbia Lake)	2000
(international boundary to head of Columbia Lake)	801
Kootenay	780
Kettle (to head of Holmes Lake)	336
Okanagan (to head of Okanagan Lake)	314
Fraser	1370
Thompson (to head of North Thompson)	489
North Thompson	338
South Thompson (to head of Shuswap)	332
Nechako (to head of Eutsuk Lake)	462
Stuart (to head of Driftwood)	415
Skeena	579
Stikine	539
Nass	380

Rivers and their tributaries	Length (km)
FLOWING INTO THE ARCTIC OCEAN	
Mackenzie (to head of Finlay)	4241
Peace (to head of Finlay)	1923
Smoky	492
Athabasca	1231
Pembina	547

Rivers and their tributaries	Length (km)
Liard	1115
South Nahanni	563
Fort Nelson (to head of Sikanni Chief)	517
Petitot	404
Hay	702
Peel (mouth of west Channel to head of Ogilvie)	684
Arctic Red	499
Slave (from Peace River to Great Slave Lake)	415
Fond du Lac (to outlet of Wollaston Lake)	277
Back (from outlet of Muskox Lake)	974
Coppermine	845
Anderson	692
Horton	618

Rivers and their tributaries	Length (km)
FLOWING INTO HUDSON BAY AND HUDSON STRAIT	
Nelson (to head of Bow)	2575
(to outlet of Lake Winnipeg)	644
Saskatchewan (to head of Bow)	1939
South Saskatchewan (to head of Bow)	1392
Red Deer	724
Bow	587
Oldman	362
North Saskatchewan	1287
Battle (to head of Pigeon Lake)	570
Red (to head of Sheyenne)	877
Assiniboine	1070

MAJOR SEA ISLANDS, BY REGION

Region and island	Area (km²)
ARCTIC ISLANDS	
Baffin Island	507,451
Queen Elizabeth Islands	
Ellesmere	196,236
Devon	55,247
Axel Heiberg	43,178
Melville	42,149
Bathurst	16,042
Prince Patrick	15,848
Ellef Ringnes	11,295
Cornwallis	6995
Amund Ringnes	5255
Mackenzie King	5048
Borden	2794
Cornwall	2258
Eglinton	1541
Graham	1378
Lougheed	1308
Byam Martin	1150
Vanier	1126
Cameron	1059
Arctic Islands, south of Queen Elizabeth Islands, but north of the Arctic Circle	
Victoria	217,291
Banks	70,028
Prince of Wales	33,339
Somerset	24,786
King William	13,111
Bylot	11,067
Prince Charles	9521
Stefansson	4463
Richards	2165
Air Force	1720
Wales	1137
Rowley	1090
Arctic Islands, south of the Arctic Circle, in Hudson Strait and Hudson Bay	
Southampton	41,214
Coats	5498
Mansel	3180
Akimski (in James Bay)	3001
Flaherty Island (part of the Belcher Islands)	1585
Nottingham	1372
Resolution	1015
PACIFIC COAST	
Vancouver	31,285
Queen Charlotte Islands	
Graham	6361
Moresby	2608
Princess Royal	2251
Pitt	1375
ATLANTIC COAST	
Newfoundland and Labrador	
Newfoundland (main island)	108,860
South Aulatsivik	456
Killinek	269
Fogo	254
Random	249
Gulf of St. Lawrence	
Cape Breton	10,311
Anticosti	7941
Prince Edward Island	5660
Bay of Fundy	
Grand Manan	137

GLACIERS

Arctic Islands	Ice area (km²)	No. of glaciers surveyed
Axel Heiberg	11,383	1121
Baffin	35,890	10,526
Bylot	4851	579
Coburg	218	106
Devon	15,714	1907
Ellesmere	77,596	n.a.
Ice shelf	484	n.a.
Meighen	83	n.a.
Melville	155	n.a.
North Kent and Calf	148	68
	146,522	14,307
Mainland		
Into Nelson River	319	1616
Into Yukon River	10,246	n.a.
Into Great Slave Lake	606	n.a.
Into Pacific Ocean	36,527	n.a.
Into Arctic Ocean	816	n.a.
Into Atlantic Ocean	n.a.	n.a.
All glaciers in Labrador	23	n.a.
	48,537	1616

Key: n.a. = not available
Estimate of total ice cover in Canada: 195,059 km²

YEAR-ROUND WEATHER OF SELECTED CANADIAN CENTRES

City	Average daily temperatures (°C)				Annual average number of days with:				Bright sunshine (hours per year)
	January	April	July	October	Rain	Snow	Thunderstorms	Winds (>63 km/h)	
St. John's	−3.9	1.2	15.5	6.9	156	88	3	23	1497
Charlottetown	−7.1	2.3	18.3	8.1	124	68	9	6	1818
Halifax	−6.0	3.3	18.2	8.6	125	64	9	3	1885
Saint John	−7.8	3.2	16.9	7.6	124	59	11	6	1865
Sept-Îles	−14.0	0.0	15.2	3.6	93	72	7	9	1990
Montréal	−10.2	5.7	20.9	8.7	114	62	25	1	2054
Toronto	−6.7	6.2	20.6	9.3	99	47	27	—	2045
Winnipeg	−19.3	3.4	19.6	6.1	72	57	27	1	2341
Churchill	−27.5	−10.1	11.8	−1.5	58	100	7	11	1827.9
Regina	−17.9	3.3	18.9	5.2	59	58	23	9	2331.1
Edmonton	−15.0	4.2	17.4	5.8	70	59	22	—	2263.7
Penticton	−2.7	8.6	20.3	8.7	78	29	12	—	2032.2
Vancouver	2.5	8.8	17.3	10.0	156	15	6	—	1919.6
Prince Rupert	−0.2	5.4	12.8	7.9	218	35	2	4	1224.1
Yellowknife	−28.8	6.9	16.3	−1.6	46	82	5	—	2276.6
Whitehorse	−20.7	0.3	14.1	0.6	52	120	6	—	1843.8
Resolute	−32.1	−23.1	4.1	−15.1	20	82	—	25	1505.1

RECORD-SETTING CLIMATIC EXTREMES

Greatest precipitation in one month: 2235.4 mm at Swanson, B.C., November 1917.

Highest wind speed (for the duration of one hour): 203 km/h at Cape Hopes Advance, Qué., Nov. 18, 1931.

Greatest annual precipitation: 8122.4 mm at Henderson Lake, B.C., 1931.

Highest temperature: 45°C at Midale and Yellow Grass, Sask., July 5, 1937.

Lowest temperature: – 63°C at Snag, N.W.T., Feb. 5, 1947.

Highest monthly snowfall: 5359 mm at Haines Apps No. 2, B.C., Dec. 1959.

Heaviest seasonal snowfall: 24465.3 mm at Revelstoke/Mt. Copeland, B.C., during the 1971–72 snowfall season.

Greatest snowfall in one day: 1181 mm at Lakelse Lake, B.C., Jan. 17, 1974.

Greatest number of hours of sunshine in one month: 621, recorded at Eureka, N.W.T., May 1972.

Lowest mean monthly temperature: – 47.9°C at Eureka, N.W.T., February 1979.

Most fogbound place: Grand Bank, Nfld., an average of 120 days of fog a year.

Northern lights: Displays have lasted up to 240 days in the Hudson Bay area.

WINDCHILL FACTOR

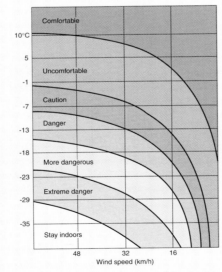

Near-freezing temperatures combined with strong winds have the same chilling effect as lower temperatures on windfree days. For example, a −15°C temperature with a 40 km/h wind has a cooling effect on the skin similar to that of −40°C on calm conditions. The windchill factor is a measure of the combined chilling effect of wind and temperature. Its calculation is based on the rate at which water cools in combined low temperature and windy conditions. Since windchill can cause frostbite and a life-threatening loss of body heat (hypothermia), the chart (*above*) serves as a guide for appropriate precautionary measures.

MEASURING WIND STRENGTH: THE BEAUFORT SCALE

In the early 1800s, Admiral Sir Francis Beaufort developed a scale from 0 to 12 to indicate wind strength (originally on ships' sails). Hurricane strength (force 12) was described in fitting naval terms as "that which no canvas could withstand." The scale was later modified for use on land. Force 6, for example, is a strong breeze (40 to 50 km/h), which causes umbrellas to turn inside out and large branches to sway.

Beaufort number	Wind name	Speed (km/h)	Observed effect of wind
0	Calm	0–1	Calm. Smoke rises straight up into the air.
1	Light air	2–5	Weather vanes remain motionless. Smoke drifts slightly with the wind.
2	Light breeze	6–11	Weather vanes active. You can feel the wind on your face. Leaves rustle.
3	Gentle breeze	12–19	Light flags fill out with wind. Twigs on trees move.
4	Moderate breeze	20–29	The wind picks up dust and loose paper. Small tree branches sway.
5	Fresh breeze	30–39	Waves break on inland waters. Small trees sway in the wind.
6	Strong breeze	40–50	Using an umbrella becomes difficult. Large tree branches sway.
7	Moderate gale	51–61	Walking against the wind is difficult. Entire large trees sway.
8	Fresh gale	62–74	Walking against the wind is almost impossible. Twigs break off trees.
9	Strong gale	75–87	Shingles blown off house roofs. Some damage to buildings.
10	Whole gale	88–102	Entire trees blown over and uprooted. Much damage to buildings.
11	Storm	103–118	Severe damage to crops, trees, and property.
12	Hurricane	119+	Widespread, violent destruction.

HUMIDITY AND COMFORT

High humidity (large amounts of water vapor in the air) and soaring temperatures produce hot, muggy and oppressive days. At high humidity, the air becomes so saturated that it cannot absorb moisture on the skin, and the cooling effect of evaporation decreases. As result, we often feel hotter on humid days than on dry days with the same or higher temperatures. The humidex (*below*) is a measure of the degree of comfort or discomfort that we experience in humid conditions. For example, if the humidity level is 75 percent and the temperature has reached 32°C, the humidex reading equals an uncomfortable 46°C.

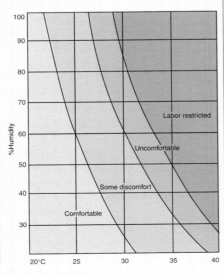

JET STREAMS

Tubular ribbons of high-speed winds—known as jet streams—circle the earth in wavelike patterns generally from west to east. Like narrow currents in a river, jet streams always travel at greater speeds than the air surrounding them. Formed in the tropopause zone at the top of the troposphere, they may be 450 km wide and 6 km high. Wind speeds can better hurricane intensities, often reaching 400 km/h and more at the core, with velocities decreasing outward from the centre.

Jet streams vary in number and differ in the paths they take over the globe according to the earth's seasons. One major jet stream over Canada follows a path over Vancouver, Winnipeg, Montréal and Halifax. Eastbound aircraft heading into this stream gain the added push of these strong winds, allowing them to cross the continent at least an hour faster than the same flight westward.

Jet-stream paths in January, at 9 km altitude

NORTH MAGNETIC POLE

Centuries of conjecture and exploration preceded the discovery of the north magnetic pole in the Canadian Arctic. Today we know that electric currents deep within the earth's molten core produce the planet's magnetic field. The north magnetic pole—like its southern counterpart in the Antarctic—is the site where the earth's magnetic field has a maximum intensity.

During the Middle Ages, navigators found that their compasses did not point exactly to the true north, but a little to one side. A legend arose that a huge magnetic mountain far in the north attracted compass needles and any ships unfortunate enough to pass close by. In a 1546 map, Gerardus Mercator erroneously located a magnetic pole near Bering Strait, while his world map of 1569 offered two positions.

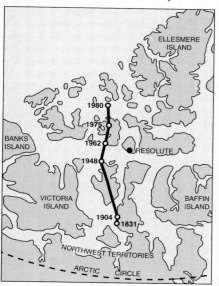

The track of the wandering north magnetic pole, from 1831 to recent times.

In 1600, the English physician and scientist William Gilbert published *De magnete*, which offered the first reliable account of magnetic phenomenon. He put forth the theory that the earth itself was the magnet and that this force, rather than a far-off northern mountain, controlled the action of the compass.

In June 1831, after several centuries of polar exploration, the north magnetic pole was finally located by the English explorer Sir James Clark Ross, who built a cairn at the spot on King William Island. At the time of Ross's discovery, the pole was fully 2100 km from the geographic north pole.

However, like the explorers and navigators it has guided, the north magnetic pole is in continuous motion, and the cairn that Ross built at Cape Adelaide no longer marks the spot. The pole is now located north of Bathurst Island, roughly 1400 km from the north geographic pole. Its average daily movement is clockwise in an ellipse centered on its mean position, which drifts from year to year.

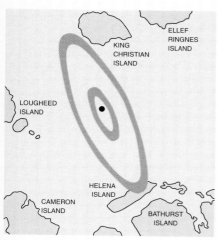

Daily motion of the north magnetic pole near Bathurst Island: the inner ring, movement on a magnetically quiet day; the outer ring, movement on an active day.

ATMOSPHERIC ZONES

The earth's atmosphere consists of several gaseous layers: the troposphere, the stratosphere, the mesosphere, and the thermosphere and exosphere, also known as the ionosphere. The layers interact with one another, and also with the sun's radiation that passes through them. They differ greatly in temperature and are subject to constant chemical and physical change.

The **troposphere** is not warmed directly by the sun's heat, which travels in wavelengths too short to be absorbed by the carbon dioxide and water vapor in this layer. Instead, it receives indirect heat that bounces off the earth's surface in longer infrared wavelengths. Temperature falls in the troposphere by about 6°C for every kilometre rise in altitude.

By contrast, the temperature of the **stratosphere** increases with height (from about −60°C to 0°C). Ozone, formed by the reaction of oxygen atoms with the sun's ultraviolet radiation, is present in the stratosphere in large amounts. The ozone traps weather in the troposphere, since the convection currents swirling about the earth cannot rise through this higher, warmer layer. It also blocks out radiation, which would otherwise destroy all living organisms.

Ozone-layer depletion, linked to the emissions of chlorofluorocarbons and other chemicals, threatens to reduce protection from radiation. In the mid-1980s, scientists discovered a vast hole in the ozone layer over Antarctica, which appears every September and fills in after two months. Lesser extensive depletion also occurs over the Arctic and has been observed in the mid-latitudes of the northern hemisphere. The 1987 Montreal Protocol was the first in a series of international agreements to control ozone-depleting emissions.

From 50 km to 80 km, in a layer called the **mesosphere**, the temperature cools again so that it reaches −100°C at its outer boundary. Beyond is the **ionosphere**, composed of nitrogen and oxygen broken down into atoms by intense solar radiation. The atoms, once stripped of their electrons, produce electrically charged particles (ions), which interact with each other as well as with earth's gravity and magnetic field.

The ionosphere and interplanetary space interact as well. The latter is affected by the earth and its magnetic field. This field deflects the constant barrage of electrically charged particles from the sun to form a region called the magnetosphere.

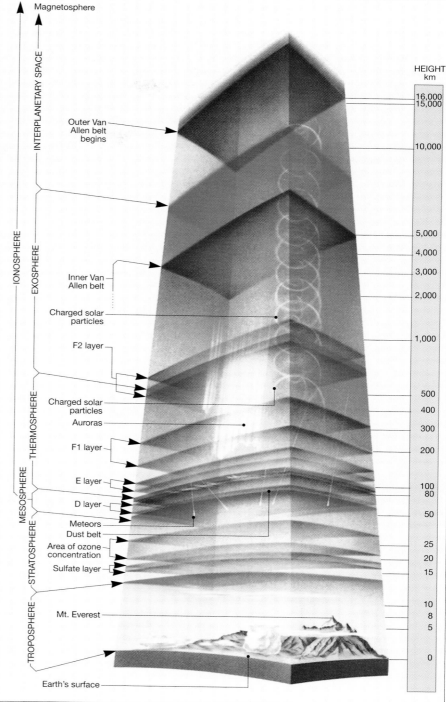

ACID RAIN

Acid precipitation is one of the major environmental problems in North America. It corrodes metals, damages forests, crops and soils, and kills lakes and streams by halting the spawning of fish and destroying other aquatic organisms. Moreover, it poses a serious hazard for human health.

Acid precipitation is caused largely by the burning of coal and oil, which release emissions of sulfur dioxide and nitrogen oxide. The emissions react with water vapor in the atmosphere to produce corrosive nitric and sulfuric acid that falls as rain or snow. The greater the acidity, the lower the pH level. A pH of 7 indicates neutrality. A drop of a point on the pH scale corresponds to a tenfold increase in acidity. Clean rain is slightly acidic with a pH of about 5.6. The acid rain that falls on Canada may be as low as 3 (about as acidic as vinegar).

One of the worst episodes of acid rain in Canada was recorded in the Muskoka-Haliburton region of Ontario between August 28 and September 4, 1981. The 200-mm rainfall represented a quarter of the region's acid rain for the entire year.

Smelting ore, generating power, refining petroleum, manufacturing pulp and paper and other industrial enterprises all contaminate the air with pollutants. The largest sources of sulfur-dioxide emissions come from the industrial heartland of the eastern United States and southwestern Ontario, and the mining operations of northeastern Ontario. During the mid-1980s, all eastern Canada produced some 4.6 million tonnes of sulfur dioxide a year.

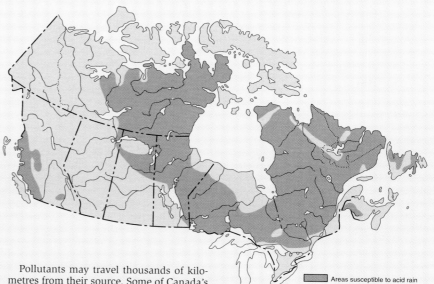

Pollutants may travel thousands of kilometres from their source. Some of Canada's acid rain comes all the way from the mills in Ohio and Pennsylvania, while heavy industry in Canada sends a portion of its acid rain to the eastern United States. Some may even be carried as far as Greenland.

Lakes situated on limestone basins are able to neutralize acid rain. But many Canadian lakes lie on granite rocks unable to counteract acidity. Ontario has been the province hardest hit, with some 19,000 dead or dying lakes. Western Canada has been less affected, but lakes in southern Québec and the Maritimes Provinces have also been damaged. The best game fish are

usually the first to disappear: acid rain has wiped out all the salmon in some rivers and streams of Nova Scotia.

During the mid-1980s, Canada initiated measures to control the acid-rain problem. In 1987, the federal government and the seven eastern provinces reached an agreement to reduce sulfur-dioxide emissions by about 50 percent from 1980 levels before 1995. In 1991, Canada and the United States signed an acid-rain accord, also with the purpose of cutting emissions by certain amounts within specific periods.

METEORITE CRATERS IN CANADA

Meteorites are fragments of rock or metal that have fallen to earth from outer space. They vary in size from that of a pinhead to masses of several tonnes. Most have formed in a belt between the orbits of Mars and Jupiter, the product of collisions between hundreds of planetlike bodies, which are called asteroids.

Meteorites consist of three major groups: stony, iron, and stony iron. The stony specimens resemble ordinary rocks and are the most commonly found. The stony irons are an almost equal mix of metal and silicate minerals, while the iron meteorites are generally heavy masses of metal containing smaller amounts of silicate minerals.

Although all meteorites resemble natural rocks and minerals, they have distinctive features that aid identification. Most possess a fusion crust, a soft outer layer, dull black to brown in color. The stony meteorites contain metallic iron and rounded granules of silicate minerals, which are called chondrules. Iron and stony iron meteorites have large amounts of nickel and are strongly magnetic.

Giant meteorites can punch sizable impact craters in the surface of the earth. Almost a third of the world's largest meteorite craters (measuring a kilometre or more in diameter) have been found in Canada. A list of these craters is given below.

Location	Diameter (km)	Age (million years)	Surface feature
1. New Quebec Crater, Qué.	3.2	5	rimmed circular lake
2. Brent, Ont.	3.8	450 ± 30	sediment-filled, shallow depression
3. Manicouagan, Qué.	70	210 ± 4	circumferential lake, central elevation
4. a) Clearwater East, Qué.	22	290 ± 20	circular lake
b) Clearwater West, Qué.	32	290 ± 20	island ring in circular lake
5. Holleford, Ont.	2	550 ± 100	sediment-filled, shallow depression
6. Deep Bay, Sask.	12	100 ± 50	discontinuous circular ridge
7. Carswell Lake, Sask.	37	485 ± 50	discontinuous circular ridge
8. Lac Couture, Qué.	8	420	circular lake
9. West Hawk Lake, Man.	2.7	100 ± 50	circular lake
10. Pilot Lake, N.W.T.	6	<300	circular lake
11. Nicholson Lake, N.W.T.	12.5	<450	irregular lake with islands
12. Steen River, Alta.	25	95 ± 7	none, buried to 200 metres
13. Sudbury, Ont.	140	1840 ± 150	elliptical basin
14. Charlevoix, Qué.	46	360 ± 25	semicircular trough, central elevation
15. Mistastin Lake, Labrador	28	38 ± 4	elliptical lake and central island
16. Lake St. Martin, Man.	23	225 ± 40	none, buried and eroded
17. Lake Wanapitei, Ont.	8.5	37 ± 2	lake-filled, partly circular
18. Gow Lake, Sask.	5	<200	lake and central island
19. Lac La Moinerie, Qué.	8	400	lake-filled, partly circular
20. Haughton, N.W.T.	20	15	shallow, circular depression
21. Slate Islands, Ont.	30	350	central uplift of submerged structure
22. Île Rouleau, Qué.	4	<300	central uplift of submerged structure

MEASURING EARTHQUAKES

In 1935, the American scientist Charles F. Richter devised a scale (*right*) that measures the magnitude of an earthquake — that is, the energy released at the source — but not the scale of surface damage. The destructiveness of a earthquake generally coincides with its magnitude. Most devastation occurs at the quake's epicentre (the point of the earth's surface directly above the quake). The damage lessens as distance increases from the epicentre.

On the Richter scale, an increase of one point indicates a tenfold jump in earthquake magnitude. Magnitude 4, for example, signifies tremors forceful enough to close open doors and awaken sleepers. Magnitude 5, with 10 times greater force than 4, denotes vibrations capable of overturning furniture and cracking masonry.

Some 300 magnitude-3 quakes occur annually in Canada. Earthquake zones include the Pacific coast, the mountainous west (where magnitude-8 quakes have been recorded), the Yukon, the High Arctic, the Atlantic coast, and eastern Canada.

The modified Richter scale of magnitude

Magnitude	Estimated number recorded each year	Estimated damage
10	Possible but never recorded	Would be felt all over the earth
9		Felt in most parts of the globe
8 to 8.6	Occur infrequently	Very great damage
7.4 to 7.9	4	Great damage
7.0 to 7.3	15	Serious damage, railway tracks and bridge members bent
6.2 to 6.9	100	Widespread damage to most structures
5.5 to 6.1	500	Moderate to slight damage
4.9 to 5.4	1400	Felt by everyone within the affected area
4.3 to 4.8	4800	Felt by most
3.5 to 4.2	30,000	Felt by a few
2.0 to 3.4	More than 150,000	Not felt but recorded

DISCOVERING NATURE

Aquariums

Sealand of the Pacific, Victoria

Undersea Gardens of Victoria

Vancouver Public Aquarium

Aquarium du Québec, Québec

Aquarium and Marine Centre, Shippigan, New Brunswick

Fisheries Museum of the Atlantic, Lunenburg, Nova Scotia

The Huntsman Marine Laboratory and Aquarium, St. Andrews, New Brunswick

P.E.I Marine Aquarium, Charlottetown

Newfoundland Freshwater Resource Centre, St. John's

Arboretums

Crown Zellerbach Arboretum and Museum, Ladysmith, British Columbia

Grant Ainscough Arboretum and Tree Improvement Centre, Nanaimo, British Columbia

Queen Elizabeth Arboretum, Vancouver

Morden Arboretum, Morden, Manitoba

Woody Plant Test Arboretum, University of Manitoba, Winnipeg

The Arboretum, Guelph, Ontario

The Arboretum, Lakehead University, Thunder Bay, Ontario

Dominion Arboretum, Ottawa

Humber Arboretum, Applied Arts Division, Humber College, Rexdale, Ontario

Laurentian University Arboretum, Sudbury, Ontario

Niagara Parks Commission, School of Horticulture, Niagara Falls, Ontario

Plum Grove Arboretum, Kakabeka Falls, Ontario

Morgan Arboretum, Macdonald College of McGill University, Ste. Anne de Bellevue, Québec

Botanical gardens

The Botanical Garden, University of British Columbia, Vancouver

Butchart Gardens, Victoria

Crystal Garden, Victoria

Minter Gardens, Chilliwack, British Columbia

Nitobe Memorial Gardens, Vancouver

Vandusen Botanical Display Garden, Vancouver

Devonian Botanic Garden, University of Alberta, Edmonton

Devonian Gardens, Calgary

Nikka Yuko Centennial Garden, Lethbridge, Alberta

Patterson Park Botanical Garden, University of Saskatchewan, Saskatoon

Agriculture Canada Research Station, Morden, Manitoba

Allan Gardens, Toronto

Botanical Gardens, Central Experimental Farm, Ottawa

Centennial Conservatory, Thunder Bay, Ontario

Royal Botanical Gardens, Hamilton

Annapolis Royal Historic Gardens, Annapolis Royal, Nova Scotia

Jardin Botanique de Montréal

Métis Gardens, Sainte-Flavie, Québec

New Brunswick Botanical Gardens, St. Jacques, New Brunswick

Malpeque Gardens, Kensington, Prince Edward Island

Memorial University Botanical Garden, St. John's

Earth science museums

Keno City Mining Museum, Keno City, Yukon

British Columbia Museum of Mining, Britannia Beach, British Columbia

M. Y. Williams Geological Museum, University of British Columbia, Vancouver

Frank Slide Interpretive Centre, Frank, Alberta

Museum of Geology, University of Alberta, Edmonton

The Royal Tyrrell Museum of Palaeontology, Drumheller, Alberta.

Geological Museum, University of Saskatchewan, Saskatoon

Biology and Earth Sciences Museum, University of Waterloo, Waterloo, Ontario

Miller Museum of Geology and Minerology, Queen's University, Kingston, Ontario

Oil Museum of Canada, Oil Springs, Ontario

Petrolia Discovery Foundation, Petrolia, Ontario

Timmins Museum, South Porcupine, Ontario

Musée de Géologie, Laval University, Sainte-Foy, Québec

Musée minéralogique et minier de la région de l'amiante, Thetford Mines, Québec

Musée minier de Malartic, Malartic, Québec

Fundy Geological Museum, Parrsboro, Nova Scotia

Inverness Miner's Museum, Inverness, Nova Scotia

Mineral and Gem Geological Museum, Parrsboro, Nova Scotia

Springhill Miner's Museum, Springhill, Nova Scotia

St. Lawrence Miner's Museum, St. Lawrence, Newfoundland

Natural history museums

British Columbia Provincial Museum, Victoria

Provincial Museum of Alberta, Edmonton

Saskatchewan Museum of Natural History, Regina

Manitoba Museum of Man and Nature, Winnipeg

Royal Ontario Museum, Toronto

The Biodome, Montréal

The New Brunswick Museum, Saint John

Nova Scotia Museum, Halifax

Newfoundland Museum, St. John's

Science centres

Pacific Geoscience Centre, Sidney, British Columbia

Science World, Vancouver

Alberta Science Centre, Calgary

Edmonton Space and Science Centre

Engergum, Calgary

Hamilton Museum of Steam and Technology

Museum of Visual Science and Optometry, University of Waterloo, Waterloo, Ontario

Ontario Science Centre, Toronto

Science North, Sudbury, Ontario

Kamloops Wildlife Park, British Columbia

Okanagan Game Farm, Kaleden, British Columbia

Stanley Park Zoological Gardens, Vancouver

Vancouver Game Farm, Aldergrove, British Columbia

Calgary Zoo, Botanical Garden, and Prehistoric Park

Valley Zoo, Edmonton

Forestry Farm Park and Zoo, Saskatoon

Moose Jaw Zoo, Moose Jaw, Saskatchewan

Sleepy Hollow Museum and Game Farm, Abernethy, Saskatchewan

Assiniboine Park Zoo, Winnipeg

African Lion Safari, Cambridge, Ontario

Bronte Creek Children's Farm, Burlington, Ontario

Chippewa Park Zoo, Thunder Bay

Jungle Cat World, Orono, Ontario

Metro Toronto Zoo, West Hill, Ontario

Riverview Park and Zoo, Peterborough

Toronto Island Park and Farm

Wasaga Fishing and Game Farm, Wasaga Beach, Ontario

Jardin zoologique de Bonaventure, Québec

Jardin zoologique de Montréal

Jardin zoologique de Québec, Charlesbourg, Québec

Parc safari africain, Hemmingford, Québec

Société zoologique de Granby, Granby, Québec

Société zoologique de Saint-Félicien Incorporée, Saint-Félicien, Québec

Nova Scotia Provincial Wildlife Park, Shubenacadie, Nova Scotia

Cherry Brook Zoo, Saint John

People and Society

HEALTH: Principal causes of death

Heart disease	38.9%
Cancer	27.6
Respiratory	8.6
Accidents	4.9
Nervous system	2.6
Diabetes	2.2
Suicide	1.8
Cirrhosis of the liver	1.1
Other	9.8

LIFE EXPECTANCY, 1986

	Male	Female
At birth	73.04	79.73
1 year	72.67	79.27
2	71.72	78.32
3	70.76	77.35
4	69.79	76.38
5	68.81	75.40
10	63.88	70.46
15	58.98	65.52
20	54.27	60.65
25	49.62	55.77
30	44.92	50.88
35	40.21	46.02
40	35.52	41.20
45	30.91	36.48
50	26.47	31.87
55	22.28	27.43
60	18.41	23.17
65	14.90	19.12
70	11.80	15.35
75	9.13	11.92
80	6.91	8.93
85	5.12	6.44
90	3.73	4.49
95	2.55	2.86
100	0.78	0.80

ETHNIC GROUPS, 1991

Country of origin	No.	%
British Isles	5,611,050	20.6
French	6,146,600	22.5
Other European	4,146,065	15.2
Austrian	27,130	0.1
Belgian	31,475	0.1
Czech and Slovak	59,125	0.2
Danish	40,640	0.1
Finnish	39,230	0.1
German	911,560	3.3
Greek	151,150	0.6
Hungarian	100,725	0.4
Icelandic	14,555	0.05
Italian	750,055	2.7
Jewish	245,840	0.9
Lithuanian	15,180	0.06
Netherlander	35,620	2.0
Norwegian	63,030	0.2
Polish	272,810	1.0
Portuguese	246,890	0.9
Romanian	28,650	0.1
Russian	38,220	0.1
Spanish	82,675	0.3
Swedish	43,345	0.2
Ukrainian	406,645	1.5
Yugoslavian	48,420	6.2
Other	493,095	1.8
Asiatic/African	1,633,660	6.0
African	26,430	0.1
Arab	144,050	0.5
Chinese	586,645	2.1
Filipino	157,250	0.6
Japanese	48,595	0.2
Korean	44,095	0.2
Lebanese	74,250	0.3
South Asian (Indian)	420,295	1.5
West Asian (Armenian)	81,660	0.3
Other	50,390	0.2
Other	875,165	3.2
Caribbean	94,395	0.3
Latin, Central, South American	85,535	0.3
Native Indian	470,615	1.7
Black	224,620	0.8
Other and not stated	8,884,360	32.5
Total	27,296,900	100.0

INDIAN POPULATION, 1992

Province or territory	Number of bands	Membership
Atlantic	31	20,584
Québec	39	52,582
Ontario	126	121,867
Manitoba	61	80,845
Saskatchewan	70	81,700
Alberta	43	66,065
British Columbia	196	90,769
Northwest Territories	22	18,341
Yukon	16	6628
CANADA	604	533,381

INUIT POPULATION, 1991

Northwest Territories	21,335
Rest of Canada	27,900
CANADA	49,255

POPULATION: Estimated population by province, June 1, 1991 (thousands)

Province or territory	0-4 years Male	0-4 years Female	5-9 years Male	5-9 years Female	10-14 years Male	10-14 years Female	15-19 years Male	15-19 years Female
Newfoundland	19.0	18.3	22.0	21.1	24.2	23.4	28.1	26.0
Prince Edward Island	4.8	4.7	5.1	4.9	5.1	4.8	5.2	4.8
Nova Scotia	31.0	29.9	31.7	30.0	31.3	30.4	34.5	32.5
New Brunswick	24.4	22.9	25.8	24.9	27.2	25.9	29.5	28.1
Québec	227.4	217.9	230.1	218.6	248.4	235.7	230.9	220.3
Ontario	362.9	344.7	253.5	335.9	337.5	320.7	349.0	330.0
Manitoba	42.0	40.1	41.3	39.1	39.5	37.8	41.5	38.8
Saskatchewan	40.0	38.2	41.5	39.7	40.2	37.9	37.2	35.9
Alberta	106.4	101.2	106.1	100.9	95.8	90.7	90.9	87.0
British Columbia	112.9	107.9	107.9	110.6	109.9	104.3	108.2	103.5
Yukon Territory	1.3	1.1		1.2	1.0	1.0	1.0	0.9
Northwest Territories	3.7	3.6	3.6	3.0			2.5	2.3
CANADA	975.8	930.7	978.2	929.8	962.9	915.1	958.4	910.2

Province or territory	20-24 years Male	20-24 years Female	25-34 years Male	25-34 years Female	35-44 years Male	35-44 years Female	45-54 years Male	45-54 years Female
Newfoundland	24.0	23.6	46.2	48.2	44.9	44.8	29.4	28.2
Prince Edward Island	4.7	4.7	10.2	10.4	9.7	9.9	6.6	6.5
Nova Scotia	33.8	33.4	77.5	79.1	69.4	70.8	47.8	47.5
New Brunswick	27.0	26.4	60.8	61.9	57.9	58.0	38.3	37.4
Québec	239.4	235.1	618.7	622.2	564.0	570.4	400.8	407.1
Ontario	370.6	370.5	901.5	918.4	787.5	810.9	550.1	549.2
Manitoba	39.9	39.1	92.3	91.3	81.0	81.3	54.4	54.2
Saskatchewan	32.3	32.2	78.6	79.4	70.7	68.7	46.0	45.6
Alberta	97.0	96.4	246.9	243.7	211.4	202.6	126.5	121.9
British Columbia	112.8	111.6	279.1	283.1	271.9	272.1	183.7	177.8
Yukon Territory	1.0	1.0	2.8	2.9	3.0	2.7	1.8	1.4
Northwest Territories	2.7	2.7	6.0	5.8	4.6	3.9	2.4	2.0
CANADA	985.2	976.7	2,420.3	2,446.4	2,175.9	2,195.5	1,487.5	1,478.8

Province or territory	55-64 years Male	55-64 years Female	65-69 years Male	65-69 years Female	70 + years Male	70 + years Female	All ages Male	All ages Female
Newfoundland	21.3	44.8	8.8	9.2	16.1	21.1	286.4	289.2
Prince Edward Island	5.3	5.4	2.4	2.6	4.9	7.2	64.0	66.2
Nova Scotia	36.9	38.9	16.2	18.8	31.7	46.9	445.8	461.5
New Brunswick	28.9	30.5	13.1	15.1	24.5	35.4	359.2	368.9
Québec	305.9	332.1	122.3	149.8	189.8	309.2	3396.3	3529.3
Ontario	447.3	461.3	187.7	223.4	305.8	466.7	4966.5	5131.5
Manitoba	45.1	46.9	20.6	24.7	41.1	60.4	539.9	556.1
Saskatchewan	42.6	42.9	19.7	21.6	42.1	56.6	492.4	501.3
Alberta	96.0	93.5	36.5	41.1	63.9	89.3	1286.0	1279.0
British Columbia	148.6	145.6	64.7	74.1	117.6	165.6	1635.2	1670.1
Yukon Territory	0.9	0.7	0.3	0.2	0.4	0.3	14.5	13.5
Northwest Territories	1.4	1.1		0.3	0.5	0.5	28.9	27.1
CANADA	1,180.0	1,219.6	492.5	580.7	837.9	1,258.8	13,515.1	13,893.8

IMMIGRATION AND EMIGRATION, 1960-1990 (thousands)

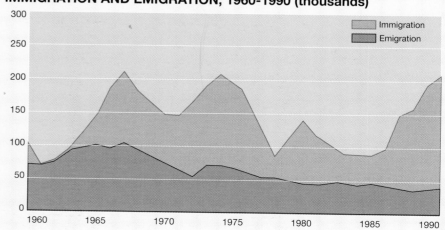

MARRIAGE RATE

Rate per 1000 persons — y-axis: 2, 4, 6, 8, 10, 12, 14
x-axis: 1921, 1931, 1941, 1951, 1961, 1971, 1981, 1991

DIVORCE RATE

Rate per 100,000 persons — y-axis: 50, 100, 150, 200, 250, 300, 350
x-axis: 1921, 1931, 1941, 1951, 1961, 1971, 1981, 1991

TOTAL FERTILITY RATE

Children per woman — y-axis: 0, 1.5, 2.0, 2.5, 3.0, 3.5, 4.0, 4.5
Replacement level of 2.1 children per woman
x-axis: 1921, 1931, 1941, 1951, 1961, 1971, 1981, 1991

INFANT MORTALITY RATE

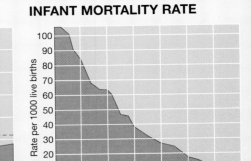

Rate per 1000 live births — y-axis: 10, 20, 30, 40, 50, 60, 70, 80, 90, 100
x-axis: 1921, 1931, 1941, 1951, 1961, 1971, 1981, 1991

AGE PYRAMID OF THE CANADIAN POPULATION, 1991 (for a total population of 100,000)

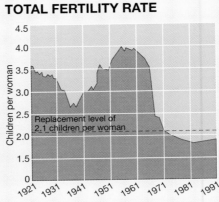

Year of birth	Age
1900-01	90+
1905-06	85
1910-11	80
1915-16	75
1920-21	70
1925-26	65
1930-31	60
1935-36	55
1940-41	50
1945-46	45
1950-51	40
1955-56	35
1960-61	30
1965-66	25
1970-71	20
1975-76	15
1980-81	10
1985-86	5
1990-91	0

Male — Female
x-axis: 900, 800, 700, 600, 500, 400, 300, 200, 100, 0, 100, 200, 300, 400, 500, 600, 700, 800, 900

❶
❷
❸
❹
❺
❻

1. Effect of excess male mortality
2. Decline in births during World War II
3. Decline in births during the Depression and disruption of immigration until the end of World War II
4. Upturn in births after World War II
5. Baby boom
6. Recent drop in fertility

NATURAL INCREASE RATE

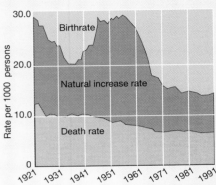
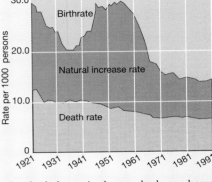

Rate per 1000 persons — y-axis: 0, 10.0, 20.0, 30.0
x-axis: 1921, 1931, 1941, 1951, 1961, 1971, 1981, 1991
Birthrate
Natural increase rate
Death rate

The shaded area in the graph above shows the difference between Canada's birth rate (number of births per 1000) and death rate (deaths per 1000); thus, the natural increase rate in population. The decline in the death rate is testimony to improved health care, hygiene and diet; the fluctuating birth rate reflects economic and social changes. The rate declined between 1929 and 1945, climbed with postwar prosperity (1947-61), and fell again in the late 1960s.

POPULATION OF CENSUS METROPOLITAN AREAS, 1951-1991

Census metropolitan areas	1951	1961	1971	1976	1981	1986	1991
Calgary	142,315	279,062	403,319	469,917	625,966	671,453	754,033
Chicoutimi–Jonquière	91,161	127,616	133,703	128,643	135,172	158,468	160,928
Edmonton	193,622	259,821	495,702	554,228	740,882	774,026	839,924
Halifax	138,427	193,353	222,637	267,991	277,727	295,922	320,521
Hamilton	281,901	401,071	489,523	529,371	542,095	557,029	599,760
Kitchener	107,474	154,864	226,846	272,158	287,801	311,195	356,421
London	167,724	226,669	286,011	270,383	326,817	342,302	381,522
Montréal	1,539,308	2,215,627	2,743,208	2,802,485	2,862,286	2,921,357	3,127,242
Oshawa			120,318	135,196	186,446	203,543	240,104
Ottawa–Hull	311,587	457,038	602,510	693,288	743,821	819,263	920,857
Québec	289,294	379,067	480,502	542,158	583,920	603,267	645,550
Regina	72,731	113,749	140,734	151,191	173,226	186,521	191,692
St. Catharines–Niagara	189,046	257,796	303,429	301,921	121,012	121,265	124,981
Saint John, N.B.	80,689	98,083	106,744	112,974	342,645	343,258	364,552
St. John's, Nfld.	80,869	106,666	131,814	143,390	154,835	161,901	171,859
Saskatoon	55,679	95,564	126,449	133,750	175,058	200,665	210,023
Sudbury	80,543	127,446	155,424	157,030	156,121	148,877	157,613
Thunder Bay	73,713	102,085	112,093	119,253	121,948	122,217	124,427
Toronto	1,261,861	1,919,409	2,628,043	2,803,101	3,130,392	3,431,981	3,893,046
Vancouver	586,172	826,798	1,082,352	1,166,348	1,268,183	1,380,729	1,602,502
Victoria	114,859	155,763	195,800	218,250	241,450	255,225	287,897
Windsor	182,619	217,215	258,643	247,582	250,885	253,988	262,075
Winnipeg	257,229	476,543	540,262	578,217	592,061	625,304	652,354

URBAN AND RURAL POPULATION, 1991 (thousands)

Province or territory	Urban No.	Urban %	Rural nonfarm No.	Rural nonfarm %	Farm No.	Farm %	Total rural No.	Total rural %	Total population No.
Newfoundland	304.5	53.6	263.3	46.3	0.7	—	264	46.3	568.5
Prince Edward Island	51.8	39.9	75.6	58.2	2.4	1.8	78	60.0	129.8
Nova Scotia	481.5	53.5	414.4	46.0	4.0	—	418.4	46.0	899.9
New Brunswick	345.2	47.7	375.3	51.8	3.3	—	378.6	51.8	723.9
Québec	5351.2	77.6	1506.7	21.8	38.1	—	1544.8	21.8	6896.0
Ontario	8253.8	81.8	1762.4	17.5	68.6	—	1831.0	17.5	10,084.9
Manitoba	787.2	72.1	279.1	25.6	25.7	2.4	304.8	28.0	1091.9
Saskatchewan	623.4	63.0	304.7	30.8	60.8	6.1	365.5	36.9	988.9
Alberta	2030.9	79.8	457.5	18.0	57.2	2.2	514.7	20.2	2545.6
British Columbia	2640.1	80.4	622.7	19.0	19.2	—	641.9	19	3282.1
Yukon-Northwest Territories	37.5	—	48.0	—	—	—	—	—	85.5
CANADA	20,907.1	76.6	6109.7	22.4	280.0	1.0	6389.7	23.4	27,297

Dominant mother tongue, 1991

Province or territory	Language	%
British Columbia	English	79.4
	Chinese	4.3
	German	2.5
	Punjabi	1.8
	French	1.4
Alberta	English	81.3
	German	2.9
	Chinese	2.1
	French	2.0
	Ukrainian	1.5
Saskatchewan	English	83.1
	German	3.8
	Native	2.8
	Ukrainian	2.5
	French	1.2
Manitoba	English	73.3
	German	5.8
	French	4.3
	Ukrainian	3.0
	Native	2.8
Ontario	English	75.1
	French	4.6
	Italian	2.8
	Chinese	2.0
	German	1.5
Québec	French	81.2
	English	8.7
	Italian	1.7
New Brunswick	English	64.1
	French	32.7
Prince Edward Island	English	93.8
	French	4.2
Nova Scotia	English	93.2
	French	3.8
Newfoundland	English	98.4
	French	0.4
Northwest Territories	English	54.2
	Native	38.3
	French	2.4
Yukon Territory	English	88.1
	French	2.9
	Native	2.6

POPULATION BY MOTHER TONGUE, 1991

Language	No.	%	Language	No.	%
English	16,516,180	60.6	Magyar (Hungarian)	72,905	0.3
French	6,505,565	23.9	Native Indian	145,585	0.5
Armenian	23,015	0.1	Netherlandic and Flemish	133,265	0.5
Baltic	19,620	0.1	Polish	171,975	0.6
Celtic	4,200	—	Portuguese	186,995	0.7
Chinese	444,940	1.6	Romanian	19,985	—
Creole	19,475	—	Russian	32,965	0.1
Croatian, Serbian, etc.	59,850	0.2	Scandinavian	46,100	0.2
Czech and Slovak	40,455	0.2	Semitic languages	132,685	0.5
Filipino	83,645	0.3	Spanish	158,655	0.6
Finnish	24,905	0.1	Ukrainian	166,830	0.6
German	424,645	1.6	Vietnamese	69,925	0.3
Greek	114,370	0.4	Yiddish	21,395	0.1
Indo-Iranian	252,930	0.9	Other	5,455	—
Inuktitut	24,030	0.1	Not stated	839,075	3.1
Italian	449,660	1.6			
Japanese	26,835	0.1	Total	27,269,860	100.0

DEMOGRAPHIC PROFILE, 1990-1991

Province or territory	Marriages 1991	Divorces 1990	Births 1991	Deaths 1991
Newfoundland	3480	1006	7510	3850
Prince Edward Island	876	276	1890	1220
Nova Scotia	5845	2414	11,990	7490
New Brunswick	4521	1695	9570	5580
Québec	28,922	20,398	97,520	50,650
Ontario	72,938	28,863	152,190	72,990
Manitoba	7032	2755	17,420	9190
Saskatchewan	5923	2354	15,430	8310
Alberta	18,612	8483	42,580	14,530
British Columbia	23,691	9735	46,040	24,800
Yukon Territory	411	173	2150	375
Northwest Territories				
CANADA	172,251	78,152	404,290	198,980

FAMILIES AND PERSONS PER FAMILY, 1981-1991

Province or territory	Families 1981	Families 1986	Families 1991	Persons per family 1981	Persons per family 1986	Persons per family 1991
Newfoundland	135.1	142.1	150.7	3.8	3.6	3.3
Prince Edward Island	30.2	32.1	33.9	3.5	3.4	3.2
Nova Scotia	216.2	230.5	244.6	3.3	3.2	3.1
New Brunswick	176.6	185.9	198.0	3.4	3.3	3.1
Québec	1671.5	1751.5	1883.2	3.3	3.1	3.0
Ontario	2279.0	2445.7	2726.7	3.2	3.1	3.1
Manitoba	262.2	276.3	285.9	3.2	3.2	3.1
Saskatchewan	245.7	260.6	257.6	3.3	3.2	3.2
Alberta	565.6	616.3	668.0	3.3	3.2	3.1
British Columbia	728.0	775.9	887.7	3.1	3.0	3.0
Yukon Territory	15.0	17.0	19.8	3.6	3.6	3.5
Northwest Territories						
CANADA	6325.6	6735.0	7356.2	3.3	3.1	3.1

Urban/rural population change in Canada, 1871-1991 (percent)

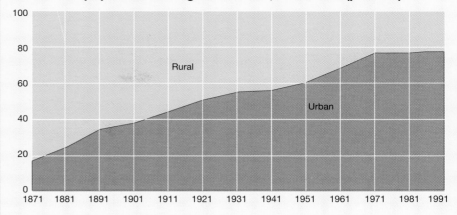

Urban population/population density in selected countries

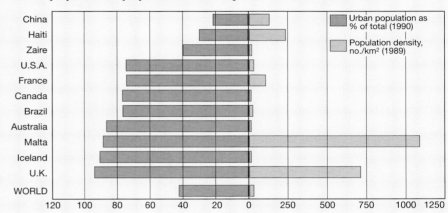

CRIME, 1988-1992

Types of crime	1988 (per 100,000 people) No.	1988 (per 100,000 people) Rate	1992 (per 100,000 people) No.	1992 (per 100,000 people) Rate	1988–92 % change Rate
All crimes of violence:	232,606	898	307,491	1122	24.9
Murder	537	2	654	2	—
Sexual assault	24,898	96	34,352	125	30.2
Robbery	24,172	93	33,186	121	30.1
All property crimes:	1,475,361	5625	1,674,362	6110	8.6
Break and enter	359,198	1386	427,152	1559	12.5
Theft over $1000	80,074	309	120,045	438	41.7
All other offenses under the criminal code:	700,040	2701	866,238	3162	14.6
Prostitution	10,721	41	10,134	37	–9.8
Offensive weapons	16,959	65	17,711	65	—
Gaming and betting	1374	5	740	3	–40.0
Total	2,854,277	11,016	3,267,300	11,923	8.2

RELIGIONS OF CANADA

The history of religion in Canada dates back to the summer day in 1534 when Jacques Cartier planted a nine-metre wooden cross on the Gaspé Coast on behalf of the King of France and in the name of Christ. Since then, the growth of Canada has been intertwined with the development of its religious faith.

Christian missionary activity did not begin until Champlain's arrival in 1603. In spite of hardships and the martyrdom of some early missionaries, the Catholic religious orders came to the New World to spread the faith, teach and heal. With the support of the French clergy and nobility, the Récollet order established itself in Quebec in 1615. The Jesuits founded their order in 1625.

Canada's largest religious faith is Roman Catholicism. The Roman Catholic hierarchy in Canada consists of an apostolic delegate representing the Pope; archbishops appointed to supervise the ecclesiastical provinces, of whom the most eminent are cardinals; and bishops appointed to govern the dioceses. In modern Canada, the Roman Catholic Church has played a major role in education and social movements.

Protestantism traces its Canadian beginnings to the late 16th and early 17th centuries when French Huguenots settled along the St. Lawrence River and the Bay of Fundy. A number of Congregationalists came to Nova Scotia from New England between 1749 and 1752. The Methodist population was significant by 1772, and most of the early Methodist clergy were circuit riders. Church services were conducted either by these itinerant ministers or by lay preachers.

The largest Protestant denomination, the United Church of Canada with 3,093,120 members, is an amalgamation of Methodist, Presbyterian and Congregationalist churches. The government of the United Church is presbyterial, its presbytery and conference courts consisting equally of ministerial and lay representatives. The chief executive officer, called a moderator, is elected biennially at a general council.

When the United Church was formed in 1925, one Presbyterian in three remained out of union, thus preserving a distinct Canadian Presbyterian denomination. Presbyterianism is a form of church government in which the church is administered by presbyters or elders. In Canada, the Presbyterian Church is headed by a moderator, committees of a general assembly, and eight synods.

The Anglican Church of Canada is part of the international Anglican communion, which became a separate stream in Christendom in the 1500s. The church is structured into ecclesiastical provinces, which are divided into dioceses. One of the archbishops is designated Primate of All Canada, but real authority rests in each diocese. The head of each diocese is a bishop in apostolic succession elected by lay and clerical representatives of all parishes at a diocesan synod.

The earliest recorded Protestant service in Canada was an Anglican Eucharist celebrated by Robert Wolfall aboard explorer Martin Frobisher's ship off Baffin Island in the summer of 1578. In 1583, Sir Humphrey Gilbert claimed Newfoundland for England, and the Church of England became its official church. Anglican clergy were associated with the Hudson's Bay Company in 1683, but it was apparently not until the early 18th century that permanent church buildings appeared—in Newfoundland and Nova Scotia. The Canadian Anglican communion became an autonomous church in 1893.

The Lutheran Church, also a product of the Reformation, appeared early in Canada. Capt. Jens Munck and 36 men from Denmark, including Rev. Rasmus Jensen, landed on Hudson Bay near the Churchill River in August 1619. By Easter, only three had survived an outbreak of scurvy. In 1740, however, Lutheran services began in Nova Scotia. More Lutherans from the United States and Europe settled in the Maritimes, Ontario and the West in the 19th century.

The church's creed is based on the theology of 16th-century reformers Martin Luther and Philip Melanchthon. In Canada, there are three branches, unified by a Lutheran council, each with a president as its chief officer.

Today, roughly 90 percent of the Canadian population is Christian. But other religious traditions, such as Judaism, have deep roots in Canada. Moreover, the 1991 census (see below) reveals new trends—the rise of Eastern non-Christian faiths, such as Buddhism, Hinduism, Sikhism, and Islam, and the revival of the religions of native peoples and the Inuit.

Denomination	1971 No.	1971 %	1991 No.	1991 %
Anglican	2,543,180	11.8	2,188,115	8.1
Baptist	667,245	3.1	663,360	2.5
Eastern Non-Christian			747,455	2.8
Greek Orthodox	316,605	1.5	231,635	0.8
Jehovah's Witnesses	174,810	0.8	168,375	0.6
Jewish	276,025	1.3	318,070	1.2
Lutheran	715,740	3.3	636,210	2.4
Mennonite	181,800	0.8	229,460	0.8
Mormon	66,635	0.3	100,770	0.3
Native and Inuit			10,840	0.03
No religious affiliations			3,386,365	12.5
Para-religious groups			28,155	0.1
Pentecostal	220,390	1.0	436,435	1.6
Presbyterian	872,335	4.0	636,295	2.4
Roman Catholic (Latin rite)	9,974,895	46.2	12,203,620	45.2
Salvation Army	119,665	0.6	112,345	0.4
Ukrainian (Greek) Catholic	227,730	1.1	128,390	0.4
United Church of Canada	3,768,800	17.5	3,093,120	11.5
Other	1,330,480	6.2	1,988,725	6.2
Total	21,568,310	100.0	27,296,900	100.0

CANADIAN COLLEGES AND UNIVERSITIES

(The list includes founding dates and enrolments)

Acadia University; Wolfville, N.S.; 1838 (4288)

Alberta, The University of; Edmonton, Alta.; 1906 (28,542)

Athabasca University; Edmonton, Alta.; 1970 (7779)

Augustana University College; Camrose, Alta.; 1910 (957)

Bishop's University; Lennoxville, Qué.; 1843 (28,670)

Brandon University; Brandon, Man.; 1899 (3748)

Brescia College (Univ. of Western Ontario); London, Ont.; 1919 (878)

British Columbia, University of; Vancouver, B.C.; 1890 (31,513)

Brock University; St. Catharines, Ont.; 1964 (11,119)

Calgary, The University of; Calgary, Alta.; 1945 (22,120)

Campion College (Univ. of Regina); Regina, Sask.; 1917 (1049)

Carleton University; Ottawa, Ont.; 1942 (20,958)

Collège universitaire de Sainte-Boniface; Winnipeg, Man.; 1818 (802)

Concordia University; Montréal, Qué.; 1974 (25,862)

Dalhousie University; Halifax, N.S.; 1818 (10,762)

Guelph, University of; Guelph, Ont.; 1964 (15,411)

Huron College (Univ. of Western Ontario); London, Ont.; 1863 (880)

The King's College; Edmonton, Alta.; 1979 (380)

King's College, University of (Dalhousie Univ.); Halifax, N.S.; 1789 (818)

King's College (Univ. of Western Ontario); London, Ont.; 1966 (2356)

Lakehead University; Thunder Bay, Ont.; 1946 (6870)

Laurentian University of Sudbury; Sudbury, Ont.; 1960 (11,483)

Laval, Université; Québec, Qué.; 1852 (27,098)

Lethbridge, University of; Lethbridge, Alta.; 1967 (4247)

McGill University; Montréal, Qué.; 1821 (27,653)

McMaster University; Hamilton, Ont.; 1887 (17,574)

Manitoba, The University of; Winnipeg, Man.; 1877 (25,085)

Memorial University of Newfoundland; St. John's, Nfld.; 1949 (17,665)

Moncton, Université de; Moncton, N.B.; 1963 (7749)

Montréal, Université de; Montréal, Qué.; 1876 (39,463)

Mount Allison University; Sackville, N.B.; 1843 (2047)

Mount Saint Vincent University; Halifax, N.S.; 1925 (3571)

New Brunswick, University of; Fredericton, N.B.; 1785 (11,952)

Ottawa, University of; Ottawa, Ont.; 1848 (25,014)

Prince Edward Island, University of; Charlottetown, P.E.I.; 1969 (3557)

Québec, Université du; Ste-Foy, Qué.; 1968 (83,100)

Queen's University at Kingston; Kingston, Ont.; 1841 (18,059)

Regina, The University of; Regina, Sask.; 1974 (9198)

Royal Military College of Canada; Kingston, Ont.; 1874 (787)

Royal Roads Military College; Victoria, B.C.; 1940 (332)

Ryerson Polytechnical Institute; Toronto, Ont.; 1948 (20,576)

Ste. Anne, University; Church Point, N.S.; 1890 (552)

St. Francis Xavier University; Antigonish, N.S.; 1853 (3665)

St. Jerome's College, The University of (Univ. of Waterloo); Waterloo, Ont.; 1864 (1056)

St. John's College (Univ. of Manitoba); Winnipeg, Man.; 1849 (enrolment included with Univ. of Manitoba)

St. Mary's University; Halifax, N.S.; 1802 (7695)

St. Michael's College, University of (Univ. of Toronto); Toronto, Ont.; 1852 (n.a.)

St. Paul University; Ottawa, Ont.; 1965 (939)

St. Paul's College (Univ. of Manitoba); Winnipeg, Man.; 1926 (enrolment included with Univ. of Manitoba)

St. Thomas More College (Univ. of Saskatchewan); Saskatoon, Sask.; 1936 (990)

St. Thomas University; Fredericton, N.B.; 1910 (1898)

Saskatchewan, The University of; Saskatoon, Sask.; 1907 (18,816)

Sherbrooke, Université de; Sherbrooke, Qué.; 1954 (18,419)

Simon Fraser University; Burnaby, B.C.; 1963 (17,165)

Sudbury, The University of; Sudbury, Ont.; 1913 (enrolment added with Laurentian Univ.)

Toronto, University of; Toronto, Ont.; 1837 (53,969)

Trent University; Peterborough, Ont.; 1963 (5793)

Trinity College, University of (Univ. of Toronto); Toronto, Ont.; 1852 (n.a.)

Trinity Western University; Langley, B.C.; 1962 (1677)

Victoria, University of; Victoria, B.C.; 1963 (14,953)

Victoria University (Univ. of Toronto); Toronto, Ont.; 1836 (n.a.)

Waterloo, University of; Waterloo, Ont.; 1959 (23,633)

Western Ontario, The University of; London, Ont.; 1878 (25,504)

Wilfrid Laurier University; Waterloo, Ont.; 1973 (8705)

Windsor, University of; Windsor, Ont.; 1963 (16,269)

Winnipeg, The University of; Winnipeg, Man.; 1967 (deriving from Manitoba College, 1871, and Wesley College, 1877), (7561)

York University; Downsview, Ont.; 1959 (41,635)

EDUCATION: Schools, teachers and enrolment, 1993-1994

	Canada	Nfld.	P.E.I.	N.S.	N.B.	Qué.	Ont.	Man.	Sask.	Alta.	B.C.	Yukon	N.W.T.
No. of schools													
Elementary/secondary	16,231	497	68	519	444	3335	5574	838	960	1830	2050	32	80
Postsecondary:													
Non-university	203	12	2	10	8	89	32	10	1	18	19	1	1
University	69	1	1	12	5	8	22	7	3	5	6	—	—
Schools for blind and deaf	18	1	1	2	—	6	4	—	—	2	—	—	—
Total	16,521	511	72	543	457	3438	5632	855	964	1855	2075	33	81
No. of teachers													
Elementary/secondary	300,797	7546	1355	10,180	8270	63,150	122,590	13,150	11,030	28,610	33,300	406	1150
Postsecondary:													
Non-university	27,260	370	110	300	430	12,560	8010	430	2300	2300	2180	40	100
University	37,880	1050	180	2100	1300	9150	14,250	1800	1500	3250	3300	—	—
Schools for blind and deaf	757	35	5	95	—	170	215	25	—	30	—	—	—
Total	366,512	9001	1650	12,675	10,000	85,030	145,065	15,405	12,960	34,190	38,780	446	1250
Enrolment													
Elementary/secondary	5,360,900	120,560	24,410	169,820	139,830	1,148,950	2,109,290	221,680	208,040	547,860	646,780	5516	17,210
Postsecondary:													
Non-university	365,065	4460	1400	2830	3800	174,510	111,170	4570	3820	27,030	30,620	290	565
University	585,200	13,720	2830	30,260	20,310	141,350	234,470	20,860	23,340	51,650	46,410	—	—
Schools for blind and deaf	2,345	130	10	660	—	510	800	140	—	95	—	—	—
Total	6,313,510	138,870	28,650	203,570	163,940	1,464,320	2,455,730	247,350	235,200	626,635	723,810	6260	17,775

CANADIAN JOURNALISM: PIONEER PUBLISHING

The first newspaper published in what is now Canada was the *Halifax Gazette*. It was founded by John Bushell, an immigrant from Boston, and the first edition came out on March 23, 1752. Two journalists from Rhode Island and New York began the second English-language newspaper, the *Royal Gazette and Nova Scotia Intelligencer*, in 1783 in what is now Saint John, N.B. Another Bostonian brought out the *Royal American Gazette* in Charlottetown in 1787, while the *Upper Canada Gazette* started in 1793 in Newark, now Niagara-on-the-Lake.

The pioneer newspapers depended, to a large degree, on government business for survival. This provided regular, lucrative work: statutes, orders, proclamations and other official documents were the bread and butter of the infant industry. The early English-language newspapers of the Maritimes and Upper Canada were in fact, if not always in name, King's printers. But in return, the authorities expected newspapers to be loyal, and did not hesitate to close down critical presses and jail offending proprietors. The idea of a free and critical press was not formulated until the mid-nineteenth century, the period marking the advent of responsible government.

The earliest newspapers were small (the *Halifax Gazette* was only the size of a half page of foolscap) and rarely more than four pages long. They were printed on imported paper using wooden flatbed handpresses with movable type. The only illustrations were the odd clumsy woodcut intended to draw attention to an advertisement for a sale of cows or to the search for a runaway slave or debtor. No attempt was made to produce the kind of eye-catching layouts that modern readers take for granted. The printer—the same man who wrote the news, solicited subscriptions and kept the accounts—simply set his material as it came to hand; the entire first section was often printed in order to reuse limited type for the next.

Apart from government-related material, pioneer newspapers contained outdated news items copied from British and American publications, literary articles, and local advertisements for such things as "choice butter by the firkin," "New England and West India rum," "sheet cork for nets," and beef at fivepence and sixpence a pound.

The first French-language journals included *La Gazette de Québec* (1764) and *La Gazette du commerce et littéraire* (1778)—later renamed the *Montreal Gazette*, which has survived to this day as Montréal's only English-language daily newspaper. Some Québec papers of the 18th and 19th centuries were published in both English and French; in the case of the *Gazette*, items written in English gradually replaced the French. On the whole, the French-language newspapers had a harder time surviving than did the English: they did not enjoy government patronage and addressed themselves to rural readers who were generally less interested in supporting them than was the urban population.

As the country opened up, pioneer newspapers mushroomed in the West. British Columbia's first newspaper was the *Victoria Gazette and Anglo-American*, founded by four Californians in 1858. Later that year the successful *British Colonist* was started by eccentric Amor de Cosmos, who was to become British Columbia's second premier. Winnipeg had the *Nor'Wester* in 1859, and Battleford the *Herald* in 1878. The early western newspapers were very different from eastern journals: an expanding, heterogeneous and literate population provided them with a healthy circulation, while advertising ensured them an income independent of government patronage. A new era had arrived; the papers were beginning to see themselves as critics of government, molders of public opinion and champions of truth.

NEWSPAPERS: Number and circulation, 1993

Province or territory	AM news- papers	PM news- papers	Daily news- papers	Total AM circulation	Total PM circulation	Number of Sunday newspapers	Total Sunday circulation
Alberta	4	5	9	461,052	76,983	6	549,971
British Columbia	4	15	19	460,555	120,354	4	339,176
Manitoba	1	3	3	49,549	178,429	3	162,194
New Brunswick	1	3	4	30,423	109,144	—	—
Newfoundland	—	2	2		51,726	2	60,204
Nova Scotia	4	3	7	149,543	75,930	1	36,218
Ontario	7	36	3	698,826	1,771,879	3	1,138,460
Prince Edward Island	1	2	3	n.a.	n.a.	—	—
Québec	9	1	10	1,002,703	53,962	6	863,707
Saskatchewan	2	2	4	135,901	19,729	—	—
Yukon–Northwest Territories	n.a.	n.a.	n.a.	n.a.		n.a.	n.a.
Total	33	72	64	2,988,552	2,458,136	25	3,151,930

RADIO AND TELEVISION, 1993

Province or territory	AM	FM	TV	Total
Newfoundland	22	18	4	44
Prince Edward Island	3	1	—	4
Nova Scotia	17	10	3	30
New Brunswick	15	14	3	32
Québec	65	64	13	142
Ontario	87	78	22	187
Manitoba	19	10	2	31
Saskatchewan	20	10	10	40
Alberta	49	20	11	80
British Columbia	63	41	8	112
Yukon Territory	1	1	0	2
Northwest Territories	4	5	1	10
Total	365	281	71	714

"HELLO MONTREAL! VANCOUVER IS SPEAKING"

Although Alexander Graham Bell was born in Scotland and died an American citizen, his life and the development of the telephone were closely associated with Canada. It was in his parents' home in Brantford, Ont., in 1874, that Bell first discussed his new invention with his father, and there in 1875 that he wrote the patent specifications for "The Electric Speaking Telephone."

On August 3, 1876, Bell tested his new invention at the Dominion Telegraph office in Mount Pleasant, Ont. In the first transmission between separate buildings, he heard his uncle recite Shakespeare's "To be, or not to be: . . ." One week later the first long-distance call was made—from Brantford to Paris, some 13 km away. Alexander Melville Bell, the inventor's father, offered a telephone service which, by November 1877, had four clients. The fifth was Prime Minister Alexander Mackenzie, whose application was predated to make him officially the first subscriber.

The Canadian telephone industry, including the Bell Telephone Company of Canada (now Bell Canada) and competing independents, took shape in the 1880s. Early development was sporadic. Rural customers in the early 1900s were even encouraged to erect their own telephone lines. But in 1916, the first Montréal to Vancouver telephone call was placed (partially on American lines) amid much pomp and ceremony. An enthusiastic Vancouver newspaper greeted the event with this headline: "Hello Montréal! Vancouver is speaking."

The privately financed TransCanada Telephone System, inaugurated in 1932, allowed voices to traverse the country for the first time without using American facilities. Today, calls are channeled by wire, cable, fibre optics, and through space. During the mid-1980s, Canadians made more than 34 billion telephone calls annually—roughly 1360 per capita.

THE PERFORMING ARTS

Theatre

British Columbia
Arts Club Theatre, Vancouver
Bastion Theatre Company, Victoria
Belfry Theatre, Victoria
Tamahnous Theatre, Vancouver
Vancouver Playhouse

Alberta
Citadel Theatre, Edmonton
Theatre Calgary

Saskatchewan
Globe Theatre, Regina
Persephone Theatre, Saskatoon
25th Street House Theatre, Saskatoon

Manitoba
Manitoba Theatre Centre, Winnipeg
Prairie Theatre Exchange, Winnipeg

Ontario
Canadian Stage Company, Toronto
Factory Theatre, Toronto
Grand Theatre, London
Great Canadian Theatre Company, Ottawa
Magnus Theatre North-West, Thunder Bay
National Arts Centre Theatre, Ottawa
O'Keefe Centre, Toronto
Pantages Theatre, Toronto
Princess of Wales, Toronto
Royal Alexandra Theatre, Toronto
St. Lawrence Centre, Toronto
Shaw Festival, Niagara-on-the-Lake
Stratford Festival, Stratford
Sudbury Theatre Centre, Sudbury
Tarragon Theatre, Toronto
Theatre Aquarius, Hamilton
Théâtre Passe Muraille, Toronto
Theatre Plus, Toronto
Toronto Free Theatre, Toronto
Toronto Truck Theatre, Toronto
Winter Garden/Elgin Theatres, Toronto
Young People's Theatre, Toronto

COMMUNICATIONS IN THE HOME, 1993

	Number of households	Percent of households
Television[1]	10,147,000	99
Color	10,015,000	97.7
Black & white	132,000	1.3
Radio (AM & FM)[2]	10,134,000	98.8
Telephone[3]	10,141,000	99
Cable television	7,414,000	72.4
VCR	7,925,000	77.3
Camcorders	1,269,000	12.4
Home computers	2,384,000	23.3
Total Canadian households	10,247,000	100.0

1 Some households have more than one television.
2 Includes households with one receiver or more.
3 Includes households with one telephone or more.

Québec
Centaur Theatre, Montréal
Compagnie Jean-Duceppe, Montréal
Piggery Theatre, North Hatley
Saidye Bronfman Centre Theatre, Montréal
Théâtre de Quat'Sous, Montréal
Théâtre du Nouveau Monde, Montréal
Théâtre du Rideau Vert, Montréal
Théâtre du Trident, Québec

New Brunswick
Theatre New Brunswick, Fredericton

Nova Scotia
Neptune Theatre, Halifax

Prince Edward Island
Charlottetown Festival

Ballet and dance

British Columbia
Ballet British Columbia

Alberta
Alberta Ballet

Manitoba
Royal Winnipeg Ballet

Ontario
Danny Grossman Dance Company, Toronto
Desrosiers Dance Theatre, Toronto
National Ballet of Canada, Toronto
Ottawa Ballet
Toronto Dance Theatre

Québec
Ballets Jazz de Montréal, Montréal
Danse-Partout, Quebec (modern dance)
Fondation de danse Margie Gillis, Montréal
Fondation Jean-Pierre Perreault, Montréal
Grands Ballets Canadiens, Montréal

Opera

British Columbia
Vancouver Opera Association

Alberta
Edmonton Opera Association
Calgary Opera Association

Manitoba
Manitoba Opera Association, Winnipeg

Ontario
Canadian Opera Company, Toronto
Opera Atelier, Toronto
Opera Hamilton
Oper Lyra, Toronto

LIBRARIES, 1993

Province or territory	Libraries reporting	Book stock	Circulation
Nfld.	32	1,263,121	1,951,127
P.E.I.	10	239,108	647,841
N.S.	95	1,777,342	5,409,343
N.B.	54	1,367,915	3,121,963
Qué.	456	12,264,583	29,700,685
Ont.	959	27,164,104	74,948,714
Man.	144	2,020,831	6,259,567
Sask.	113	2,615,667	9,637,117
Alta.	340	6,799,947	24,338,489
B.C.	236	8,852,810	27,039,989
Yukon	61	118,300	160,506
N.W.T.	21	138,000	147,036
CANADA	2471	64,621,728	183,362,377

Québec
Opéra de Montréal
Opéra de Québec

Orchestras

British Columbia
Civic Orchestra of Victoria
Prince George Symphony Orchestra
Vancouver Philharmonic Orchestra
Vancouver Symphony Orchestra
Victoria Symphony Orchestra

Alberta
Calgary Philharmonic Orchestra
Edmonton Symphony Orchestra

Saskatchewan
Regina Symphony
Saskatoon Symphony

Manitoba
Manitoba Chamber Orchestra, Winnipeg
Winnipeg Symphony Orchestra

Ontario
Fanshaw Community Orchestra, London
Hamilton Philharmonic Orchestra
Kitchener-Waterloo Symphony Orchestra
National Arts Centre Orchestra, Ottawa
National Youth Orchestra, Ottawa
Ottawa Symphony Orchestra
Peterborough Symphony Orchestra
Pro Arte Orchestra, Toronto
Sault Symphony Orchestra, Sault Ste. Marie
Tafelmusik Baroque Orchestra, Toronto
Thunder Bay Symphony Orchestra
Toronto Philharmonic Orchestra
Toronto Sinfonietta
Toronto Symphony

Québec
McGill Chamber Orchestra, Montréal
Montréal Symphony Orchestra
Orchestre metropolitain, Montréal
Orchestre symphonique de Québec

New Brunswick
Symphony New Brunswick, Saint John

Nova Scotia
Symphony Nova Scotia, Halifax

Prince Edward Island
Prince Edward Island Symphony Orchestra, Charlottetown

Newfoundland
Newfoundland Symphony Orchestra, St. John's

PERFORMING ARTS: Companies, attendance, and performances

	1984-85	1988-89	1990-91
Theatre			
Companies	146	202	226
Attendance	6,771,165	9,402.032	8,651,199
Performances	25,182	33,421	31,999
Music			
Companies	62	91	100
Attendance	2,455,318	3,420,589	3,070,439
Performances	2,568	3,319	4,046
Dance			
Companies	32	48	54
Attendance	1,180,761	1,428,994	1,311,435
Performances	1,803	2,164	2,028
Opera			
Companies	9	13	15
Attendance[1]	475,836	276,883	554,265
Performances[1]	571	269	616
Total			
Companies	249	354	395
Attendance	10,883,080	14,528,498	13,587,338
Performances	30,124	39,173	38,689

1 The 1988-89 figures are only for Ontario and Quebec

MAJOR MUSEUMS AND GALLERIES

National museums (Ottawa-Hull)

Canadian Museum of Civilization (Art and displays about our cultural heritage)

Canadian Museum of Contemporary Photography (Canadian photographs displayed as art or social documentation)

Canadian Museum of Nature (Exhibits relating to botany, geology, paleontology, and zoology)

Canadian War Museum (Objects and displays relating to Canada's military past)

Currency Museum (Exhibits about the history of Canadian currency)

National Aviation Museum (Exhibits of historic aircraft and other objects)

National Gallery of Canada (Canada's most extensive art collection)

National Museum of Science and Technology (Agriculture, astronomy, industrial technology, physics, and transportation)

Provincial museums

British Columbia
Art Gallery of Greater Victoria
British Columbia Provincial
   Museum, Victoria
Museum of Anthropology, Vancouver
Vancouver Art Gallery
Vancouver Museum

Alberta
Glenbow Museum, Calgary
Edmonton Art Gallery
Olympic Hall of Fame, Calgary
Provincial Museum of Alberta, Edmonton
Royal Tyrrell Museum, Drumheller

Saskatchewan
Dunlop Art Gallery, Regina
Mackenzie Art Gallery, Regina
Mendel Art Gallery, Saskatoon
Royal Saskatchewan Museum, Regina
Saskatchewan Museum of Natural History,
   Regina
Western Development Museum, Saskatoon

Manitoba
Eskimo Museum, Churchill
Manitoba Museum of Man and Nature,
   Winnipeg
Winnipeg Art Gallery

Ontario
Art Gallery of Hamilton
Art Gallery of Ontario, Toronto
McMichael Canadian Collection,
   Kleinburg
Ontario Science Centre, Toronto
Royal Ontario Museum, Toronto
Thunder Bay Art Gallery

Québec
Canadian Centre for Architecture,
   Montréal
McCord Museum, Montréal
Montréal Museum of Fine Arts, Montréal
Musée d'art contemporain, Montréal

Musée d'arts décoratifs, Montréal
Musée de la civilisation, Québec
Musée du Québec, Québec
Musée du séminaire, Québec
Pointe-à-Callière Museum of Archaeology
   and History, Montréal

New Brunswick
Acadian Historical Village, Caraquet
Beaverbrook Art Gallery, Fredericton
New Brunswick Museum, Saint John
Owens Art Gallery, Sackville.

Nova Scotia
Art Gallery of Nova Scotia, Halifax
Fisheries Museum of the Atlantic,
   Lunenberg
Maritime Museum of the Atlantic, Halifax
Nova Scotia Museum, Halifax

Prince Edward Island
Acadian Museum, Miscouche
Confederation Centre Art Gallery and
   Museum, Charlottetown

Newfoundland
Memorial University Art Gallery,
   St. John's
Newfoundland Museum, St. John's

Yukon and Northwest Territories
MacBride Museum, Whitehorse, Yukon
Northern Life Museum and National
   Exhibition Centre, Fort Smith, N.W.T.
Prince of Wales Northern Heritage
   Museum, Yellowknife, N.W.T.

HOW CANADIANS TRAVEL

The chart below shows how car travel declined in popularity with vacationing Canadians after 1966, only to revive in the mid-1980s. The decline in car vacations occurred with an expansion of the airline industry, which began to offer vacationers a wide range of inexpensive flights and more destinations in the late 1960s. But the faltering of the economy in the early 1980s and 1990s prompted many Canadians to vacation closer to home, using the family car. A number of other factors, such as increases in the cost of air travel and cuts in train services, have reinforced this trend.

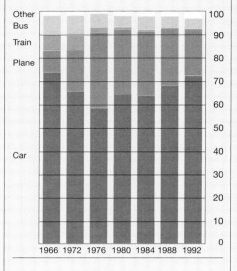

WHERE CANADIANS TRAVEL (thousands)[1]

Country/region	1980	1985	1989
United States	24,594	23,886	33,969
New York	3,623	3,700	5,299
Michigan	2,099	2,052	2,549
Washington	1,833	1,642	2,388
Florida	1,482	1,536	2,234
Vermont	1,273	1,189	1,506
Maine	1,098	974	1,333
Pennsylvania	873	867	1,331
California	826	763	1,047
Europe	1,591	2,578	2,764
United Kingdom	446	644	667
France	205	377	380
Germany	169	259	293
Netherlands	120	187	231
Switzerland	117	200	175
Italy	105	190	169
Caribbean	621	776	929
Dominican Republic	n.a.	n.a.	186
Bahamas	125	100	103
Jamaica	70	77	96
Cuba	33	60	68
Barbados	110	87	64
Bermuda	42	40	62
Mexico and Central America	236	290	514
Asia	159	274	382
Hong Kong	24	53	75
Japan	27	47	52
Australasia[2]	66	108	131
Africa	66	86	100
South America	56	108	204

[1] Includes visits which lasted less than a day.
[2] Includes islands in the Pacific and Indian oceans.
n.a.—not available.

WILBY'S 1912 CAR JOURNEY—ACROSS CANADA IN 52 DAYS

Completion of the Trans-Canada Highway in 1967 has made cross-country travel safe and enjoyable. It was more difficult in 1912, when Englishman Thomas Wilby attempted the journey. On August 27, the wheels of his spanking new Reo automobile were backed into the Atlantic Ocean near Halifax, and Wilby and his chauffeur F.V. Haney were off.

The trip was a series of mishaps and near-disasters. In Québec, the heavily packed Reo was unable to climb a steep, cobbled street. Haney calmly turned the car around and inched up the hill backwards. Near North Bay, a pair of horses were hitched to the car to pull it from a sandy ditch. Later, the roadless wilderness north of Lake Superior blocked their way. Wilby transported the car to Sudbury by rail, and across Lake Superior by boat.

The Prairies awed Wilby, who wrote, "It was grand and large . . . the real West at last!" In contrast to the flat Prairie tracks, the roads of British Columbia were winding, dangerous trails. While Wilby was driving along the Fraser River at night, the acetylene headlights of the car went out. A young hitchhiker had to lie on the hood of the car dangling an oil lamp to guide the way. Finally, 52 days from Halifax, the wheels of the Reo were edged close to the ocean near Port Alberni on Vancouver Island, and a flask of Atlantic water was emptied into the Pacific.

THE GREY CUP CHAMPIONSHIP GAMES, 1954-1994

1954	Nov. 27	Edmonton	26	Montreal	25	
1955	Nov. 26	Edmonton	34	Montreal	19	
1956	Nov. 24	Edmonton	50	Montreal	27	
1957	Nov. 30	Hamilton	32	Winnipeg	7	
1958	Nov. 29	Winnipeg	35	Hamilton	2	
1959	Nov. 28	Winnipeg	21	Hamilton	7	
1960	Nov. 26	Ottawa	16	Edmonton	6	
1961	Dec. 2	Winnipeg	21	Hamilton	14	
1962	Dec. 1-2	Winnipeg	28	Hamilton	27	
1963	Nov. 30	Hamilton	21	B.C.	10	
1964	Nov. 28	B.C.	34	Hamilton	24	
1965	Nov. 27	Hamilton	22	Winnipeg	16	
1966	Nov. 26	Saskatchewan	29	Ottawa	14	
1967	Dec. 2	Hamilton	24	Saskatchewan	1	
1968	Nov. 30	Ottawa	24	Calgary	21	
1969	Nov. 30	Ottawa	29	Saskatchewan	11	
1970	Nov. 28	Montreal	23	Calgary	10	
1971	Nov. 28	Calgary	14	Toronto	11	
1972	Dec. 3	Hamilton	13	Saskatchewan	10	
1973	Nov. 25	Ottawa	22	Edmonton	18	
1974	Nov. 24	Montreal	20	Edmonton	7	
1975	Nov. 23	Edmonton	9	Montreal	8	
1976	Nov. 28	Ottawa	23	Saskatchewan	6	
1977	Nov. 27	Montreal	41	Edmonton	6	
1978	Nov. 26	Edmonton	20	Montreal	13	
1979	Nov. 25	Edmonton	17	Montreal	9	
1980	Nov. 23	Edmonton	48	Hamilton	10	
1981	Nov. 22	Edmonton	26	Ottawa	23	
1982	Nov. 28	Edmonton	32	Toronto	16	
1983	Nov. 27	Toronto	18	B.C.	17	
1984	Nov. 18	Winnipeg	47	Hamilton	17	
1985	Nov. 24	B.C.	37	Hamilton	24	
1986	Nov. 30	Hamilton	39	Edmonton	15	
1987	Nov. 29	Edmonton	38	Toronto	36	
1988	Nov. 27	Winnipeg	22	B.C.	21	
1989	Nov. 26	Saskatchewan	43	Hamilton	40	
1990	Nov. 25	Winnipeg	50	Edmonton	11	
1991	Nov. 24	Toronto	36	Calgary	21	
1992	Nov. 29	Calgary	24	Winnipeg	10	
1993	Nov. 28	Edmonton	33	Winnipeg	23	
1994	Nov. 27	B.C.	26	Baltimore	23	

CANADIAN-BORN SPORTS

Canada's long sporting tradition has borrowed much from Indian and European games. Lacrosse, adopted as our national sport in 1867, evolved from the Indian game called *baggataway*. Contests between tribes involved as many as 400 players, lasted several days and resulted in broken limbs, even death. Settlers began to play a scaled-down, less violent version in the 1840s, and during the last half of the 19th century, it became Canada's most popular sport.

The first organized hockey game was probably played in 1855 at Kingston by members of a regiment of the Royal Canadian Rifles, although English troops had played a variation of the game, called shinny, as early as 1783. About 1880, McGill University students wrote the first official rules, which changed greatly through the years. A position called rover has been eliminated, for example, and forward passes were legalized in the early 1900s. In 1893, Governor General Lord Stanley presented a cup to Canada's top amateur team. Since 1912, the cup has been awarded to professionals, and since 1926, to the champions of the National Hockey League.

Canoeing and snowshoeing—practical means of transportation invented by native Indians—were turned into sports by early Canadians. Voyageurs took time out from the fur trade to run rapids and race for fun. An annual challenge match on Lake Winnipeg drew as many as 100 canoes to compete in contests that sometimes lasted 40 hours. In the 1870s, canoe clubs were founded in Montréal and Toronto; annual regattas featured singles, doubles and half-mile war canoe races. The sport was made an Olympic event in 1936.

The Montréal Snowshoe Club, founded in 1840, attracted hundreds to torchlight parades, snowball battles and treks to outlying villages. The standard garb was a tuque, blanket coat and sash; the top speed, 11 km an hour.

STANLEY CUP WINNERS
Prior to the formation of N.H.L. in 1917

Season	Champions	Coach
1892-93	Montreal A.A.A.	
1893-94	Montreal A.A.A.	
1894-95	Montreal Victorias	Mike Grant*
1895-96	Winnipeg Victorias (February) J. C. G.	Armytage
1895-96	Montreal Victorias (December, 1896)	Mike Grant*
1896-97	Montreal Victorias	Mike Grant*
1897-98	Montreal Victorias	F. Richardson
1898-99	Montreal Shamrocks	H. J. Trihey*
1899-1900	Montreal Shamrocks	H. J. Trihey*
1900-01	Winnipeg Victorias	D. H. Bain
1901-02	Montreal A.A.A.	C. McKerrow
1902-03	Ottawa Silver Seven	A. T. Smith
1903-04	Ottawa Silver Seven	A. T. Smith
1904-05	Ottawa Silver Seven	A. T. Smith
1905-06	Montreal Wanderers	Cecil Blachford*
1906-07	Kenora Thistles (January)	Tommy Phillips*
1906-07	Montreal Wanderers (March)	Cecil Blachford
1907-08	Montreal Wanderers	Cecil Blachford
1908-09	Ottawa Senators	Bruce Stuart*
1909-10	Montreal Wanderers	Pud Glass*
1910-11	Ottawa Senators	Bruce Stuart*
1911-12	Quebec Bulldogs	C. Nolan
**1912-13	Quebec Bulldogs	Joe Malone*
1913-14	Toronto Blueshirts	Scotty Davidson*
1914-15	Vancouver Millionaires	Frank Patrick
1915-16	Montreal Canadiens	George Kennedy
1916-17	Seattle Metropolitans	Pete Muldoon

* In the early years the teams were frequently run by the Captain.
** Victoria defeated Québec in challenge series. No official recognition.

STANLEY CUP WINNERS

Season	Champions	Coach
1917-18	Toronto Arenas	Dick Carroll
1918-19	No decision	
1919-20	Ottawa Senators	Pete Green
1920-21	Ottawa Senators	Pete Green
1921-22	Toronto St. Pats	Eddie Powers
1922-23	Ottawa Senators	Pete Green
1923-24	Montreal Canadiens	Leo Dandurand
1924-25	Victoria Cougars	Lester Patrick
1925-26	Montreal Maroons	Eddie Gerard
1926-27	Ottawa Senators	Dave Gill
1927-28	New York Rangers	Lester Patrick
1928-29	Boston Bruins	Cy Denneny
1929-30	Montreal Canadiens	Cecil Hart
1930-31	Montreal Canadiens	Cecil Hart
1931-32	Toronto Maple Leafs	Dick Irvin
1932-33	New York Rangers	Lester Patrick
1933-34	Chicago Black Hawks	Tommy Gorman
1934-35	Montreal Maroons	Tommy Gorman
1935-36	Detroit Red Wings	Jack Adams
1936-37	Detroit Red Wings	Jack Adams
1937-38	Chicago Black Hawks	Bill Stewart
1938-39	Boston Bruins	Art Ross
1939-40	New York Rangers	Frank Boucher
1940-41	Boston Bruins	Cooney Weiland
1941-42	Toronto Maple Leafs	Hap Day
1942-43	Detroit Red Wings	Jack Adams
1943-44	Montreal Canadiens	Dick Irvin
1944-45	Toronto Maple Leafs	Hap Day
1945-46	Montreal Canadiens	Dick Irvin
1946-47	Toronto Maple Leafs	Hap Day
1947-48	Toronto Maple Leafs	Hap Day
1948-49	Toronto Maple Leafs	Hap Day
1949-50	Detroit Red Wings	Tommy Ivan
1950-51	Toronto Maple Leafs	Joe Primeau
1951-52	Detroit Red Wings	Tommy Ivan
1952-53	Montreal Canadiens	Dick Irvin
1953-54	Detroit Red Wings	Tommy Ivan
1954-55	Detroit Red Wings	Jimmy Skinner
1955-56	Montreal Canadiens	Toe Blake
1956-57	Montreal Canadiens	Toe Blake
1957-58	Montreal Canadiens	Toe Blake
1958-59	Montreal Canadiens	Toe Blake
1959-60	Montreal Canadiens	Toe Blake
1960-61	Chicago Black Hawks	Rudy Pilous
1961-62	Toronto Maple Leafs	Punch Imlach
1962-63	Toronto Maple Leafs	Punch Imlach
1963-64	Toronto Maple Leafs	Punch Imlach
1964-65	Montreal Canadiens	Toe Blake
1965-66	Montreal Canadiens	Toe Blake
1966-67	Toronto Maple Leafs	Punch Imlach
1967-68	Montreal Canadiens	Toe Blake
1968-69	Montreal Canadiens	Claude Ruel
1969-70	Boston Bruins	Harry Sinden
1970-71	Montreal Canadiens	Al MacNeil
1971-72	Boston Bruins	Tom Johnson
1972-73	Montreal Canadiens	Scotty Bowman
1973-74	Philadelphia Flyers	Fred Shero

CANADIAN OLYMPIC GOLD MEDALISTS

SUMMER GAMES

Athens 1896
No Canadian representation

Paris 1900
3000 m steeplechase,
George Orton (for the USA)

St. Louis 1904
56-lb weight,
Etienne Desmarteau

Football, Galt Football Club
Golf, George S. Lyon
Lacrosse, Winnipeg Shamrocks

London 1908
200 m, Robert Kerr

Shooting, clay pigeon,
W.H. Ewing Lacrosse,
Canadian team

Stockholm 1912
10,000-m walk,
George Goulding

Swimming, 400 m,
George Ritchie Hodgson

Swimming, 1500 m,
George Ritchie Hodgson

Antwerp 1920
110-m hurdles,
Earl Thompson

Boxing, welterweight,
Albert Schneider

Paris 1924
No gold medal winner

Amsterdam 1928
100 m, Percy Williams

200 m, Percy Williams

400-m relay, women,
Canadian team

High jump, women,
Ethel Catherwood

Los Angeles 1932
High jump,
Duncan McNaughton

Boxing, bantamweight,
Horace Gwynne

Berlin 1936
Canoeing, Canadian
singles, Francis Amyot

London 1948
No gold medal winner

Helsinki 1952
Shooting, clay pigeon,
George Patrick Généreux

Stockholm-Melbourne 1956
Rowing, coxswainless fours,
University of British Columbia

Shooting, small-bore rifle,
Gerard Ouellette

Rome 1960
No gold medal winner

Tokyo 1964
Rowing, coxswainless pairs,
George Hungerford,
Roger Charles Jackson

Mexico 1968
Equestrian, prix des nations
jumping event,
James Day, Jim Elder,
Tom Gayford

Munich 1972
No gold medal winner

Montréal 1976
No gold medal winner

Moscow 1980
No Canadian representation

Los Angeles 1984
Swimming, men's 200 m
individual medley,
Alex Baumann

Swimming, men's 400 m
individual medley,
Alex Baumann

Women's springboard diving,
Sylvie Bernier

Canoeing, Canadian singles 500 m,
Larry Cain

Swimming, 200-m breaststroke,
Victor Davis

Canoeing, kayak pairs 1000 m,
Hugh Fisher,
Alwyn Morris

Rhythmic Gymnastics, all around,
Lori Fung

Women's 200-m breaststroke,
Anne Offenbrite

Women's sport pistol,
Linda Thom

Eight-oared shell
with coxswain,
National team

Seoul 1988
Boxing, super heavyweight,
Lennox Lewis

Synchronized swimming, solo,
Carolyn Waldo

Synchronized swimming, duet,
Carolyn Waldo,
Michelle Cameron

Barcelona 1992
Rowing, women's pairs,
Marnie McBean,
Kathleen Heddle

Track, men's 110-m hurdles,
Mark McKoy

Swimming, men's 100-m
backstroke,
Mark Tewksbury

Rowing, women's fours,
Kirsten Barnes,
Brenda Taylor,
Jessica Monroe,
Kay Worthington

Rowing, men's eights,
John Wallace,
Bruce Robertson,
Michael Forgeron,
Darren Barber,
Robert Marland,
Michael Rascher,
Andy Crosby,
Derek Porter,
Terry Paul

Rowing, women's eights,
Kirsten Barnes,
Brenda Taylor,
Megan Delehanty,
Shannon Crawford,
Marnie McBean,
Kay Worthington,
Jessica Monroe,
Kathleen Heddle,
Lesley Thompson

Synchronized
swimming solo,
Sylvie Fréchette

WINTER GAMES

Antwerp 1920
Ice hockey
Winnipeg Falcons

Chamonix 1924
(First Official Winter Games)
Ice hockey,
Toronto Granites

Saint-Moritz 1928
Ice hockey,
University of Toronto Grads

Lake Placid 1932
Figure skating, men,
Montgomery Wilson

Speed skating, women, 500 m,
Jean Wilson

Ice hockey,
Winnipeg Monarchs

Garmisch-Partenkirchen 1936
No gold medal winner

Saint-Moritz 1948
Figure skating, women,
Barbara Ann Scott

Ice hockey,
R.C.A.F. Flyers

Oslo 1952
Ice hockey,
Edmonton Mercurys

Cortina D'Ampezzo 1956
No gold medal winner

Squaw Valley 1960
Skiing, slalom, women
Anne Heggveit

Figure skating, pairs,
Barbara Wagner,
Bob Paul

Innsbruck 1964
Bobsled, four-man,
Canadian team

Grenoble 1968
Skiing, giant slalom, women,
Nancy Greene

Sapporo 1972
No gold medal winner

Innsbruck 1976
Skiing, giant slalom,
women,
Kathy Kreiner

Lake Placid 1980
No gold medal winner

Sarajevo 1984
Speed skating, men's 1000 m,
Gaétan Boucher

Speed skating, men's 1500 m,
Gaétan Boucher

Calgary 1988
No gold medal winner

Albertville 1992
Alpine skiing, women's downhill,
Kerrin Lee Gartner

Speed skating, women's
short track relay,
Sylvie Daigle,
Nathalie Lambert,
Annie Perreault,
Angela Cutrone

Freestyle Skiing, men's aerials (demo)
Philippe Laroche

Lillehammer 1994
Biathlon, women's 7.5 km,
Myriam Bédard

Biathlon, women's 15 km,
Myriam Bédard

Freestyle skiing, men's moguls,
Jean-Luc Brassard

Season	Champions	Coach	Season	Champions	Coach
1974-75	Philadelphia Flyers	Fred Shero	1984-85	Edmonton Oilers	Glen Sather
1975-76	Montreal Canadiens	Scotty Bowman	1985-86	Montreal Canadiens	Jean Perron
1976-77	Montreal Canadiens	Scotty Bowman	1986-87	Edmonton Oilers	Glen Sather
1977-78	Montreal Canadiens	Scotty Bowman	1987-88	Edmonton Oilers	Glen Sather
1978-79	Montreal Canadiens	Scotty Bowman	1988-89	Calgary Flames	Terry Crisp
1979-80	New York Islanders	Al Arbour	1989-90	Edmonton Oilers	John Muckler
1980-81	New York Islanders	Al Arbour	1990-91	Pittsburgh Penguins	Bob Johnson
1981-82	New York Islanders	Al Arbour	1991-92	Pittsburgh Penguins	Scotty Bowman
1982-83	New York Islanders	Al Arbour	1992-93	Montreal Canadiens	Jacques Demers
1983-84	Edmonton Oilers	Glen Sather	1993-94	New York Rangers	Mike Keenan

Economy and Industry

SELECTED ECONOMIC INDICATORS, 1986-1993

	1986 ($'000)	1987 ($'000)	1988 ($'000)	1989 ($'000)	1990 ($'000)	1991 ($'000)	1992 ($'000)	1993 ($'000)
Gross domestic product	505,666	551,597	605,906	650,748	670,952	675,928	688,541	711,658
Personal disposable income	338,093	361,435	394,235	432,135	453,615	466,013	476,920	487,651
Retail sales	153,786	168,894	181,652	189,302	192,558	181,208	185,049	193,815
Manufacturing shipments	253,343	272,037	297,693	308,987	299,195	280,968	280,479	309,852
Mineral production	n.a.	n.a.	36,955	39,333	40,778	35,204	35,411	n.a.

Other selected statistics								
Employment (thousands)	11,531	11,861	12,245	12,486	12,572	12,340	12,240	12,383
Unemployment rate (percent)	9.5	8.8	7.8	7.5	8.1	10.3	11.3	11.2
Personal savings rate (percent)	10.5	9.1	9.5	10.2	9.7	10.1	10.6	9.2
Consumer price index (1986 = 100 percent)	100	104.4	108.6	114.0	119.5	126.2	128.1	130.4
Housing starts	197,000	245,000	222,562	215,382	181,630	156,197	168,271	156,000

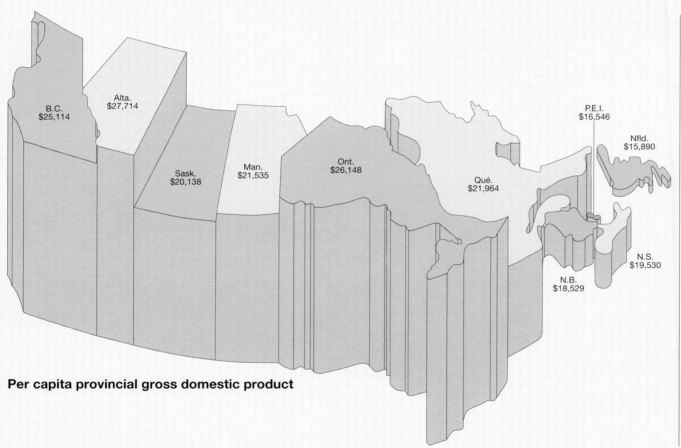

Per capita provincial gross domestic product

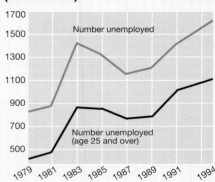

Unemployment, 1979-1994 (thousands)

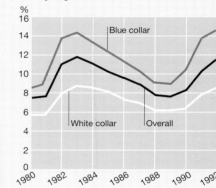

Unemployment rate 1980-1992

PROVINCIAL GROSS DOMESTIC PRODUCT, 1992

Province or territory	Provincial GDP (million dollars)	Population (thousands)	Per capita GDP (dollars)
Newfoundland	9,232	581	15,890
Prince Edward Island	2,151	130	16,546
Nova Scotia	17,987	921	19,530
New Brunswick	13,878	749	18,529
Québec	157,065	7151	21,964
Ontario	277,454	10,611	26,148
Manitoba	23,969	1113	21,535
Saskatchewan	20,239	1005	20,138
Alberta	72,942	2632	27,714
British Columbia	86,669	3451	25,114
Yukon and Northwest Territories	3,125	92	33,965
Total GDP	684,711	Total 27,296	Average GDP $22,461

LABOR FORCE, 1994 (thousands)

Province or territory	Labor force	Employed	Unemployed	Unemployment rate	Participation rate
Newfoundland	216	170	46	21.5	48.6
Prince Edward Island	63	49	14	22.7	63.0
Nova Scotia	406	342	64	15.8	57.7
New Brunswick	307	265	42	13.8	54.2
Québec	3343	2873	470	14.1	60.7
Ontario	5248	4649	599	11.4	64.9
Manitoba	533	472	61	11.5	65.6
Saskatchewan	464	423	41	8.9	64.6
Alberta	1368	1231	137	10.0	70.2
British Columbia	1742	1547	195	11.2	65.1
CANADA	13,691	12,020	1671	12.2	63.5

LABOR FORCE—OCCUPATION GROUPS, 1991

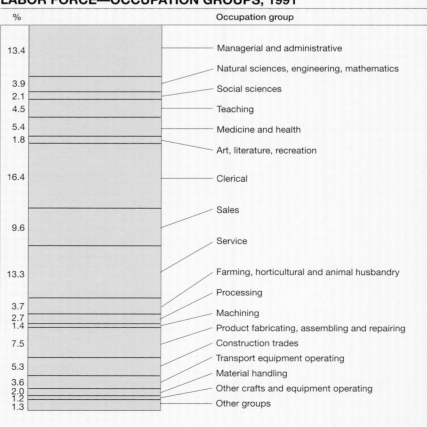

%	Occupation group
13.4	Managerial and administrative
	Natural sciences, engineering, mathematics
3.9	Social sciences
2.1	Teaching
4.5	Medicine and health
5.4	Art, literature, recreation
1.8	
16.4	Clerical
	Sales
9.6	Service
13.3	Farming, horticultural and animal husbandry
	Processing
3.7	Machining
2.7	Product fabricating, assembling and repairing
1.4	Construction trades
7.5	Transport equipment operating
5.3	Material handling
3.6	Other crafts and equipment operating
2.0	Other groups
1.2	
1.3	

MEN AND WOMEN IN CANADA'S LABOR FORCE

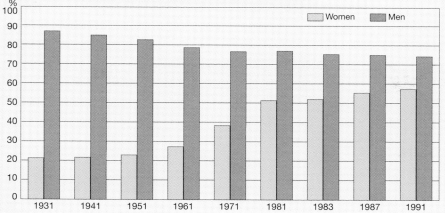

LABOR FORCE—EDUCATIONAL ATTAINMENT, 1991

Percentages by level of schooling

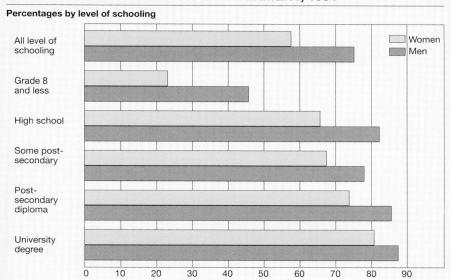

FEDERAL GOVERNMENT REVENUE SOURCES

	1970-71 %	1990-91 %
Other	7.5	8.5
Sales of goods and services	3.9	4.0
Return on investment	7.2	7.5
Health, social service levies	5.3	8.0
Property tax	11.8	8.4
Consumption taxes	23.8	20.3
Corporate income tax	10.5	6.7
Personal income tax	29.9	36.6

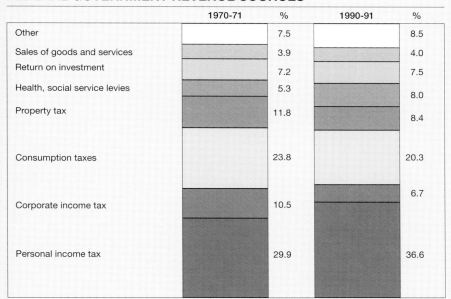

FEDERAL GOVERNMENT EXPENDITURES

	1970-71 %	1990-91 %
Other	8.2	10.1
Debt charges	10.4	20.3
Protection of people and property	9.6	7.6
Education	19.0	11.9
Resource conservation, industrial development	4.9	4.1
Transportation, communications	8.8	4.9
Health	13.4	13.4
Social services	18.6	21.7
General services	7.1	6.0

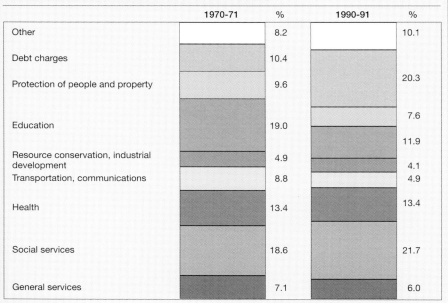

INFLATION RATES, 1915-1990

EXCHANGE RATE, 1984-1994

Value of the Canadian dollar in US currency

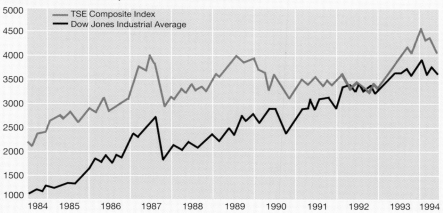

STOCK MARKETS, June 1984-June 1994

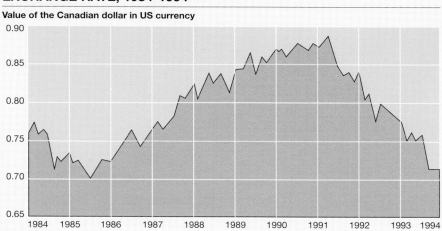

CONSUMER INCOME AND SPENDING (billion dollars)

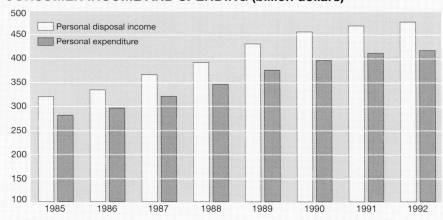

HOUSING STARTS IN URBAN CENTRES, 1982-1992 (thousands)

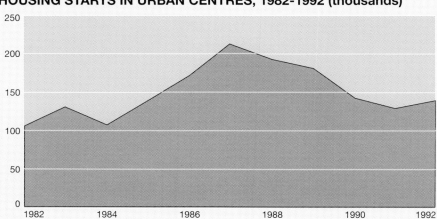

AVERAGE WEEKLY EARNINGS, 1981-1991

Source and region	Average weekly earnings (dollars)				
	1981	1986	1989	1990	1991
Industry:					
Forestry	452.87	564.61	628.91	646.73	685.84
Mining and milling	534.35	711.05	819.69	863.13	908.78
Manufacturing	383.75	504.04	572.85	601.72	627.24
Durables	408.72	536.50	594.45	626.71	652.57
Nondurables	360.23	474.21	546.73	572.64	598.94
Construction	521.31	510.40	594.71	627.24	639.03
Transportation, communications and other utilities	427.47	558.80	623.67	646.13	684.34
Trade	262.56	317.50	359.80	375.17	391.19
Finance, insurance and real estate	353.71	452.59	540.89	542.15	562.82
Service	234.86	364.54	406.42	431.67	459.52
Province or territory:					
Newfoundland	328.08	408.11	523.46	537.48	577.33
Prince Edward Island	250.83	348.31	424.44	436.09	447.45
Nova Scotia	296.35	390.31	487.94	509.55	533.48
New Brunswick	313.37	399.93	508.98	524.24	545.88
Québec	351.57	420.25	548.00	579.79	605.82
Ontario	347.92	439.79	592.34	625.47	657.93
Manitoba	314.42	402.16	338.00	560.11	570.56
Saskatchewan	336.76	402.15	484.53	523.22	546.33
Alberta	390.40	444.90	563.16	589.51	611.94
British Columbia	407.03	449.88	590.22	617.19	636.28
Yukon	—	—	566.36	590.67	645.88
Northwest Territories	—	—	603.72	605.09	642.88

CANADA'S LARGEST COMPANIES, 1993

Company (head office)	Sales or operating revenue (million dollars)	Foreign ownership (%)
BCE Inc. (Montréal)	20,784	—
General Motors of Canada Ltd. (Oshawa, Ont.)	18,347	100
Ford Motor Co. of Canada (Oakville, Ont.)	14,443	96
George Weston Ltd. (Toronto)	11,599	
Chrysler Canada Ltd. (Windsor, Ont.)	9,453	100
Alcan Aluminium Ltd. (Montréal)	9,183	31
Canadian Pacific Ltd. (Montréal)	8,963	
Noranda Inc. (Toronto)	8,538	
Imasco Ltd. (Montréal)	7,989	42
Imperial Oil Ltd. (Toronto)	7,968	73
Ontario Hydro (Toronto)	7,768	
Seagram Co. (Montréal)	7,431	
Thomson Corp. (Toronto)	7,229	
Hydro-Québec (Montréal)	6,807	
IBM Canada Ltd. (Markham)	6,760	100
Univa Inc. (Montréal)	6,701	
Power Corp. of Canada (Montréal)	6,181	
Brascan Ltd. (Toronto)	5,951	
Hudson's Bay Co. (Toronto)	5,152	
Oshawa Group Ltd. (Islington, Ont.)	5,011	
Petro-Canada (Calgary)	4,551	
Shell Canada Ltd. (Calgary)	4,492	78
Bombardier Inc. (Montréal)	4,448	
Canada Safeway Ltd. (Calgary)	4,357	100
Canadian National Railway Co. (Montréal)	4,051	

CANADA'S LARGEST UNIONS, 1993

Union	Members
Canadian Union of Public Employees	412,242
National Union of Public and General Employees	307,592
Public Service Alliance of Canada	171,091
United Food and Commercial Workers' International Union	170,000
National Automobile, Aerospace and Agricultural Implement Workers Union of Canada	170,000
United Steel Workers of America	161,232
Communications, Energy and Paperworkers Union of Canada	143,000
International Brotherhood of Teamsters, Chauffeurs, Warehousemen and Helpers of America	95,000
Fédération des affaires sociales inc.	94,675
Fédération des enseignantes et enseignants des commissions scolaires	75,000
Service Employees International Union	75,000

INTERNATIONAL TRADE

The value of Canadian exports is sightly less than 25 percent of the country's gross domestic product. Our dependence on imports is great, too. The Canadian climate is unsuitable for the production of a wide range of everyday items and foodstuffs such as sugar, coffee, vegetables and tropical fruits. To maintain our high material standard of living requires an immense influx of imports of finished products, ranging from computer equipment to paperback books.

Imports, 1993 (million dollars)

Live animals	174.0
Food, feed, beverages, tobacco	10,084.3
Inedible crude materials Including iron ores, crude petroleum, natural gas, coal, aluminium ores, etc.	8715.4
Inedible fabricated materials Including wood and paper, textiles, chemicals, iron, steel and nonferrous metals	31,595.0
Inedible end products Including industrial machinery, agricultural machinery, transportation equipment, etc.	114,167.1
Special transactions Including unclassifiable imports, shipments of less than $500 each, and goods returned within 5 years	4325.0
Total imports	169,316.1

Exports, 1993 (million dollars)

Live animals	1382.1
Food, feed, beverages, tobacco	12,608.7
Inedible crude materials, including iron ores, crude petroleum, natural gas, coal, aluminium ores, etc.	20,495.7
Inedible fabricated materials, including wood and paper, chemicals, iron, steel and nonferrous metals	53,835.0
Inedible end products, including industrial machinery, agricultural machinery, transportation equipment, etc.	89,321.2
Special transactions, including settlers' effects, private donations and gifts, exports for exhibit or competition, exports to Canadian diplomats and forces	3864.3
Total exports	181,026.3

PERSONAL EXPENDITURE, 1982-1991 (per person)

Goods and services	(Million dollars)				
	1982	1984	1986	1989	1991
Food, beverages and tobacco	39,924	44,478	50,420	59,265	64,725
Clothing and footwear	13,230	15,225	17,982	21,116	21,345
Gross rent, fuel and power	47,323	56.056	64,230	83,087	95,774
Furniture, furnishings, household equipment and operation	19,278	22,877	27,484	34,508	34,825
Medical care and health service	7985	10,314	14,425	15,905	17,213
Transportation and communication	30,524	37,757	45,602	57,707	58,239
Recreation, entertainment, education and cultural services	21,667	26,235	31,926	41,973	44,058
Personal goods and services	31,910	37,439	46,622	62,360	68,219
Other	627	1,263	1819	3,012	27,360
Total	212,468	251,645	296,810	378,933	410,413

CANADIAN BANKS, 1994

	Nfld.	P.E.I.	N.S.	N.B.	Qué.	Ont.	Man.	Sask.	Alta.	B.C.	Yukon	N.W.T.	Can. Total	Outside Can.	Total
Bank of Montreal	← 88 →				205	478	← 114 →		124	151	n.a.	n.a.	1160	—	1160
Banque Nationale du Canada	1	2	4	28	484	97	4	2	2	1	—	—	625	—	625
Bank of Nova Scotia (1993)	62	9	75	54	97	474	35	51	117	112	1	1	1088	—	1088
Canadian Imperial Bank of Commerce	16	8	39	23	175	658	80	89	163	190	11	6	1458	—	1458
Royal Bank of Canada	20	5	75	29	223	521	86	94	134	← 164 →		n.a.	1351	96	1447
Toronto Dominion Bank	8	4	20	17	89	593	57	45	117	116	1	1	1068	—	1068
Canadian Western Bank	—	—	—	—	—	1	2	5	5	—	—	13	—	13	—
Laurentian Bank of Canada	—	—	1	—	175	68	—	—	1	2	—	—	247	1	248
Total													6984		7094

TYPE OF DWELLING—BY PROVINCE AND CITY, 1991

Province or territory	Total private dwellings	Single detached	Apartments	Single detached %	Apartments %
Newfoundland	174,495	133,130	810	76.3	0.5
Prince Edward Island	44,475	32,475	35	73.0	0.1
Nova Scotia	324,375	219,630	12,095	67.7	3.7
New Brunswick	253,710	181,650	3600	71.6	1.4
Québec	2,634,300	1,175,086	137,105	44.6	5.2
Ontario	3,638,365	2,094,970	595,385	57.6	16.4
Manitoba	405,120	275,915	35,675	68.1	8.8
Saskatchewan	363,150	275,935	10,085	76.0	2.8
Alberta	910,390	569,430	45,635	62.5	5.0
British Columbia	1,243,895	728,745	69,060	58.6	5.6
Yukon Territory	9915	5970	5	60.2	0.1
Northwest Territories	16,075	9980	520	62.1	3.2
CANADA	10,018,265	5,702,915	910,015	56.9	9.1

Metropolitan area					
Calgary, Alta.	277,290	157,565	21,960	56.7	7.9
Chicoutimi/Jonquière, Qué.	57,250	27,600	765	48.2	1.3
Edmonton, Alta.	307,960	175,620	21,460	57.0	7.0
Halifax, N.S.	119,795	57,800	11,765	48.2	9.8
Hamilton, Ont.	222,135	132,275	39,780	59.5	17.9
Kitchener, Ont.	129,305	70,295	13,485	54.4	10.4
London, Ont.	149,265	80,495	25,470	54.3	17.2
Montréal, Qué.	1,244,485	368,150	109,965	29.6	8.8
Oshawa, Ont.	83,255	53,225	7695	63.9	9.2
Ottawa-Hull, Ont., Qué.	353,070	154,110	62,660	43.6	17.7
Québec, Qué.	255,675	105,585	14,545	41.3	5.7
Regina, Sask.	72,110	50,100	3635	69.5	5.0
Saint John, N.B.	45,520	24,710	1830	54.3	4.0
St. Catharines, Ont.	138,890	95,290	8630	68.6	6.2
St John's, Nfld.	55,915	32,450	645	58.0	1.2
Saskatoon, Sask.	40,020	49,805	4490	62.2	5.6
Sudbury, Ont.	57,460	20,840	4100	36.0	7.0
Thunder Bay, Ont.	47,155	31,985	2520	67.8	5.3
Toronto, Ont.	1,374,930	607,445	386,130	44.1	28.0
Vancouver, B.C.	613,995	302,135	58,985	49.2	9.6
Victoria, B.C.	120,365	64,585	5755	53.7	4.8
Windsor, Ont.	97,940	66,325	10,945	67.7	11.1
Winnipeg, Man.	253,560	183,025	33,680	60.4	13.3

AGRICULTURE: Farm cash receipts, 1991 (million dollars)

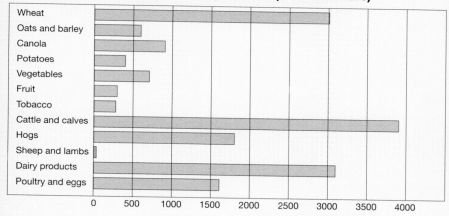

AGRICULTURE: Percentage of farms by product

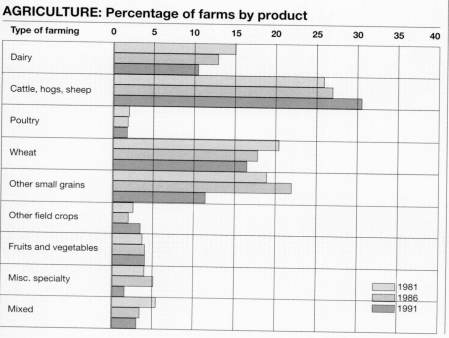

HOUSING TYPES, 1981-1991 (thousands of units)

Type		1981	1986	1991
Total occupied private dwellings	No.	8026	9331	10,018
	%	100.0	100.0	100.0
Single detached	No.	4711.3	5234.7	5710.3
	%	58.7	56.1	57.0
Single attached	No.	698.3	811.8	851.5
	%	8.7	8.7	8.5
Apartment and duplex	No.	2632.5	3060.6	3245.8
	%	32.8	32.8	32.4
Mobile	No.	n.a.	223.9	210.4
	%	n.a.	2.4	2.1
Tenure Owned	No.	5104.5	5841.2	6341.4
	%	63.6	62.6	63.3
Rented	No.	2921.5	3489.8	3676.6
	%	36.4	37.4	36.7

HOUSEHOLDS WITH SELECTED FACILITIES, 1953-1993

Year	Refrig- erators %	Home freezers %	Washing machines %	Clothes dryers %	Dish- washers %	Sewing machines %	Vacuum cleaners %	Air condi- tioners %
1953	66.3	2.2	—	—	—	23.4	48.0	—
1961	92.0	13.1	14.2	14.7	1.5	44.8	69.0	1.7
1965	95.8	22.6	23.1	27.4	2.7	52.4	74.9	2.2
1971	98.2	34.0	39.4	43.1	8.6	64.3	82.8	5.3
1975	99.3	41.8	52.1	51.6	15.2	65.4	86.5	12.4
1978	99.4	47.2	59.1	56.0	23.8	—	—	15.3
1981	99.4	52.8	76.7	63.9	31.3	—	—	5.7
1986	99.3	57.7	76.4	68.6	37.9	—	—	18.1
1993	99.8	58.7	79.2	75.1	45.2	—	—	25.7

FISHERIES: Catches and value, 1986-1989

Region and type	1986 Nominal catches (tonnes)	Marketed value (thousand $)	1989 Nominal catches (tonnes)	Marketed value (thousand $)
BY REGION				
Atlantic Coast	1,244,957	880,145	497,515	1,284,036
Pacific Coast	225,738	401,959	272,305	416,294
Freshwater Fisheries	45,507	76,826	51,198	82,690
CANADA	1,516,202	1,358,930	816,018	1,783,020
BY PROVINCE—SEA FISHERIES				
Nova Scotia	450,720	422,738	475,998	524,194
New Brunswick	143,033	88,167	152,526	119,004
Prince Edward Island	45,802	62,154	42,812	68,312
Québec	91,190	100,163	97,161	126,195
Newfoundland	515,464	209,603	499,086	292,697
Atlantic	1,246,209	882,825	1,267,583	1,130,402
British Columbia	225,738	401,959	251,336	422,296
Sea fisheries	1,471,947	1,284,784	1,518,919	1,552,698
BY PROVINCE—FRESHWATER FISHERIES				
Ontario	25,180	46,317	27,757	48,340
Manitoba	12,143	20,564	11,997	25,415
Saskatchewan	3789	3968	3835	5385
Alberta	1613	1891	1887	2330
Yukon and Northwest Territories	1530	1406	1513	2258
Freshwater fisheries	44,255	74,146	46,989	83,728

MINING: Value of production, 1980-1991 (billion dollars)

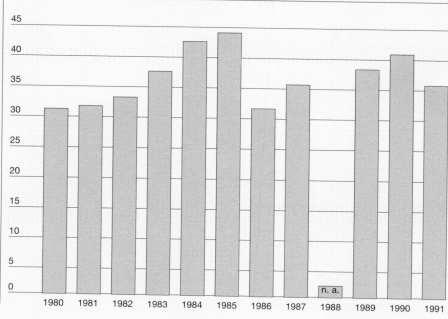

CANADA'S FOREST AREA (square kilometres)
National total: 4,364,000 km²

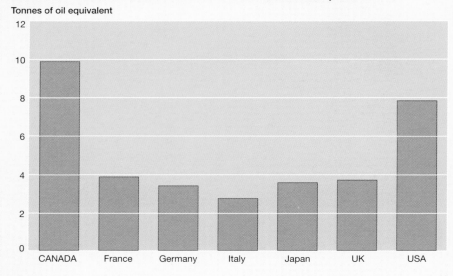

PROVINCIAL FOREST AREA
National total: 44 percent

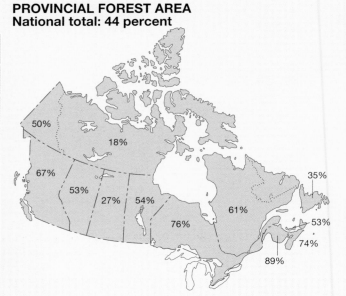

FORESTRY:
Volume of wood, 1991 (million m³)

Province or territory	Soft-woods	Hard-woods	Total
Newfoundland	487	38	525
Prince Edward Island	16	10	26
Nova Scotia	150	94	244
New Brunswick	362	209	571
Québec	3020	1204	4225
Ontario	2205	1325	3529
Manitoba	444	236	680
Saskatchewan	536	370	905
Alberta	1684	972	2656
British Columbia	8180	688	8867
Yukon	436	44	480
Northwest Territories	315	131	446
CANADA	17,834	5320	23,154

ENERGY CONSUMPTION BY THE G7 COUNTRIES, 1990
Tonnes of oil equivalent

PRIMARY ENERGY PRODUCTION BY FUEL, 1973-2010
Petajoules

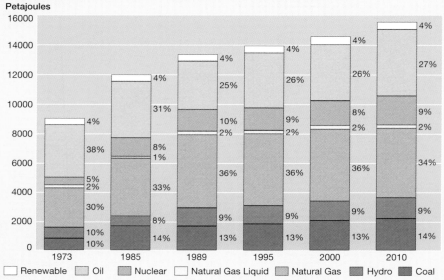

☐ Renewable ☐ Oil ☐ Nuclear ☐ Natural Gas Liquid ☐ Natural Gas ☐ Hydro ☐ Coal

DOMESTIC DEMAND FOR PRIMARY ENERGY BY FUEL, 1973-2010
Petajoules

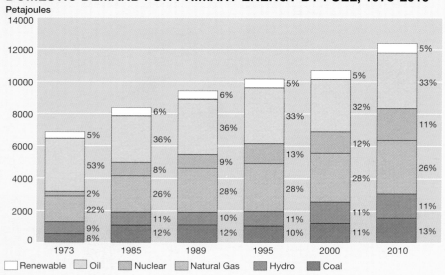

☐ Renewable ☐ Oil ☐ Nuclear ☐ Natural Gas ☐ Hydro ☐ Coal

VESSELS AND TONNAGE AT SPECIFIC PORTS, 1987-1991

PORT	Number vessel arrivals 1987	1991	Cargo handled ('000 tonnes) 1987	1991
St. John's	1027	875	866	947
Halifax	2054	2054	15,791	14,892
Saint John	1618	1472	13,043	17,094
Belledune	47	34	425	329
Sept-Iles	609	640	19,343	21,919
Saguenay	n.a.	112	n.a.	513
Baie de Ha! Ha!	198	193	3287	4133
Québec	1416	1099	18,320	18,536
Trois-Rivières	348	270	2209	1397
Montréal	2616	2247	21,867	17,470
Prescott	25	31	349	472
Port Colborne	n.a.	2	93	21
Churchill	71	44	597	265
Vancouver	10,399	9,614	63,957	70,714
Prince Rupert	1613	1597	13,405	13,256
Total	22,041	20,284	173,552	181,958

CANADIAN AIR CARRIERS, 1955-1991

	Passengers ('000)	Passenger kilometres ('000 000)	Cargo kilograms ('000)	Hours flown ('000)
1955	2763	1983	105,163	623
1960	4830	4507	95,401	879
1965	6832	8729	128,618	1128
1970	12,031	18,605	256,420	1669
1975	20,493	31,539	362,711	2466
1980	28,554	46,996	399,418	3091
1985	29,056	49,580	498,706	2273
1990	36,813	66,791	654,483	2267
1991	32,302	57,873	639,778	2083

LENGTH OF RAILWAY TRACK OPERATED[1], 1986-1990 (kilometres)

	1986	1989	1990
Class I			
Canadian National	50 708	47 242	46 205
Canadian Pacific	33 458	31 720	30 367
Sub-total	84 166	78 963	76 572
Classes II and III	9 378	10 141	10 308
Total	93 544	89 104	86 880

[1] As of December 31st.

REGISTERED MOTOR VEHICLES, 1984-1990

	1984	1985	1986	1989	1990
Newfoundland	236,454	257,693	273,192	301,152	305,851
Prince Edward Island	73,802	76,126	78,619	88,377	84,716
Nova Scotia	508,859	529,267	505,116	566,902	603,615
New Brunswick	403,637	416,805	426,482	455,252	475,671
Québec	2,921,223	2,974,099	3,145,116	3,527,732	3,580,765
Ontario	4,941,245	5,179,918	5,367,277	5,943,747	6,000,322
Manitoba	705,902	739,488	758,947	775,267	779,069
Saskatchewan	699,050	697,160	669,256	736,638	735,964
Alberta	1,745,162	1,729,287	1,739,472	1,850,771	1,861,662
British Columbia	2,129,427	2,175,032	2,222,717	2,420,890	2,499,485
Yukon	19,798	20,479	20,866	27,072	30,909
Northwest Territories	20,953	23,271	20,231	25,729	23,058
Canada	14,405,512	14,818.625	15,227,311	16,719,529	16,981,087

Cities and towns with populations of 5000 or more (1991)

These abbreviations specify the status of the places listed below.

BOR	Borough
C	City
CM	County (municipality)
COM	Community
CT	Canton (municipalité de)
DM	District municipality
ID	Improvement district
MD	Municipal district
MUN	Municipality
P	Paroisse (municipalité de)
PAR	Parish
RM	Rural municipality
SCM	Subdivision of county municipality
SD	Sans designation (municipalité)
SRD	Subdivision of regional district
T	Town
TP	Township
UNO	Unorganized—Non organisé
V	Ville/City
VL	Village

BRITISH COLUMBIA	Type	Pop.
Vancouver	C	471,844
Surrey	DM	245,173
Burnaby	DM	158,858
Richmond	DM	126,624
Saanich	DM	95,577
Delta	DM	88,978
Coquitlam	DM	84,021
Kelowna	C	75,950
North Vancouver	DM	75,157
Victoria	C	71,228
Prince George	C	69,653
Matsqui	DM	68,064
Kamloops	C	67,057
Langley	DM	66,040
Nanaimo	C	60,129
Chilliwack	DM	49,531
Maple Ridge	DM	48,422
New Westminster	C	43,585
West Vancouver	DM	38,783
North Vancouver	C	38,436
Port Coquitlam	C	36,773
Penticton	C	27,258
Mission	DM	26,202
Vernon	C	23,514
Comox-Strathcona, Subd. C	SRD	22,186
North Cowichan	DM	21,373
Campbell River	DM	21,175
Langley	C	21,175
Terrace	DM	19,765
Abbotsford	DM	18,864
Port Alberni	C	18,403
Oak Bay	DM	17,815
Central Okanagan, Subd. B	SRD	17,770
Kitimat	DM	17,712
Capital, Subd. B	SRD	17,276
Port Moody	C	16,981
Prince Rupert	C	16,620
Cranbrook	C	16,447
Nanaimo, Subd. B	SRD	16,413
White Rock	C	16,314
Esquimalt	DM	16,192
Cariboo, Subd. A	SRD	14,866
Fort St. John	C	14,156
North Okanagan, Subd. B	SRD	14,088
Central Saanich	DM	13,684
Colwood	C	13,468
Central Kootenay, Subd. B	SRD	13,167
Powell River	DM	12,991
Nanaimo, Subd. A	SRD	12,780
Salmon Arm	DM	12,115
Squamish	DM	11,709
Courtenay	C	11,652
Cowichan Valley, Subd. C	SRD	11,598
Fraser-Fort George	SRD	11,526
Capital, Subd. A	SRD	11,474
Dawson Creek	C	11,433
Campbell River	DM	11,305
Pitt Meadows	DM	11,147
Columbia-Shuswap, Subd.C	SRD	11,017
Sunshine Coast, Subd. A	SRD	10,819
Cowichan Valley, Subd. B	SRD	10,564
Williams Lake	T	10,385
Central Okanagan, Subd. A.	SRD	10,093
Sidney	T	10,082
North Saanich	DM	9645
Summerland	DM	9253
Comox-Strathcona, Subd. B	SRD	9139
Peace River, Subd. B	SRD	8820
Nelson	C	8760
Peace River, Subd. C	SRD	8429
Comox	T	8253
Okanagan-Similkameen, Subd. B	SRD	8248
Quesnel	T	8179
Coldstream	DM	7999
Trail	C	7919
Revelstoke	C	7729
Alberni-Clayoquot, Subd. A	SRD	7706
Okanagan-Similkameen, Subd. B	SRD	7657
Thompson-Nicola, Subd. A	SRD	7641
Parksville	C	7306
Central Kootenay, Subd. A	SRD	7164
Kitimat-Stikine	SRD	7143
East Kootenay, Subd. B	SRD	6914
Central Kootenay, Subd. C	SRD	6721
Castlegar	C	6579
Kimberley	C	6531
Bulkley-Nechako, Subd. A	SRD	6346
Merritt	T	6253
Sechelt	DM	6123
Bulkley-Nechako, Subd. B	SRD	5996
Kootenay Boundary, Subd. B	SRD	5945
View Royal	T	5925
Mackenzie	DM	5796
Port Hardy	DM	5082
Smithers	T	5029
Fernie	C	5012

ALBERTA	Type	Pop.
Calgary	C	710,677
Edmonton	C	616,741
Lethbridge	C	60,974
Red Deer	C	58,134
Strathcona, County No. 20	CM	56,573
Medicine Hat	C	43,625
St. Albert	T	42,146
Fort McMurray	T	34,706
Grande Prairie	C	28,271
Parkland, County No. 31	CM	22,550
Rocky View No. 44	MD	19,888
Sturgeon No. 90	MD	15,465
Red Deer County No. 23	CM	15,049
Leduc	T	13,970
Camrose	C	13,420
Spruce Grove	C	12,884
Airdrie	C	12,456
Grande Prairie County No. 1	CM	12,314
Improvement District 17	ID	12,299
Fort Saskatchewan	T	12,078
Leduc County No. 25	CM	11,503
Improvement District 18 (part)	ID	11,388
Foothills No. 31	MD	10,912
Wetaskiwin	C	10,634
Bonnyville No. 87	MD	10,269
Clearwater No. 99	MD	10,133
Lloydminster (Part)	C	10,042
Mountain View County No. 17	CM	9951
Wetaskiwin County No. 10	CM	9816
Brooks	T	9433
Hinton	T	9046
Improvement District No. 14	ID	8692
Lethbridge County No. 26	CM	8442

	Type	Pop.
Lac Ste. Anne, County No. 28	CM	8059
Ponoka County No. 3	CM	7896
Camrose County No. 22	CM	7475
Edson	T	7323
Improvement District 23	ID	7260
Stony Plain	T	7226
Westlock No. 92	MD	6994
Whitecourt	T	6938
Okotoks	T	6720
Peace River	T	6717
Crowsnest Pass	T	6679
Taber	T	6660
St. Paul, County No. 19	CM	6489
Brazeau	MD	6301
Drumheller	C	6277
High River	T	6269
Morinville	T	6104
Athabasca, County No. 12	CM	6049
Newell County No. 4	CM	6014
Drayton Valley	T	5983
Ponoka	T	5861
Wheatland County No. 16	CM	5779
Innisfail	T	5700
Banff	T	5688
Canmore	T	5681
Slave Lake	T	5607
Barrhead County No. 11	CM	5591
Olds	T	5542
Rocky Mountain House	T	5461
Beaver County No. 9	CM	5430
Taber No. 14	MD	5317
Coaldale	T	5310
Improvement District No. 16	ID	5269
Cochrane	T	5265
Stettler County No. 6	CM	5251
Vegreville	T	5138
Bonnyville	T	5132
Beaumont	T	5042

SASKATCHEWAN	Type	Pop.
Saskatoon	C	186,058
Regina	C	179,178
Prince Albert	C	34,181
Moose Jaw	C	33,593
Yorkton	C	15,315
Swift Current	C	14,815
North Battleford	C	14,350
Estevan	C	10,240
Weyburn	C	9673
Lloydminster (Part)	C	7241
Corman Park	RM	6809
Melfort	C	5628

MANITOBA	Type	Pop.
Winnipeg	C	616,790
Brandon	C	38,567
Thompson	C	14,977
Portage La Prairie	C	13,186
Springfield	RM	11,102
Selkirk	T	9815
St. Andrews	RM	9461
Hanover	RM	8905
Dauphin	T	8453
Steinbach	T	8213
Tache	RM	7576
Portage La Prairie	RM	7156
Flin Flon (Part)	C	7119
Rockwood	RM	6990
Winkler	T	6397
The Pas	T	6166
East St. Paul	RM	5820
Morden	T	5273
Richot	RM	5146

ONTARIO	Type	Pop.
Toronto	C	635,395
York, North	C	562,564
Scarborough	C	524,598
Mississauga	C	463,388
Hamilton	C	318,499
Ottawa	C	313,987
Etobicoke	BOR	309,993
London	C	303,165
Brampton	C	234,445
Windsor	C	191,435
Kitchener	C	168,282
Markham	T	153,811
York	C	140,525
Burlington	C	129,575
Oshawa	C	129,344
St. Catharines	C	129,300
Oakville	T	114,670
Thunder Bay	C	113,946
Vaughan	T	111,359
Nepean	TP	107,627
York, East	BOR	102,696
Gloucester	TP	101,677
Sudbury	C	92,884
Cambridge	C	92,772
Guelph	C	87,976
Brantford	C	81,997
Sault Ste. Marie	C	81,476
Richmond Hill	T	80,142
Niagara Falls	C	75,399
Sarnia-Clearwater	C	74,376
Waterloo	C	71,181
Pickering	T	68,631
Peterborough	C	68,371
Barrie	C	62,728
Whitby	T	61,281
Ajax	T	57,350
Kingston	C	56,597
North Bay	C	55,405
Stoney Creek	T	49,968
Newcastle	T	49,479
Welland	C	47,914
Timmins	C	47,461
Cornwall	C	47,137
Newmarket	T	45,474
Chatham	C	43,557
Cumberland	TP	40,697
Kingston	TP	39,791
Kanata	C	37,344
Belleville	C	37,243
Halton Hills	T	36,816
Caledon	T	34,965
Milton	T	32,075
Woodstock	C	30,075
St. Thomas	C	29,990
Georgina	TP	29,746
Flamborough	TP	29,616
Aurora	T	29,454
Stratford	C	27,666
Fort Erie	T	26,006
Orillia	C	25,925
Nanticoke	C	22,727
Ancaster	T	21,988
Valley East	T	21,939
Dundas	T	21,868
Owen Sound	C	21,674
Innisfil	TP	21,667
Brockville	C	21,582
Haldimand	T	20,573
Allston, Beeton, Tecumseth and Tittenham	T	20,239
Port Colborne	C	18,766
Grimsby	T	18,520
Gwilliambury, East	TP	18,367
Whitchurch-Stouffville	T	18,357
Vanier	C	18,150
King	TP	18,121
Orangeville	T	17,921
Scugog	TP	17,810
Bradford West Gwilliambury	T	17,702
Thorold	C	17,542
Woolwich	TP	17,365
Lincoln	T	17,149
Trenton	T	16,908

	Type	Pop.
Sidney	TP	16,702
Lindsay	T	16,696
Sandwich (West)	TP	16,628
Goulbourn	TP	16,151
Delhi	TP	15,852
Simcoe	T	15,539
Cobourg	T	15,079
Rayside-Balfour	T	15,039
Huntsville	T	14,997
West Carleton	TP	14,647
Leamington	T	14,182
Essa	TP	14,177
Uxbridge	TP	14,092
Elliot Lake	T	14,089
Pembroke	C	13,997
Osgoode	TP	13,976
Midland	T	13,865
Collingwood	T	13,505
Pelham	T	13,328
Wilmot	TP	13,107
Niagara-on-the-Lake	T	12,945
Nickel Centre	T	12,332
Bracebridge	T	12,308
Ermestown	TP	12,229
Dunnville	T	12,131
Tillsonburg	T	12,019
Wallaceburg	T	11,846
Norfolk	TP	11,804
Rideau	TP	11,778
Port Hope	T	11,505
Pittsburgh	TP	11,447
Brock	TP	11,057
Lincoln West	TP	10,864
Moore	TP	10,664
Russell	TP	10,659
Strathroy	T	10,566
Tecumseth	TP	10,495
Kirkland Lake	T	10,440
Norwich	TP	10,416
Kapuskasing	T	10,344
Maidstone	TP	9992
Gravenhurst	T	9988
Walden	T	9805
Kenora	T	9782
Glandbrook	TP	9726
Kenora	UNO	9723
Hawkesbury	T	9706
Hamilton	TP	9616
Smiths Falls	T	9396
Ingersoll	T	9378
Kenora	UNO	9231
Oro	TP	9073
Tiny	TP	9035
Smith	TP	8997
Clarence	TP	8982
Amherstburg	T	8921
Fort Frances	T	8891
Paris	T	8600
Mersea	TP	8514
South-West Oxford	TP	8514
Zorra	TP	8239
Wellesley	TP	8234
Petawawa	TP	8191
Orillia	TP	8142
Renfrew	T	8134
Yarmouth	TP	7987
Fergus	T	7940
Dorchester, North	TP	7865
Vespra	TP	7770
Charlottenburgh	TP	7651
Thurlow	TP	7615
Erin	TP	7561
Sudbury, Unorganized, North Part	UNO	7463
Goderich	T	7452
Algoma	UNO	7450
Elizabethtown	TP	7439
Carleton Place	T	7432
Gosfield South	TP	7380
Blandford-Blenheim	TP	7266
East Zorra-Tavistock	TP	7251
Augusta	TP	7176
Tay	TP	7017
Murray	TP	6921
Mariposa	TP	6906
Port Elgin	T	6857
Westminster	TP	6826
Dumfries North	TP	6821
Rockland	T	6771
Essex	T	6759
Hanover	T	6711
Arnprior	T	6679
Chatham	TP	6655
Penetanguishene	T	6643
Kincardine	T	6585
Brantford	TP	6509
Dryden	T	6505
Harwich	TP	6450
Cornwall	TP	6408
Emily	TP	6311
Aylmer	T	6244
Wasaga Beach	T	6224
Wainfleet	TP	6203
Caradoc	TP	6147
Parry Sound	T	6125
Hearst	T	6079
Malahide	TP	6000
Iroquois Falls	T	5999
Eramosa	TP	5949
Cambridge	TP	5915
London	TP	5877
Medonte	TP	5848
Sturgeon Falls	T	5837
Petawawa	VL	5793
Mono	TP	5782
Raleigh	TP	5749
Burford	TP	5733
Kingsville	T	5716
Fenelon	TP	5710
Oxford (on Rideau)	TP	5690
Cavan	TP	5633
Perth	T	5574
Lobo	TP	5529
Espanola	T	5527
Anderdon	TP	5502
Muskoka Lakes	TP	5498
St. Marys	T	5496
McNab	TP	5464
New Liskeard	T	5431
Listowel	T	5404
Onaping Falls	T	5402
Puslinch	TP	5397
Ameliasburgh	TP	5357
Sandwich South	TP	5349
Nottawasaga	TP	5311
Plympton	TP	5304
Colchester South	TP	5292
Bosanquet	TP	5249
Gananoque	T	5209
Napanee	T	5179
Manvers	TP	5166
Marathon	T	5064

QUÉBEC	Type	Pop.
Montréal	V	1,017,666
Laval	V	314,398
Québec	V	167,517
Longueuil	V	129,874
Gatineau	V	92,284
Montréal-Nord	V	85,616
Sherbrooke	V	76,429
St-Hubert	V	74,027
Lasalle	V	73,804
St-Léonard	V	73,120
St-Laurent	V	72,402
Ste-Foy	V	71,133
Charlesbourg	V	70,788
Beauport	V	69,158
Brossard	V	64,793
Chicoutimi	V	62,670
Verdun	V	61,307
Hull	V	60,707
Jonquière	V	57,933
Repentigny	V	49,630
Trois-Rivières	V	49,426
Pierrefonds	V	48,735
Dollard-des-Ormeaux	V	46,922
Granby	V	42,804
Châteauguay	V	39,833
Terrebonne	V	39,678
Lévis-Lauzon	V	39,452
St-Hyacinthe	V	39,292
St-Jean-sur-Richelieu	V	37,607
St-Eustache	V	37,278
Anjou	V	37,210
Drummondville	V	35,462
Lachine	V	35,266
Boucherville	V	33,796
Cap-de-la-Madeleine	V	33,716
Aylmer	V	32,244
Rimouski	V	30,873
Côte-St-Luc	V	28,700
Pointe-Claire	V	27,647
Salaberry-de-Valleyfield	V	27,598
Rouyn-Noranda	V	26,448
Baie-Comeau	V	26,012
Alma	V	25,910
Mascouche	V	25,828
Sept-Îles	V	24,848
Ste-Thérèse	V	24,158
Val-d'Or	V	23,842
St-Jérôme	V	23,384
St-Bruno-de-Montarville	V	23,103
Outremont	V	22,935
Blainville	V	22,679
Victoriaville	V	21,495
Boisbriand	V	21,124
La Baie	V	20,995
St-Lambert	V	20,976
Ste-Julie	V	20,632
Westmount	V	20,239
Trois-Rivières-Ouest	V	20,076
Shawinigan	V	19,931
Beaconsfield	V	19,616
St-Georges	V	19,583
Sorel	V	18,786
Beloeil	V	18,516
St-Constant	V	18,423
Mont-Royal	V	18,212
Mirabel	V	17,971
Greenfield Park	V	17,652
Kirkland	V	17,495
Joliette	V	17,396
Thetford Mines	V	17,273
Dorval	V	17,249
Val-Bélair	V	17,181
Gaspé	V	16,402
Chambly	V	15,893
L'Ancienne-Lorette	V	15,242
Lachenaie	V	15,074
St-Luc	V	15,008
La Prairie	V	14,938
Varennes	V	14,758
Fleurimont	SD	14,727
Rock Forest	V	14,551
Grand-Mère	V	14,287
Loretteville	V	14,219
Cap-Rouge	V	14,105
Magog	V	14,034
Rivière-du-Loup	V	14,017
La Gardeur	V	13,814
Tracy	V	13,181
Deux-Montagnes	V	13,035
Matane	V	12,756
St-Jean-Chrysostome	V	12,717
St-Augustin-de-Desmaures	P	12,680
Sillery	V	12,519
Mont-St-Hilaire	V	12,341
Cowansville	V	11,982
Montmagny	V	11,861
Lachute	V	11,730
Roberval	V	11,628
Shawinigan-Sud	V	11,584
St-Raphaël-de-l'Île-Bizard	P	11,352
Rosemère	V	11,198
Vaudreuil	V	11,187
Candiac	V	11,064
Bellefeuille	P	11,005
Bécancour	V	10,911
Vanier	V	10,833
Granby	CT	10,623
La Plaine	P	10,576
Buckingham	V	10,548
Ste-Marie	V	10,542
Charny	V	10,239
St-Antoine	T	10,232
St-Basile-le-Grand	V	10,127
La Tuque	V	10,003
St-Romuald-d'Etchemin	V	9830
Ste-Catherine	V	9805
St-Charles-Borromée	SD	9658
Pincourt	V	9639
Iberville	V	9352
St-Félicien	V	9340
Ascot	SD	9085
St-Lazare	P	9057
Chibougamau	V	8855
Hampstead	V	8645
Lorraine	V	8410
St-Timothée	SD	8292
Mercier	V	8227
Dolbeau	V	8181
La Sarre	V	8153
St-Nicéphore	SD	8093
L'Île-Perrot	V	8064
Louiseville	V	8000
Mont-Laurier	V	7862
Grantham-Ouest	SD	7709
St-Nicolas	V	7600
Arthabaska	V	7584
Lac-Saint-Charles	SD	7520
Ste-Marthe-sur-le-Lac	V	7410
Port-Cartier	V	7383
Ste-Sophie	SD	7377
Lafontaine	VL	7365
Ste-Victoire-d'Arthabaska	P	7313
St-Étienne-de-Lauzon	SD	7256
Plessisville	V	6952
Mistassini	V	6842
Bernières	SD	6831
St-Louis-de-France	P	6747
St-Lin	P	6734
Coaticook	V	6637
Asbestos	V	6487
Beauharnois	V	6449
St-Athanèse	P	6411
Mont-Joli	V	6265
Farnham	V	6146
Ste-Julienne	P	6092
Delson	V	6063
Otterburn Park	V	6046
Prévost	SD	6024
Dorion	V	5920
Roxboro	V	5879
St-Rédempteur	V	5862
Lac-Mégantic	V	5838
St-Amable	V	5804
Ste-Marie-du-Cap-de-la-Madeleine	SD	5798
St-Rémi	V	5768
Masson	V	5753
L'Assomption	V	5706
Donnacona	V	5659
Ste-Anne-des-Monts	V	5652
Charlemagne	V	5598
Contrecœur	VL	5501
St-Pierre-de-Sorel	P	5467
Notre-Dame-des-Prairies	P	5455
Ste-Agathe-des-Monts	V	5452
Lemoyne	V	5412
La Pêche	SD	5394
Carignan	V	5386
Notre-Dame-de-l'Île-Perrot	P	5372
Montréal-Ouest	V	5180
Marleville	V	5164
L'Assomption	P	5124
L'Acadie	SD	5074
Pintendre	SD	5028

NEW BRUNSWICK	Type	Pop.
Saint John	C	74,969
Moncton	C	57,010
Fredericton	C	46,466
Riverview	T	16,270
Bathurst	C	14,409
Edmundston	C	10,835
Dieppe	T	10,463

Oromocto	T	9325
Campbellton	C	8699
Quispamsis	T	8446
Moncton	PAR	8268
Shediac	PAR	8249
Saumarez	PAR	7862
Alnwick	PAR	6988
Beresford	PAR	6764
Chatham	T	6544
Grand Falls	T	6083
Dundas	PAR	5951
New Maryland	PAR	5751
Newcastle	T	5711
Sackville	T	5494
Douglas	PAR	5237
Kingsclear	PAR	5055
Fairvale	VL	5041

NOVA SCOTIA	Type	Pop.
Halifax	C	114,445
Dartmouth	C	67,798
Halifax, Subd. C	SCM	45,667
Halifax, Subd. D	SCM	37,289
Sydney	C	26,063
Lunenburg	MD	25,720
Cape Breton, Subd. B	SCM	25,385
Kings, Subd. A	SCM	21,253
Glace Bay	T	19,501
East Hants	MD	18,560
Halifax, Subd. E	SCM	18,211
Colchester	SCM	17,782
Cape Breton, Subd. A	SCM	17,433
Halifax, Subd. B	SCM	14,611
West Hants	MD	13,611
Colchester	SCM	12,031
Truro	T	11,683
Bedford	T	11,618
Kings, subd. B	SCM	11,076
Yarmouth	MD	10,827
Halifax, Subd. A	SCM	10,814
Chester	MD	10,762
New Glasgow	T	9905
Amherst	T	9742
Clare	MD	9654
Pictou, Subd. C	SCM	9502
Digby	MD	9230
Argyle	MD	9215
Annapolis, Subd. A	SCM	8554
Yarmouth	T	7781
Barrington	MD	7774
New Waterford	T	7695
Sydney Mines	T	7551
Kings, Subd. C	SCM	7498
North Sydney	T	7260
Bridgewater	T	7248
Antigonish, Subd. A	SCM	7221
Inverness, Subd. A	SCM	6947
Antigonish, Subd. B	SCM	6854
Pictou, Subd. A	SCM	6841
Pictou, Subd. B	SCM	6598
Queens, Subd. B	SCM	6528
Guysborough	MD	6518
Inverness, Subd. B	SCM	6352
Halifax, Subd. F	SCM	6130
Kentville	T	5506
Shelburne	MD	5450
Kings, Subd. D	SCM	5268
Stellarton	T	5237
Cumberland	SCM	5200

PRINCE EDWARD ISLAND	Type	Pop.
Charlottetown	C	15,396
Summerside	T	7474
Sherwood	COM	6006

NEWFOUNDLAND	Type	Pop.
St. John's	C	95,770
Mount Pearl	C	23,689
Corner Brook	C	22,410
Conception Bay South	T	17,590
Grand Falls-Windsor	T	14,693
Gander	T	10,339
Labrador City	T	9061
Happy Valley-Goose Bay	T	8610
Stephenville	T	7621
Marystown	T	6739
Goulds	T	6162
Channel-Port aux Basques	T	5644
Bay Roberts	T	5474
Carbonear	T	5259

YUKON TERRITORY	Type	Pop.
Whitehorse	C	17,925

NORTHWEST TERRITORIES	Type	Pop.
Yellowknife	C	15,179

KILOMETRE GUIDE

1 KM = 0.6 MI

	BANFF	BRANDON	CALGARY	CHARLOTTETOWN	CHICOUTIMI	DAWSON CREEK	EDMONTON	FLIN FLON	FREDERICTON	GASPÉ	HALIFAX	HAMILTON	JASPER	KENORA	MONCTON	MONTRÉAL	NIAGARA FALLS
BANFF	•	1259	129	5079	4348	1019	428	1362	4706	4823	5121	3631	286	1669	4904	3872	3700
BOSTON	4471	3212	4342	999	835	4954	4363	3899	652	1223	921	840	4731	2802	824	546	771
BRANDON	1259	•	1130	3864	3090	1741	1151	726	3447	3565	3862	2372	1519	410	3689	2614	2441
CALGARY	129	1130	•	4931	4220	890	299	1233	4558	4694	4973	3502	415	1540	4756	3743	3571
CHARLOTTETOWN	5079	3864	4931	•	935	5554	4963	4500	373	845	280	1854	5332	3402	175	1199	1860
CHICAGO	2905	1646	2776	2577	1846	3388	2797	2334	2203	2321	2618	784	3166	1236	2401	1370	853
CHICOUTIMI	4348	3090	4220	935	•	4831	4241	3777	562	679	977	1083	4609	2680	760	476	1152
CINCINNATI	3402	2144	3273	2409	1794	3885	3294	2831	2062	2271	2371	763	3663	1733	2234	1318	734
CLEVELAND	3467	2208	3338	2025	1410	3949	3359	2895	1677	1886	1986	418	3727	1798	1849	933	349
DAWSON CREEK	1019	1741	890	5554	4831	•	591	1642	5189	5306	5684	4113	752	2152	5378	4355	4183
DETROIT	3367	2108	3238	2115	1384	3850	3259	2795	1741	1859	2157	322	3627	1698	1939	908	391
EDMONTON	428	1151	299	4963	4241	591	•	1051	4598	4715	5013	3523	369	1561	4788	3764	3592
FAIRBANKS	3495	4218	3367	8031	7308	2477	3067	4118	7665	7783	8081	6590	3228	4628	7885	6832	6659
FLIN FLON	1362	726	1233	4500	3777	1642	1051	•	4134	4252	4550	3059	1419	1098	4324	3301	3129
FREDERICTON	4706	3447	4588	373	562	5189	4598	4134	•	700	415	1440	4966	3037	198	834	1510
GASPÉ	4823	3565	4694	845	679	5306	4715	4252	700	•	945	1558	5084	3154	669	951	1627
HALIFAX	5121	3862	4973	280	997	5604	5013	4550	415	945	•	1856	5382	3452	275	1249	1925
HAMILTON	3631	2372	3502	1854	1083	4113	3523	3059	1440	1558	1856	•	3891	1962	1630	607	69
INDIANAPOLIS	3217	1959	3088	2543	1846	3700	3109	2646	2195	2321	2504	787	3478	1548	2367	1370	853
JASPER	286	1519	415	5332	4609	752	369	1419	4966	5084	5382	3891	•	1930	5156	4133	3961
KENORA	1669	410	1540	3402	2680	2152	1561	1098	3037	3154	3452	1962	1930	•	3227	2203	2031
LOS ANGELES	2723	3513	2707	6136	5406	3399	3006	3899	5763	5881	6178	4344	2874	3605	5961	4929	4413
MINNEAPOLIS	2190	932	2062	3058	2335	2673	2082	1619	2692	2810	3108	1447	2451	708	2882	1859	1516
MONCTON	4904	3689	4756	175	760	5378	4788	4324	198	669	275	1630	5156	3227	•	1024	1699
MONTRÉAL	3872	2614	3743	1199	476	4355	3764	3301	834	951	1249	607	4133	2203	1084	•	676
NEW YORK	4448	3190	4319	1353	1070	4931	4340	3877	1009	1540	1278	818	4709	2779	1181	613	748
NORTH BAY	3314	2055	3185	1757	1035	3796	3206	2742	1392	1510	1807	402	3574	1645	1582	558	472
OTTAWA	3682	2424	3553	1389	666	4165	3574	3111	1024	1141	1439	467	3943	3013	1213	190	536
PHILADELPHIE	4093	2834	3964	1506	1202	4575	3985	3521	1159	1672	1427	813	4353	2424	1331	745	744
PORT AUX BASQUES	5555	4297	5407	521	1411	6030	5440	4976	850	1321	576	2282	5808	3879	652	1675	2351
PRINCE ALBERT	912	731	784	4543	3821	1193	602	449	4178	4295	4593	3103	970	1141	4368	3344	3172
PRINCE GEORGE	632	1865	761	5678	4955	406	715	1765	5312	5430	5728	4237	346	2276	5502	4479	4307
QUÉBEC	4142	2884	4014	959	206	4625	4035	3571	586	703	982	877	4403	2474	784	270	949
RÉGINA	893	365	764	4178	3455	1376	785	752	3813	3930	4228	2737	1154	776	4002	2979	2807
RIVIÈRE-DU-LOUP	4324	3066	4196	755	180	4807	4216	3753	381	499	797	1059	4585	2655	579	452	1128
ROCHESTER	3829	2570	3700	1625	1012	4311	3721	3257	1278	1487	1587	200	4089	2160	1450	536	143
ROUYN-NORANDA	3154	1896	3026	1843	1120	3637	3046	2583	1477	1595	1893	694	3415	1485	1667	644	763
SAINT-JOHN	4812	3553	4664	323	649	5295	4704	4241	106	806	309	1547	5073	3143	148	940	1616
ST. JOHN'S	6482	5224	6334	1448	2338	6957	6367	5903	1777	2248	1503	3209	6735	4806	1579	2602	3278
SAN FRANCISCO	2050	3090	2179	5181	5451	2717	2478	3476	5808	5926	6223	4389	2634	3634	6006	4974	4458
SASKATOON	748	623	620	4435	3713	1118	528	613	4070	4188	4485	2995	896	1033	4260	3236	3064
SAULT STE. MARIE	2887	1629	2758	2184	1461	3370	2779	2316	1819	1936	2234	744	3148	1218	2008	985	813
SEATTLE	1081	2340	1210	5811	5089	1318	1360	2411	5446	5564	5861	4027	1236	2750	5636	4612	4096
SHERBROOKE	4028	2770	3899	1151	420	4511	39204	3457	777	895	1193	763	4289	2359	975	156	832
SUMMERSIDE	5053	3795	4925	63	909	5528	937	4474	348	819	317	1780	5306	3376	150	1173	1849
SYDNEY	5401	4142	5253	367	1257	5876	5285	4822	695	1167	422	2128	5654	3724	497	1521	2197
THUNDER BAY	2179	921	2050	2892	2169	2662	2071	1608	2527	2644	2942	1452	2440	510	2717	1693	1521
TORONTO	3563	2305	3434	1738	1015	4046	3455	2992	1373	1490	1788	68	3824	1894	1563	539	137
VANCOUVER	929	2187	1057	6000	5277	1202	1244	2290	5634	5752	6050	4559	875	2597	5824	4801	4628
VICTORIA	1033	2292	1162	6104	5382	1307	1349	2395	5739	5856	6154	4664	980	2702	5929	4905	4733
WASHINGTON	4105	2847	3977	1719	1384	4588	3998	3534	1371	1902	1640	832	4366	2437	1543	932	763
WHITEHORSE	2514	3236	2385	7049	6326	1495	2086	3137	6684	6801	7099	5609	2247	3647	6874	5850	5678
WINDSOR	3370	2111	3241	2111	1381	3853	3262	2799	1738	1856	2153	319	3631	1701	1936	904	388
WINNIPEG	1465	206	1336	3607	2884	1947	1357	893	3241	3359	3656	2166	1725	204	3431	2408	2235
YARMOUTH	4986	3727	4838	497	842	5449	4878	4414	280	980	345	1720	5246	3317	322	1114	1790

	OTTAWA	PORT AUX BASQUES	PRINCE ALBERT	PRINCE GEORGE	QUÉBEC	RÉGINA	RIVIÈRE-DU-LOUP	ROUYN-NORANDA	SAINT-JOHN	ST. JOHN'S	SASKATOON	SAULT STE. MARIE	SHERBROOKE	SUMMERSIDE	SYDNEY	THUNDER BAY	TORONTO	VANCOUVER	VICTORIA	WHITEHORSE	WINDSOR	WINNIPEG	YARMOUTH
BANFF	3682	5555	912	632	4142	893	4324	3154	4812	6482	748	2887	4028	5053	5401	2179	3563	929	1033	2514	3370	1465	4986
BOSTON	735	1476	3943	5077	629	3578	811	1189	676	2403	3835	1584	423	974	1321	2292	908	5399	5504	6396	1159	2953	571
BRANDON	2424	4297	731	1865	2884	365	3066	1896	3553	5224	623	1629	2770	3795	4142	921	2305	2187	2292	3236	2111	206	3727
CALGARY	3553	5407	784	761	4014	764	4196	3026	4664	6334	620	2758	3899	4925	5253	2050	3434	1057	1162	2385	3241	1336	4838
CHARLOTTETOWN	1389	521	4543	5678	959	4178	755	1843	323	1448	4435	2184	1151	63	367	2892	1738	6000	604	7049	2111	3607	497
CHICAGO	1230	3053	2377	3512	1640	2012	1822	1444	2309	3980	2269	726	1520	2551	2898	1070	830	3833	3938	4883	465	1440	2483
CHICOUTIMI	666	1411	3821	4955	206	3455	180	1120	649	2338	3713	1461	420	909	1257	2169	1015	5277	5382	6326	1381	2884	842
CINCINNATI	1218	2886	2874	4009	1590	2509	1770	1436	2086	3813	2766	900	1474	2383	2731	1567	809	4331	4435	5380	444	1938	2021
CLEVELAND	834	2501	2939	4073	1205	2573	1386	1112	1701	3428	2831	856	1090	1999	2346	1564	486	4395	4500	5444	282	2002	1637
DAWSON CREEK	4165	6030	1193	406	4625	1376	4807	3637	5295	6957	1118	3370	4511	5528	5876	2662	4046	1202	1307	1495	3853	1947	5449
DETROIT	768	2591	2839	3973	1178	2474	1360	995	1848	3518	2731	566	1064	2089	2437	1286	369	4295	4400	5345	3	1902	2021
EDMONTON	3574	5440	602	715	4035	785	4216	3046	4704	6367	528	2779	3920	4937	5285	2071	3455	1244	1349	2086	3262	1357	4878
FAIRBANKS	6642	8507	3669	2882	7102	3853	7284	6114	7772	9434	3595	5847	6988	8005	8352	5139	6523	3679	3784	982	6330	4424	7926
FLIN FLON	3111	4976	449	1765	3571	752	3753	2583	4241	5903	613	2316	3457	4474	4822	1608	2992	2290	239	3137	279	893	4414
FREDERICTON	1024	850	4178	5312	586	3813	381	1477	106	1777	4070	1819	777	348	695	2527	1373	5634	5739	6684	1738	3241	280
GASPÉ	1141	1321	4295	5430	703	3930	499	1595	806	2248	4188	1936	895	819	117	2644	1490	5752	5856	6801	1856	3359	980
HALIFAX	1439	576	4593	5728	982	4228	797	1893	309	1503	4485	2234	1193	317	422	2942	1788	6050	6154	7099	2153	3656	345
HAMILTON	467	2282	3103	4237	877	2737	1059	694	1547	3209	2995	744	763	1780	2128	1452	68	4559	4664	5609	319	2166	1720
INDIANAPOLIS	1230	3019	2689	3824	1640	2324	1822	1456	2219	3946	2581	978	1526	2517	2865	1382	830	4146	4250	5195	465	1753	2155
JASPER	3943	5808	970	346	4403	1154	4585	3415	5073	6735	896	3148	4289	5306	5654	2440	3824	875	980	2247	3631	1725	5246
KENORA	2013	3879	1141	2276	2474	776	2655	1485	3143	4806	1033	1218	2359	3376	3724	510	1894	2597	2702	3647	1701	204	3317
LOS ANGELES	4789	5613	3513	2993	5200	3148	5382	5003	5869	7540	3405	4286	5086	6111	6458	3756	4390	2313	2211	4894	4025	3401	6043
MINNEAPOLIS	1669	3534	1662	2797	2129	1297	2311	1592	2799	4461	1555	874	2015	3032	3380	560	1493	2812	2710	4168	1128	726	2972
MONCTON	1213	652	4368	5502	784	4002	579	1667	148	1579	4260	2008	975	150	497	2717	1563	5824	5929	6874	1936	3431	322
MONTRÉAL	190	1675	3344	4479	270	2979	452	644	940	2602	3236	985	156	1173	1521	1693	539	4801	4905	5850	904	2408	1114
NEW YORK	777	1833	3920	5055	864	3555	1041	1257	1033	2760	3813	1561	657	1331	1679	22691	885	5414	5518	6463	1136	2984	929
NORTH BAY	369	2234	2786	3920	829	2420	1011	291	1498	3161	2678	426	715	1732	2709	135	335	4242	4347	5279	700	1849	1672
OTTAWA	•	1865	3154	4289	460	2789	642	552	1130	2792	3046	795	346	1363	1711	1503	399	4611	4715	5660	764	2218	1304
PHILADELPHIE	772	1983	3565	4699	961	3199	1143	1389	1183	2752	3457	1556	806	1481	1828	2264	880	5021	5126	6070	921	2623	1078
PORT AUX BASQUES	1865	•	5020	6154	1436	4654	13	2319	800	927	4912	2660	1627	584	154	3368	2214	6476	6581	7225	2588	4083	840
PRINCE ALBERT	3154	5020	•	1316	3615	365	3796	2626	4284	5947	164	2359	3500	4517	4865	1651	3051	1841	1946	2688	2842	937	4458
PRINCE GEORGE	4289	6154	1316	•	4749	1500	4931	3761	5419	7081	1242	3481	4635	5652	6000	2786	4170	797	901	1901	3977	2071	5592
QUÉBEC	460	1436	3615	4749	•	3249	204	914	673	2363	3507	1255	214	933	1281	1963	809	5071	5176	6120	1175	2678	866
RÉGINA	2789	4654	365	1500	3249	•	3431	2261	3919	5581	257	1981	3135	4152	4500	1286	2670	1822	1926	2871	2477	571	4104
RIVIÈRE-DU-LOUP	642	1231	3796	4931	204	3431	•	1096	488	2158	3689	1437	396	729	1077	2145	991	5253	5358	6302	1357	2860	661
ROCHESTER	436	2102	3301	4435	806	2935	988	893	1302	3029	3193	941	692	1600	1947	1650	266	4757	4862	5807	517	2364	1238
ROUYN-NORANDA	52	2319	2626	3761	914	2261	1096	•	1584	3246	2519	718	800	1817	2165	975	626	4083	4188	5132	991	1690	1757
SAINT-JOHN	1130	800	4284	5419	673	3919	488	1584	•	1727	4176	1925	864	298	645	2633	1479	5741	5845	6790	1844	3347	174
ST. JOHN'S	2792	927	5947	7081	2363	5581	2158	3246	1727	•	5839	3587	2554	1511	1081	4295	3141	7403	7775	8452	3515	5010	1783
SAN FRANCISCO	4834	6658	3050	2311	5245	2858	5427	5049	5914	7585	2886	4331	5131	6156	6503	3964	4435	1630	1529	4212	4070	3430	6088
SASKATOON	3046	4912	164	1242	3507	257	3689	2519	4176	5839	•	2239	3392	4410	4757	1543	2927	1677	1782	2614	2734	829	4350
SAULT STE. MARIE	795	2660	2359	3481	1255	1981	1437	718	1925	3587	2239	•	1141	2158	2506	708	676	3803	3907	4852	581	1423	2099
SEATTLE	4472	6288	1962	912	4899	1975	5065	4199	5552	7215	1830	3454	4768	5786	6133	3261	4073	232	130	2813	3703	2546	5726
SHERBROOKE	346	1627	3500	4635	214	3135	396	800	864	2554	3392	1141	•	1125	1473	1849	695	4957	5061	6006	1061	2564	1057
SUMMERSIDE	1363	584	4517	5652	933	4152	729	1817	298	1511	4410	2158	1125	•	430	2866	1709	5974	6078	7023	2086	3581	472
SYDNEY	1711	154	4865	6000	1281	4500	1077	2165	645	1081	4757	2506	1473	430	•	3214	2060	6322	6426	7371	2433	3928	702
THUNDER BAY	1503	3368	1651	2786	1963	1286	2145	975	2633	4295	1543	708	1849	2866	3214	•	1384	3108	3212	4157	1289	715	2807
TORONTO	399	2214	3051	4170	809	2670	991	626	1479	3141	2927	676	695	1709	2060	1384	•	4492	4596	5528	369	2099	1653
VANCOUVER	4611	6476	1841	797	5071	1822	5253	4083	5741	7403	1677	3803	4957	5974	6322	3108	4492	•	105	2697	4299	2232	5914
VICTORIA	4715	6581	1946	901	5176	1926	5358	4188	5845	7775	1782	3907	5061	6078	6426	3212	4596	105	•	2802	4403	2337	6019
WASHINGTON	1014	2195	3578	4712	1178	3112	1360	1576	1395	3122	3454	1394	1048	1693	2041	2271	900	5034	5139	6083	1014	2641	1291
WHITEHORSE	5660	7525	2688	1901	6120	2871	6302	5132	6790	8452	2614	4852	6006	7023	7371	4157	5528	2697	2802	•	5348	3524	6964
WINDSOR	764	2588	2842	3977	1175	2477	1357	991	1844	3515	2734	581	1061	2086	2433	1289	369	4299	4403	5348	•	1905	2018
WINNIPEG	2218	4083	937	2071	2678	571	2860	1690	3347	5010	829	1423	2564	3581	3928	715	2099	2232	2337	3524	1905	•	3521
YARMOUTH	1304	840	4458	5592	866	4104	661	1757	174	1783	4350	2099	1057	472	702	2807	1653	5914	6019	6964	2018	3521	•

Kilometres are calculated along main highways and include ferry distances.

MAPS OF CANADA

MAP SYMBOLS

Maps of Canada is an easy-to-read and up-to-date series of 28 maps —to every region of this country— specially adapted for this book by Schwerdt Graphic Arts Ltd. Altogether, the maps locate almost 9,000 populated places and more than 8,000 physical features. For easy reference, see the map index on pages 154–175. The scales of the maps vary according to the density of the named places and features. The legend here lists map symbols as follows: roads, road signs, distances, transportation, boundaries, cities and towns, physical features, and sites.

Provinces, territories, national parks and national historic sites, and major physical features, such as oceans, seas, and rivers, are identified in both official languages. The authority for virtually all the Canadian names comes from provincial government sources.

Maps of Canada is an information source that can also be used for travel planning. The Canadian road network is completely mapped. The maps also show the road system in areas of the northern United States and Alaska adjacent to the international boundary. An additional feature, *Cities of Canada*, offers maps of more than 30 important Canadian centres, which appear on pages 140–151.

ROADS

Multilane divided expressway/autoroute with interchange (limited access)

Undivided expressway/autoroute with interchange (limited access)

Toll expressway/autoroute

Multilane principal highway with interchange

Principal highway with interchange

Secondary highway

Local road

N-813   Forest or ZEC¹ road

ROAD SIGNS

Trans-Canada Highway

16   Yellowhead Highway

3   Crowsnest Highway

416   Provincial or state highway

27   U.S. interstate highway

88   Other U.S. highways

69   U.S. county or rural road

231   County or regional road (Ont.)

416   Interchange number

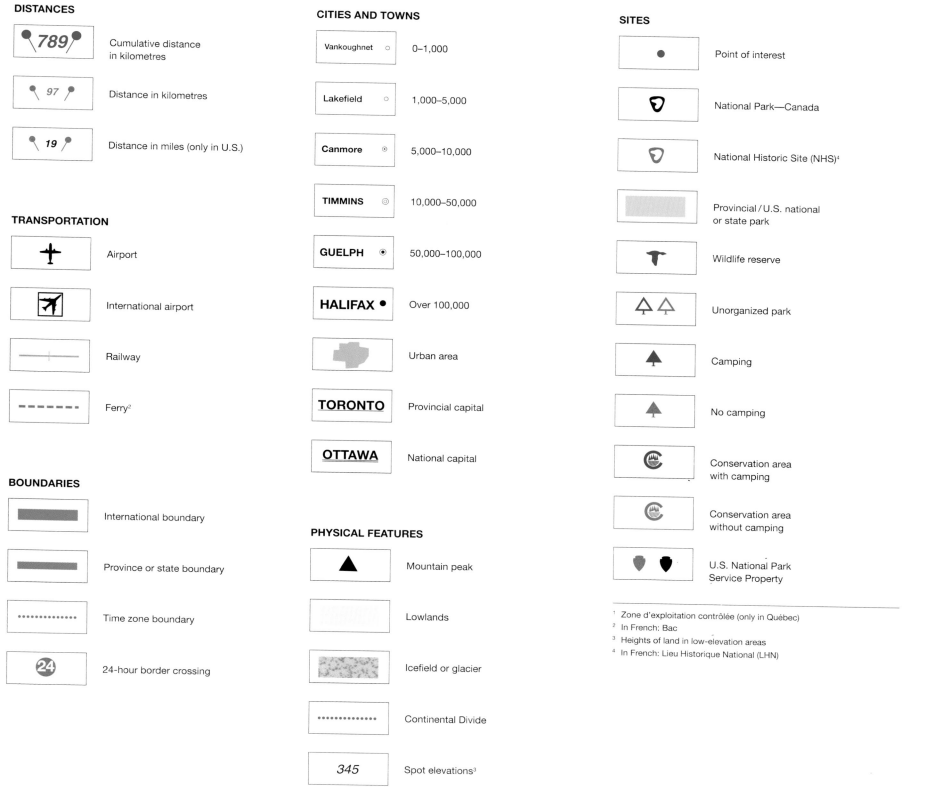

DISTANCES

789 Cumulative distance in kilometres

97 Distance in kilometres

19 Distance in miles (only in U.S.)

TRANSPORTATION

Airport

International airport

Railway

Ferry[2]

BOUNDARIES

International boundary

Province or state boundary

Time zone boundary

24-hour border crossing

CITIES AND TOWNS

Vankoughnet 0–1,000

Lakefield 1,000–5,000

Canmore 5,000–10,000

TIMMINS 10,000–50,000

GUELPH 50,000–100,000

HALIFAX Over 100,000

Urban area

TORONTO Provincial capital

OTTAWA National capital

PHYSICAL FEATURES

Mountain peak

Lowlands

Icefield or glacier

Continental Divide

345 Spot elevations[3]

SITES

Point of interest

National Park—Canada

National Historic Site (NHS)[4]

Provincial/U.S. national or state park

Wildlife reserve

Unorganized park

Camping

No camping

Conservation area with camping

Conservation area without camping

U.S. National Park Service Property

---

[1] Zone d'exploitation contrôlée (only in Québec)
[2] In French: Bac
[3] Heights of land in low-elevation areas
[4] In French: Lieu Historique National (LHN)

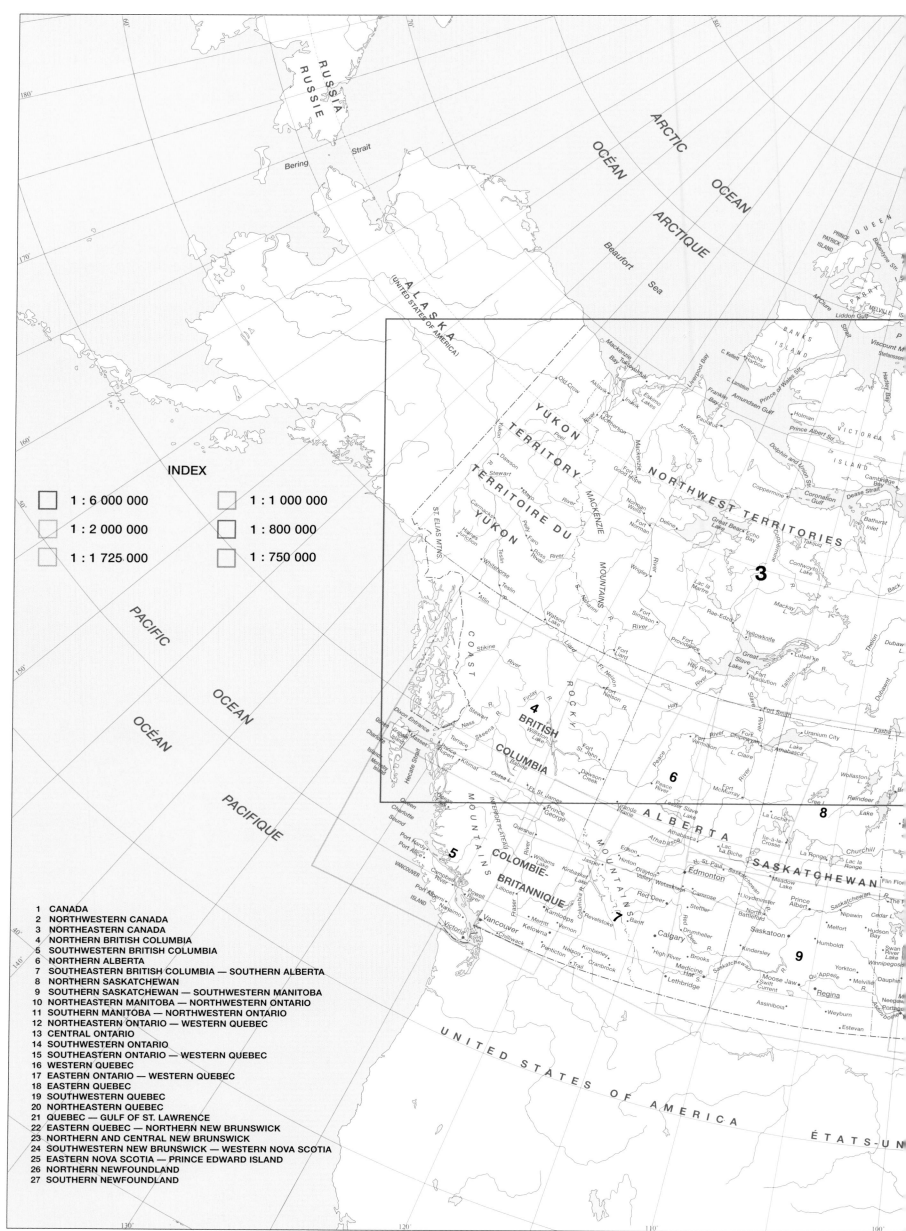

INDEX

☐ 1 : 6 000 000	☐ 1 : 1 000 000
☐ 1 : 2 000 000	☐ 1 : 800 000
☐ 1 : 1 725 000	☐ 1 : 750 000

1 CANADA
2 NORTHWESTERN CANADA
3 NORTHEASTERN CANADA
4 NORTHERN BRITISH COLUMBIA
5 SOUTHWESTERN BRITISH COLUMBIA
6 NORTHERN ALBERTA
7 SOUTHEASTERN BRITISH COLUMBIA — SOUTHERN ALBERTA
8 NORTHERN SASKATCHEWAN
9 SOUTHERN SASKATCHEWAN — SOUTHWESTERN MANITOBA
10 NORTHEASTERN MANITOBA — NORTHWESTERN ONTARIO
11 SOUTHERN MANITOBA — NORTHWESTERN ONTARIO
12 NORTHEASTERN ONTARIO — WESTERN QUEBEC
13 CENTRAL ONTARIO
14 SOUTHWESTERN ONTARIO
15 SOUTHEASTERN ONTARIO — WESTERN QUEBEC
16 WESTERN QUEBEC
17 EASTERN ONTARIO — WESTERN QUEBEC
18 EASTERN QUEBEC
19 SOUTHWESTERN QUEBEC
20 NORTHEASTERN QUEBEC
21 QUEBEC — GULF OF ST. LAWRENCE
22 EASTERN QUEBEC — NORTHERN NEW BRUNSWICK
23 NORTHERN AND CENTRAL NEW BRUNSWICK
24 SOUTHWESTERN NEW BRUNSWICK — WESTERN NOVA SCOTIA
25 EASTERN NOVA SCOTIA — PRINCE EDWARD ISLAND
26 NORTHERN NEWFOUNDLAND
27 SOUTHERN NEWFOUNDLAND

RUSSIA
RUSSIE

ARCTIC OCÉAN OCEAN ARCTIQUE

Bering Strait

Beaufort Sea

A L A S K A
(UNITED STATES OF AMERICA)

PRINCE
PATRICK
ISLAND

MELVILLE

QUEEN

Liddon Gulf

McClure Strait

C. Kellett

BANKS ISLAND

Sachs
Harbour

C. Lambton

Amundsen Gulf

VICTORIA

Prince Albert Sd.

Holman

ISLAND

Dolphin and Union Str.

Coppermine

Cambridge
Bay

Coronation Gulf

Dease Strait

Old Crow

Inuvik
Eskimo
Lakes

Aklavik

Fort
McPherson

Mackenzie
Bay
Tuktoyaktuk

Franklin Bay

Prince of Wales Str.

Bathurst
Inlet

YUKON TERRITORY
TERRITOIRE DU YUKON

NORTHWEST TERRITORIES

Dawson

Fort
Good Hope

Norman
Wells

Deline

Takijuq

Contwoyto
Lake

Mayo

Pelly

Fort
Norman

Great Bear
Lake

Echo
Bay

Faro

Ross River

Carmacks

Rae-Edzo

Mackay
L.

Yellowknife

MACKENZIE MOUNTAINS

Whitehorse

Teslin

Watson
Lake

Fort
Simpson

Thelon

Fort
Providence

ST. ELIAS MTS.

Haines
Junction

Great
Slave
Lake

Lutselke

Hay River

Fort
Resolution

Atlin

COAST

Fort
Liard

Fort Nelson

Fort
Smith

Uranium City

Stikine

Fort
Liard

Hay R.

Dease L.

Fort
Vermilion

Fort
Chipewyan

Telegraph
Creek

Finlay

ROCKY

Peace R.

Lake
Athabasca

PACIFIC OCEAN OCÉAN PACIFIQUE

Dixon Entrance

Queen Charlotte

Graham I.

Masset

Hecate Strait

BRITISH COLUMBIA
COLOMBIE-BRITANNIQUE

Williston
L.

Hazelton

Fort St. James

Fort
St. John

Dawson
Creek

McMurray

Fort
McMurray

La Loche

Grande
Prairie

ALBERTA

SASKATCHEWAN

Moresby
Island

Smithers

Terrace

Kitimat

Prince
Rupert

Queen Charlotte Sound

Prince
George

Athabasca

Île-à-la-
Crosse

La Ronge

Churchill

Skeena

Peace River

MOUNTAINS

INTERIOR PLATEAU

Quesnel

Grande
Cache

Edson

Hinton

Drayton
Valley

St. Paul

Meadow
Lake

Prince
Albert

Nipawin

Hudson
Bay

Port Hardy

Port Alice

Campbell
River

Williams
Lake

Edmonton

Wetaskiwin

Camrose

Lloydminster

North
Battleford

Melfort

Humboldt

VANCOUVER ISLAND

Port Alberni

Nanaimo

Kamloops

Revelstoke

Merritt

Vernon

Red Deer

Stettler

Saskatoon

Swan
River

Yorkton

Melville

Victoria

Vancouver

Chilliwack

Kelowna

Penticton

Nelson

Kimberley

Kindersley

Calgary

Drumheller

Medicine
Hat

Dauphin

Fraser River

Hope

Trail

Cranbrook

High River

Brooks

Saskatchewan R.

Moose Jaw

Swift
Current

Regina

Neepawa

Portage

Lethbridge

Assiniboia

Weyburn

Estevan

Qu'Appelle

U N I T E D   S T A T E S   O F   A M E R I C A

É T A T S - U

86

GREENLAND
(DENMARK)

GROENLAND
(DANEMARK)

ICELAND
ISLANDE

ELLESMERE ISLAND

Alert

Eureka

AXEL
HEIBERG
ISLAND

Amund
Ringnes

Norwegian
Bay

Grise Fiord

Jones Sound

DEVON ISLAND

Clarence
Head

Baffin Bay

Barrow Strait

Lancaster Sound

Somerset Island

Bylot

Nanisivik
Arctic Bay

C. Graham
Moore

Brodeur
Peninsula

Pond Inlet

Boothia
Peninsula

Clyde River

Gulf
of
Boothia

Taloyoak

Igloolik

Hall
Beach

Parry
Bay

Prince
Charles
Island

Broughton
Island

BAFFIN ISLAND

Pangnirtung

Cumberland Sound

Committee
Bay

Repulse
Bay

PENINSULA

Foxe
Basin

Nettilling

Amadjuak

TERRITOIRES DU NORD-OUEST

Atlantic Time Zone
Heure de l'Atlantique

Davis Strait

Wager
Bay

C. Dorcester

Southampton
Island

Coral
Harbour

Cape
Dorset

Foxe Channel

Frobisher Bay

Iqaluit

*Note : All islands in Ungava Bay, Hudson
Bay and James Bay lie within the
Northwest Territories.

*Note : Toutes les îles de la baie d'Ungava,
de la baie d'Hudson et de la baie
James font partie des Territoires du
Nord-Ouest.

Baker Lake

Baker
Inlet

Chesterfield

Evans
Strait

Coats
Island

Hudson Strait

Resolution
Island

C. Chidley

ATLANTIC   ATLANTIQUE

OCEAN

Rankin Inlet

Mansel I.

Salluit

Akpatok I.

Labrador

Sea

Arviat

Péninsule

Ungava
Bay

Nain

Hopedale

OCÉAN

Churchill

Hudson

Bay

Povungnituk
d'Ungava

Ottawa
Islands

L. Minto

Kuujjuaq

Inukjuak

Lake Melville
Goose Bay

Cartwright

NEWFOUNDLAND   TERRE-NEUVE

St. Anthony

Newfoundland Time Zone
Heure de Terre-Neuve

Gillam

C. Henrietta
Maria

Belcher
Islands

Kuujjuarapik

L. à l'Eau
Claire

Schefferville

Smallwood
Res.

Happy Valley-
Goose Bay

Churchill Falls
Churchill

Blanc-Sablon

Pahastashoo

Strait of Belle Isle
Détroit de Belle-Isle

Baie Verte

St. John's

Gods
Lake

Sandy
Lake

Red
Lake

C. Chisasibi

La

Riv.

QUÉBEC

Gagnon

Natashquan

Labrador City

Corner
Brook

Grand Falls-
Windsor

Gander

Bonavista

Carbonear

James

Bay

Attawapiskat

Akimiski
I.

Moosonee

Chibougamau

Riv.

Sept-Îles

Havre-
St-Pierre

Île d'Anticosti

Channel-Port-
aux-Basques

St-Pierre et
Grand Banks
St. Pierre et Miquelon
and Miquelon
(FRANCE)

Stephenville

CAPE
BRETON

Sioux
Lookout

Dryden

ONTARIO

Timmins

Kirkland
Lake

Rouyn-
Noranda

Val-d'Or

Chisasibi

Baie-
Comeau

Cap-
Chat

Gaspé

Îles-de-
la-Madeleine

Gulf of St. Lawrence
Golfe du Saint-Laurent

Cabot Strait

Sydney

Canso

Atikokan

Geraldton

Nipigon

Hearst

Kapuskasing

Iroquois
Falls

Matagami

Amos

St-Félicien

Roberval

Chicoutimi

La Tuque

Matane

Rimouski

Edmundston

Campbellton

Bathurst

PRINCE EDWARD
ISLAND
ÎLE-DU-PRINCE-
ÉDOUARD

Charlottetown
Summerside

Moncton

Amherst

New Glasgow

Sable I.

Thunder
Bay

Chapleau

Wawa

Sudbury

North
Bay

Mont-
Laurier

Shawinigan

Trois-Rivières

Drummondville

Sherbrooke

Alma

Québec

Montmagny

APPALACHES

LAURENTIDES

Edmundston

NEW
BRUNSWICK
NOUVEAU-
BRUNSWICK

Fredericton

Saint
John

Kentville

NOVA SCOTIA
NOUVELLE-ÉCOSSE

Halifax

Bridgewater

Liverpool

Kenora

Fort
Frances

Manitouwadge

Elliot
Lake

Sault Ste.
Marie

Georgian
Bay

Parry
Sound

Huntsville

Ottawa

Hull

Granby

St-Jérôme

Montréal

Cornwall

Brockville

Kingston

Belleville

Bay of Fundy
Baie de Fundy

Yarmouth

Baccaro Pt.

Manitoulin

Owen
Sound

Barrie

Peterborough

Oshawa

Lake Ontario

MÉRIQUE

Lake
Michigan

Lake Huron

Toronto

Hamilton

Kitchener

St. Catharines
Niagara Falls

Lake Superior

Woodstock

Brantford

Sarnia

London

Chatham

Windsor

125   0   125   250   375   500

kilometres   kilomètres

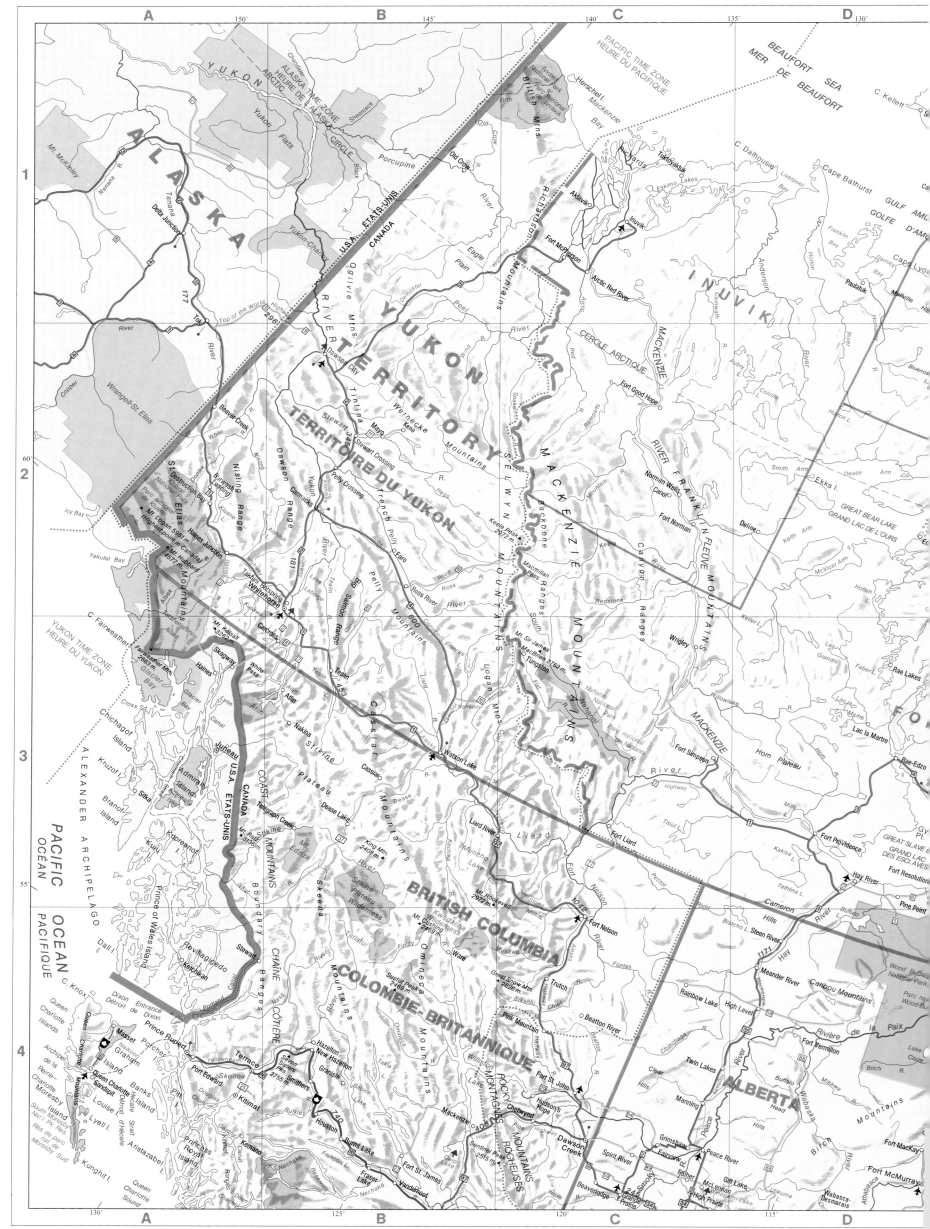

E 120° 115° 75° 110° F 105° 100° 95° G 90° 85° H 80° 75°

Aulavik National Park
Parc national de Aulavik
Mercy Bay
M'Clure Strait
BANKS
Thomsen River
Prince of Wales Strait
Passage Point

MELVILLE ISLAND
Byam Martin I.
Bathurst Island
Cornwallis Island
Kaujuitoq
DEVON ISLAND
Maxwell Bay

VISCOUNT MELVILLE SOUND
DÉTROIT DU VICOMTE-DE-MELVILLE
Lowther I.
Barrow Strait
Russell
Prince Leopold I.
LANCASTER SOUND
DÉTROIT DE LANCASTER
EASTERN TIME ZONE
HEURE DE L'EST

Dundas Peninsula
Peel Pt.
MOUNTAIN TIME ZONE
HEURE DES ROCHEUSES
Kilian I.
Stefansson Island
Minto Head
Ommanney Bay
CENTRAL TIME ZONE
HEURE DU CENTRE
C. Clarence
Cape Crauford
Arctic Bay
Adams Sd.
Borden
Bylot Island
Mittimatalik

Barnard Pt.
Richard Collinson Inlet
Wynniatt Bay
Hadley Bay
Prince Albert Peninsula
Shaler Mtns.
Storkerson Peninsula

Presoott
PRINCE OF WALES ISLAND
SOMERSET ISLAND
Creswell Bay
BRODEUR PENINSULA
Admiralty Inlet
BAFFIN ISLAND
ÎLE BAFFIN
Navy Board Inlet
Eclipse Sd.

Cape Gaston
Minto Inlet
Diamond Jenness Peninsula
Holman
Prince Albert Sound

KITIKMEOT
VICTORIA ISLAND
ÎLE VICTORIA
M'Clintock Détroit de Channel M'Clintock
C. Swinburne
Franklin Strait
Peel Sound
Prince Regent Inlet
Bernier Bay
Gifford R.
Erichsen L.

Wollaston Peninsula
Prince Albert Sound
Zela L.
Gateshead I.
Larsen Sound
Pelly Pt.
BOOTHIA PENINSULA
C. Margaret
Crown Prince Frederik I.
Fury and Hecla Str.
Jens Munk I.
Igloolik

Dolphin and Union Strait
Krusenstern C.
Washburn L.
C. Felix
James Ross Str.
Pelly Bay
Harrison Islands
C. Chapman
Sanirajaq

Coronation Gulf
Richardson I.
Cambridge Bay
Admiralty I.
Albert Edward Bay
Victoria Strait
King William Island
Matty I.
Taloyoak
Simpson Peninsula
Committee Bay
MELVILLE PENINSULA

Coppermine
Kent Peninsula
Dease Strait
Melbourne I.
Jenny Lind I.
Gjoa Haven
Rae Str.
Pelly
Simpson Str.
Simoson
Pelly Bay
Wales I.
Parry Bay

Bathurst Inlet
Melville Sound
Queen Maud Gulf
Adelaide Peninsula
Sherman Basin
Charney Inlet

Bowes Pt.
Hayes R.

ARCTIC CIRCLE
Hood
Takijuq L.
Burnside
MacAlpine L.
CERCLE ARCTIQUE
Rae Isthmus
Repulse Bay
ARCTIC CIRCLE
Winter I.
Vansittart I.

NORTHWEST TERRITOIRES
Point L.
Contwoyto
Back R.
Garry L.
TERRITORIES
DU NORD-OUEST
White I.
Frozen Str.
C. Comfort

Lac de Gras
Mackay
Aylmer
Clinton-Colden
Artillery L.
Thelon
Schultz L.
Tehek
Baker Lake
Baker L.
Wager Bay
Roes Welcome Sound
SOUTHAMPTON ISLAND
Coral Harbour

SMITH
McLeod B.
Christie B.
Reliance
Whitefish L.
Wharton L.
Mallery L.
Chesterfield Inlet
Cape Fullerton
Cape Kendall
Bay of Gods Mercy
Cape Low
Fisher Strait

Lutsel'ke
Snowdrift
Lynx L.
KEEWATIN
Dubawnt Lake
Kaminuriak
Chesterfield Inlet
Kangiqcliniq
Rankin Inlet
Marble I.
Coats Island

Rutledge L.
Nonacho River
Yathkyed Lake
Kaminak L.
Whale Cove

Taltson
Thoa
Whoidaia Lake
Snowbird Lake
Ennadai Lake
Angikuni L.
Kazan R.
Baker R.
Dawson Inlet
Maguse
Arviat

Tazin L.
Uranium City
Kasba Lake
Nueltin Lake
Selwyn L.
Edehon L.
Thlewiaza River
South Henik L.
Tha-anne R.
HUDSON BAY
BAIE D'HUDSON

Lake Athabasca
Fond-du-Lac Fond
Stony Rapids
Black Lake
Wollaston L.
Cree L.
Cochrane R.
Nejanilini L.
Caribou R.

SASKATCHEWAN
955
Wollaston Lake
Brochet
MANITOBA
Reindeer Lake
Big Sand L.
Tadoule L.
Seal River
Churchill
Cape Churchill
Flekwe R.
North Knife L.
Churchill River
Owl R.
905

50 0 50 100 150 200 250
kilometres 1:6 000 000 kilomètres

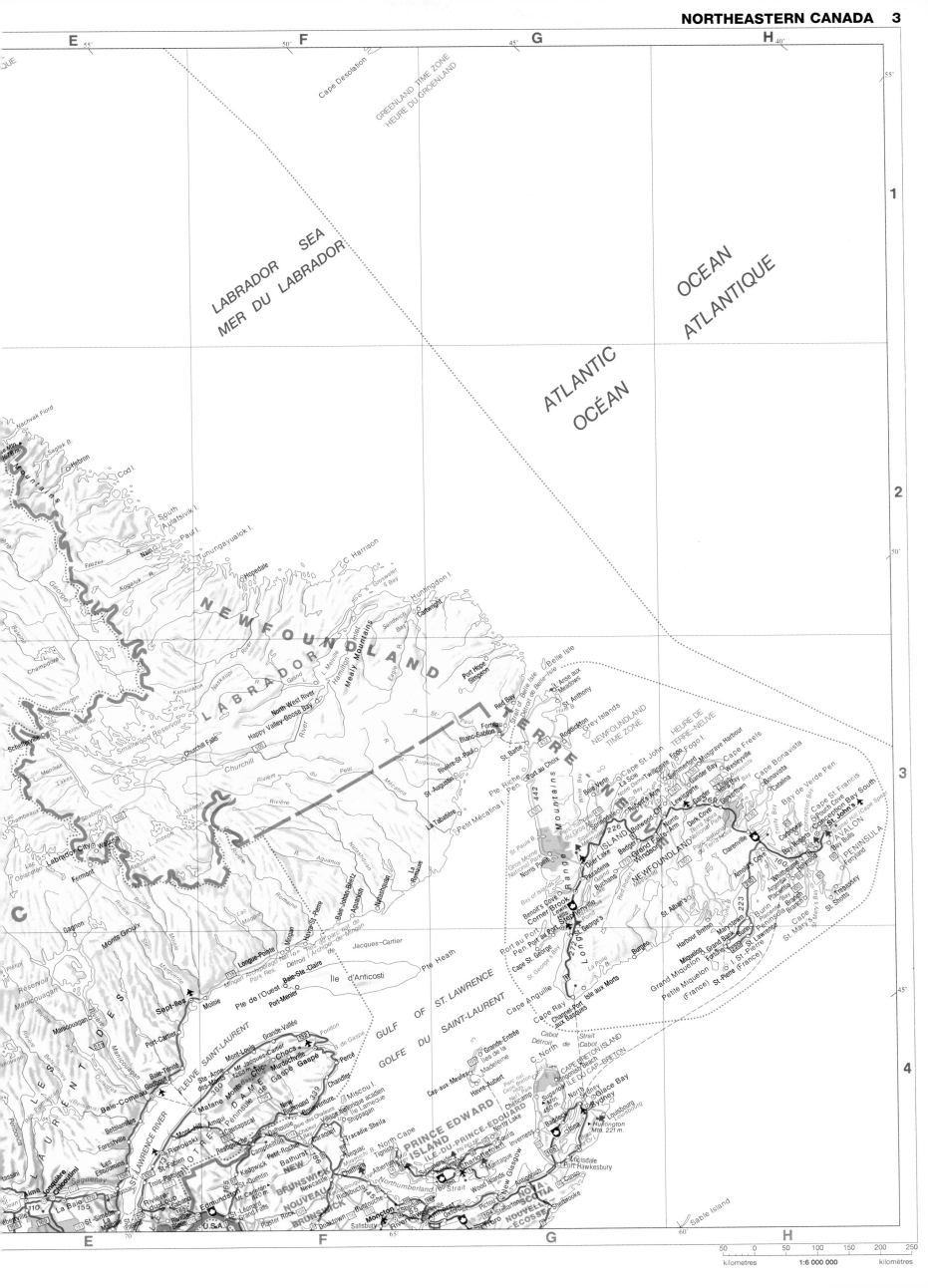

LABRADOR SEA
MER DU LABRADOR

OCEAN ATLANTIQUE

ATLANTIC OCÉAN

GREENLAND TIME ZONE
HEURE DU GROENLAND

Cape Desolation

NEWFOUNDLAND

LABRADOR

NEWFOUNDLAND TIME ZONE
HEURE DE TERRE-NEUVE

GULF OF ST. LAWRENCE
GOLFE DU SAINT-LAURENT

Île d'Anticosti

PRINCE EDWARD ISLAND
ÎLE-DU-PRINCE-ÉDOUARD

NEW BRUNSWICK
NOUVEAU BRUNSWICK

NOVA SCOTIA
NOUVELLE-ÉCOSSE

St. John's

Sable Island

50   0   50   100   150   200   250
kilometres   1:6 000 000   kilomètres

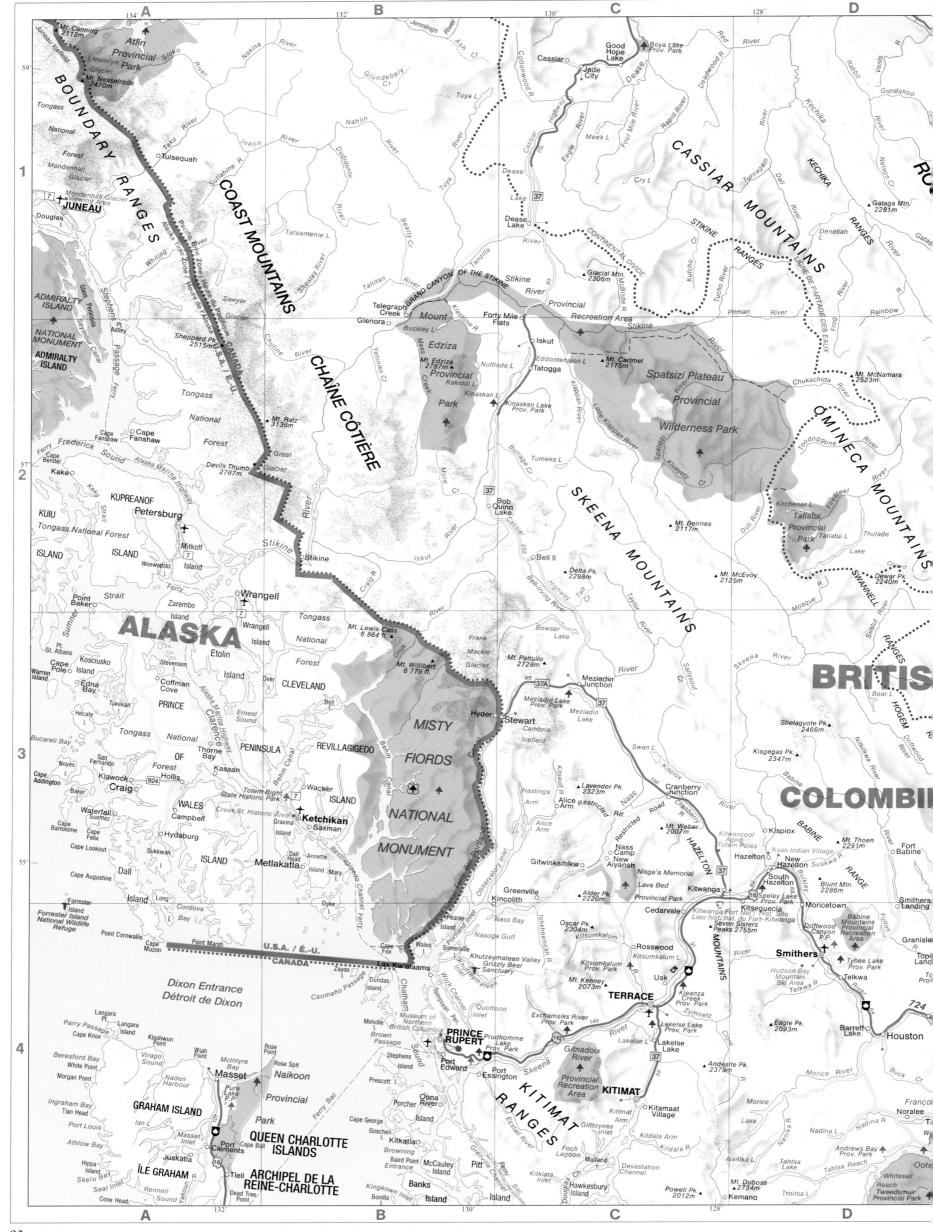

E 124° F 122° G 120° H 118°

Grayling R
River
Springs Park
Liard
Nelson Forks
River
Fort 77
Nelson
Muncho Lake Provincial Park
Muncho L
Muncho Lake
Toad River
97 Alaska Summit Pass Highway
Stone Mountain Provincial Park
219
115 Creek Prov. Park
Racing R
Wokkpash Provincial Recreation Area
Schiga
Churchill Pk. 2819m
Tuchodi
Mt. Sylvia 2942m
Creek
Fort Nelson
28
Andy Bailey Prov. Rec. Area
Muskwa
Cheves Cr
Elleh
Kyklo Cr
Kotcho Lake
735m
Kwokullie L
Thetlaandoa Cr
Shekilie
Zama Lake
Meander River
59°
35
Hay L
Zama L
Habay
Chateh
141
58
1

Kwadacha Provincial Wilderness Park
Prophet River
97
Prophet River Prov. Rec. Area
River
Trutch
Trutch Cr
Conroy Cr
Beatton River
Fontas River
1082m
Amber River
Mega R
Hay River
Rainbow Lake
Paddle Prairie
Keg River
35 695
Kemp R
Chinchaga River

ROCKY MOUNTAIN FOOTHILLS
Great Snow Mtn. 2896m
Deserters Pk. 2265m
Mica Pk. 2065m
FINLAY RANGES
Mt. Laurier 2351m
Chowade River
Halfway River
Graham River
Buckinghorse River Prov. Park
Buckinghorse River
Sikanni Chief
Pink Mountain
Besa River
Sikanni
Chief River
Beatton River
Prespatou
Altona
Dolg River
1120m
CLEAR HILLS
Whitemud River
ALBERTA
57° 2

INTERIOR PLAINS / PLAINES DE L'INTÉRIEUR
Pacific Time Zone / Heure du Pacifique
Mountain Time Zone / Heure des Rocheuses

COLUMBIA
MONTAGNES ROCHEUSES
ROCKY MOUNTAIN RANGES
Williston Lake
Wonowon
Blueberry River
Buick
Rose Prairie
Montney
North Pine
Goodlow
Cleardale
Worsley
Eureka
Eureka River
726 730
120
64 685 737
Hines Creek
732 735 Brownvale
729 Whitelaw 2
Fairview 682
Bluesky

CRITANNIQUE
Germansen Landing
Manson Creek
Omineca River
Osilinka River
Finlay Reach
Dunlevy Prov. Rec. Area
W.A.C. Bennett Dam
Hudson's Hope
Peace Reach
Charlie Lake Prov. Park
Charlie Lake
FORT ST. JOHN
Baldonnel
Taylor
Cecil Lake
Beatton
North Pine
67
Clayhurst
Cherry Point
Peace River
Taylor Landing Prov. Park
Kiskatinaw Prov. Park
Farmington
97
Rolla
73
Silver Valley
Bonanza
Gordondale
Moonshine Lake Provincial Park
725 Blueberry Mountain
681 680 Dunvegan
727 Rycroft
Dunvegan Historical Village
Dunvegan Prov. Park
Spirit River 731
Wanham 733
Woking
677 2
3

HART RANGES
MISINCHINKA RANGES
Germansen L
Chuchi Lake
Tchentlo Lake
Led Creek
Witch L
Klawli R
Nation River
Pine Pass
Azu Mountain Ski Area
Mackenzie
39 29
Bijoux Falls Prov. Park
Tudyah Lake Prov. Park
McLeod Lake
McLeod
406
Pine River
Chetwynd
Moberly Lake
Moberly Lake Prov. Park
29
Lone Prairie
Murray River
Sukunka Falls Prov. Park
Gwillim Lake Prov. Park
29
Bullmoose Mtn. 2020m
Tumbler Ridge
Sunset Prairie
Progress
Groundbirch
98
East Pine Prov. Park
Arras
Mile 0 Alaska Highway
DAWSON CREEK
Pouce Coupe
Pouce Coupe 1033m
49
Swan Lake Prov. Park
Sudeten P.P.
Tupper
Tomslake
Demmitt
720 721 719
105
Gordondale
Bay Tree
Bear Canyon
717
Lymburn
Goodfare
Beaverlodge
Saskatoon Island Prov. Park
Hythe
724
672
La Glace
59
Valhalla Centre
Buffalo Lake
Clairmont
Huallen
SEXSMITH
674
GRANDE PRAIRIE
Teepee Creek
Bezanson
104
736
55° 3

CONTREFORTS DES ROCHEUSES
CONTINENTAL DIVIDE / LIGNE DE PARTAGE DES EAUX
Middle River
Kazchek L
Inzana L
Tezzeron Cr
Carp Lake Provincial Park
Carp Lake
Whiskers Point Prov. Park
Parsnip River
152
Crooked River
Sentinel Pk. 2499m
Mountain Time Zone / Heure des Rocheuses
Pacific Time Zone / Heure du Pacifique
Monkman Provincial Park
Ice Mtn. 2286m
Wapiti River
Narraway River
Cutbank River
Kakwa River
40
734
4

Trembl.eur Lake
Tachie
Pinchi Lake
Stuart Lake Prov. Park
Tezzeron Cr
Fort St. James National Historic Site
Lieu historique national du Fort-St-James
Stuart Lake
Sowchea Bay Prov. Rec. Area
Fort St. James
Raarens Beach Prov. Park
Salmon River
Great Beaver L
Crooked River Prov. Park
Bear Lake
97
Summit Lake
Summit L
Fraser River
Upper Fraser
McGregor River
Sinclair Mills
Herrick Creek
Mt. Sir Alexander 3274m
Monkman Provincial Recreation Area
Kakwa Provincial Recreation Area
Mt. May 2450m
Mt. Buchanan 2735m
Intersection Mtn. 2461m
Grande Cache
143

Burns Lake
Endako
128
Beaumont Prov. Park
Fort Fraser
27
Nechako River National Wildlife Reserve
Eskers Prov. Park
Willow River
Purden Lake Prov. Park
Longworth
Penny
CN
Fleuve Fraser River
Dome Creek
Crescent Spur
Morkill River
Mt. De Veber 2577m
Willmore Wilderness Provincial Park
162

Fraser Lake
Fraser Lake
Lejac
Engen
Tachick
Vanderhoof
16
Isle Pierre
Reid Lake
Shelley
PRINCE GEORGE
18
Mt. Bagg 2384m
Mt. Chown 3351m
Resthaven Mtn. 3098m
Resthaven Icefield
JASPER N.P.
P.N. JASPER

Southbank
Tchesinkut Lake
Francois Lake
Nulki L
Cluculz L
Dahl Lake Prov. Park
Baldy Hughes
West Lake P.P.
97A
Red Rock
Stoner
97
Kenney Dam
Nechako River
Cheslatta Lake
Intata Reach
Finger L
Willow River
Bowron River

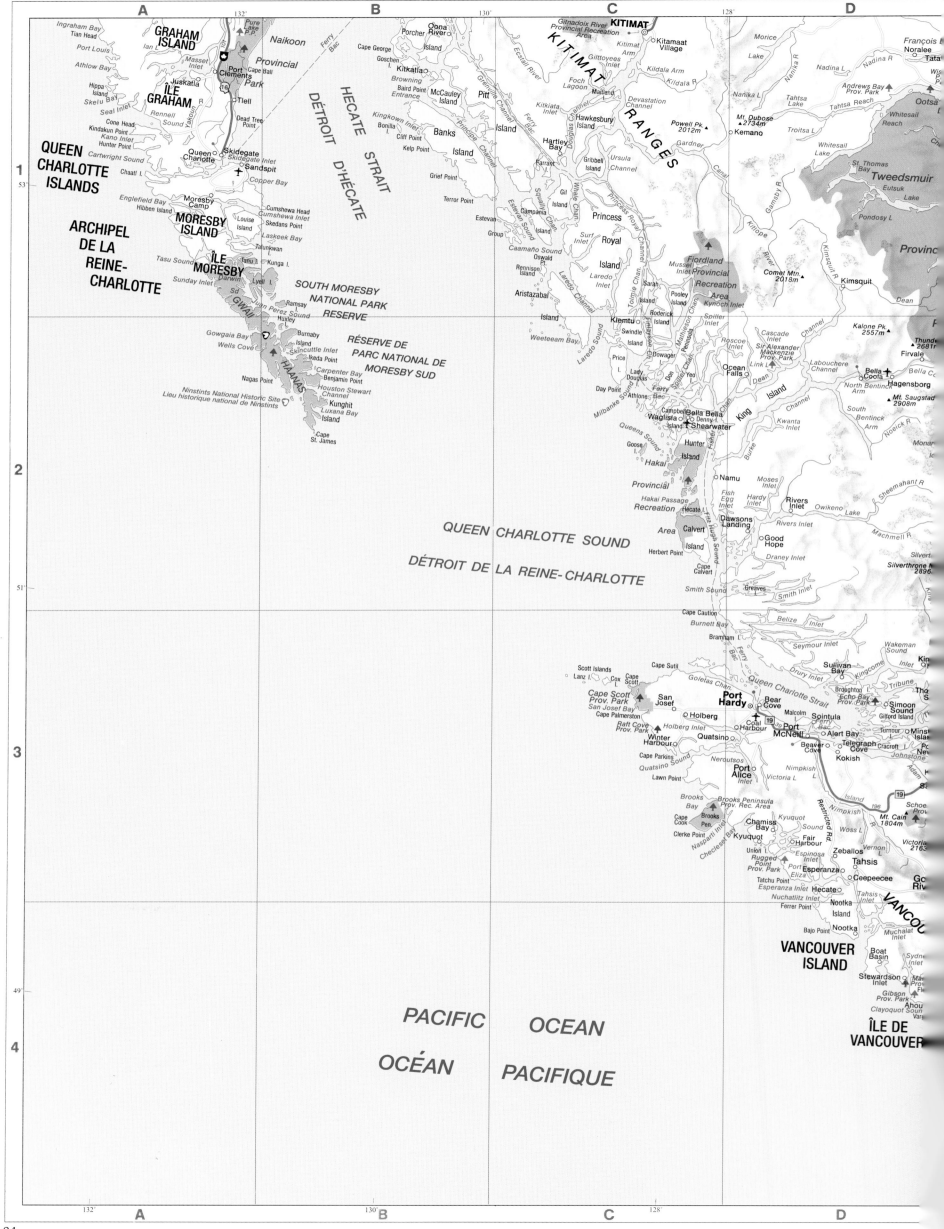

BRITISH COLUMBIA
COLOMBIE-BRITANNIQUE

INTERIOR PLATEAU
PLATEAU DE L'INTÉRIEUR

ALBERTA

WASHINGTON

CHAÎNE CÔTIÈRE

COLUMBIA MOUNTAINS

MONASHEE MOUNTAINS

CASCADE RANGE

CANADA
U.S.A. / É.U.

Major places: Prince George, Quesnel, Williams Lake, Vanderhoof, Fort Fraser, Endako, McBride, Valemount, Kamloops, Salmon Arm, Vernon, Kelowna, Penticton, Merritt, Cache Creek, Ashcroft, Clinton, Lytton, Hope, Princeton, Chilliwack, Abbotsford, Mission, Maple Ridge, Port Coquitlam, Coquitlam, Port Moody, Surrey, Langley, Delta, Richmond, Burnaby, VANCOUVER, North Vancouver, W. Vancouver, White Rock, Squamish, Whistler, Pemberton, Lillooet, Powell River, Comox, Courtenay, Campbell River, Parksville, Port Alberni, Nanaimo, Ladysmith, Duncan, Sidney, VICTORIA, Esquimalt, Colwood, Oak Bay, Saanich, Bellingham, Mount Vernon, Anacortes, Oak Harbor, Sedro Woolley, Osoyoos, Oliver, Keremeos, Summerland, Peachland, Westbank

Mt. Robson 3954m, Mt. Waddington 4016m, Mt. Sir Alexander 3274m, Mt. Chown 3331m, Mt. Sir Wilfred Laurier 3505m, Mt. Baker 3285m / 10 778 ft.

Provincial Parks: Bowron Lake Provincial Park, Wells Gray Provincial Park, Garibaldi Provincial Park, Manning Provincial Park, Pacific Rim, Jasper National Park / Parc National de Jasper, Willmore Wilderness Provincial Park

Rivers: Fraser River, Nechako River, Thompson, Chilcotin, Chilako, Quesnel River, Columbia River

53° 51° 49°

124° 122° 120°

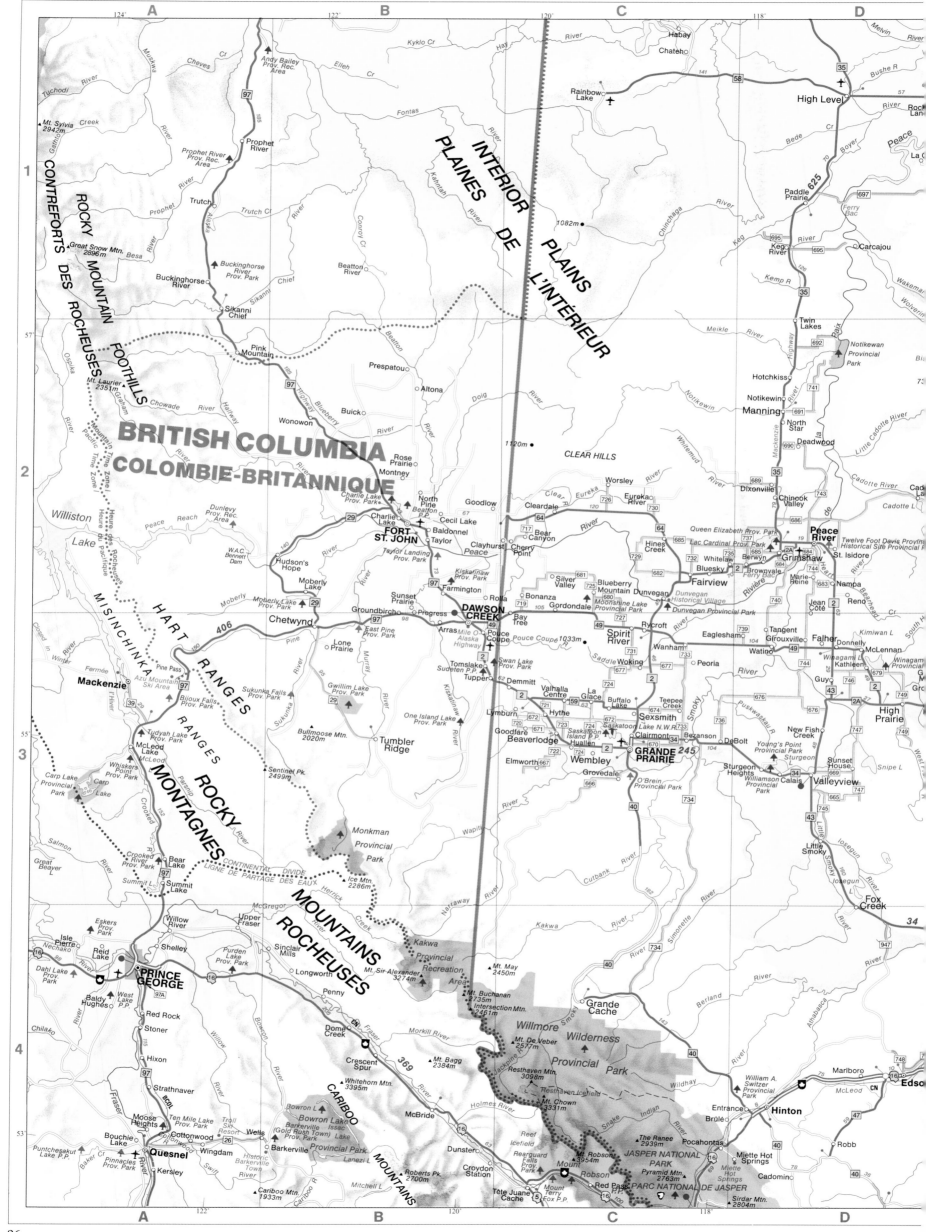

NORTHERN ALBERTA

ALBERTA

SASKATCHEWAN

WOOD BUFFALO NATIONAL PARK / PARC NATIONAL WOOD BUFFALO

Lake Athabasca / Lac Athabasca
Fort Chipewyan
Old Fort Bay
Carswell Lake
Lake Claire / Lac Claire
Mamawi Lake
Baril Lake
Snare River
William River
Charles Lake

John D'oro Prairie
Fox Lake
Eva L
Riviêre
de la Paix

BIRCH MOUNTAINS
Gardiner Lakes
Namur L
Legend L
Mink L
Grew
Chipewyan L
776m

BUFFALO HEAD HILLS
Lafond Cr

Richardson Lake National Wildlife Reserve
Richardson Lake
Douglas R
Cluff Lake
McTaggart L

Fort MacKay
Steepbank River
955
Descharme River
Descharme Lake
Preston L
Lloyd L
Careen L
Roe L
Black Birch Lake
Wasekamio Lake

FORT McMURRAY
Fort McMurray Oil Sands Interpretive Centre
Clearwater
Clearwater River Provincial Park
955
Turnor Lake
Frobisher Lake
La Loche
Lac La Loche
Black Point
Bear Creek
Turnor Lake
Waskwei I

Gregoire Lake Provincial Park
Anzac
Gordon Lake
Gipsy L
Garson Lake
Garson Lake
Kimowin R
GRIZZLY BEAR HILLS
St. George's Hill
Dillon
Michel
Peter Pond Lake
Landing
Churchill Lake
155
Buffalo Narrows

Loon Lake
Red Earth Creek
Peerless Lake
Trout Lake
Graham L
Tepee L
63
CHEECHAM HILLS
881
Chard
Bohn L
Dillon L
925
Dillon

88
686
91
Peerless Lake
Muskwa L
North Wabasca Lake
Wabasca-Desmarais
Mariana Lake
63
Christina L
Conklin
Christina Lake
Winefred River
Vermette L
Niska L
Upper Cummins
MOSTOOS HILLS
Kazan L
Aubichon Arm

PELICAN MOUNTAINS
1023m
South Wabasca Lake
Sandy Lake
754
813
Rock Island
Orloff L
Fawcett L
McMillan L
Wandering River
WATAPI L
Wiau L
SASKATCHEWAN
773m
904
Flotten L
Waterhen Lake

Lesser Slave Lake Provincial Park
Petit Lac des Esclaves
Canyon Creek
Widewater
Kinuso
Faust
Slave Lake
2
Smith
Hondo
Calling Lake
Calling Lake Provincial Park
Breynat
Wandering River
Imperial Mills
881
Logan L
Heart L
Sand River
COLD LAKE AIR WEAPONS RANGE
PRIMROSE LAKE
Primrose Lake
Cole Bay
Jans Bay
Canoe Lake
Canoe Narrows
Macallum
Arsenault L

ALBERTA
33
House Mtn. 1067m
Swan Hills
Saulteaux River
Chisholm
Island Lake
2
813
Grassland
Plamondon
Churchill Provincial Park
Lac la Biche
Lakeland Provincial Park
Beaver River
Touchwood
Spencer L
Wolf L
Marie Lake
Cold Lake
919
Meadow Lake Provincial Park
Lac des Iles
224
Waterhen Lake
941
Dorintosh

Swan Ridge Ski Area
Freeman River
44
Fawcett
663
Atmore
Buck
Hylo
North Missawawi L
858
Pinehurst Recreation Area
Seibert
Lakeland Provincial Park
Cold Lake Prov. Park
Cold Lake
892
950
Goodsoil
Beaver

Flatbush
West Baptiste
White Gull
Sunset Beach
Cross Lake Prov. Park
812
Athabasca
63
Boyle
Caslan
Fork Lake
55
Goodridge
Iron River
41
Medley
La Corey
Grand Centre
Piercland
55
Peerless L
Rapid View
Meadow Lake

Jarvie
801
Colinton
663
Bondiss
Boyle
89
866
867
Goodridge
McRae
Moose Lake Prov. Park
Ardmore
Beaver Crossing
21
Makwa Lake Provincial Park
304

Vega
661
Larkspur
Perryvale
Rochester
76
Kikino
Long Lake Prov. Park
Whitefish L
36
Goodfish Lake
St. Lina
Franchere
Glendon
Bonnyville
897
Beaverdam
699
Loon Lake
10
Meadow Lake

Fort Assiniboine
769
776
Pibroch
Tawatinaw
Tawatinaw Valley Ski Area
Abee
Bellis
Boyne
Garner Lake Prov. Park
Therien
882
Hoselaw
Gurneyville
557
Steele Narrows Provincial Historic Park
Makwa

Whitecourt
658
Camp Creek
Neerlandia
Bloomsbury
Rossington
18
Westlock
Clyde
Egremont
Radway
827
Warspite
Waskatenau
857
Smoky Lake
859
Vilna
28
St. Brides
St. Paul
Horseshoe
Flat Lake
Sputinow
Barthel
4

Blue Ridge
655
Tiger Lily
763
Manola
777
Pickardville
Busby
11
18
Thorhild
656
Radway
Andrew
Hamlin
652
Saddle Lake
Lafond
881
Elk Point
41
Lindbergh
897
Bronson L
Onion Lake
26
Brightsand
795

Green Court
751
Rochfort Bridge
654
764
Sangudo
Birch Cove
651
Legal
Alcomdale
Sandy Beach
794
803
Redwater
38
St. Michael
830
Star
637
Wostok
Willingdon
860
Brosseau
Duvernay
Musidora
Myrnam
640
893
Dewberry
Fort Pitt Prov. Hist. Park
641
Tulliby Lake
797
Frenchman Butte
Paradise Hill
21
Spruce Lake

Barrhead
Gunn
Alberta Beach
Darwell
633
Morinville
Calahoo
Namao
28A
Bon Accord
Gibbons
643
Bruderheim
644
Lamont
855
Chipman
645
Hairy Hill
Two Hills
Beauvallon
870
Derwent
Marwayne
631
Greenstreet
45
Hillmond
21
Turtle Lake
South Bay

Morinville
Onoway
Villeneuve
ST. ALBERT
FORT SASKATCHEWAN
21
P.N. ELK ISLAND N.P.
15
Hilliard
Mundare
Warwick
631
Lavoy
Ranfurly
Innisfree
Minburn
Mannville
16
Vermilion
897
LLOYDMINSTER
Streamstown
Kitscoty
Blackfoot
684
Marshall
303
Mervin
794
697

SPRUCE GROVE
Wabamun
16X
EDMONTON
Wabamun Lake Provincial Park
SHERWOOD PARK
Cooking Lake
Vegreville
Beaverhill L
Lindbrook
626
855
857
Poe
Holden
870
Musidora
251
Vermilion Provincial Park
Islay
CN
760m
Clandonald
Marwayne
Rivercourse
675
Maidstone
Waseca

Stony Plain
Devon
Nisku
625
Beaumont
New Sarepta
Miquelon Lake P.P.
Kingman
617
Round Hill
Bruce
Viking
615
Kinsella
619
Paradise Valley
614
McLaughlin
675
21
Neilburg
40
Cut Knife

Drayton Valley
621
St. Francis
Lindale
622
Telfordville
39
LEDUC
Kavanagh
814
Tofield
Ryley
855
14
Holden
654
870
Fabyan
881
Heath
Marsden
17
Wilbert

Cynthia
753
Rocky Rapids
Geneseo
654
Warburg
778
Thorsby
Calmar
CAMROSE
Ohaton
26
Daysland
Bawlf
13
Wainwright
17

Lodgepole
620
Breton
616
Sundance Beach
Pigeon Lake Prov. Park
Buck L
Pipestone P.P.
Westerose
Gwynne
Armena
834
854
WETASKIWIN
56
2A
822
Bittern L
Millet
Mulhurst
Falun

20   0   20   40   60   80   100
kilometres   1:2 000 000   kilomètres

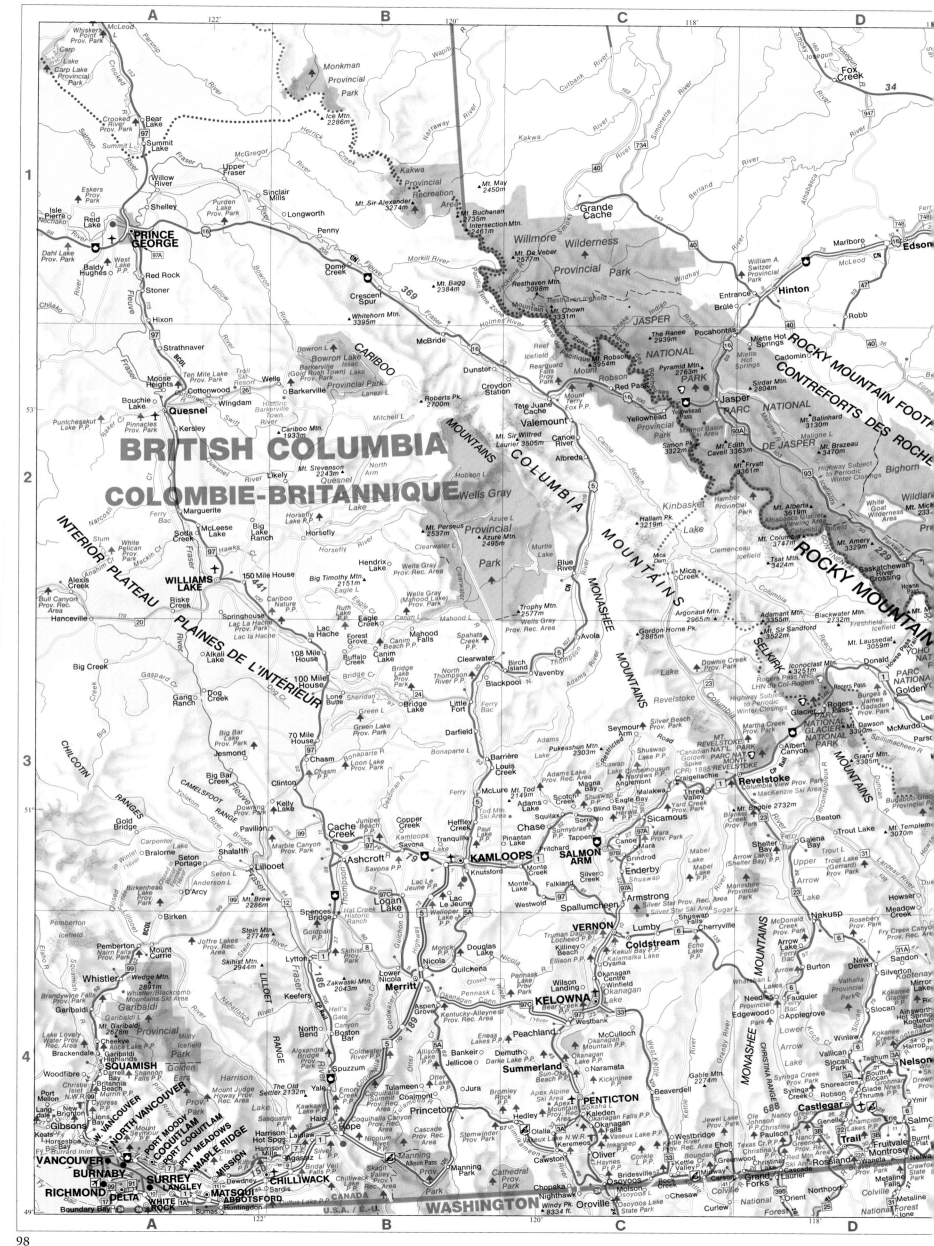

ALBERTA

MONTAGNES ROCHEUSES

SASKATCHEWAN

MONTANA

CANADA
U.S.A. / É.-U.

Major places:

- EDMONTON
- ST. ALBERT
- FORT SASKATCHEWAN
- SHERWOOD PARK
- SPRUCE GROVE
- Stony Plain
- Beaumont
- LEDUC
- CAMROSE
- WETASKIWIN
- Ponoka
- Lacombe
- Blackfalds
- RED DEER
- Sylvan Lake
- Penhold
- Innisfail
- Olds
- Didsbury
- Carstairs
- Crossfield
- AIRDRIE
- Cochrane
- CALGARY
- Strathmore
- Okotoks
- High River
- Nanton
- Claresholm
- Fort Macleod
- LETHBRIDGE
- Coaldale
- Taber
- Coalhurst
- Magrath
- Raymond
- Cardston
- Pincher Creek
- Crowsnest Pass
- Coleman
- Blairmore
- Bellevue
- Fernie
- CRANBROOK
- Kimberley
- Sparwood
- Banff
- Canmore
- Brooks
- MEDICINE HAT
- Redcliff
- Bow Island
- LLOYDMINSTER
- St. Paul
- Elk Point
- Vegreville
- Vermilion
- Wainwright
- Stettler
- Hanna
- Drumheller
- Rosedale
- Coronation
- Consort
- Oyen
- Vulcan
- Three Hills
- WATERTON-GLACIER INTERNATIONAL PEACE PARK
- WATERTON LAKES NAT'L PARK / PARC NAT. DES LACS-WATERTON
- NATIONAL PARK / PARC NATIONAL DE BANFF
- KOOTENAY NATIONAL PARK
- CYPRESS HILLS
- THE MIDDLE SAND HILLS
- Canadian Forces Base Suffield
- Sweetgrass
- Coutts
- Shelby
- Cut Bank
- Browning

TERRITOIRES DU NORD-OUEST
Heure des Rocheuses
Heure du Centre

MANITOBA

HEWAN

Lakes and places (partial):

Lacusta L, Opescal L, Sovereign L, Dodge Lake, Selwyn Lake, Faraud L, Grollier Lake, Bompas L, Young L, Herbert Lake, Hawkins L, Wapiyao L, Keseechewun L, Bonokoski L, Misaw Lake, Wayow L, Bailey L, Patterson L, Kasba Lake, Hasbala L, Schwandt R, Snyder L, Putahow Lake, Nahili L, Nueltin L, Nejanilini Lake

Chipman R, Stony Lake, Black Lake, Fir I, Porcupine R, Ochak L, Fanson L, Franklin L, Walker L, Nunim L, Kohn L, Hara L, Burnett L, Kasmere Lake, Partridge River, Little Duck L, Wolverine R

Black Lake, Giles Lake, Wapata L, Hawrock L, Fond du Lac River, Misekumaw L, Hannah L, Nordbye L, Walsh L, Kingston L, Bannock L, Charcoal Lake, Misty Lake, Lac Brochet, Munroe Lake, MacLeod L, Dufflin Lakes, Egenolf L, Seal L

Forsyth L, Hatchet L, Bentley L, Waspison Lake, Kingsley L, Whiskey Jack L, Sprott L, Seal River, North R, Stony Lake, Shethanei L, Negassa L, Tadoule Lake

Pasfield Lake, Theriau Lake, Cunning Bay, Snowshoe L, Collins Bay, Rabbabou Bay, Clark Bay, Wollaston, George I, Fidler Bay, Blue I, Zangeza Bay, Zengle L, Cochrane R, Chipewyan R, Big Sand Lake, Trout L, Little Sand L, Currie L

Points North Landing, Rabbit Lake Mine, Wollaston Lake, Hidden Bay, Loranger Island, Mackenzie L, Nekweaga Bay, Compulsion Bay, Cumines I, Boundary Island, Brochet, Waterbury Lake, Close L, Micheal L

Keefe L, Morell L, Cairns L, Reindeer Lake, Bedford Island, Swan Bay, Beaver I, Eyrie L, Jordan Lake, MacKerracher L, Moss L, Wood L, Muskwesi R, Southern Indian Lake

Wheeler L, Russell Lake, Peter L, Lac du Caribou, Wells Lake, Melvin L, James L, Denison L, Long Pt, Gauer Lake, Partridge Breast Lake

Key Lake Mine, Wathaman L, Wepusko Bay, Kinoosao, Malcolm Island, Vandekerckhove Lake, Goldsand L, Torrance L, Chapman L, Cousins L

Upper Foster Lake, Oliver L, Nokomis Lake, McMillan L, Zed L, Lynn Lake, Hughes River, Barrington L, Opachuanau Lake, South Indian Lake, Bac Ferry, Uhlman Lake, Baldock L

Middle Foster L, Deception Lake, Davin Lake, Numabin Bay, Lawrence Bay, Dunphy Lakes, McVeigh, Fox Mine, Eden Lake, Rusty L, Barnes L, Roe L

Lower Foster L, Pink River, Macoun Lake, Laurie Lake, Tod L, Eager L, McGavock L, Drybrough, Chicken L, Granville Lake, Karsakuwigamak L, Pemichigamau L, Harding Lake

Gow L, Missi L, May L, Deep Bay, Shaw L, Kamuchawie Lake, Russell L, Herriot, Hone, Leaf Rapids, Costello L, Leftrook Lake

Hickson L, Maribelli L, Kyaska L, Harriott R, Pagato L, Kamatsi L, McCallum L, Jetait, McKnight Lake, Suwannee Lake, Raft Lake, Rat River, Nelson House, Footprint L

Paull L, Jewett L, Brabant Lake, Harriott L, Steephill Lake, Pagato River, Wapisu L, Highrock L, Nelson L, Wapisu Lake, Odei River

Keith L, McTavish Lake, Hepburn L, Versailles L, Colin L, Loon River, Britton L, Pukatawagan L, Heaman L, Highrock L, Threepoint Lake, Wuskwatim L, Ospwagan L

Shadd L, McLennan Lake, Brabant Lake, Wiskau R, Okipwatsikew L, Loon Lake, Pukatawagan, Pawistik, Flatrock L, Apeganau L, Paint Lake Prov. Rec. Area

Campbell L, Grandmother's Bay, Missinipe, Mountain L, Iskwatam L, Wintego Lake, Flanagan L, Sisipuk Lake, Morin L, Rafter L, Charles L, Wimapedi River

Black Bear Island Lake, North Bay, Otter L, Stanley Mission Provincial Historic Site, Nistowiak L, Trade Lake, Manawan Lake, Sandy Bay, Kipahigan Lake, Takipy, Burntwood Lake, Setting L, Halfway L

Stanley Mission, Iskwatikan L, Keg L, Churchill River, Kississing, Guthrie L, Ruddock L, Wimapedi L, Ferguson Creek, Lyddal, Grass R

Sucker River, Lac la Ronge Provincial Park, Nunn L, Sadler L, Wood Lake, Chachukew L, Pelican Narrows, Mari L, Kississing Lake, Moose L, Big I, Sherridon, Limestone Point L, File L, Wabowden, Pipun, Duck L

La Ronge, Air Ronge, Lac la Ronge, Hunter Bay, Wapawekka Lake, Brownell L, Mirond L, Corneille L, Wildnest L, Kisseynew L, Fay Lake, Loonhead L, Snow Lake, Herblet L, Herb Lake, Wekusko Lake, Hargrave L

Bigstone R, Deschambault Lake, Jan Lake, Jan Lake Prov. Rec. Site, Hanson L, Embury L, Flin Flon, Optic Lake, Naosap L, Heming Lake, Woosey L, Herb Lake Landing, Kiski L, Dunlop, Button

Deschambault Lake, Lac Deschambault, WAPAWEKKA HILLS, Amisk Lake, Amisk Lake Prov. Rec. Site, Creighton, Bakers Narrows, Sherritt Jct, Grass River Provincial Park, Reed Lake, Tyrrell, Ponton, Turnbull, Wekusko, Paterson

Bear River, Meeyoomoot L, East Trout L, Montréal L, Twigge L, Bigstone L, Acheninni L, Denare Beach, Schist Lake, Payuk L, Athapap L, Cranberry Portage, Simonhouse L, McClarty L, Dering, Cormorant, Dyce, Kiskitto Lake

Timber Bay, Suggi Lake, Windy L, Seager Wheeler L, Mossy River, McKenzie L, Namew Lake, Sturgeon Landing, Maraiche L, Goose L, Egg L, Simonhouse, Dering L, North Moose Lake, Kiskittogisu L

Cumberland Lake, Rocky Lake, Atik L, Wanless, Clearwater L, Halcrow, Mawdesley L, Budd, Clearwater Lake P.P., Root Lake, William L, Minago R

Highways (partial): 905, 247, 102, 22, 915, 36, 912, 2, 20, 969, 927, 913, 165, 911, 106, 122, 135, 69, 167, 10, 394, 396, 391, 204, 375, 123, 393, 395, 392, 39, 596, 373, 30, 6, 101, 596, 175

449 m, 469 m, 796 m

20 0 20 40 60 80 100
kilometres   1:2 000 000   kilomètres

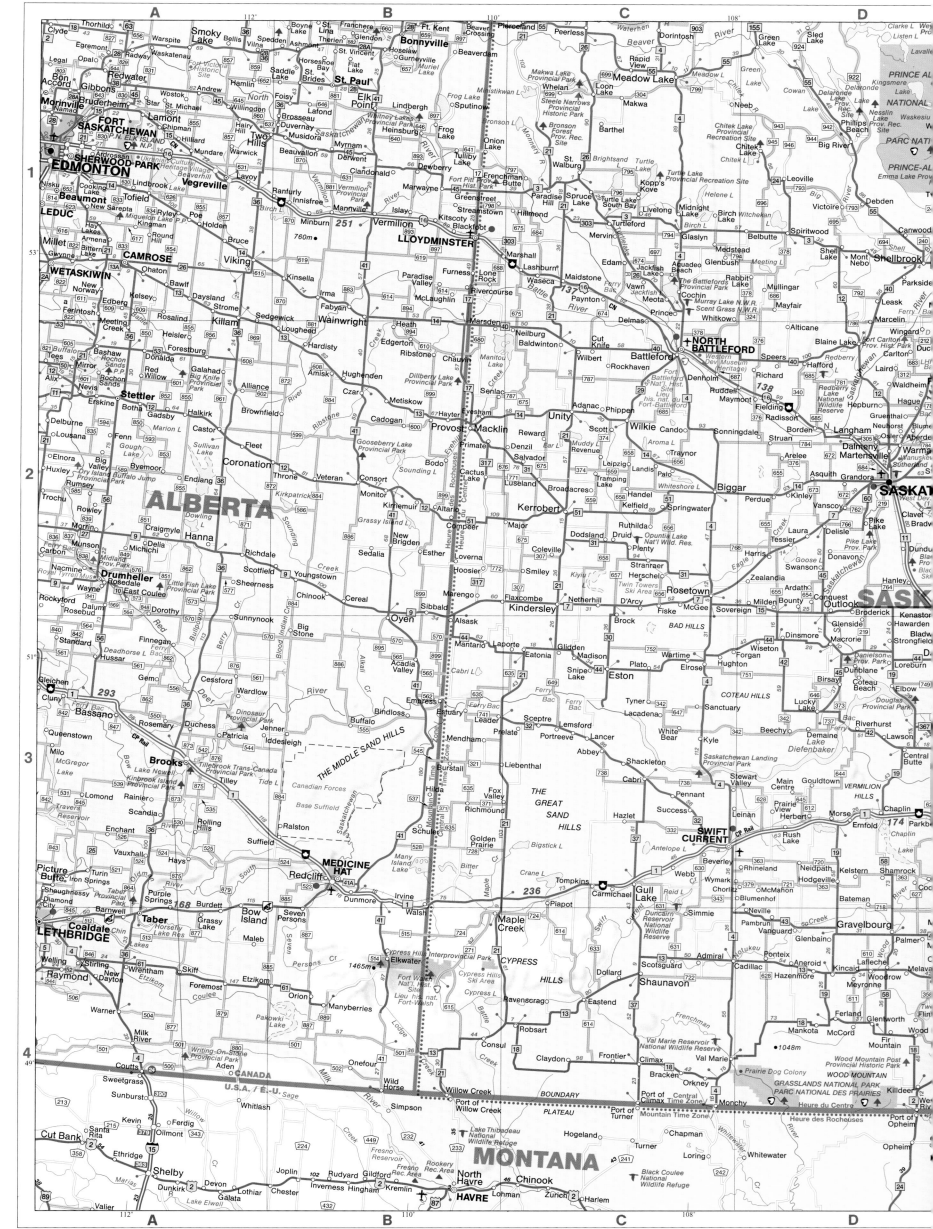

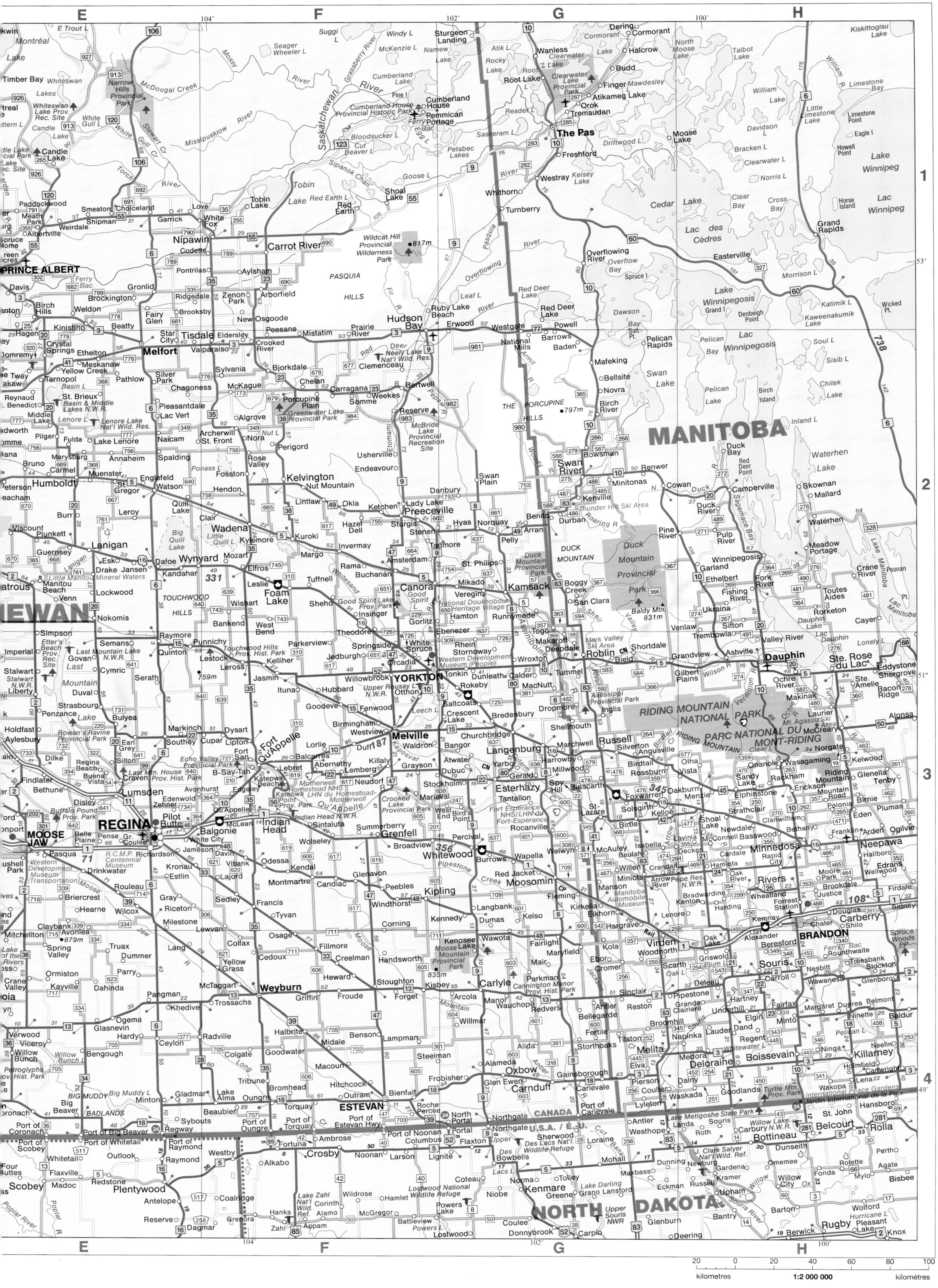

MANITOBA

NORTH DAKOTA

U.S.A. / É.U.

CANADA

RIDING MOUNTAIN NATIONAL PARK

PARC NATIONAL DU MONT-RIDING

DUCK MOUNTAIN

Duck Mountain Provincial Park

THE PORCUPINE HILLS

PASQUIA HILLS

TOUCHWOOD HILLS

BADLANDS

kilometres   20   0   20   40   60   80   100   kilometres

1:2 000 000

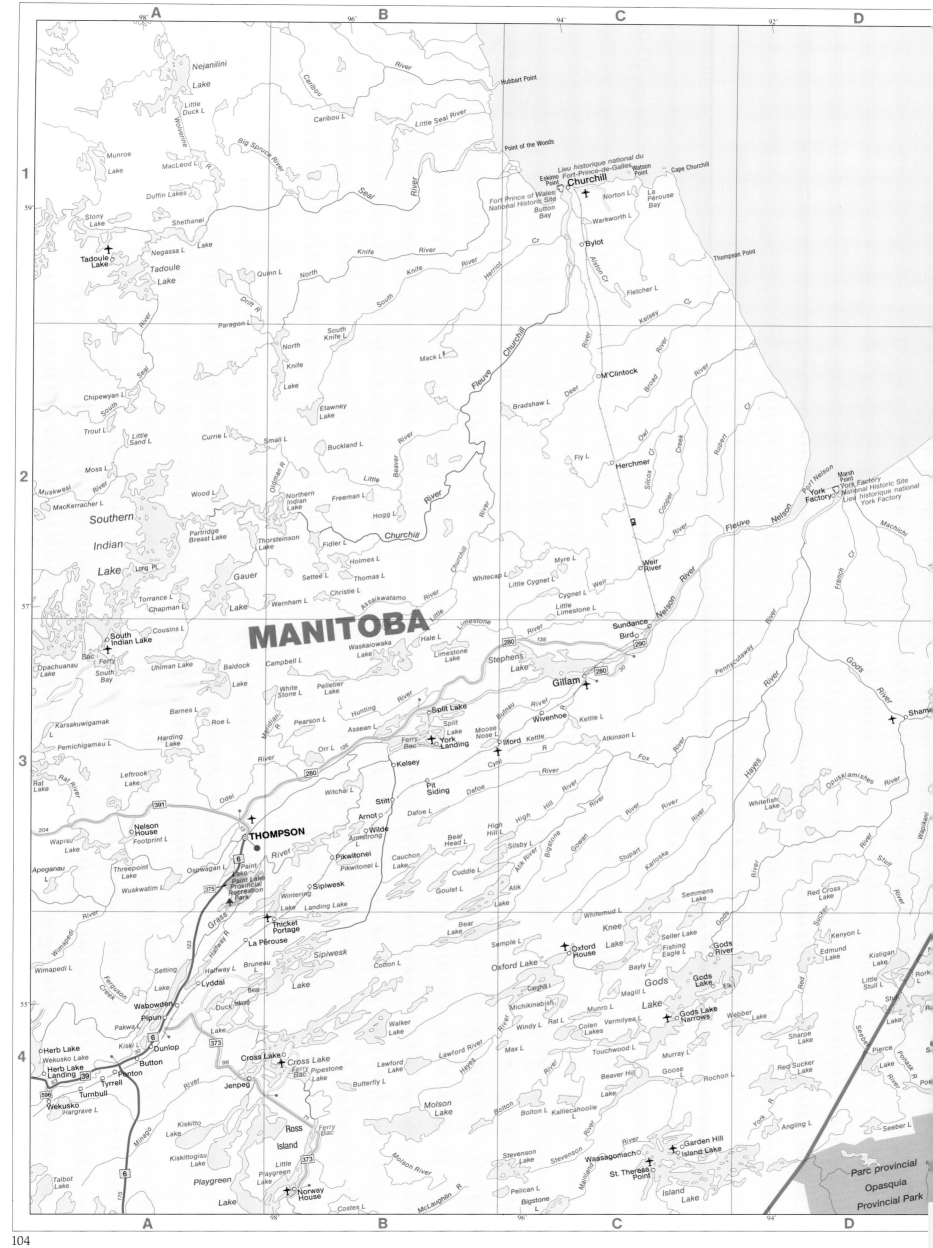

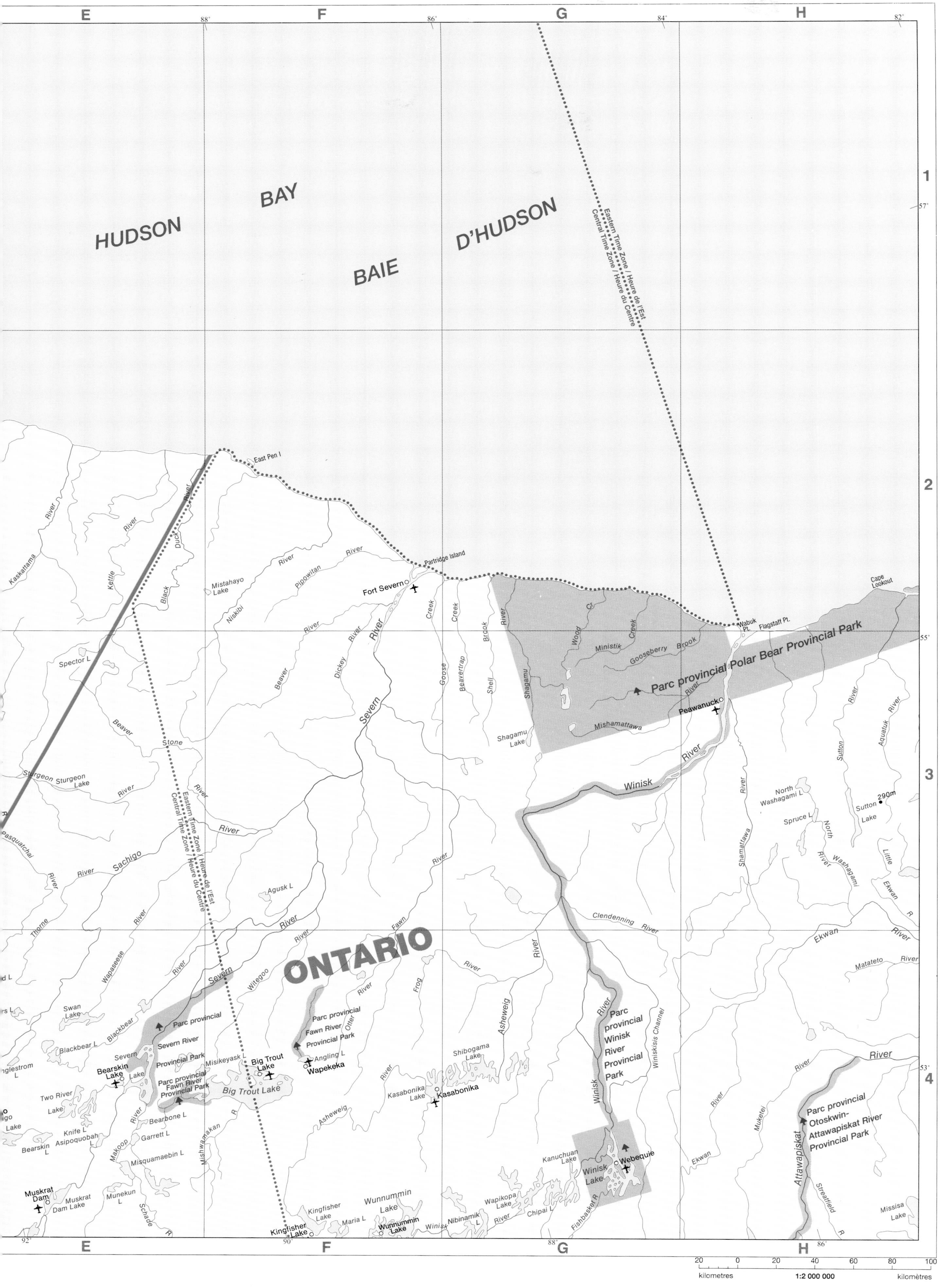

E · 88° · F · 86° · G · 84° · H · 82°

HUDSON BAY

BAIE D'HUDSON

Eastern Time Zone / Heure de l'Est
Central Time Zone / Heure du Centre

East Pen I

Kaskattama River

Kettle River

Black River

Duck River

Mistahayo Lake

Niskibi River

Pipowitan River

River

Partridge Island

Fort Severn

Creek

Creek

Goose Creek

Beavertrap Creek

Brook

Shell Brook

Shagamu River

Wood Cr.

Ministik Creek

Gooseberry Brook

Wabuk Pt. Flagstaff Pt.

Cape Lookout

Parc provincial Polar Bear Provincial Park

Spector L

Beaver River

Dickey River

Severn River

Shagamu Lake

Mishamattawa

Peawanuck

Sutton River

Aquatuk River

Stone River

Sturgeon Sturgeon Lake

Eastern Time Zone / Heure de l'Est
Central Time Zone / Heure du Centre

Winisk River

North Washagami L

Spruce L

North Washagami River

North Washagami River

Little Ekwan R

Sutton Lake

290m

Sachigo River

Beaver River

Pasquatchai River

River

Agusk L

Fawn River

River

Clendenning River

Shamattawa River

Ekwan River

Ekwan River

Thorne River

Wapaseese River

Severn River

Witegoo River

ONTARIO

Otter River

Frog River

Asheweig River

River

Winiskisis Channel

Matateto River

Swan Lake

Blackbear River

Blackbear L

Parc provincial Severn River Provincial Park

Parc provincial Fawn River Provincial Park

Angling L

Wapekeka

Shibogama Lake

Parc provincial Winisk River Provincial Park

River

River

Bearskin Lake

Severn Lake

Misikeyask L

Big Trout Lake

Asheweig River

Kasabonika Lake

Kasabonika

Winisk River

Two River Lake

Mishwakan R

Big Trout Lake

Bearbone L

Knife L Asipoquobah L

Garrett L

Parc provincial Otoskwin-Attawapiskat River Provincial Park

Attawapiskat River

Muketei River

Ekwan River

Bearskin L

Makoop River

Misquamaebin L

Kanuchuan Lake

Winisk Lake

Webequie

Fishbasket R

Muskrat Dam

Muskrat Dam Lake

Munekun Lake

Schade R

Kingfisher Lake

Wunnummin Lake

Maria L

Wunnummin Lake

Winisk River

Nibinamik L

Wapikopa Lake

Chipai L

Streatfield R

Missisa Lake

Kingfisher Lake

1:2 000 000

20 0 20 40 60 80 100

kilometres   kilomètres

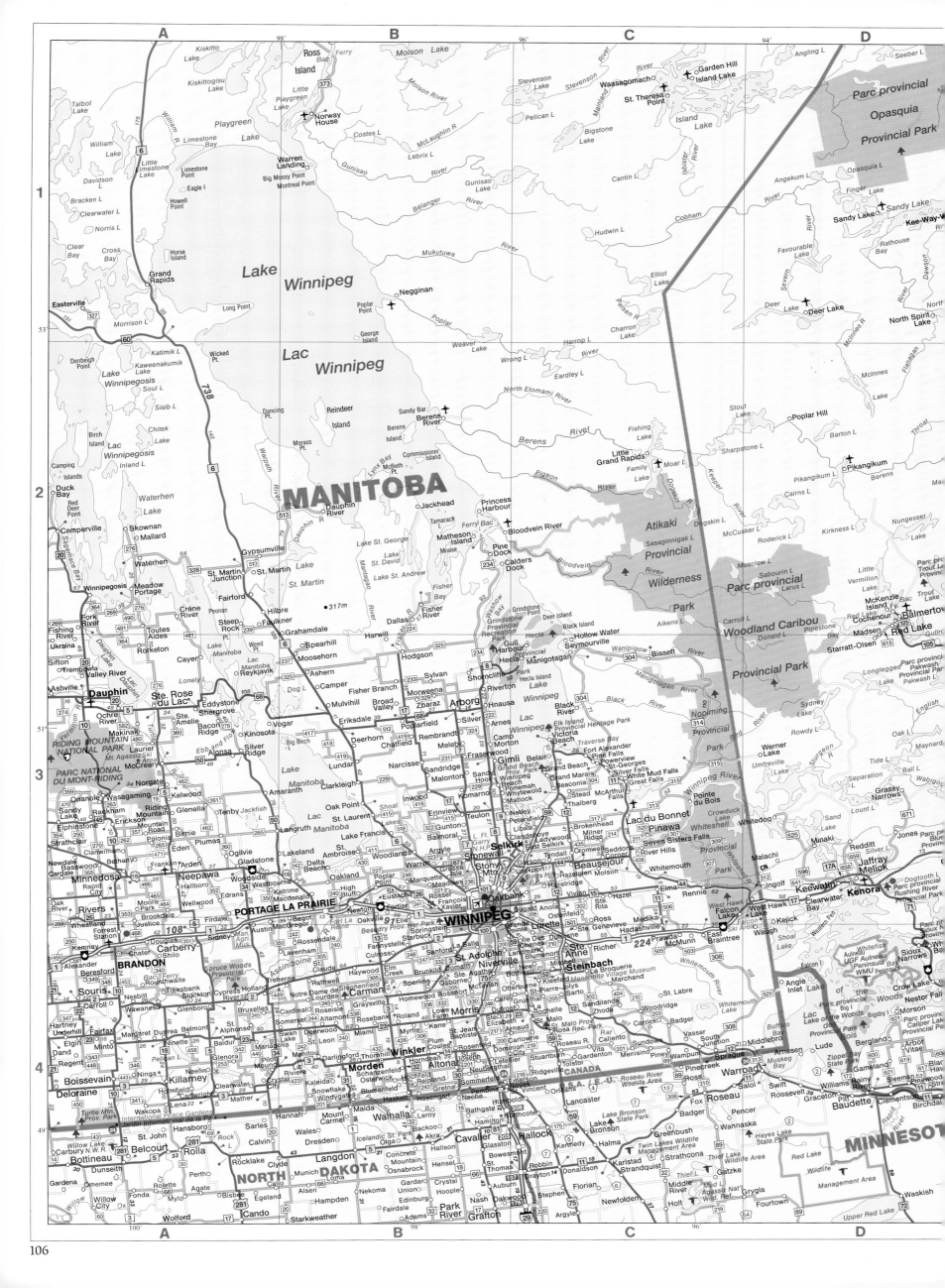

ONTARIO

THUNDER BAY

LAKE SUPERIOR

LAC SUPÉRIEUR

MICHIGAN

CANADA
U.S.A. / É.-U.

Muskrat Dam · Muskrat Dam Lake · Munekun L · Makoop R · Misquamaebin L
Lower Bearskin L · Misamikwash L · Kingfisher Lake · Kingfisher · Maria L · Wunnummin Lake
Winisk Lake · Webequie · Parc provincial Winisk River Provincial Park
Kanuchuan R · Wapikopa Lake · Chipai R · Fishbasket R · River · Streatfield
Magiss L · Weagamow Lake · Eyapamikama L · Wunnummin Lake · Nibinamik L · Lofte · Summer Beaver · Chipai L · Mameigwess Lake
Nikip L · Opakopa L · North Caribou Lake · Skinner · Pipestone River Provincial Park
Kabanja L · Lansdowne House · Parc provincial Otoskwin-Attawapiskat River Provincial Park · Attawapiskat R
Windigo River · Windigo Lake · Opapimiskan L · Pipemuta · Attawapiskat · Marten Falls · Ogoki
Upper Windigo Lake · Horseshoe Lake · Dumond R · Ozhiski Lake · Machawaian L · Wabassi R · Albany River
Whitestone L · Pipestone · River · Williams L · Totogan L · Machawaian L · Parc provincial Albany River Provincial Park
Cat L · Cat Lake · Gitchie · Central Patricia · Pickle · Keezhik Lake · Miminiska L · Petawanga L · Fort Hope · Eabamet Lake · Washi Lake · Makokibatan Lake
Upper Goose · Kapikik L · Pickle Lake · Pickle L · Opikeigen L · Triangular L · Dusey R · Ogoki R
Birch L · Zionz L · Fawcett L · New Osnaburgh · Osnaburgh L · Pashkokogan L · Greenbush L · Grayson L · Kagianagami Lake · Ogoki Lake · Little Current R
State Falls · Gull L · Sesikinaga L · Bamaji L · Doran L · McCrea L · Whitewater Lake · Ogoki Reservoir · Melchett L · Parc provincial Little Current River Provincial Park
South Bay · Wenasaga R · Lake St. Joseph · Miniss Lake · Wabakimi Lake · Parc provincial Wabakimi Wilderness Provincial Park · Smoothrock · Abamasagi L · O'Sullivan L · Esnagami Lake · Nakina · Lower Twin L
Bluffy L · Churchill R · DeLesseps L · Savant L · Pikitigushi River · Caribou Lake · Armstrong · Ombabika R · Aroland · Upper Twin L
Confederation L · Hooker L · Vincent L · Savant · Allan L · Collins · Wabinosh L · Ferland · North Pen Bay · Fleming R · Onaman · Longlac · Long Lake
434m · Allanwater Bridge · Kawaweogama L · Logan L · South Pen Bay · Humboldt · Murchison · Geraldton · Geraldton East
Lac Seul · Lac Seul · 516 · Savant Lake · Sesegonago L · Wapikaimaski Lake · Parc provincial Kopka River Provincial Park · Geikie L · RCC Geikie Island CGP · Lake Nipigon · Parc provincial Livingstone Point Provincial Park · Parc provincial MacLeod Provincial Park · Long Lake
Sioux Lookout · Hudson · O'Briens Landing · Silver Dollar · Bell L · Sparkling L · Harmon L · RNP West Bay PNR · Obonga L · Kelvin · Shakespeare · Lac Nipigon · Jellicoe · Beardmore · Wintering L
Parc provincial Ojibway Provincial Park · Minniaki L · Parc provincial Minniaki Kames Provincial Park · Shikag L · Metionga L · Park prov. Pantagruel Creek Prov. Park · 527 · Gull Bay · RNP Kabitotikwia River PNR · Grand Bay · Parc provincial Lake Nipigon Provincial Park · Rocky Bay · Macdiarmid · Barbara L · Roslyn L
Eton-Rugby · Dryden · Oxdrift · Wabigoon · Dinorwic · Basket L · Paguchi L · Sowden L · Wawang L · Parc provincial Brightsand River Provincial Park · Kashishibog L · Holinshead L · Chief Bay · McIntyre Bay · Black Sturgeon L · Frazer L · Nipigon R · Helen L · RNP Kama Hills PNR 593m · RNP Gravel River PNR · Rainbow Falls Provincial Park
Borups Corners · Dyment · Mameigwous L · Indian L · Parc provincial Sandbar Lake Provincial Park · Réserve naturelle provinciale Bonheur River Kame Provincial Nature Reserve · Graham · Parc prov. Kaiashk Prov. Park · 811 · Garden L · Pakashkan L · 585 · Nipigon · Red Rock · Rossport · CP Rail · Schreiber · Terrace Bay · Parc provincial Slate Islands Provincial Park
Ignace · 466 · English River · Upsala · Dog R · Muskeg L · Dog L · RNP Albert Lake Mesa PNR · Greenwich · 582 · RNP Cavern Lake PNR · Dorion · Hurkett · Black Bay · Black Bay Peninsula · RNP Puff Island PNR · Simpson Island · St. Ignace Island
502 · Sandford L · White Otter L · Upper Scotch L · 180 · Lac des Mille Lacs · Raith · Parc provincial Lake Silver Falls Provincial Park · 589 · Ouimet Canyon PNR · RNP Shesheeb Bay PNR
Turtle L · Parc provincial Turtle River Provincial Park · Clearwater West L · Finlayson L · Marmion L · Kashabowie · Shebandowan · Shabaqua Corners · Finmark · 591 · Lappe · Terry Fox Memorial · Pass Lake · 587 · Wild Goose PNR · RNP Edward Island PNR · Parc provincial Sleeping Giant (Sibley) Provincial Park
Atikokan · Sapawe · 335 · Eva L · Burchell L · Shebandowan · Shebandowan · Kakabeka Park · Murillo · 102 · 566m · 130 · RNP Edward Island · Thunder Bay · Isle Royale · MICHIGAN
Mine Centre · Seine River Village · Pickerel L · RNP Little Greenwater PNR · 802 · Parc provincial Kakabeka Falls Provincial Park · Kakabeka Falls · Stanley · Rosslyn Village · Pie Island · RNP Le Pate PNR · Thunder Cape
Fort Frances · International Falls · South International Falls · VOYAGEURS NATIONAL PARK · Parc provincial Sand Point Provincial Park · Beaverhouse L · Parc provincial Quetico Provincial Park · McKenzie L · Parc provincial Matawin River Provincial Park Weikwabinoaw · Nolalu · Suomi · South Gillies · Hymers · 595 · 588 · RNP Thompson Island PNR · ISLE ROYALE NATIONAL PARK · Rock Harbor
Couchiching · Kabetogama · Namakan L · Quetico · Sturgeon L · Kawnipi L · RNP Arrowhead Peninsula PNR · Saganagons L · Saganaga Lake · Northern Light L · PP Arrowhead L PP · Whitefish L · Parc prov. Middle Falls Prov. Park · 593 · Cloud Bay · Siskiwit Bay · LAC SUPÉRIEUR
Pelland · Ericsburg · Ray · Kabetogama · Lac la Croix · Hunter Island · Sand Point L · Crooked L · Sea Gull L · Parc provincial La Vérendrye River Provincial Park · Pigeon River · Grand Portage · Grand Portage National Monument · Passenger Ferry
Littlefork · 217 · Crane Lake · 24 · Superior National Forest · 116 · Basswood L · Snowbank L · Brule L · Eagle Mtn. 2301 ft. · Kodonce River State Park · Hovland · 12 · Greenwood · Grand Portage Pass. Fy · LAKE SUPERIOR
Ash Lake · Buyck · Nett L · Pelican L · Cusson · Orr · 23 · Trout L · Superior National Forest · Judge C.R. Magney State Park · Grand Marais · Cascade River State Park · Copper Harbor · Fort Wilkins State Park · Bete Grise
Silverdale · Rauch · Gheen · Burntside L · Ely · Winton · Vermilion L · Isabella R · Sawbill Landing · 61 · Eagle River · Phoenix · Central · Keweenaw Peninsula · Lake Linden
Cook · Soudan · Soudan Underground Mine State Park · Tower · 45 · 169 · 1 · Lutsen · Ray Berglund State Park · Tofte · Calumet · Mohawk · Laurium · Gay · MICHIGAN

QUÉBEC

ONTARIO

Major places:

Hearst, Hallebourg, Val Côté, Mattice, Lowther, Opasatika, Harty, Val Rita, KAPUSKASING, Moonbeam, Fauquier, Departure Lake, Smooth Rock Falls, Grégoires Mill, Driftwood, Hunta, Clute, Cochrane, Fraserdale

Peterbell, Elsas, Kapuskasing Lake, Missinaibi, Foleyet, TIMMINS, Porcupine, South Porcupine, Schumacher, Gold Centre, Connaught, Hoyle, Shillington, Porquis Junction, Iroquois Falls, Nellie Lake, Tunis, Monteith, Barbers Bay, Val Gagné, Matheson, Ramore, Holtyre

Chapleau, Nemegosis, Kormak, Sultan, Ramsey, Westree, Gogama, Shining Tree, Matachewan, Elk Lake, Gowganda, Kenabeek, Charlton, Earlton, Englehart, Tomstown, Kirkland Lake, Chaput Hughes, Swastika, Larder Lake, Tarzwell, Boston Creek, Kenogami Lake, Sesekinika, King Kirkland, Kearns, Virginiatown, Montbeillard

ROUYN-NORANDA, Évain, McWatters, Cadillac, Arntfield, D'Alembert, Destor, Preissac, Duparquet, Rapide-Danseur, Roquemaure, Palmarolle, La Sarre, Macamic, Authier, Taschereau, Launay, Villemontel, Languedoc, Guyenne, Normétal, Val-St-Gilles, Villebois, Val-Paradis, Beaucanton, La Reine, Dupuy, Clerval, Île-Népawa

New Liskeard, Haileybury, North Cobalt, Cobalt, Latchford, Temagami, Marten River, Thornloe, Hilliardton, Dymond, Belle Vallée, Guérin, Notre-Dame-du-Nord, Angliers, St-Eugène-de-Guigues, St-Bruno-de-Guigues, Ville-Marie, Fabre, Laniel, Kipawa, Témiscaming, Fugèreville, Latulipe, Belleterre, Laforce, Moffet, Laforce, Winneway, Rémigny

SUDBURY, Garson, Chelmsford, Copper Cliff, Lively, Coniston, Wahnapitae, Hanmer, Val Caron, Val Therese, Blezard Valley, Capreol, Skead, Falconbridge, Markstay, Warren, Verner, Sturgeon Falls, Garden Village, NORTH BAY, Callander, Corbeil, Bonfield, Mattawa, Rutherglen, Redbridge, Balsam Creek, Crystal Falls, Field, Desaulniers, Tilden Lake

ELLIOT LAKE, Espanola, Massey, Spanish, Blind River, Algoma Mills, Iron Bridge, Thessalon, Sowerby, Bruce Sta., Rydal Bank, Wharncliffe, Dunns Valley, Poplar Dale, Ophir, McKerrow, Webbwood, Walford, Naughton, Whitefish, Nairn Centre, Worthington, Agnew, Cartier, Levack, Onaping, Dowling, Azilda

Chapleau, West Bay, Little Current, Sucker Creek, Sheguiandah, Gore Bay, Manitoulin Island, Silver Water, Meldrum Bay, Cockburn I., Drummond Island, Île Manitoulin, Killarney, Whitefish Falls, Birch Island, Bigwood, Alban, Noëlville, French River, Loring, Port Loring, Arnstein, Commanda, Powassan, Trout Creek, South River, Sundridge, Golden Valley, Restoule

North Channel, Georgian Bay, Baie Georgienne

Scale 1:1 725 000

kilomètres 20 0 20 40 60 80 100 kilometres

MANITOULIN ISLAND
ÎLE MANITOULIN

GEORGIA

LAKE HURON

LAC HURON

M I C H I G A N

BRUCE PENINSULA
PÉNINSULE DE BRUCE

PARC MARIN NATIONAL
FATHOM FIVE
NATIONAL MARINE PARK

BRUCE PENINSULA NATIONAL PARK
PARC NATIONAL DE LA PÉNINSULE-DE-BRUCE

Algonquin Provincial Park
Parc provincial Algonquin

ONTARIO

BAIE GEORGIENNE

Thirty Thousand Islands

Trente Mille Îles

Parry Sound

HUNTSVILLE

Bracebridge

Gravenhurst

ORILLIA

Lake Simcoe
Lac Simcoe

Penetanguishene
MIDLAND
Coldwater

COLLINGWOOD
Wasaga Beach
Stayner
Creemore
Angus

BARRIE

NEWMARKET
AURORA
Bradford
Uxbridge

ORANGEVILLE

Keswick
Sutton
Beaverton

LINDSAY
Fenelon Falls
Minden

Cannington
Sunderland

RICHMOND HILL
MARKHAM
Thornhill
PICKERING
AJAX
WHITBY
OSHAWA

LAKE ONTARIO
LAC ONTARIO

1:750 000
kilometres 10 0 10 20 30 40 50

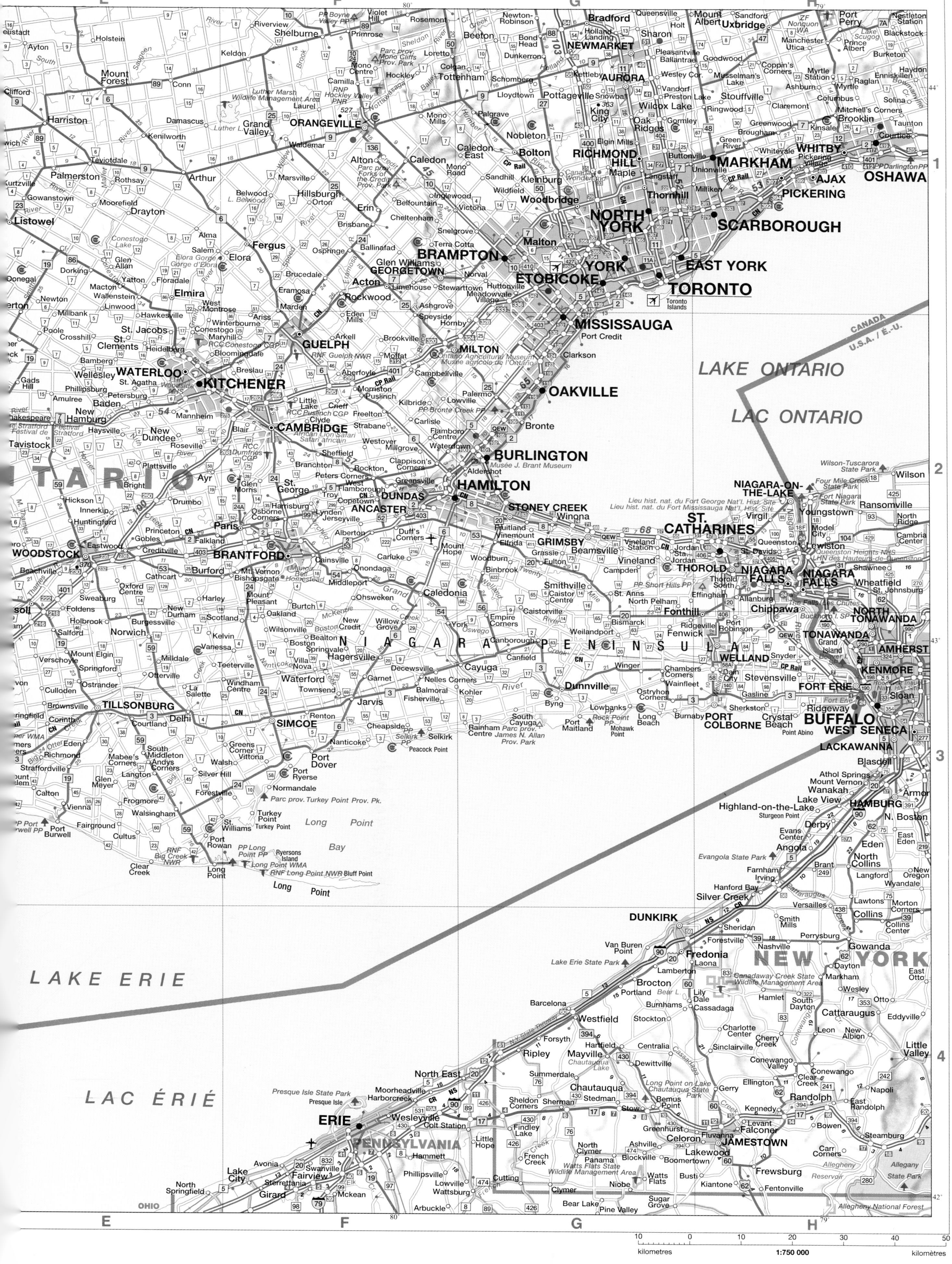

LAKE ONTARIO
LAC ONTARIO
LAKE ERIE
LAC ÉRIÉ
NIAGARA PENINSULA
NEW YORK
PENNSYLVANIA
OHIO
CANADA
U.S.A. / É.-U.
TORONTO
NORTH YORK
SCARBOROUGH
EAST YORK
YORK
ETOBICOKE
MISSISSAUGA
BRAMPTON
OAKVILLE
BURLINGTON
HAMILTON
STONEY CREEK
DUNDAS
ANCASTER
ST. CATHARINES
NIAGARA FALLS
NIAGARA-ON-THE-LAKE
THOROLD
WELLAND
FORT ERIE
BUFFALO
WEST SENECA
LACKAWANNA
TONAWANDA
NORTH TONAWANDA
AMHERST
KENMORE
KITCHENER
WATERLOO
CAMBRIDGE
GUELPH
BRANTFORD
WOODSTOCK
TILLSONBURG
SIMCOE
ORANGEVILLE
MILTON
GEORGETOWN
RICHMOND HILL
MARKHAM
PICKERING
AJAX
WHITBY
OSHAWA
NEWMARKET
AURORA
DUNKIRK
ERIE
JAMESTOWN
Long Point Bay
E
F
G
H
1
2
3
4
10 0 10 20 30 40 50
kilometres 1:750 000 kilomètres

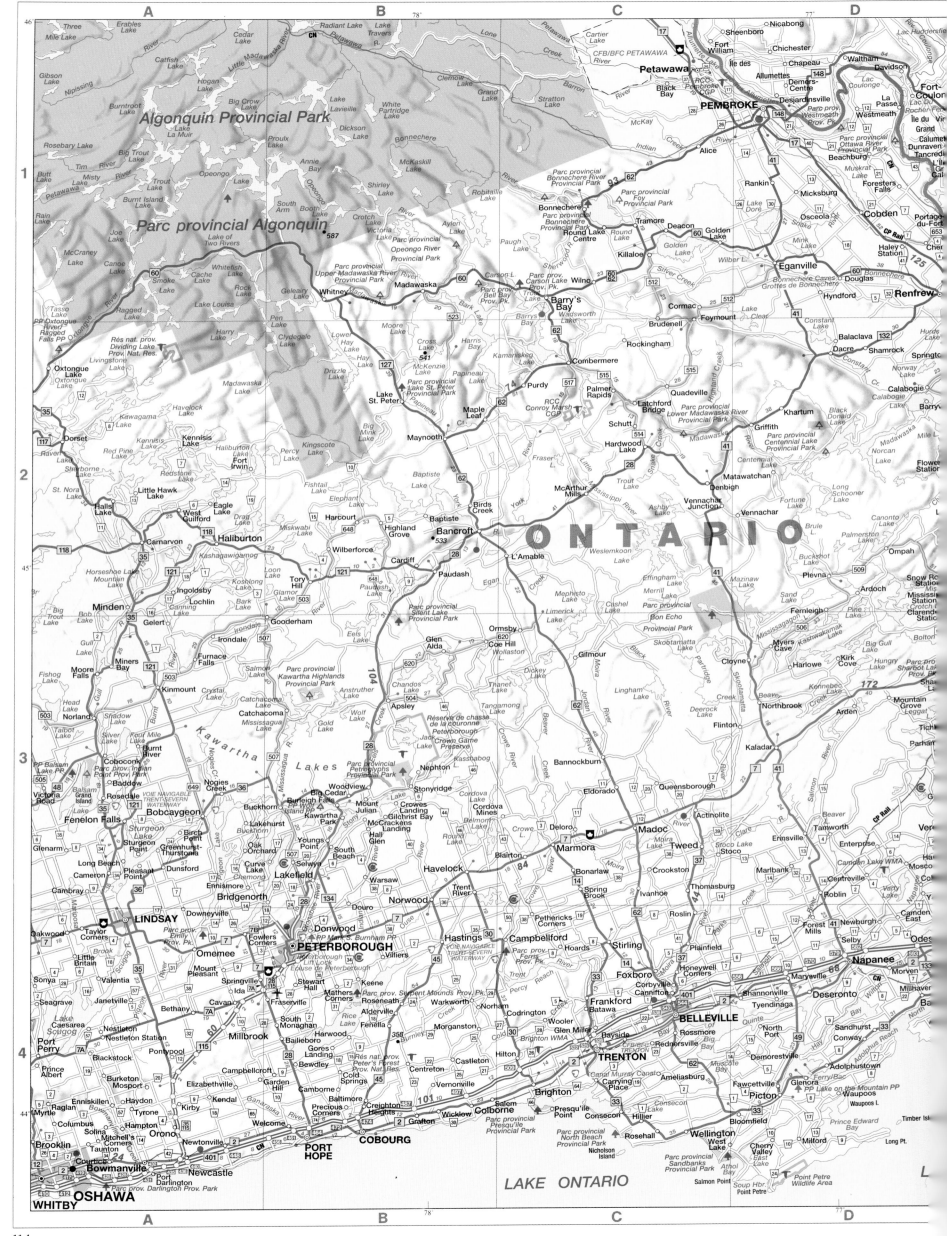

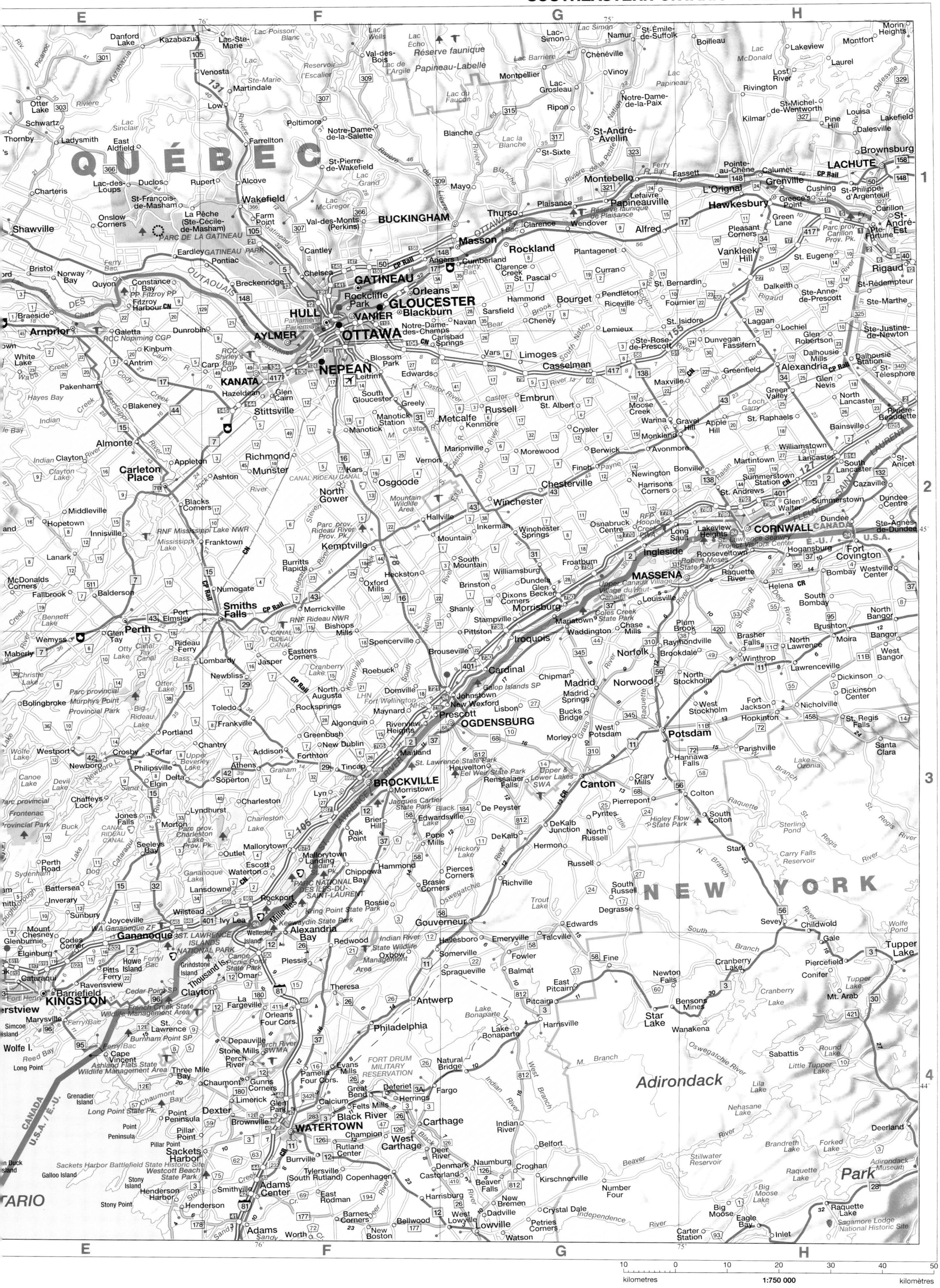

QUÉBEC

NEW YORK

ONTARIO

Adirondack Park

BUCKINGHAM
GATINEAU
HULL
AYLMER
OTTAWA
VANIER
GLOUCESTER
NEPEAN
KANATA
LACHUTE
Hawkesbury
L'Orignal
Grenville
CORNWALL
MASSENA
OGDENSBURG
Prescott
BROCKVILLE
Potsdam
Canton
Gouverneur
KINGSTON
Gananoque
Alexandria Bay
Carleton Place
Smiths Falls
Perth
Almonte
Arnprior
Watertown
Philadelphia
Carthage
West Carthage
Lowville

CANADA
U.S.A. / E.-U.

10   0   10   20   30   40   50
kilometres
1:750 000
kilomètres

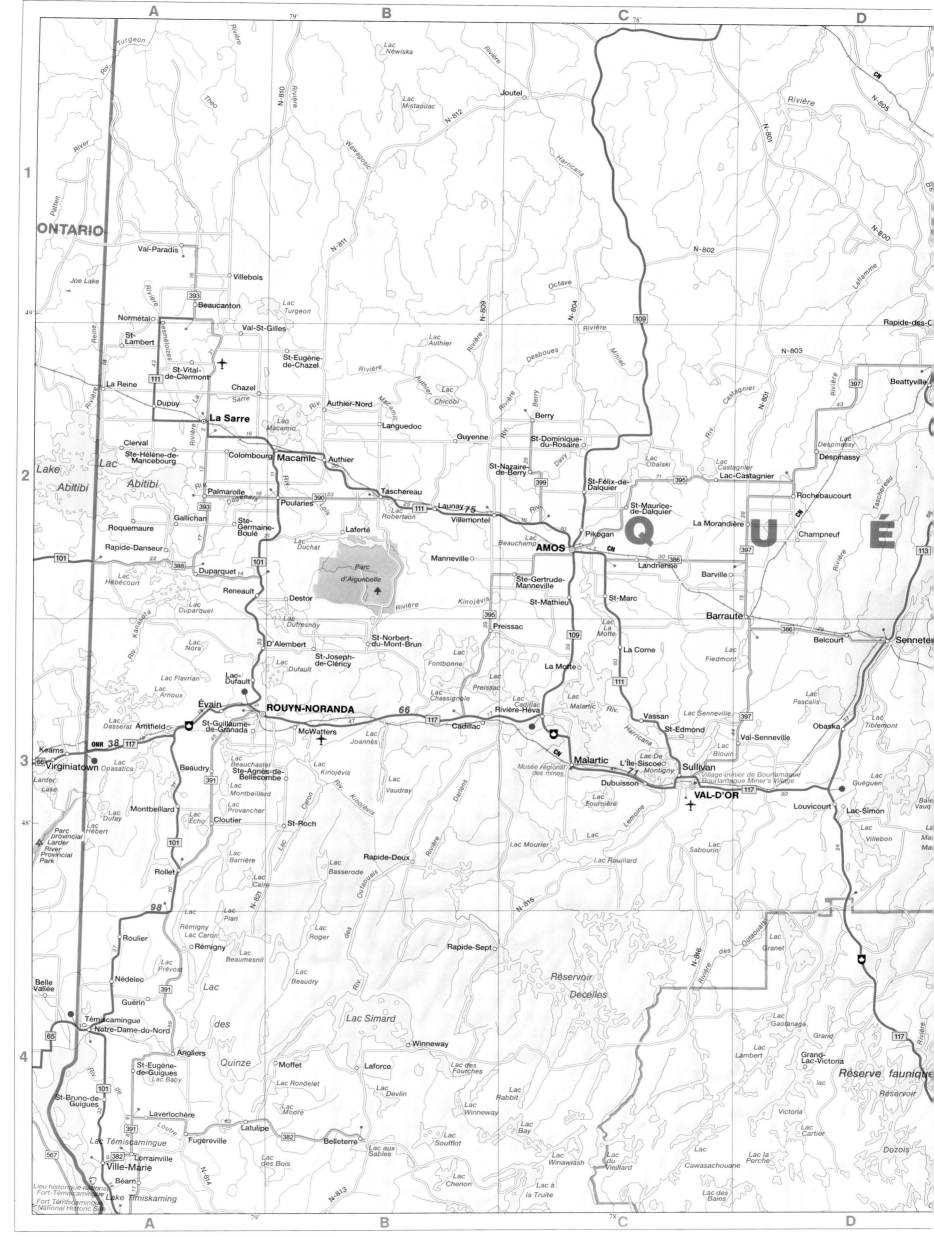

E F G H

Lac du Bras
Coupé
Lac la
Dauversière
Lac
Opawica
Lac
Irène
Obatagamau
L-226
Lac
Ronde
CN
Lac
Bachelor
Lac
La Ronde
Rivière
de la Baie
Lac
Râne
L-209
Lac
Verneuil
Desmaraisville
Lac Wachigabau
Rivière
Lac
des Vents
Lac
Coapatina
Lac
Mannard
Waswanipi
Lac Lessard
Opawica
Rivière
d'Eau
Opawica
Lac
Malouin
Lac Lichen
Lac
Pougnet
Lac
Doda
Lac
Rohault
Miquelon
Lac
Pusticamica
Lac Margry
Lac de la
Surprise
Lac
Pambrun
Lac
Gabriel
113
Lac
Rochester
Lac Nicobi
Lac
Crisafy
Lac
Monaco
Lac
Esther
Lac
Pierrefonds
Lac
Rouge
Lac
Crisafy
Lac
Némégouse
Lac
Robert
N-851
Lac
Hébert
de
Rivière
Lac
Roméo
l'Aigle
Lac
Roy
Lac
Beaucours
Lac Wilson
Rivière
Petit
lac Hébert
Rivière
Lac
Compton
Lac
Novellet
au
Lac Oliva
Lac de
la Ligne
Lac
Périgny
Panache
Lac
Lacroix
Lac
Augusta
Lac Ventadour
Lac
Nelson
N-853
Lac
Barry
Pascagama
Lac
Baptiste
Lac Pfister
Lac
Nairn
Riv.
Cuvillier
Lac aux
Loutres
Lac
Bailly
Toursaint
T-453
Lac Dubois
Riv.
Robin
Lac
Wétetnagami
Lac
Robertine
Lac Perrier
Lac
Froid
Lac du
Principal
Lac
Cuvillier
Rivière
Lac
Masères
Lac
Mathieu
Riv.
Lecompte
Lac
Castonguay
Lac
St-Père
Lac
Mesplet
Lac
St-Cyr
Rivière
Lac
Lindsay
Lac
Desforges
Lecompte
Rivière
Lac
Cherrier
Lac de la
Rencontre
Lac Louison
Lac des
Terrasses
Réservoir Gouin
Riv.
Augier
Lac
Achepabanca
Lac
Charette
Lac
Maricourt
Lac
Mégiscane
Lac
du
Mâle
Rivière
Delestres
Lac
Tuillé
Mégiscane
Lac
Berthelot
Lac
Canusio
Lac
Deschamps
Lac
Wiashgamic
Lac
Valets
Lac
Girouard
Lac
Ouiscatis
Lac
Pascagama
Lac de
la Tête
Lac
Lepage
Nemio
Rivière
Lac
Martin
N-830
Lac
Valmy
Serpent
Lac aux
Cedres
Lac
Bernier
Lac des
Cinq Milles
Kekek
Lac
Bongard
Lac
Brécourt
Lac des
Garancières
Lac
Huguenin
Lac
Faillon
Lac
Maude
Rivière
Trévet
Lac
Frigon
Lac
Sulte
Lac
Francoeur
Lac
Delâge
Lac
Serpent
Lac
Lacoursière
Lac
Tessier
Lac
Achintre
Lac
Benjamin
Lac
Dugué
Lac
Tassé
Press
CN
Forsythe
Gagnon-Siding
Riv.
Langlade
Lac
Bourgmont
Lac
Médera
Chassaigne
Lac
Jaux
Lac
Oskélanéo
Lac
Lajoie
T-402
T-400
Paradis
Rivière
Lac
Choiseul
Monet
Lac
Buies
Lac
Carmen
Lac
Trévet
Lac
Chênevert
Lac
Tamarac
Lac
Neault
Clova
Oskélanéo
Lac
Parker
Lac de
l'Ours
Blanc
Lac
Decelles
Lac
Capitachouane
Lac
Jalobert
Lac des Neiges
Lac du
Brouillard
Lac
Gaston
Lac Lorette
Lac
Péronne
Lac Mirande
Lac
Tomney
Lac
Obabcata
Lac Shannon
Lac
Primeau
Lac Jeune
CN
Parent
Lac
Dumais
Lac
Cambrai
O-751
Lac de la
Fourche
Lac des
Dix Milles
Lac
Landry
Lac
Mauser
Lac
Yprès
Lac
Festubert
Lac
Robson
Lac
Gosselin
Lac
Thaumur
Lac
Choquette
Bleuets
Lac
Dandurand
Lac
Niverville
Lac
Yser
Lac
Camachigama
Lac
Indian
Lac
Chaume
Riv.
Rivière
Bazin
Rochocouane
Rivière
Lac
Abos
Lac
Blavet
Festubert
Riv.
aux
Lac
Harris
Lac
Pikianikijuan
Lac Farbus
Lac
Échouani
Rivière
Lac
Long
Lac Pierre
Lac
Esden
Lac des
Augustines
O-752
Lac des
Outaouais
Choiart
du
Lac
Wagwabika
Lac
Seymour
Lac
Bouchette
Lac
Landron
Lac
Capimitchigama
Canot
Lac
Lajoue
Rivière
MitchinaméCus
Riv.
Lac
Doré
Lac
Gaudois
Lac
O'Sullivan
Lac
Winchell
O-752
Lac
Girène
Lac
Nasigon
Lac
Leluau
Némiscachingue
Lac
Rodin
Lac
Duchastel
Lac
Turnbull
Lac
Bazinet
Lac
Adonis
Réservoir
La Vérendrye
Cabonga
Lac
Séguin
O-764
Lac
Lenôtre
Lac
Maxime
Lac
McLennan
Wapus
Lac Vimont
Lac
Lecointre
Lac De La
Bidière
Lac du
Pin Rouge
Lac
Mitchinamécus
Lac
Duplessis
Lac
Badajoz
Lac
Waterloo
Lac à la
Culotte
Lac
St-Amour
Rivière

B E C

kilometres   1:800 000   kilomètres
10 0 10 20 30 40 50

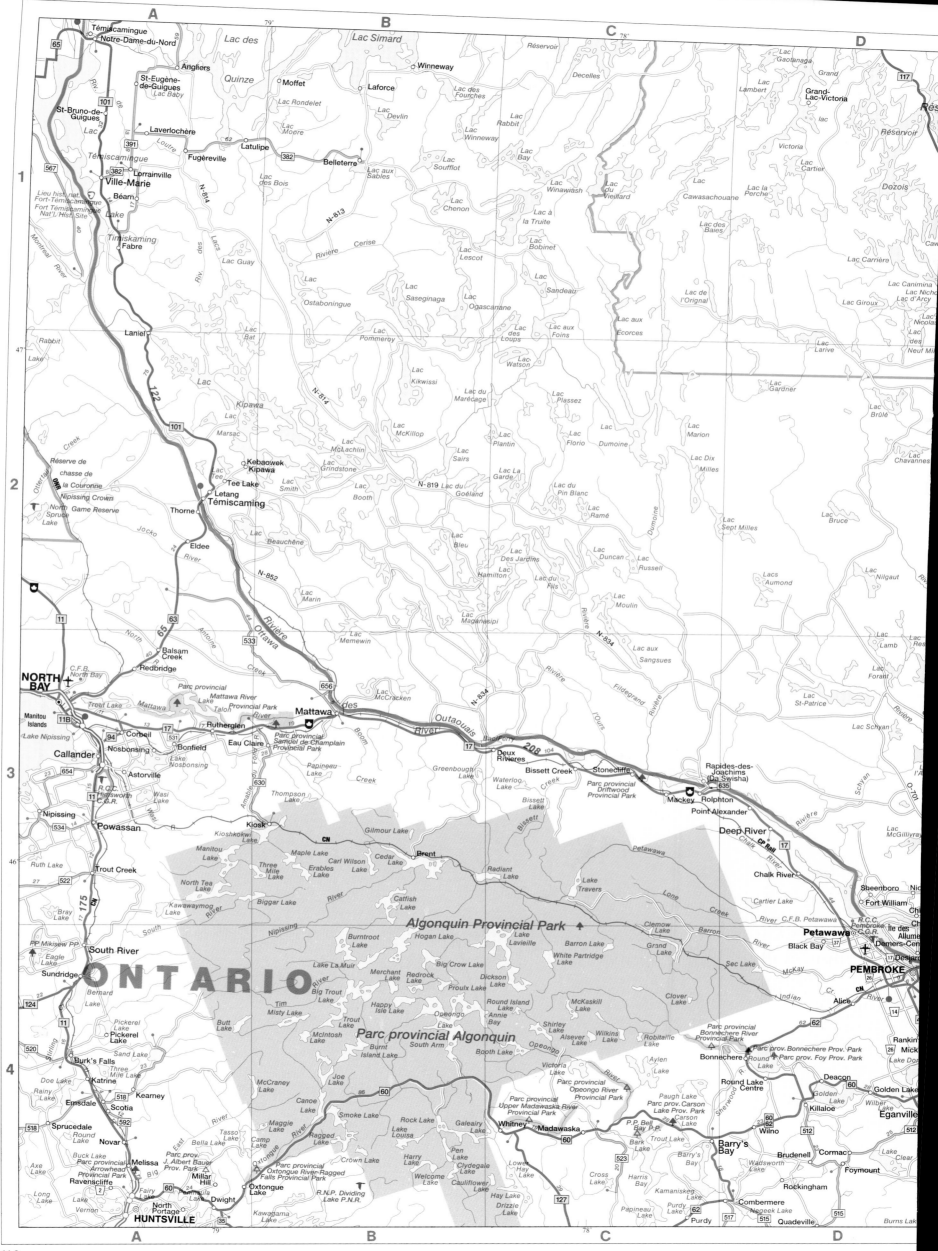

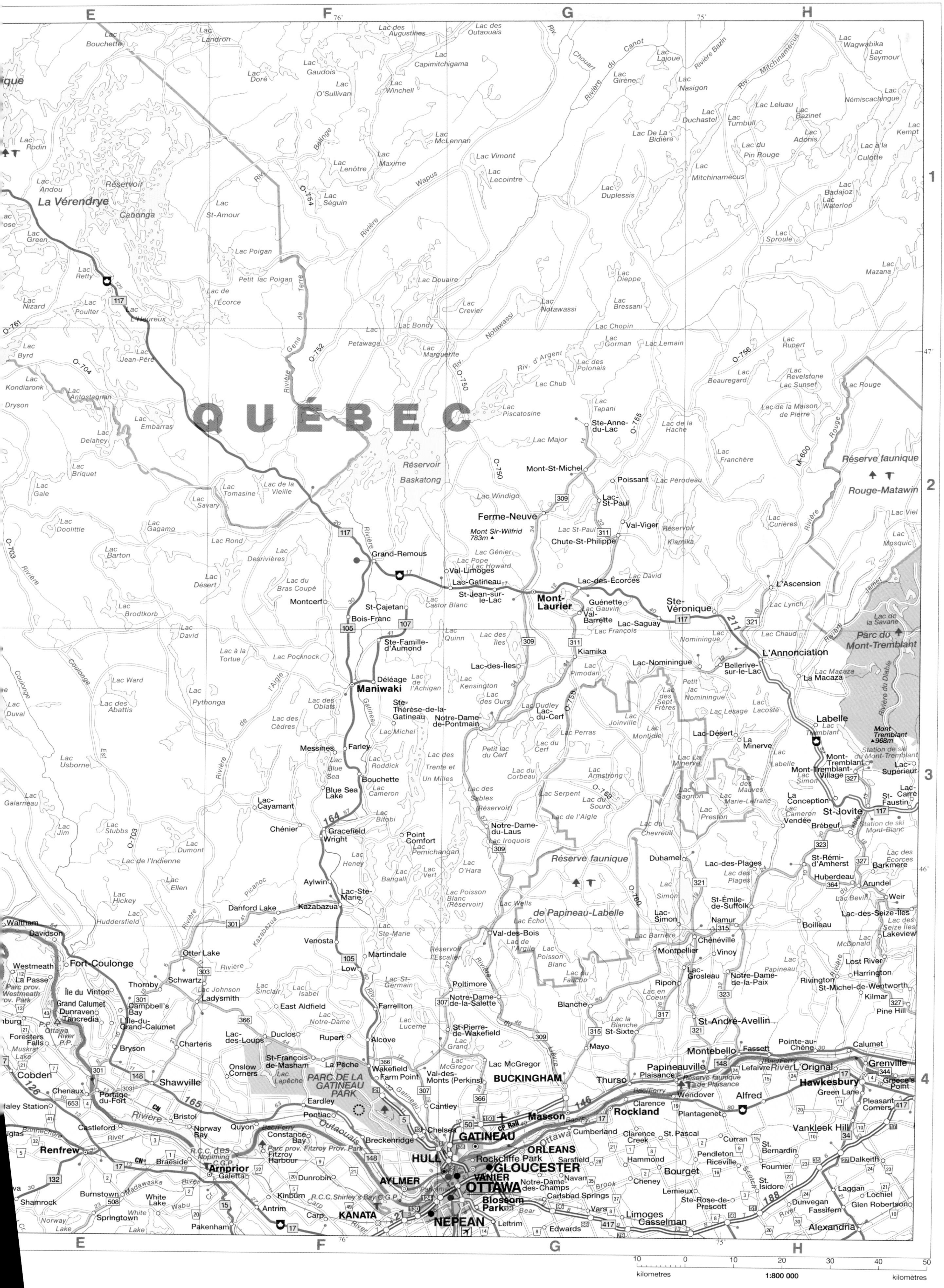

QUÉBEC

La Vérendrye

Réservoir Cabonga

Réservoir Baskatong

Parc du Mont-Tremblant

Réserve faunique Rouge-Matawin

Réserve faunique de Papineau-Labelle

PARC DE LA GATINEAU PARK

Mont Sir-Wilfrid 783m
Mont Tremblant 968m

Ste-Anne-du-Lac, Mont-St-Michel, Poissant, Ferme-Neuve, Val-Viger, L'Ascension, Chute-St-Philippe, Lac-des-Écorces, Ste-Véronique, Grand-Remous, Val-Limoges, Lac-Gatineau, St-Jean-sur-le-Lac, Mont-Laurier, Guénette, Val-Gauvin, Val-Barrette, Lac-Saguay, Montcerf, St-Cajetan, Bois-Franc, Ste-Famille-d'Aumond, Kiamika, Lac-Nominingue, Belleriive-sur-le-Lac, La Macaza, Labelle, Déléage, Maniwaki, Ste-Thérèse-de-la-Gatineau, Notre-Dame-de-Pontmain, Lac-du-Cerf, Lac-Désert, La Minerve, Mont-Tremblant, Mont-Tremblant-Village, La Conception, St-Jovite, St-Faustin, Messines, Farley, Bouchette, Blue Sea Lake, Lac-Cayamant, Chénier, Gracefield, Wright, Notre-Dame-du-Laus, Duhamel, Lac-des-Plages, St-Rémi-d'Amherst, Huberdeau, Barkmere, Arundel, Weir, Aylwin, Lac-Ste-Marie, Kazabazua, Danford Lake, Val-des-Bois, St-Émile-de-Suffolk, Namur, Lac-des-Seize-Îles, Boileau, Lakeview, Venosta, Martindale, Low, Poltimore, Notre-Dame-de-la-Salette, Ripon, Lac-Simon, Chénéville, Montpellier, Vinoy, Lost River, Harrington, Rivington, St-Michel-de-Wentworth, Kilmar, Pine Hill, Otter Lake, Thornby, Schwartz, Ladysmith, East Aldfield, St-Germain, Farrellton, St-Pierre-de-Wakefield, Blanche, Lac-Grosleau, Notre-Dame-de-la-Paix, St-André-Avellin, St-Sixte, Montebello, Fassett, Pointe-au-Chêne, Calumet, Grenville

Fort-Coulonge, Westmeath, La Passe, Île du Vinton, Grand Calumet, Dunraven, Tancredia, L'Île-du-Grand-Calumet, Campbell's Bay, Bryson, Charteris, Lac-des-Loups, Duclos, Rupert, Alcove, Wakefield, Farm Point, Val-des-Monts (Perkins), Buckingham, Mayo, Thurso, Papineauville, Plaisance, Wendover, Alfred, Hawkesbury, L'Orignal, Green Lane, Pleasant Corners, Vankleek Hill

Cobden, Chenaux, Portage-du-Fort, Shawville, Bristol, Norway Bay, Quyon, Pontiac, Eardley, Breckenridge, Chelsea, Cantley, Masson, Rockland, Clarence, Clarence Creek, Plantagenet, Curran, St. Bernardin, Fournier, Dalkeith

Renfrew, Braeside, Arnprior, Galetta, Dunrobin, Kinburn, Antrim, Carp, Kanata, Aylmer, Hull, Gatineau, Orleans, Rockcliffe Park, Vanier, Gloucester, Ottawa, Nepean, Blossom Park, Navan, Cumberland, Sarsfield, St. Pascal, Pendleton, Riceville, Bourget, Cheney, Hammond, Limoges, Casselman, Edwards, Leitrim, Vars, Cartsbad Springs, Notre-Dame-des-Champs, St. Isidore, Ste-Rose-de-Prescott, Lemieux, Laggan, Dunvegan, Fassifern, Glen Robertson, Lochiel, Alexandria

1:800 000

kilometres 10 0 10 20 30 40 50 kilometres

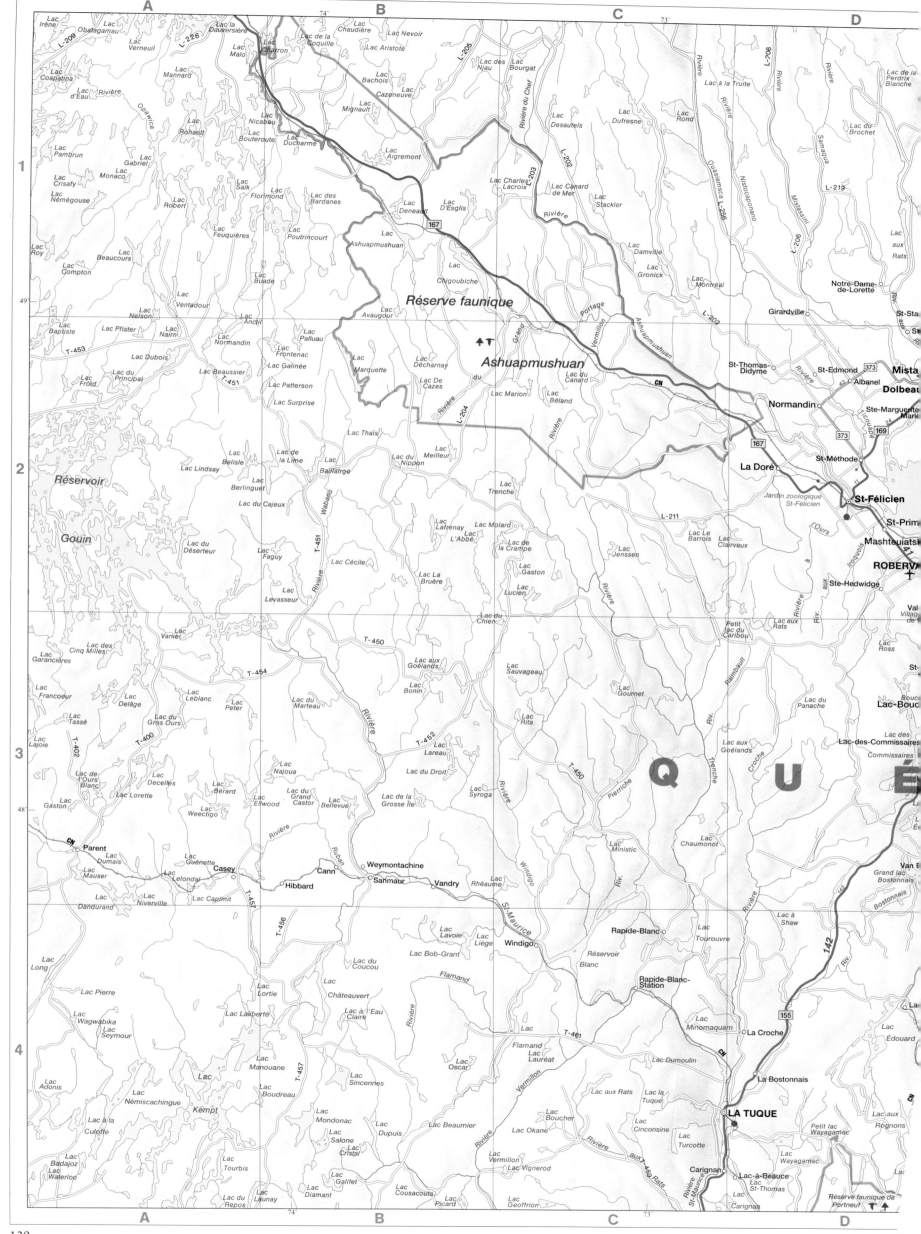

E | F | 71° | G | 70° | H

Lac Gicopec
Lac Laliberté
Lac d'Alleboust
Brûle-Neige
Lac Brûle-Neige
Lac Étienniche
Lac Melonèze
Réservoir
Pipmuacan
Lac à Paul
Lac Gouin
Labrieville
Lac Cabituquimats
Rivière

Lac Pelletier
Rivière
Lac Chausson
L-222
Lac Doucet
Lac St-Jacques
Lac de Mun
Lac du Porc-Épic
Lac au Menton
Lac Riverin
Lac Daluzeau
Lac Andrieux
Lac Catherine
Lac Klemka
Lac Bayeuville
Lac du Sault aux Cochons
Lac Cacuscanus
385
Lac Leman

L-250
Lac Lemoine
Lac Alex
Alex
Lac aux Canots
Lac Rouvray
Lac aux Huards
Lac Rond
Lac Tétu
Lac Maria-Chapdelaine
Lac la Sorbière
Lac Barma
Lac des Baies
Lac la Saulx
Lac Portneuf
Lac Isidore

Lac de l'Ouest
Lac des Aigles
Lac aux Grandes Pointes
L-253
Petit lac Onatchiway
Lac Bergeron
Lac au Poivre
Lac Vanel
Lac Brazza
Lac de l'Île Verte
Lac Itomamo
49°

Lac Noir
Lac Proulx
Élisabeth-Proulx
Rivière
Péribonca
L-250
Lac Bernabé
Lac de la Boiteuse
Lac Vermont
Lac Onatchiway
Lac Mirepoix
Lac Beauséjour
Lac Emmuraillé
Lac Laflamme
Lac Albert
Rivière

St-Ludger-de-Milot
Jeanne-
St-Augustin
éribonka
Lac Tchitogama
Bac/Fy.
Lac de la Grande Décharge
Lac la Mothe
Lac des Huit Chutes
Lac Moncouche
Lac Doumic
Lac Morin
Lac le Marié
Lac Tremblay
Lac le Breton
Lac Gosselin
Lac Jalobert
Lac Larrey
Lac Gorgotton

169 73
Ste-Monique
Parc de la Pointe-Taillon
L'Ascension
St-Henri-de-Taillon
Lac Labrecque
St-Léon
Bégin
St-David-de-Falardeau
L-201
L-200
Ste-Marguerite

Delisle
St-Nazaire
St-Ambroise
St-Honoré
Lac Laurent
Riv. du Sault-au-Mouton

ALMA
169
St-Gédéon
St-Bruno
St-Charles-de-Bourget
Shipshaw
Valin
St-Fulgence
Lac St-Germains
Rivière
Escoumins

Hébertville-Station
Métabetchouan
CN
Larouche
34
170
47
372
70
Shipshaw
CHICOUTIMI
Ste-Rose-du-Nord
Lac Fortin
119
St-Basile-de-Tableau
172
Lac des Sables
138

Desbiens
Lac-à-la-Croix
Hébertville
JONQUIÈRE
Arvida
Lac Long
372
19
LA BAIE
170
Saguenay
Lac Otis
Saguenay
Rivière-Ste-Marguerite
Sacré-Cœur
Grandes-Bergeronnes
Petites-Bergeronnes

St-André-du-Lac-St-Jean
Lac Kénogami
St-Cyriac
Laterrière
147
St-Félix-d'Otis
Rivière-Éternité
L'Anse-St-Jean
River
Petit-Saguenay
L'Anse-de-Roche
Parc marin du Saguenay

Lac à la Carpe
Lac de la Belle
Lac des Îlots
Lac Huard
Lac Éternité
Lac Brébeuf
Rivière
123
Réserve faunique de la Rivière-Petit-Saguenay
Tadoussac
Bac/Fy.
St-Paul
Écorces
175
Ferland
381
St-Jean
Baie-Ste-Catherine
Pointe aux Alouettes

B
E
C
LAURENTIDES
169
Chicoutimi
Boilleau
Q-356
Lac Ha! Ha!
Q-358
Sagard
Lac Buteux
138
Saguenay Marine Park
48°

Mont-Apica
Lac aux Montagnais
Lac aux Écorces
L-215
Mars
Lac au Porc-Épic
Lac Bazile
Rivière
Lac Onésime
Lac aux Canards
Lac Deschênes
Baie-des-Rochers
Cacouna
132

Réserve faunique
Lac Métascouac
Lac Décoigne
Lac des Martres
Lac au Sable
Lac aux Îlots
Lac au Plongeon
Port-aux-Quilles
St-Siméon
Île aux Lièvres
RIVIÈRE-DU-LOUP
St-Patrice
507

des Laurentides
Métabetchouane
Lac Pikauba
Rivière
Port-au-Persil
Cap au Saumon
Notre-Dame-du-Portage
St-Antonin
185
499

Lac Brûlé
Lac Ventadour
175
Parc des Grands-Jardins
381
Grand-Fonds
St-Fidèle-de-Mont-Murray
Les Pèlerins
St-Alexandre
St-André
230
289

Lac aux Rognons
Lac à Moïse
Montmorency
Lac des Neiges
138
St-Urbain
St-Hilarion
Notre-Dame-des-Monts
St-Aimé-des-Lacs
Ste-Agnès
Clermont
Cap-à-l'Aigle
La Malbaie
Pointe-au-Pic
33
Îles de St-Germain
Kamouraska
St-Joseph-de-Kamouraska
Ste-Hélène
485
471

Petit lac Jacques-Cartier
Parc de la Jacques-Cartier
Lac à l'Épaule
Lac Sautauriski
Cartier
Lac Malbaie
Lac Ripault
St-Urbain
362
Cap aux Oies
Les Éboulements
St-Joseph-de-la-Rive
Pointe Iroquois
La Baleine
Île aux Coudres
Baie-St-Paul
St-Placide-de-Charlevoix
St-Bernard-sur-Mer
St-Louis-de-l'Isle-aux-Coudres
Petite-Rivière-St-François
St-Cassien-des-Caps
185
CN
Cap au Diable
Saint-Laurent
St-Denis
20
132
495
St-Pascal
St-Philippe-de-Néri
Mont-Carmel
St-Pacôme
Rivière-Ouelle
Village-des-Aulnaies
St-Roch-des-Aulnaies
Ste-Louise
430
La Pocatière
287
St-Gabriel-Lalemant
St-Onésime

Lac Aaron

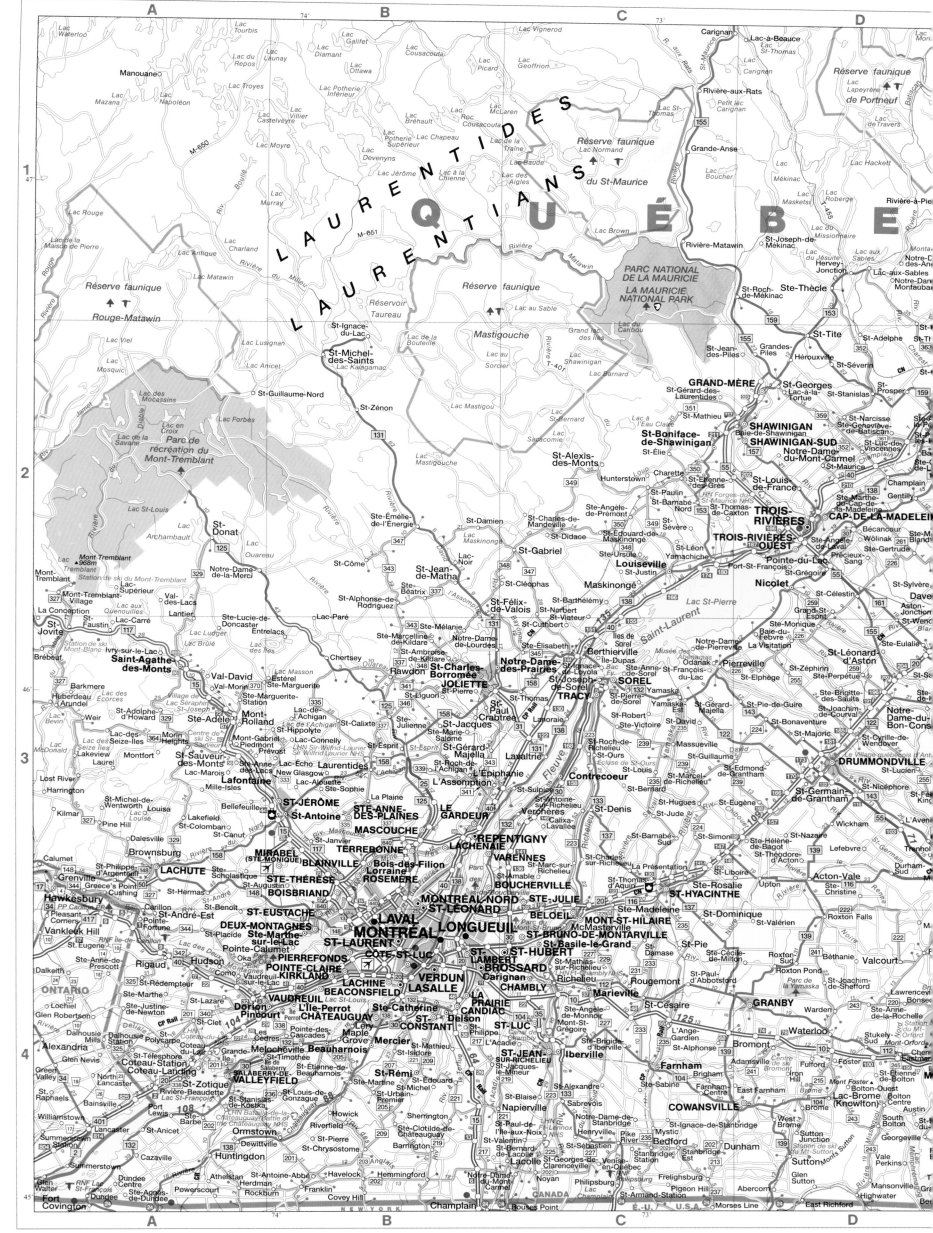

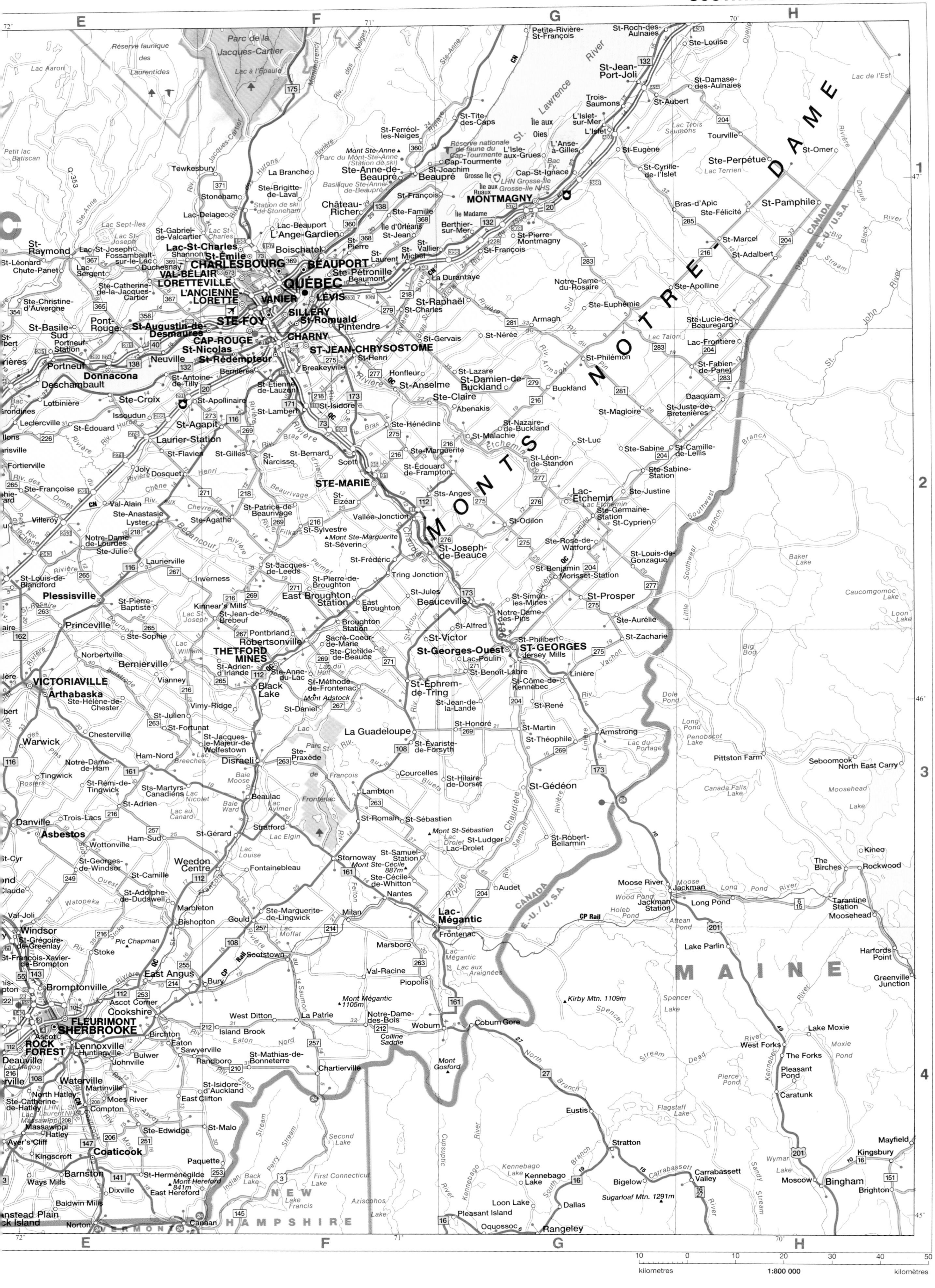

NOTRE-DAME

MONTS NOTRE-DAME

MAINE

MONTMAGNY
QUÉBEC
LÉVIS
STE-FOY
CHARLESBOURG
BEAUPORT
VANIER
SILLERY
CAP-ROUGE
ST-NICOLAS
CHARNY
ST-JEAN-CHRYSOSTOME
STE-MARIE
ST-GEORGES
ST-GEORGES-OUEST
THETFORD MINES
VICTORIAVILLE
Arthabaska
Plessisville
Princeville
Asbestos
Danville
Warwick
SHERBROOKE
FLEURIMONT
ROCK FOREST
Coaticook
Lac-Mégantic
Black Lake
Disraeli
Beauceville

Parc de la Jacques-Cartier
Réserve faunique des Laurentides
Réserve nationale de faune de Cap-Tourmente
Parc du Mont-Ste-Anne

St-Raymond
Ste-Louise
St-Jean-Port-Joli
St-Damase-des-Aulnaies
St-Omer
St-Pamphile
St-Marcel
St-Adalbert

Lac à l'Épaule
Lac St-Charles
Lac Sept-Îles
Île d'Orléans
Île aux Grues
Île aux Oies

Lawrence River
Rivière Chaudière
Rivière Etchemin

1:800 000

kilometres   10   0   10   20   30   40   50   kilometres

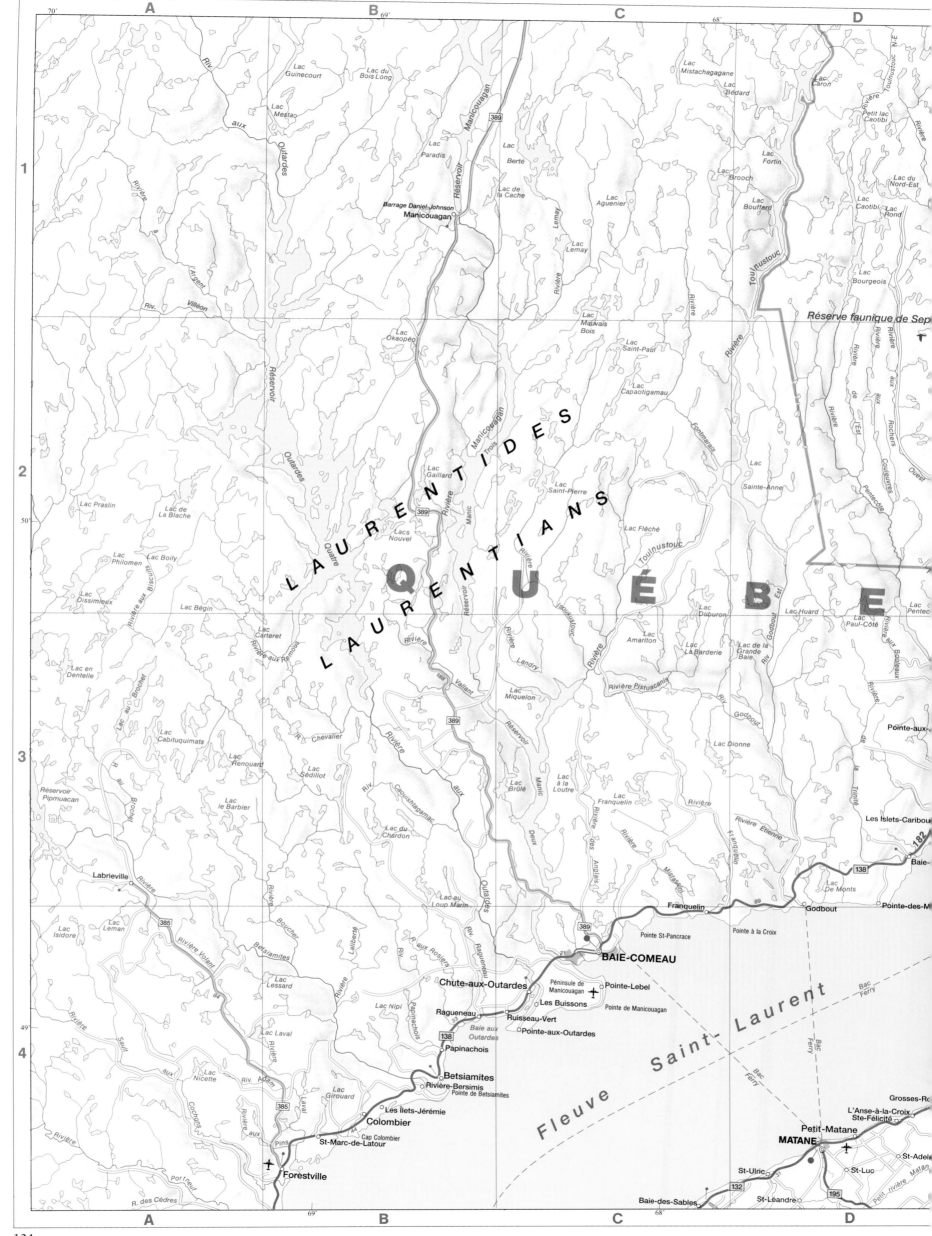

E F G H

1

2

3

4

67° 66° 65°

51°

50°

49°

Lac Nipissis
Lac Franchetot
Lac à l'Aigle
Lac Tortue
• 998m
Lac Nipisso
Magpie
Ouest
Lac
Lac de la Mine
Magpie
Lac Manitou
Lac Nouël

Grand lac du Nord
Lac Cacaoui
Rivière Sainte
Rivière
Rivière
Lac à Renard

Riv.
Rivière Manitou
Rivière Sheldrake
Rivière au Tonnerre
Rivière
Rivière Jupitagon
Magpie

Marguerite
Lac Catista
Lac Picard
Rivière Vallée
Moisie
Lac Dollard
Rivière Nipisso
Lac Tchinicaman
Lac Travers
Lac des Eudistes
Lac Brézel
Lac Touzel
Lac à Renard

Grand lac des Rapides
Matamec
Riv. aux Loups
Rivière aux Marins
Rivière Tortue
Rivière au

Lac Asquiche
Lac Brûlé
Lac Curot
Lac des Rapides
Lac Matamec
Baie Moisie
Pointe-St-Charles
Rivière-Pigou
Manitou
Rivière-aux-Graines
Sheldrake
Rivière-au-Tonnerre
Magpie

Lac Pasteur
Lac Morin
SEPT-ÎLES
Baie de Sept-Îles
Clarke City
Maliotenam
Moisie
138
61
ONSL
5e

Pasteur
Gallix
138
71
Rivière-Brochu
Baie de Ste-Marguerite
Pointe à la Chasse
Île Grosse Boule
Refuge d'oiseaux migrateurs de l'Île-du-Corossol
41

Port-Cartier
Pointe Ste-Marguerite
Pointe Jambon
Rochers
39

Bac Ferry
Bac Ferry

Pointe Sproule
Baie-Ste-Claire
Pointe de l'Ouest
ÎLE D'ANTICOSTI
ANTICOSTI ISLAND
Réserve faunique de l'Île-d'Anticosti

glais

St. Lawrence River

Cap-au-Renard
Marsoui
Ruisseau-à-Rebours
Rivière-à-Claude
Mont-St-Pierre
Mont-Louis
L'Anse-Pleureuse
Gros-Morne
Manche-d'Épée
Madeleine-Centre
Cap de la Madeleine
Rivière-la-Madeleine
Cap Barré
Grande-Vallée
Petite-Vallée
Pointe-à-la-Frégate
Petite-Anse

Ruisseau-Castor
La Martre
132
68
Rivière à Claude
Rivière Mont-St-Pierre
13
45
27
Cloridorme
St-Yvon
132
110
22

Tourelle
Ste-Anne-des-Monts
Pointe Ste-Anne
Cap-Chat
34
Marsoui
Rivière de Mont-Louis
198
Madeleine
Rivière
L'Anse-à-Valleau
St-Maurice-de-l'Échouerie
Pointe-Jaune

Capucins
Pointe du Cap Chat
132
299
Cap Chat
Réserve faunique des Chic-Chocs
Mt Jacques-Cartier
• 1268m
Réserve faunique des Chic-Chocs
Lac York
128
Rivière Dartmouth
PARC NATIONAL FORILLON
Morris NATIONAL PARK
Petit Cap
197

Méchins
132
Cap-Seize
Murdochville
Rivière Béland
Rivière de la Petite Fourche
Fontenelle

de-Cherbourg
MONTS CHIC- CHOCS
299
Rivière Cascapédia
Rivière York
88
Lac York
198
Wakeham
York Centre
GASPÉ
13

faunique de Matane

10 0 10 20 30 40 50
kilomètres 1:800 000 kilomètres

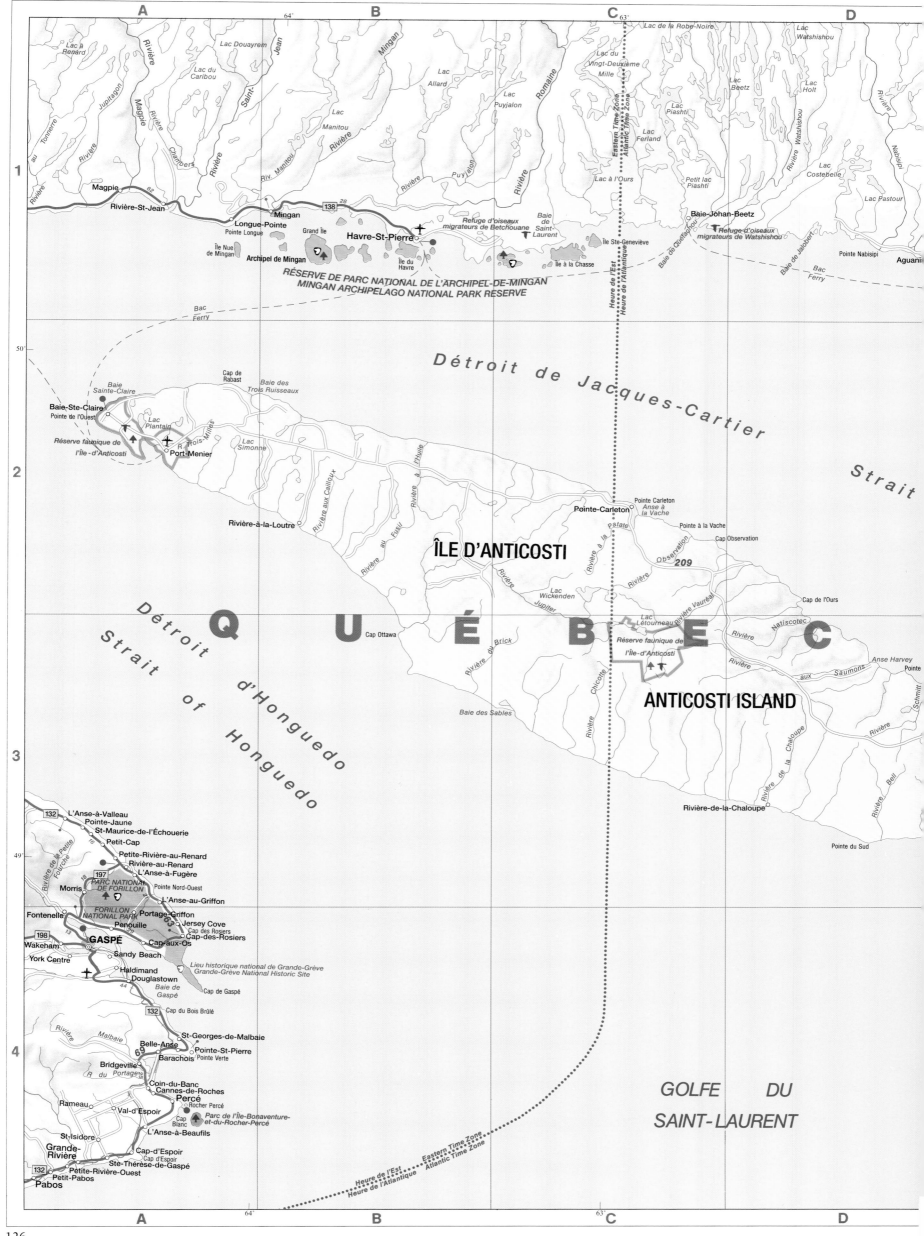

A   64'   **B**   **C** 63'   **D**

Lac de la Robe-Noire
Lac Watshishou

Lac à Renard
Lac Douayrem
Lac
Lac Allard
Lac du Vingt-Deuxième Mille
Lac Beetz
Lac Holt

1

Lac du Caribou
Lac Manitou
Lac Puyjalon
Lac Ferland
Lac Piashti
Petit lac Piashti
Lac Costebelle
Lac Pastour

Magpie
Rivière-St-Jean
62
138 28
Mingan
Longue-Pointe
Pointe Longue
Grand Île
Havre-St-Pierre
Refuge d'oiseaux migrateurs de Betchouane
Baie de Saint-Laurent
Baie-Johan-Beetz
Refuge d'oiseaux migrateurs de Watshishou
Pointe Nabisipi
Aguani

Île Nue de Mingan
Archipel de Mingan
Île du Havre
Île Ste-Geneviève
Île à la Chasse

RÉSERVE DE PARC NATIONAL DE L'ARCHIPEL-DE-MINGAN
MINGAN ARCHIPELAGO NATIONAL PARK RESERVE

Bac Ferry

Détroit de Jacques-Cartier   *Strait*

50'

Baie Sainte-Claire
Cap de Rabast
Baie des Trois Ruisseaux
Baie-Ste-Claire
Pointe de l'Ouest
Lac Plantain
R. Trois-Milles
Port-Menier
Réserve faunique de l'Île-d'Anticosti
Lac Simonne

Pointe Carleton
Anse à la Vache
Pointe à la Vache
Cap Observation

2

Rivière-à-la-Loutre
Pointe-Carleton

ÎLE D'ANTICOSTI
209

Cap de l'Ours

Q U É B E C

Réserve faunique de l'Île-d'Anticosti
Rivière Natiscotec
Anse Harvey
Pointe

Cap Ottawa
Lac Wickenden
Lac Létourneau Rivière Vauréal

ANTICOSTI ISLAND

Détroit   *d'Honguedo*
Strait   *of*   *Honguedo*

Baie des Sables

3

Rivière-de-la-Chaloupe

Pointe du Sud

L'Anse-à-Valleau
132
Pointe-Jaune
St-Maurice-de-l'Échouerie
Petit-Cap
Petite-Rivière-au-Renard
197
Rivière-au-Renard
L'Anse-à-Fugère
Morris
PARC NATIONAL DE FORILLON
Pointe Nord-Ouest
49'
L'Anse-au-Griffon
Fontenelle
FORILLON NATIONAL PARK
Portage-Griffon
Penouille
Jersey Cove
198
Cap des Rosiers
GASPÉ
Cap-des-Rosiers
Wakeham
Cap-aux-Os
York Centre
Sandy Beach
Haldimand
Lieu historique national de Grande-Grève
Douglastown
Grande-Grève National Historic Site
Baie de Gaspé
Cap de Gaspé
132
Cap du Bois Brûlé

4

Rivière Malbaie
St-Georges-de-Malbaie
69
Belle-Anse
Pointe-St-Pierre
Barachois
Pointe Verte
Bridgeville
Coin-du-Banc
Cannes-de-Roches
Rameau
Percé
Rocher Percé
Val-d'Espoir
Cap Blanc
Parc de l'Île-Bonaventure-et-du-Rocher-Percé
St-Isidore
L'Anse-à-Beaufils
Grande-Rivière
Cap-d'Espoir
Ste-Thérèse-de-Gaspé
132
Petite-Rivière-Ouest
Petit-Pabos
Pabos

GOLFE   **DU**
SAINT-LAURENT

Eastern Time Zone / Atlantic Time Zone
Heure de l'Est / Heure de l'Atlantique

A   64'   **B**   **C** 63'   **D**

E   F   G   H

Lac Victor
Lac Landry
Rivière
Lac d'Auteuil
Lac Musquaro
Lac
Couchy
Lac
Noirclair
Lac Triquet
R. Étamamiou
Île du Petit Mécatina

Lac Paimpont
Natashquan
Rivière
Lac Marie-Claire
Rivière Olomane
Lac Musquanousse
Lac Coacoachu
Chevery
Harrington Harbour
Îles Harrington

Lac Kégashka
Île Watageistic
Lac Salé

Kégashka
Lac
Îles Ste-Marie
Refuge d'oiseaux migrateurs des Îles-Ste-Marie

Baie des Loups
Wolf Bay
Étamamiou
Bac Ferry

Musquaro
La Romaine
Île du Lac

Natashquan
Kegaska
Pointe Chicoutai
Bac Ferry
Refuge d'oiseaux migrateurs de l'Île-à-la-Brume
Refuge d'oiseaux migrateurs de la Baie-des-Loups

Poste
Pointe de Natashquan
—50°

1

62°   61°

Rochers aux Oiseaux

Île Brion

G O L F E   D U

S A I N T - L A U R E N T

Île de l'Est
Leslie
Grosse-Île
Réserve nationale de faune de la Pointe-de-l'Est
Old Harry
Pointe de l'Est
20   199
Île de la Grande Entrée
Pointe-aux-Loups
Grande-Entrée
87

Île du Havre aux Maisons
ÎLES DE LA MADELEINE
QUÉBEC

ques Cartier

Fatima
Les Caps
L'Étang-du-Nord
La Vernière
Havre-aux-Maisons
Cap-aux-Meules
Île du Cap aux Meules

2

G U L F   O F

S T.   L A W R E N C E

199
Baie de Plaisance
Île d'Entrée
L'Île-d'Entrée

Île du Havre Aubert
Étang-des-Caps
Bac Ferry
Vers Montréal
To Montréal
Cap du Sud-Ouest
Millerand
Bassin
Havre-Aubert

de la Table
Baie du Renard
Baie-du-Renard

47°
Cape St. Lawrence
Meat Cove
47°

3

Pointe de l'Est
Réserve faunique de l'Île-d'Anticosti
Baie du Naufrage
Pointe Heath

49°

au
ormoran

Red River
Pleasant Bay
CAPE BRETON ISLAND
CT
CAPE BRETON HIGHLANDS NATIONAL PARK
44
White Hill 532 m

ÎLE DU CAP-BRETON
Presqu'île
PARC NATIONAL DES HAUTES-TERRES-DU-CAP-BRETON

Cheticamp
Petit Etang
Belle Marche
Cheticamp Island
Cheticamp Lake
Ingon

Point Cross
CAPE BRETON HIGHLANDS

Grand Etang
Bac Ferry

St. Joseph du Moine
HAUTES TERRES DU CAP-BRETON

4

PRINCE EDWARD ISLAND
ÎLE-DU-PRINCE-ÉDOUARD

Campbell's Cove Provincial Park
Hermanville
Fairfield
North Lake
16
East Point
East Point

St. Margarets
Elmira
302
16

NOVA SCOTIA
NOUVELLE-ÉCOSSE
CT
Margaree Harbour
Belle Cote
Kingross

Bear River
307
305
Baltic
Margaree Valley
North River Provincial Park

Kingsboro
Basin Head Fisheries Museum
East Margaree
Portree

Red Point
16
Chimney Corner
219
Margaree Centre
Museum of Cape Breton Heritage

2
Rollo Bay
Souris
Red Point Provincial Park
St. Rose
Margaree Forks
Northeast Margaree

Fortune Bridge
Howe Point
Souris Beach Provincial Park
Dunvegan
Southwest Margaree
Lake O'Law Provincial Park
North River Bridge
CT
St. Ann's

Little Pond
19
Inverness
Finlayson

Boughton Bay

GULF   OF
ST.   LAWRENCE

E   F   G   H
62°   61°

kilomètres   1:800 000   kilomètres
10   0   10   20   30   40   50

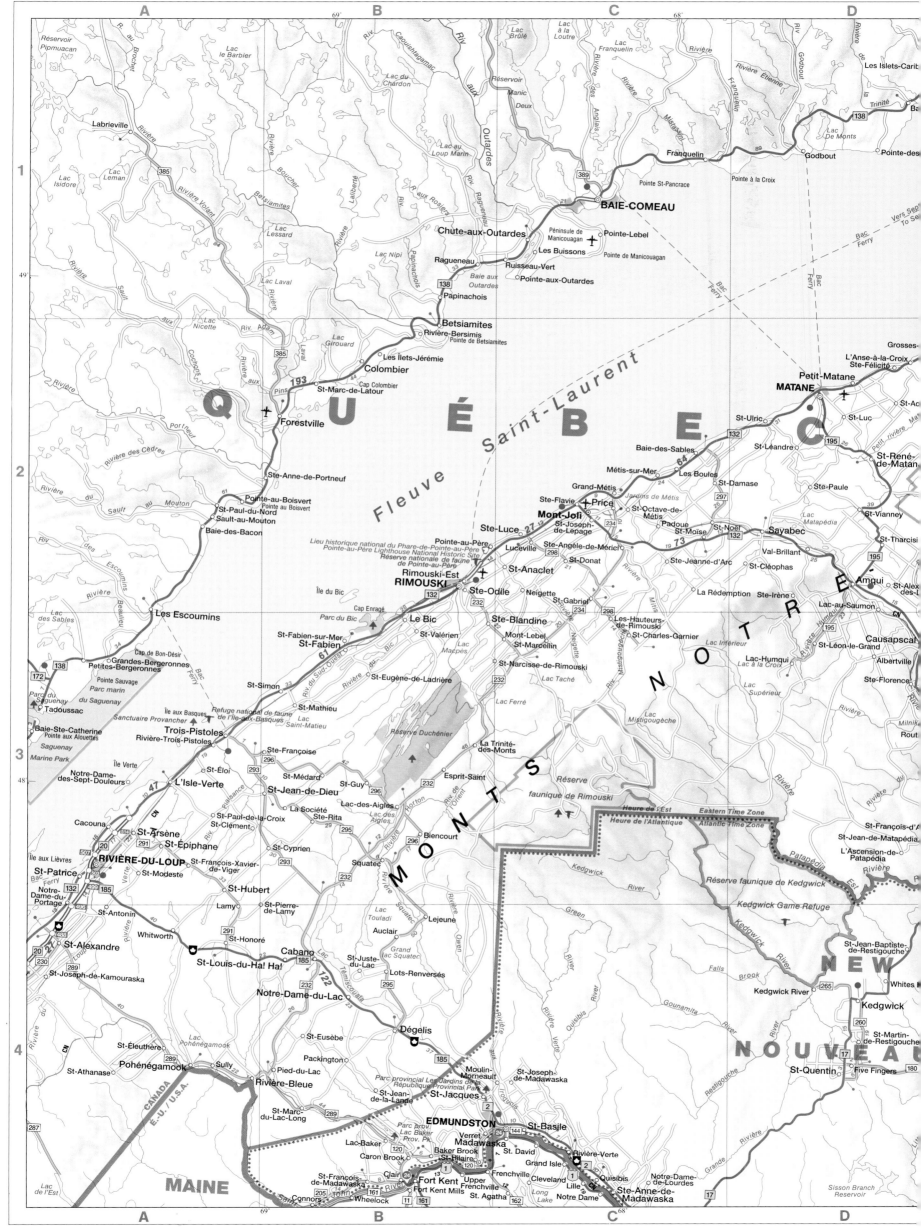

St. Lawrence River

Lawrence River

Ste-Anne-des-Monts
Pointe Ste-Anne
Cap-Chat
Pointe du Cap Chat
Capucins
132
échins
Ruisseau-Castor
Cap-au-Renard
La Martre
Tourelle
34
Cap-Seize
299
Marsoui
68
132
21
Ruisseau-à-Rebours
Rivière-à-Claude
Mont-St-Pierre
Mont-Louis
13
L'Anse-Pleureuse
Gros-Morne
Manche-d'Épée
Madeleine-Centre
Cap de la Madeleine
Rivière-la-Madeleine
45
Cap Barré
Grande-Vallée
Petite-Vallée
Pointe-à-la-Frégate
Petite-Anse
27
Cloridorme
St-Yvon
170
132
22
L'Anse-à-Valleau
Pointe-Jaune
St-Maurice-de-l'Échouerie
Petit-Cap
49°

Réserve faunique
des Chic-Chocs
Mt Jacques-Cartier
▲1268m
Réserve faunique
des Chic-Chocs
Murdochville
Lac York
198
128
York
Rivière
PARC NATIONAL
Morris
DE FORILLON
NATIONAL PARK
Fontenelle
197
GASPÉ
Wakeham
York Centre

-Cherbourg
MONTS CHIC-CHOCS
299
faunique de Matane
DAME
Réserve faunique
de Dunière
Automne
299
143
Cascapédia

Rameau
St-Isidore

Grande-Rivière
Petite-Rivière-Ouest
Pabos
Petit-Pabos
Chandler
Réserve faunique
de Port-Daniel
Pabos Mills
Pointe de Newport
Newport
132
170
36
Pointe au Maquereau
St-Jules
299
Grande-Cascapédia
St-Edgar
Clemville
L'Anse-aux-Gascons
Gesgapegiag
Maria
St-Alphonse
St-Jogues
Port-Daniel
Pointe de l'Ouest
Nouvelle
132
72
29
New Richmond
Kelly
Marcil
Drapeau
Black-Cape
St-Elzéar
Shigawake
St-Godefroi
Escuminac
St-Omer
Rivière-Paspébiac
L'Alverne
Pointe-à-la-Garde
Miguasha-Ouest
Miguasha
Parc de Miguasha
Carleton
Pointe Tracadigache
Caplan
St-Siméon
132
Bonaventure
Hope Town
Paspébiac
New Carlisle
Pointe Bonaventure
St-Fidèle-de-Restigouche
St-André-de-Restigouche
Oak Bay
Point
Restigouche
Pointe-à-la-Croix
La Nim
134
Dalhousie
de la
Île/la Île de
Dalhousie
Junction
280
Eel River Crossing
Charlo
BAIE DES CHALEURS
Île Miscou Island
Miscou Centre
Atholville
Tide Head
Dundee
River Charlo
Parc prov. Sugarloaf Prov. Park
Heron Island
CHALEUR BAY
Petit-Shippagan
Île Lamèque Island
Campbellton
Glen Livet
Balmoral
275
Blackland
New Mills
53
Pigeon Hill
Val-d'Amour
17
Glencoe
270
Maltais
134
Durham Centre
Pointe Belledune Point
Belledune
Anse-Bleue
303
Maisonnette
Caraquet I.
P.P. Maisonnette P.P.
Bas-Caraquet
310
Ste-Marie-St-Raphaël
305
Dawsonville
275
St-Arthur
Nash Creek
Jacquet
River
344
Grande-Anse
Pokeshaw
330
Caraquet
145
Lamèque
Robinsonville
Lorne
Sunnyside
Pointe-Verte
333
Petit-Rocher
BAIE
P.P. Pokeshaw
Le Village historique acadien/Acadian Historical Village
St-Léonlin
Bertrand
335
St-Simon
Shippagan
PP Shippagan PP
Upsalquitch
61
134
NEPISIGUIT
New Bandon
11
325
St-Léonin
Haut-Pokemouche
Aquarium and Marine
Centre l L'Aquarium et
Centre marin
Nigadoo
Beresford
315
Stonehaven
Clifton
135
14
Maltampec
15
Pokemouche
345
Inkerman
Nicholas-Denys
Robertville
BAY
Janeville
65
Burnsville
Rang-St-Georges
355
North Tetagouche
322
Parc prov. Youghall Prov. Park
11
Salmon Beach
340
Notre-Dame-des-Érables
Paquetville
350
Pokemouche
135
Parc provincial Tetagouche Falls
Provincial Park
BATHURST
South Tetagouche
180
Réserve faunique
de Tracadie
Val-Doucet
Pont-Landry
St-Isidore
160
Losier Settlement
11
Brunswick Mines
430
134
Tracadie Game Refuge
8
St-Sauveur
160
St-Irénée
365
Tracadie-Sheila
Parc provincial Val Comeau Provincial Park
Parc provincial
Mont Carleton
Mount Carleton
Provincial Park
820m
Mt. Carleton
Nepisiguit
River
360
Allardville
Val-Comeau
370
Pont-Lafrance
Rivière-du-Portage
Brunswick Mines
40
Daulnay
Brantville
460
Bathurst Mines
430
Jeanne-Mance
8
Price Settlement
Wishart Point
Tabusintac
Heath Steele
Allainville
455
Fairisle
445
11
Layillette

1:800 000
kilomètres 10 0 10 20 30 40 50 kilomètres

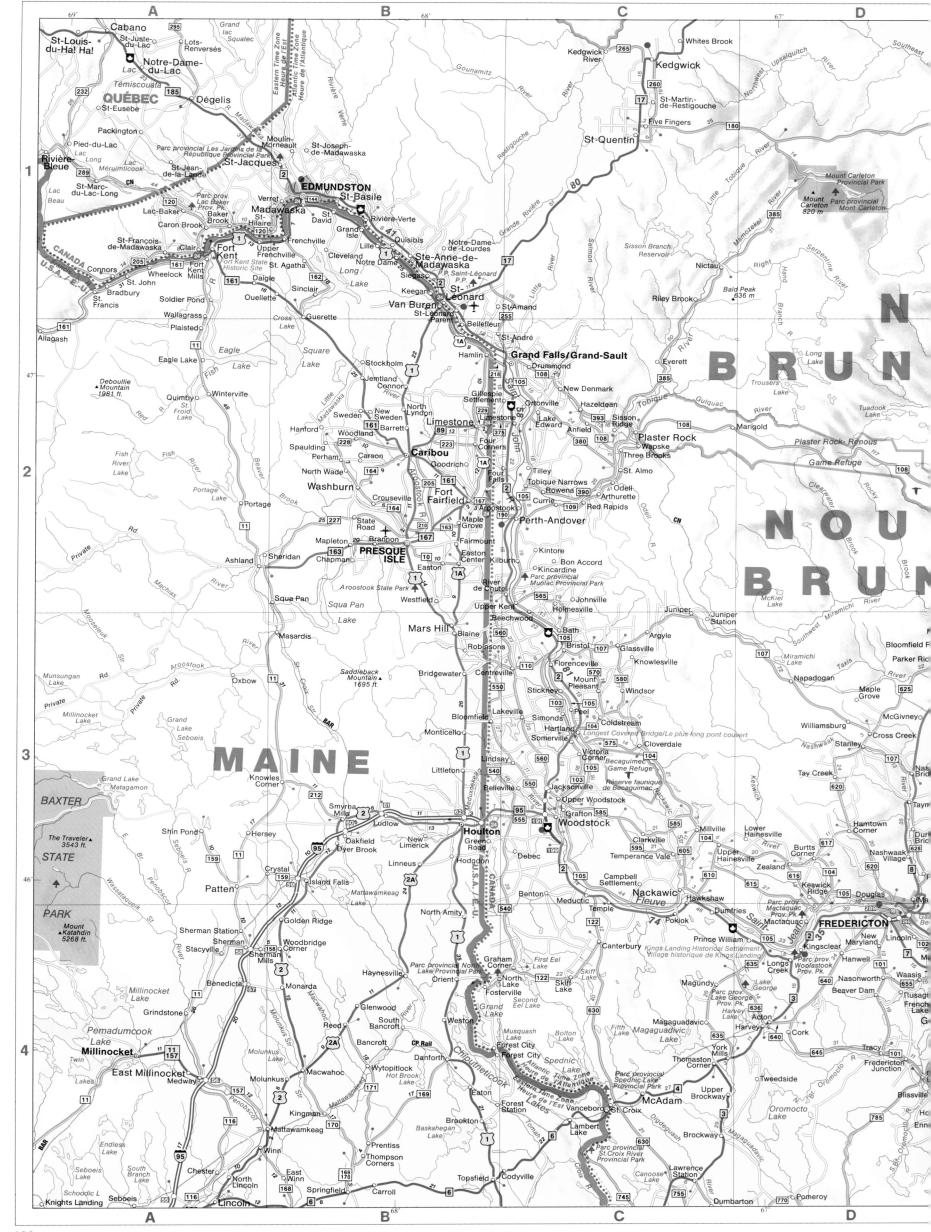

Nicholas-Denys, Beresford, Janeville, Burnsville, Haut-Pokemouche, Maltampec, Le Goulet, Inkerman
Robertville, North Tetagouche, Paquetville, Pokemouche, Rang-St-Georges, Notre-Dame-des-Erables, Pont Landry, Losier Settlement
Tetagouche River, Parc provincial Youghall, Salmon Beach, Val-Doucet, St-Isidore, St-Irénée, Tracadie-Sheila
BATHURST, Réserve faunique de Tracadie, Tracadie Game Refuge, Val-Comeau, Parc provincial Val Comeau Provincial Park
Brunswick Mines, Allardville, St-Sauveur, Pont Lafrance, Rivière-du-Portage, Brantville
Bathurst Mines, Daulnay, Jeanne Mance, Price Settlement, Wishart Point
Heath Steele, Allainville, Lavillette, Fairisle, Tabusintac, Neguac Beach
Nepisiguit River, Bartibog, Lagacéville, Neguac, Parc provincial Neguac Provincial Park, Burnt Church
Wayerton, Beaver Brook Station, Bartibog Bridge, Loggieville, Hardwicke, Escuminac, Point Escuminac
Sevogle, Parc provincial Middle Island Provincial Park, Historic McDonald Farm, Ferme historique McDonald, Miramichi Bay, Baie de Miramichi
Douglastown, Chatham, Centre Napan, Miramichi, Bay du Vin, Baie-Ste-Anne
Newcastle, Chatham Head, Nelson-Miramichi, Black River, Pointe-Sapin
Whitney, Derby Junction, Beaubears Island N.H.S., Barnaby River, St. Margarets, Parc provincial Redmondville Provincial Park
Silikers, Sunny Corner, Millerton, Derby, Chelmsford, Barnaby, Fontaine
Red Bank, Quarryville, McKinleyville, Rosaireville, Laketon
McGraw Brook, White Rapids, Collette, Shediac Ridge, Kouchibouguac
Renous River, Blackville, Rogersville, Acadieville, St-Louis-de-Kent, PARC NATIONAL KOUCHIBOUGUAC
Howard, Acadie Siding, St-Ignace, Grande-Aldouane, Richibucto, Indian Island
Upper Blackville, Kent Lake, Richibucto Cape, Richibucto-Village, Cap-Lumière
Blissfield, Kent Junction, St-Charles, Rexton, Ste-Anne-de-Kent
Doaktown, Big Cove, Molus River, South Branch, St-Edouard-de-Kent, Dune de Buctouche
Carrolls Crossing, New Bandon, Bass River, Smiths Corner, Pine Ridge, Bouctouche, St-Thomas
Harcourt, Beersville, Fords Mills, St-Norbert, McKees Mills, Cormierville
Adamsville, Ste-Marie-de-Kent, Haut-Bouctouche, Île Cocagne Island
Coal Branch, McLean Settlement, Coates Mills, St-Antoine, Pointe aux Renards, Cap-des-Caissie
St-Paul, Hébert, Notre-Dame, Cocagne, Grande-Digue, Baie de Shediac
Gaspereau Forks, Canaan, Shediac Bridge, Shediac Cape, Pointe-du-Chêne
Salmon Creek, Canaan Game Refuge, Réserve faunique de Canaan, Irishtown, Barachois, Cap-Pelé
Chipman, Coal Creek, Lutes Mountain, Shediac, Dorchester Crossing, Robichaud, Petit-Cap
Minto, Newcastle Bridge, New Canaan, Scoudouc, Aboujagane, Little Shemogue
Ripples, Cumberland Bay, Canaan Road, Berry Mills, Dieppe, Meadow Brook, Port Elgin, Upper Cape
Grand Lake, Canaan Forks, MONCTON, RIVERVIEW, Coverdale, Fox Creek, Calhoun, Baie Verte, Tidnish
Youngs Cove Road, Salisbury, River Glade, Turtle Creek, Pré-d'en-Haut, Memramcook, College Bridge, Jolicure
Princess Park, Youngs Cove, Coles Island, Petitcodiac, Havelock, Hillsborough, Dorchester, Middle Sackville, Tidnish Bridge
Lakeville Corner, Douglas Harbour, Waterborough, Cornhill, The Glades, Parkindale, Albert Mines, Frosty Hollow, Sackville, Point de Bute
Scotchtown, Whites Cove, Codys, Newtown, Anagance, Portage Vale, Prosser Brook, Hopewell Cape, Wood Point, Aulac, Amherst
Jemseg, Cambridge-Narrows, Pearsonville, Elgin, Hillside, Hopewell Cape, Les rochers en pots de fleurs, Shepody, Johnson Mills
Gagetown, Lower Jemseg, Berwick, Penobsquis, Goshen, Parc prov. The Rocks, Riverside-Albert, Lower Rockport, Amherst Point
Queenstown, Belleisle Creek, Smiths Creek, Roachville, Mechanic Settlement, Harvey, Cape Maringouin, Maccan, Nappan
Hatfield Point, Springfield, Sussex, Sussex Corner, Waterford, Joggins, River Hebert, Barronsfield
Shannon, Apohaqui, Jeffries Corner, PARC NATIONAL DE FUNDY, Minudie, Athol, Springhill Junction
Wickham, Norton, Poodiac, Waterside, Alma, Shulie, South Brook, Springhill
Hampstead, Hampton, Bloomfield, Hammondvale, Hillsdale, Cape Enrage, Chignecto Game Sanctuary, West Brook, Mapleton
Evandale, Oak Point, Kingston, Lakeside, Upham, Hanford Brook, Sand River, Harrison Settlement, Halfway River
Long Reach, Gondola Point, Nauwigewauk, New Salem, Apple River, Port Greville, Kirkhill, Moose River, Lakelands, Lynn
Morrisdale, Quispamsis, Fairvale, Rothesay, East Riverside-Kingshurst, New Yarmouth, Fox River, Diligent River, Parrsboro, Five Islands, Lower Economy

TIGNISH, Skinners Pond, Fisherman's Haven P.P., St. Louis, Kildare Capes, Cape Kildare
Norway, Mimnegash, St. Edward, Jacques Cartier Provincial Park, Montrose
PRINCE EDWARD ISLAND, Campbellton, Elmsdale, Mill River East, Alberton, Cascumpec
Cape Wolfe, O'Leary, Mill River Provincial Park, Carleton, Freeland
West Cape, Knutsford, Coleman, Inverness, Mount Pleasant, Mount Ellerslie
Cedar Dunes Provincial Park, West Point, Glenwood, Enmore, Tyne Valley, Richmond
ÎLE-DU-PRINCE-ÉDOUARD, St-Chrysostome, Abram-Village, Wellington
NORTHUMBERLAND STRAIT, DÉTROIT DE NORTHUMBERLAND, Cape Egmont, Mont-Carmel, Union Corner Provincial Park, Egmont Bay, Baie d'Egmont

NOVA SCOTIA, NOUVELLE-ÉCOSSE, CHIGNECTO, Baie de Chignectou, Chignecto Bay, Amherst, West Leicester, Mansfield, Little River, Salem, Collingwood Corner, Wyvern, East Mapleton, Five Islands P.P., Lower Economy

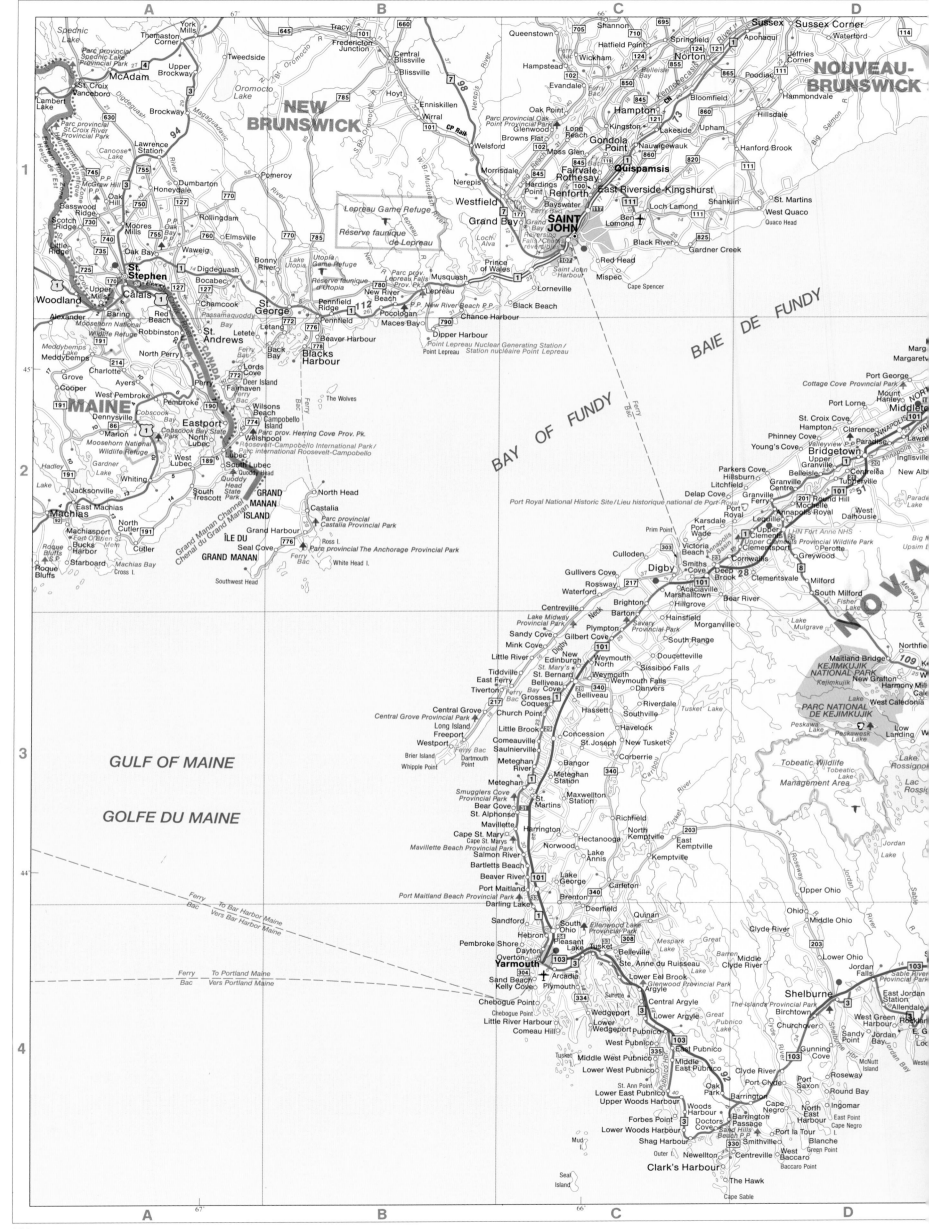

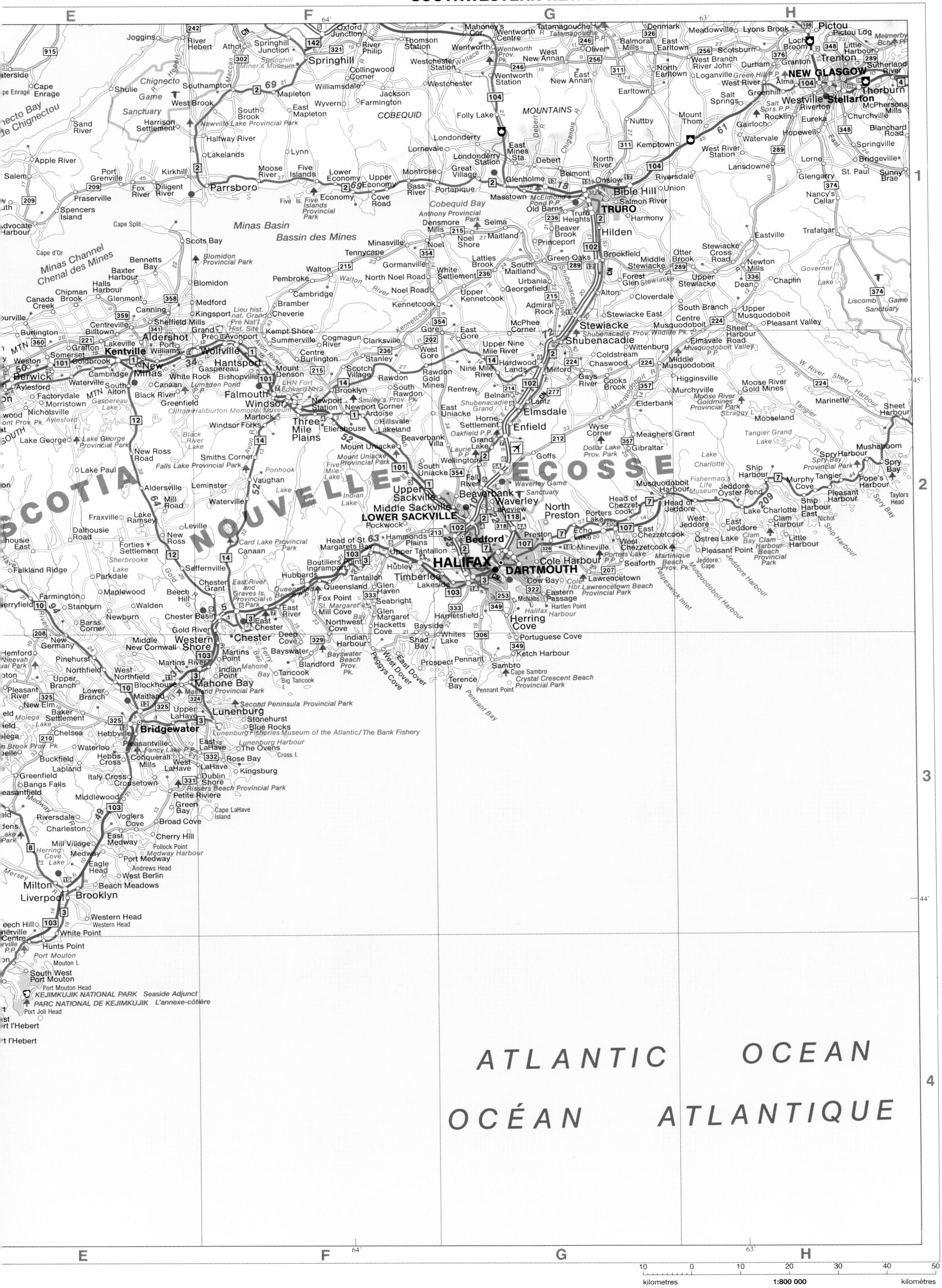

E
F
G
H
1
2
3
4
ATLANTIC OCEAN
OCÉAN ATLANTIQUE
NOUVELLE-ÉCOSSE
SCOTIA
Minas Basin
Bassin des Mines
Minas Channel
Chenal des Mines
Cobequid Bay
COBEQUID
MOUNTAINS
Chignecto Game Sanctuary
HALIFAX
DARTMOUTH
TRURO
NEW GLASGOW
Stellarton
Westville
Trenton
Pictou
Thorburn
Bible Hill
Stewiacke
Shubenacadie
Elmsdale
Enfield
Bedford
LOWER SACKVILLE
Middle Sackville
Upper Sackville
Windsor
Falmouth
Hantsport
Wolfville
Kentville
New Minas
Aldershot
Berwick
Springhill
Parrsboro
Oxford Junction
Chester
Mahone Bay
Lunenburg
Bridgewater
Liverpool
Milton
Brooklyn
Hubbards
Timberlea
Cole Harbour
Herring Cove
Musquodoboit Harbour
Jeddore Oyster Pond
Sheet Harbour
Spry Harbour
Liscomb Game Sanctuary
KEJIMKUJIK NATIONAL PARK Seaside Adjunct
PARC NATIONAL DE KEJIMKUJIK L'annexe-côtière
Port Joli Head
Cape LaHave Island
Crystal Crescent Beach Provincial Park
Cape Sambro
Peggys Cove
10 0 10 20 30 40 50
kilometres 1:800 000 kilomètres

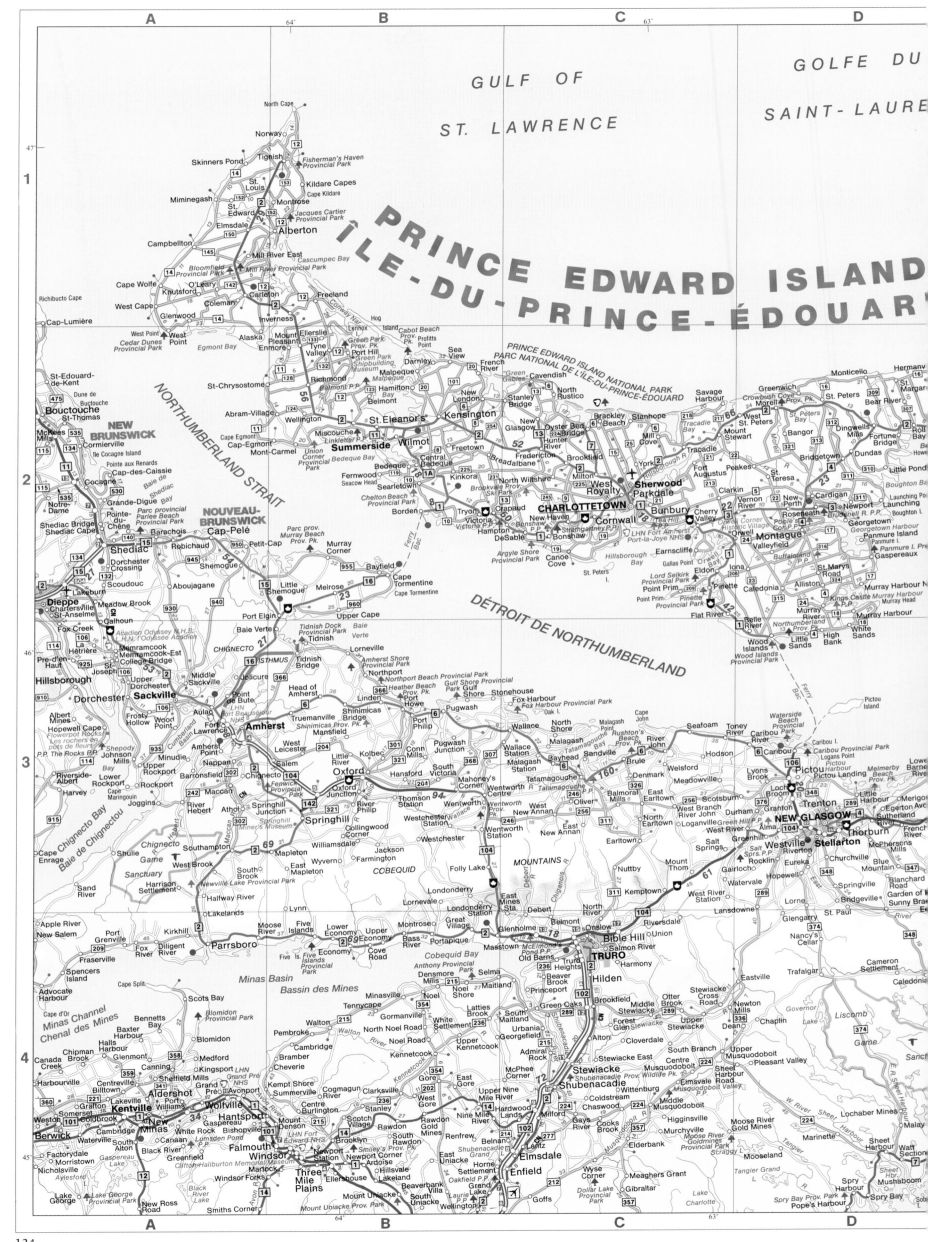

CABOT STRAIT / DÉTROIT DE CABOT

To Channel-Port aux Basques Nfld. / Vers Channel-Port aux Basques T.-N.
To Argentia Nfld. / Vers Argentia T.-N.
Ferry / Bac

Cape St. Lawrence
Meat Cove
St. Lawrence Bay
Cape North
Bay St. Lawrence
Capstick
Cabot's Landing Provincial Park
Aspy Bay
North Harbour
Cape North
Dingwall
Smelt Brook
South Harbour
Long Point
Neil Harbour
Pleasant Bay
Red River
Ingonish
CAPE BRETON HIGHLANDS NATIONAL PARK
White Hill 532 m
North Bay Ingonish
Middle Head
South Bay Ingonish
Presqu'île
PARC NATIONAL DES HAUTES-TERRES-DE-CAP-BRETON
Ingonish Beach
Ingonish Ferry
Cape Smoky
Cape Smokey Provincial Park
Petit Etang
Belle Marche
Cheticamp
Cheticamp Island
Cheticamp Lake
Wreck Cove
Wreck Cove Lakes
Point Cross
French River
Skir Dhu
Grand Etang
St. Joseph du Moine
Breton Cove
North Shore
Plaster Provincial Park
Margaree Harbour
Belle Cote
Kingross
Indian Brook
Cape Dauphin
Point Anconi

CAPE BRETON ISLAND
ÎLE DU CAP-BRETON

East Margaree
Portree
Margaree Valley
Margaree Centre
Northeast Margaree
Museum of Cape Breton Heritage
North River Provincial Park
North River Bridge
St. Ann's
Tarbotvale
Englishtown
Dalem Lake
Big Bras d'Or
Little Bras d'Or
Sydney Mines
New Victoria
New Waterford
Scotchtown
Dominion
Chimney Corner
St. Rose
Dunvegan
South West Margaree Provincial Park
Finlayson
North Gut St. Ann's
St. Ann's Prov. Pk.
Florence
GLACE BAY
Miners Museum
Inverness
Strathlorne
Upper Margaree
Scotsville
Upper Middle River
Baddeck Forks
Big Hill
Georges River
North Sydney
Donkin
Port Morien
Cape Percé
LHN Marconi NHS
Lake Ainslie East Side
Middle River
Hunters Mountain
Big Harbour
Barachois
Boularderie
SYDNEY
Westmount
Cape Morien
Black River
Nyanza
Baddeck
Ross Ferry
Barachois Prov. Pk.
Andrews
Boisdale
Sydney River
Howie Centre
Birch Grove
Homeville
Round Island
Scaterie Island
Mabou Mines
Glendyer
Mason Point
Trout River
Trout Brook
LHN Alexander Graham Bell NHS
Beaver Cove
Hornes Road
Mira Road
Mira River
Mira Bay
Main-à-Dieu
Mabou Harbour Mouth
West Mabou Harbour
Mabou
Brook Village
Lake Ainslie South Side
Churchview
Washabuck Centre
Shunacadie
Sydney Forks
East Bay
Marion Bridge
Albert Bridge
Trout Brook
Catalone
Cape Breton
Port Hood
Port Hood I.
Henry
Glencoe Station
Glencoe Mills
Blues Mills
West Alba
Whycocomagh
Little Narrows
Iona
Christmas Island
MacCormack Prov. Pk.
Ben Eoin
Ben Eoin Provincial Wildlife Park
Louisbourg
Maryville
Orangedale
Melford
Denys Basin
Bucklaw
McKinnons Harbour
Estmere
Eskasoni
East Bay
Big Pond
Salmon River Road
Two Rivers Provincial Wildlife Park
LOUISBOURG NATIONAL HISTORIC PARK
PARC HISTORIQUE NATIONAL DE LA FORTERESSE-DE-LOUISBOURG
Gabarus Bay
Judique
Big Harbour Island
Militia Point
Malagawatch
Marble Mountain
West Bay
Middle Cape
Irish Cove
Salem
Lake Uist
Enon
Victoria Bridge
Gabarus Lake
Gabarus
Cape Gabarus
Campbell
Long Point Provincial Park
Craigmore
Glendale
River Denys
Lime Hill
Johnstown
Irish Cove Prov. Pk.
Loch Lomond
L. Uist
Fourchu Bay
Livingstone Cove
Ballantynes Cove
Cape George
Georgeville
Lakevale
St. Georges Bay
Baie de Saint-Georges
Kingsville
West Bay Road
St. Georges Channel
West Bay
Cape George Harbour
Red Islands
Hay Cove
Soldiers Cove
Lake Uist
Loch Lomond
Head of Loch Lomond
Framboise
Fourchu
Malignant Cove
Big Marsh
Morristown
Crystal Cliffs
Antigonish Harbour
Queensville
Dundee
Sporting Mountain
St. Peters Canal
French Cove
Chapel Island
Barra Head
Grand River
Lower L'Esprit
Framboise Cove
North Grant
Southside Antigonish Harbour
Cape Blue
Bayfield Beach P.P.
Pomquet
Pomquet Beach P.P.
Linwood
Tracadie
Havre Boucher
Troy
Creignish
St. Georges Channel
Grand Anse
Bourgeois
Grande Greve
L'Ardoise
Grand River
L'Archeveque
St. Esprit
Antigonish
Afton
Lower South River
Mulgrave
Frankville
Auld Cove
Port Hastings
Granville
Cleveland
Louisdale
St. Peters
Point Michaud
Michaud Point
Point Michaud Provincial Park
Brierly Brook
James River
Salt Springs
Monastery
Upper Big Tracadie
Mattie Settlement
Point Tupper
PORT HAWKESBURY
Evanston
D'Escousse
Red Point
St. Joseph
Glen Road
St. Andrews
New France
Port Malcolm
ISLE MADAME
Arichat
West Arichat
Petit-de-Grat Island
Petit-de-Grat Bridge
Little Anse
Heatherton
Caledonia Mills
Lincolnville
Sand Point
Melford
Janvrin Island
Arichat Provincial Park
Cape Argos
Glen Road
Fraser Mills
Upper South River
Boylston
Boylston Provincial Park
Port Shoreham
St. Francis Harbour
Ashdale
Glen Alpine
North Lochaber
Lochaber
Roman Valley
Glencoe
Guysborough
Halfway Cove
Philips Harbour
Fox Island Main
Canso
Cape Canso
Grassy Island National Historic Site
Lieu historic national de l'île-Grassy
Andrew I.
Goshen
Giant Lake
Eight Island Lake
Forest Hill
Salmon River Lake
Erinville
Ogden
Roachvale
Queensport
Hazel Hill
Little Dover
Dover Bay
Lochiel Lake Prov. Pk.
Denver
Smithfield
Melrose
Aspen
Country Harbour Cross Roads
Country Harbour
Country Harbour Mines
Isaac's Harbour
Salmon River
Lundy
Loon L.
Charlos Cove
Cole Harbour
Port Felix
Whitehead
Crows Nest
Waternish
Stillwater
Glenelg
Sherbrooke Provincial Park
Sherbrooke
Miner's Museum
Sherbrooke Village
Jordanville
Indian Harbour Lake
Port Bickerton
Drumhead
Goldboro
Seal Harbour
New Harbour
Larrys River
Tor Bay
Berry Head
Flying Point
Tor Bay Atlantic Provincial Park
Whitehaven Harbour
Goldenville
St. Mary's River
Spanish Ship Bay
Sonora
Indian Harbour
Harpellville
Wine Harbour
Cape St. Marys
Gegogan Harbour
Country Harbour
Cape Harbour
Mocodome
Liscomb
Liscomb Mills
Liscomb I.
Marie Joseph
Ecum Secum
Marie Joseph Provincial Park
Barren

NOVA SCOTIA
NOUVELLE-ÉCOSSE

ATLANTIC OCEAN
OCÉAN ATLANTIQUE

Chedabucto Bay
Milford Haven R.
Goose Harbour
Salmon River Lake
Country Harbour
Salsman Prov. Pk.

Campbell's Cove Prov. Park
North Lake
East Point
Kingsboro
Basin Head Fisheries Museum
East Point Provincial Park

Ferry / Bac
To îles de la Madeleine Québec / Vers îles de la Madeleine Québec

10 0 10 20 30 40 50
kilometres   1:800 000   kilomètres

E   F   G   H

LABRADOR SEA
(ATLANTIC OCEAN)

MER DU LABRADOR
(OCEAN ATLANTIQUE)

Ferry To Cartwright and Goose Bay
Bac Vers Cartwright et Goose Bay

Freighter
Cargo

Wild Bight
Cook's Harbour
Pistolet Bay Prov. Pk.
Raleigh
435
437
436
L'Anse aux Meadows
Viking Settlement Hist. Site
LHN L'Anse aux Meadows NHS
Quirpon Island
Straitsview
Quirpon
Gunners Cove
St. Lunaire Griquet
Cape Onion

Pistolet Bay

Little Brehat
Great Brehat

St. Anthony
Grenfell House
430
St. Anthony Bight
St. Carols

Hare Bay
Hare Bay Islands Ecological Reserve
Maiden Point
Main Brook

Goose Cove
Fichot Islands

Grandois
St. Juliens
Croque
Pond
Crouse
Cape Rouge
Conche
Groais I.
Grey
Islands
Bell Island
French Cove

IDLAND
EUVE

Horse I.
Western I.
Eastern I.
Islands

Cape Corbin
Pacquet
417
Confusion Bay
Brent's Cove
La Scie
Manful Bight
414
416
Harbour Round
Tilt Cove
Snooks Arm
Round Harbour
415
Bobby Cove
Nippers Harbour
Smith's Harbour
King's Cove
Harry's Harbour
Jackson's Cove
392
Little Bay Islands
Beaumont
Long Island
Lushes Bight
Suley
Little Ann's Bay Cove
Coffee Cove
Miles Cove
Brighton
Triton
Pilley's Island
Jim's Cove
Card's Harbour
Robert's Arm
380
Leading Tickles

Notre Dame Bay
Baie de Notre-Dame

Crow Head
Durrell
Wild Cove
Back Harbour
Twillingate
340
Herring Neck
Bayview
Pikes Arm
Toogood Arm
Change
Tizzard's Harbour
346
Cobbs Arm
Change Islands
Fogo
Barr'd Islands
Joe Batt's Arm
334
Sandy Cove
Tilting
Shoal Bay
Cape Cove
Seldom
Little Seldom
Fogo Head
Hare Bay
Deep Bay
Fogo Island
Cape Fogo
333
Little Fogo Islands
Funk Island Ecological Reserve
Funk Island

Valley Pond
Moreton's Harbour
Bridgeport
345
Fairbank
Kettle Cove
Black Duck Cove
Newville
New World Island
Dildo Run Prov. Pk.
Stag Harbour
Ferry Bac
Wadham Islands

Exploits
Chanceport
Cottlesville
Cottle's Island
Summerford
344
Carter's Cove
Virgin Arm
Farewell
Port Albert

Fortune Harbour
Cottrell's Cove
Cull's Island
Fleury Bight

Hamilton Sound

Aspen Cove
Ladle Cove
Musgrave Harbour
Doting Cove
330

Village Cove
340
Stoneville
Horwood

Point Leamington
Comfort Cove
Newstead
Boyd's Cove
331
Dog Bay Pond Prov. Pk.
Beaver Cove
Frederickton
Noggin Cove
Carmanville
Ragged Harbour
330
Anchor Harbour
Deadman's Bay

Pleasantview
352
Little Burnt Bay
343
Birchy Bay
Rodgers Cove
332
Davidsville
330
Deadman's Bay Prov. Pk.
Lumsden
Windmill Bight Prov. Pk.

South West Arm
350
Indian Neck
Baytona
Victoria Cove
Wings Point
Dormans Cove
Main Point
Banting Lake

Embree
342
Thwart Island
Campbellton
340
Clarkes Head
Gander Bay
Island Pond
Cape Freels North
Cape Freels South

Point of Bay
Stanhope
341
Loon Bay
Ten Mile Lake
Burnt Lake
109
Weirs Pond
330
Templeman
Newtown
Pound Cove

Phillips Head
Porterville
Lewisporte
Gander River
320
Valleyfield
Wesleyville
Brookfield
Badger's Quay
Greenspond

Northern Arm
Laurenceton
340
Notre Dame Junction
Ten Mile Pond
Wing Pond
Shamblers Cove
Shoe Cove Point

New Bay Pond
Botwood
Norris Arm Northside
350
Lake O'Brien
Jonathan's Pond Prov. Pk.
Jonathan's Pond
Indian Bay Pond
North West Arm
Centreville
Indian Bay
Trinity
Lewis Island

Hodges Hill 569m
Peterview
Rattling Brook
Norris Arm
351
Bishop's Falls
Jumpers Brook
Glenwood
Appleton
Monchy
1
GANDER
Benton
Home Pond

Aspen Brook Prov. Pk.
Beothuck Prov. Pk.
1
Red Cliff
360
GRAND FALLS-WINDSOR
96
Glenwood Prov. Park
Gander Lake
Souls Pond
Gull Pond

Bonavista Bay
Baie de Bonavista

E   F   G   H

10 0 10 20 30 40 50
kilometres   1:1 000 000   kilomètres

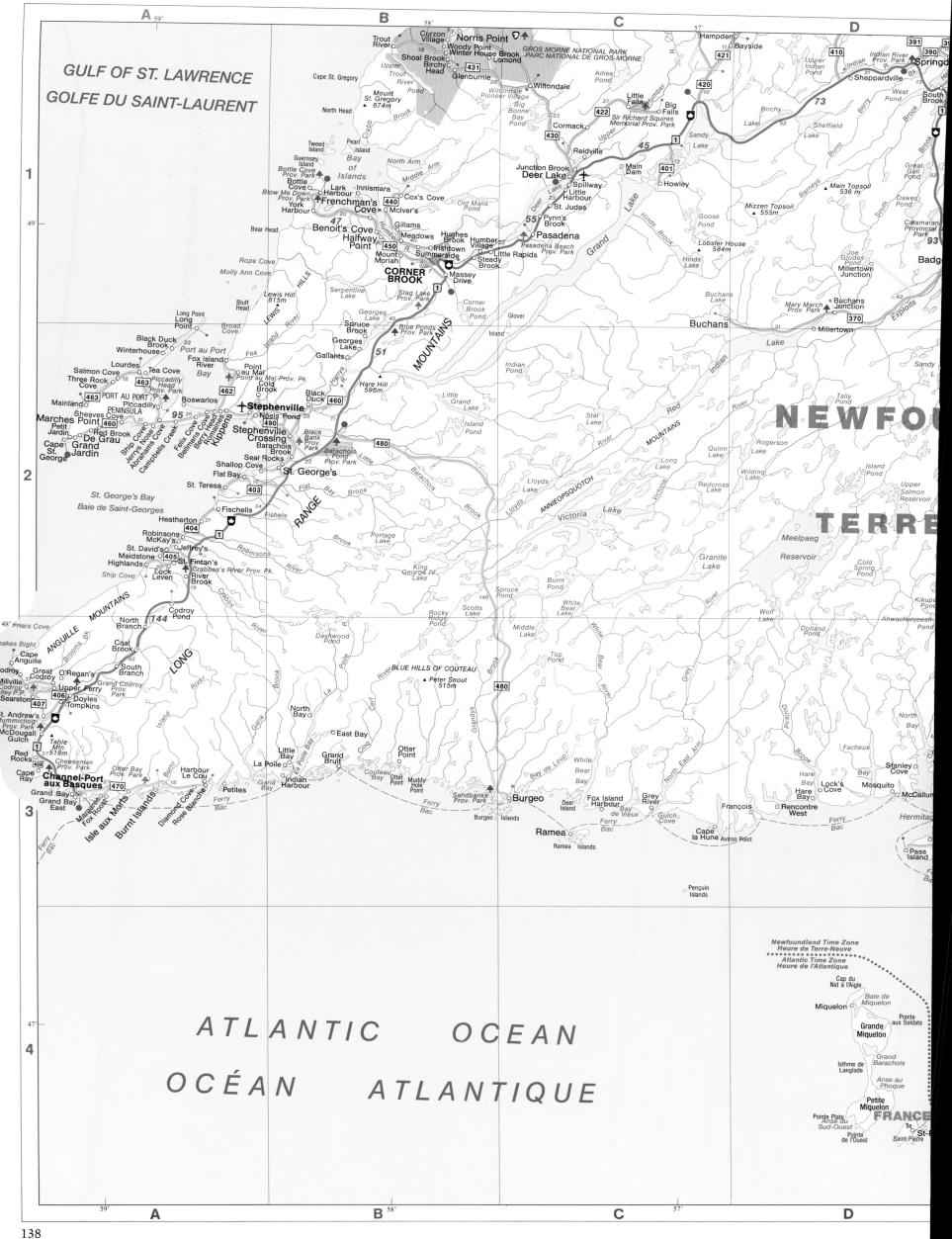

GULF OF ST. LAWRENCE
GOLFE DU SAINT-LAURENT

GROS MORNE NATIONAL PARK
PARC NATIONAL DE GROS-MORNE

NEWFOU

TERRE

ATLANTIC OCEAN

OCÉAN ATLANTIQUE

Newfoundland Time Zone
Heure de Terre-Neuve
Atlantic Time Zone
Heure de l'Atlantique

FRANCE

Triton Brighton Miles Cove Cull's Island Fluery Bight Chanceport Carter's Cove Virgin Arm Port Albert Summerford Cottlesville Cottle's Island Stoneville 335 Horwood Fredrickton Aspen Cove Ladle Cove Musgrave Harbour Doting Cove Ragged Harbour

Robert's Arm Pilley's Island Jim's Cove Card's Harbour Leading Tickles 344 Cottrell's Cove Village Cove 340 Boyd's Cove Birchy Bay Dog Bay Pond Prov. Park Rodgers Cove 332 Victoria Cove Davidsville Carmanville Noggin Cove Deadman's Bay Lumsden

Pleasantview 352 350 Seal Bay Badger Bay Exploits Islands Comfort Cove Newstead 343 Baytona Main Point Wesleyville Cape Freels North Cape Freels South Newtown Templeman

Embree 342 341 Stanhope Campbellton Dormans Cove Clarkes Head Gander Bay 330 Valleyfield Brookfield Badger's Quay Greenspond

Lewisporte 340 Notre Dame Junction 109 Gander River Benton Hare Bay Dover St. Brendan's Shambler's Cove Shoe Cove Point

Botwood 350 Norris Arm Northside 340 Lake O'Brien Glenwood 330 96 Appleton Monchy 601 GANDER Shalloway Cove Centreville Trinity Indian Bay

Peterview Phillips Head Point of Bay Laurenceton Glenwood Prov. Park Middle Brook 320 Dark Cove Saunders Cove Culls Harbour St. Chads Sandringham Salvage Burnside Bonavista Bay Baie de Bonavista Bonavista

Bishop's Falls 351 Norris Arm Gambo Glovertown Traytown Happy Adventure Sandy Cove Eastport Blackhead Spillars Cove Lancaster Elliston Maberly

GRAND FALLS-WINDSOR 1 360 Square Pond Prov. Park TERRA NOVA NATIONAL PARK 149 PARC NATIONAL DE TERRA-NOVA 301 Tickle Cove Red Cliff Open Hall Plate Cove Keels Duntura King's Cove Amherst Cove Catalina Port Union

Charlottetown Musgravetown 233 Jamestown 234 Portland Brooklyn Lethbridge Princeton Lockston Summerville Trinity East Champney's English Harbour Trinity Trouty Old Bonaventure New Bonaventure

Bunyan's Cove Bloomfield 230 BONAVISTA Rattle Falls Prov. Park 239 PENINSULA Port Blandford Thorburn Lake 232 Georges Brook Harcourt Monroe Waterville Clifton Burgoynes Cove Ireland's Eye

Shoal Harbour Clarenville 231 Milton Gin Cove Snook's Harbour Petley Britannia Random Grates Cove Baccalieu Island Red Head Cove

Deep Bight 28 Hillview Adeytown Hatchet Cove St. Jones Within Weybridge Lady Cove Hickman's Harbour Daniel's Cove 70 Bay de Verde

North West Brook 205 Queen's Cove 204 Southport Gooseberry Cove Butter Cove Caplin Cove New Melbourne Lead Cove 80 Caplin Cove

Swift Current Goobies 210 1 Garden Cove North Harbour St. Jones Without Hant's Harbour New Chelsea Brownsdale Gull Island Cove Long Beach

Glenview Come By Chance Sunnyside Winterton Turks Cove New Perlican Northern Bay Job's Cove Orchre Pit Cove Bradleys Cove

Arnold's Cove 201 Southern Harbour Rantem Bellevue Green's Harbour Hearts Content Cable Sta. Prov. Hist. Heart's Content 80 Western Bay Blackhead Adams Cove Broad Cove

Bar Haven Island Best's Harbour Chance Cove Whiteway Heart's Desire 74 Kingston Small Point Biscayan Cove Pouch Cove Shoe Cove

Norman's Cove 203 Tickle Harbour Fair Haven Hopeall Thornlea New Harbour Heart's Delight Islington 114 Victoria 70 Perry's Cove Salmon Cove 20 Flat Rock

Chapel Arm 202 Long Harbour Old Shop South Dildo Dildo Carbonear Harbour Grace Upper Island Cove Bristol's Hope 21 Bauline Torbay Portugal Cove St. Philip's 41 ST. JOHN'S

Blaketown 80 Spaniard's Bay 72 Bay Roberts Shearstown Tilton Country Road Port de Grave Bishop's Cove Clarke's Beach Cupids Brigus 50 Paradise 60 MT. PEARL St. Thomas

Whitbourne 1 Conception Harbour Colliers Avondale 71 Marysvale South River North River Makinsons Bacon Cove Gallows Cove 70 60 Conception Bay South 61 Maddox Cove Goulds 10

Placentia Junction 101 100 Markland Lakeview 79 Holyrood 62 Chapels Cove Harbour Main Cochrane Pond Prov. Park Petty Hbr. 11 Motion Head

Argentia Freshwater Jerseyside Dunville 91 Placentia 100 PENINSULA Father Duffy's Well Prov. Park Bay Bulls 13 Witless Bay

Point Verde North Harbour 92 St. Catherines 93 Salmonier Forest Field 90 Mobile Tors Cove La Manche Prov. Park Burnt Cove Bauline East

Little Barasway Great Barasway Ship Cove Mount Carmel Mitchells Brook New Bridge 94 St. Joseph's 140 O'Donnells Mount Carmel AVALON 10 Shores Cove Brigus S. Island Cove

Gooseberry Cove Patrick's Cove Angels Cove Reginaville Mosquito Admiral's Beach 90 Mall Bay Gulch Riverhead Wilderness Admiral's Cove Cape Broyle 142 Calvert

Point Breme Cuslett St. Bride's 100 Branch Colinet Island St. Mary's Reserve Aquaforte Port Kirwan Ferryland

Cape St. Mary's Ecological Reserve Cape St. Mary's Point Lance 90 St. Vincent's Path End Holyrood Gaskiers St. Stephens Renews Kingman's

Gull Island Pt. St. Shotts Cape Pine 10 Trepassey Peter's River Biscay Bay Cappahayden Chance Cove Prov. Park Cape Race Lighthouse Portugal Cove South Long Beach Mistaken Point Eco. Res.

BURIN PENINSULA Marystown 210 213 Garnish Frenchman's Cove Grand Beach Winterland 222 Creston 221 Burin Epworth St. Lawrence 220 Lawn Corbin

Grand Bank Fortune Molliers Lewin's Cove Bay View Salmonier Mortier Black Duck Cove Collins Cove Little St. Lawrence Lawn Bay Taylors Bay Lord's Cove Point au Gaul Allan's Island

Fortune Bay Baie de Fortune Mercer's Cove Jean de Baie Mooring Cove Spanish Room Rock Harbour Little Bay Beau Bois Tides Point Red Harbour Jude Island Placentia Bay Baie de Plaisance

Head of Bay d'Espoir 360 361 Milltown Morrisville Conne River Camp Boggy Jipujijkuei Kuespem Prov. Park Big Blue Hill Pond Pool's Cove Rencontre East

Belle Bay 362 Doctors Harbour Corbin Bay English Harbour East Terrenceville Harbour Mille Little Harbour East Monkstown Davis Cove Merasheen Island

St. Bernard's 212 Jacques Fontaine Little Bay East Brookside Boat Harbour Baine Harbour Parkers Cove Petit Forte South East Bight Toslow Isle Valen St. Leonards St. Kyran's

Belleoram 363 St. Jacques English Harbour West Point Rosie Rushoon Port Anne Great Paradise Little Paradise Little Bona Red Island

Jersey Harbour Wreck Cove Boxey Combes Cove St. John Harbour 364 360 Miller's Passage Ship Harbour Fox Harbour

Wilderness Meta Pond Reserve Bay du Nord **Wilderness** Reserve 206 Kaegudeck Lake Medonnegonix Lake Koskaecodde Lake

Castle Hill Nat'l. Hist. Site / Lieu hist. nat. de Castle Hill

1:1 000 000 kilometres 10 0 10 20 30 40 50 kilometres

CITIES (

CANADA

ROADS AND STREETS

- Expressway/autoroute
- Provincial highway
- Arterial road
- Main street
- Other street
- **232** Exit number
- → One-way street

TRANSPORTATION

- Railway line with station
- GO station (Ont.)
- Metro station (Montréal)
- Skytrain (Vancouver)
- Bus terminal

PUBLIC PLACES

- Tourist information
- Hotel/motel
- Point of interest
- Museum or art gallery
- Theatre or concert hall
- Park
- Building
- Built-up area
- Cemetery
- Cinema
- City Hall
- *360* Civic address
- Community centre
- Fire hall
- Hospital
- Industrial area
- Government/Institutional Area

- Municipal boundary
- Place of worship
- Police station
- Post office
- School
- Public library
- Shopping centre

RECREATIONS

- Arena
- Bicycle path
- Marina
- Indoor pool
- Outdoor pool
- Outdoor rink
- Running track
- Tennis court

Vancouver Area

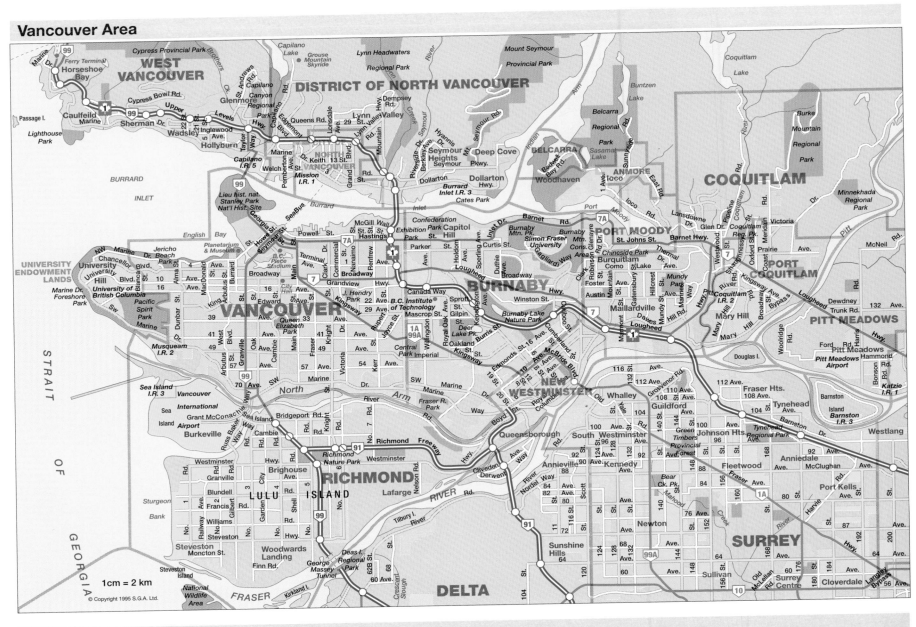

1cm = 2 km

© Copyright 1995 S.G.A. Ltd.

Vancouver Downtown

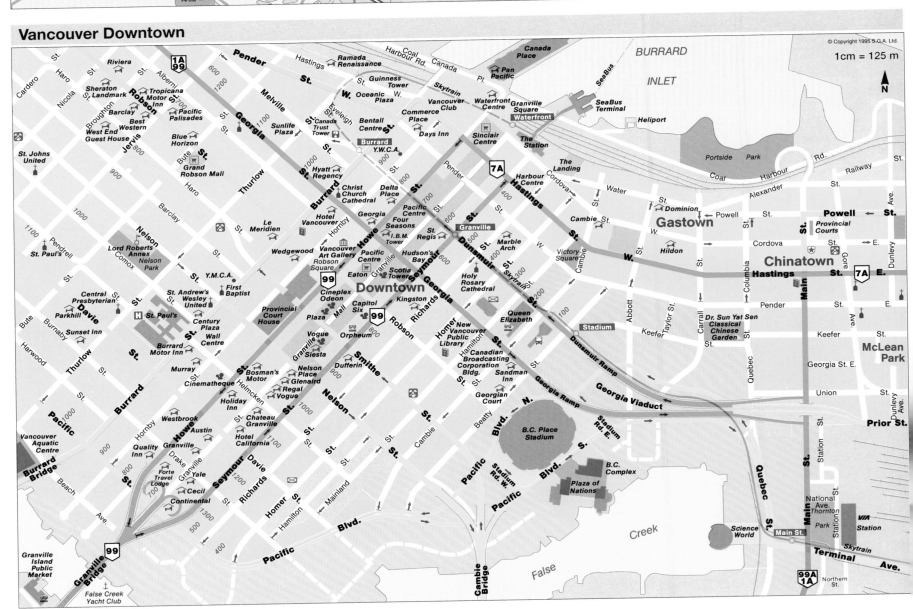

© Copyright 1995 S.G.A. Ltd.

1cm = 125 m

Victoria

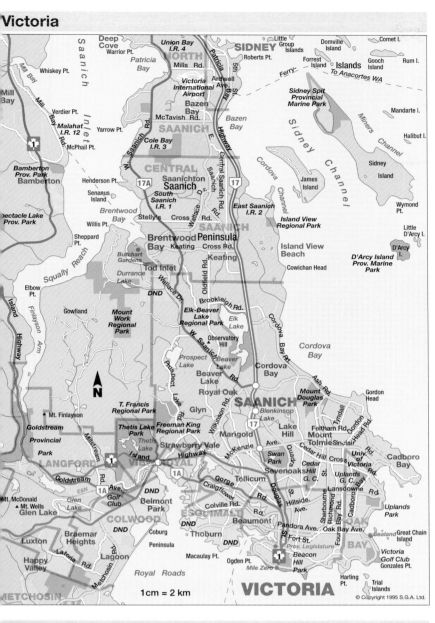

1cm = 2 km

© Copyright 1995 S.G.A. Ltd.

Whitehorse

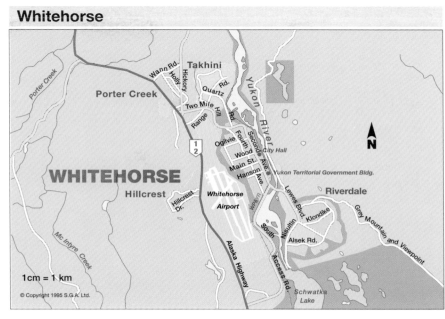

1cm = 1 km

© Copyright 1995 S.G.A. Ltd.

Yellowknife

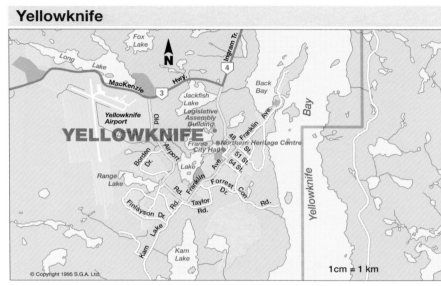

1cm = 1 km

© Copyright 1995 S.G.A. Ltd.

Calgary

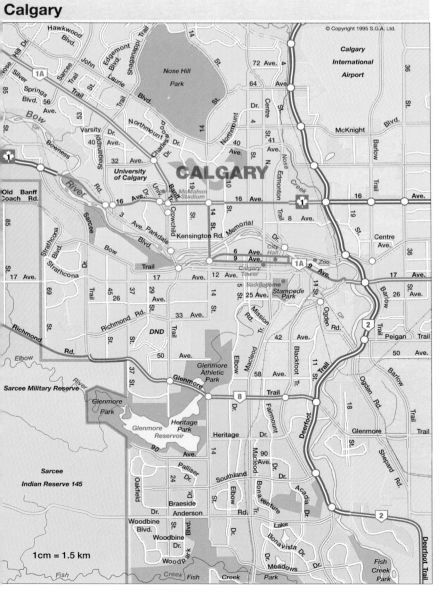

1cm = 1.5 km

© Copyright 1995 S.G.A. Ltd.

Edmonton

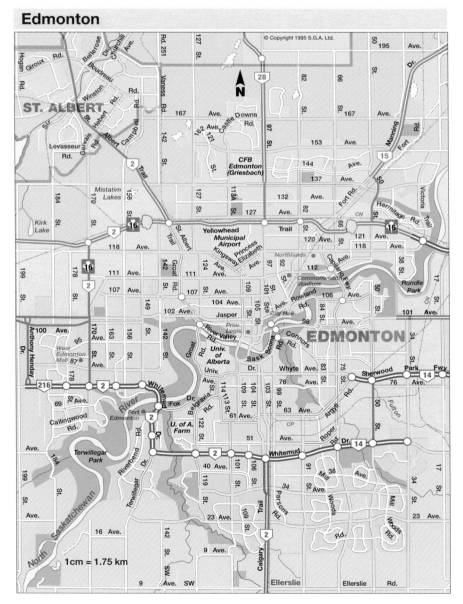

1cm = 1.75 km

© Copyright 1995 S.G.A. Ltd.

Regina

1cm = 1 km

Winnipeg

1cm = 1.5 km

Saskatoon

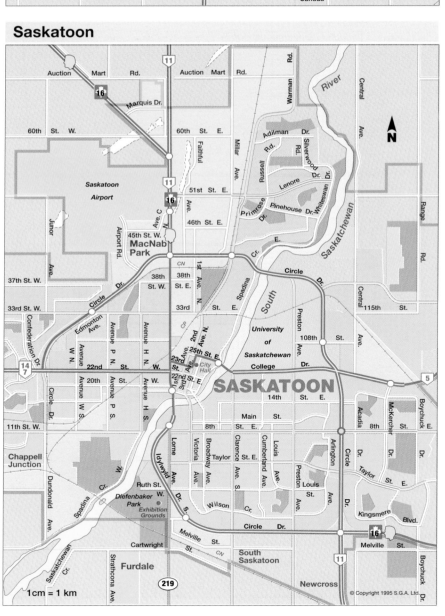

1cm = 1 km

Thunder Bay

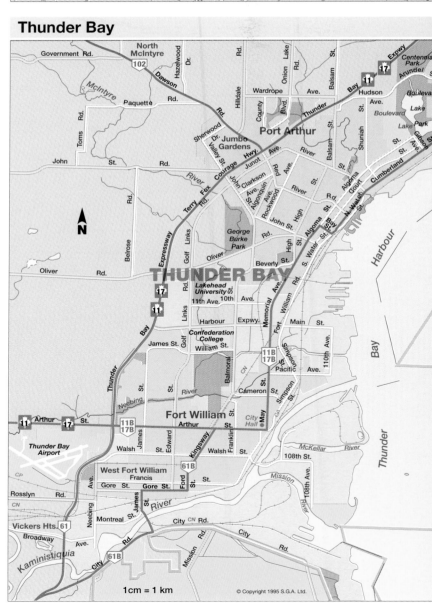

1cm = 1 km

Toronto Area

1cm = 1.66 km

© Copyright 1995 S.G.A. Ltd.

Toronto Downtown

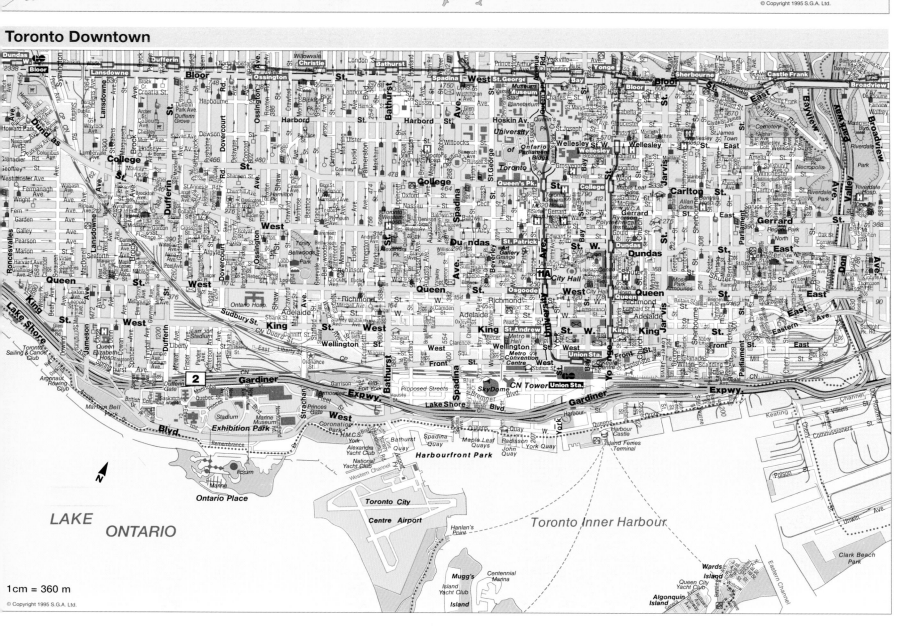

1cm = 360 m

© Copyright 1995 S.G.A. Ltd.

145

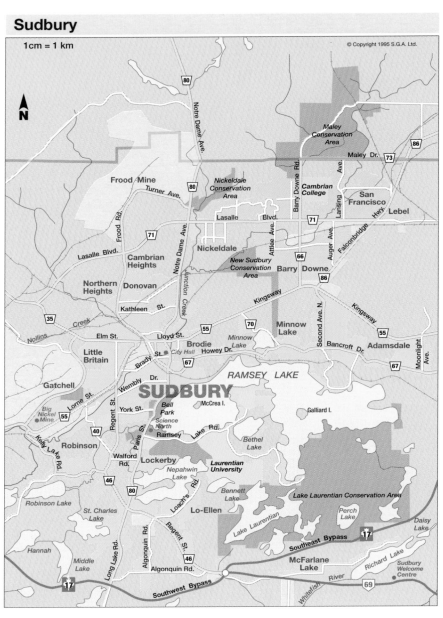

1cm = 1 km

© Copyright 1995 S.G.A. Ltd.

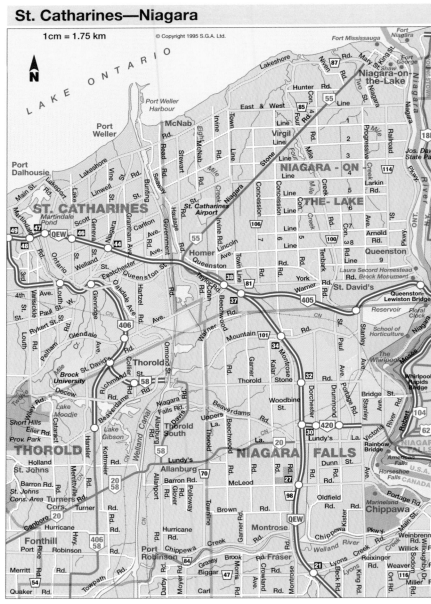

1cm = 1.75 km

© Copyright 1995 S.G.A. Ltd.

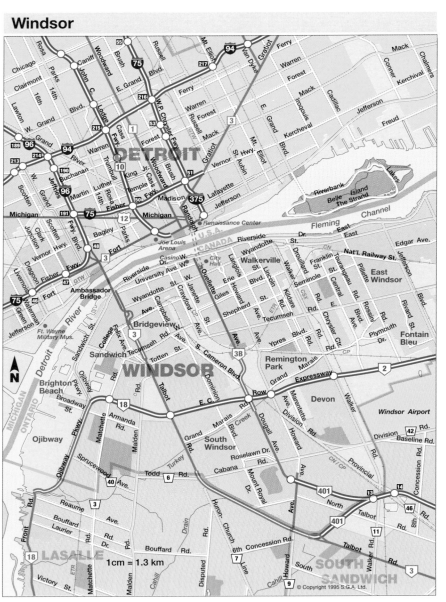

1cm = 1.3 km

© Copyright 1995 S.G.A. Ltd.

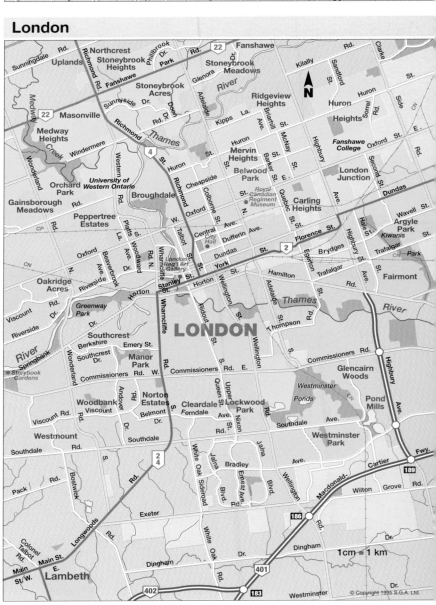

1cm = 1 km

© Copyright 1995 S.G.A. Ltd.

Ottawa Area

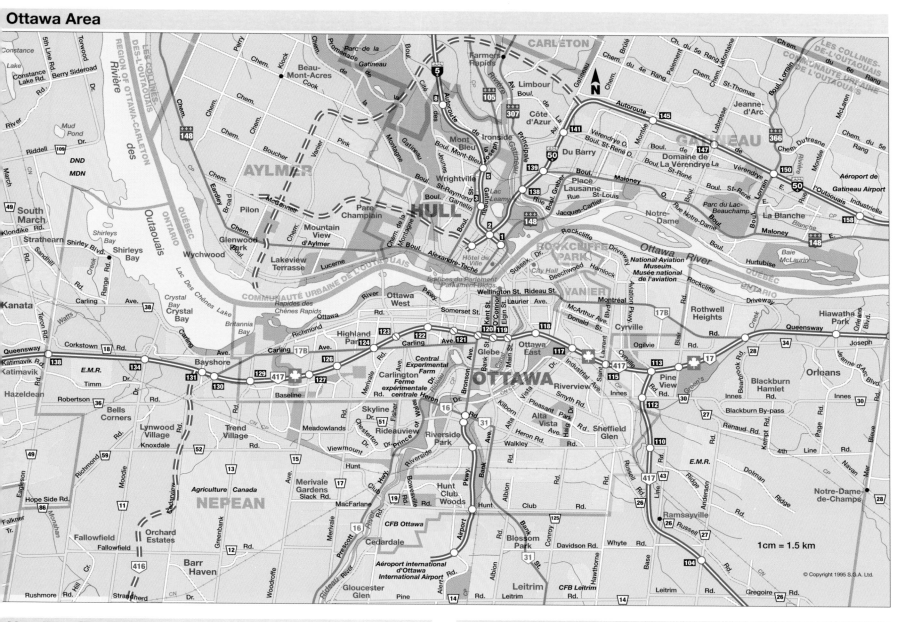

1cm = 1.5 km

© Copyright 1995 S.G.A. Ltd.

Hamilton/Burlington

1cm = 1.75 km

© Copyright 1995 S.G.A. Ltd.

Ottawa Downtown

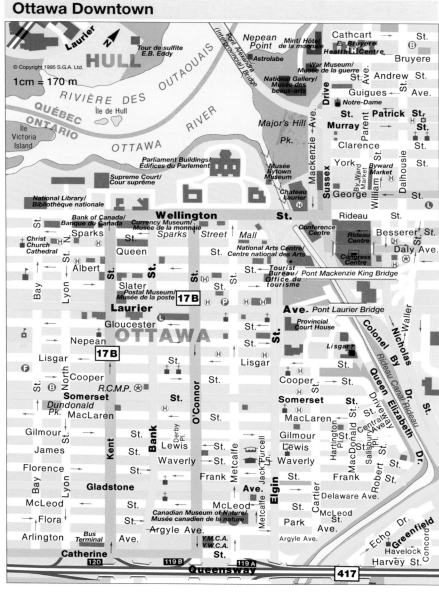

© Copyright 1995 S.G.A. Ltd.

1cm = 170 m

Kitchener/Waterloo

1cm = 1 km

Kingston

1cm = 1 km

Oshawa

1cm = 1.25 km

Trois-Rivières

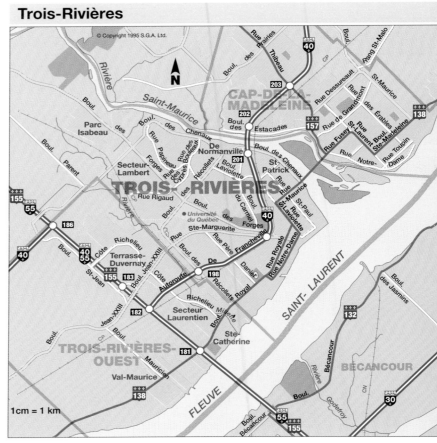

1cm = 1 km

Chicoutimi—Jonquière

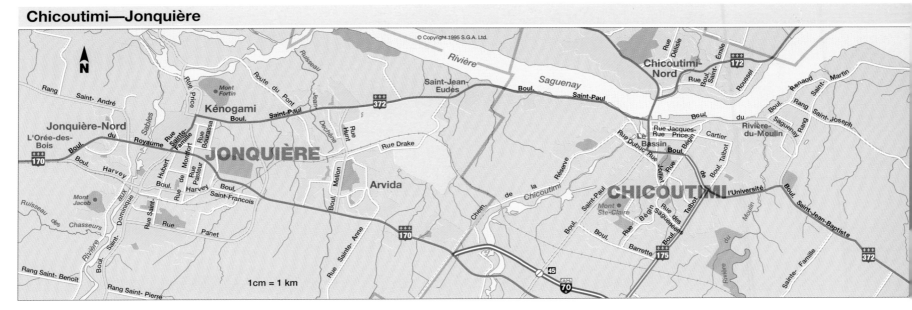

1cm = 1 km

Montréal Area

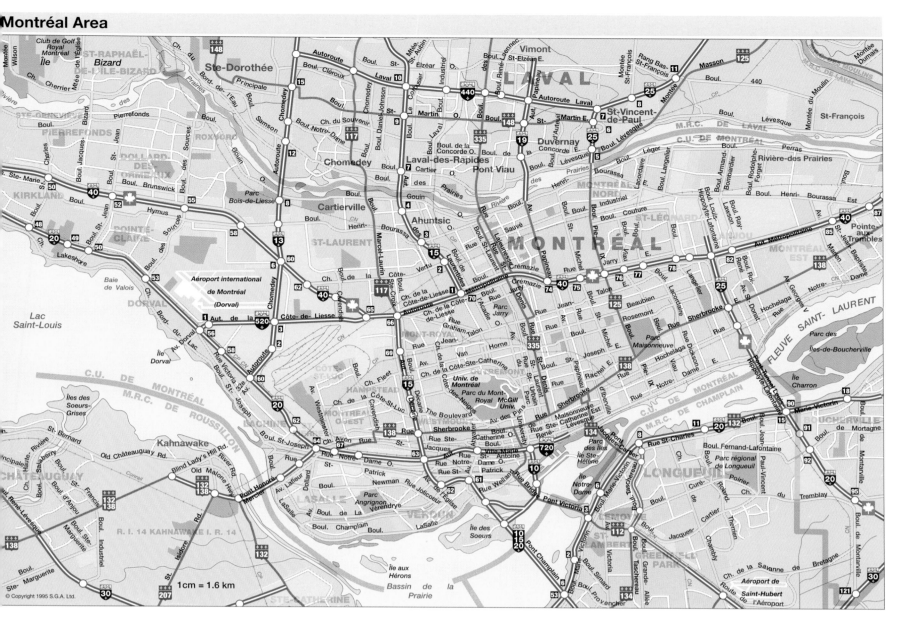

1cm = 1.6 km

© Copyright 1995 S.G.A. Ltd.

Montréal Downtown

1cm = 125 m

© Copyright 1995 S.G.A. Ltd.

Québec City Area

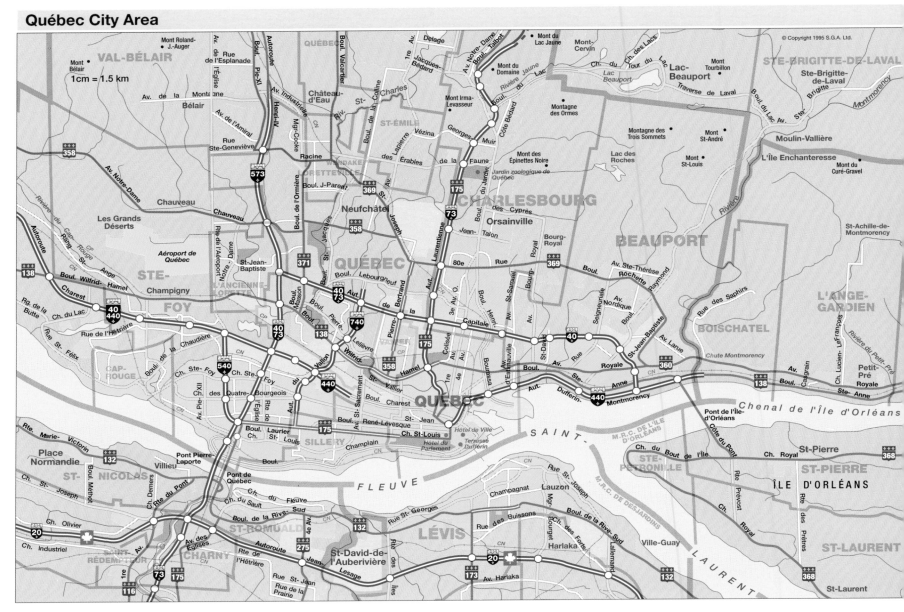

Québec City Downtown

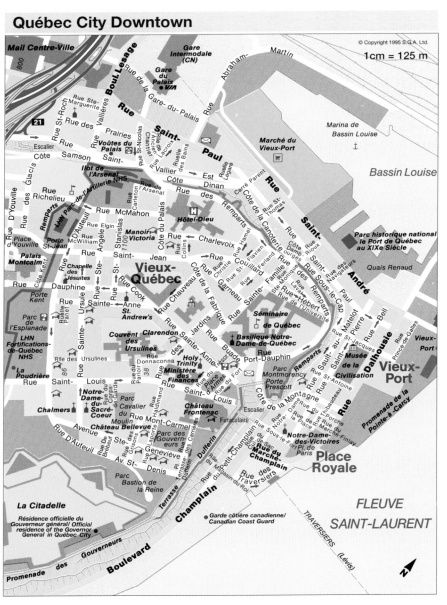

Sherbrooke

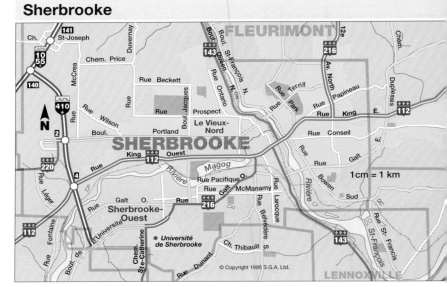

Fredericton

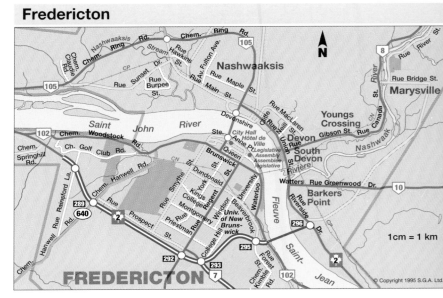

Saint John

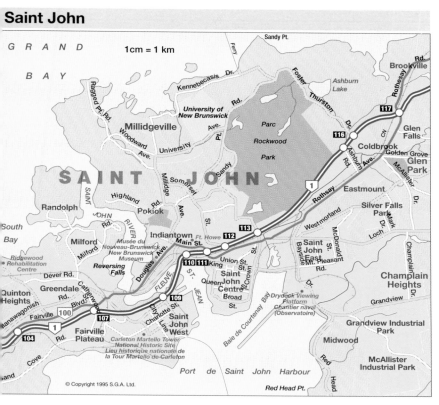

Halifax

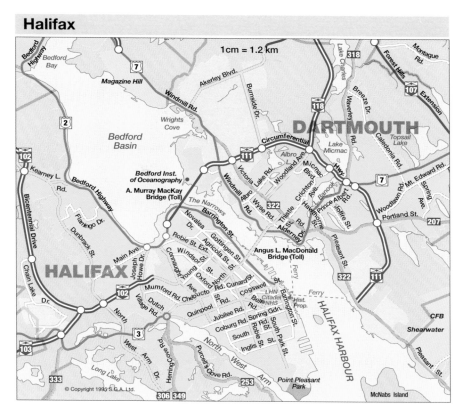

Moncton

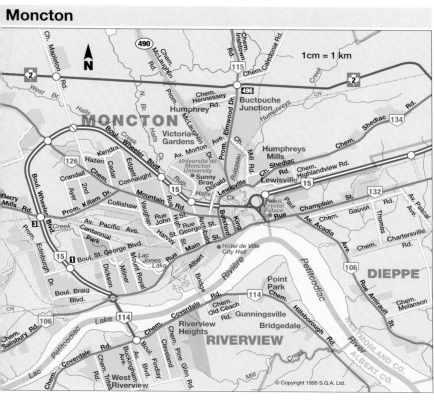

Sydney

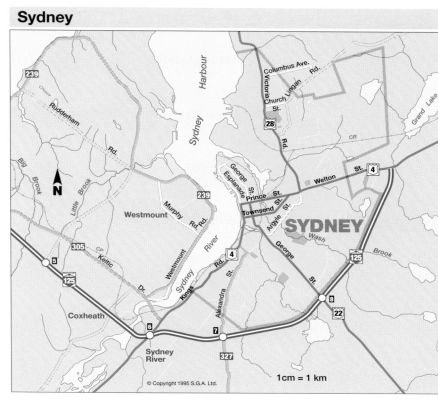

Charlottetown

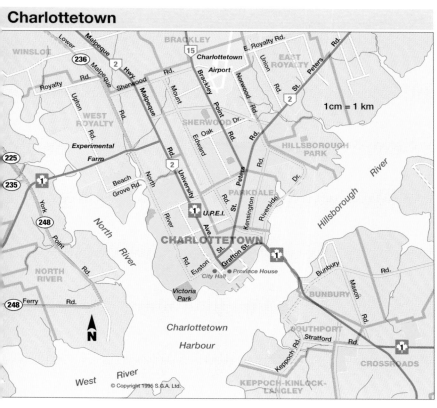

St. John's

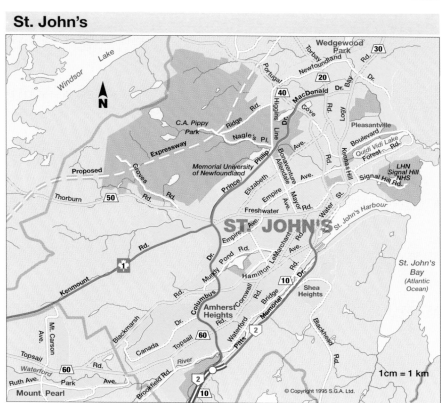

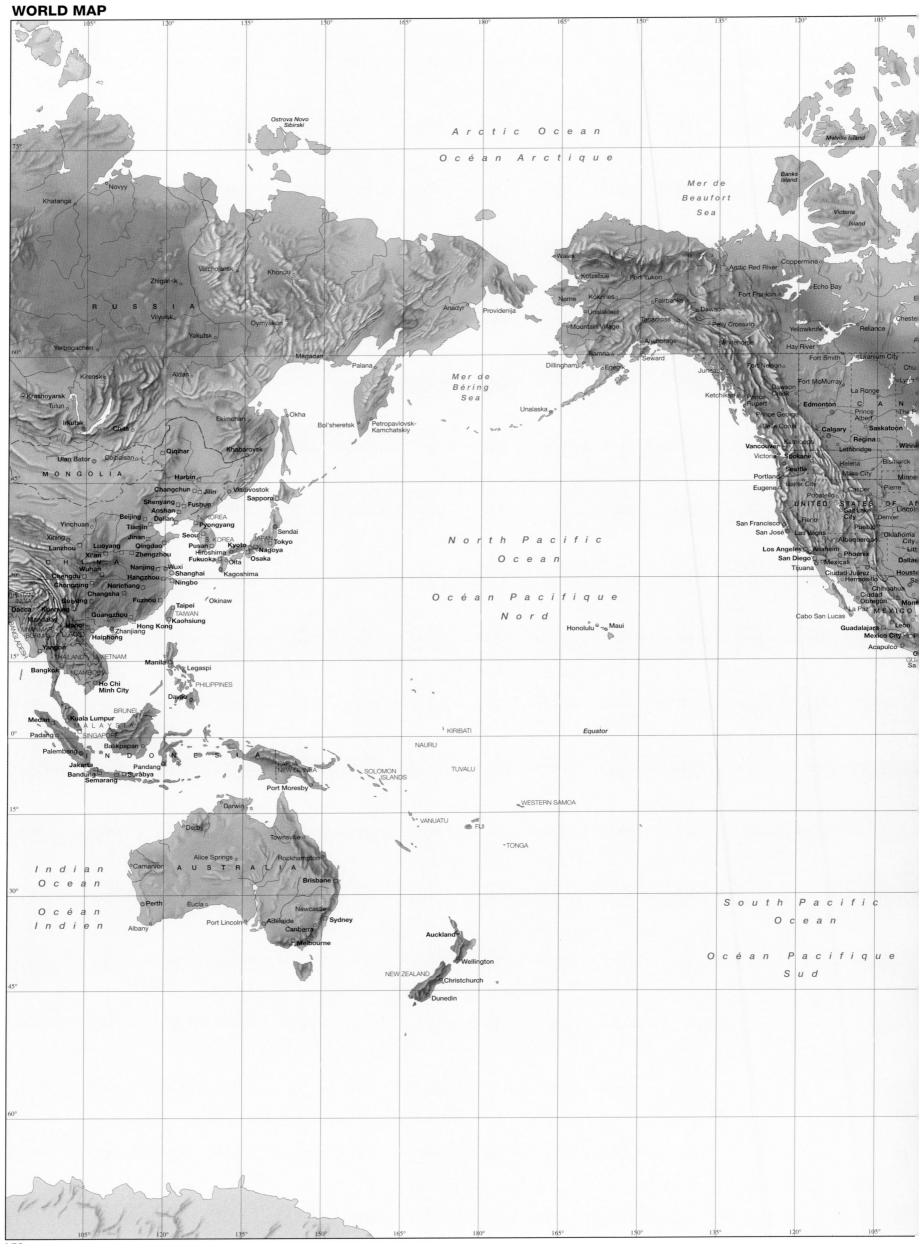

MAP INDEX

Populated Places

The index lists more than 17,000 names that appear on the preceding maps. The first section of the index lists populated places, such as cities, towns and villages; the second section, physical features such as rivers and lakes, as well as parks. Each name is followed by a figure (the map number) and the map coordinates—the letters at the top and bottom of the map, and the numbers at the sides. Use the coordinates to find the appropriate area on the map, then scan the area for the name. For example, to find Kent Junction, search through the list of populated places for the name of this New Brunswick community. After noting the references—23 F2—go to Map 23 and use the coordinates F2 to pinpoint the map area where Kent Junction appears.

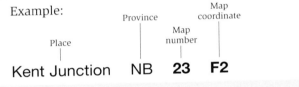

Example:

Place	Province	Map number	Map coordinate
Kent Junction	NB	23	F2

A

Abbey SASK 9 C3
Abbotsford BC 5 G4
Abee ALTA 7 F1
Abenakis QUÉ 19 G2
Abercorn QUÉ 19 D4
Aberdeen SASK 9 D2
Aberfoyle ONT 14 F2
Abernethy SASK 9 F3
Abert Mines NB 23 G4
Aboujagane NB 23 H3
Abrahams Cove NFLD 27 A2
Acaciaville NS 24 C2
Acadia Valley ALTA 7 H2
Acadie Siding NB 23 F2
Acadieville NB 23 F2
Acme ALTA 7 F2
Actinolite ONT 15 C3
Acton NB 23 D4
Acton ONT 14 F1
Acton-Vale QUÉ 19 D3
Adams Cove NFLD 27 H3
Adams Lake BC 7 C3
Adamsville NB 23 F3
Adamsville QUÉ 19 C4
Adanac SASK 9 C2
Addington Forks NS 25 E3
Addison ONT 15 F3
Adelaide ONT 14 C3
Aden ALTA 7 H4
Adeytown NFLD 27 G2
Admiral SASK 9 C4
Admiral Rock NS 24 G1
Admiral's Beach NFLD 27 G4
Admiral's Cove NFLD 27 H4
Adolphustown ONT 15 D4
Advocate Harbour NS 24 E1
Aetna ALTA 7 G4
Afton NS 25 E3
Agassiz BC 5 G4
Aguanish QUÉ 21 D1
Ahmic Harbour ONT 13 G1
Ahousat BC 5 D4
Ailsa Craig ONT 14 D2
Ainsworth Hot Springs BC 7 D4
Air Ronge SASK 8 E4
Airdrie ALTA 7 F3
Ajax ONT 14 H1
Aklavik NWT 2 C1
Akulivik QUÉ 3 C2
Alameda SASK 9 G4
Alaska PEI 25 A2
Alban ONT 12 G4
Albanel QUÉ 18 D2
Albany Cross NS 24 D2
Albert Bridge NS 25 H2
Albert Canyon BC 7 D3
Alberta Beach ALTA 7 E1
Alberton ONT 14 F2
Alberton PEI 25 B1
Albertville QUÉ 22 D3
Albertville SASK 9 E1
Albreda BC 7 C2
Alcomdale ALTA 7 F1
Alcona ONT 13 G4
Alcove QUÉ 17 F4
Alder Flats ALTA 7 E2
Aldershot NS 24 E2
Aldershot ONT 14 G2
Aldersville NS 24 E2
Aldersyde ALTA 7 F3
Alderville ONT 15 B4
Alert Bay BC 5 D3
Alexander MAN 11 A4
Alexandria ONT 15 H2
Alexis Creek BC 5 F2
Alfred ONT 15 G1
Algoma Mills ONT 12 E4
Algonquin ONT 15 F3
Algrove SASK 9 F2
Alice ONT 15 C1
Alice Arm BC 4 C3
Alida SASK 9 G4
Alingly SASK 9 E1
Alix ALTA 7 F2
Alkali Lake BC 5 G2
Allainville NB 23 F1
Allan SASK 9 D2
Allan Park ONT 13 E4
Allan's Island NFLD 27 E4
Allanburg ONT 14 H2
Allanwater Bridge ONT 11 F3
Allardville NB 23 F1
Allendale NS 24 D4
Allenford ONT 13 D3
Alliance ALTA 7 G2
Alliston ONT 13 F4
Alliston PEI 25 D2
Alma NB 23 G4
Alma NS 24 H1
Alma ONT 14 E1
Alma QUÉ 18 E2
Almonte ONT 15 E2
Alonsa MAN 11 A3
Alsask SASK 9 B3
Alsike ALTA 7 E1
Altamont MAN 11 B4
Altario ALTA 7 H2
Alticane SASK 9 D2
Alton NS 24 G1
Alton ONT 14 F1
Altona BC 4 G2
Altona MAN 11 B4
Alvanley ONT 13 D3
Alvena SASK 9 D2
Alvinston ONT 14 C3
Amaranth MAN 11 A3
Amberley ONT 14 C1
Ameliasburg ONT 15 C4
Amherst NS 25 A3
Amherst Cove NFLD 27 H2
Amherst Point NS 25 A3
Amherstburg ONT 14 A4
Amherstview ONT 15 E4
Amisk ALTA 7 G2
Amos QUÉ 16 C2
Amqui QUÉ 22 D2
Amsterdam SASK 9 F2
Amulree ONT 14 E2
Amyot ONT 12 D2
Anagance NB 23 F4
Anahim Lake BC 5 E2
Ancaster ONT 14 F2
Anchor Point NFLD 26 D1
Andersons Cove NFLD 27 F3
Andrew ALTA 7 F1
Andys Corners ONT 14 E3
Aneroid SASK 9 D4
Anfield NB 23 C2
Angels Cove NFLD 27 G4
Anglemont BC 7 C3
Angliers QUÉ 17 A1
Angus ONT 13 F4
Angusville MAN 9 G3
Annaheim SASK 9 E2
Annan ONT 13 E3
Annapolis Royal NS 24 D2
Anola MAN 11 C3
Anse-Bleue NB 22 H4
Anten Mills ONT 13 G3
Antigonish NS 25 E3
Antler SASK 9 G4
Antrim ONT 15 E2
Anzac ALTA 6 G2
Apohaqui NB 23 F4
Appin ONT 14 C3
Apple Hill ONT 15 H2
Apple River NS 24 E1
Applegrove BC 7 D4
Appleton NFLD 27 F1
Appleton ONT 15 E2
Apsley ONT 15 B3
Apto ONT 13 G3
Aquadeo Beach SASK 9 C1
Aquaforte NFLD 27 H4
Arbor Vitae ONT 11 D4
Arborfield SASK 9 F1
Arborg MAN 11 B3
Arcadia NS 24 C4
Archerwill SASK 9 F2
Arcola SASK 9 G4
Arctic Bay NWT 2 H1
Arctic Red River NWT 2 C1
Ardath SASK 9 D2
Ardbeg ONT 13 F1
Arden MAN 11 A3
Arden ONT 15 D3
Ardenode ALTA 7 F3
Ardill SASK 9 E4
Ardmore ALTA 6 G3
Ardoch ONT 15 D2
Ardoise NS 24 F2
Ardrossan ALTA 7 F1
Ardtrea ONT 13 G3
Arelee SASK 9 D2
Argenta BC 7 D4
Argentia NFLD 27 G4
Argyle MAN 11 B3
Argyle NB 23 C3
Argyle NS 24 C4
Argyle ONT 13 H3
Arichat NS 25 F3
Arisaig NS 25 E3
Ariss ONT 14 F2
Arkell ONT 14 F2
Arkona ONT 14 C2
Armagh QUÉ 19 G1
Armena ALTA 7 F1
Armstrong BC 7 C3
Armstrong ONT 12 A4
Armstrong QUÉ 19 G3
Arnaud MAN 11 C4
Arnes MAN 11 B3
Arnold's Cove NFLD 27 G3
Arnot MAN 10 B3
Arnprior ONT 15 E1
Arnstein ONT 13 F1
Arntfield QUÉ 16 A3
Aroland ONT 12 B1
Aroostook NB 23 C2
Arran SASK 9 G2
Arras BC 4 G3
Arrow Lake BC 7 D4
Arrow River MAN 9 G3
Arrowwood ALTA 7 F3
Arthabaska QUÉ 19 E3
Arthur ONT 14 E1
Arthurette NB 23 C2
Arundel QUÉ 19 A3
Arva ONT 14 D2
Arviat NWT 2 G4
Arvida QUÉ 18 F3
Asbestos QUÉ 19 E3
Ascot QUÉ 19 E4
Ascot Corner QUÉ 19 E4
Ashburn ONT 14 H1
Ashcroft BC 5 G3
Ashdale NS 25 E3
Ashern MAN 11 B3
Ashgrove ONT 14 F1
Ashmont ALTA 7 G1
Ashton ONT 15 F2
Ashville MAN 11 A3
Aspen NS 25 E4
Aspen Brook NFLD 27 E1
Aspen Cove NFLD 27 G1
Aspen Grove BC 5 H3
Asquith SASK 9 D2
Assiniboia SASK 9 E4
Astle NB 23 D3
Aston-Jonction QUÉ 19 D2
Astorville ONT 12 H4
Athabasca ALTA 6 F3
Athalmer BC 7 E3
Athapap MAN 8 G4
Athelstan QUÉ 19 A4
Athens ONT 15 F3
Atherley ONT 13 G3
Athol NS 24 F1
Atholville NB 22 E3
Atikameg ALTA 6 E2
Atikameg Lake MAN 9 G1
Atikokan ONT 11 F4
Atlin BC 2 B3
Atmore ALTA 6 F3
Attawapiskat ONT 3 B4
Atwater SASK 9 G3
Atwood ONT 14 D1
Aubert-Gallion (see St-Georges-Ouest) QUÉ 19 G3
Auburn NS 24 E2
Auburn ONT 14 D1
Auclair QUÉ 22 B4
Auden ONT 12 B1
Audet QUÉ 19 G3
Aulac NB 23 H4
Auld Cove NS 25 F3
Aurora ONT 14 G1
Austin MAN 11 A3-4
Austin QUÉ 19 D4
Authier QUÉ 16 B2
Authier-Nord QUÉ 16 B2
Avening ONT 13 F4
Avola BC 7 C3
Avon ONT 14 E3
Avondale NFLD 27 H3
Avondale NS 25 D3
Avonhurst SASK 9 F3
Avonlea SASK 9 E3
Avonmore ONT 15 G2
Avonport NS 24 F2
Ayer's Cliff QUÉ 19 E4
Aylesbury SASK 9 E3
Aylesford NS 24 E2
Aylmer ONT 14 D3
Aylmer QUÉ 17 F4
Aylsham SASK 9 F1
Aylwin QUÉ 17 F3
Ayr ONT 14 E2
Ayton ONT 14 E1
Azilda ONT 12 G4

B

Back Bay NB 24 B2
Back Harbour NFLD 26 F3
Bacon Cove NFLD 27 H3
Bacon Ridge MAN 11 A3
Baddeck NS 25 G2
Baddeck Forks NS 25 G2
Baddow ONT 13 H3
Baden MAN 9 G2
Baden ONT 14 E2
Badger MAN 11 C4
Badger NFLD 27 D1
Badger's Quay NFLD 27 G1
Badjeros ONT 13 F4
Bagot MAN 11 B3
Baie Verte NB 23 H3
Baie Verte NFLD 26 D3
Baie-Comeau QUÉ 22 C1
Baie-de-Shawinigan QUÉ 19 D2
Baie-des-Bacon QUÉ 22 A2
Baie-des-Ha!-Ha! QUÉ 26 A2
Baie-des-Moutons QUÉ 26 A2
Baie-des-Rochers QUÉ 18 H3
Baie-des-Sables QUÉ 22 C2
Baie-du-Febvre QUÉ 19 D3
Baie-du-Poste QUÉ 3 D4
Baie-du-Renard QUÉ 21 E3
Baie-James (see Matagami) QUÉ 3 C4
Baie-Johan-Beetz QUÉ 21 C1
Baie-Ste-Anne NB 23 G2
Baie-Ste-Catherine QUÉ 18 H3
Baie-Ste-Claire QUÉ 21 A2
Baie-St-Paul QUÉ 18 G4
Baie-Trinité QUÉ 22 D1
Bailey Brook NS 25 D3
Bailieboro ONT 15 B4
Baine Harbour NFLD 27 F3
Bainsville ONT 15 H2
Baker Brook NB 23 A8
Baker Lake NWT 2 G3
Baker Settlement NS 24 E3
Bakers Brook NFLD 26 B3
Bakers Narrows MAN 8 G4
Bala ONT 13 G2
Balaclava ONT 15 D2
Balcarres SASK 9 F3
Balderson ONT 15 E2
Baldonnel BC 4 G3
Baldur MAN 11 A4
Baldwin ONT 13 G4
Baldwin Mills QUÉ 19 E4
Baldwinton SASK 9 C2
Baldy Hughes BC 5 F1
Balfour BC 7 D4
Balgonie SASK 9 E3
Ballantrae ONT 14 H1
Ballantynes Cove NS 25 E3
Ballinafad ONT 14 F1
Ballymote ONT 14 D2
Balm Beach ONT 13 F3
Balmertown ONT 11 D2
Balmoral MAN 11 B3
Balmoral NB 22 E3
Balmoral ONT 14 F3
Balmoral Mills NS 24 G1
Balmy Beach ONT 13 E3
Balsam Creek ONT 12 H4
Baltic PEI 25 E2
Baltimore ONT 15 B4
Balzac ALTA 7 F3
Bamberg ONT 14 E2
Bamfield BC 5 E4
Bancroft ONT 15 B2
Banff ALTA 7 E3
Bangor NS 24 C3
Bangor PEI 25 D2
Bangor SASK 9 G3
Bangs Falls NS 24 E3
Bankeir BC 5 H3
Bankend SASK 9 F2
Bannockburn ONT 15 C3
Baptiste ONT 15 B2
Barachois NB 23 H3
Barachois QUÉ 21 A4
Barachois Brook NFLD 27 B2
Barachois Harbour NS 25 G2
Barbers Bay ONT 12 G2
Barclay ONT 13 G4
Bareneed NFLD 27 H3
Barge Bay NFLD 26 D1
Barkerville BC 5 G1
Barkmere QUÉ 19 A3
Barkway ONT 13 H2
Barnaby River NB 23 F2
Barney's River NS 25 D3
Barnston QUÉ 19 E4
Barnwell ALTA 7 G3
Barons ALTA 7 G3
Barr'd Harbour NFLD 26 C2
Barr'd Islands NFLD 26 G3
Barra Head NS 25 G3
Barraute QUÉ 16 D2
Barrett Lake BC 4 D4
Barrhead ALTA 7 E1
Barrie ONT 13 G3
Barriefield ONT 15 E4
Barrière BC 5 H2
Barrington NS 24 D4
Barrington QUÉ 19 B4
Barrington Passage NS 24 C4
Barronsfield NS 25 A3
Barrow Bay ONT 13 D2
Barrows MAN 9 G2
Barry's Bay ONT 15 C1
Barryvale ONT 15 D2
Barthel SASK 9 C1
Bartibog NB 23 F1
Bartibog Bridge NB 23 F2
Bartletts Beach NS 24 C3
Bartletts Harbour NFLD 26 C2
Barton NS 24 C3
Barville QUÉ 16 C2
Barwick ONT 11 D4
Bas-Caraquet NB 22 H4
Bashaw ALTA 7 F2
Bass River NB 23 G2
Bass River NS 24 F1
Bassano ALTA 7 G3
Bassin QUÉ 21 F3
Basswood MAN 11 A3
Basswood Ridge NB 24 A1
Batawa ONT 15 C4
Batchawana Bay ONT 12 D4
Bateman SASK 9 D3
Bath NB 23 C3
Bath ONT 15 D4
Bathurst NB 22 G4
Bathurst Mines NB 23 F1
Batiscan QUÉ 19 D2
Batoche SASK 9 D2
Battersea ONT 15 E3
Battleford SASK 9 C2
Bauline NFLD 27 H3
Bauline East NFLD 27 H4
Bawlf ALTA 7 F1
Baxter ONT 13 G4
Baxter Harbour NS 24 E1
Bay Bulls NFLD 27 H3
Bay de Verde NFLD 27 H2
Bay du Vin NB 23 G2
Bay Roberts NFLD 27 H3
Bay St Lawrence NS 25 G1
Bay Tree ALTA 6 C2-3
Bay View NFLD 27 E4
Bayfield NB 25 B2
Bayfield NS 25 E3
Bayfield ONT 14 C1
Bayfield Inlet ONT 13 E1
Bayhead NS 25 C3
Bayshore Village ONT 13 G3
Bayside NFLD 27 C1
Bayside NS 24 F2
Bayside ONT 15 C4
Baysville ONT 13 H2
Bayswater NB 24 C1
Bayswater NS 24 F3
Baytona NFLD 27 F1
Bayview NFLD 26 F4
Beach Meadows NS 24 E3
Beachburg ONT 15 D1
Beachside NFLD 26 E4
Beachville ONT 14 E2
Beaconia MAN 11 C3
Beaconsfield QUÉ 19 B4
Bealton ONT 14 F3
Béam QUÉ 17 A1
Beamsville ONT 14 G2
Bear Canyon ALTA 6 C2
Bear Cove BC 5 D3
Bear Cove NFLD 26 B4
Bear Cove NFLD 26 D3
Bear Cove NS 24 C3
Bear Creek SASK 8 C3
Bear Island ONT 12 G4
Bear Lake BC 4 F4
Bear Lake ONT 13 G1
Bear River NS 24 C2
Bear River PEI 25 D2
Bearberry ALTA 7 E2
Beardmore ONT 12 B1
Bearskin Lake ONT 10 E4
Beaton BC 7 D3
Beatrice ONT 13 G2
Beatton River BC 4 G2
Beatty SASK 9 E1-2
Beattyville QUÉ 16 D2
Beau Bois NFLD 27 F4
Beaubier SASK 9 F4
Beaucanton QUÉ 16 A1
Beauceville QUÉ 19 G2
Beaudry QUÉ 16 A3
Beauharnois QUÉ 19 B4
Beaulac QUÉ 19 F3
Beaumont ALTA 7 F1
Beaumont NFLD 26 E4
Beaumont QUÉ 19 F1
Beauport QUÉ 19 F1
Beaupré QUÉ 19 F1
Beausejour MAN 11 C3
Beauval SASK 8 D4
Beauvallon ALTA 7 G1
Beaver Brook NS 24 G1
Beaver Brook Station NB 23 F1
Beaver Cove BC 5 D3
Beaver Cove NFLD 27 F1
Beaver Cove NS 25 G2
Beaver Creek YK 2 A2
Beaver Crossing ALTA 6 G3
Beaver Dam NB 23 D4
Beaver Harbour NB 24 B2
Beaver Harbour NS 25 D4
Beaver Lake ALTA 6 G3
Beaver Lake SASK 8 C1
Beaver Mines ALTA 7 F4
Beaver River NS 24 C3
Beaverbank NS 24 G2
Beaverbank Villa NS 24 G2
Beaverdam ALTA 6 G4
Beaverdell BC 7 C4
Beaverlodge ALTA 6 C3
Beaverton ONT 13 H3
Bécancour QUÉ 19 D2
Bedeque PEI 25 B2
Bedford NS 24 G2
Bedford QUÉ 19 C4
Beebe Plain QUÉ 19 D4
Beech Hill NS 24 E2
Beech Hill NS 24 E3
Beechwood NB 23 C2
Beechy SASK 9 D3
Beersville NB 23 G3
Beeton ONT 14 G1
Bégin QUÉ 18 F2
Beiseker ALTA 7 F2
Belair MAN 11 C3
Belbutte SASK 9 D1
Belcourt QUÉ 16 D3
Belfountain ONT 14 F1
Belgrave ONT 14 D1
Bell Ewart ONT 13 G4
Bell II BC 4 C2
Bella Bella BC 5 C2
Bella Coola BC 5 D2
Bellburns NFLD 26 C3
Belldowns Point NFLD 26 B3
Belle Cote NS 25 F2
Belle Marche NS 25 F1
Belle Plaine SASK 9 E3
Belle River ONT 14 A4
Belle River PEI 25 D3
Belle Vallée ONT 12 H3
Belle-Anse QUÉ 21 A4
Belledune NB 22 F3
Bellefeuille QUÉ 19 A3
Bellefleur NB 23 B2
Bellegarde SASK 9 G4
Belleisle NS 24 D2
Belleisle Creek NB 23 F4
Belleoram NFLD 27 E3
Bellerive-sur-le-Lac QUÉ 17 H3
Belleterre QUÉ 17 B1
Belleville NB 23 C3
Belleville NS 24 C4
Belleville ONT 15 C4
Bellevue ALTA 7 F4
Bellevue NFLD 27 G3
Bellis ALTA 7 F1
Belliveau NS 24 C3
Belliveau Cove NS 24 C3
Bellmans Cove NFLD 27 A2
Bellsite MAN 9 G2
Belmont MAN 11 A4
Belmont NS 24 G1
Belmont ONT 14 D3
Belmont PEI 25 B2
Belmore ONT 14 D1
Belnan NS 24 G2
Beloeil QUÉ 19 C4
Belwood ONT 14 F1
Ben Eoin NS 25 G2
Ben Lomond NB 24 C1
Benalto ALTA 7 F2
Bengough SASK 9 E4
Benito MAN 9 G2
Benmiller ONT 14 C1
Bennetts Bay NS 24 E1
Benoit's Cove NFLD 27 B1
Benson SASK 9 F4
Bent River ONT 13 G2
Bentley ALTA 7 F2
Benton NB 23 C3
Benton NFLD 27 F1
Berens River MAN 11 B2
Beresford MAN 11 A4
Beresford NB 22 G4
Bergen ALTA 7 E2
Bergland ONT 11 D4
Berkeley ONT 13 E3
Bernières QUÉ 19 F2
Bernierville QUÉ 19 E3
Berry QUÉ 16 C2
Berry Head NFLD 27 A2
Berry Mills NB 23 G3
Berthier-sur-Mer QUÉ 19 G1
Berthierville QUÉ 19 C3
Bertrand NB 22 H4
Bertwell SASK 9 F2
Bervie ONT 13 D4
Berwick NB 23 F4
Berwick NS 24 E2
Berwick ONT 15 G2
Berwyn ALTA 6 D2
Best's Harbour NFLD 27 G3
Béthanie QUÉ 19 D4
Bethany MAN 11 A3
Bethany ONT 15 A4
Bethune SASK 9 E3
Betsiamites QUÉ 22 B2
Beulah MAN 9 G3
Beverley SASK 9 C3
Bewdley ONT 15 B4
Bezanson ALTA 6 C3
Bible Hill NS 24 G1
Bide Arm NFLD 26 D2
Bield MAN 9 G3
Biencourt QUÉ 22 B3
Bienfait SASK 9 F4
Big Bar Creek BC 5 G3
Big Bay BC 5 E3
Big Bay ONT 13 E3
Big Bay Point ONT 13 G3
Big Beaver SASK 9 E4
Big Bras d'Or NS 25 G2
Big Brook NFLD 26 D1
Big Cedar ONT 15 B3
Big Cedar Point ONT 13 G4
Big Chute ONT 13 G2-3
Big Cove NB 23 G2
Big Creek BC 5 F2
Big Falls NFLD 27 C1
Big Harbour NS 25 G2
Big Harbour Island NS 25 F3
Big Hill NS 25 G2
Big Lake Ranch BC 5 G2
Big Marsh NS 25 E3
Big Pond NS 25 G2
Big River SASK 9 D1
Big Stone ALTA 7 G2
Big Trout Lake ONT 10 F4
Big Valley ALTA 7 F2
Biggar SASK 9 C2
Bigwood ONT 12 G4
Billtown NS 24 E2
Binbrook ONT 14 G2
Bindloss ALTA 7 H3
Binscarth MAN 9 G3
Birch Cove ALTA 7 E1
Birch Grove NS 25 H2
Birch Hills SASK 9 E1
Birch Island BC 7 C3
Birch Island ONT 12 F4
Birch Lake SASK 9 C1
Birch Point ONT 15 A3
Birch River MAN 9 G2
Birchton QUÉ 19 E4
Birchtown NS 24 D4
Birchy Bay NFLD 27 F1
Birchy Cove NFLD 26 E3
Birchy Head NFLD 27 B1
Bird MAN 10 C3
Bird Cove NFLD 26 D2
Birds Creek ONT 15 B2
Bird's Point SASK 9 G3
Birdtail MAN 9 G3
Birken BC 5 F3
Birmingham SASK 9 F3
Birnie MAN 11 A3
Birr ONT 14 D2
Birsay SASK 9 D3
Birtle MAN 9 G3
Biscay Bay NFLD 27 H4
Biscayan Cove NFLD 27 H3
Biscotasing ONT 12 F3
Bishop's Cove NFLD 27 H3
Bishop's Falls NFLD 27 E1
Bishops Mills ONT 15 F2
Bishopsgate ONT 14 F2
Bishopton QUÉ 19 E3
Bishopville NS 24 F2
Bismarck ONT 14 G3
Bissett MAN 11 C3
Bissett Creek ONT 17 C3
Bittern Lake ALTA 7 F1
Bjorkdale SASK 9 F2
Black Bay ONT 15 C1
Black Beach NB 24 C1
Black Cove NFLD 26 D3
Black Creek BC 5 E3
Black Diamond ALTA 7 F3
Black Duck NFLD 27 B2
Black Duck Brook NFLD 27 A2
Black Duck Cove NFLD 27 F4
Black Duck Cove NFLD 26 D1
Black Duck Cove NFLD 26 F4

Black Hawk ONT 11 D4
Black Lake QUÉ 19 F3
Black Lake SASK 8 E1
Black Point SASK 8 C3
Black River MAN 11 C3
Black River NB 24 C1
Black River NB 23 F2
Black River NS 25 F2
Black River NS 24 E2
Black-Cape QUÉ 22 F3
Blackburn ONT 15 F1
Blackfalds ALTA 7 F2
Blackfoot ALTA 7 H1
Blackhead NFLD 27 H3
Blackie ALTA 7 F3
Blackland NB 22 F3
Blackpool BC 5 H2
Blacks Corners ONT 15 E2
Blacks Harbour NB 24 B2
Blackstock ONT 14 H1
Blackville NB 23 E2
Blackwater ONT 13 H4
Bladworth SASK 9 D3
Blaine Lake SASK 9 D2
Blainville QUÉ 19 B3
Blair ONT 14 F2
Blairmore ALTA 7 F4
Blairton ONT 15 C3
Blakeney ONT 15 E2
Blaketown NFLD 27 H3
Blanc-Sablon QUÉ 26 C1
Blanchard Road NS 24 H1
Blanche NS 24 D4
Blanche QUÉ 17 G4
Blandford NS 24 F3
Blenheim ONT 14 C4
Blezard Valley ONT 12 G4
Blind Bay BC 7 C3
Blind Channel BC 5 E3
Blind River ONT 12 E4
Bliss Landing BC 5 E3
Blissfield NB 23 E2
Blissville NB 23 D4
Blockhouse NS 24 E3
Bloedel BC 5 E3
Blomidon NS 24 E1
Bloodvein River MAN 11 B2
Bloomfield NB 23 F4
Bloomfield NB 23 B3
Bloomfield NFLD 27 G2
Bloomfield ONT 15 D4
Bloomfield Ridge NB 23 D3
Bloomingdale ONT 14 E2
Bloomington NS 24 E2
Bloomsbury ALTA 7 E1
Blossom Park ONT 15 F2
Blubber Bay BC 5 E3
Blue Ridge ALTA 7 E1
Blue River BC 7 C2
Blue Rocks NS 24 F3
Blue Sea Lake QUÉ 17 F3
Blueberry Mountain ALTA 6 C2
Blues Mills NS 25 F2
Bluesky ALTA 6 C2
Bluevale ONT 14 D1
Bluewater Beach ONT 13 F3
Bluffton ALTA 7 E2
Blumenfeld MAN 11 B4
Blumenheim SASK 9 D2
Blumenhof SASK 9 D3
Blumenort MAN 11 C4
Blythe ONT 14 D1
Blytheswood ONT 14 B4
Boat Basin BC 5 D4
Boat Harbour NFLD 27 F3
Boat Harbour NFLD 26 E1
Bob Quinn Lake BC 4 B2
Bobby Cove NFLD 26 E3
Bobcaygeon ONT 15 A3
Bocabec NB 24 A1
Bodo ALTA 7 H2
Boggy Creek MAN 9 G2
Bognor ONT 13 E3
Boharm SASK 9 E3
Boiestown NB 23 E3
Boilleau QUÉ 18 F3
Boilleau QUÉ 17 H3
Bois-des-Filion QUÉ 19 B3
Bois-Franc QUÉ 17 F2
Boisbriand QUÉ 19 B3
Boischatel QUÉ 19 F1
Boisdale NS 25 G2
Boissevain MAN 11 A4
Bolingbroke ONT 15 E3
Bolsover ONT 13 H3
Bolton ONT 14 G1
Bolton Centre QUÉ 19 D4
Bolton-Ouest QUÉ 19 D4
Bon Accord ALTA 7 F1
Bon Accord NB 23 C2
Bonanza ALTA 6 C2
Bonarlaw ONT 15 C3
Bonaventure QUÉ 22 G3
Bonavista NFLD 27 H2
Bond Head ONT 14 G1
Bondiss ALTA 6 F3
Bonfield ONT 12 H4
Bonnechere ONT 15 C1
Bonny River NB 24 B1
Bonnyville ALTA 6 G4
Bonsecours QUÉ 19 D4
Bonshaw PEI 25 C2
Bonville ONT 15 H2
Borden PEI 25 B2
Borden SASK 9 D2
Bornholm ONT 14 D2
Borups Corners ONT 11 E3
Boston ONT 14 F3
Boston Bar BC 5 G3
Boston Creek ONT 12 G3
Boswarlos NFLD 27 A2
Boswell BC 7 E4
Botha ALTA 7 F2
Bothwell ONT 14 C3
Bottle Cove NFLD 27 B1
Bottrell ALTA 7 F3
Botwood NFLD 27 E1
Boucher (see St-Joseph-de-Mékinac) QUÉ 19 D1
Boucherville QUÉ 19 B3
Bouchette QUÉ 17 F3
Bouchie Lake BC 5 F1
Bouctouche NB 23 G3
Boularderie NS 25 G2
Boundary Bay BC 5 F4
Bounty SASK 9 D2
Bourget ONT 15 G1
Boutilliers Point NS 24 F2
Bow Island ALTA 7 H3
Bowden ALTA 7 F2
Bowen Island BC 5 F4
Bowland's Bay ONT 12 G4
Bowman (see Val-des-Bois) QUÉ 17 G4
Bowmanville ONT 15 A4
Bowser BC 5 E4
Bowsman MAN 9 G2
Boxey Harbour NFLD 27 E3
Boyd's Cove NFLD 27 F1
Boyle ALTA 6 F3
Boylston NS 25 F3
Boyne Lake ALTA 6 G4
Brabant Lake SASK 8 F3
Bracebridge ONT 13 G2
Bracken SASK 9 C4
Brackendale BC 5 F3
Brackley Beach PEI 25 C2
Bradford ONT 14 G1
Bradford West Gwillimbury (see Bradford) ONT 14 G1
Bradleys Cove NFLD 27 H3
Brador QUÉ 26 C1
Bradwardine MAN 9 H3
Bradwell SASK 9 D2
Braeside ONT 15 E1
Bragg Creek ALTA 7 F3
Bralorne BC 5 F3
Bramber NS 24 F1
Brampton ONT 14 G1
Branch NFLD 27 G4
Branchton ONT 14 F2
Brandon MAN 11 A4
Brant ALTA 7 F3
Brantford ONT 14 F2
Brantville NB 23 G1
Bras-d'Apic QUÉ 19 G1
Breadalbane PEI 25 B2
Breakeyville QUÉ 19 F2
Brébeuf QUÉ 17 H3
Brechin ONT 13 H3
Breckenridge QUÉ 17 F4
Bredenbury SASK 9 G3
Brent QUÉ 17 B3
Brent's Cove NFLD 26 E3
Brenton NS 24 C3
Brentwood ONT 13 F4
Breslau ONT 14 F2
Breton ALTA 7 E1
Breton Cove NS 25 G2
Breynat ALTA 6 F3
Bridesville BC 7 C4
Bridge Lake BC 5 G2
Bridgenorth ONT 15 B3
Bridgeport NFLD 26 F4
Bridgetown NS 24 D2
Bridgetown PEI 25 D2
Bridgeville NS 24 H1
Bridgeville QUÉ 21 A4
Bridgewater NS 24 E3
Briercrest SASK 9 E3
Brierly Brook NS 25 E3
Brig Bay NFLD 26 D2
Brigden ONT 14 B3
Brigham QUÉ 19 C4
Bright ONT 14 E2
Brighton NFLD 27 E1
Brighton NS 24 C2
Brighton ONT 15 C4
Brights Grove ONT 14 B2
Brigus NFLD 27 H3
Brigus South NFLD 27 H4
Brinston ONT 15 G2
Brisbane ONT 14 F1
Brisco BC 7 E3
Bristol NB 23 C3
Bristol QUÉ 17 E4
Bristol's Hope NFLD 27 H3
Britannia NFLD 27 G2
Britannia Beach BC 5 F4
Britt ONT 13 E1
Broad Cove NFLD 27 H3
Broad Cove NS 24 E3
Broad Valley MAN 11 B3
Broadacres SASK 9 C2
Broadview SASK 9 F3
Brochet MAN 8 G2
Brock SASK 9 C2
Brocket ALTA 7 F4
Brockington SASK 9 E1
Brockville ONT 15 F3
Brockway NB 24 A1
Broderick SASK 9 D2
Brodhagen ONT 14 D2
Brokenhead MAN 11 C3
Brome QUÉ 19 D4
Bromhead SASK 9 F4
Bromont QUÉ 19 D4
Bromptonville QUÉ 19 E4
Bronte ONT 14 G2
Brook Village NS 25 F2
Brookdale MAN 11 A3
Brookfield NFLD 27 G1
Brookfield NS 24 G1
Brookfield PEI 25 C2
Brooklin ONT 14 H1
Brooklyn NFLD 27 G2
Brooklyn NS 24 F2
Brooklyn NS 24 E3
Brooks ALTA 7 G3
Brooksby SASK 9 E1
Brookside NFLD 27 F3
Brookville ONT 14 F2
Broomhill MAN 9 G4
Brossard QUÉ 19 B4
Brosseau ALTA 7 G1
Brougham ONT 14 H1
Broughton Station QUÉ 19 F2
Brouseville ONT 15 G3
Brown Hill ONT 13 G4
Brown's Cove NFLD 26 D4
Brownfield ALTA 7 G2
Brownlee SASK 9 D3
Browns Flat NB 23 E4
Brownsburg QUÉ 19 A3
Brownsdale NFLD 27 H3
Brownsville ONT 14 E3
Brownvale ALTA 6 D2
Bruce ALTA 7 G1
Bruce Mines ONT 12 E4
Bruce Station ONT 12 E4
Brucedale ONT 14 F1
Brucefield ONT 14 D2
Brudenell ONT 15 C1-2
Bruderheim ALTA 7 F1
Brûlé ALTA 7 C1
Brule NS 25 C3
Brunkild MAN 11 B4
Brunner ONT 14 E2
Bruno SASK 9 E2
Brunswick Mines NB 23 E1
Brussels ONT 14 D1
Bruxelles MAN 11 A4
Bryanston ONT 14 D2
Bryson QUÉ 17 E4
B-Say-Tah SASK 9 F3
Buchanan SASK 9 F2
Buchans NFLD 27 C1
Buchans Junction NFLD 27 D1
Buck Creek ALTA 7 E1
Buck Lake ALTA 7 E2
Buckfield NS 24 E3
Buckhorn ONT 15 B3
Buckingham QUÉ 17 G4
Buckinghorse River BC 4 F2
Buckland QUÉ 19 G2
Bucklaw NS 25 F2
Budd MAN 9 G1
Buena Vista SASK 9 E3
Buffalo ALTA 7 H3
Buffalo Creek BC 5 G2
Buffalo Head Prairie ALTA 6 D1
Buffalo Lake ALTA 6 C3
Buffalo Narrows SASK 8 C3
Buick BC 4 G2
Bull Cove NFLD 27 F4
Bulwer QUÉ 19 E4
Bulyea SASK 9 E3
Bunbury PEI 25 C2
Bunyan's Cove NFLD 27 G2
Burdett ALTA 7 G3
Burford ONT 14 F2
Burgeo NFLD 27 C3
Burgessville ONT 14 E3
Burgoynes Cove NFLD 27 G2
Burin NFLD 27 F4
Burk's Falls ONT 13 G1
Burketon ONT 14 H1
Burleigh Falls ONT 15 B3
Burlington NFLD 26 E3
Burlington NS 24 E2
Burlington ONT 14 G2
Burmis ALTA 7 F4
Burnaby BC 5 F4
Burnaby ONT 14 G3
Burns Lake BC 4 E4
Burnside NFLD 27 G2
Burnstown ONT 15 E2
Burnsville NB 22 G4
Burnt Church NB 23 G1
Burnt Cove NFLD 27 H4
Burnt Flat BC 7 D4
Burnt Islands NFLD 27 A3
Burnt River ONT 13 H3
Burr SASK 9 E2
Burrits Rapids ONT 15 F2
Burrows SASK 9 G3
Burstall SASK 9 B3
Burtch ONT 14 F2
Burton BC 7 D4
Burton NB 23 E4
Burtts Corner NB 23 D3
Burwash Landing YK 2 A2
Bury QUÉ 19 F4
Busby ALTA 7 E1
Bushell Park SASK 9 E3
Butter Cove NFLD 27 G3
Button MAN 10 A4
Buttonville ONT 14 G1
Byemoor ALTA 7 G2
Bylot MAN 10 C1
Byng ONT 14 G3
Byng Inlet ONT 13 E1

C

Cabano QUÉ 22 B4
Cabri SASK 9 C3
Cache Bay ONT 12 G4
Cache Creek BC 5 G3
Cacouna QUÉ 18 H3
Cactus Lake SASK 9 B2
Cadillac QUÉ 16 B3
Cadillac SASK 9 C4
Cadogan ALTA 7 H2
Cadomin ALTA 7 D2
Cadotte Lake ALTA 6 D2
Caesarea ONT 13 H4
Cainsville ONT 14 F2
Cairngorm ONT 14 C3
Cairo ONT 14 C3
Caistor Centre ONT 14 G2
Caistorville ONT 14 G2
Calabogie ONT 15 D2
Calahoo ALTA 7 E1
Calais ALTA 6 D3
Calder SASK 9 G3
Calders Rock MAN 11 B2
Caledon ONT 14 F1
Caledon East ONT 14 G1
Caledonia NS 25 D4
Caledonia NS 24 D3
Caledonia ONT 14 F2
Caledonia PEI 25 D2
Caledonia Mills NS 25 E3
Calgary ALTA 7 F3
Calhoun NB 23 G3
Caliento MAN 11 C4
Caliper Lake ONT 11 D4
Calixa-Lavallée QUÉ 19 C3
Callander ONT 12 H4
Calling Lake ALTA 6 F3
Calmar ALTA 7 F1
Calstock ONT 12 D1
Calton ONT 14 E3
Calumet QUÉ 19 A3
Calvert NFLD 27 H4
Camborne ONT 15 B4
Cambray ONT 13 H3
Cambridge NS 24 F1
Cambridge NS 24 E2
Cambridge ONT 14 F2
Cambridge Bay NWT 2 F2
Cambridge-Narrows NB 23 E4
Camden East ONT 15 D4
Cameron ONT 13 H3
Cameron Settlement NS 25 D4
Camilla ONT 14 F1
Camlachie ONT 14 B2
Camp Boggy NFLD 27 E3
Camp Creek ALTA 7 E1
Camp Morton MAN 11 B3
Campbell NS 25 F3
Campbell River BC 5 E3
Campbell Settlement NB 23 C3
Campbell's Bay QUÉ 17 E4
Campbellcroft ONT 15 B4
Campbellford ONT 15 C4
Campbells Creek NFLD 27 A2
Campbellton NB 22 E3
Campbellton NFLD 27 F1
Campbellton PEI 25 A1
Campbellville ONT 14 F2
Campden ONT 14 G2
Camper MAN 11 B3
Camperville MAN 11 A2
Camrose ALTA 7 F1
Camsell Portage SASK 8 C1
Canaan NB 23 G3
Canaan NS 24 E2
Canaan NS 24 F2
Canaan Forks NB 23 F3
Canaan Road NB 23 F3
Canada Creek NS 24 E1
Canal Flats BC 7 E3
Canborough ONT 14 G3
Candiac QUÉ 19 B4
Candiac SASK 9 F3
Candle Lake SASK 9 E1
Cando SASK 9 C2
Canfield ONT 14 G3
Canim Lake BC 5 G2
Canmore ALTA 7 E3
Cann QUÉ 18 B3
Cannes-de-Roches QUÉ 21 A4
Cannifton ONT 15 C4
Canning NS 24 E1
Cannings Cove NFLD 27 G2
Cannington ONT 13 H3
Canoe BC 7 C3
Canoe Cove PEI 25 C2
Canoe Narrows SASK 8 C4
Canoe River BC 7 C2
Canol NWT 2 C2
Canora SASK 9 F2
Canso NS 25 G3
Canterbury NB 23 C4
Cantley QUÉ 17 F4
Canwood SASK 9 D1
Canyon BC 7 E4
Canyon Creek ALTA 6 E3
Cap-à-L'Aigle QUÉ 18 H4
Cap-au-Renard QUÉ 22 F1
Cap-aux-Meules QUÉ 21 F3
Cap-aux-Os QUÉ 21 A4
Cap-Chat QUÉ 22 E1
Cap-d'Espoir QUÉ 21 A4
Cap-de-la-Madeleine QUÉ 19 D2
Cap-des-Caissie NB 23 G3
Cap-des-Rosiers QUÉ 21 A4
Cap-Egmont PEI 25 B2
Cap-Lumière NB 23 G2
Cap-Pelé NB 23 H3
Cap-Rouge QUÉ 19 F1
Cap-St-Ignace QUÉ 19 G1
Cap-Seize QUÉ 22 F1
Cap-Tourmente QUÉ 19 G1
Cape Anguille NFLD 27 A3
Cape Broyle NFLD 27 H4
Cape Cove NFLD 26 G3
Cape Croker ONT 13 D2
Cape Dorset NWT 3 C1
Cape Enrage NB 23 G4
Cape Freels NFLD 27 G1
Cape Freels North NFLD 27 G1
Cape Freels South NFLD 27 G1
Cape George NS 25 E3
Cape George Harbour NS 25 G3
Cape la Hune NFLD 27 C3
Cape Negro NS 24 D4
Cape North NS 25 G1
Cape Onion NFLD 26 E1
Cape Race NFLD 27 H4
Cape Ray NFLD 27 A3
Cape St George NFLD 27 A2
Cape St Mary NS 24 C3
Cape Tormentine NB 25 B2
Cape Wolfe PEI 25 A1
Caplan QUÉ 22 G3
Caplin Cove NFLD 27 G3
Caplin Cove NFLD 27 H3
Cappahayden NFLD 27 H4
Capreol ONT 12 G4
Capstick NS 25 G1
Capucins QUÉ 22 E1
Caramat ONT 12 C1
Caraquet NB 23 G1
Carberry MAN 11 A4
Carbon ALTA 7 F2
Carbonear NFLD 27 H3
Carcajou ALTA 6 D1
Carcross YK 2 B3
Cardale MAN 11 A3
Cardiff ONT 15 B2
Cardigan PEI 25 D2
Cardinal MAN 11 B4
Cardinal ONT 15 G3
Cardross SASK 9 E4
Card's Harbour NFLD 27 E1
Cardston ALTA 7 G4
Carey MAN 11 C4
Cargill ONT 13 D4
Caribou NS 25 D3
Caribou River NS 25 D3
Carievale SASK 9 G4
Carignan QUÉ 19 C1
Carignan QUÉ 19 C4
Carillon QUÉ 19 A4
Carleton NS 24 C3
Carleton PEI 25 A1
Carleton QUÉ 22 F3
Carleton Place ONT 15 E2
Carling ONT 13 F2
Carlisle ONT 14 F2
Carlow ONT 14 C1
Carlowrie MAN 11 C4
Carlsbad Springs ONT 15 F2
Carlsruhe ONT 14 D1
Carlton SASK 9 D2
Carluke ONT 14 F2
Carlyle SASK 9 G4
Carmacks YK 2 B2
Carman MAN 11 B4
Carmangay ALTA 7 G3
Carmanville NFLD 27 G1
Carmel SASK 9 E2
Carmichael SASK 9 C3
Carnarvon ONT 13 H2
Carnduff SASK 9 G4
Carnwood ALTA 7 E1
Caroline ALTA 7 E2
Caron SASK 9 E3
Caron Brook NB 23 A1
Caronport SASK 9 E3
Carp ONT 15 F2
Carragana SASK 9 F2
Carrick MAN 11 C4
Carroll MAN 11 A4
Carrolls Crossing NB 23 E3
Carrot River SASK 9 F1
Carrying Place ONT 15 C4
Carseland ALTA 7 F3
Carson BC 7 D4
Carstairs ALTA 7 F2
Carter's Cove NFLD 27 F1
Cartier ONT 12 F4
Cartwright MAN 11 A4
Cartwright NFLD 3 F2
Carway ALTA 7 G4
Cascade BC 7 D4
Casey QUÉ 18 A3
Caslan ALTA 6 F3
Casselman ONT 15 G2
Cassiar BC 4 C1
Castalia NB 24 B2
Castle Mountain ALTA 7 E3
Castleford ONT 15 E1
Castlegar BC 7 D4
Castleton ONT 15 B4
Castor ALTA 7 G2
Castors River NFLD 26 C2
Cat Lake ONT 11 E2
Catalina NFLD 27 H2
Catalone NS 25 H2
Cataraqui ONT 15 E4
Catchacoma ONT 15 B3
Cathcart ONT 14 E2
Causapscal QUÉ 22 D3
Cavan ONT 15 A4
Cavendish NFLD 27 H3
Cavendish PEI 25 C2
Cawaja Beach ONT 13 F3
Cawston BC 7 C4
Caycuse BC 5 E4
Cayer MAN 11 A3
Cayley ALTA 7 F3
Cayuga ONT 14 G3
Cazaville QUÉ 19 A4
Cecebe ONT 13 G1
Cecil Lake BC 4 G3
Cedar BC 5 F4
Cedar Beach ONT 14 A4
Cedar Point ONT 13 F3
Cedar Springs ONT 14 C4
Cedarhurst Park ONT 14 A4
Cedarvale BC 4 C4
Cedoux SASK 9 F4
Ceepeecee BC 5 D3
Central Argyle NS 24 C4
Central Bedeque PEI 25 B2
Central Blissville NB 23 D4
Central Butte SASK 9 D3
Central Grove NS 24 B3
Central Patricia ONT 11 F1
Central Saanich BC 5 F4
Centralia ONT 14 D2
Centre Burlington NS 24 F2
Centre Musquodoboit NS 24 H1-2
Centre Napan NB 23 F2
Centrelea NS 24 D2
Centreton ONT 15 B4
Centreville NB 23 C3
Centreville NFLD 27 G1
Centreville NS 24 C2
Centreville NS 24 D4
Centreville NS 24 E1
Centreville ONT 15 D3
Cereal ALTA 7 H2
Cessford ALTA 7 G3
Ceylon ONT 13 E4
Ceylon SASK 9 E4
Chaffeys Lock ONT 15 E3
Chagoness SASK 9 F1
Chalk River ONT 17 D3
Chamberlain SASK 9 E3
Chambers Corners ONT 14 G3
Chambly QUÉ 19 C4
Chambord QUÉ 18 E2
Chamcook NB 24 A1
Chamiss Bay BC 5 D3
Champion ALTA 7 F3
Champlain QUÉ 19 D2
Champneuf QUÉ 16 D2
Champney's NFLD 27 H2
Chance Cove NFLD 27 G3
Chance Harbour NB 24 B1
Chanceport NFLD 27 F1
Chandler QUÉ 22 H3
Change Islands NFLD 26 F3
Channel-Port aux Basques NFLD 27 A3
Chantry ONT 15 E3
Chapais QUÉ 3 D4
Chapeau QUÉ 17 D4
Chapel Arm NFLD 27 G3
Chapel Island NS 25 G3
Chapels Cove NFLD 27 H3
Chapleau ONT 12 E3
Chaplin NS 24 H1
Chaplin SASK 9 D3
Chaput Hughes ONT 12 G3
Chard ALTA 6 G2
Charette QUÉ 19 C2
Charing Cross ONT 14 B4
Charles MAN 8 G4
Charlesbourg QUÉ 19 F1
Charleston NS 24 E3
Charleston ONT 15 F3
Charlie Lake BC 4 G3
Charlo NB 22 F3
Charlos Cove NS 25 F4
Charlottetown NFLD 27 G2
Charlottetown PEI 25 C2
Charlton ONT 12 G3
Charny QUÉ 19 F2
Charteris QUÉ 17 E4
Chartersville NB 23 G3
Chartierville QUÉ 19 F4
Chase BC 7 C3
Chasm BC 5 G2
Chaswood NS 24 G2
Château-Richer QUÉ 19 F1
Châteauguay QUÉ 19 B4
Chateh ALTA 6 C1
Chater MAN 11 A4
Chatfield MAN 11 B3
Chatham NB 23 F2
Chatham ONT 14 B4
Chatham Head NB 23 F2
Chatsworth ONT 13 E3
Chauvin ALTA 7 H1
Chazel QUÉ 16 A2
Cheapside ONT 14 F3
Chebogue Point NS 24 C4
Cheekye BC 5 F3
Chelan SASK 9 F2
Chelmsford NB 23 F2
Chelmsford ONT 12 G4
Chelsea NS 24 E3
Chelsea QUÉ 17 F4
Cheltenham ONT 14 F1
Chemainus BC 5 F4
Chenaux ONT 15 D1
Chénéville QUÉ 17 H4
Cheney ONT 15 G1
Chénier QUÉ 17 F3
Chepstow ONT 13 D4
Cherhill ALTA 7 E1
Cherry Hill NS 24 E3
Cherry Point ALTA 6 C2
Cherry River QUÉ 19 D4
Cherry Valley ONT 15 D4
Cherry Valley PEI 25 C2
Cherryfield NS 24 E2
Cherryville BC 7 C4
Chertsey QUÉ 19 B3
Chesley ONT 13 D4
Chester NS 24 F2
Chester Basin NS 24 F2
Chester Grant NS 24 F2
Chesterfield Inlet NWT 2 H2
Chesterville ONT 15 G2
Chesterville QUÉ 19 E3
Cheticamp NS 25 F1
Chetwynd BC 4 G3
Cheverie NS 24 F1
Chevery QUÉ 21 H1
Chezacut BC 5 F2
Chibougamau QUÉ 3 D4
Chichester QUÉ 17 D3
Chicoutimi QUÉ 18 F2
Chignecto NS 25 A3
Chilanko Forks BC 5 F2
Chilliwack BC 5 G4
Chimney Corner NS 25 F2
Chinook ALTA 7 G2
Chinook Valley ALTA 6 D2
Chipman ALTA 7 F1
Chipman NB 23 E3
Chipman Brook NS 24 E1
Chippawa ONT 14 H2
Chippawa Hill ONT 13 D3
Chisasibi QUÉ 3 C4
Chisholm ALTA 6 E3
Chitek Lake SASK 9 D1
Choiceland SASK 9 E1
Chopaka BC 7 C4
Chorlitz SASK 9 D3
Christian Island ONT 13 F3
Christina Lake BC 7 D4
Christmas Island NS 25 G2
Christopher Lake SASK 9 E1
Church Point NS 24 C3
Churchbridge SASK 9 G3
Churchill MAN 10 C1
Churchill ONT 13 G4
Churchill Falls NFLD 3 E3
Churchover NS 24 D4
Churchview NS 25 F2
Churchville NS 24 H1
Chute-aux-Outardes QUÉ 22 C1
Chute-Panet QUÉ 19 E1
Chute-St-Philippe QUÉ 17 G2
Clair NB 23 A1
Clair SASK 9 F2
Clairmont ALTA 6 C3
Clam Harbour NS 24 H2
Clandeboye MAN 11 B3
Clandeboye ONT 14 D2
Clandonald ALTA 7 G1
Clanwilliam MAN 11 A3
Clappison's Corners ONT 14 F2
Claremont ONT 14 H1
Clarence NS 24 D2
Clarence ONT 15 G1
Clarence Creek ONT 15 G1
Clarendon Station ONT 15 D3
Clarenville NFLD 27 G2
Claresholm ALTA 7 F3
Clarington (see Bowmanville) ONT 15 A4
Clark's Harbour NS 24 C4
Clarke City QUÉ 20 E2
Clarke's Beach NFLD 27 H3
Clarke's Corners ONT 13 D2
Clarkes Head NFLD 27 F1
Clarkin PEI 25 C2
Clarkleigh MAN 11 B3
Clarksburg ONT 13 E3
Clarkson ONT 14 G2
Clarksville NS 24 F2
Clarkville NB 23 C3
Clavering ONT 13 D3
Clavet SASK 9 D2
Claybank SASK 9 E3
Claydon SASK 9 C4
Clayhurst BC 4 G3
Clayton ONT 15 E2
Clear Creek ONT 14 E3
Cleardale ALTA 6 C2
Clearwater BC 5 H2
Clearwater MAN 11 A4
Clearwater Bay ONT 11 D3
Clemenceau SASK 9 F2
Clementsport NS 24 D2
Clementsvale NS 24 D2
Clemville QUÉ 22 H3
Clermont QUÉ 18 G4
Clerval QUÉ 16 A2
Cleveland NS 25 F3
Clifford ONT 14 E1
Clifton NB 22 G4
Clifton NFLD 27 G2
Climax SASK 9 C4
Clinton BC 5 G3
Clinton ONT 14 D1
Clive ALTA 7 F2
Clo-oose BC 5 E4
Cloridorme QUÉ 22 H1
Cloud Bay ONT 12 A3
Cloutier QUÉ 16 A3
Clova QUÉ 16 G3
Cloverdale NB 23 C3
Cloverdale NS 24 G1
Cloyne ONT 15 D3
Cluff Lake SASK 8 C2
Cluny ALTA 7 G3
Clute ONT 12 G2
Clyde ALTA 7 F1
Clyde ONT 14 F2
Clyde River NS 24 D4
Clydesdale NS 25 E3
Coachman's Cove NFLD 26 D3
Coal Branch NB 23 G3
Coal Brook NFLD 27 A3
Coal Creek NB 23 E3
Coal Harbour BC 5 D3
Coaldale ALTA 7 G4
Coalhurst ALTA 7 G4
Coalmont BC 5 H4
Coates Mills NB 23 G3
Coaticook QUÉ 19 E4
Cobalt ONT 12 H3
Cobbs Arm NFLD 26 F4
Cobden ONT 15 D1
Coboconk ONT 13 H3
Cobourg ONT 15 B4
Cocagne NB 23 G3
Cochenour ONT 11 D2
Cochin SASK 9 C1
Cochrane ALTA 7 F3
Cochrane ONT 12 G2
Coddle Harbour NS 25 F4
Coderre SASK 9 D3
Codes Corner ONT 15 E4
Codette SASK 9 F1
Codrington ONT 15 C4
Codroy NFLD 27 A3
Codroy Pond NFLD 27 A2
Codys NB 23 E4
Coe Hill ONT 15 B3
Coffee Cove NFLD 26 E4
Cogmagun River NS 24 F2
Coin-du-Banc QUÉ 21 A4
Colborne ONT 15 B4
Colchester ONT 14 A4
Cold Brook NFLD 27 A2
Cold Lake ALTA 6 G3
Cold Springs ONT 15 B4
Coldbrook NS 24 E2
Coldstream BC 7 C4
Coldstream NB 23 C3
Coldstream NS 24 G2
Coldstream ONT 14 D2-3
Coldwater ONT 13 G3
Cole Bay SASK 8 C4
Cole Harbour NS 25 F4
Cole Harbour NS 24 G2
Colebrook ONT 15 D3
Coleman ALTA 7 F4
Coleman PEI 25 A1
Coles Island NB 23 F4
Coleville SASK 9 C2
Colfax SASK 9 F4
Colgan ONT 14 G1
Colgate SASK 9 F4
Colinet NFLD 27 H4
Colinton ALTA 6 F3
College Bridge NB 23 G3
College Heights ALTA 7 F2
Collette NB 23 F2
Colliers NFLD 27 H3
Collingwood ONT 13 F3
Collingwood Corner NS 24 F1
Collins ONT 12 A1
Collins Bay ONT 15 E4
Collins Cove NFLD 27 F4
Colombier QUÉ 22 B2
Colombourg QUÉ 16 A2
Colonsay SASK 9 E2
Colpton NS 24 E3
Columbus ONT 14 H1
Colwood BC 5 F4
Comber ONT 14 B4
Combermere ONT 15 C2
Combes Cove NFLD 27 E3
Come by Chance NFLD 27 G3
Comeau Hill NS 24 C4
Comeauville NS 24 C3
Comfort Cove NFLD 27 F1
Commanda ONT 13 G1
Como QUÉ 19 A4
Comox BC 5 E4
Compeer ALTA 7 H2
Compton QUÉ 19 E4
Conception Bay South NFLD 27 H3
Conception Harbour NFLD 27 H3
Concession NS 24 C3
Conche NFLD 26 E2
Condor ALTA 7 E2
Conestogo ONT 14 E2
Congress SASK 9 D4
Coniston ONT 12 G4
Conklin ALTA 6 G3
Conn ONT 14 E1
Conn Mills NS 25 B3
Connaught ONT 12 G2
Conne River NFLD 27 E3
Connors NB 23 A1
Conquerall Mills NS 24 E3
Conquest SASK 9 D2
Conrich ALTA 7 F3
Consecon ONT 15 C4
Consort ALTA 7 G2
Constance Bay ONT 15 E1
Constance Lake ONT 12 D1
Consul SASK 9 B4
Contrecoeur QUÉ 19 C3
Conway ONT 15 D4
Cooking Lake ALTA 7 F1
Cooks Brook NS 24 G2
Cook's Harbour NFLD 26 E1
Cookshire QUÉ 19 E4
Cookstown ONT 13 G4
Coombs BC 5 E4
Copenhagen ONT 14 D3
Copetown ONT 14 F2
Copper Cliff ONT 12 G4
Copper Creek BC 5 G3
Coppermine NWT 2 E2
Coppin's Corners ONT 14 H1
Coquitlam BC 5 F4
Coral Harbour NWT 3 B1
Corbeil ONT 12 H4
Corberrie NS 24 C3
Corbett ONT 14 C2
Corbetton ONT 13 F4
Corbin BC 7 F4
Corbin NFLD 27 E4
Corbyville ONT 15 C4
Cordova Mines ONT 15 C3
Corinth ONT 14 E3
Cork NB 23 D4
Cormac ONT 15 C1
Cormack NFLD 27 C1
Cormierville NB 23 G3
Cormorant MAN 9 G1
Corner Brook NFLD 27 B1
Cornhill NB 23 F4
Corning SASK 9 F3

Cornwall ONT 15 H2
Cornwall PEI 25 C2
Cornwallis NS 24 C2
Coronach SASK 9 E4
Coronation ALTA 7 G2
Corunna ONT 14 B3
Coteau Beach SASK 9 D3
Coteau-du-Lac QUÉ 19 A4
Coteau-Landing QUÉ 19 A4
Coteau-Station QUÉ 19 A4
Côte-Nord-du-Golfe-Saint-Laurent (see Chevery) QUÉ 21 H1
Côte-St-Luc QUÉ 19 B4
Cottam ONT 14 A4
Cottle's Island NFLD 27 F1
Cottlesville NFLD 27 F1
Cottonwood BC 5 G1
Cottrell's Cove NFLD 27 E1
Couchiching ONT 11 E4
Coulson ONT 13 G3
Coulter MAN 9 G4
Country Harbour Cross Roads NS 25 E4
Country Harbour Mines NS 25 E4
Country Road NFLD 27 H3
Courcelles QUÉ 19 F3
Courtenay BC 5 E4
Courtice ONT 14 H1
Courtland ONT 14 E3
Courtright ONT 14 B3
Courval SASK 9 D3
Coutts ALTA 7 G4
Cove Road NS 24 F1
Coverdale NB 23 G3
Covey Hill QUÉ 19 B4
Cow Bay NS 24 G2
Cow Head NFLD 26 B3
Cowan MAN 9 G2
Cowansville QUÉ 19 D4
Cowichan Bay BC 5 F4
Cowley ALTA 7 F4
Cox's Cove NFLD 27 B1
Crabtree QUÉ 19 B3
Craigellachie BC 7 C3
Craighurst ONT 13 G3
Craigleith ONT 13 F3
Craigmore NS 25 F3
Craigmyle ALTA 7 G2
Craik SASK 9 E3
Cranberry Junction BC 4 C3
Cranberry Portage MAN 8 G4
Cranbrook BC 7 E4
Crandall MAN 9 G3
Crane River MAN 11 A2
Crane Valley SASK 9 E4
Crapaud PEI 25 B2
Craven SASK 9 E3
Crawford Bay BC 7 D4
Crediton ONT 14 D2
Creditville ONT 14 E2
Cree Lake SASK 8 D2
Creelman SASK 9 F4
Creemore ONT 13 F4
Creighton SASK 8 G4
Creighton Heights ONT 15 B4
Creignish NS 25 F3
Cremona ALTA 7 F2
Crescent Lake SASK 9 G3
Crescent Spur BC 5 G1
Crestomere ALTA 7 F2
Creston BC 7 E4
Creston NFLD 27 E-F4
Crestwynd SASK 9 E3
Crieff ONT 14 F2
Cromer MAN 9 G4
Cromwell MAN 11 C3
Crooked Bay ONT 13 G2
Crooked River SASK 9 F2
Crookston ONT 15 C3
Croque NFLD 26 E2
Crosby ONT 15 E3
Cross Creek NB 23 D3
Cross Lake MAN 10 B4
Crossfield ALTA 7 F2
Crosshill ONT 14 E2
Croton ONT 14 C3
Crouse NFLD 26 E2
Crousetown NS 24 E3
Crow Head NFLD 26 F3
Crow Lake ONT 11 D4
Crow Lake ONT 15 E3
Crowes Landing ONT 15 B3
Crown Hill ONT 13 G3
Crows Nest NS 25 E4
Crowsnest Pass ALTA 7 F4
Croydon Station BC 7 C2
Crumlin ONT 14 D3
Crutwell SASK 9 D1
Crysler ONT 15 G2
Crystal Beach ONT 14 H3
Crystal City MAN 11 A4
Crystal Cliffs NS 25 E3
Crystal Falls ONT 12 H4
Crystal Springs SASK 9 E2
Cudworth SASK 9 E2
Culloden NS 24 C2
Culloden ONT 14 E3
Culls Harbour NFLD 27 G2
Cull's Island NFLD 27 E1
Culross MAN 11 B4
Cultus ONT 14 E3
Cumberland BC 5 E4
Cumberland ONT 15 G1
Cumberland Bay NB 23 E3
Cumberland Beach ONT 13 G3
Cumberland House SASK 9 F1
Cupar SASK 9 F3
Cupids NFLD 27 H3
Curran ONT 15 G1
Currie NB 23 C2
Curve Lake ONT 15 B3
Curzon Village NFLD 27 B1
Cushing QUÉ 19 A3
Cuslett NFLD 27 G4
Cut Knife SASK 9 C2
Cutler ONT 12 F4
Cymric SASK 9 E3
Cynthia ALTA 7 E1
Cypress River MAN 11 A4
Czar ALTA 7 G2

D

Da Swisha QUÉ 17 C3
Daaquam QUÉ 19 H2
Dacre ONT 15 D2
Dafoe SASK 9 E2
Dahinda SASK 9 E4
Dain City ONT 14 H3
D'Alembert QUÉ 16 A3
Dalemead ALTA 7 F3
Dalesville QUÉ 19 A3
Dalhousie NB 22 F3
Dalhousie East NS 24 E2
Dalhousie Junction NB 22 E3
Dalhousie Mills ONT 15 H2
Dalhousie Road NS 24 E2
Dalhousie Station QUÉ 19 A4
Dalkeith ONT 15 H1
Dallas MAN 11 B2
Dalmeny SASK 9 D2
Dalny MAN 9 H4
Dalrymple ONT 13 H3
Dalston ONT 13 G3
Dalton ONT 12 D3
Dalum ALTA 7 G2
Damascus ONT 14 E1
Dana SASK 9 E2
Danbury SASK 9 G2
Dand MAN 11 A4
Danford Lake QUÉ 17 F3
Daniel's Cove NFLD 27 H2
Daniel's Harbour NFLD 26 C3
Danvers NS 24 C3
Danville QUÉ 19 E3
Dapp ALTA 7 E1
Darby Harbour NFLD 27 F3
D'Arcy BC 5 F3
D'Arcy SASK 9 C2
Darfield BC 5 F2
Dark Cove NFLD 27 G2
Darling Lake NS 24 C4
Darlingford MAN 11 B4
Darnley PEI 25 B2
Darrell Bay BC 5 F4
Dartmouth NS 24 G2
Dashwood ONT 14 C2
Daulnay NB 23 F1
Dauphin MAN 11 A3
Dauphin River MAN 11 B2
Daveluyville QUÉ 19 D2
Davidson QUÉ 17 E4
Davidson SASK 9 D3
Davidsville NFLD 27 F1
Davin SASK 9 F3
Davis SASK 9 E1
Davis Cove NFLD 27 G3
Dawson City YK 2 B2
Dawson Creek BC 4 G3
Dawsons Landing BC 5 D2
Dawsonville NB 22 E3
Daysland ALTA 7 G1
Dayton NS 24 C4
De Grau NFLD 27 A2
De Winton ALTA 7 F3
Deacon ONT 15 C1
Deadman's Bay NFLD 27 G1
Deadmans Cove NFLD 26 D1
Deadwood ALTA 6 D2
Dealtown ONT 14 B4
Dean NS 24 H1
Deanlea Beach ONT 13 F3
Dease Lake BC 4 C1
Deauville QUÉ 19 E4
Debden SASK 9 D1
Debec NB 23 C3
Debert NS 24 G1
DeBolt ALTA 6 C3
Decewsville ONT 14 F3
Decker MAN 9 G3
Deep Bay NFLD 26 G3
Deep Bight NFLD 27 G2
Deep Brook NS 24 C2
Deep Cove NS 24 F3
Deep River ONT 17 D3
Deepdale MAN 9 G3
Deer Lake NFLD 27 C1
Deer Lake ONT 11 D1
Deerbrook ONT 14 B4
Deerfield NS 24 C4
Deerhorn MAN 11 B3
Deerwood MAN 11 B4
Defoy QUÉ 19 D3
Dégelis QUÉ 22 B4
Del Bonita ALTA 7 G4
Delacour ALTA 7 F2
Delap Cove NS 24 C2
Delaware ONT 14 D3
Delburne ALTA 7 F2
Déléage QUÉ 17 F3
Deleau MAN 9 H4
Delhi ONT 14 E3
Delia ALTA 7 G2
Deline NWT 2 D2
Delisle QUÉ 18 E2
Delisle SASK 9 D2
Delmas SASK 9 C1
Deloraine MAN 11 A4
Deloro ONT 15 C3
Delson QUÉ 19 B4
Delta BC 5 F4
Delta ONT 15 E3
Delta Beach MAN 11 B3
Demaine SASK 9 D3
Demers-Centre QUÉ 17 D4
Demmitt ALTA 6 C3
Demorestville ONT 15 D4
Dempsey Corners NS 24 E2
Demremy SASK 9 E2
Demuth BC 7 C4
Denare Beach SASK 8 G4
Denbigh ONT 15 C2
Denfield ONT 14 D2
Denholm SASK 9 C2
Denman Island BC 5 E4
Denmark NS 24 G1
Densmore Mills NS 24 G1
Denver NS 25 E4
Denzil SASK 9 C2
Departure Lake ONT 12 F2
Derby NB 23 F2
Derby Junction NB 23 F2
Dering MAN 9 G1
Derwent ALTA 7 G1
DeSable PEI 25 C2
Desaulniers ONT 12 G4
Desbarats ONT 12 E4
Desbiens QUÉ 18 E2
Desboro ONT 13 D3
Deschaillons QUÉ 19 E2
Deschambault QUÉ 19 E2
Deschambault Lake SASK 8 F4
Descharme Lake SASK 8 C2-3
D'Escousse NS 25 G3
Deseronto ONT 15 D4
Desjardinsville QUÉ 17 D4
Desmaraisville QUÉ 16 F1
Despinassy QUÉ 16 D2
Destor QUÉ 16 B2
Destruction Bay YK 2 A2
Deux Rivieres ONT 17 C3
Deux-Montagnes QUÉ 19 B4
Devlin ONT 11 E4
Devon ALTA 7 F1
Dewberry ALTA 7 G1
Dewdney BC 5 G4
Dewittville QUÉ 19 A4
Diamond City ALTA 7 G4
Diamond Cove NFLD 27 A3
Dickson ALTA 7 F2
Didsbury ALTA 7 F2
Dieppe NB 23 G3
Digby NS 24 C2
Digdeguash NB 24 A1
Dildo NFLD 27 H3
Diligent River NS 24 E1
Dilke SASK 9 E3
Dillon ONT 13 F2
Dillon SASK 8 C3
Dingwall NS 25 G1
Dingwells Mills PEI 25 D2
Dinorwic ONT 11 E3
Dinsmore SASK 9 D3
Dipper Harbour NB 24 B2
Dipper Lake SASK 8 D3
Disley SASK 9 E3
Disraeli QUÉ 19 F3
Dixons Corners ONT 15 G2
Dixonville ALTA 6 D2
Dixville QUÉ 19 E4
Doaktown NB 23 E3
Dobbinton ONT 13 D3
Dock Cove NFLD 27 G1
Doctors Brook NS 25 E3
Doctors Cove NS 24 C4
Doctors Harbour NFLD 27 E3
Dodsland SASK 9 C2
Dog Creek BC 5 G2
Dokis ONT 12 G4
Dolbeau QUÉ 18 D2
Dollard SASK 9 C4
Domain MAN 11 B4
Dome Creek BC 5 G1
Dominion NS 25 H2
Dominion City MAN 11 B-C4
Domville ONT 15 F3
Donald BC 7 D3
Donalda ALTA 7 F2
Donavon SASK 9 D2
Donegal ONT 14 E1
Donkin NS 25 H2
Donnacona QUÉ 19 E2
Donnelly ALTA 6 D3
Donwood ONT 15 B4
Dorchester NB 23 H3
Dorchester ONT 14 D3
Dorchester Crossing NB 23 G3
Dore Lake SASK 8 D4
Dorintosh SASK 9 C1
Dorion ONT 12 A2
Dorion QUÉ 19 B4
Dorking ONT 14 E1
Dormans Cove NFLD 27 F1
Dornoch ONT 13 E4
Dorothy ALTA 7 G2
Dorset ONT 13 H2
Dosquet QUÉ 19 E2
Doting Cove NFLD 27 G1
Doucetteville NS 24 C3
Douglas MAN 11 A4
Douglas NB 23 D3
Douglas ONT 15 D1
Douglas Harbour NB 23 E4
Douglas Lake BC 5 H3
Douglastown NB 23 F2
Douglastown QUÉ 21 A4
Douro ONT 15 B3
Dover NFLD 27 G1
Dover Centre ONT 14 B3
Dowling ONT 12 F4
Downeyville ONT 15 A4
Doyles NFLD 27 A3
Drake SASK 9 E2
Drapeau QUÉ 22 F3
Drayton ONT 14 E1
Drayton Valley ALTA 7 E1
Dresden ONT 14 B3
Driftpile ALTA 6 E3
Driftwood ONT 12 F2
Drinkwater SASK 9 E3
Dropmore MAN 9 G3
Druid SASK 9 C2
Drumbo ONT 14 E2
Drumhead NS 25 F4
Drumheller ALTA 7 G2
Drummond NB 23 C2
Drummondville QUÉ 19 D3
Drybrough MAN 8 G3
Dryden ONT 11 E3
Duart ONT 14 C3
Dublin ONT 14 D2
Dublin Shore NS 24 F3
Dubreuilville ONT 12 D2
Dubuc SASK 9 F3
Dubuisson QUÉ 16 C3
Duchesnay QUÉ 19 E1
Duchess ALTA 7 G3
Duck Bay MAN 11 A2
Duck Lake SASK 9 D2
Duck River MAN 9 H2
Duclos QUÉ 17 F4
Duclos Point ONT 13 H3
Duff SASK 9 F3
Duff's Corners ONT 14 F2
Dufresne MAN 11 C4
Dugald MAN 11 C3
Duhamel QUÉ 17 H3
Dumas SASK 9 G3
Dumbarton NB 24 A1
Dumfries NB 23 C4
Dummer SASK 9 E4
Dunblane SASK 9 D3
Duncan BC 5 F4
Dunchurch ONT 13 F1
Dundalk ONT 13 F4
Dundas ONT 14 F2
Dundas PEI 25 D2
Dundee NB 22 E3
Dundee NS 25 F3
Dundee QUÉ 19 A4
Dundee Centre QUÉ 19 A4
Dundonald ONT 15 G2
Dundurn SASK 9 D2
Dunedin ONT 13 F4
Dunfield NFLD 27 H2
Dungannon ONT 14 C1
Dunham QUÉ 19 C4
Dunkerron ONT 14 G1
Dunleath SASK 9 G3
Dunlop MAN 10 A4
Dunmore ALTA 7 H3
Dunns Valley ONT 12 E4
Dunnville ONT 14 G3
Dunraven QUÉ 17 E4
Dunrea MAN 11 A4
Dunrobin ONT 15 F1
Dunsford ONT 15 A3
Dunster BC 5 H1
Duntroon ONT 13 F3
Duntura NFLD 27 H2
Dunvegan ALTA 6 C2
Dunvegan NS 25 F2
Dunvegan ONT 15 H2
Dunville NFLD 27 G4
Duparquet QUÉ 16 A2
Dupuy QUÉ 16 A2
Durban MAN 9 G2
Durham NS 24 H1
Durham ONT 13 E4
Durham Bridge NB 23 D3
Durham Centre NB 22 F3
Durham-Sud QUÉ 19 D3
Durrell NFLD 26 F3
Dutton ONT 14 D3
Duttona Beach ONT 14 D3
Duval SASK 9 E3
Duvernay ALTA 7 G1
Dwight ONT 13 H2
Dyce MAN 8 G4
Dyer's Bay ONT 13 D2
Dyment ONT 11 E3
Dymond ONT 12 H3
Dysart SASK 9 F3

E

Eagle ONT 14 C3
Eagle Bay BC 7 C3
Eagle Creek BC 5 G2
Eagle Head NS 24 E3
Eagle Lake ONT 11 E3
Eagle Lake ONT 15 A2
Eagle River ONT 11 E3
Eaglesham ALTA 6 D3
Ear Falls ONT 11 E3
Eardley QUÉ 17 F4
Earl Grey SASK 9 E3
Earls Cove BC 5 F4
Earlton ONT 12 G3
Earltown NS 24 G1
Earnscliffe PEI 25 C2
East Aldfield QUÉ 17 F4
East Angus QUÉ 19 E4
East Bay NFLD 27 B3
East Bay NS 25 G2
East Braintree MAN 11 C4
East Broughton QUÉ 19 F2
East Broughton Station QUÉ 19 F2
East Chester NS 24 F2
East Chezzetcook NS 24 G2
East Clifton QUÉ 19 E4
East Coulee ALTA 7 G2
East Dover NS 24 F3
East Earltown NS 24 G1
East Farnham QUÉ 19 D4
East Ferry NS 24 C3
East Gore NS 24 G2
East Green Harbour NS 24 D4
East Gwillimbury (see Sharon) ONT 14 G1
East Hereford QUÉ 19 E4
East Jeddore NS 24 H2
East Jordan Station NS 24 D4
East Kemptville NS 24 C3
East LaHave NS 24 F3
East Linton ONT 13 E3
East Mapleton NS 24 F1
East Margaree NS 25 F2
East Margaretville NS 24 D2
East Medway NS 24 E3
East Mines Station NS 24 G1
East New Annan NS 24 G1
East Point PEI 25 E2
East Port l'Hebert NS 24 E4
East Pubnico NS 24 C4
East Quoddy NS 25 D4
East River NS 24 F2
East River St Marys NS 25 E3
East Riverside-Kingshurst NB 24 C1
East Selkirk MAN 11 C3
East Uniacke NS 24 G2
East York ONT 14 G1
Eastend SASK 9 C4
Eastern Passage NS 24 G2
Easterville MAN 11 A1
Eastmain QUÉ 3 C4
Eastman QUÉ 19 D4
Eastons Corners ONT 15 F3
Eastport NFLD 27 G2
Eastville NS 24 H1
Eastwood ONT 14 E2
Eaton QUÉ 19 E4
Eatonia SASK 9 C3
Eatonville ONT 14 C4
Eau Claire ONT 12 H4
Ebenezer SASK 9 F3
Eberts ONT 14 B3
Ebor MAN 9 G4
Echo Bay NWT 2 D2
Echo Bay ONT 12 D4
Echo Lake NS 24 G2
Eckville ALTA 7 E2
Economy NS 24 F1
Ecum Secum NS 25 E4
Edam SASK 9 C1
Edberg ALTA 7 F2
Eddies Cove NFLD 26 D1
Eddies Cove West NFLD 26 C2
Eddystone MAN 11 A3
Eden MAN 11 A3
Eden ONT 14 E3
Eden Lake NS 25 D3
Eden Mills ONT 14 F2
Edenvale ONT 13 F3
Edenwold SASK 9 E3
Edgar ONT 13 G3
Edgeley SASK 9 F3
Edgerton ALTA 7 G1
Edgewater BC 7 E3
Edgewood BC 7 D4
Edmonton ALTA 7 F1
Edmonton Beach ALTA 7 E1
Edmundston NB 23 B1
Edrans MAN 11 A3
Edson ALTA 7 D1
Edwards ONT 15 F2
Edys Mills ONT 14 B3
Eel River Crossing NB 22 F3
Effingham ONT 14 G2
Eganville ONT 15 D1
Egerton NS 25 D3
Egmondville ONT 14 D2
Egmont BC 5 F4
Egremont ALTA 7 F1
Eholt BC 7 C4
Eight Island Lake NS 25 E4
Elak Dase SASK 8 D3
Elbow SASK 9 D3
Eldee ONT 12 H4
Elderbank NS 24 G2
Eldersley SASK 9 F2
Eldon PEI 25 C2
Eldorado ONT 15 C3
Elfrida ONT 14 G2
Elfros SASK 9 F2
Elgin MAN 11 A4
Elgin NB 23 G4
Elgin ONT 15 E3
Elgin Mills ONT 14 G1
Elginburg ONT 15 E4
Elginfield ONT 14 D2
Elie MAN 11 B3
Elizabethville ONT 15 A4
Elk Lake ONT 12 G3
Elk Point ALTA 7 G1
Elkford BC 7 E4
Elkhorn MAN 9 G3
Elko BC 7 E4
Elkton ALTA 7 E-F2
Elkwater ALTA 7 H3
Ellershouse NS 24 F2
Ellerslie PEI 25 B2
Elliot Lake ONT 12 E4
Elliston NFLD 27 H2
Ellscott ALTA 6 F3
Elm Creek MAN 11 B4
Elma MAN 11 C3
Elmira ONT 14 E1
Elmira PEI 25 E2
Elmsdale NS 24 G2
Elmsdale PEI 25 A1
Elmstead ONT 14 A4
Elmsvale NS 24 H2
Elmsville NB 24 A1
Elmvale ONT 13 F3
Elmwood ONT 13 D4
Elmworth ALTA 6 C3
Elnora ALTA 7 F2
Elora ONT 14 F1
Elphin ONT 15 E2
Elphinstone MAN 11 A3
Elrose SASK 9 C3
Elsas ONT 12 E2
Elsinore ONT 13 D3
Elstow SASK 9 D2
Elva MAN 9 G4
Embree NFLD 27 F1
Embro ONT 14 E2
Embrun ONT 15 G2
Emerson MAN 11 B4
Emeryville ONT 14 A4
Emo ONT 11 E4
Empire Corners ONT 14 G3
Empress ALTA 7 H3
Emsdale ONT 13 G1
Enchant ALTA 7 G3
Endako BC 5 E1
Endeavour SASK 9 F2
Enderby BC 7 C3
Endiang ALTA 7 G2
Enfield NS 24 G2
Engen BC 5 E1
Englee NFLD 26 D2
Englefeld SASK 9 E2
Englehart ONT 12 G3
English Harbour NFLD 27 H2
English Harbour East NFLD 27 F3
English Harbour West NFLD 27 E3
English River ONT 11 F3
Englishtown NS 25 G2
Enilda ALTA 6 D3
Enmore PEI 25 B2
Enniskillen NB 23 D4
Enniskillen ONT 14 H1
Ennismore ONT 15 A3
Enon NS 25 G3
Ensign ALTA 7 F3
Enterprise ONT 15 D3
Entrance ALTA 7 D1
Entrelacs QUÉ 19 B3
Entwistle ALTA 7 E1
Epworth NFLD 27 E4
Eramosa ONT 14 F1
Erickson BC 7 E4
Erickson MAN 11 A3
Erie BC 7 D4
Erie Beach ONT 14 C4
Erieau ONT 14 C4
Eriksdale MAN 11 B3
Erin ONT 14 F1
Erinsville ONT 15 D3
Erinview MAN 11 B3
Erinville NS 25 E3
Ernfold SASK 9 D3
Erskine ALTA 7 F2
Erwood SASK 9 G2
Escott ONT 15 F3
Escuminac NB 23 G2
Escuminac QUÉ 22 E3
Esk SASK 9 E2
Eskasoni NS 25 G2
Espanola ONT 12 F4
Esperanza BC 5 D3
Esprit-Saint QUÉ 22 B3
Esquimalt BC 5 F4
Essex ONT 14 A4
Estaire ONT 12 G4
Estérel QUÉ 19 B3
Esterhazy SASK 9 G3
Estevan SASK 9 F4
Estevan Group BC 5 C1
Esther ALTA 7 H2
Estlin SASK 9 E3
Estmere NS 25 F2
Eston SASK 9 C3
Estuary SASK 9 B3
Étamamiou QUÉ 21 G1
Étang-des-Caps QUÉ 21 F3
Ethel ONT 14 D1
Ethelbert MAN 9 H2
Ethelton SASK 9 E2
Etobicoke ONT 14 G1
Eton-Rugby ONT 11 E3
Etzikom ALTA 7 H4
Eugenia ONT 13 E4
Eureka NS 24 H1
Eureka River ALTA 6 C2
Évain QUÉ 16 A3
Evandale NB 23 E4
Evansburg ALTA 7 E1
Evanston NS 25 F3
Evansville ONT 13 B1
Everett NB 23 C2
Everett ONT 13 F4
Evesham SASK 9 B2
Exeter ONT 14 D2
Exshaw ALTA 7 E3
Eyebrow SASK 9 D3

F

Fabre QUÉ 17 A1
Fabyan ALTA 7 G1
Factorydale NS 24 E2
Fair Harbour BC 5 D3
Fair Haven NFLD 27 G3
Fairfax MAN 11 A4
Fairfield PEI 25 E2
Fairford MAN 11 A2
Fairground ONT 14 E3
Fairhaven NB 24 A2
Fairisle NB 23 G1
Fairlight SASK 9 G4
Fairmont Hot Springs BC 7 E3
Fairvale NB 24 C1
Fairview ALTA 6 C2
Fairy Glen SASK 9 E1
Falcon Lake MAN 11 C3
Falconbridge ONT 12 G4
Falher ALTA 6 D3
Falkland BC 7 C3
Falkland ONT 14 E2
Falkland Ridge NS 24 E2
Fall River NS 24 G2
Fallbrook ONT 15 E2
Fallis ALTA 7 E1
Falmouth NS 24 F2
False Bay BC 5 E4
Falun ALTA 7 F1
Fanny Bay BC 5 E4
Fannystelle MAN 11 B4
Farewell NFLD 26 F4
Farley QUÉ 17 F3
Farm Point QUÉ 17 F4
Farmington BC 4 G3
Farmington NS 24 E2
Farmington NS 24 F1
Farnham QUÉ 19 C4
Farnham-Centre QUÉ 19 C4
Faro YK 2 B2
Farrellton QUÉ 17 F4
Fassett QUÉ 17 H4
Fassifern ONT 15 H2
Fatima QUÉ 21 F3
Faulkner MAN 11 A2
Fauquier BC 7 D4
Fauquier ONT 12 F2
Faust ALTA 6 E3
Fawcett ALTA 6 E3
Fawcett Lake ALTA 6 F3
Fawcettville ONT 15 D4
Fay Lake MAN 8 G4
Felix Cove NFLD 27 A2
Fenella ONT 15 B4
Fenelon Falls ONT 13 H3
Fenn ALTA 7 F2
Fennell ONT 13 G4
Fenton SASK 9 E1
Fenwick ONT 14 G3
Fenwood SASK 9 F3
Fergus ONT 14 F1
Fergusonvale ONT 13 G3
Ferintosh ALTA 7 F2
Ferland ONT 12 B1
Ferland QUÉ 18 F3
Ferland SASK 9 D4
Ferme-Neuve QUÉ 17 G2
Fermeuse NFLD 27 H4
Fermont QUÉ 3 E3
Ferndale ONT 13 D2
Fernie BC 7 E4
Fernleigh ONT 15 D2
Fernwood PEI 25 B2
Ferry Road NB 23 F2
Ferryland NFLD 27 H4
Fertile SASK 9 G4
Fesserton ONT 13 G3
Feversham ONT 13 F4
Fichot Islands NFLD 26 E1
Field BC 7 D3
Field ONT 12 G4
Fielding SASK 9 D2
Fife Lake SASK 9 E4
Fillmore SASK 9 F4
Finch ONT 15 G2
Findlater SASK 9 E3
Fingal ONT 14 D3
Finger MAN 9 G1
Finlayson NS 25 F2
Finmark ONT 11 G4
Finnegan ALTA 7 G3
Fir Mountain SASK 9 D4
Firdale MAN 11 A3
Fire River ONT 12 E2
Firvale BC 5 D2
Fischells NFLD 27 A2
Fisher Branch MAN 11 B3
Fisher Home ALTA 7 E1
Fisher River MAN 11 B2
Fisherville ONT 14 F3
Fishing River MAN 11 A3
Fiske SASK 9 C2
Fitch Bay QUÉ 19 D4
Fitzgerald ALTA 8 B1
Fitzroy Harbour ONT 15 E1
Five Fingers NB 22 D4
Five Islands NS 24 F1
Flamboro Centre ONT 14 F2
Flamborough (see Waterdown) ONT 14 F2
Flat Bay NFLD 27 A2
Flat Lake ALTA 6 G4
Flat River PEI 25 C2
Flat Rock NFLD 27 H3
Flatbush ALTA 6 E3
Flathead BC 7 F4
Flaxcombe SASK 9 B2
Fleet ALTA 7 G2
Fleming SASK 9 G3
Flesherton ONT 13 E4
Fleur de Lys NFLD 26 D3
Fleurimont QUÉ 19 E4
Flin Flon MAN 8 G4
Flintoft SASK 9 D4
Flinton ONT 15 D3
Floradale ONT 14 E1
Floral Park ONT 13 G3
Florence NS 25 G2
Florence ONT 14 C3
Florenceville NB 23 C3
Flower Station ONT 15 D2
Flower's Cove NFLD 26 D1
Fluery Bight NFLD 27 E1
Foam Lake SASK 9 F2
Fogo NFLD 26 G3
Foisy ALTA 7 G1
Foldens ONT 14 E2-3
Foleyet ONT 12 F3
Folly Lake NS 24 G1
Fond-du-Lac SASK 8 D1
Fontaine NB 23 G2
Fontainebleau QUÉ 19 F3
Fontenelle QUÉ 22 H2
Fonthill ONT 14 H3
Foot's Bay ONT 13 G2
Forbes Point NS 24 C4
Fords Mills NB 23 G3
Fordwich ONT 14 D1
Foremost ALTA 7 H4
Forest ONT 14 C2
Forest City NB 23 B4
Forest Field NFLD 27 H4
Forest Glen NS 24 G1
Forest Grove BC 5 G2
Forest Hill NS 25 E4
Forest Home ONT 13 G3
Forest Mills ONT 15 D4
Forestburg ALTA 7 G2
Foresters Falls ONT 15 D1
Forestville ONT 14 F3
Forestville QUÉ 22 B2
Forfar ONT 15 E3
Forgan SASK 9 C3
Forget SASK 9 F4
Fork Lake ALTA 6 G3
Fork River MAN 11 A2
Formosa ONT 14 D1
Forrest Station MAN 11 A4
Forresters Point NFLD 26 D1
Forsythe QUÉ 16 E3
Fort Albany ONT 3 C4
Fort Alexander MAN 11 C3
Fort Assiniboine ALTA 7 E1
Fort Augustus PEI 25 C2
Fort Babine BC 4 D3
Fort Chipewyan ALTA 6 G1
Fort Coulonge QUÉ 17 E4
Fort Erie ONT 14 H3
Fort Frances ONT 11 E4
Fort Fraser BC 5 E1
Fort Good Hope NWT 2 C2
Fort Hope ONT 11 G2
Fort Irwin ONT 15 A2
Fort Kent ALTA 6 G3
Fort Lawrence NS 25 A3
Fort Liard NWT 2 C3
Fort MacKay ALTA 6 G2
Fort Mcleod ALTA 7 F4
Fort McMurray ALTA 6 G2
Fort McPherson NWT 2 C1
Fort Nelson BC 4 F1
Fort Norman NWT 2 C2
Fort Providence NWT 2 D3
Fort Qu'Appelle SASK 9 F3
Fort Resolution NWT 2 D3
Fort St James BC 4 E4
Fort St John BC 4 G3
Fort San SASK 9 F3
Fort Saskatchewan ALTA 7 F1
Fort Severn ONT 10 F2
Fort Simpson NWT 2 C3
Fort Smith NWT 2 E4
Fort Steele BC 7 E4
Fort Vermilion ALTA 6 D1
Fort William QUÉ 17 D3
Forteau NFLD 26 D1
Forthton ONT 15 F3
Fortier MAN 11 B3
Fortierville QUÉ 19 E2
Forties Settlement NS 24 E2
Fortune NFLD 27 E4
Fortune Bridge PEI 25 D2
Fortune Harbour NFLD 27 E1
Forty Mile Flats BC 4 C2
Fossambault-sur-le-Lac QUÉ 19 E1
Fosston SASK 9 F2
Foster QUÉ 19 D4
Fosterville NB 23 B4
Four Falls NB 23 C2
Fourchu NS 25 H3
Fournier ONT 15 G1
Fowlers Corners ONT 15 A4
Fox Creek ALTA 7 D1
Fox Creek NB 23 G3
Fox Harbour NFLD 27 G4
Fox Harbour NS 25 C3
Fox Island Harbour NFLD 27 C3
Fox Island Main NS 25 F3-4
Fox Island River NFLD 27 A2
Fox Lake ALTA 6 E1
Fox Mine MAN 8 G3
Fox Point NS 24 F2
Fox River NS 24 E1
Fox Roost NFLD 27 A3
Fox Valley SASK 9 C3
Foxboro ONT 15 C4
Foxwarren MAN 9 G3
Foymount ONT 15 C2
Framboise NS 25 G3
Franchere ALTA 6 G4
Francis SASK 9 F3
François NFLD 27 D3
Francois Lake BC 5 E1
Frankford ONT 15 C4
Franklin MAN 11 A3
Franklin QUÉ 19 B4
Franklin Beach ONT 13 G4
Franktown ONT 15 E2
Frankville NS 25 F3
Frankville ONT 15 F3
Franquelin QUÉ 22 C1
Fraser Lake BC 5 E1

aser Mills NS **25 E3**
aserdale ONT **12 F1**
aserville NS **24 E1**
aserville ONT **15 B4**
aserwood MAN **11 B3**
ater ONT **12 D3**
axville NS **24 E2**
edericton NFLD **27 F1**
edericton NB **23 D4**
edericton PEI **25 C2**
edericton Junction NB **23 D4**
eeland PEI **25 B1**
eelton ONT **14 F2**
eeport NS **24 B3**
eetown PEI **25 B2**
elighsburg QUÉ **19 C4**
ench Cove NFLD **26 E2**
ench Cove NS **25 G3**
ench Lake NB **23 D4**
ench River NS **25 G1**
ench River NS **25 D3**
ench River PEI **25 B2**
enchman Butte SASK **9 C1**
enchman's Cove NFLD **27 B1**
enchman's Cove NFLD **27 E4**
eshford MAN **9 G1**
eshwater NFLD **27 G4**
oatburn ONT **15 G2**
obisher SASK **9 G4**
og Lake ALTA **7 G1**
ogmore ONT **14 E3**
ontenac QUÉ **19 G3-4**
ontier SASK **9 C4**
osty Hollow NB **23 H4**
oude SASK **9 F4**
uitland ONT **14 G2**
uitvale BC **7 D4**
ugèreville QUÉ **17 A1**
ulda SASK **9 E2**
ulford QUÉ **19 D4**
ulford Harbour BC **5 F4**
ullarton ONT **14 D2**
ulton ONT **14 G2**
urby's Cove NFLD **27 E3**
urnace Falls ONT **15 A3**
urness SASK **9 B1**

G

abarus NS **25 H3**
abarus Lake NS **25 H3**
abriola BC **5 F4**
ads Hill ONT **14 E2**
adsby ALTA **7 G2**
agetown NB **23 E4**
agnon QUÉ **3 E4**
agnon-Siding QUÉ **16 F3**
ainsborough SASK **9 G4**
airloch NS **24 H1**
alahad ALTA **7 G2**
alena Bay BC **7 D3**
aletta ONT **15 E1**
aleville NFLD **26 D4**
alix QUÉ **20 E2**
allants NFLD **27 B2**
allichan QUÉ **16 A2**
alloway BC **7 E4**
allows Cove NFLD **27 H3**
ambo NFLD **27 G2**
amebridge ONT **13 H3**
ameland ONT **11 D4**
ananoque ONT **15 E4**
ander NFLD **27 F1**
ander Bay NFLD **27 F1**
ang Ranch BC **5 G2**
arden Cove NFLD **27 G3**
arden Hill MAN **11 C1**
arden Hill ONT **15 A4**
arden of Eden NS **25 D3**
arden River ONT **12 D4**
arden Village ONT **12 H4**
ardenton MAN **11 C4**
ardiner Mines NS **25 H2**
Gardner Creek NB **24 C1**
Gargamelle NFLD **26 C2**
Garibaldi Highlands BC **5 F3-4**
Garland MAN **9 H2**
Garnet ONT **14 F3**
Garnish NFLD **27 E4**
Garrick SASK **9 E1**
Garson MAN **11 C3**
Garson ONT **12 G4**
Garson Lake SASK **8 C3**
Gaskiers NFLD **27 G4**
Gasline ONT **14 H3**
Gaspé QUÉ **22 H2**
Gaspereau NS **24 F2**
Gaspereau Forks NB **23 E3**
Gaspereaux PEI **25 D2**
Gatineau QUÉ **17 G4**
Gaultois NFLD **27 E3**
Gays River NS **24 G2**
Geary NB **23 D4**
Gelert ONT **15 A3**
Gem ALTA **7 G3**
Genelle BC **7 D4**
Genesee ALTA **7 E1**
Gentilly QUÉ **19 D2**
Georgefield NS **24 G1**
Georges Brook NFLD **27 G2**
Georges Lake NFLD **27 B2**
Georges River NS **25 G2**
Georgetown ONT **14 F1**
Georgetown PEI **25 D2**
Georgeville NS **25 E3**
Georgeville QUÉ **19 D4**
Georgina (see Keswick) ONT **13 G4**
Gerald SASK **9 G3**
Geraldton ONT **12 B1**
Geraldton East ONT **12 C1**
Germansen Landing BC **4 E3**
Gesgapegiag QUÉ **22 F3**
Gesto ONT **14 A4**
Ghost Lake ALTA **7 E3**
Giant Lake NS **25 E3**
Gibbons ALTA **7 F1**
Gibraltar NS **24 G2**
Gibsons BC **5 F4**
Gift Lake ALTA **6 E3**
Gilbert Cove NS **24 C3**
Gilbert Plains MAN **9 H3**
Gilchrist Bay ONT **15 B3**
Gilford ONT **13 G4**
Gillam MAN **10 C3**
Gillams NFLD **27 B1**
Gillespie Settlement NB **23 C2**
Gillies Bay BC **5 E4**
Gilmour ONT **15 C3**
Gimli MAN **11 B3**
Gin Cove NFLD **27 G2**
Girardville QUÉ **18 D1**
Girouxville ALTA **6 D3**
Girvin SASK **9 E3**
Gitwinksihlkw BC **4 C3**
Gjoa Haven NWT **2 G2**
Glace Bay NS **25 H2**
Glacier BC **7 D3**
Glade BC **7 D4**
Gladmar SASK **9 E4**
Gladstone MAN **11 A3**
Glammis ONT **13 D4**
Glanworth ONT **14 D3**
Glaslyn SASK **9 C1**
Glasnevin SASK **9 E4**
Glassville NB **23 C3**
Gleichen ALTA **7 F3**
Glen Alda ONT **15 B3**
Glen Allen ONT **14 E1**
Glen Alpine NS **25 E3**
Glen Becker ONT **15 G2**
Glen Cairn ONT **15 F2**
Glen Ewen SASK **9 G4**
Glen Haven NS **24 F2**
Glen Huron ONT **13 F4**
Glen Livet NB **22 E3**
Glen Margaret NS **24 F2**
Glen Meyer ONT **14 E3**
Glen Miller ONT **15 C4**
Glen Morris ONT **14 F2**
Glen Nevis ONT **15 H2**
Glen Orchard ONT **13 G2**
Glen Road NS **25 E3**
Glen Robertson ONT **15 H2**
Glen Sutton QUÉ **19 D4**
Glen Tay ONT **15 E2-3**
Glen Walter ONT **15 H2**
Glen Williams ONT **14 F1**
Glenarm ONT **13 H3**
Glenavon SASK **9 F3**
Glenbain SASK **9 D4**
Glenboro MAN **11 A4**
Glenburnie NFLD **27 B1**
Glenburnie ONT **15 E4**
Glenbush SASK **9 C1**
Glencairn ONT **13 F4**
Glencoe NB **22 E3**
Glencoe NS **25 E3**
Glencoe ONT **14 C3**
Glencoe Mills NS **25 F2**
Glencoe Station NS **25 F2**
Glendale NS **25 F3**
Glendale Cove BC **5 E3**
Glendon ALTA **6 G4**
Glendyer NS **25 F2**
Glenelg NS **25 E4**
Glenella MAN **11 A3**
Glenevis ALTA **7 E1**
Glengarry NS **24 H1**
Glenholme NS **24 G1**
Glenmont NS **24 E1**
Glenora BC **4 B2**
Glenora MAN **11 A4**
Glenora ONT **15 D4**
Glenside SASK **9 D3**
Glentworth SASK **9 D4**
Glenview NFLD **27 G3**
Glenwood ALTA **7 F4**
Glenwood NB **23 E4**
Glenwood NFLD **27 F1**
Glenwood PEI **25 A1**
Glidden SASK **9 C3**
Gloucester ONT **15 F1**
Glovertown NFLD **27 G2**
Gobles ONT **14 E2**
Goblin NFLD **27 D3**
Godbout QUÉ **22 D1**
Goderich ONT **14 C1**
Godfrey ONT **15 D3**
Gods Lake MAN **0 C4**
Gods Lake Narrows MAN **10 C4**
Gods River MAN **10 C4**
Goffs NS **24 G2**
Gogama ONT **12 F3**
Gold Bridge BC **5 F3**
Gold Centre ONT **12 F2**
Gold River BC **5 D3**
Gold River NS **24 F2**
Goldboro NS **25 F4**
Golden BC **7 D3**
Golden Lake ONT **15 C1**
Golden Prairie SASK **9 B3**
Golden Valley ONT **13 G1**
Goldenville NS **25 E4**
Gondola Point NB **24 C1**
Goobies NFLD **27 G3**
Good Hope BC **5 D2**
Good Hope Lake BC **4 C1**
Gooderham ONT **15 B3**
Goodeve SASK **9 F3**
Goodfare ALTA **6 C3**
Goodfish Lake ALTA **6 G4**
Goodlands MAN **9 H4**
Goodlow BC **4 G3**
Goodridge ALTA **6 G3**
Goodsoil SASK **8 C4**
Goodwater SASK **9 F4**
Goodwood ONT **14 H1**
Goose Cove NFLD **27 H2**
Goose Cove NFLD **26 E1**
Gooseberry Cove NFLD **27 G3**
Gooseberry Cove NFLD **27 G4**
Gordon Bay ONT **13 G2**
Gordondale ALTA **6 C2**
Gore NS **24 G1-2**
Gore Bay ONT **13 B1**
Gores Landing ONT **15 B4**
Gorlitz SASK **9 F2**
Gormanville NS **24 F1**
Gormley ONT **14 G1**
Gorrie ONT **14 D1**
Goshen NB **23 G4**
Goshen NS **25 E4**
Goudreau ONT **12 D3**
Goulais River ONT **12 D4**
Gould QUÉ **19 F3**
Goulds NFLD **27 H3**
Gouldtown SASK **9 D3**
Govan SASK **9 E3**
Government Landing ONT **11 E4**
Gowanstown ONT **14 E1**
Gowganda ONT **12 G3**
Gracefield QUÉ **17 F3**
Grafton NB **23 C3**
Grafton NS **24 E2**
Grafton ONT **15 B4**
Graham ONT **11 F3**
Graham Corner NB **23 C4**
Grahamdale MAN **11 B2**
Granby QUÉ **19 D4**
Grand Anse NS **25 F3**
Grand Bank NFLD **27 E4**
Grand Bay NB **24 C1**
Grand Bay NFLD **27 A3**
Grand Bay East NFLD **27 A3**
Grand Beach MAN **11 C3**
Grand Beach NFLD **27 E4**
Grand Bend ONT **14 C2**
Grand Bruit NFLD **27 B3**
Grand Centre ALTA **6 G3**
Grand Coulee SASK **9 E3**
Grand Etang NS **25 F1**
Grand Falls NB **23 C2**
Grand Falls-Windsor NFLD **27 E1**
Grand Forks BC **7 D4**
Grand Greve NS **25 G3**
Grand Harbour NB **24 B2**
Grand Jardin NFLD **27 A2**
Grand Lake NS **24 G2**
Grand Le Pierre NFLD **27 F3**
Grand Marais MAN **11 C3**
Grand Pointe ONT **14 B4**
Grand Pré NS **24 F2**
Grand Rapids MAN **11 A1**
Grand River NS **25 G3**
Grand Valley ONT **14 F1**
Grand-Digue NB **23 G3**
Grand-Fonds QUÉ **18 H4**
Grand-Lac-Victoria QUÉ **16 D4**
Grand-Mère QUÉ **19 D2**
Grand-Métis QUÉ **22 C2**
Grand-Remous QUÉ **17 F2**
Grand-Sault NB **23 C2**
Grand-St-Esprit QUÉ **19 D2**
Grande Cache ALTA **7 C1**
Grande Clairiere MAN **9 H4**
Grande Pointe MAN **11 B4**
Grande Prairie ALTA **6 C3**
Grande-Aldouane NB **23 G2**
Grande-Anse NB **22 G4**
Grande-Anse QUÉ **19 C1**
Grande-Cascapédia QUÉ **22 F3**
Grande-Entrée QUÉ **21 G2**
Grande-Île QUÉ **19 A4**
Grande-Rivière QUÉ **22 H3**
Grande-Vallée QUÉ **22 G1**
Grandes-Bergeronnes QUÉ **18 H3**
Grandes-Piles QUÉ **19 D2**
Grandmother's Bay SASK **8 E4**
Grandois NFLD **26 E1-2**
Grandora SASK **9 D2**
Grandview MAN **9 G3**
Granges BC **5 F4**
Granisle BC **4 D4**
Granite Bay BC **5 E3**
Graniteville QUÉ **19 D4**
Granton NS **24 H1**
Granton ONT **14 D2**
Grantville NS **25 F3**
Granum ALTA **7 F4**
Granville Centre NS **24 D2**
Granville Ferry NS **24 D2**
Grasmere BC **7 F4**
Grassie ONT **14 G2**
Grassland ALTA **6 F3**
Grassy Lake ALTA **7 G3**
Grassy Narrows ONT **11 D3**
Grassy Plains BC **5 E1**
Grates Cove NFLD **27 H2**
Gravel Hill ONT **15 G2**
Gravelbourg SASK **9 D4**
Gravenhurst ONT **13 G2**
Gray SASK **9 E3**
Gray Creek BC **7 D4**
Grayson SASK **9 F3**
Graysville MAN **11 B4**
Great Barasway NFLD **27 G4**
Great Codroy NFLD **27 A3**
Great Falls MAN **11 C3**
Great Paradise NFLD **27 F3**
Great Village NS **24 G1**
Greece's Point QUÉ **19 A3**
Greely ONT **15 F2**
Green Acres SASK **9 E1**
Green Bay NS **24 E3**
Green Court ALTA **7 E1**
Green Island Brook NFLD **26 D1**
Green Island Cove NFLD **26 D1**
Green Lake SASK **9 D1**
Green Lane ONT **15 H1**
Green Oaks NS **24 G1**
Green Point NFLD **26 B3**
Green River ONT **14 H1**
Green Road NB **23 B3**
Green Valley ONT **15 H2**
Greenbank ONT **13 H4**
Greenbush ONT **15 F3**
Greenfield NS **24 F2**
Greenfield NS **24 E3**
Greenfield ONT **15 H2**
Greenhurst-Thurstonia ONT **15 A3**
Greenock ONT **14 D1**
Greens Corner ONT **14 F3**
Green's Harbour NFLD **27 H3**
Greenspond NFLD **27 G1**
Greenstreet SASK **9 B1**
Greensville ONT **14 F2**
Greenville BC **4 C3**
Greenwich PEI **25 D2**
Greenwood BC **7 C4**
Greenwood NS **24 E2**
Greenwood ONT **14 H1**
Grégoires Mill ONT **12 F2**
Grenfell SASK **9 F3**
Grenville QUÉ **19 A3**
Gretna MAN **11 B4**
Grey River NFLD **27 C3**
Greywood NS **24 D2**
Griffin SASK **9 F4**
Griffith ONT **15 D2**
Grimsby ONT **14 G2**
Grimshaw ALTA **6 D2**
Grindrod BC **7 C3**
Griquet NFLD **26 E1**
Griswold MAN **9 H4**
Grole NFLD **27 D3**
Grondines QUÉ **19 E2**
Gronlid SASK **9 E1**
Gros Cap ONT **12 D4**
Gros-Morne QUÉ **22 G1**
Grosse Isle MAN **11 B3**
Grosse-Île QUÉ **21 G2**
Grosses Coques NS **24 C3**
Grosses-Roches QUÉ **22 D2**
Grouard Mission ALTA **6 D3**
Groundbirch BC **4 G3**
Grovedale ALTA **6 C3**
Gruenthal SASK **9 D2**
Grunthal MAN **11 C4**
Guelph ONT **14 F2**
Guénette QUÉ **17 G2**
Guérin QUÉ **16 A4**
Guernsey SASK **9 E2**
Guilds ONT **14 C4**
Gulch Riverhead NFLD **27 H4**
Gulf Shore NS **25 B3**
Gull Bay ONT **12 A1**
Gull Harbour MAN **11 C3**
Gull Island NFLD **27 H3**
Gull Lake ALTA **7 F2**
Gull Lake SASK **9 C3**
Gullivers Cove NS **24 C2**
Gunn ALTA **7 E1**
Gunners Cove NFLD **26 E1**
Gunning Cove NS **24 D4**
Gunton MAN **11 B3**
Gurneyville ALTA **6 G4**
Guthrie ONT **13 G3**
Guy ALTA **6 D3**
Guyenne QUÉ **16 B2**
Guysborough NS **25 F3**
Gwynne ALTA **7 F1**
Gypsumville MAN **11 A2**

H

Habay ALTA **6 C1**
Hacketts Cove NS **24 F2**
Hadashville MAN **11 C4**
Hafford SASK **9 D2**
Hagar ONT **12 G4**
Hagen SASK **9 E1**
Hagensborg BC **5 D2**
Hagersville ONT **14 F3**
Hague SASK **9 D2**
Haig BC **5 G4**
Haileybury ONT **12 H3**
Haines Junction YK **2 A2**
Hainsfield NS **24 C3**
Hairy Hill ALTA **7 G1**
Halbrite SASK **9 F4**
Halcrow MAN **9 G1**
Haldimand QUÉ **21 A4**
Haldimand (see Cayuga) ONT **14 G3**
Haley Station ONT **15 D1**
Halfmoon Bay BC **5 F4**
Halfway Cove NS **25 F4**
Halfway Point NFLD **27 B1**
Halfway River NS **24 F1**
Haliburton ONT **15 A2**
Halifax NS **24 G2**
Halkirk ALTA **7 G2**
Hall Glen ONT **15 B3**
Hallboro MAN **11 A3**
Hallebourg ONT **12 E1**
Halls Harbour NS **24 E1**
Halls Lake ONT **13 H2**
Hallville ONT **15 F2**
Halton Hills (see Georgetown) ONT **14 F1**
Hamer Bay ONT **13 G2**
Hamilton ONT **14 F-G2**
Hamilton PEI **25 B2**
Hamiota MAN **9 H3**
Hamlin ALTA **7 G1**
Hammond ONT **15 G1**
Hammonds Plains NS **24 F2**
Hammondvale NB **23 F4**
Ham-Nord QUÉ **19 E3**
Hampden NFLD **27 D1**
Hampstead NB **23 E4**
Hampton NB **23 E4**
Hampton NS **24 D2**
Hampton PEI **25 C2**
Ham-Sud QUÉ **19 E3**
Hamton SASK **9 G2**
Hamtown Corner NB **23 D3**
Hanceville BC **5 F2**
Handel SASK **9 C2**
Handsworth SASK **9 F4**
Hanford Brook NB **24 D1**
Hanley SASK **9 D2**
Hanmer ONT **12 G4**
Hanna ALTA **7 G2**
Hanover ONT **13 D4**
Hansford NS **25 B3**
Hant's Harbour NFLD **27 H3**
Hantsport NS **24 F2**
Hanwell NB **23 D4**
Happy Adventure NFLD **27 G2**
Happy Valley–Goose Bay NFLD **3 F3**
Harbour Breton NFLD **27 E3**
Harbour Buffett NFLD **27 G3**
Harbour Deep NFLD **26 D2**
Harbour Grace NFLD **27 H3**
Harbour Le Cou NFLD **27 A3**
Harbour Main NFLD **27 H3**
Harbour Mille NFLD **27 F3**
Harbour Round NFLD **26 E3**
Harbourville NS **24 E1**
Harcourt NB **23 F3**
Harcourt NFLD **27 G2**
Harcourt ONT **15 B2**
Harding MAN **9 H3**
Hardings Point NB **24 C1**
Hardisty ALTA **7 G1**
Hardwicke NB **23 G2**
Hardwood Lake ONT **15 C2**
Hardwood Lands NS **24 G2**
Hardwood Ridge NB **23 E3**
Hardy SASK **9 E4**
Hare Bay NFLD **27 D3**
Hare Bay NFLD **27 G1**
Hare Bay NFLD **26 G3**
Hargrave MAN **9 G3**
Harley ONT **14 E2**
Harlowe ONT **15 D3**
Harmony NS **24 G1**
Harmony Mills NS **24 D3**
Harpellville NS **25 E4**
Harricott NFLD **27 H4**
Harrietsfield NS **24 G2**
Harrietsville ONT **14 D3**
Harrigan Cove NS **25 E4**
Harrington NS **24 C3**
Harrington ONT **14 D-E2**
Harrington QUÉ **19 A3**
Harrington Harbour QUÉ **21 H1**
Harris SASK **9 D2**
Harrisburg ONT **14 F2**
Harrison Hot Springs BC **5 G4**
Harrison Mills BC **5 G4**
Harrison Settlement NS **24 E1**
Harrisons Corners ONT **15 G2**
Harriston ONT **14 E1**
Harrogate BC **7 D3**
Harrop BC **7 D4**
Harrow ONT **14 A4**
Harrowby MAN **9 G3**
Harrowsmith ONT **15 E3**
Harry's Harbour NFLD **26 E3**
Hartington ONT **15 D-E3**
Hartland NB **23 C3**
Hartley Bay BC **5 C1**
Hartney MAN **11 A4**
Harty ONT **12 E2**
Harvey NB **23 D4**
Harvey NB **23 G4**
Harvie Heights ALTA **7 E3**
Harwill MAN **11 B3**
Harwood ONT **15 B4**
Haskett MAN **11 B4**
Hassett NS **24 C3**
Hastings ONT **15 B4**
Hatchet Cove NFLD **27 G3**
Hatfield Point NB **23 E4**
Hatley QUÉ **19 E4**
Haut-Bouctouche NB **23 G3**
Haut-Pokemouche NB **22 H4**
Havelock NB **23 F3**
Havelock NS **24 C3**
Havelock ONT **15 B3**
Havelock QUÉ **19 B4**
Havre Boucher NS **25 F3**
Havre-Aubert QUÉ **21 G3**
Havre-aux-Maisons QUÉ **21 G3**
Havre-St-Pierre QUÉ **21 B1**
Hawarden SASK **9 D3**
Hawk Junction ONT **12 D3**
Hawke's Bay NFLD **26 C2**
Hawkesbury ONT **15 H1**
Hawkestone ONT **13 G3**
Hawkesville ONT **14 E2**
Hawkins Corner ONT **13 G3**
Hawkshaw NB **23 C3**
Hay Camp ALTA **8 B1**
Hay Cove NS **25 G3**
Hay Lakes ALTA **7 F1**
Hay River NWT **2 D3**
Hays ALTA **7 G3**
Haysville ONT **14 E2**
Hayter ALTA **7 H2**
Haywood MAN **11 B4**
Hazel MAN **11 C3**
Hazel Dell SASK **9 F2**
Hazel Hill NS **25 F4**
Hazeldean NB **23 C2**
Hazeldean ONT **15 F2**
Hazelglen MAN **11 C3**
Hazelridge MAN **11 C3**
Hazelton BC **4 D3**
Hazenmore SASK **9 D4**
Hazlet SASK **9 C3**
Head of Amherst NS **25 B3**
Head of Bay d'Espoir NFLD **27 E3**
Head of Chezzetcook NS **24 G2**
Head of Loch Lomond NS **25 G3**
Head of Millstream NB **23 F4**
Head of St Margarets Bay NS **24 F2**
Heaman MAN **8 G3**
Hearne SASK **9 E3**
Hearst ONT **12 E1**
Heart's Content NFLD **27 H3**
Heart's Delight NFLD **27 H3**
Heart's Desire NFLD **27 H3**
Heath ALTA **7 G1**
Heath Steele NB **23 E1**
Heathcote ONT **13 E3**
Heatherton NFLD **27 A2**
Heatherton NS **25 E3**
Hebbs Cross NS **24 E3**
Hebbville NS **24 E3**
Hébert NB **23 G3**
Hébertville QUÉ **18 E3**
Hébertville-Station QUÉ **18 E2**
Hebron NFLD **3 E2**
Hebron NS **24 C4**
Hecate BC **5 D3**
Heckston ONT **15 F2**
Hecla MAN **11 C3**
Hectanooga NS **24 C3**
Hedley BC **7 C4**
Heffley Creek BC **5 H3**
Heidelberg ONT **14 E2**
Heinsburg ALTA **7 G1**
Heisler ALTA **7 G2**
Hemford NS **24 E3**
Heming Lake MAN **8 G4**
Hemmingford QUÉ **19 B4**
Hendon SASK **9 F2**
Hendrix Lake BC **5 G2**
Henribourg SASK **9 E1**
Henryville QUÉ **19 C4**
Hensall ONT **14 D2**
Hepburn SASK **9 D2**
Hepworth ONT **13 D3**
Herb Lake MAN **8 H4**
Herb Lake Landing MAN **8 H4**
Herbert SASK **9 D3**
Herchmer MAN **10 C2**
Herdman QUÉ **19 A4**
Heriot Bay BC **5 E3**
Hermanville PEI **25 D2**
Hermitage-Sandyville NFLD **27 E3**
Heron Bay ONT **12 C2**
Hérouxville QUÉ **19 D2**
Herring Cove NS **24 G2**
Herring Neck NFLD **26 F4**
Herriot MAN **8 G3**
Herschel SASK **9 C2**
Hervey-Jonction QUÉ **19 D1**
Heward SASK **9 F4**
Heyden ONT **12 D4**
Hibbard QUÉ **18 B3**
Hibbs Cove NFLD **27 H3**
Hibernia NS **24 E3**
Hickman's Harbour NFLD **27 G2**
Hickory Corner ONT **14 C3**
Hickson ONT **14 E2**
Higginsville NS **24 H2**
High Bank PEI **25 D3**
High Beach NFLD **27 E4**
High Bluff MAN **11 B3**
High Level ALTA **6 D1**
High Prairie ALTA **6 D3**
High River ALTA **7 F3**
Highgate ONT **14 C3**
Highland Grove ONT **15 B2**
Highlands NFLD **27 A2**
Highrock MAN **8 G3**
Highwater QUÉ **19 D4**
Hilbre MAN **11 A2**
Hilda ALTA **7 H3**
Hilden NS **24 G1**
Hillcrest Mines ALTA **7 F4**
Hillers BC **5 E4**
Hillgrove NS **24 C2**
Hilliard ALTA **7 F1**
Hilliardton ONT **12 H3**
Hillier ONT **15 C4**
Hillmond SASK **9 C1**
Hillsborough NB **23 G4**
Hillsburgh ONT **14 F1**
Hillsburn NS **24 D2**
Hillsdale NB **23 F4**
Hillsdale ONT **13 G3**
Hillside NB **23 G4**
Hillsport ONT **12 C2**
Hillspring ALTA **7 F4**
Hillsvale NS **24 F2**
Hillview NFLD **27 G3**
Hilton ONT **15 C4**
Hilton Beach ONT **12 E4**
Hines Creek ALTA **6 C2**
Hinton ALTA **7 D1**
Hitchcock SASK **9 F4**
Hixon BC **5 F1**
Hnausa MAN **11 B3**
Hoadley ALTA **7 E2**
Hoards ONT **15 C4**
Hobbema ALTA **7 F2**
Hochfeld MAN **11 B4**
Hockley ONT **14 F1**
Hodgeville SASK **9 D3**
Hodgson MAN **11 B3**
Hodson NS **25 C3**
Hoey SASK **9 E2**
Holbein SASK **9 D1**
Holberg BC **5 C3**
Holbrook ONT **14 E3**
Holden ALTA **7 F1**
Holdfast SASK **9 E3**
Holland MAN **11 A4**
Holland Centre ONT **13 E3**
Holland Landing ONT **14 G1**
Hollow Water MAN **11 C3**
Holly ONT **13 G4**
Holman NWT **2 E1**
Holmesville NB **23 C2**
Holmesville ONT **14 C1**
Holmfield MAN **11 A4**
Holstein ONT **14 E1**
Holt ONT **14 G1**
Holtville NB **23 D3**
Holtyre ONT **12 G2**
Holyrood NFLD **27 H3**
Holyrood ONT **14 D1**
Homeville NS **25 H2**
Homewood MAN **11 B4**
Hondo ALTA **6 E3**
Hone MAN **8 G3**
Honey Harbour ONT **13 G3**
Honeydale NB **24 A1**
Honeymoon Bay BC **5 F4**
Honeywell Corners ONT **15 C4**
Honeywood ONT **13 F4**
Honfleur QUÉ **19 F2**
Hooping Harbour NFLD **26 D2**
Hoosier SASK **9 B2**
Hope BC **5 G4**
Hope Bay ONT **13 D2**
Hope Town QUÉ **22 G3**
Hopeall NFLD **27 H3**
Hopedale NFLD **3 F2**
Hopetown ONT **15 E2**
Hopewell NS **24 H1**
Hopewell Cape NB **23 G4**
Hornby ONT **14 G2**
Hornby Island BC **5 E4**
Horndean MAN **11 B4**
Horne Settlement NS **24 G2**
Hornepayne ONT **12 D2**
Hornes Road NS **25 H2**
Horning's Mills ONT **13 F4**
Horsefly BC **5 G2**
Horseshoe Bay ALTA **7 G1**
Horseshoe Bay BC **5 F4**
Horseshoe Lake ONT **13 F2**
Horseshoe Valley ONT **13 G3**
Horwood NFLD **27 F1**
Hoselaw ALTA **6 G4**
Hotchkiss ALTA **6 D2**
Houston BC **4 D4**
Howard NB **23 F2**
Howdenvale ONT **13 D3**
Howick QUÉ **19 B4**
Howie Centre NS **25 H2**
Howley NFLD **27 C1**
Howser BC **7 D3**
Hoyle ONT **12 G2**
Hoyt NB **23 D4**
Huallen ALTA **6 C3**
Hubbard SASK **9 F3**
Hubbards NS **24 F2**
Huberdeau QUÉ **19 A3**
Hubley NS **24 F2**
Hudson ONT **11 E3**
Hudson QUÉ **19 A4**
Hudson Bay SASK **9 F2**
Hudson's Hope BC **4 F3**
Hughenden ALTA **7 G2**
Hughes Brook NFLD **27 B1**
Hughton SASK **9 C3**
Hull QUÉ **17 G4**
Humber Village NFLD **27 B1**
Humboldt SASK **9 E2**
Humphrey ONT **13 G2**
Hunta ONT **12 F2**
Hunter River PEI **25 C2**
Hunters Mountain NS **25 G2**
Hunterstown QUÉ **19 C2**
Huntingdon BC **5 G4**
Huntingdon QUÉ **19 A4**
Huntingford ONT **14 E2**
Huntingville QUÉ **19 E4**
Hunts Point NS **24 E4**
Huntsville ONT **13 H2**
Hurkett ONT **12 A2**
Huron Park ONT **14 D2**
Hussar ALTA **7 G3**
Huttonville ONT **14 G1**
Huxley ALTA **7 F2**
Hyas SASK **9 G2**
Hyde Park ONT **14 D3**
Hylo ALTA **6 F3**
Hymers ONT **11 G4**
Hyndford ONT **15 D1**
Hythe ALTA **6 C3**

I

Iberville QUÉ **19 C4**
Ida ONT **15 A4**
Iddesleigh ALTA **7 G3**
Igloolik NWT **2 H2**
Ignace ONT **11 F3**
Ilderton ONT **14 D2**
Île des Chênes MAN **11 C4**
Île-Dupas QUÉ **19 C3**
Île-à-la-Crosse SASK **8 D4**
Ilford MAN **10 C3**
Imperial SASK **9 E3**
Imperial Mills ALTA **6 G3**
Indian Bay NFLD **27 G1**
Indian Brook NS **25 G2**
Indian Gardens NS **24 E3**
Indian Harbour NFLD **27 B3**
Indian Harbour NS **24 F3**
Indian Harbour Lake NS **25 E4**
Indian Head SASK **9 F3**
Indian Island NB **23 G2**
Indian Point NS **24 F3**
Ingersoll ONT **14 E2**
Ingleside ONT **15 G2**
Inglewood ONT **14 F1**
Inglis MAN **9 G3**
Inglisville NS **24 D2**
Ingoldsby ONT **15 A2**
Ingolf ONT **11 D3**
Ingomar NS **24 D4**
Ingonish NS **25 G1**
Ingonish Beach NS **25 G1**
Ingonish Ferry NS **25 G1**
Ingramport NS **24 F2**
Inkerman NB **22 H4**
Inkerman ONT **15 G2**
Innerkip ONT **14 E2**
Innisfail ALTA **7 F2**
Innisfil (see Stroud) ONT **13 G4**
Innismara NFLD **27 B1**
Innisville ONT **15 E2**
Insinger SASK **9 F2**
Inukjuak QUÉ **3 C3**
Inuvik NWT **2 C1**
Inverary ONT **15 E3**
Inverhuron ONT **13 C4**
Invermay SASK **9 F2**
Invermere BC **7 E3**
Inverness NS **25 F2**
Inverness PEI **25 B1**
Inverness QUÉ **19 E2**
Inwood MAN **11 B3**
Inwood ONT **14 C3**
Iona NS **25 G2**
Iona ONT **14 D3**
Iona PEI **25 D2**
Iona Station ONT **14 D3**
Ipperwash Beach ONT **14 C2**
Iqaluit NWT **3 D1**
Ireland NS **25 E3**
Irish Cove NS **25 G3**
Irish Lake ONT **13 E4**
Irishtown NB **23 G3**
Irishtown NFLD **27 B1**
Irma ALTA **7 G1**
Iron Bridge ONT **12 E4**
Iron Hill QUÉ **19 D4**
Iron River ALTA **6 G3**
Iron Springs ALTA **7 G3**
Irondale ONT **15 A3**
Iroquois ONT **15 G3**
Iroquois Falls ONT **12 G2**
Irricana ALTA **7 F3**
Irvine ALTA **7 H3**
Irvines Landing BC **5 F4**
Isaac's Harbour NS **25 E4**
Isaac's Harbour North NS **25 E4**
Isabella MAN **9 G3**
Iskut BC **4 C2**
Island Brook QUÉ **19 F4**
Island Cove NFLD **27 G3**
Island Cove NFLD **27 H4**
Island Grove ONT **13 G4**
Island Harbour NFLD **26 G4**
Island Lake ALTA **6 F3**
Island Lake MAN **11 C1**
Islay ALTA **7 G1**
Isle aux Morts NFLD **27 A3**
Isle Pierre BC **5 F1**
Isle Valen NFLD **27 F3**
Islington NFLD **27 H3**
Issoudun QUÉ **19 E2**
Italy Cross NS **24 E3**
Ituna SASK **9 F3**
Ivanhoe ONT **15 C3**
Ivry-sur-le-Lac QUÉ **19 A3**
Ivujivik QUÉ **3 B2**
Ivy Lea ONT **15 F3**

J

Jackfish Lake SASK **9 C1**
Jackhead MAN **11 B2**
Jackson NS **24 F1**
Jackson ONT **13 D3**
Jackson's Arm NFLD **26 D3**
Jackson's Cove NFLD **26 E3**
Jacksons Point ONT **13 G4**
Jacksonville NB **23 C3**
Jacques Fontaine NFLD **27 F3**
Jacquet River NB **22 F3**
Jade City BC **4 C1**
Jaffray BC **7 E4**
Jaffray Melick ONT **11 D3**
James River NS **25 E3**
James River Bridge ALTA **7 E2**
Jameson SASK **9 E3**
Jamestown NFLD **27 G2**
Jan Lake SASK **8 F4**
Janetville ONT **13 H4**
Janeville NB **22 G4**
Jans Bay SASK **8 C4**
Jansen SASK **9 E2**
Jaratt ONT **13 G3**
Jarvie ALTA **6 F3**

Notre-Dame-de-Pontmain QUÉ 17 G3
Notre-Dame-de-Stanbridge QUÉ 19 C4
Notre-Dame-des-Anges QUÉ 19 D1
Notre-Dame-des-Bois QUÉ 19 F4
Notre-Dame-des-Champs ONT 15 F1
Notre-Dame-des-Érables NB 22 G4
Notre-Dame-des-Monts QUÉ 18 G4
Notre-Dame-des-Pins QUÉ 19 G2
Notre-Dame-des-Prairies QUÉ 19 B3
Notre-Dame-des-Sept-Douleurs QUÉ 22 A3
Notre-Dame-du-Bon-Conseil QUÉ 19 D3
Notre-Dame-du-Lac QUÉ 22 B4
Notre-Dame-du-Laus QUÉ 17 G3
Notre-Dame-du-Mont-Carmel QUÉ 19 D2
Notre-Dame-du-Mont-Carmel QUÉ 19 C4
Notre-Dame-du-Nord QUÉ 17 A1
Notre-Dame-du-Portage QUÉ 18 H4
Notre-Dame-du-Rosaire QUÉ 19 G1
Nottawa ONT 13 F3
Nottawaga Beach ONT 13 F3
Nouvelle QUÉ 22 F3
Novar ONT 13 G1
Novra MAN 9 G2
Noyan QUÉ 19 C4
Numogate ONT 15 F2
Nut Mountain SASK 9 F2
Nuttby NS 24 G1
Nyanza NS 25 G2

O

Oak Bay BC 5 F4
Oak Bay NB 24 A1
Oak Bay QUÉ 22 E3
Oak Hill NB 24 A1
Oak Lake MAN 9 H4
Oak Orchard ONT 15 A3
Oak Park NS 24 C4
Oak Point MAN 11 B3
Oak Point NB 23 E4
Oak Ridges ONT 14 G1
Oak River MAN 11 A3
Oakbank MAN 11 C3
Oakburn MAN 9 H3
Oakdale ONT 14 C3
Oakland MAN 11 B3
Oakland ONT 14 F3
Oakville MAN 11 B3
Oakville ONT 14 G2
Oakwood ONT 13 H4
Oba ONT 12 D2
Obaska QUÉ 16 D3
O'Briens Landing ONT 11 F3
Ocean Falls BC 5 D2
Ochre River MAN 11 A3
Odanak QUÉ 19 C3
Odell NB 23 C2
Odessa ONT 15 D4
Odessa SASK 9 F3
O'Donnells NFLD 27 H4
Ogden NS 25 F4
Ogden (see Tomifobia) QUÉ 19 E4
Ogema SASK 9 E4
Ogilvie MAN 11 A3
Ogoki ONT 11 H1
Ohaton ALTA 7 F1
Ohio NS 25 E3
Ohio NS 24 D4
Ohsweken ONT 14 F2
Oil City ONT 14 B3
Oil Springs ONT 14 B3
Oka QUÉ 19 A4
Okanagan Centre BC 7 C4
Okanagan Falls BC 7 C4
Okla SASK 9 F2
Okotoks ALTA 7 F3
Olalla BC 7 C4
Old Barns NS 24 G1
Old Bonaventure NFLD 27 H2
Old Crow YK 2 B1
Old Harry QUÉ 21 G2
Old Perlican NFLD 27 H2
Old Shop NFLD 27 G3
Oldcastle ONT 14 A4
Olds ALTA 7 F2
O'Leary PEI 25 A1
Olha MAN 9 H3
Oliphant ONT 13 D3
Oliver BC 7 C4
Oliver NS 24 G1
Oliver ONT 14 A4
Omemee ONT 15 A4
Omerville QUÉ 19 E4
Ompah ONT 15 D2
Onanole MAN 11 A3
Onaping ONT 12 F4
Onaping Falls (see Dowling) ONT 12 F4
Onefour ALTA 7 H4
100 Mile House BC 5 G2
108 Mile House BC 5 G2
150 Mile House BC 5 G2
Onion Lake SASK 9 B1
Onondaga ONT 14 F2
Onoway ALTA 7 E1
Onslow NS 24 G1
Onslow Corners QUÉ 17 F4
Oona River BC 5 B1
Ootsa Lake BC 5 E1
Opal ALTA 7 F1
Opasatika ONT 12 E1-2
Open Hall NFLD 27 H2
Ophir ONT 12 E4
Optic Lake MAN 8 G4
Orangedale NS 25 F3
Orangeville ONT 14 F1
Orcadia SASK 9 F3
Orchre Pit Cove NFLD 27 H3
O'Regan's NFLD 27 A3
Orillia ONT 13 G3
Orion ALTA 7 H4
Orkney SASK 9 C4
Orleans ONT 15 F1
Ormiston SASK 9 E4
Ormsby ONT 15 C3
Ormstown QUÉ 19 B4
Oro Station ONT 13 G3
Orok MAN 9 G1
Oromocto NB 23 D4
Orono ONT 15 A4
Orr Lake ONT 13 G3
Orrville ONT 13 G2
Orton ONT 14 F1
Ortonville NB 23 C2
Orwell ONT 14 D3
Orwell PEI 25 C-D2
Osage SASK 9 F4
Osborne MAN 11 B4
Osborne Corners ONT 14 F2
Osceola ONT 15 D1
Osgoode ONT 15 F2
Oshawa ONT 14 H1
Oskélanéo QUÉ 16 G3
Osler SASK 9 D2
Osnabruck Centre ONT 15 G2
Osoyoos BC 7 C4
Ospringe ONT 14 F1
Ossossane Beach ONT 13 F3
Ostenfeld MAN 11 C3
Osterwick MAN 11 B4
Ostrander ONT 14 E3
Ostrea Lake NS 24 H2
Ostryhon Corners ONT 14 G3
Ottawa ONT 15 F1-2
Otter Bay BC 5 F4
Otter Brook NS 24 H1
Otter Lake ONT 13 F2
Otter Lake QUÉ 17 E4
Otter Point NFLD 27 B3
Otterburne MAN 11 C4
Otterville ONT 14 E3
Otthon SASK 9 F3
Ouellette ONT 12 G4
Oungre SASK 9 F4
Outer Cove NFLD 27 H3
Outlet ONT 15 F3
Outlook SASK 9 D2
Outram SASK 9 F4
Overflowing River MAN 9 G1
Overton NS 24 C4
Owen Sound ONT 13 E3
Oxbow SASK 9 G4
Oxdrift ONT 11 E3
Oxford NS 25 B3
Oxford Centre ONT 14 E2
Oxford House MAN 10 C4
Oxford Junction NS 24 F1
Oxford Mills ONT 15 F2
Oxley ONT 14 A4
Oxtongue Lake ONT 13 H2
Oyama BC 7 C4
Oyen ALTA 7 H2
Oyster Bed Bridge PEI 25 C2

P

Pabos QUÉ 22 H3
Pabos Mills QUÉ 22 H3
Packington QUÉ 22 B4
Pacquet NFLD 26 E3
Paddle Prairie ALTA 6 D1
Paddockwood SASK 9 E1
Padoue QUÉ 22 C2
Pagwa River ONT 12 D1
Pain Court ONT 14 B4
Paisley ONT 13 D4
Pakenham ONT 15 E2
Pakuashipi QUÉ 26 B1
Palermo ONT 14 G2
Palgrave ONT 14 G1
Palmarolle QUÉ 16 A2
Palmer SASK 9 D4
Palmer Rapids ONT 15 C2
Palmerston ONT 14 E1
Palmyra ONT 14 C4
Palo SASK 9 C2
Pambrun SASK 9 D4
Pangman SASK 9 E4
Pangnirtung NWT 3 D1
Panmure Island PEI 25 D2
Papinachois QUÉ 22 B1
Papineauville QUÉ 17 H4
Paquette QUÉ 19 F4
Paquette Corners ONT 14 A4
Paquetville NB 22 G4
Paradis QUÉ 16 E3
Paradise NFLD 27 H2
Paradise NFLD 27 H3
Paradise NS 24 D2
Paradise Hill SASK 9 C1
Paradise Point ONT 13 F3
Paradise Valley ALTA 7 H1
Parent QUÉ 18 A3
Parham ONT 15 D3
Paris ONT 14 F2
Parisville QUÉ 19 E2
Park Head ONT 13 D3
Parkbeg SASK 9 D3
Parkdale NS 24 E2
Parkdale PEI 25 C2
Parker Ridge NB 23 D3
Parkers Cove NFLD 27 F3
Parkers Cove NS 24 D2
Parkerview SASK 9 F3
Parkhill ONT 14 C2
Parkindale NB 23 G4
Parkland ALTA 7 F3
Parkman SASK 9 G4
Parkside SASK 9 D1
Parksville BC 5 E4
Parrsboro NS 24 F1
Parry SASK 9 E4
Parry Island ONT 13 F2
Parry Sound ONT 13 F2
Parson BC 7 D3
Parson's Pond NFLD 26 C3
Pasadena NFLD 27 C1
Paspébiac QUÉ 22 G3
Pasqua SASK 9 E3
Pass Island NFLD 27 D3
Pass Lake ONT 12 A2
Paterson MAN 8 H4
Path End NFLD 27 H4
Pathlow SASK 9 E2
Patricia ALTA 7 G3
Patrick's Cove NFLD 27 G4
Patuanak SASK 8 D3
Paudash ONT 15 B2
Paulatuk NWT 2 D1
Paulson BC 7 D4
Pavilion BC 5 G3
Pawistik MAN 8 G3
Paynton SASK 9 C1
Payuk MAN 8 G4
Peace Point ALTA 8 B1
Peace River ALTA 6 D2
Peachland BC 7 C4
Peakes PEI 25 D2
Pearsonville NB 23 F4
Peawanuck ONT 10 H3
Peebles SASK 9 F3
Peel NB 23 C3
Peerless SASK 9 C1
Peerless Lake ALTA 6 E2
Peers ALTA 7 D1
Peesane SASK 9 F2
Pefferlaw ONT 13 H4
Peggys Cove NS 24 F3
Pelee Island ONT 14 D4
Pelham (see Fonthill) ONT 14 H3
Pelican Narrows SASK 8 F4
Pelican Rapids MAN 9 G2
Pelly SASK 9 G2
Pelly Bay NWT 2 H2
Pelly Crossing YK 2 B2
Pemberton BC 5 F3
Pembroke NS 24 F1
Pembroke ONT 15 D1
Pembroke Shore NS 24 C4
Pemmican Portage SASK 9 F1
Pendleton ONT 15 G1
Penetanguishene ONT 13 F3
Penhold ALTA 7 F2
Pennant NS 24 G3
Pennant SASK 9 C3
Pennfield NB 24 B1
Pennfield Ridge NB 24 B1
Penniac NB 23 D3
Penny BC 5 G1
Penobsquis NB 23 F4
Penouille QUÉ 21 A4
Pense SASK 9 E3
Penticton BC 7 C4
Penzance SASK 9 E3
Peoria ALTA 6 C3
Percé QUÉ 21 A4
Percival SASK 9 G3
Perdue SASK 9 D2
Péribonka QUÉ 18 E2
Perigord SASK 9 F2
Perkins QUÉ 17 G4
Perkinsfield ONT 13 F3
Perotte NS 24 D2
Perrault Falls ONT 11 E3
Perry's Cove NFLD 27 H3
Perryvale ALTA 6 F3
Perth ONT 15 E2
Perth Road ONT 15 E3
Perth-Andover NB 23 C2
Petawawa ONT 15 C1
Peter's River NFLD 27 G4
Peterbell ONT 12 E2
Peterborough ONT 15 B4
Peters Corners ONT 14 F2
Petersburg ONT 14 E2
Petersfield MAN 11 B3
Peterson SASK 9 E2
Peterview NFLD 27 E1
Pethericks Corners ONT 15 C4
Petit Etang NS 25 F1
Petit Forte NFLD 27 F3
Petit Jardin NFLD 27 A2
Petit-Cap QUÉ 22 H1
Petitcodiac NB 23 F4
Petit-de-Grat Bridge NS 25 G3
Petite Rivière NS 24 E3
Petite-Anse QUÉ 22 H1
Petite-Rivière-au-Renard QUÉ 21 A3
Petite-Rivière-Ouest QUÉ 22 H3
Petite-Rivière-St-François QUÉ 18 G4
Petite-Rivière-St-François QUÉ 19 G1
Petite-Vallée QUÉ 22 H1
Petites NFLD 27 A3
Petites-Bergeronnes QUÉ 18 H3
Petit-Matane QUÉ 22 D2
Petit-Pabos QUÉ 22 H3
Petit-Rocher NB 22 G4
Petit-Saguenay QUÉ 18 H3
Petit-Shippagan NB 22 H3
Petley NFLD 27 G2
Petrolia ONT 14 B3
Petty Harbour NFLD 27 H3
Phelpston ONT 13 F3
Philips Harbour NS 25 F4
Philipsburg QUÉ 19 C4
Philipsville ONT 15 E3
Phillips Arm BC 5 E3
Phillips Beach SASK 9 D1
Phillips Head NFLD 27 E1
Phillipsburg ONT 14 E2
Phinney Cove NS 24 D2
Phippen SASK 9 C2
Piapot SASK 9 C3
Pibroch ALTA 7 E1
Pic Mobert South ONT 12 C2
Pic River ONT 12 C2
Piccadilly NFLD 27 A2
Pickardville ALTA 7 E1
Pickerel Lake ONT 13 G1
Pickering ONT 14 H1
Pickering Village ONT 14 H1
Pickle Lake ONT 11 F1
Picton ONT 15 D4
Pictou NS 24 H1
Pictou Landing NS 24 H1
Picture Butte ALTA 7 G3
Pied-du-Lac QUÉ 22 B4
Piedmont QUÉ 19 A3
Pierceland SASK 9 C1
Pierrefonds QUÉ 19 B4
Pierreville QUÉ 19 C3
Pierson MAN 9 G4
Pigeon Cove NFLD 26 D1
Pigeon Hill NB 22 H4
Pigeon Hill QUÉ 19 C4
Pikangikum ONT 11 D2
Pike Bay ONT 13 D3
Pike Lake SASK 9 D2
Pike River QUÉ 19 C4
Pikes Arm NFLD 26 F3
Pikogan QUÉ 16 C2
Pikwitonei MAN 10 B3
Pilger SASK 9 E2
Pilley's Island NFLD 27 E1
Pilot Butte SASK 9 E3
Pilot Mound MAN 11 A4
Pinantan Lake BC 7 C3
Pinawa MAN 11 C3
Pincher ALTA 7 F4
Pincher Creek ALTA 7 F4
Pincourt QUÉ 19 B4
Pine Dock MAN 11 B2
Pine Falls MAN 11 C3
Pine Hill QUÉ 19 A3
Pine Lake ALTA 7 F2
Pine Point NWT 2 D3
Pine Ridge NB 23 G3
Pine River MAN 9 H2
Pine River ONT 13 C4
Pinehouse Lake SASK 8 D4
Pinehurst NS 24 E3
Pinette PEI 25 C2
Pinewood ONT 11 D4
Piney MAN 11 C4
Pink Mountain BC 4 F2
Pinkerton ONT 13 D4
Pintendre QUÉ 19 F1
Pinware NFLD 26 D1
Piopolis QUÉ 19 F4
Pipestone ALTA 7 F1
Pipestone MAN 9 G4
Pipun MAN 10 A4
Pit Siding MAN 10 B3
Pitt Meadows BC 5 F4
Pitts Ferry ONT 15 E4
Pittston ONT 15 G2
Placentia NFLD 27 G4
Placentia Junction NFLD 27 G3
Plainfield ONT 15 C4
Plaisance QUÉ 17 G-H4
Plamondon ALTA 6 F3
Plantagenet ONT 15 G1
Plaster Rock NB 23 C2
Plate Cove East NFLD 27 H2
Plate Cove West NFLD 27 G2
Plato SASK 9 C3
Plattsville ONT 14 E2
Pleasant Bay NS 25 G1
Pleasant Corners ONT 15 H1
Pleasant Harbour NS 24 H2
Pleasant Lake NS 24 C4
Pleasant Point NS 24 H2
Pleasant Point ONT 15 A3
Pleasant River NS 24 E3
Pleasant Valley NS 24 H1
Pleasantdale SASK 9 E2
Pleasantfield NS 24 E3
Pleasantview NFLD 27 E1
Pleasantville NS 24 E3
Pleasantville ONT 14 G1
Plenty SASK 9 C2
Plessisville QUÉ 19 E2
Plevna ONT 15 D2
Plum Coulee MAN 11 B4
Plum Point NFLD 26 D2
Plumas MAN 11 A3
Plunkett SASK 9 E2
Plymouth NS 24 C4
Plympton NS 24 C3
Pocahontas ALTA 7 C2
Pockwock NS 24 F2
Pocologan NB 24 B1
Poe ALTA 7 F1
Pohénégamook QUÉ 22 A4
Point Alexander ONT 17 D3
Point au Gaul NFLD 27 E4
Point au Mal NFLD 27 A2
Point Clark ONT 14 C1
Point Comfort QUÉ 17 F3
Point Cross NS 25 F1
Point de Bute NB 23 H4
Point Edward ONT 14 B2
Point Escuminac NB 23 G2
Point La Haye NFLD 27 G4
Point La Nim NB 22 E3
Point Lance NFLD 27 G4
Point Leamington NFLD 27 E1
Point May NFLD 27 E4
Point Michaud NS 25 G3
Point of Bay NFLD 27 E1
Point Prim PEI 25 C2
Point Rosie NFLD 27 E3
Point Tupper NS 25 F3
Point Verde NFLD 27 G4
Pointe au Baril ONT 13 E1
Pointe au Baril Station ONT 13 F1
Pointe aux Pins ONT 12 D4
Pointe du Bois MAN 11 C3
Pointe-à-la-Croix QUÉ 22 E3
Pointe-à-la-Frégate QUÉ 22 H1
Pointe-à-la-Garde QUÉ 22 E3
Pointe-au-Boisvert QUÉ 22 A2
Pointe-au-Chêne QUÉ 17 H4
Pointe-au-Père QUÉ 22 B2
Pointe-au-Pic QUÉ 18 H4
Pointe-aux-Anglais QUÉ 20 D3
Pointe-aux-Loups QUÉ 21 G2
Pointe-aux-Outardes QUÉ 22 C1
Pointe-Calumet QUÉ 19 B4
Pointe-Carleton QUÉ 21 C2
Pointe-Claire QUÉ 19 B4
Pointe-des-Cascades QUÉ 19 B4
Pointe-des-Monts QUÉ 22 D1
Pointe-du-Chêne NB 23 H3
Pointe-du-Lac QUÉ 19 D2
Pointe-Fortune QUÉ 19 A4
Pointe-Jaune QUÉ 22 H1
Pointe-Lebel QUÉ 22 C1
Pointe-Parent QUÉ 21 E1
Pointe-St-Pierre QUÉ 21 A4
Pointe-Sapin NB 23 G2
Pointe-Verte NB 22 F-G4
Points North Landing SASK 8 E2
Poissant QUÉ 17 G2
Pokemouche NB 22 H4
Pokeshaw NB 22 G4
Pokiok NB 23 C4
Poland ONT 15 E2
Pollards Point NFLD 26 D3
Pollett River NB 23 G4
Polonia MAN 11 A3
Poltimore QUÉ 17 G4
Pomeroy NB 24 A1
Pomquet NS 25 E3
Pond Cove NFLD 26 D1
Ponemah MAN 11 B3
Ponoka ALTA 7 F2
Pont Lafrance NB 23 G1
Pont Landry NB 23 G1
Pontbriand QUÉ 19 F3
Ponteix SASK 9 D4
Pontiac QUÉ 17 F4
Ponton MAN 8 H4
Pontrilas SASK 9 F1
Pont-Rouge QUÉ 19 E1
Pontypool ONT 15 A4
Poodiac NB 23 F4
Poole ONT 14 E2
Pool's Cove NFLD 27 E3
Pope's Harbour NS 24 H2
Poplar Dale ONT 12 E4
Poplar Hill ONT 11 D2
Poplar Hill ONT 14 D3
Poplar Point MAN 11 B3
Poplarfield MAN 11 B3
Porcupine ONT 12 G2
Porcupine Plain SASK 9 F2
Porquis Junction ONT 12 G2
Port Alberni BC 5 E4
Port Albert NFLD 27 F1
Port Albert ONT 14 C1
Port Albion BC 5 E4
Port Alice BC 5 D3
Port Alma ONT 14 B4
Port Anne NFLD 27 F3
Port Anson NFLD 27 E1
Port au Choix NFLD 26 C2
Port Bickerton NS 25 E4
Port Blandford NFLD 27 G2
Port Bolster ONT 13 H3
Port Bruce ONT 14 D3
Port Burwell ONT 14 E3
Port Carling ONT 13 G2
Port Carmen ONT 13 G1
Port Clements BC 5 A1
Port Clyde NS 24 D4
Port Colborne ONT 14 H3
Port Coquitlam BC 5 F4
Port Credit ONT 14 G2
Port Cunnington ONT 13 H2
Port Darlington ONT 15 A4
Port de Grave NFLD 27 H3
Port Dover ONT 14 F3
Port Dufferin NS 25 D4
Port Edward BC 4 B4
Port Elgin NB 23 H3
Port Elgin ONT 13 D3
Port Elmsley ONT 15 E2
Port Essington BC 4 B4
Port Felix NS 25 E3
Port Franks ONT 14 C2
Port George NS 24 D2
Port Glasgow ONT 14 C3
Port Grenville NS 24 E1
Port Hardy BC 5 D3
Port Hastings NS 25 F3
Port Hawkesbury NS 25 F3
Port Hill PEI 25 B2
Port Hillford NS 25 E4
Port Hood NS 25 F2
Port Hope ONT 15 B4
Port Hope Simpson NFLD 3 G3
Port Howe NS 25 B3
Port Joli NS 24 E4
Port Kirwan NFLD 27 H4
Port la Tour NS 24 D4
Port Lambton ONT 14 B3
Port Lewis QUÉ 19 A4
Port l'Hebert NS 24 E4
Port Loring ONT 13 F1
Port Lorne NS 24 D2
Port McNeill BC 5 D3
Port McNicoll ONT 13 G3
Port Maitland NS 24 C3
Port Maitland ONT 14 G3
Port Malcolm NS 25 F3
Port Medway NS 24 E3
Port Mellon BC 5 F4
Port Moody BC 5 F4
Port Morien NS 25 H2
Port Mouton NS 24 E4
Port Neville BC 5 D3
Port of Big Beaver SASK 9 E4
Port of Carievale SASK 9 G4
Port of Climax SASK 9 C4
Port of Coronach SASK 9 E4
Port of Estevan Highway SASK 9 F4
Port of Oungre SASK 9 F4
Port of Torquay SASK 9 F4
Port Perry ONT 14 H1
Port Philip NS 25 B3
Port Renfrew BC 5 E4
Port Rexton NFLD 27 H2
Port Robinson ONT 14 H3
Port Rowan ONT 14 E3
Port Royal NS 24 D2
Port Ryerse ONT 14 F3
Port Sandfield ONT 13 G2
Port Saunders NFLD 26 C2
Port Saxon NS 24 D4
Port Severn ONT 13 G3
Port Shoreham NS 25 F3
Port Stanley ONT 14 D3
Port Stanton ONT 13 G3
Port Sydney ONT 13 G2
Port Union NFLD 27 H2
Port Wade NS 24 C2
Port Williams NS 24 E2
Portage la Prairie MAN 11 B3
Portage Vale NB 23 F4
Portage-du-Fort QUÉ 17 E4
Portage-Griffon QUÉ 21 A4
Portapique NS 24 G1
Port-au-Persil QUÉ 18 H3-4
Port-aux-Quilles QUÉ 18 H3
Port-Cartier QUÉ 20 E2
Port-Daniel QUÉ 22 H3
Porters Lake NS 24 G2
Porterville NFLD 27 E1
Portland NFLD 27 G2
Portland ONT 15 E3
Portland Creek NFLD 26 C3
Port-Menier QUÉ 21 A2
Portneuf QUÉ 19 E2
Portneuf-Station QUÉ 19 E2
Portree NS 25 F2
Portreeve SASK 9 C3
Port-St-François QUÉ 19 D2
Portugal Cove NFLD 27 H3
Portugal Cove South NFLD 27 H4
Portuguese Cove NS 24 G3
Pottageville ONT 14 G1
Pouce Coupe BC 4 G3
Pouch Cove NFLD 27 H3
Poularies QUÉ 16 B2
Pound Cove NFLD 27 G1
Povungnituk QUÉ 3 C2
Powassen ONT 12 H4
Powell MAN 9 H2
Powell River BC 5 E3
Powerscourt QUÉ 19 A4
Powerview MAN 11 C3
Prairie River SASK 9 F2
Prairie Siding ONT 14 B4
Prairie View SASK 9 D3
Prawda MAN 11 C4
Précieux-Sang QUÉ 19 D2
Precious Corners ONT 15 B4
Pré-d'en-Haut NB 23 G3
Preeceville SASK 9 F2
Preissac QUÉ 16 B3
Prelate SASK 9 C3
Prescott ONT 15 F3
Prespatou BC 4 G2
Presqu'ile NS 25 F1
Presqu'ile Point ONT 15 C4
Press QUÉ 16 E3
Preston NS 24 G2
Preston Lake ONT 14 G1
Prévost QUÉ 19 A3
Price QUÉ 22 C2
Price Settlement NB 23 G1
Prices Corner ONT 13 G3
Priceville ONT 13 E4
Priddis ALTA 7 F3
Primate SASK 9 B2
Primeau Lake SASK 8 D3
Primrose ONT 14 F1
Prince SASK 9 C1
Prince Albert ONT 14 H1
Prince Albert SASK 9 E1
Prince George BC 5 F1
Prince of Wales NB 24 B1
Prince Rupert BC 4 B4
Prince William NB 23 D4
Princeport NS 24 G1
Princess Harbour MAN 11 B2
Princess Park NB 23 E4
Princeton BC 5 H4
Princeton NFLD 27 G2
Princeton ONT 14 E2
Princeville QUÉ 19 E2
Pritchard BC 7 C3
Procter BC 7 D4
Progress BC 4 G3
Prophet River BC 4 F1
Prospect NS 24 F3
Prosser Brook NB 23 G4
Proton Station ONT 13 E4
Providence Bay ONT 13 B1
Provost ALTA 7 H2
Prud'homme SASK 9 E2
Pubnico NS 24 C4
Puce ONT 14 A4
Pugwash NS 25 B3
Pugwash Junction NS 25 B3
Pukatawagan MAN 8 G3
Pulp River MAN 9 H2
Punnichy SASK 9 E3
Purbeck's Cove NFLD 26 D3
Purdy ONT 15 C2
Purple Springs ALTA 7 G3
Puslinch ONT 14 F2
Putnam ONT 14 E3
Pynn's Brook NFLD 27 C1

Q

Quadeville ONT 15 C2
Qualicum Beach BC 5 E4
Qu'Appelle SASK 9 F3
Quaqtaq QUÉ 3 D2
Quarryville NB 23 F2
Quathiaski Cove BC 5 E3
Quatsino BC 5 D3
Québec QUÉ 19 F1
Queen Charlotte BC 5 A1
Queen's Cove NFLD 27 G3
Queensborough ONT 15 C3
Queensland NS 24 F2
Queensport NS 25 F4
Queenston ONT 14 H2
Queenstown ALTA 7 G3
Queenstown NB 23 E4
Queensville NS 25 F3
Queensville ONT 14 G1
Quesnel BC 5 F1
Quilchena BC 5 H3
Quill Lake SASK 9 E2
Quinan NS 24 C4
Quinton SASK 9 E3
Quirpon NFLD 26 E1
Quisibis NB 23 B1
Quispamsis NB 24 C1
Quyon QUÉ 17 F4

R

Rabbit Lake SASK 9 D1
Rabbit Lake Mine SASK 8 F2
Racine QUÉ 19 D4
Rackham MAN 11 A3
Radisson QUÉ 3 C4
Radisson SASK 9 D2
Radium Hot Springs BC 7 E3
Radville SASK 9 E4
Radway ALTA 7 F1
Rae Lakes NWT 2 D3
Rae-Edzo NWT 2 D3
Rafter MAN 8 G3
Ragged Harbour NFLD 27 G1
Raglin ONT 14 H1
Ragueneau QUÉ 22 B1
Rainbow Lake ALTA 6 C1
Rainham Centre ONT 14 G3
Rainier ALTA 7 G3
Rainy River ONT 11 D4
Raith ONT 11 G4
Raleigh NFLD 26 E1
Ralston ALTA 7 H3
Rama SASK 9 F2
Ramea NFLD 27 C3
Rameau QUÉ 22 H2
Ramore ONT 12 G2
Ramsay ONT 12 F3
Randboro QUÉ 19 E4
Ranfurly ALTA 7 G1
Rang-St-Georges NB 22 H4
Ranger Lake ONT 12 E4
Rankin ONT 15 D1
Rantem NFLD 27 G3
Rapid City MAN 11 A3
Rapid View SASK 9 C1
Rapide-Blanc QUÉ 18 C4
Rapide-Blanc-Station QUÉ 18 C4
Rapide-Danseur QUÉ 16 A2
Rapide-des-Cèdres QUÉ 16 D1
Rapide-Deux QUÉ 16 B3
Rapide-Sept QUÉ 16 B4
Rapides-des-Joachims QUÉ 17 C3
Rathwell MAN 11 B4
Rattling Brook NFLD 27 E1
Rattling Brook NFLD 26 D4
Raven ALTA 7 E2
Ravenna ONT 13 E3
Ravenscliffe ONT 13 G2
Ravenscrag SASK 9 C4
Ravenshoe ONT 13 G4
Ravensview ONT 15 E4
Ravenswood ONT 14 C2
Rawdon NS 24 F2
Rawdon QUÉ 19 B3
Rawdon Gold Mines NS 24 F2
Raymond ALTA 7 G4
Raymond ONT 13 G2
Raymore SASK 9 E3
Rayside-Balfour (see Chelmsford) ONT 12 G4
Readlyn SASK 9 E4
Red Bank NB 23 E2
Red Bay NFLD 26 D1
Red Bay ONT 13 D3
Red Brook NFLD 27 A2
Red Cliff NFLD 27 H2
Red Cliff NFLD 27 E1
Red Deer ALTA 7 F2
Red Deer Lake MAN 9 G1
Red Earth SASK 9 F1
Red Earth Creek ALTA 6 E2
Red Harbour NFLD 27 F4
Red Head NB 24 C1
Red Head Cove NFLD 27 H2
Red Island NFLD 27 G3
Red Islands NS 25 G3
Red Jacket SASK 9 G3
Red Lake ONT 11 D2
Red Lake Road ONT 11 E3
Red Pass BC 7 C2
Red Point PEI 25 E2
Red Rapids NB 23 C2
Red River NS 25 G1
Red Rock BC 5 F1
Red Rock ONT 12 B2
Red Rocks NFLD 27 A3
Red Willow ALTA 7 F2
Redbridge ONT 12 H4
Redcliffe ALTA 7 H3
Redditt ONT 11 D3
Redickville ONT 13 F4
Rednersville ONT 15 C4
Redonda Bay BC 5 E3
Redstone BC 5 F2
Redvers SASK 9 G4
Redwater ALTA 7 F1
Reeces Corners ONT 14 B3
Reefs Harbour NFLD 26 C2
Regent MAN 11 A4
Regina SASK 9 E3
Regina Beach SASK 9 E3
Reginaville NFLD 27 G4
Regway SASK 9 E4
Reid Lake BC 5 F1
Reidville NFLD 27 C1
Reinland MAN 11 B4
Reliance NWT 2 E3
Rembrandt MAN 11 B3
Rémigny QUÉ 16 A4
Rencontre East NFLD 27 E3
Rencontre West NFLD 27 D3
Reneault QUÉ 16 A2
Renews NFLD 27 H4
Renforth NB 24 C1
Renfrew NS 24 G2
Renfrew ONT 15 D1
Rennie MAN 11 C3
Reno ALTA 6 D2
Renous NB 23 F2
Renton ONT 14 F3
Renwer MAN 9 G2
Repentigny QUÉ 19 B3
Repulse Bay NWT 2 H2
Reserve SASK 9 F2
Reserve Mines NS 25 H2
Restigouche QUÉ 22 E3
Reston MAN 9 G4
Restoule ONT 12 H4
Revelstoke BC 7 D3
Revenue SASK 9 C2
Reward SASK 9 C2
Rexton NB 23 G2
Reykjavik MAN 11 A3
Reynaud SASK 9 E2
Rhineland SASK 9 D3
Ribstone ALTA 7 H1
Riceton SASK 9 E3
Riceville ONT 15 G1
Rich Lake ALTA 6 G3
Rich Valley ALTA 7 E1
Richard SASK 9 D2
Richards Landing ONT 12 D4
Richardson SASK 9 E3
Richdale ALTA 7 G2
Richelieu QUÉ 19 C4
Richer MAN 11 C4
Richfield NS 24 C3
Richibouctou-Village NB 23 G2
Richibucto NB 23 G2
Richmond BC 5 F4
Richmond ONT 14 E3
Richmond ONT 15 F2
Richmond PEI 25 B2
Richmond QUÉ 19 D3
Richmond Hill ONT 14 G1
Richmound SASK 9 B3
Rideau Ferry ONT 15 E3
Ridgedale SASK 9 E1
Ridgetown ONT 14 C4
Ridgeville MAN 11 C4
Ridgeville ONT 14 G3
Ridgeway ONT 14 H3
Riding Mountain MAN 11 A3
Rigaud QUÉ 19 A4
Riley Brook NB 23 C1
Rimbey ALTA 7 F2
Rimouski QUÉ 22 B2

Rimouski-Est QUÉ 22 B2
Ringwood ONT 14 H1
Riondel BC 7 D4
Ripley ONT 14 D1
Ripon QUÉ 17 H4
Ripples NB 23 E3
Riske Creek BC 5 F2
River Bourgeois NS 25 G3
River Brook NFLD 27 A2
River Charlo NB 22 F3
River de Chute NB 23 C2
River Denys NS 25 F3
River Glade NB 23 G3
River Hebert NS 24 E1
River Hills MAN 11 C3
River John NS 25 C3
River of Ponds NFLD 26 C2
River Philip NS 24 F1
River Valley ONT 12 G4
Rivercourse ALTA 7 H1
Riverdale NS 24 C3
Riverfield QUÉ 19 B4
Riverhead NFLD 27 H3
Riverhurst SASK 9 D3
Rivers MAN 11 A3
Rivers Inlet BC 5 D2
Riversdale NS 24 H1
Riversdale NS 24 E3
Riversdale ONT 14 D1
Riverside-Albert NB 23 G4
Riverton MAN 11 B3
Riverton NS 24 H1
Riverview NB 23 G3
Riverview ONT 14 F1
Riverview Heights ONT 15 F3
Rivière-à-Claude QUÉ 22 F1
Rivière-à-la-Loutre QUÉ 21 B2
Rivière-à-Pierre QUÉ 19 D1
Rivière-au-Renard QUÉ 21 A3
Rivière-au-Tonnerre QUÉ 20 H2
Rivière-aux-Graines QUÉ 20 G2
Rivière-aux-Rats QUÉ 19 C1
Rivière-Beaudette QUÉ 19 A4
Rivière-Bersimis QUÉ 22 B2
Rivière-Bleue QUÉ 22 A4
Rivière-Brochu QUÉ 20 E2
Rivière-de-la-Chaloupe QUÉ 21 D3
Rivière-du-Loup QUÉ 18 H3
Rivière-du-Portage NB 23 G1
Rivière-Éternité QUÉ 18 G3
Rivière-Héva QUÉ 16 C3
Rivière-la-Madeleine QUÉ 22 G1
Rivière-Matawin QUÉ 19 C1
Rivière-Ouelle QUÉ 18 H4
Rivière-Paspébiac QUÉ 22 G3
Rivière-Pentecôte QUÉ 20 E3
Rivière-Pigou QUÉ 20 G2
Rivière-St-Jean QUÉ 21 A1
Rivière-St-Paul QUÉ 26 C1
Rivière-Ste-Marguerite QUÉ 18 H3
Rivière-Trois-Pistoles QUÉ 22 A3
Rivière-Verte NB 23 B1
Rivington QUÉ 17 H4
Roachvale NS 25 F4
Roachville NB 23 F4
Robb ALTA 7 D1
Robert's Arm NFLD 27 E1
Robertsonville QUÉ 19 F3
Robertville NB 22 F4
Roberval QUÉ 18 D2
Robichaud NB 23 H3
Robinsons NFLD 27 A2
Robinsonville NB 22 E3
Roblin MAN 9 G3
Roblin ONT 15 D3
Robsart SASK 9 C4
Robson BC 7 D4
Rocanville SASK 9 G3
Roche Percee SASK 9 F4
Rochebaucourt QUÉ 16 D2
Roches Point ONT 13 G4
Rochester ALTA 7 F1
Rochfort Bridge ALTA 7 E1
Rochon Sands ALTA 7 F2
Rock Bay BC 5 E3
Rock Creek BC 7 C4
Rock Forest QUÉ 19 E4
Rock Harbour NFLD 27 F4
Rock Island QUÉ 19 E4
Rock Lake ONT 12 E4
Rockburn QUÉ 19 B4
Rockcliffe Park ONT 15 F1
Rockford ONT 13 E3
Rockglen SASK 9 E4
Rockhaven SASK 9 C2
Rockingham ONT 15 C2
Rockland NS 24 D4
Rockland ONT 15 G1
Rocklin NS 24 H1
Rocklyn ONT 13 E3
Rockport NB 23 H4
Rockport ONT 15 F3
Rocksprings ONT 15 F3
Rockton ONT 14 F2
Rockwood ONT 14 F1
Rocky Bay ONT 12 B2
Rocky Harbour NFLD 26 B4
Rocky Lane ALTA 6 D1
Rocky Mountain House ALTA 7 E2
Rocky Point BC 5 F4
Rocky Rapids ALTA 7 E1
Rockyford ALTA 7 F3
Roddickton NFLD 26 D2
Rodgers Cove NFLD 27 F1
Rodney ONT 14 C3
Roebuck ONT 15 F3
Rogers Pass BC 7 D3
Rogersville NB 23 F2
Rokeby SASK 9 G3
Roland MAN 11 B4
Rolla BC 4 G3
Rollet QUÉ 16 A3
Rolling Hills ALTA 7 G3
Rollingdam NB 24 A1
Rollo Bay PEI 25 D2
Rolphton ONT 17 C3
Romaines NFLD 27 A2
Roman Valley NS 25 E3
Rooms NFLD 26 D4
Roosville BC 7 F4
Root Lake MAN 9 G1
Roquemaure QUÉ 16 A2
Rorketon MAN 11 A3
Rosa MAN 11 C4
Rosaireville NB 23 F2
Rosalind ALTA 7 F1
Rose Bay NS 24 F3
Rose Blanche NFLD 27 A3
Rose Prairie BC 4 G2
Rose Valley SASK 9 F2
Roseau River MAN 11 C4
Rosebank MAN 11 B4
Rosebud ALTA 7 F2-3
Rosedale ALTA 7 G2
Rosedale ONT 13 H3
Rosehall ONT 15 C4
Roseisle MAN 11 B4
Rosemary ALTA 7 G3
Rosemère QUÉ 19 B3
Rosemont ONT 14 F1
Roseneath ONT 15 B4
Roseneath PEI 25 D2
Rosenfeld MAN 11 B4
Rosengart MAN 11 B4
Rosenort MAN 11 B4
Rosetown SASK 9 C2
Roseville ONT 14 E2
Roseway NS 24 D4
Roslin ONT 15 C4
Ross Ferry NS 25 G2
Ross River YK 2 B2
Rossburn MAN 9 G3
Rosseau ONT 13 G2
Rosseau Road ONT 13 F2
Rossendale MAN 11 B4
Rosser MAN 11 B3
Rossfield NS 25 D3
Rossington ALTA 7 E1
Rossland BC 7 D4
Rosslyn Village ONT 12 A2
Rossmore ONT 15 C4
Rossport ONT 12 B2
Rossway NS 24 C2
Rosswood BC 4 C4
Rosthern SASK 9 D2
Rostock ONT 14 D-E2
Rothesay NB 24 C1
Rothsay ONT 14 E1
Rougemont QUÉ 19 C4
Rouleau SASK 9 E3
Roulier QUÉ 16 A4
Round Bay NS 24 D4
Round Harbour NFLD 26 E3
Round Hill ALTA 7 F1
Round Hill NS 24 D2
Round Island NS 25 H2
Round Lake Centre ONT 15 C1
Roundabout NFLD 27 E4
Rounthwaite MAN 11 A4
Routhierville QUÉ 22 D3
Rouyn-Noranda QUÉ 16 A3
Rowena NB 23 C2
Rowley ALTA 7 F2
Roxton Falls QUÉ 19 D4
Roxton Pond QUÉ 19 D4
Roxton-Sud QUÉ 19 D4
Royston BC 5 E4
Ruby Lake Beach SASK 9 F1
Ruddell SASK 9 C-D2
Ruddock MAN 8 G4
Ruisseau-à-Rebours QUÉ 22 F1
Ruisseau-Castor QUÉ 22 F1
Ruisseau-Vert QUÉ 22 C1
Rumsey ALTA 7 F2
Runnymede SASK 9 G2
Rupert QUÉ 17 F4
Rusagonis NB 23 D4
Ruscom Station ONT 14 A4
Rush Lake SASK 9 D3
Rushoon NFLD 27 F3
Russel MAN 9 G3
Russell ONT 15 G2
Rusty Pond Siding NFLD 27 E1
Rutherford ONT 14 B3
Rutherglen ONT 12 H4
Ruthilda SASK 9 C2
Ruthven ONT 14 A4
Rycroft ALTA 6 C3
Rydal Bank ONT 12 E4
Rykerts BC 7 E4
Ryley ALTA 7 F1

S

Places with saints' names listed below are ordered in the following way: **St** Adolphe, **St**-Adalbert, **Ste** Agathe, **Ste**-Adèle.

Saanich BC 5 F4
Sable River NS 24 D4
Sabrevois QUÉ 19 C4
Sachigo ONT 10 E4
Sachs Harbour NWT 2 D1
Sackville NB 23 H4
Sacré-Coeur QUÉ 18 H3
Sacré-Coeur-de-Marie QUÉ 19 F3
Saddle Lake ALTA 7 G1
Saganaga Lake ONT 11 F4
Sagard QUÉ 18 H3
Sagehill SASK 9 E2
St Adolphe MAN 11 B4
St Agatha ONT 14 E2
St Alban's NFLD 27 E3
St Albert ALTA 7 F1
St Albert ONT 15 G1
St Almo NB 23 C2
St Alphonse MAN 11 A4
St Alphonse NS 24 C3
St Ambroise MAN 11 B3
St Andrew's NFLD 27 A3
St Andrews NB 24 A2
St Andrews NS 25 E3
St Andrews ONT 15 H2
St Ann's NS 25 G2
St Anns ONT 14 G2
St Anthony NFLD 26 E1
St Anthony Bight NFLD 26 E1
St Barbe NFLD 26 D1
St Benedict SASK 9 E2
St Bernard NS 24 C3
St Bernardin ONT 15 H1
St Bernard's NFLD 27 F3
St Brendan's NFLD 27 G1
St Brides ALTA 7 G1
St Bride's NFLD 27 G4
St Brieux SASK 9 E2
St Carols NFLD 26 E1
St Catharines ONT 14 H2
St Catherines NFLD 27 H4
St Chads NFLD 27 G2
St Charles ONT 12 G4
St Clair Beach ONT 14 A4
St Claude MAN 11 B4
St Clements ONT 14 E2
St Columban ONT 14 D2
St Croix NB 23 C4
St Croix Cove NS 24 D2
St David's NFLD 27 A2
St Davids ONT 14 H2
St Denis SASK 9 D2
St Edward PEI 25 A1
St Eleanor's PEI 25 B2
St Esprit NS 25 G3
St Eugene ONT 15 H1
St Eustache MAN 11 B3
St Francis ALTA 7 E1
St Francis Harbour NS 25 F3
St François Xavier MAN 11 B3
St Front SASK 9 E2
St George NB 24 B1
St George ONT 14 F2
St George's NFLD 27 B2
St Georges Channel NS 25 F3
St George's Hill SASK 8 C3
St Gregor SASK 9 E2
St Isidore ALTA 6 D2
St Isidore ONT 15 G1
St Isidore-de-Bellevue SASK 9 E2
St Jacobs ONT 14 E2
St Jacques NFLD 27 E3
St Jean Baptiste MAN 11 B4
St Joachim ONT 14 A4
Saint John NB 24 C1
St John Harbour NFLD 27 E3
St John's NFLD 27 H3
St Jones Within NFLD 27 G3
St Jones Without NFLD 27 G3
St Joseph MAN 11 B4
St Joseph NS 25 E3
St Joseph NS 24 C3
St Joseph ONT 14 C2
St Joseph du Moine NS 25 F1
St Joseph's NFLD 27 H4
St Joseph's NFLD 27 F3
St Joseph's Cove NFLD 27 E3
St Judes NFLD 27 C1
St Juliens NFLD 26 E2
St Kyran's NFLD 27 F3
St Labre MAN 11 C4
St Laurent MAN 11 B3
St Lawrence NFLD 27 E4
St Lazare MAN 9 G3
St Leon MAN 11 B4
St Leonards NFLD 27 F3
St Lina ALTA 6 G4
St Louis PEI 25 A1
St Louis SASK 9 E2
St Lunaire NFLD 26 E1
St Malo MAN 11 C4
St Margarets NB 23 F2
St Margarets PEI 25 D2
St Martin MAN 11 A2
St Martin Junction MAN 11 A2
St Martins NB 24 D1
St Martins NS 24 C3
St Mary's NFLD 27 G4
St Marys ONT 14 D2
St Mary's River NS 25 E4
St Marys Road PEI 25 D2
St Michael ALTA 7 F1
St Pascal ONT 15 G1
St Patricks NFLD 26 E4
St Paul ALTA 7 G1
St Paul NS 24 H1
St Pauls NFLD 26 B3
St Pauls Station ONT 14 D2
St Peters NS 25 G3
St Peters PEI 25 D2
St Philips SASK 9 G2
St Phillip's NFLD 27 H3
St Raphaels ONT 15 H2
St Rose NS 25 F2
St Shotts NFLD 27 H4
St Stephen NB 24 A1
St Stephens NFLD 27 G4
St Teresa NFLD 27 A2
St Teresa PEI 25 D2
St Theresa Point MAN 11 C1
St Thomas NFLD 27 H3
St Thomas ONT 14 D3
St Veronica's NFLD 27 E3
St Victor SASK 9 E4
St Vincent ALTA 6 G4
St Vincent's NFLD 27 G4
St Walburg SASK 9 C1
St Williams ONT 14 E-F3
St-Adalbert QUÉ 19 H1
St-Adelme QUÉ 22 D2
St-Adelphe QUÉ 19 D2
St-Adolphe-d'Howard QUÉ 19 A3
St-Adolphe-de-Dudswell QUÉ 19 E3
St-Adrien QUÉ 19 E3
St-Adrien-d'Irlande QUÉ 19 F3
St-Agapit QUÉ 19 F2
St-Aimé-des-Lacs QUÉ 18 G4
St-Alban QUÉ 19 E1
St-Albert QUÉ 19 E3
St-Alexandre QUÉ 18 H4
St-Alexandre QUÉ 19 C4
St-Alexandre-des-Lacs QUÉ 22 D2
St-Alexis-de-Matapédia QUÉ 22 E3
St-Alexis-des-Monts QUÉ 19 C2
St-Alfred QUÉ 19 G2
St-Alphonse QUÉ 22 G3
St-Alphonse QUÉ 19 C4
St-Alphonse-de-Rodriguez QUÉ 19 B2
St-Amable QUÉ 19 C3
St-Amand NB 23 B1
St-Ambroise QUÉ 18 F2
St-Ambroise-de-Kildare QUÉ 19 B3
St-Anaclet QUÉ 22 C2
St-André NB 23 B2
St-André QUÉ 18 H4
St-André-Avellin QUÉ 17 H4
St-André-de-Restigouche QUÉ 22 E3
St-André-du-Lac-St-Jean QUÉ 18 E3
St-André-Est QUÉ 19 A4
St-Angès-de-Dundee QUÉ 19 A4
St-Anicet QUÉ 19 A4
St-Anselme NB 23 G3
St-Anselme QUÉ 19 F2
St-Antoine NB 23 G3
St-Antoine QUÉ 19 B3
St-Antoine-Abbé QUÉ 19 B4
St-Antoine-de-Tilly QUÉ 19 E2
St-Antoine-sur-Richelieu QUÉ 19 C3
St-Antonin QUÉ 18 H4
St-Apollinaire QUÉ 19 E2
St-Armand-Station QUÉ 19 C4
St-Arsène QUÉ 22 A3
St-Arthur NB 22 E3
St-Athanase QUÉ 22 A4
St-Aubert QUÉ 19 G1
St-Augustin QUÉ 26 B1
St-Augustin QUÉ 18 E2
St-Augustin QUÉ 19 B3
St-Augustin-de-Desmaures QUÉ 19 F1
St-Barbe QUÉ 19 A4
St-Barnabé-Nord QUÉ 19 C2
St-Barnabé-Sud QUÉ 19 C3
St-Barthélémy QUÉ 19 C2
St-Basile NB 23 B1
St-Basile-de-Tableau QUÉ 18 G3
St-Basile-le-Grand QUÉ 19 C4
St-Basile-Sud QUÉ 19 E1
St-Benjamin QUÉ 19 G2
St-Benoît QUÉ 19 A4
St-Benoît-du-Lac QUÉ 19 D4
St-Benoît-Labre QUÉ 19 G3
St-Bernard QUÉ 19 F2
St-Bernard QUÉ 19 C3
St-Bernard-de-Lacolle QUÉ 19 B4
St-Bernard-sur-Mer QUÉ 18 G4
St-Blaise QUÉ 19 C4
St-Bonaventure QUÉ 19 D3
St-Boniface-de-Shawinigan QUÉ 19 C2
St-Bruno QUÉ 18 E2
St-Bruno-de-Guigues QUÉ 17 A1
St-Bruno-de-Kamouraska QUÉ 18 H4
St-Bruno-de-Montarville QUÉ 19 C4
St-Cajetan QUÉ 17 F2
St-Calixte QUÉ 19 B3
St-Camille QUÉ 19 E3
St-Camille-de-Lellis QUÉ 19 G2
St-Canut QUÉ 19 A3
St-Casimir QUÉ 19 D2
St-Cassien-des-Caps QUÉ 18 G4
St-Célestin QUÉ 19 D2
St-Césaire QUÉ 19 C4
St-Charles NB 23 G2
St-Charles QUÉ 19 F1
St-Charles-Borromée QUÉ 19 B3
St-Charles-de-Bourget QUÉ 18 F2
St-Charles-de-Mandeville QUÉ 19 C2
St-Charles-Garnier QUÉ 22 C3
St-Charles-sur-Richelieu QUÉ 19 C3
St-Chrysostome PEI 25 A2
St-Chrysostome QUÉ 19 B4
St-Claude QUÉ 19 E3
St-Clément QUÉ 22 A3
St-Cléophas QUÉ 22 D2
St-Cléophas QUÉ 19 C2
St-Clet QUÉ 19 A4
St-Colomban QUÉ 19 A3
St-Côme QUÉ 19 B2
St-Côme-de-Kennebec QUÉ 19 G3
St-Constant QUÉ 19 B4
St-Cuthbert QUÉ 19 C3
St-Cyprien QUÉ 22 B3
St-Cyprien QUÉ 19 G2
St-Cyr QUÉ 19 E3
St-Cyriac QUÉ 18 F3
St-Cyrille-de-l'Islet QUÉ 19 G1
St-Cyrille-de-Wendover QUÉ 19 D3
St-Damase QUÉ 22 C2
St-Damase QUÉ 19 C4
St-Damase-des-Aulnaies QUÉ 19 H1
St-Damien QUÉ 19 B2
St-Damien-de-Buckland QUÉ 19 G2
St-Daniel QUÉ 19 F3
St-David QUÉ 19 C3
St-David-de-Falardeau QUÉ 18 F2
St-Denis QUÉ 18 H4
St-Denis QUÉ 19 C3
St-Denis-de-Brompton QUÉ 19 E4
St-Didace QUÉ 19 C2
St-Dominique QUÉ 19 C4
St-Dominique-du-Rosaire QUÉ 16 C2
St-Donat QUÉ 22 C2
St-Donat QUÉ 19 A2
St-Edgar QUÉ 22 G3
St-Edmond QUÉ 18 D2
St-Edmond QUÉ 16 C3
St-Edmond-de-Grantham QUÉ 19 D3
St-Édouard QUÉ 19 E2
St-Édouard QUÉ 19 B4
St-Édouard-de-Frampton QUÉ 19 G2
St-Edouard-de-Kent NB 23 G3
St-Édouard-de-Maskinongé QUÉ 19 C2
St-Éleuthère QUÉ 22 A4
St-Élie QUÉ 19 C2
St-Élie-d'Orford QUÉ 19 E4
St-Éloi QUÉ 22 A3
St-Elphège QUÉ 19 D3
St-Elzéar QUÉ 22 G3
St-Elzéar QUÉ 19 F2
St-Émile QUÉ 19 F1
St-Émile-de-Suffolk QUÉ 17 H3
St-Éphrem-de-Tring QUÉ 19 F3
St-Épiphane QUÉ 22 A3
St-Esprit QUÉ 19 B3
St-Étienne-de-Beauharnois QUÉ 19 B4
St-Étienne-de-Bolton QUÉ 19 D4
St-Étienne-de-Lauzon QUÉ 19 F2
St-Etienne-des-Grès QUÉ 19 C2
St-Eugène QUÉ 18 D2
St-Eugène QUÉ 19 G1
St-Eugène QUÉ 19 D3
St-Eugène-de-Chazel QUÉ 16 B2
St-Eugène-de-Guigues QUÉ 17 A1
St-Eugène-de-Ladrière QUÉ 22 B3
St-Eusèbe QUÉ 22 B4
St-Eustache QUÉ 19 B4
St-Évariste-de-Forsyth QUÉ 19 F3
St-Fabien QUÉ 22 B3
St-Fabien-de-Panet QUÉ 19 H2
St-Fabien-sur-Mer QUÉ 22 B3
St-Faustin QUÉ 19 A3
St-Félicien QUÉ 18 D2
St-Félix-d'Otis QUÉ 18 G3
St-Félix-de-Dalquier QUÉ 16 C2
St-Félix-de-Kingsey QUÉ 19 D3
St-Félix-de-Valois QUÉ 19 B2
St-Ferréol-les-Neiges QUÉ 19 F1
St-Fidèle-de-Mont-Murray QUÉ 18 H4
St-Fidèle-de-Restigouche QUÉ 22 E3
St-Flavien QUÉ 19 E2
St-Fortunat QUÉ 19 E3
St-François QUÉ 19 G1
St-François-d'Assise QUÉ 22 D3
St-François-de-Madawaska NB 23 A1
St-François-de-Masham QUÉ 17 F4
St-François-de-Sales QUÉ 18 D3
St-François-du-Lac QUÉ 19 C3
St-François-Xavier-de-Brompton QUÉ 19 E4
St-François-Xavier-de-Viger QUÉ 22 A3
St-Frédéric QUÉ 19 F2
St-Fulgence QUÉ 18 F2
St-Gabriel QUÉ 22 C2
St-Gabriel QUÉ 19 C2
St-Gabriel-de-Valcartier QUÉ 19 F1
St-Gabriel-Lalemant QUÉ 18 H4
St-Gédéon QUÉ 18 E2
St-Gédéon QUÉ 19 G3
St-Georges MAN 11 C3
St-Georges QUÉ 19 D2
St-Georges QUÉ 19 G3
St-Georges-de-Clarenceville QUÉ 19 C4
St-Georges-de-Malbaie QUÉ 21 A4
St-Georges-de-Windsor QUÉ 19 E3
St-Georges-Ouest QUÉ 19 G3
St-Gérard QUÉ 19 F3
St-Gérard-des-Laurentides QUÉ 19 C2
St-Gérard-Majella QUÉ 19 B3
St-Gérard-Majella QUÉ 19 C3
St-Germain QUÉ 18 H4
St-Germain-de-Grantham QUÉ 19 D3
St-Gervais QUÉ 19 F2
St-Gilbert QUÉ 19 E2
St-Gilles QUÉ 19 F2
St-Godefroi QUÉ 22 G3
St-Grégoire QUÉ 19 D2
St-Grégoire-de-Greenlay QUÉ 19 E4
St-Guillaume QUÉ 19 D3
St-Guillaume-de-Granada QUÉ 16 A3
St-Guillaume-Nord QUÉ 19 A2
St-Guy QUÉ 22 B3
St-Henri QUÉ 19 F2
St-Henri-de-Taillon QUÉ 18 E2
St-Hermas QUÉ 19 A3
St-Herménégilde QUÉ 19 E4
St-Hilaire NB 23 B1
St-Hilaire-de-Dorset QUÉ 19 G3
St-Hilarion QUÉ 18 G4
St-Hippolyte QUÉ 19 B3
St-Honoré QUÉ 18 F2
St-Honoré QUÉ 22 A4
St-Honoré QUÉ 19 G3
St-Hubert QUÉ 22 A3
St-Hubert QUÉ 19 C4
St-Hugues QUÉ 19 C3
St-Hyacinthe QUÉ 19 C3
St-Ignace NB 23 G2
St-Ignace-de-Loyola QUÉ 19 C3
St-Ignace-de-Stanbridge QUÉ 19 C4
St-Ignace-du-Lac QUÉ 19 B2
St-Irénée NB 23 G1
St-Irénée QUÉ 18 G4
St-Isidore NB 23 G1
St-Isidore QUÉ 22 H2
St-Isidore QUÉ 19 F2
St-Isidore QUÉ 19 B4
St-Isidore-d'Aukland QUÉ 19 E4
St-Jacques NB 23 B1
St-Jacques QUÉ 19 B3
St-Jacques-de-Dupuy (see Dupuy) QUÉ 16 A2
St-Jacques-de-Leeds QUÉ 19 F2
St-Jacques-le-Majeur-de-Wolfestown QUÉ 19 E3
St-Jacques-le-Mineur QUÉ 19 B4
St-Janvier QUÉ 19 B3
St-Jean QUÉ 19 F1
St-Jean-Baptiste-de-Restigouche NB 22 D4
St-Jean-Chrysostome QUÉ 19 F2
St-Jean-de-Brébeuf QUÉ 19 F2
St-Jean-de-Cherbourg QUÉ 22 E2
St-Jean-de-Dieu QUÉ 22 B3
St-Jean-de-la-Lande QUÉ 22 B4
St-Jean-de-la-Lande QUÉ 19 G3
St-Jean-de-Matapédia QUÉ 22 D3
St-Jean-de-Matha QUÉ 19 B2
St-Jean-des-Piles QUÉ 19 D2
St-Jean-Port-Joli QUÉ 19 G1
St-Jean-sur-le-Lac QUÉ 17 G2
St-Jean-sur-Richelieu QUÉ 19 C4
St-Jérôme QUÉ 19 B3
St-Joachim QUÉ 19 F1
St-Joachim-de-Courval QUÉ 19 D3
St-Joachim-de-Shefford QUÉ 19 D4
St-Jogues QUÉ 22 G3
St-Joseph NB 23 G3
St-Joseph-de-Beauce QUÉ 19 F2
St-Joseph-de-Cléricy QUÉ 16 B3
St-Joseph-de-Kamouraska QUÉ 18 H4
St-Joseph-de-la-Rive QUÉ 18 G4
St-Joseph-de-Lepage QUÉ 22 C2
St-Joseph-de-Madawaska NB 23 B1
St-Joseph-de-Mékinac QUÉ 19 D1
St-Joseph-de-Sorel QUÉ 19 C3
St-Jovite QUÉ 19 A3
St-Jude QUÉ 19 C3
St-Jules QUÉ 22 F3
St-Jules QUÉ 19 F2
St-Julien QUÉ 19 E3
St-Juste-de-Brentenières QUÉ 19 H2
St-Juste-du-Lac QUÉ 22 B4
St-Justin QUÉ 19 C2
St-Lambert QUÉ 19 F2
St-Lambert QUÉ 19 B4
St-Lambert QUÉ 16 A2
St-Laurent QUÉ 19 F1
St-Laurent QUÉ 19 B4
St-Lazare QUÉ 19 G2
St-Lazare QUÉ 19 A4
St-Léandre QUÉ 22 D2
St-Léon QUÉ 18 E2
St-Léon QUÉ 19 C2
St-Léon-de-Standon QUÉ 19 G2
St-Léon-le-Grand QUÉ 22 D3
St-Léonard NB 23 B1
St-Léonard QUÉ 19 E1
St-Léonard QUÉ 19 B3
St-Léonard-d'Aston QUÉ 19 D3
St-Léonard-Parent NB 23 B1
St-Léonlin NB 22 G4
St-Liboire QUÉ 19 D3
St-Liguori QUÉ 19 B3
St-Louis QUÉ 19 C3
St-Louis-de-Blandford QUÉ 19 E2
St-Louis-de-France QUÉ 19 D2
St-Louis-de-Gonzague QUÉ 19 G2
St-Louis-de-Gonzague QUÉ 19 B4
St-Louis-de-Kent NB 23 G2
St-Louis-de-l'Isle-aux-Coudres QUÉ 18 G4
St-Louis-du-Ha! Ha! QUÉ 22 B4
St-Luc QUÉ 22 D2
St-Luc QUÉ 19 G2
St-Luc QUÉ 19 C4
St-Luc-de-Vincennes QUÉ 19 D2
St-Lucien QUÉ 19 D3
St-Ludger QUÉ 19 G3
St-Ludger-de-Milot QUÉ 18 E2
St-Magloire QUÉ 19 G2
St-Majoric QUÉ 19 D3
St-Malachie QUÉ 19 G2
St-Malo QUÉ 19 F4
St-Marc QUÉ 16 C2
St-Marc-de-Latour QUÉ 22 B2
St-Marc-des-Carrières QUÉ 19 E2
St-Marc-du-Lac-Long QUÉ 22 B4
St-Marc-sur-Richelieu QUÉ 19 C3
St-Marcel QUÉ 19 H1
St-Marcel-de-Richelieu QUÉ 19 C3
St-Marcellin QUÉ 22 C3
St-Martin QUÉ 19 G3
St-Martin-de-Restigouche NB 22 D4
St-Mathias-de-Bonneterre QUÉ 19 F4
St-Mathias-sur-Richelieu QUÉ 19 C4
St-Mathieu QUÉ 22 B3
St-Mathieu QUÉ 19 C2
St-Mathieu QUÉ 19 B4
St-Mathieu QUÉ 16 C2
St-Maurice QUÉ 19 D2
St-Maurice-de-Dalquier QUÉ 16 C2
St-Maurice-de-l'Échouerie QUÉ 22 H1
St-Médard QUÉ 22 B3
St-Méthode QUÉ 18 D2
St-Méthode-de-Frontenac QUÉ 19 F3
St-Michel QUÉ 19 F1
St-Michel QUÉ 19 B4
St-Michel-de-Wentworth QUÉ 19 A3
St-Michel-des-Saints QUÉ 19 B2
St-Modeste QUÉ 22 A3
St-Moïse QUÉ 22 C2
St-Narcisse QUÉ 19 F2
St-Narcisse QUÉ 19 D2
St-Narcisse-de-Rimouski QUÉ 22 C3
St-Nazaire QUÉ 18 E2
St-Nazaire QUÉ 19 D3
St-Nazaire-de-Berry QUÉ 16 C2
St-Nazaire-de-Buckland QUÉ 19 G2
St-Nérée QUÉ 19 G2
St-Nicéphore QUÉ 19 D3
St-Nicolas QUÉ 19 F2
St-Noël QUÉ 22 C2
St-Norbert NB 23 G3
St-Norbert QUÉ 19 C2
St-Norbert-du-Mont-Brun QUÉ 16 B3
St-Octave-de-Métis QUÉ 22 C2
St-Odilon QUÉ 19 G2
St-Omer QUÉ 22 F3
St-Omer QUÉ 19 H1
St-Onésime QUÉ 18 H4
St-Ours QUÉ 19 C3
St-Pacôme QUÉ 18 H4
St-Pamphile QUÉ 19 H1
St-Pascal QUÉ 18 H4
St-Patrice QUÉ 18 H3
St-Patrice-de-Beaurivage QUÉ 19 F2
St-Paul NB 23 G3
St-Paul QUÉ 19 B3
St-Paul-d'Abbotsford QUÉ 19 C4
St-Paul-de-la-Croix QUÉ 22 A3
St-Paul-de-l'Île-aux-Noix QUÉ 19 C4
St-Paul-du-Nord QUÉ 22 A2
St-Paulin QUÉ 19 C2
St-Philémon QUÉ 19 G2
St-Philibert QUÉ 19 G3
St-Philippe QUÉ 19 B4
St-Philippe-d'Argenteuil QUÉ 19 A3
St-Philippe-de-Néri QUÉ 18 H4
St-Pie QUÉ 19 C4
St-Pie-de-Guire QUÉ 19 D3
St-Pierre QUÉ 19 F1
St-Pierre QUÉ 19 B3
St-Pierre QUÉ 19 B4
St-Pierre-Baptiste QUÉ 19 E2
St-Pierre-de-Broughton QUÉ 19 F2
St-Pierre-de-Lamy QUÉ 22 B3
St-Pierre-de-Sorel QUÉ 19 C3
St-Pierre-de-Wakefield QUÉ 17 G4
St-Pierre-Jolys MAN 11 C4
St-Pierre-les-Becquets QUÉ 19 D2
St-Pierre-Montmagny QUÉ 19 G1
St-Placide QUÉ 19 A4
St-Placide-de-Charlevoix QUÉ 18 G4
St-Polycarpe QUÉ 19 A4
St-Praxède QUÉ 19 F3
St-Prime QUÉ 18 D2
St-Prosper QUÉ 19 G2
St-Prosper QUÉ 19 D2
St-Quentin NB 22 D4
St-Raphaël QUÉ 19 G1
St-Raymond QUÉ 19 E1
St-Rédempteur QUÉ 19 F2
St-Rédempteur QUÉ 19 A4
St-Rémi QUÉ 19 B4
St-Rémi-d'Amherst QUÉ 17 H3
St-Rémi-de-Tingwick QUÉ 19 E3
St-René QUÉ 19 G3
St-René-de-Matane QUÉ 22 D2
St-Robert QUÉ 19 C3
St-Robert-Bellarmin QUÉ 19 G3
St-Roch QUÉ 16 B3
St-Roch-de-l'Achigan QUÉ 19 B3
St-Roch-de-Mékinac QUÉ 19 D1
St-Roch-de-Richelieu QUÉ 19 C3
St-Roch-des-Aulnaies QUÉ 19 G1
St-Romain QUÉ 19 F3
St-Romuald QUÉ 19 F1
St-Rosaire QUÉ 19 E3
St-Samuel QUÉ 19 D3
St-Samuel-Station QUÉ 19 F3
St-Sauveur NB 23 F1
St-Sauveur-des-Monts QUÉ 19 A3
St-Sébastien QUÉ 19 F3

St-Sébastien QUÉ **19 C4**
St-Sévère QUÉ **19 C2**
St-Séverin QUÉ **19 F2**
St-Séverin QUÉ **19 D2**
St-Siméon QUÉ **18 H3**
St-Siméon QUÉ **22 G3**
St-Simon NB **22 H4**
St-Simon QUÉ **22 B3**
St-Simon QUÉ **19 C3**
St-Simon-les-Mines QUÉ **19 G2**
St-Sixte QUÉ **17 G4**
St-Stanislas QUÉ **18 D1**
St-Stanislas QUÉ **19 D2**
St-Stanislas-de-Kostka QUÉ **19 A4**
St-Sulpice QUÉ **19 C3**
St-Sylvère QUÉ **19 D2**
St-Sylvestre QUÉ **19 F2**
St-Télesphore QUÉ **19 A4**
St-Tharcisius QUÉ **22 D2**
St-Théodore-d'Acton QUÉ **19 D3**
St-Théophile QUÉ **19 G3**
St-Thomas NB **23 G3**
St-Thomas QUÉ **19 C3**
St-Thomas-d'Aquin QUÉ **19 C3**
St-Thomas-de-Caxton QUÉ **19 C2**
St-Thomas-Didyme QUÉ **18 D2**
St-Thuribe QUÉ **19 D2**
St-Timothée QUÉ **19 A4**
St-Tite QUÉ **19 D2**
St-Tite-des-Caps QUÉ **19 G1**
St-Ubalde QUÉ **19 D1**
St-Ulric QUÉ **22 D2**
St-Urbain QUÉ **18 G4**
St-Urbain-Premier QUÉ **19 B4**
St-Valentin QUÉ **19 C4**
St-Valère QUÉ **19 E3**
St-Valérien QUÉ **22 B3**
St-Valérien QUÉ **19 D4**
St-Vallier QUÉ **19 G1**
St-Vianney QUÉ **22 D2**
St-Viateur QUÉ **19 C2**
St-Victoire QUÉ **19 C3**
St-Victor QUÉ **19 F3**
St-Vital-de-Clermont QUÉ **16 A2**
St-Wenceslas QUÉ **19 D3**
St-Yvon QUÉ **22 H1**
St-Zacharie QUÉ **19 G3**
St-Zénon QUÉ **19 B2**
St-Zéphirin QUÉ **19 D3**
St-Zotique QUÉ **19 A4**
Ste Agathe MAN **11 B4**
Ste Amelie MAN **11 A3**
Ste Anne MAN **11 C4**
Ste Anne du Ruisseau NS **24 C4**
Ste Elizabeth MAN **11 B4**
Ste Genevieve MAN **11 C4**
Ste Rita MAN **11 C3**
Ste Rose du Lac MAN **11 A3**
Ste-Adèle QUÉ **19 A3**
Ste-Agathe QUÉ **19 F2**
Ste-Agathe-des-Monts QUÉ **19 A3**
Ste-Agnès QUÉ **18 G4**
Ste-Agnès-de-Bellecombe QUÉ **16 B3**
Ste-Anastasie QUÉ **19 E2**
Ste-Angèle-de-Laval QUÉ **19 D2**
Ste-Angèle-de-Mérici QUÉ **22 C2**
Ste-Angèle-de-Monnoir QUÉ **19 C4**
Ste-Angèle-de-Prémont QUÉ **19 C2**
Ste-Anne-de-Beaupré QUÉ **19 F1**
Ste-Anne-de-Kent NB **23 G2**
Ste-Anne-de-la-Pérade QUÉ **19 D2**
Ste-Anne-de-la-Rochelle QUÉ **19 D4**
Ste-Anne-de-Madawaska NB **23 B1**
Ste-Anne-de-Portneuf QUÉ **22 B2**
Ste-Anne-de-Prescott ONT **15 H1**
Ste-Anne-des-Lacs QUÉ **19 A3**
Ste-Anne-des-Monts QUÉ **22 E1**
Ste-Anne-de-Sorel QUÉ **19 C3**
Ste-Anne-des-Plaines QUÉ **19 B3**
Ste-Anne-du-Lac QUÉ **17 G2**
Ste-Anne-du-Lac QUÉ **19 F3**
Ste-Apolline QUÉ **19 G1**
Ste-Aurélie QUÉ **19 G2**
Ste-Béatrix QUÉ **19 B2**
Ste-Blandine QUÉ **22 B3**
Ste-Brigide-d'Iberville QUÉ **19 C4**
Ste-Brigitte-de-Laval QUÉ **19 F1**
Ste-Brigitte-des-Saults QUÉ **19 D3**
Ste-Catherine QUÉ **19 B4**
Ste-Catherine-de-Hatley QUÉ **19 E4**
Ste-Catherine-de-la-Jacques-Cartier QUÉ **19 E1**
Ste-Cécile-de-Lévrard QUÉ **19 D2**
Ste-Cécile-de-Milton QUÉ **19 D4**
Ste-Cécile-de-Whitton QUÉ **19 F3**
Ste-Christine QUÉ **19 D3**
Ste-Christine-d'Auvergne QUÉ **19 E1**
Ste-Claire QUÉ **19 F2**
Ste-Clotilde-de-Beauce QUÉ **19 F3**
Ste-Clotilde-de-Châteauguay QUÉ **19 B4**
Ste-Clotilde-de-Horton QUÉ **19 D3**
Ste-Croix QUÉ **19 E2**
Ste-Edwidge QUÉ **19 E4**
Ste-Élisabeth QUÉ **19 C3**
Ste-Élisabeth-de-Proulx QUÉ **18 E2**
Ste-Émélie-de-l'Énergie QUÉ **19 B2**
Ste-Eulalie QUÉ **19 D3**
Ste-Euphémie QUÉ **19 G1**
Ste-Famille QUÉ **19 F1**
Ste-Famille-d'Aumond QUÉ **17 F3**
Ste-Félicité QUÉ **22 D2**
Ste-Félicité QUÉ **19 H1**
Ste-Flavie QUÉ **22 C2**
Ste-Florence QUÉ **22 D3**
Ste-Foy QUÉ **19 F1**
Ste-Françoise QUÉ **22 B3**
Ste-Françoise QUÉ **19 E2**
Ste-Geneviève-de-Batiscan QUÉ **19 D2**
Ste-Germaine-Boulé QUÉ **16 A2**
Ste-Germaine-Station QUÉ **19 G2**
Ste-Gertrude QUÉ **19 D2**
Ste-Gertrude-Manneville QUÉ **16 C2**
Ste-Hedgwidge QUÉ **18 D2**
Ste-Hélène QUÉ **18 H4**
Ste-Hélène-de-Bagot QUÉ **19 D3**
Ste-Hélène-de-Chester QUÉ **19 E3**
Ste-Hélène-de-Mancebourg QUÉ **16 A2**
Ste-Hénédine QUÉ **19 F2**
Ste-Irène QUÉ **22 D2**
Ste-Jeanne-d'Arc QUÉ **18 E2**
Ste-Jeanne-d'Arc QUÉ **22 C2**
Ste-Julie QUÉ **19 C3**
Ste-Julie QUÉ **19 E2**
Ste-Julienne QUÉ **19 B3**
Ste-Justine QUÉ **19 G2**
Ste-Justine-de-Newton QUÉ **19 A4**
Ste-Louise QUÉ **19 H1**
Ste-Luce QUÉ **22 C2**
Ste-Lucie-de-Beauregard QUÉ **19 H1**
Ste-Lucie-de-Doncaster QUÉ **19 A3**
Ste-Madeleine QUÉ **19 C3**
Ste-Marcelline-de-Kildare QUÉ **19 B3**
Ste-Marguerite QUÉ **19 A3**
Ste-Marguerite QUÉ **19 F2**
Ste-Marguerite QUÉ **22 E3**
Ste-Marguerite-de-Lingwick QUÉ **19 F3**
Ste-Marguerite-Marie QUÉ **18 D2**
Ste-Marguerite-Station QUÉ **19 A3**
Ste-Marie QUÉ **19 F2**
Ste-Marie-de-Blandford QUÉ **19 D2**
Ste-Marie-de-Kent NB **23 G3**
Ste-Marie-St-Raphaël NB **22 H4**
Ste-Marie-Salomé QUÉ **19 B3**
Ste-Marthe QUÉ **19 A4**
Ste-Marthe-du-Cap-de-la-Madeleine QUÉ **19 D2**
Ste-Marthe-sur-le-Lac QUÉ **19 B4**
Ste-Martine QUÉ **19 B4**
Ste-Mélanie QUÉ **19 B3**
Ste-Monique QUÉ **18 E2**
Ste-Monique QUÉ **19 B3**
Ste-Monique QUÉ **19 D3**
Ste-Odile QUÉ **22 B2**
Ste-Paule QUÉ **22 D2**
Ste-Perpétue QUÉ **19 D3**
Ste-Perpétue QUÉ **19 H1**
Ste-Pétronille QUÉ **19 F1**
Ste-Rita QUÉ **22 B3**
Ste-Rosalie QUÉ **19 C3**
Ste-Rose-de-Prescott ONT **15 G2**
Ste-Rose-de-Watford QUÉ **19 G2**
Ste-Rose-du-Nord QUÉ **18 G3**
Ste-Sabine QUÉ **19 C4**
Ste-Sabine QUÉ **19 G2**
Ste-Sabine-Station QUÉ **19 G2**
Ste-Scholastique QUÉ **19 A3**
Ste-Sophie QUÉ **19 B3**
Ste-Sophie QUÉ **19 E3**
Ste-Sophie-de-Lévrard QUÉ **19 E2**
Ste-Thècle QUÉ **19 D1**
Ste-Thérèse QUÉ **19 B3**
Ste-Thérèse-de-Gaspé QUÉ **21 A4**
Ste-Thérèse-de-la-Gatineau QUÉ **17 F3**
Ste-Ursule QUÉ **19 C2**
Ste-Véronique QUÉ **17 H2**
Saintfield ONT **13 H4**
Saints-Anges QUÉ **19 F2**
Saints-Martyrs-Canadiens QUÉ **19 E3**
Salaberry-de-Valleyfield QUÉ **19 A4**
Salem NS **25 B3**
Salem ONT **14 E1**
Salem ONT **15 B4**
Salem Road NS **25 G3**
Salford ONT **14 E3**
Salisbury NB **23 G3**
Salluit QUÉ **3 C2**
Sally's Cove NFLD **26 B3**
Salmo BC **7 D4**
Salmon Arm BC **7 C3**
Salmon Bay QUÉ **26 C1**
Salmon Beach NB **22 G4**
Salmon Cove NFLD **27 A2**
Salmon Cove NFLD **27 H3**
Salmon Creek NB **23 E3**
Salmon River NS **24 C3**
Salmon River NS **24 G1**
Salmon River Lake NS **25 E4**
Salmon River Road NS **25 G2**
Salmonier NFLD **27 H4**
Salmonier NFLD **27 E4**
Salt Pond NFLD **27 E4**
Salt Springs NS **25 E3**
Salt Springs NS **24 H1**
Saltcoats SASK **9 G3**
Saltery Bay BC **5 F3**
Saltford ONT **14 C1**
Salvador SASK **9 C2**
Salvage NFLD **27 G2**
Sambro NS **24 G3**
San Clara MAN **9 G2**
San Josef BC **5 C3**
Sanca BC **7 E4**
Sanctuary SASK **9 C3**
Sand Beach NS **24 C4**
Sand Point NS **25 F3**
Sand River NS **24 E1**
Sandfield ONT **13 C1**
Sandford NS **24 C4**
Sandford ONT **14 H1**
Sandhill ONT **14 G1**
Sandhurst ONT **15 D4**
Sandilands MAN **11 C4**
Sandon BC **7 D4**
Sandridge MAN **11 B3**
Sandringham NFLD **27 G2**
Sandspit BC **5 A1**
Sandville NS **25 C3**
Sandy Bay SASK **8 F4**
Sandy Beach ALTA **7 E1**
Sandy Beach QUÉ **21 A4**
Sandy Cove NFLD **27 G2**
Sandy Cove NFLD **26 D1**
Sandy Cove NFLD **26 G3**
Sandy Cove NS **24 C3**
Sandy Cove ONT **13 G3**
Sandy Hook MAN **11 B3**
Sandy Lake ALTA **6 F3**
Sandy Lake MAN **11 A3**
Sandy Lake ONT **11 D1**
Sandy Point NS **24 D4**
Sanford MAN **11 B4**
Sangudo ALTA **7 E1**
Sanikiluaq NWT **3 C3**
Sanirajaq NWT **2 H2**
Sanmaur QUÉ **18 B3**
Sans Souci ONT **13 F2**
Sapawe ONT **11 F4**
Saratoga Beach BC **5 E3**
Sardis BC **5 G4**
Sarita BC **5 E4**
Sarnia ONT **14 B3**
Sarsfield ONT **15 G1**
Sarto MAN **11 C4**
Saskatchewan River Crossing ALTA **7 D2**
Saskatoon SASK **9 D2**
Saturna BC **5 F4**
Sauble Beach ONT **13 D3**
Sauble Beach North ONT **13 D3**
Sauble Beach South ONT **13 D3**
Sauble Falls ONT **13 D3**
Saulnierville NS **24 C3**
Sault Ste Marie ONT **12 D4**
Sault-au-Mouton QUÉ **22 A2**
Saunders Cove NFLD **27 G2**
Savage Cove NFLD **26 D1**
Savage Harbour PEI **25 C2**
Savant Lake ONT **11 F3**
Savona BC **5 G3**
Sawlog Bay ONT **13 F3**
Sawyerville QUÉ **19 E4**
Sayabec QUÉ **22 D2**
Sayward BC **5 D3**
Scandia ALTA **7 G3**
Scarborough ONT **14 H1**
Scarth MAN **9 G4**
Sceptre SASK **9 C3**
Schanzenfeld MAN **11 B4**
Schefferville NFLD **3 E3**
Schefferville QUÉ **3 E3**
Schist Lake MAN **8 G4**
Schomberg ONT **14 G1**
Schreiber ONT **12 B2**
Schuler ALTA **7 H3**
Schumacher ONT **12 F2**
Schutt ONT **15 C2**
Schwartz QUÉ **17 F4**
Scone ONT **13 D4**
Scotch Creek BC **7 C3**
Scotch Ridge NB **24 A1**
Scotch Village NS **24 F2**
Scotchtown NB **23 E4**
Scotchtown NS **25 H2**
Scotfield ALTA **7 G2**
Scotia ONT **13 G1**
Scotland ONT **14 F3**
Scots Bay NS **24 E1**
Scotsburn NS **24 H1**
Scotsguard SASK **9 C4**
Scotstown QUÉ **19 F4**
Scotsville NS **25 F2**
Scott QUÉ **19 F2**
Scott SASK **9 C2**
Scottsville ONT **14 D3**
Scoudouc NB **23 G3**
Scout Lake SASK **9 D4**
Scudder ONT **14 D4**
Sea View PEI **25 B2**
Seabright NS **24 F2**
Seacliffe ONT **14 A4**
Seafoam NS **25 C3**
Seaforth NS **24 G2**
Seaforth ONT **14 D2**
Seagrave ONT **13 H4**
Seal Cove NB **24 B2**
Seal Cove NFLD **27 D3**
Seal Cove NFLD **26 D3**
Seal Harbour NS **25 F4**
Seal Rocks NFLD **27 B2**
Searchmont ONT **12 D4**
Searletown PEI **25 B2**
Searston NFLD **27 A3**
Seba Beach ALTA **7 E1**
Sebright ONT **13 H3**
Sebringville ONT **14 D2**
Sechelt BC **5 F4**
Sedalia ALTA **7 H2**
Seddons Corner MAN **11 C3**
Sedgewick ALTA **7 G1**
Sedley SASK **9 F3**
Seebe ALTA **7 E3**
Seeleys Bay ONT **15 E3**
Seffernville NS **24 E2**
Seine River Village ONT **11 E4**
Selby ONT **15 D4**
Seldom NFLD **26 G4**
Selkirk MAN **11 C3**
Selkirk ONT **14 F3**
Selma NS **24 G1**
Selwyn ONT **15 B3**
Semans SASK **9 E3**
Senlac SASK **9 B2**
Senneterre QUÉ **16 D3**
Sept-Îles QUÉ **20 F2**
Serath SASK **9 E3**
Serpent River ONT **12 F4**
Sesekinika ONT **12 G3**
Seton Portage BC **5 G3**
Seven Persons ALTA **7 H3**
Seven Sisters Falls MAN **11 C3**
70 Mile House BC **5 G2**
Severn Bridge ONT **13 G3**
Severn Falls ONT **13 G3**
Sevogle NB **23 E2**
Sexsmith ALTA **6 C3**
Seymour Arm BC **7 C3**
Seymourville MAN **11 C3**
Shabaqua Corners ONT **11 G4**
Shackleton SASK **9 C3**
Shad Bay NS **24 F2-3**
Shag Harbour NS **24 C4**
Shakespeare ONT **14 E2**
Shalalth BC **5 G3**
Shallop Cove NFLD **27 A2**
Shallow Lake ONT **13 D3**
Shalloway Cove NFLD **27 G1**
Shamattawa MAN **10 C4**
Shambles Cove NFLD **27 G1**
Shamrock ONT **15 D2**
Shamrock SASK **9 D3**
Shanklin NB **24 D1**
Shanly ONT **15 G2**
Shannon NB **23 E4**
Shannon QUÉ **19 E1**
Shannonville ONT **15 D4**
Shanty Bay ONT **13 G3**
Sharbot Lake ONT **15 D3**
Sharon ONT **14 G1**
Shaughnessy ALTA **7 G3**
Shaunavon SASK **9 C4**
Shawanaga ONT **13 F1**
Shawinigan QUÉ **19 D2**
Shawinigan-Sud QUÉ **19 D2**
Shawnigan Lake BC **5 F4**
Shawville QUÉ **17 E4**
Shearstown NFLD **27 H3**
Shearwater BC **5 C2**
Sheaves Cove NFLD **27 A2**
Shebandowan ONT **11 G4**
Shedden ONT **14 D3**
Shediac NB **23 G3**
Shediac Bridge NB **23 G3**
Shediac Cape NB **23 G3**
Shediac Ridge NB **23 F2**
Sheenboro QUÉ **17 D3**
Sheerness ALTA **7 G2**
Sheet Harbour NS **24 H2**
Sheet Harbour Road NS **24 H1**
Sheffield NB **23 E4**
Sheffield ONT **14 F2**
Sheffield Mills NS **24 E1**
Sheguiandah ONT **13 C1**
Sheho SASK **9 F2**
Shekatika QUÉ **26 B1**
Shelburne NS **24 D4**
Shelburne ONT **14 F1**
Sheldrake QUÉ **20 H2**
Shell Lake SASK **9 D1**
Shellbrook SASK **9 D1**
Shelley BC **5 F1**
Shellmouth MAN **9 G3**
Shelter Bay BC **7 D3**
Shemogue NB **23 H3**
Sheppardville NFLD **27 D1**
Sherbrooke NS **25 E4**
Sherbrooke QUÉ **19 E4**
Shergrove MAN **11 A3**
Sherkston ONT **14 H3**
Sherridon MAN **8 G4**
Sherrington QUÉ **19 B4**
Sherritt Junction MAN **8 G4**
Sherwood PEI **25 C2**
Sherwood Park ALTA **7 F1**
Sheshegwaning ONT **13 A1**
Shetland ONT **14 C3**
Shigawake QUÉ **22 H3**
Shillington ONT **12 G2**
Shilo MAN **11 A4**
Shinimicas Bridge NS **25 B3**
Shining Tree ONT **12 F3**
Ship Cove NFLD **27 A2**
Ship Cove NFLD **27 G4**
Ship Harbour NFLD **27 G3**
Ship Harbour NS **24 H2**
Ship Harbour East NS **24 H2**
Shipka ONT **14 C2**
Shipman SASK **9 E1**
Shippagan NB **22 H4**
Shipshaw QUÉ **18 F2**
Shoal Arm NFLD **26 E4**
Shoal Bay NFLD **26 G3**
Shoal Brook NFLD **27 B1**
Shoal Cove NFLD **26 C2**
Shoal Harbour NFLD **27 G2**
Shoal Lake MAN **9 H3**
Shoal Lake SASK **9 F1**
Shoe Cove NFLD **27 H3**
Shoreacres BC **7 D4**
Shores Cove NFLD **27 H4**
Shorncliffe MAN **11 B3**
Shortdale MAN **9 G3**
Shrewsbury ONT **14 C4**
Shubenacadie NS **24 G2**
Shulie NS **24 E1**
Shunacadie NS **25 G2**
Shuswap Falls BC **7 C4**
Sibbald ALTA **7 H2**
Sicamous BC **7 C3**
Sidney BC **5 F4**
Sidney MAN **11 A4**
Siegas NB **23 B1**
Sifton MAN **11 A3**
Sikanni Chief BC **4 F2**
Sillery QUÉ **19 F1**
Sillikers NB **23 E2**
Silton SASK **9 E3**
Silver MAN **11 B3**
Silver Creek BC **7 C3**
Silver Dollar ONT **11 F3**
Silver Falls MAN **11 C3**
Silver Hill ONT **14 E3**
Silver Park SASK **9 E2**
Silver Ridge MAN **11 A3**
Silver Valley ALTA **6 C2**
Silver Water ONT **13 A1**
Silverton BC **7 D4**
Silverton MAN **9 G3**
Simcoe ONT **14 F3**
Simmie SASK **9 C4**
Simonds NB **23 C3**
Simonhouse MAN **8 G4**
Simoon Sound BC **5 D3**
Simpson SASK **9 E3**
Sinclair MAN **9 G4**
Sinclair Mills BC **5 G1**
Singhampton ONT **13 F4**
Sintaluta SASK **9 F3**
Sioux Lookout ONT **11 E3**
Sioux Narrows ONT **11 D4**
Sipiwesk MAN **10 B3**
Sirdar BC **7 E4**
Sissiboo Falls NS **24 C3**
Sisson Ridge NB **23 C2**
Skead ONT **12 G4**
Skidegate BC **5 A1**
Skiff ALTA **7 G4**
Skiff Lake NB **23 C4**
Skinners Pond PEI **25 A1**
Skir Dhu NS **25 G1**
Skookumchuck BC **7 E4**
Skownan MAN **11 A2**
Slate Falls ONT **11 E2**
Slave Lake ALTA **6 E3**
Sled Lake SASK **8 D4**
Sleeman ONT **11 D4**
Slocan BC **7 D4**
Slocan Park BC **7 D4**
Small Point NFLD **27 H3**
Smeaton SASK **9 E1**
Smelt Brook NS **25 G1**
Smiley SASK **9 C2**
Smith ALTA **6 E3**
Smithers BC **4 D4**
Smithers Landing BC **4 D4**
Smithfield NS **25 E4**
Smiths Corner NB **23 F3**
Smiths Corners NS **24 F2**
Smiths Cove NS **24 C2**
Smiths Creek NB **23 F4**
Smiths Falls ONT **15 F2**
Smith's Harbour NFLD **26 E3**
Smithville NS **24 D4**
Smithville ONT **14 G2**
Smoky Lake ALTA **7 F1**
Smooth Rock Falls ONT **12 F2**
Smuts SASK **9 D2**
Snelgrove ONT **14 G1**
Snipe Lake SASK **9 C3**
Snooks Arm NFLD **26 E3**
Snook's Harbour NFLD **27 G2**
Snow Lake MAN **8 H4**
Snow Road Station ONT **15 D2**
Snowball ONT **14 G1**
Snowflake MAN **11 B4**
Snug Harbour ONT **13 F2**
Snyder ONT **14 H3**
Soda Creek BC **5 G2**
Sointula BC **5 D3**
Soldiers Cove NS **25 G3**
Solina ONT **14 H1**
Solsgirth MAN **9 G3**
Sombra ONT **14 B3**
Somerset MAN **11 B4**
Somerset NS **24 E2**
Somerville NB **23 C3**
Somme SASK **9 F2**
Sommerfeld MAN **11 B4**
Sonningdale SASK **9 D2**
Sonora NS **25 E4**
Sonya ONT **13 H4**
Sooke BC **5 F4**
Soperton ONT **15 F3**
Sop's Arm NFLD **26 D3**
Sorel QUÉ **19 C3**
Sorrento BC **7 C3**
Souris MAN **11 A4**
Souris PEI **25 D2**
South Alton NS **24 E2**
South Bar NS **25 H2**
South Bay ONT **11 E2**
South Bay ONT **13 G3**
South Baymouth ONT **13 C1**
South Beach ONT **15 B3**
South Bolton QUÉ **19 D4**
South Branch NB **23 G3**
South Branch NFLD **27 A3**
South Branch NS **24 H1**
South Brook NFLD **27 D1**
South Brook NS **24 F1**
South Brookfield NS **24 E3**
South Cayuga ONT **14 G3**
South Dildo NFLD **27 H3**
South East Bight NFLD **27 F3**
South Gillies ONT **11 G4**
South Gloucester ONT **15 F2**
South Gut St Ann's NS **25 G2**
South Hazelton BC **4 D3**
South Indian Lake MAN **8 H3**
South Junction MAN **11 C4**
South Lancaster ONT **15 H2**
South Maitland NS **24 G1**
South Middleton ONT **14 E3**
South Milford NS **24 D2**
South Monaghan ONT **15 B4**
South Mountain ONT **15 G2**
South Ohio NS **24 C4**
South Porcupine ONT **12 F2**
South Range NS **24 C3**
South Rawdon NS **24 F2**
South River NFLD **27 H3**
South River ONT **13 G1**
South Slocan BC **7 D4**
South Tetagouche NB **22 F4**
South Uniacke NS **24 F2**
South Victoria NS **25 B3**
South West Port Mouton NS **24 E4**
South Woodslee ONT **14 A4**
Southampton NS **24 F1**
Southampton ONT **13 D3**
Southbank BC **5 E1**
Southend SASK **8 F3**
Southern Bay NFLD **27 G2**
Southern Harbour NFLD **27 G3**
Southey SASK **9 E3**
Southport NFLD **27 G3**
Southside Antigonish Harbour NS **25 E3**
Southville NS **24 C3**
Southwest Margaree NS **25 F2**
Southwold ONT **14 D3**
Sovereign SASK **9 D2**
Sowerby ONT **12 E4**
Spalding SASK **9 E2**
Spallumcheen BC **7 C3**
Spaniard's Bay NFLD **27 H3**
Spanish ONT **12 F4**
Spanish Room NFLD **27 F4**
Spanish Ship Bay NS **25 E4**
Sparta ONT **14 D3**
Sparwood BC **7 F4**
Spearhill MAN **11 B3**
Spedden ALTA **7 G1**
Speers SASK **9 D2**
Spencers Island NS **24 E1**
Spencerville ONT **15 F3**
Spences Bridge BC **5 G3**
Sperling MAN **11 B4**
Speyside ONT **14 F2**
Spillars Cove NFLD **27 H2**
Spillimacheen BC **7 E3**
Spillway NFLD **27 C1**
Spirit River ALTA **6 C3**
Spiritwood SASK **9 D1**
Split Lake MAN **10 B3**
Sporting Mountain NS **25 F3**
Spragge ONT **12 E4**
Sprague MAN **11 C4**
Spring Bay ONT **13 B1**
Spring Brook ONT **15 C3**
Spring Coulee ALTA **7 G4**
Spring Valley SASK **9 E4**
Springdale NFLD **27 D1**
Springfield NB **23 E4**
Springfield NS **24 E2**
Springfield ONT **14 E3**
Springford ONT **14 E3**
Springhill NS **24 F1**
Springhill Junction NS **24 F1**
Springmount ONT **13 D3**
Springside SASK **9 F3**
Springstein MAN **11 B4**
Springtown ONT **15 D2**
Springvale ONT **14 F3**
Springville NS **24 H1**
Springville ONT **15 A4**
Springwater SASK **9 C2**
Sproat Lake BC **5 E4**
Spruce Brook NFLD **27 B2**
Spruce Grove ALTA **7 F1**
Spruce Home SASK **9 E1**
Spruce Lake SASK **9 C1**
Spruce View ALTA **7 F2**
Sprucedale ONT **13 G1**
Spry Bay NS **24 H2**
Spry Harbour NS **24 H2**
Sputinow ALTA **7 G1**
Spuzzum BC **5 G4**
Spy Hill SASK **9 G3**
Squamish BC **5 F4**
Squatec QUÉ **22 B3**
Squilax BC **7 C3**
Staffa ONT **14 D2**
Stag Harbour NFLD **26 G4**
Stalwart SASK **9 E3**
Stampville ONT **15 G2**
Stanbridge-Est QUÉ **19 C4**
Stanbridge-Station QUÉ **19 C4**
Stanburn NS **24 E2**
Stand Off ALTA **7 G4**
Standard ALTA **7 F3**
Stanhope NFLD **27 F1**
Stanhope PEI **25 C2**
Stanley NB **23 D3**
Stanley NS **24 F2**
Stanley ONT **12 A2**
Stanley Bridge PEI **25 C2**
Stanley Cove NFLD **27 D3**
Stanley Mission SASK **8 E4**
Stanstead Plain QUÉ **19 E4**
Staples ONT **14 B4**
Star ALTA **7 F1**
Star City SASK **9 E2**
Starbuck MAN **11 B4**
Starratt-Olsen ONT **11 D3**
Stauffer ALTA **7 E2**
Stavely ALTA **7 F3**
Stayner ONT **13 F3**
Stead MAN **11 C3**
Steady Brook NFLD **27 B1**
Steelman SASK **9 F4**
Steen River ALTA **2 D4**
Steep Rock MAN **11 A2**
Steinbach MAN **11 C4**
Stella ONT **15 D4**
Stellarton NS **24 H1**
Stenen SASK **9 F2**
Stephenville NFLD **27 A2**
Stephenville Crossing NFLD **27 B2**
Stettler ALTA **7 F2**
Stevensville ONT **14 H3**
Stewardson Inlet BC **5 D4**
Stewart BC **4 C3**
Stewart Crossing YK **2 B2**
Stewart Hall ONT **15 B4**
Stewart Valley SASK **9 C3**
Stewarttown ONT **14 F1**
Stewiacke NS **24 G1**
Stewiacke Cross Road NS **24 H1**
Stewiacke East NS **24 G1**
Stickney NB **23 C3**
Stikine BC **4 B2**
Stillwater BC **5 E3**
Stillwater NS **25 E4**
Stirling ALTA **7 G4**
Stirling ONT **15 C4**
Stitt MAN **10 B3**
Stittsville ONT **15 F2**
Stock Cove NFLD **27 H2**
Stockholm SASK **9 G3**
Stockton MAN **11 A4**
Stoco ONT **15 C3**
Stoke QUÉ **19 E4**
Stokes Bay ONT **13 D2**
Stone Valley NFLD **27 D3**
Stonecliffe ONT **17 C3**
Stoneham QUÉ **19 F1**
Stonehaven NB **22 G4**
Stonehouse NS **25 B3**
Stonehurst NS **24 F3**
Stoner BC **5 F1**
Stone's Cove NFLD **27 F3**
Stoneville NFLD **27 F1**
Stonewall MAN **11 B3**
Stoney Creek ONT **14 G2**
Stoney Point ONT **14 B4**
Stony Lake SASK **8 E1**
Stony Mountain MAN **11 B3**
Stony Plain ALTA **7 F1**
Stony Rapids SASK **8 E1**
Stonyridge ONT **15 B3**
Stormont NS **25 E4**
Stornoway QUÉ **19 F3**
Stornoway SASK **9 G3**
Storthoaks SASK **9 G4**
Stouffville ONT **14 H1**
Stoughton SASK **9 F4**
Strabane ONT **14 F2**
Straffordville ONT **14 E3**
Straitsview NFLD **26 E1**
Stranraer SASK **9 C2**
Strasbourg SASK **9 E3**
Stratford ONT **14 E2**
Stratford QUÉ **19 F3**
Strathburn ONT **14 C3**
Strathclair MAN **11 A3**
Strathlorne NS **25 F2**
Strathmore ALTA **7 F3**
Strathnaver BC **5 F1**
Strathroy ONT **14 C3**
Stratton ONT **11 D4**
Streamstown ALTA **7 H1**
Strome ALTA **7 G1**
Strongfield SASK **9 D3**
Stroud ONT **13 G4**
Struan SASK **9 D2**
Stuart Island BC **5 E3**
Stuartburn MAN **11 C4**
Stuie BC **5 D2**
Stukely-Sud QUÉ **19 D4**
Sturdies Bay BC **5 F4**
Sturgeon Bay ONT **13 G3**
Sturgeon Falls ONT **12 H4**
Sturgeon Heights ALTA **6 D3**
Sturgeon Landing SASK **9 G1**
Sturgeon Point ONT **15 A3**
Sturgis SASK **9 F2**
Success SASK **9 C3**
Sucker Creek ONT **13 C1**
Sucker River SASK **8 E4**
Sudbury ONT **12 G4**
Suffield ALTA **7 H3**
Suley Ann's Cove NFLD **26 E4**
Sullivan QUÉ **16 C3**
Sullivan Bay BC **5 D3**
Sully QUÉ **22 A4**
Sultan ONT **12 E3**
Summer Beaver ONT **11 G1**
Summerberry SASK **9 F3**
Summerford NFLD **27 F1**
Summerland BC **7 C4**
Summers Corners ONT **14 E3**
Summerside NFLD **27 B1**
Summerside PEI **25 B2**
Summerstown ONT **15 H2**
Summerstown Station ONT **15 H2**
Summerville NFLD **27 G2**
Summerville NS **24 F2**
Summerville Centre NS **24 E4**
Summit Lake BC **4 F4**
Sunbury ONT **15 E3**
Sundance MAN **10 C3**
Sundance Beach ALTA **7 F1**
Sunderland ONT **13 H4**
Sundown MAN **11 C4**
Sundre ALTA **7 E2**
Sundridge ONT **13 G1**
Sunnidale Corners ONT **13 F3**
Sunny Brae NS **25 D3**
Sunny Corner NB **23 E2**
Sunnynook ALTA **7 G2**
Sunnyside NB **22 F3**
Sunnyside NFLD **27 G3**
Sunset House ALTA **6 D3**
Sunset Prairie BC **4 G3**
Suomi ONT **11 G4**
Surrey BC **5 F4**
Sussex NB **23 F4**
Sussex Corner NB **23 F4**
Sutherland River NS **25 D3**
Sutton ONT **13 G4**
Sutton QUÉ **19 D4**
Sutton Junction QUÉ **19 D4**
Swalwell ALTA **7 F2**
Swan Hills ALTA **6 E3**
Swan Lake MAN **11 B4**
Swan Plain SASK **9 G2**
Swan River MAN **9 G2**
Swanger Cove NFLD **27 E3**
Swanson SASK **9 D2**
Swartz Bay BC **5 F4**
Swastika ONT **12 G3**
Sweaburg ONT **14 E2**
Sweet Bay NFLD **27 G2**
Swift Current NFLD **27 G3**
Swift Current SASK **9 C3**
Swift Rapids ONT **13 G3**
Swinton Park ONT **13 E4**
Sybouts SASK **9 E4**
Sydenham ONT **15 E3**
Sydney NS **25 H2**
Sydney Forks NS **25 H2**
Sydney Mines NS **25 H2**
Sydney River NS **25 H2**
Sylvan MAN **11 B3**
Sylvan ONT **14 C2**
Sylvan Lake ALTA **7 F2**
Sylvania SASK **9 F2**
Syringa Creek BC **7 D4**

T

Ta Ta Creek BC **7 E4**
Taber ALTA **7 G3**
Tabusintac NB **23 G1**
Tachie BC **4 E4**
Tadmore SASK **9 F2**
Tadoule Lake MAN **8 H1**
Tadoussac QUÉ **18 H3**
Taghum BC **7 D4**
Tahsis BC **5 D3**
Takhini Hotspring YK **2 B2**
Takipy MAN **8 G4**
Takla Landing BC **4 E3**
Takysie Lake BC **5 E1**
Talbotville Royal ONT **14 D3**
Taloyoak NWT **2 G2**
Tamworth ONT **15 D3**
Tancook NS **24 F3**
Tancredia QUÉ **17 E4**
Tangent ALTA **6 D3**
Tangier NS **24 H2**
Tantallon NS **24 F2**
Tantallon SASK **9 G3**
Tappen BC **7 C3**
Tara ONT **13 D3**
Tarbotvale NS **25 G2**
Tarnopol SASK **9 E2**
Tarzwell ONT **12 G3**
Taschereau QUÉ **16 B2**
Tasiujaq QUÉ **3 D2**
Tatalrose BC **5 E1**

Physical Features

A

Aaron, Lac QUÉ 19 E1
Aaron, Parc provincial ONT 11 E3
Aaron Provincial Park ONT 11 E3
Abamasagi Lake ONT 12 B1
Abattis, Lac des QUÉ 17 E3
Aberdeen Lake NWT 2 F3
Abino, Point ONT 14 H3
Abitibi, Lac ONT 12 G-H2
Abitibi, Lac QUÉ 16 A2
Abitibi, Lake ONT 16 A2
Abitibi, Lake QUÉ 12 G-H2
Abitibi de Troyes, Parc provincial ONT 12 G2
Abitibi de Troyes Provincial Park ONT 12 G2
Abitibi River ONT 12 F1
Abos, Lac QUÉ 16 E4
Acadie, Rivière l' QUÉ 19 B4
Acadien Historical Village NB 22 G4
Acadien Odyssey National Historic Site NB 23 G3
Achapapuskow Lake MAN 8 G4
Acheninni Lake SASK 8 F4
Achepabanca, Lac QUÉ 16 F2
Achigan, Lac de l' QUÉ 19 B3
Achigan, Lac de l' QUÉ 17 D3
Achigan, Lac de l' QUÉ 17 F3
Achigan, Rivière de l' QUÉ 19 B3
Achintre, Lac QUÉ 16 G3
Adam, Rivière QUÉ 22 A-B2
Adam Creek, Réserve naturelle provinciale ONT 12 F1
Adam Creek Provincial Nature Reserve ONT 12 F1
Adam River BC 5 D3
Adamant Mountain BC 7 D2
Adams Lake BC 7 C3
Adams Lake Provincial Recreation Area BC 7 C3
Adams River BC 7 C3
Adams Sound NWT 2 H1
Adanac Ski Area SASK 9 E1
Adelaide Peninsula NWT 2 G2
Adies Pond NFLD 27 C1
Admiralty Inlet NWT 2 H1
Admiralty Island NWT 2 F2
Adolphus Reach ONT 15 D4
Adonis, Lac QUÉ 16 H4
Adstock, Mont QUÉ 19 F3
African Lion Safari ONT 14 F2
Agawa Bay ONT 12 D3
Agawa Canyon ONT 12 D3
Agawa River ONT 12 D3
Agnes Lake ONT 11 F4
Agnew Lake ONT 12 F4
Aguanus, Rivière QUÉ 3 F3
Aguasabon River ONT 12 B2
Aguenier, Lac QUÉ 20 C1
Agusk Lake ONT 10 F3
Ahmic Lake ONT 13 G1
Ahwachanjeesh Pond NFLD 27 D3
Aigle, Lac à l' QUÉ 20 G1
Aigle, Lac de l' QUÉ 17 G3
Aigle, Rivière de l' QUÉ 16 G1
Aigle, Rivière de l' QUÉ 17 F3
Aigles, Lac des QUÉ 18 E1
Aigles, Lac des QUÉ 22 B3
Aigles, Lac des QUÉ 19 B1
Aigremont, Lac QUÉ 18 B1
Aiguebelle, Parc d' QUÉ 16 B2
Aikens Lake MAN 11 C2
Ailleboust, Lac d' QUÉ 18 E1
Ainslie, Lake NS 25 F2
Aishihik Lake YK 2 A2
Akamina-Kishinena Provincial Recreation Area BC 7 F4
Akie River BC 4 E2
Akimiski Island NWT 3 C4
Akpatok Island NWT 3 D2
Alaska Highway BC 4 E1
Alaska Highway YK 2 A2
Albanel, Lac QUÉ 3 D4
Albany River ONT 3 B4
Albany River, Parc provincial ONT 11 H1
Albany River Provincial Park ONT 11 H1
Albert, Lac QUÉ 18 G2
Albert Edward Bay NWT 2 F2
Albert Lake Mesa, Réserve naturelle provinciale ONT 12 A2
Albert Lake Mesa Provincial Nature Reserve ONT 12 A2
Alberta, Mount ALTA 7 D2
Alder Peak BC 4 C3
Alex, Lac QUÉ 18 E1
Alex, Rivière QUÉ 18 E1
Alexander Bay NFLD 27 G2
Alexander Graham Bell National Historic Site NS 25 G2
Alexander-Graham-Bell, Lieu historique national NS 25 G2
Alexandra Bridge Provincial Park BC 5 G3
Algonquin, Parc provincial ONT 17 B-C4
Algonquin Provincial Park ONT 17 B-C4
Alice Arm BC 4 C3
Alice Creek ALTA 6 F1
Alice Lake Provincial Park BC 5 F3
Alkali Creek ALTA 7 H2
Allan, Mount ALTA 7 E3
Allan Water River ONT 11 F3
Allard, Lac QUÉ 21 B1
Alliés, Lac des QUÉ 18 F4
Allison Lake Provincial Park BC 5 H4
Allison Pass BC 5 H4
Allumette Lake ONT 15 C1
Allumettes, Île des QUÉ 17 D4
Allumettes, Lac aux ONT 15 D1
Alouettes, Pointe aux QUÉ 18 H3
Alsek River YK 2 A2
Alstead River SASK 8 D3
Alston Creek MAN 10 C1
Alva, Loch NB 24 B1
Amable du Fond River ONT 17 A-B3
Amadjuak Lake NWT 3 C1
Amariton, Lac QUÉ 20 C3
Amery, Mount ALTA 7 D2
Amherst Island ONT 15 D4
Amherst Shore Provincial Park NS 25 B3
Amisk Lake SASK 8 F4
Amisk Lake Provincial Recreation Site SASK 8 F4
Amisk River ALTA 6 F3
Amour Point NFLD 26 D1
Amphitrite Point BC 5 E4
Amundsen, Golfe d' NWT 2 D1
Amundsen Gulf NWT 2 D1
Anabusko River MAN 10 E2
Anaharea Lake ONT 12 D2
Anahim Creek BC 5 F2
Anchor Harbour NFLD 27 G1
Anconi, Point NS 25 G2
Anctil, Lac QUÉ 18 A2
Anderson Lake BC 5 G3
Anderson River NWT 2 D1
Andesite Peak BC 4 C4
Andou, Lac QUÉ 17 E1
Andrew Lake ALTA 8 B1
Andrews Bay Provincial Park BC 5 D1
Andrews Head NS 24 E3
Andrieux, Lac QUÉ 18 G1
Andy Bailey Provincial Recreation Area BC 4 F1
Angekum Lake ONT 11 D1
Angers, Rivière QUÉ 22 F3
Angikuni Lake NWT 2 F3
Anglais, Pointe aux QUÉ 20 E3
Anglais, Rivière des QUÉ 20 C3
Anglais, Rivière des QUÉ 19 B4
Anglin Lake Provincial Recreation Site SASK 9 E1
Angling Lake MAN 10 D4
Angling River ONT 10 F4
Anguille Mountains NFLD 27 A2
Anicet, Lac QUÉ 19 A2
Anima Nipissing Lake ONT 12 G3
Anjigami Lake ONT 12 D3
Annapolis Basin NS 24 C2
Annapolis River NS 24 D2
Annapolis Valley NS 24 D2
Annie Bay ONT 15 B1
Annieopsquotch Mountains NFLD 27 C2
Anse aux Meadows, Lieu historique national de l' NFLD 26 E1
Anse aux Meadows National Historic Site NFLD 26 E1
Anson Creek ONT 13 H3
Anstruther Lake ONT 15 B3
Antelope Lake SASK 9 C3
Anthony Provincial Park NS 24 G1
Anticosti, Île d' QUÉ 21 C2
Anticosti Island QUÉ 21 C2
Antigonish Harbour NS 25 E3
Antique, Lac QUÉ 19 A2
Antler River SASK 9 G4
Antoine, Lac QUÉ 17 E3
Antoine Creek ONT 17 A3
Antostagnan, Lac QUÉ 17 E2
Apeganau Lake MAN 8 H3
Apex Alpine Ski Area BC 7 C4
Apex Mountain Provincial Recreation Area BC 7 C4
Aquarium and Marine Centre NB 22 H4
Aquarium et Centre marin NB 22 H4
Aquatuk River ONT 10 H3
Ara Lake ONT 12 B1
Araignées, Lac aux QUÉ 19 G4
Archambault, Lac QUÉ 19 A2
Archibald Lake SASK 8 C1
Archipel-de-Mingan, Réserve du parc national de l' QUÉ 21 B1
Arctic Red River NWT 2 C1-2
Arcy, Lac d' QUÉ 17 D1
Argent, Rivière d' QUÉ 17 G2
Argent, Rivière l' QUÉ 20 A3
Argile, Lac de l' QUÉ 17 G4
Argonaut Mountain BC 7 C2
Argos, Cape NS 25 F3
Argyle Shore Provincial Park PEI 25 C2
Arichat Provincial Park NS 25 F3
Aristazabal Island BC 5 C1
Aristote, Lac QUÉ 18 B1
Armagh, Rivière QUÉ 19 G2
Armit River MAN 9 G2
Armit River SASK 9 G2
Armstrong, Lac QUÉ 17 G3
Armstrong Lake MAN 10 B3
Arnaud, Rivière QUÉ 3 C2
Arnoux, Lac QUÉ 16 A3
Aroma Lake SASK 9 C2
Arran Lake ONT 13 D3
Arrow Lake ONT 11 G4
Arrow Lake, Parc provincial ONT 11 G4
Arrow Lake Provincial Park ONT 11 G4
Arrow Lakes Provincial Park BC 7 D4
Arrow Lakes (Shelter Bay Unit) Provincial Park BC 7 D3
Arrow River MAN 9 G3
Arrowhead, Parc provincial ONT 13 H2
Arrowhead Lake ALTA 8 A1
Arrowhead Peninsula, Réserve naturelle provinciale ONT 11 F4
Arrowhead Peninsula Provincial Nature Reserve ONT 11 F4
Arrowhead Provincial Park ONT 13 H2
Arsenault Lake SASK 8 C4
Artillery Lake NWT 2 E3
Ascot, Rivière QUÉ 19 E4
Asessippi Provincial Park MAN 9 G3
Ash Creek BC 4 B1
Ashby Lake ONT 15 C2
Asheweig River ONT 10 G4
Ashuanipi Lake QUÉ 3 E3
Ashuapmushuan, Lac QUÉ 18 B1
Ashuapmushuan, Réserve faunique QUÉ 18 B2
Ashuapmushuan, Rivière QUÉ 18 C2
Asipoquobah Lake ONT 10 E4
Aspen Beach Provincial Park ALTA 7 F2
Aspen Brook Provincial Park NFLD 27 E1
Aspy Bay NS 25 G1
Asquiche, Lac QUÉ 20 E2
Assaikwatamo River MAN 10 B2
Assean Lake MAN 10 B3
Assemetquagan, Rivière QUÉ 22 E3
Assiniboine, Mount ALTA 7 E3
Assiniboine, Mount BC 7 E3
Assiniboine River MAN 11 A-B4
Assiniboine River SASK 9 G3
Assinica, Lac QUÉ 3 D4
Assomption, Rivière l' QUÉ 19 B2
Athabasca, Lac ALTA 8 C1
Athabasca, Lac SASK 8 C1
Athabasca, Lake ALTA 8 C1
Athabasca, Lake SASK 8 C1
Athabasca Glacier Viewing Area ALTA 7 D2
Athabasca River ALTA 6 G1
Athabasca Sand Dunes Provincial Wilderness Park SASK 8 C1
Athlone Island BC 5 C2
Athlow Bay BC 5 A5
Athol Bay ONT 15 D4
Atik Lake MAN 9 G1
Atik Lake MAN 10 B3
Atik River MAN 10 C3
Atikaki Provincial Wilderness Park MAN 11 C2
Atikonak Lake NFLD 3 E3
Atikwa Lake ONT 11 E3-4
Atkinson Lake MAN 10 C3
Atlin Lake BC 2 B3
Atlin Provincial Park BC 4 A6
Attawapiskat Lake ONT 11 G1
Attawapiskat River ONT 3 B4
Attikamagen Lake NFLD 3 E3
Attwood Lake ONT 11 G2
Attwood River ONT 11 G2
Aubichon Arm SASK 8 D4
Aubrey Falls, Parc provincial ONT 12 E4
Aubrey Falls Provincial Park ONT 12 E4
Aubry Lake NWT 2 D2
Augier, Lac QUÉ 16 E2
Augusta, Lac QUÉ 16 H1
Augustines, Lac des QUÉ 17 F1
Aulavik, Parc national de NWT 2 E1
Aulavik National Park NWT 2 E1
Aulneau Peninsula ONT 11 D4
Aulneau Peninsula, Unité de gestion de la faune ONT 11 D4
Aulneau Peninsula Wildlife Management Unit ONT 11 D4
Aumond, Lacs QUÉ 17 D2
Ausable River ONT 14 C2
Auteuil, Lac d' QUÉ 21 E1
Authier, Lac QUÉ 16 B2
Authier, Rivière QUÉ 16 B2
Avalon Peninsula NFLD 27 G-H4
Avalon Wilderness Reserve NFLD 27 H4
Avaugour, Lac QUÉ 18 B1
Aviron Point NFLD 27 C3
Avon River NS 24 F2
Avon River ONT 14 D2
Awenda, Parc provincial ONT 13 F3
Awenda Provincial Park ONT 13 F3
Axe Lake ONT 13 G2
Aylen Lake ONT 15 B1
Aylesford Lake NS 24 E2
Aylmer, Lac QUÉ 19 F3
Aylmer, Mount ALTA 7 E3
Aylmer Lake NWT 2 E3
Aylmer Wildlife Management Area ONT 14 E3
Azu Mountain Ski Area BC 4 F3
Azure Lake BC 5 H2
Azure Mountain BC 5 H2

B

Babine Lake BC 4 D-E4
Babine Mountains Provincial Recreation Area BC 4 D4
Babine Range BC 4 D3
Babine River BC 4 D3
Baby, Lac QUÉ 17 A7
Baccalieu Island NFLD 27 H2
Baccaro Point NS 24 D4
Bachelor, Lac QUÉ 16 F1
Bachois, Lac QUÉ 18 B1
Back River NWT 2 F3
Backbone Ranges NWT 2 C2
Backside Pond Provincial Park NFLD 27 H3
Bad Hills SASK 9 C3
Badajoz, Lac QUÉ 17 H1
Badgeley Island ONT 13 C1
Badgeley Point ONT 13 C1
Badger Bay NFLD 26 E4
Badwater River SASK 8 E1
Bae River NWT 2 E2
Baezaeko River BC 5 F1
Baffin, Île NWT 2 H1
Baffin, Île NWT 3 C1
Baffin Island NWT 2 H1
Baffin Island NWT 3 C1
Bagg, Mount BC 5 H1
Baie, Lac de la QUÉ 16 H1
Baie-des-Loups, Refuge d'oiseaux migrateurs de la QUÉ 21 G1
Baies, Lac des QUÉ 18 G-H1
Baies, Lac des QUÉ 17 C-D1
Bailey Creek ONT 14 F1
Bailey Lake SASK 8 F1
Baillairgé, Lac QUÉ 18 B2
Bailly, Lac QUÉ 16 G2
Baird Point BC 5 B1
Bajo Point BC 5 D4
Baker Creek BC 5 F1
Baker Lake NWT 2 G3
Bald Peak NB 23 C1
Baldock Lake MAN 10 A3
Baldy Mountain MAN 9 G2
Baleine, Grande Rivière de la QUÉ 3 C3
Baleine, Petite Rivière de la QUÉ 3 C3
Baleine, Rivière à la QUÉ 3 E2
Balinhard Mount ALTA 7 D2
Ball Lake ONT 11 D3
Ballantyne River SASK 8 F4
Ballard, Cape NFLD 27 H4
Balsam Lake ONT 13 H3
Balsam Lake, Parc provincial ONT 13 H3
Balsam Lake Provincial Park ONT 13 H3
Bamaji Lake ONT 11 E2
Bamberton Provincial Park BC 5 F4
Banff, Parc national de ALTA 7 E3
Banff National Park ALTA 7 E3
Bangall, Lac QUÉ 17 F3
Bank Fishery Exhibit, The NS 24 F3
Banks Island BC 5 B1
Banks Island NWT 2 E1
Bannock Lake SASK 8 F1
Bantalor, Réserve faunique de NB 23 E3
Bantalor Game Refuge NB 23 E3
Banting Lake NFLD 27 G1
Baptiste, Lac QUÉ 16 H2
Baptiste Lake ONT 15 B2
Bar Haven Island NFLD 27 G3
Bar Lake SASK 8 D4
Barachois Pond Provincial Park NFLD 27 B2
Barachois Provincial Park NS 25 G2
Barbara Lake ONT 12 B2
Barbier, Lac le QUÉ 22 A9
Bardanes, Lac des QUÉ 18 B1
Baril Lake ALTA 6 F1
Bark Lake ONT 12 F4
Bark Lake ONT 15 A2
Bark Lake ONT 15 B1-2
Barkerville (Gold Rush Town) Provincial Park BC 5 G1
Barkley Sound BC 5 E4
Barma, Lac QUÉ 18 G1
Barnaby River NB 23 F2
Barnard Point NWT 2 E1
Barnes Lake MAN 10 A3
Barneys Brook NFLD 27 D1
Barré, Cap QUÉ 22 G1
Barrel Lake ONT 11 F3
Barren Island NS 25 E4
Barrie Island ONT 13 B1
Barrière, Lac QUÉ 16 A3
Barrière, Lac QUÉ 17 G-H4
Barrington River MAN 8 G3
Barron River ONT 15 C1
Barrow Bay ONT 13 D2
Barrow Strait NWT 2 G1
Barry, Lac QUÉ 16 B4
Barrys Bay ONT 15 C1
Bartholomew River NB 23 E2
Bartibog River NB 23 F1
Barton, Lac QUÉ 17 E2
Barton Lake ONT 11 D2
Basilique Ste-Anne-de-Beaupré QUÉ 19 F1
Basin Head Fisheries Museum PEI 25 E2
Basin Lake SASK 9 E2
Basin & Middle Lakes National Wildlife Reserve SASK 9 E2
Baskatong, Réservoir QUÉ 17 F2
Basket Lake ONT 11 E3
Basques, Île aux QUÉ 22 A3
Bass Lake ONT 13 C1
Bass Lake ONT 13 D3
Bass Lake ONT 15 E3
Bass Lake, Parc provincial ONT 13 G3
Bass Lake Provincial Park ONT 13 G3
Bass River NB 23 F1
Basserode, Lac QUÉ 16 B3
Basswood Lake ONT 11 F4
Bat, Lac QUÉ 17 A2
Bataille-de-la-Châteauguay, Lieu historique national de la QUÉ 19 B4
Bataille-de-la-Ristigouche, Lieu historique national de la QUÉ 22 E3
Batchawana Bay ONT 12 D4
Batchawana Bay, Parc provincial ONT 12 D4
Batchawana Bay Provincial Park ONT 12 D4
Batchawana River ONT 12 D3
Bateau Cove NFLD 26 C2
Bateau Island ONT 13 F2
Bathurst, Cape NWT 2 D1
Bathurst Inlet NWT 2 E2
Bathurst Island NWT 2 G1
Batiscan, Petit lac QUÉ 19 E1
Batiscan, Rivière QUÉ 19 D1
Batoche, Lieu historique national de SASK 9 D2
Batoche National Historic Site SASK 9 D2
Battery Provincial Park NS 25 G3
Battle Creek SASK 9 B4
Battle of the Châteauguay National Historic Site QUÉ 19 B4
Battle of the Restigouche National Historic Site QUÉ 22 E3
Battle River ALTA 7 F2
Battle River SASK 9 C1
Batty Lake MAN 8 G4
Baude, Lac QUÉ 19 C1
Bay, Lac QUÉ 17 C1
Bay du Nord River NFLD 27 E3
Bay du Nord Wilderness Reserve NFLD 27 F2
Bay du Vin River NB 23 F2
Bayeuville, Lac QUÉ 18 G1
Bayfield, Île QUÉ 26 B1
Bayfield Beach Provincial Park NS 25 E3
Bayfield River ONT 14 C1
Bayfield Sound ONT 13 B1
Bayly Lake MAN 10 C4
Bayonne, Rivière QUÉ 19 C3
Bays, Lake of ONT 13 H2
Bayswater Beach Provincial Park NS 24 F3
Bayview Escarpment, Réserve naturelle provinciale ONT 13 E3
Bayview Escarpment Provincial Nature Reserve ONT 13 E3
Bazile, Lac QUÉ 18 G3
Bazin, Rivière QUÉ 16 H4
Bazinet, Lac QUÉ 16 H4
Beale, Cape BC 5 E4
Bear Brook ONT 15 G1
Bear Creek ONT 14 C3
Bear Creek Provincial Park BC 7 C4
Bear Head NFLD 27 B1
Bear Head Lake MAN 10 B3
Bear Lake BC 4 D3
Bear Lake MAN 10 B4
Bear Lake ONT 13 G1
Bear River ALTA 6 D1
Bear River SASK 8 E4
Bearbone Lake ONT 10 E4
Bears Rump Island ONT 13 C-D2
Bearskin Lake ONT 10 E4
Beatton Provincial Park BC 4 G3
Beatton River BC 4 G2
Beatty Creek BC 4 B1
Beatty Saugeen River ONT 13 E4
Beaubears Island National Historic Site NB 23 F2
Beauchamp, Lac QUÉ 16 C2
Beauchastel, Lac QUÉ 16 A3
Beauchêne, Lac QUÉ 17 B2
Beaucours, Lac QUÉ 16 H1
Beaudry, Lac QUÉ 16 B4
Beaudry Provincial Heritage Park MAN 11 B3
Beaufort, Mer de NWT 2 D1
Beaufort Sea NWT 2 D1
Beaulieu, Rivière QUÉ 22 A2-3
Beaumesnil, Lac QUÉ 16 A4
Beaumier, Lac QUÉ 18 B4
Beaumont Provincial Marine Park BC 5 F4
Beaumont Provincial Park BC 5 E1
Beaupré Lake SASK 8 D4
Beauregard, Lac QUÉ 17 H2
Beaurivage, Rivière QUÉ 19 F2
Beauséjour, Lac QUÉ 18 G2
Beauséjour, Lac QUÉ 18 F4
Beausoleil Island ONT 13 F3
Beaussier, Lac QUÉ 18 A2
Beauvais Lake Provincial Park ALTA 7 F4
Beaver Brook NFLD 26 D2
Beaver Creek ONT 15 D3
Beaver Creek ONT 15 C3
Beaver Creek Provincial Park BC 7 D4
Beaver Hill Lake MAN 10 C4
Beaver Island SASK 8 F2
Beaver Lake ALTA 6 G3
Beaver Lake ONT 15 D3
Beaver Lake ONT 13 F1
Beaver Mountain Provincial Park NS 25 E3
Beaver River ALTA 6 G3
Beaver River ONT 10 F3
Beaver River ONT 13 E4
Beaver River ONT 13 H4
Beaver River SASK 8 C4
Beaver Stone River ONT 10 E3
Beaverbrook Art Gallery NB 23 D4
Beaverhill Lake ALTA 7 F1
Beaverhouse Lake ONT 11 F4
Beaverlodge Lake SASK 8 C1
Beaverstone Bay ONT 13 D1
Beavertrap Creek ONT 10 G3
Becaguimec, Réserve faunique de NB 23 C3
Becaguimec Game Refuge NB 23 C3
Bécancour, Rivière QUÉ 19 E2
Beckwith Island ONT 13 F3
Bédard, Lac QUÉ 20 C1
Bede Creek ALTA 6 D1
Bedeque Bay PEI 25 B2
Bedford Island ONT 12 F4
Bedford Island SASK 8 F2
Bedwell Sound BC 5 E4
Beetz, Lac QUÉ 21 C1
Begbie, Mount BC 7 D3
Bégin, Lac QUÉ 20 A2
Beirnes, Mount BC 4 C2
Béland, Lac QUÉ 18 C2
Béland, Rivière QUÉ 22 G2
Belanger Bay ONT 13 A1
Bélanger River MAN 11 B1
Bélanger River SASK 8 D3
Belcher Islands NWT 3 C3
Bélinge, Rivière QUÉ 17 F1
Belisle, Lac QUÉ 18 A2
Belize Inlet BC 5 D3
Bell, Rivière QUÉ 21 D3
Bell, Rivière QUÉ 16 D1
Bell Bay, Parc provincial ONT 15 B1
Bell Bay Provincial Park ONT 15 B1
Bell Homestead ONT 14 F2
Bell Island NFLD 26 E2
Bell Island NFLD 27 H3
Bell Lake ONT 11 F3
Bell Peninsula NWT 3 B1
Bella Coola River BC 5 D2
Bella Lake ONT 13 H1
Belle, Lac de la QUÉ 18 E3
Belle Bay NFLD 27 E3
Belle Isle, Strait of NFLD 26 D1
Belle River ONT 14 A4
Belledune, Pointe NB 22 F3
Belledune Point NB 22 F3
Belle-Isle, Détroit de NFLD 26 D1
Belleisle Bay NB 24 C1
Bellemare, Lac QUÉ 18 E1
Bellevue, Lac QUÉ 18 B3
Bellevue Beach Provincial Park NFLD 27 G3
Bell-Irving River BC 4 C2
Belly River ALTA 7 F4
Belmont Lake ONT 15 B3
Belmont Provincial Park PEI 25 B2
Belwood Lake ONT 14 F1
Ben Eoin Provincial Park NS 25 G2
Benjamin, Lac QUÉ 16 G3
Benjamin Point BC 5 B2
Bennett Lake ONT 15 E2
Bentley Lake SASK 8 F1
Beothuck Provincial Park NFLD 27 E1
Bérard, Lac QUÉ 18 A3
Berens Island MAN 11 B2
Berens River MAN 11 C2
Berens River ONT 11 D2
Beresford Bay BC 4 A4
Berford Lake ONT 13 D3
Bergeron, Lac QUÉ 18 G1
Berland River ALTA 7 C1
Berlinguet, Lac QUÉ 18 B2
Bernabé, Lac QUÉ 18 E2
Bernard, Lac QUÉ 19 C2
Bernard Lake ONT 13 G1
Bernier, Lac QUÉ 16 G2
Bernier Bay NWT 2 H1
Berry, Rivière QUÉ 16 C2
Berry Creek ALTA 7 G2
Berry Creek ALTA 8 A1
Berry Head NS 25 F4
Berry Hill Pond NFLD 27 E2
Bersimis, Rivière QUÉ 3 E4
Berté, Lac QUÉ 20 C1
Berthelot, Lac QUÉ 16 F2
Besa River BC 4 F2
Besnard Lake SASK 8 E4
Betchouane, Refuge d'oiseaux migrateurs de QUÉ 21 C1
Bethune Memorial House ONT 13 G2
Betsiamites, Pointe de QUÉ 22 B2
Betsiamites, Rivière QUÉ 3 E4
Bevin, Lac QUÉ 19 A3
Bic, Île du QUÉ 22 B2
Bic, Parc du QUÉ 22 B3
Bic, Rivière du QUÉ 22 B3
Biche, Lac la ALTA 6 F3
Bienville, Lac QUÉ 3 D3
Big Bald Mountain NB 23 E1
Big Bar Lake Provincial Park BC 5 G2
Big Bay ONT 15 C4
Big Birch Island MAN 11 B3
Big Black River QUÉ 19 H1
Big Blue Hill Pond NFLD 27 E3
Big Bonne Bay Pond NFLD 27 E3
Big Burnt Island ONT 13 C1
Big Caribou Lake ONT 13 F1
Big Chute, Ber roulant de ONT 13 G2
Big Chute Marine Railway ONT 13 G2
Big Creek BC 5 F2
Big Creek ONT 14 B4
Big Creek ONT 14 E3
Big Creek, Réserve nationale de faune ONT 14 E3
Big Creek National Wildlife Reserve ONT 14 E3
Big Crow Lake ONT 15 A1
Big East River ONT 13 H1
Big Forks Brook NB 23 F3
Big Gull Lake ONT 15 D3
Big Hill Springs Provincial Park ALTA 7 F3
Big Island MAN 8 G4
Big Island NWT 3 C1
Big Island ONT 11 D4
Big Island SASK 8 D4
Big Knife Provincial Park ALTA 7 G2
Big LaHave Lake NS 24 E2
Big Lake ONT 13 C1
Big Mink Lake ONT 15 B2
Big Molly Upsim Lake NS 24 D2
Big Mossy Point MAN 11 B1
Big Muddy Badlands SASK 9 E4
Big Muddy Lake SASK 9 E4
Big Otter Creek ONT 14 E3
Big Pond NFLD 27 H4
Big Quill Lake SASK 9 E2
Big Rideau Lake ONT 15 E3
Big Ridge, The NS 25 F2
Big River SASK 9 D1
Big Salmon Range YK 2 B2
Big Salmon River NB 24 D1

165

167

H

I

J

K

CREDITS

Abbreviations used for credits below are:

ROM Royal Ontario Museum
NA National Archives of Canada
WNB Webster Collection of Pictorial Canadiana, New Brunswick Museum

Credits are left to right, top to bottom, with supplementary information as needed.

6–7 Globe at National Museum of Science & Technology © Rand McNally & Co., R.L. 80-GP-21/photo by John Evans.

9 Crespi-Madrid; Crombie McNeil; Geological Survey of Canada, G.S.C. 202872-G.

10 Courtesy of the Field Museum of Natural History, Chicago (3).

11 Susanne M. Swibold; National Museum of Man, National Museums of Canada.

12 From the *Reader's Digest Complete Atlas of the British Isles;* Smithsonian Institute #72-5994.

13 Harold V. Green; from "Field Guide to Snow Crystals," by Edward R. Lachapelle, University of Washington Press (2).

15 *Weather-Making Oceans,* courtesy National Geographical Mapping Division, Surveys & Mapping Branch, Energy, Mines & Resources Canada.

16 *Length of High Summer,* courtesy Canadian Climate Centre, Atmospheric Environment Services, Environment Canada; *Hours of Bright Sunshine,* used by permission of Nelson Canada, A Division of Thomson Canada Limited.

17 *Montreal in March,* from Oke (1978); "Boundary Layer Climates," Methuen, London.

18 *Length of Snow Cover Season,* courtesy Canadian Climate Centre, Atmospheric Environment Services, Environment Canada; (bottom 3) *Snow Accumulation,* from Oke (1978); "Boundary Layer Climates," Methuen, London.

19 Robert J. Cheng, Atmospheric Sciences Research Center, State University of New York at Albany (3); Atmospheric Environment Services; Robert J. Cheng, Atmospheric Sciences Research Center, State University of New York at Albany; from "Clouds, Rain & Rainmaking," by B. J. Mason, Cambridge University Press/photo by U. Makaya; National Hydrology Research Institute (3); © Dave Timewell/Image Finders; Patrick Morrow; © J. Lama/Publiphoto.

22 BM 2683-Brian Milne/Valan Naturefotos; Mark K. Peck; Leonard Lee Rue III; R.N. Smith; (bottom) Mary Ferguson; Harold V. Green.

23 Norman R. Lightfoot; Leonard Lee Rue III; Maxime St-Amour; Leonard Lee Rue III; Edgar T. Jones.

24 Doris Mowry; Cynthia Chalk; Mary Ferguson.

25 (Bottom left) Doris Mowry; (top right) Barbara K. Deans; MT 654-Mark Tomalty/Valan Naturefotos.

26 Richard Wright; © Jack Fields/Photo Researchers; Susanne M. Swibold; Menno Fieguth; © Bill Brooks/Bruce Coleman Inc.

27 (Top) Rick Filler; Paul von Baich.

28 ROM (2); courtesy Glenbow Museum, Calgary.

29 (Top) courtesy National Museum of Man, National Museums of Canada (2); Lande Collection Dept. of Rare Books, McGill University Libraries/photo Mike Haimes; ROM; (bottom) courtesy Glenbow Museum, Calgary.

30 (Top right) Mary Evans Picture Library, London; Aldus Books Ltd., London; Naval Museum of Madrid/photo by Oronoz; NA C-16105; National Art Gallery, Wellington, New Zealand.

30–31 National Museum of Science & Technology © Rand McNally & Co., R.L. 79-GP-19/photo by John Evans.

31 Bodleian Library, Oxford; Aldus Books Ltd., London; National Gallery of Canada, Ottawa; National Portrait Gallery, London (2); BBC Hulton Picture Library, London.

32 Parks Canada; Ron Webber; NA C-1080.

33 Alan Daniel; WNB/photo Rod Stears; WNB.

34 WNB #429/photo Rod Stears; Canadian Pacific Corporate Archives; NA C-605.

35 Glenbow–Alberta Institute; detail "The Taking of Vimy Ridge, Easter Monday, 1917," by Richard Jack, Canadian War Museum.

36 Agriculture Canada; courtesy Agco Corporate Group.

39 Vancouver Public Library; Canadian Forestry Service.

42–43 Courtesy Placer Development Ltd.

43 Courtesy Inco.

44–45 NA C-82808 (top); MacMillan Bloedel; Canada Packers/photo Robert C. Ragsdale; courtesy Visual Services, Dofasco Inc.; courtesy GM of Canada; © Daniel Wiener; Connors Bros. Ltd.

63 Reader's Digest Library of Modern Knowledge.

COVER © Imtek Imagineering/Masterfile.

ILLUSTRATORS: Jim Bruce, George Buctel, Peter Buerschaper, Alan Daniel, Louise Delorme, Diane Desrosiers, Howard S. Friedman, Jean-Claude Gagnon, Réal Lefebvre, Andris Leimanis, Anker Odum, Elayne Sears.

PRINTING: Transcontinental Printing Inc.

BINDING: Harpell's Press Co-operative

PAPER: Westvaco